LETTERS OF HART CRANE AND HIS FAMILY

LETTERS

OF

HART CRANE

AND

HIS FAMILY

Edited By

THOMAS S.W. LEWIS

NEW YORK AND LONDON 1974
COLUMBIA UNIVERSITY PRESS

Library of Congress Cataloging in Publication Data

Crane, Hart, 1899–1932.
  Letters of Hart Crane and his family.
  Includes bibliographical references.
  1. Crane, Hart, 1899–1932—Biography. 2. Crane family. I. Title.
PS3505.R272Z54 1974   811'.5'2 [B]   73-21675
            ISBN 0-231-03740-6

FOR JILL

CONTENTS

PREFACE

❦

Six years ago, after reading the materials in the Hart Crane collection at Columbia University Libraries, I decided that a complete edition of Crane's correspondence with his family would put much of the poet's life into a proper perspective. With generous encouragement from Kenneth Lohf, Curator of Rare Books and Manuscripts at Columbia, and John Unterecker, Crane's biographer, I began the project. This edition of the correspondence between Crane, his mother, Grace Hart Crane, his father, Clarence Arthur Crane, and his grandmother, Elizabeth Belden Hart, forms a coherent narrative of the poet's life with his family. Although some of the letters have been published in *The Letters of Hart Crane,* edited by Brom Weber (Berkeley and Los Angeles: University of California Press, 1965), they were not always printed in their entirety. My edition restores the complete text of the letters in Weber's volume, includes letters that have never before been published, and presents both sides of the correspondence.

These letters may be read on several levels. On the surface they record the events in the correspondents' lives: whom they meet, where they travel, what they are doing—information that is necessary to anyone concerned with biography. On another level these letters may be analyzed for those sentences, phrases, and paragraphs that parallel passages in Crane's poetry. Perhaps most importantly, this correspondence documents Hart Crane's remarkable relationship with his parents and his emergence as a poet from a typical Midwestern background. An understanding of Crane's relationship with his parents is essential to any real appreciation of his tortured life.

The marriage of Clarence Arthur Crane and Grace Edna Hart seems to have been doomed from the start. They quarreled, sometimes bitterly, through eighteen years of marriage; it was only natural that their son, Harold Hart Crane, became the focus of their at-

tention. Even before their divorce in 1917, Harold Crane (as he was
known then) was subtly pulled in two directions; after the final
separation, tensions among the family became more pronounced.
Perhaps unconsciously, but nonetheless dramatically, Grace Crane
tried to alienate her son from his father by having him change his
first name from Harold to her maiden name, Hart; by telling him
in her letters that Clarence Crane was a callous man who cared little for his son's welfare; and by encouraging his desire to write poetry. Clarence Crane, whose interest in literature stopped at Edgar
Guest and Elbert Hubbard, wanted only for his son, "Harold," to
work with him in his own business—the manufacture and distribu-
tion of candy. His letters often contained warnings of the financial
difficulties Crane would face as a poet.

Emotionally Harold Hart Crane was inextricably bound to each
parent, and though he tried in vain to please both, he met with little success. While sentences like: "Mother you do not appreciate
how much I love you," written in 1917, helped to meet Grace
Crane's demands of an unfailing devotion to her, he was unable at
the same time to be a dutiful son to his father. Clarence Crane's
early letters reveal an angry, uncomprehending father who wants
only what is best for his son, and who feels that somehow by circumstances over which he has little control he is being prevented
from providing it. It was not until later in his life that Harold (as
he was always known to his father) and Clarence developed a mutual respect. Clarence helped his son with monthly, semimonthly,
and sometimes weekly checks. In the meantime Grace continued to
demand her son's unmitigated love, and sometimes, as these letters
show, she resorted to emotional blackmail to get it: Hart must always write her frequently; Hart must remain devoted to her; Hart
must never fall in love, for "love is a *sickness*."

Viewing Hart Crane's bondage of "sundered parentage" with
greater objectivity and the wisdom that comes through experience
was the poet's maternal grandmother, Elizabeth Belden Hart. From
the time that Crane left his home in Cleveland in late 1916, until
her death in 1927, Mrs. Hart was almost constantly with her daughter, Grace Crane—and her correspondence with Crane reveals just
how intimately she knew her daughter's mind. She frequently (and

sometimes secretly) filled her letters to Hart with her astute observations and advice for achieving a more stable relationship with his parents.

On August 12, 1924, Hart wrote to his mother about his family situation: "I'm in a trap that will probably confine me the rest of my life, so I might as well laugh at such a world as my imagination qualifies me for." This correspondence repeatedly confirms that Crane had good reason to believe that he was trapped—and his struggle to be free takes on almost mythic proportions. History reminds us of the Sicilian tyrant Phalaris who had constructed for torture an enormous, hollow, bronze bull. Phalaris would place his victims inside the brazen beast and roast it over an open fire. Not one for discord, the tyrant had his bull so constructed that the screams of those inside came out as melodious sounds. Much of Hart Crane's correspondence with his family records the torment of one inside the bull; Crane's poetry records the beauty of his screams.

No edition of this size could be completed without the assistance of many persons, and it is a pleasant task to name just a few of them. John Unterecker has given me an extraordinary amount of his time and advice. In addition to reading the manuscript in its early stages and offering innumerable suggestions, he has made available to me his extensive files of Crane materials. Herbert Leibowitz and Elizabeth Donno also read the manuscript in its early stages and offered valuable suggestions. The Special Collections of Columbia University Libraries has made available its Crane collection and given me permission to use the letters in this book. Kenneth Lohf at Special Collections has helped me frequently both with his interest and with his knowledge. I wish to thank as well the University of Texas Library and Ohio State University Library for permission to use various letters that they own. (A calendar of letters at the end of the volume gives the location of all manuscripts.)

For permission to print letters in which they hold the literary rights, I wish to thank Mrs. Donald Hise, Mrs. Helen Hart Hurlbert, and Columbia University. Several sections of this book appeared in a different form in *Salmagundi*.

I would like also to thank Mrs. Jean Frank, Mrs. Maria Jolas, and Mrs. B. W. Huebsch for permission to reprint letters by Waldo Frank, Eugene Jolas, and B. W. Huebsch, respectively. Acknowledgment is made to The Viking Press, Inc., for permission to quote from Malcolm Cowley's poem "The Flower and the Leaf," published in *Blue Juniata: Collected Poems,* by Malcolm Cowley (copyright © 1968 by Malcolm Cowley; reprinted by permission of The Viking Press, Inc.).

It is especially pleasant to acknowledge the substantial financial assistance I have received from the Woodrow Wilson Fellowship Foundation, the Committee on Research Grants at Skidmore College, and the American Philosophical Society. To each of these institutions I offer my sincere thanks.

Librarians in reference departments at The New York Public Library, Columbia University Libraries, and the Lucy Scribner Library at Skidmore College have helped me with the identification of many people, places, and events mentioned in the letters. I want to thank especially Eugene Sheehey, Marilyn Goldstein, and Gillian Lewis.

People from New York, Cleveland, and Warren, Ohio, who have patiently given me their recollections of the Cranes and the Harts include Samuel Loveman, Elizabeth Madden, Claire Spencer Evans, Harley McHugh, Helen Hart Hurlbert, and Mrs. Donald Hise. My editor at Columbia University Press, William Bernhardt, has substantially improved this manuscript by making wise observations and offering excellent suggestions for changes. Others with whom I have had long conversations about Crane, his poetry, and his life have indirectly contributed to this edition. These include Ellin Sarot, Michael Moore, Daniel O'Day, Martha Franson, Jan Young, and Harry Segessman. I also want to thank Edwin M. Moseley, Robert Boyers, and my parents, Mr. and Mrs. William Draper Lewis, Jr., for their splendid assistance and encouragement. But my greatest debt is to the person to whom I have dedicated this book.

Saratoga Springs, New York   THOMAS S. W. LEWIS
September, 1973

EDITORIAL PRINCIPLES & ABBREVIATIONS

All letters have been transcribed directly from the manuscripts or from xerox copies of the originals. I have made every effort to present the text of each letter exactly as it was written; however, at times I have resorted to silent emendations of insignificant typographical errors (especially in those letters typed by Clarence Crane's secretaries). I have endeavored to keep such changes to a minimum.

Any additions to the letters appear in brackets.

I have tampered very little with the punctuation in these letters. Mrs. Hart's letters—especially those written in her later years—often had a comma in the place of a period and vice versa. In the interest of the reader's sanity I have silently corrected these mistakes.

When an address or date (or any part of these) is not given by the author or is not a part of the author's stationery, I have included this information in brackets at the head of the letter. Salutations which in the letters might be spread over several lines have been run on and separated by a virgule.

When necessary, a description of the author's stationery appears at the top of the letter on the left. Except in establishing the date of a letter I have taken no account of any of the envelopes which survive with the letter.

The following abbreviations have been used in the description of the letters:

AL	autograph letter
ALS	autograph letter signed
TL	typed letter
TLC	typed letter copy
TLD	typed letter draft
TLS	typed letter signed
TMS	typed manuscript

When I have felt it necessary, I have included brief biographical connecting links between the letters to help the reader better understand events in the correspondents' lives. Wishing, however, to have the letters speak for themselves, I have kept such intrusions to a minimum.

I have attempted to identify all persons, places, and events alluded to in the letters. I have, of course, not always been successful.

CHRONOLOGY

1898
JUNE 1   Marriage of Clarence Arthur Crane and Grace
          Edna Hart in Chicago. They settle in Garretts-
          ville, Ohio, where Clarence works in his father's
          maple syrup cannery.

1899
JULY 21   Birth of Harold Hart Crane.

1903
EARLY   Grace Crane's parents, Clinton and Elizabeth
          Belden Hart, move from Chicago to Cleveland.
          They settle at 1709 East 115th Street.

NOVEMBER? Clarence Crane moves his family to Warren,
          Ohio. There he establishes his own maple syrup
          cannery.

1908
EARLY   Clarence Crane sells his cannery to the Corn
          Products Refining Company and takes a job as
          salesman for the new owners.

MIDDLE   Clarence and Grace Crane separate. Mrs.
          Crane goes to a sanitarium. Clarence moves to
          the Chicago office of the Corn Products Refin-
          ing Company. Harold is sent to live with his
          maternal grandparents in Cleveland.

1909
EARLY   The Crane family is reunited in Cleveland at
          the Hart's house. Grace Crane develops a fer-
          vent interest in Christian Science.

1911
APRIL?   Clarence Crane establishes the Crane Chocolate
          Company.

1913
JANUARY 23 Clinton Hart, the poet's grandfather, dies. He
          leaves a legacy of $5000 to his grandson, which

is to be held in trust until Elizabeth Belden Hart's death.

APRIL 30

Clarence Crane's parents, Arthur Edward and Ella Melissa Crane, who had moved to Cleveland in 1910, buy a house across from the Harts on East 115th Street.

1914
JANUARY

Harold enrolls in Cleveland's East High School, which he attends intermittently for the next three years.

JANUARY–
FEBRUARY

Mrs. Crane visits her mother at the Harts' winter home on the Isle of Pines.

SUMMER

Harold and his mother take a tour through the eastern United States.

1915
JANUARY–
FEBRUARY

Mr. and Mrs. Crane and their son travel to the Isle of Pines. Upon their arrival Clarence quarrels with his wife and returns to Cleveland. Grace and Harold return at the end of February.

1916
SUMMER

Mrs. Crane and her son tour the western United States.

EARLY NOVEMBER

Clarence and Grace Crane separate. He takes a room at the Cleveland Athletic Club. They enlist the aid of John J. Sullivan, a lawyer and family friend, to file a petition for divorce.

DECEMBER 29

Harold Hart Crane moves to New York. He settles at 139 East 15th Street. Grace Crane travels to Chicago and Oak Park, Illinois, to visit her friends Blanche and Frank Ross.

1917
JANUARY

Harold begins tutoring with M. Tardy preparatory to entering college in the fall.

JANUARY 20

Mrs. Crane travels to Palm Beach, Florida.

FEBRUARY

Clarence Crane travels to California on business.

FEBRUARY 19

Mrs. Crane returns to Cleveland.

MARCH 4–24

Grace Crane visits Harold in New York.

APRIL	Harold returns to Cleveland in the second week of April for a brief visit.
APRIL 19	Grace and Clarence Crane are divorced.
MAY	Grace Crane and Mrs. Hart arrive in New York on May 1. Two weeks later they sublet a small apartment at 44 Gramercy Park. Mrs. Hart returns to Cleveland about May 20.
JUNE	Clarence Crane begins to correspond with Grace.
JULY 15	Grace and Harold return to Cleveland to prepare for Grace's remarriage to Clarence.
JULY 31	Clarence and Grace quarrel over Harold's wish to live in New York. Harold returns to New York. Shortly after this Harold Hart Crane begins calling himself "Hart Crane."
MID-AUGUST	Grace Crane attempts another reconciliation with Clarence, but is rebuffed. She goes to New York with her mother. There she suffers a nervous collapse.
LATE SEPTEMBER	The lease on the apartment at 44 Gramercy Park expires. Grace and Mrs. Hart return to Cleveland. Hart moves to a rooming house at 25 East 11th Street.
NOVEMBER	Grace visits Hart in New York shortly before Thanksgiving. Both Hart and Mrs. Crane become seriously ill.
MID-DECEMBER	Grace and Hart return to Cleveland for Christmas. They are "guests of honor" at a New Year's Eve party given by Clarence Crane.
1918 JANUARY	Hart and his mother return to New York.
FEBRUARY	Clarence threatens to withhold Hart's allowance if he does not have evidence that his son is employed. Grace urges Hart to take a job with the Crane company, but Hart refuses.
EARLY MARCH	After suffering another nervous collapse, Grace Crane returns to Cleveland.
EARLY JUNE	Hart returns to Cleveland to take a job in a munitions plant.

JULY 4	Grace and Mrs. Hart begin a motor tour to New York and New England.
JULY 18	Hart quits his job at the munitions plant.
AUGUST 8	Grace and Mrs. Hart return from their motor tour.
MID-AUGUST	Clarence Crane marries Frances Kelley.
MID-NOVEMBER	Hart takes a job as a reporter for the Cleveland *Plain Dealer*.

1919

EARLY JANUARY	Hart leaves his job on the *Plain Dealer*.
LATE FEBRUARY	Hart returns to New York. He takes a room at 119 West 76th Street.
EARLY MARCH	Hart moves to 307 West 70th Street.
EARLY APRIL	Hart becomes "Advertising Manager" of *The Little Review*.
EARLY MAY	Hart moves to 24 West 16th Street to rooms directly over *The Little Review*.
JULY 11	Hart moves to Brookhaven, Long Island, to live with Claire Spencer and her husband Harrison Smith.
MID-AUGUST	Hart returns to New York and takes a job as a shipping clerk with the Rheinthal and Newman Company.
NOVEMBER 6	Hart goes to Cleveland to work for his father.
DECEMBER	Hart sells chocolates for his father in Akron, Ohio.

1920

JANUARY	Hart returns to Cleveland to work in his father's chocolate factory. Grace and Mrs. Hart leave for the Isle of Pines where they spend the winter. They return in March.
EARLY SEPTEMBER	Hart moves to Washington to sell his father's chocolates.
OCTOBER 15	Hart returns to Cleveland to resume work in his father's factory.

1921

JANUARY	Mrs. Hart and Grace Crane spend the winter on the Isle of Pines.

APRIL 20	Clarence and Hart argue and Hart quits his job. He continues to live with his mother, searching unsuccessfully for employment.
LATE AUTUMN	Hart enrolls in an advertising course at Western Reserve University.
1922	
EARLY JANUARY	Hart takes a position as advertising copywriter for the Corday and Gross Company in Cleveland.
JULY	Hart leaves Corday and Gross to work for Stanley Patno, who runs a direct mail advertising service in Cleveland.
1923	
EARLY MARCH	Crane is dismissed by Patno because of the lack of business.
LATE MARCH	Hart returns to New York to look for a job. He lives with Gorham Munson and his wife, Elizabeth, for two months.
LATE MAY	Hart is hired as copywriter for the J. Walter Thompson Company.
JUNE	Crane sublets a room from Louis Kantor at 45 Grove Street.
LATE OCTOBER	Hart leaves his job at J. Walter Thompson.
EARLY NOVEMBER	Hart moves to Edward Nagle's and Slater Brown's house in Woodstock, New York, where he spends the winter.
DECEMBER	Grace Crane takes a position as a saleslady for the Josephine Shop, a small gift shop in Cleveland. She works there until Christmas.
1924	
JANUARY 2	Hart returns to New York, staying at 45 Grove Street.
JANUARY 7	Clarence Crane offers his son a position with the Crane Chocolate Company. Hart refuses the offer in a letter of January 12.
JANUARY 28	Hart takes a job with the Pratt and Lindsay advertising firm. He is dismissed from the job on February 11.
FEBRUARY 27	Hart moves to 15 Van Nest Place.

MARCH	Hart considers taking a job on a West Indian merchant ship.
APRIL 2	Hart moves to James Light's apartment at 30 Jones Street.
APRIL 7	Hart begins work at Sweet's Catalogue Service in New York.
APRIL 14?	Hart moves to 110 Columbia Heights, Brooklyn.
LATE SUMMER	Grace Crane begins seeing Charles Curtis.
LATE DECEMBER	Hart travels to Cleveland for Christmas at East 115th Street. He returns to New York on December 26.

1925

JUNE 6	Hart leaves Sweet's Catalogue Service and goes to Slater Brown's house at Patterson, New York.
EARLY JUNE	Grace visits her friends the Rosses in Oak Park, Illinois.
JULY 27	The Hart house at 1709 East 115th Street in Cleveland is sold. Hart returns to Cleveland to help his mother and grandmother dispose of the property. Grace and her mother move to the Wade Park Manor, an apartment building in Cleveland.
EARLY SEPTEMBER	Hart borrows $200 from his friends Richard and Charlotte Rychtarik to buy land in Patterson, New York.
SEPTEMBER 18	Hart returns to Patterson.
OCTOBER 6	Grace travels to Miami, Florida to consider taking a job as a real-estate saleslady. Shortly after this Mrs. Hart travels to Winter Haven, Florida, to visit a friend there. By early November, both Mrs. Hart and Mrs. Crane become ill.
OCTOBER 11	Hart returns to New York City to look for work.
EARLY DECEMBER	Mrs. Hart returns to Cleveland.
DECEMBER 6	Still out of work, Hart appeals to the financier Otto Kahn for financial assistance. Kahn agrees to give Crane an immediate loan of $1000. On December 12, Hart goes to Patterson to spend

the winter with Allen Tate and his wife, Caroline Gordon.

MID-DECEMBER Mrs. Crane is well enough to return to Cleveland.

1926
MID-MARCH Hart makes a brief visit to Cleveland to see his grandmother, who is still ill.

MID-APRIL Hart quarrels with Allen Tate and his wife. He prepares to go to the Isle of Pines.

APRIL 29 Grace Hart Crane marries Charles Curtis in New York City.

APRIL 30 Hart sails for the Isle of Pines with the author Waldo Frank. They arrive at the island on May 5. Frank leaves Crane after a few days' visit.

EARLY SEPTEMBER Hart learns that his mother's marriage to Mr. Curtis is foundering.

LATE OCTOBER Hart leaves the Isle of Pines and returns to New York.

EARLY NOVEMBER Hart goes to Patterson, New York. On November 9 Grace Hart Curtis files a petition for a divorce.

1927
JANUARY 3 Frances Kelley Crane, Clarence's second wife, dies.

EARLY APRIL Hart returns to Cleveland to visit his father. Clarence and his son travel to New York City on April 18. Hart goes on to Patterson, N.Y., on April 20. The hearing for Mrs. Curtis's divorce is held on April 19.

APRIL 29 Grace Curtis is granted a divorce from Charles Curtis. She resumes calling herself Grace Hart Crane.

MAY 19 Clarence Crane buys two houses at Chagrin Falls, Ohio. Through the summer and fall he renovates the structures for an inn to be known as Crane's Canary Cottage.

SEPTEMBER Grace Crane and Mrs. Hart prepare to move to California.

SEPTEMBER 19 Otto Kahn gives Hart another $500.

EARLY OCTOBER	Hart plans to spend the winter in Martinique. Grace, who had moved to Hollywood in mid-October, objects to her son being so far away. Hart abandons his plans.
NOVEMBER 14	Hart goes to Altadena, California, as a secretary and companion to Herbert A. Wise.

1928

MARCH 20	Hart leaves Wise's employment in Altadena and joins his mother in Hollywood. He looks without success for work in Hollywood writing movie scenarios.
LATE MAY	Hart Crane breaks with his mother. He leaves her and Mrs. Hart late one night, never to see either again. He travels by train to New Orleans and then takes a boat to New York. After several days in New York he travels to Patterson, staying at Mrs. Addie Turner's farmhouse in Patterson.
JULY 26	Hart moves to Eleanor Fitzgerald's house in Gaylordsville, Connecticut.
AUGUST 2	Hart stays with the Habichts at Croton-on-Hudson.
AUGUST 9	Hart stays at Malcolm Cowley's apartment in New York.
AUGUST 16	Hart takes a part-time position at a bookstore in New York City.
AUGUST 20	Hart takes a temporary position with the Griffin, Johnson, and Mann advertising firm in New York. He moves to 77 Willow Street about September 1.
SEPTEMBER 6	Elizabeth Belden Hart dies in California.
OCTOBER 15	Grace Crane becomes ill in California. Hart refuses to visit her.
MID-OCTOBER	Hart moves back to 110 Columbia Heights in Brooklyn. He takes a job with the Henry L. Doherty brokerage firm. He leaves this job in November.
LATE NOVEMBER AND EARLY DECEMBER	Grace Crane signs the necessary legal papers for Hart to receive the $5000 that Mrs. Hart had held in trust since her husband's death in

1913. Hart sails on December 8 on the *Tuscania* to London. He arrives in London on December 22.

1929
JANUARY 6

Hart goes to Paris. While there he spends much of his time with Harry and Caresse Crosby. Hart and the Crosbys make plans to publish a special edition of *The Bridge*.

APRIL AND MAY

Hart visits Collioure and Marseilles. He returns to Paris in late June.

EARLY JULY

Hart has a fight in the Café Select. After a trial on July 10 he decides to return to New York. He embarks on the *Homeric* on July 18.

JULY 24

Hart arrives in New York. He takes a room at 130 Columbia Heights in Brooklyn.

OCTOBER 21–26

Hart spends the week in Patterson, New York.

EARLY NOVEMBER

Hart visits Clarence Crane at Chagrin Falls. In the middle of the month he learns that his mother is coming to Ohio from California to be with her son at Thanksgiving. Hart leaves immediately for New York. From Thanksgiving to Christmas Hart divides his time between 130 Columbia Heights, Brooklyn, and Patterson.

1930
EARLY?

Mrs. Crane is employed by the Carleton Hotel in Oak Park, Illinois.

JANUARY 1

Hart moves to a room at 190 Columbia Heights.

JANUARY 25

Clarence Crane marries Bessie Meachem, an employee of the Crane company, in Cleveland.

MID-APRIL

Hart spends two weeks at Patterson and then returns to 190 Columbia Heights.

SUMMER AND FALL

Hart lives in Patterson, Columbia Heights, Gaylordsville, Connecticut, and at the Hotel Albert in New York City.

DECEMBER 12

Hart returns to Chagrin Falls for Christmas with his father. He stays in Chagrin Falls for the winter.

1931
MARCH 15

Hart receives a $2000 fellowship from the John Simon Guggenheim Memorial Foundation.

MARCH 20?   Hart returns to New York. He makes plans to
                   spend his fellowship year in Mexico.

APRIL 4   Hart sails for Vera Cruz on the *Orizaba*. He
                   arrives on April 10. On April 11 he travels to
                   Mexico City.

JULY 6   Clarence Crane dies in Chagrin Falls. Hart re-
                   turns to Chagrin Falls on July 11. Clarence
                   Crane is buried in Garrettsville, Ohio, on July
                   12.

AUGUST 29   Hart returns to Vera Cruz on the *Orizaba*. He
                   arrives on September 5. On September 6 he
                   travels to Mexico City.

SEPTEMBER 12   Hart travels to Tepotzlan for five days.

1932
APRIL 24   Hart leaves Vera Cruz on the *Orizaba*. He
                   jumps from the deck of the *Orizaba* at noon on
                   April 27.

1947
AUGUST 30   Grace Hart Crane dies in Teaneck, New Jer-
                   sey.

LETTERS OF HART CRANE AND HIS FAMILY

Clarence Arthur Crane and Grace Edna Hart were married in Chicago on June 1, 1898. An only daughter of Clinton and Elizabeth Belden Hart, Grace Crane was descended on both sides of her family from early New England settlers. Mr. Hart, who had lived much of his early life in Warren, Ohio, was an executive with the Sykes Roofing Company in Chicago. Clarence Crane was the only son of a well-to-do family that had been one of the first to settle in the Western Reserve. His parents, Arthur Edward and Ella Melissa Crane, lived in Garrettsville, Ohio, where Mr. Crane operated a small but highly successful maple syrup cannery. Clarence was a rugged and independent person, a near genius in business affairs, who firmly believed that hard and honest work was the only way to achieve happiness and success. After attending Allegheny College for two years, he took a job for a short while with the National Biscuit Company, and then became a salesman for his father's company in Garrettsville. It was in Garrettsville in a house his father had built for them that Clarence and Grace Crane began their married life; and it was there the Cranes' only child, Harold Hart Crane, was born on July 21, 1899.

While working for his father, Clarence Crane made the business prosper, but he soon became impatient with the small size of the operation. In late 1903, with financial help from his parents and Grace's, Clarence moved his family to Warren, to begin his own maple syrup cannery. This venture was so successful that Clarence sold the cannery five years later to the Corn Products Refining Company, becoming manager and salesman for the new owners. Three years later, in April, 1911, Clarence Crane began in Cleveland what soon became his most successful venture—manufacturing and retailing chocolates. The Crane Chocolate Company expanded rapidly; soon Clarence operated restaurants in Cleveland and Akron, and distributed his brand of "Mary Garden Chocolates" (named after the singer) through wholesale outlets in New York and Kansas City. Clarence took a particular interest in retailing his products, often writing his own advertising copy: "Music by Mary Garden, Candies by Crane." And for a new product he invented and first marketed, the Life Saver, Clarence designed a wrapper showing a sailor throwing a life ring to a pretty girl in distress. Beneath the picture the caption read: "For that stormy breath." In a few years after beginning his confectionery business "C.A.," as he was known to both friends and employees, was thought by many to be a millionaire.

Unfortunately Clarence Crane was much more successful conducting his business than his personal affairs, for his marriage to Grace was a disaster from the beginning. Grace found Garrettsville, Warren, and even Cleveland—as well as C.A.'s circle of friends—to be much slower paced than the society she had been accustomed to in Chicago. There she had lived in a world of parties, with attention lavished on her by both family and friends. First attracted to Grace by her beauty, Clarence wrote long, emotional letters during their courtship pleading for marriage; Grace, who had resisted these protestations of love before the wedding, resisted them even more after it. While she wanted a husband who would lead her into society, Clarence wanted a wife who would take an interest in the problems and successes of his business. Neither was satisfied. Clarence increasingly channeled his energy into his work, often traveling to the Crane company offices in New York and Kansas City, while Grace spent much of her time visiting friends in Chicago and New York or traveling with her son on long vacation trips. C.A. and Grace found that they had little in common; neither one was happy, yet neither one wanted the marriage to be dissolved.

As a consequence of his parents' problems, Harold, as he was called then, spent much of his childhood visiting his relatives—his paternal aunts Alice (later Mrs. Loring Williams) and Bess (later Mrs. Newton Byron Madden) in Garrettsville, and his mother's sister-in-law, Zell Hart Deming,[1] and her daughter, Helen Hart, in Warren. A particularly bitter quarrel in 1908 had its effect on all

---

[1] Mrs. Deming was married first to Grace's brother, Frank. After his death she married William Deming, publisher of the Cheyenne (Wyoming) *Tribune*.

three members of the family. Harold was sent to live in Cleveland with his grandmother and grandfather Hart, who had moved there from Chicago in 1903. Suffering from a nervous breakdown, Grace entered a sanitarium. Clarence, as mentioned above, went to work for the Chicago office of the Corn Products Refining Company. By 1909 Harold's parents were together once again at the Harts' house in Cleveland; Clarence was now busy organizing his chocolate company, while Grace became interested in Christian Science. Soon she persuaded C.A., Harold, and her parents to attend the religious services with her.

The first two extant letters, both by Harold, were written to his parents while they were traveling.

To Clarence Arthur Crane

June 2 1910
Cleveland, O.

TLS, 1 p.

My dear Father:—[1]

I had written to Mother so many times that I thought I would write to you this time. It is raining very hard out doors. I just came home from the Library with a new book called Mr. Wind and Madm. Rain [.] [2] The day before yesterday I had my test in Spelling, and stood 100. I got your little note the other day and Mothers letter this morning and I am expecting you home Sunday morning to eat breakfast with us. It will seem good to have you back again. Tell Mother that I am brushing my teeth every day. With much love to you and Mother.

Sincerely your son/ Harold

[1] Clarence and Grace were staying at the Hotel Metropole in Chicago.
[2] Harold very likely read P. E. Musset's classic children's book in an edition translated by Emily Makepeace and illustrated by Charles Bennett that Putnam published in 1905.

To Grace Hart Crane

Cleveland O
Nov. 5, 1910.

TLS, 1 p.
LETTERHEAD: CLARENCE A. CRANE/WARREN, OHIO

My dear Mother—

I have been going to write you for a long time but I have been so busy with my home work that I have not had time.

This afternoon we all went to the Hipp. and I never saw a better show [.] Eva Tangua [1] was the princepul feature of the show. She was even better than I thought she would be. She had seven new gowns and they were beautiful just the kind I like.

I got your letter and we were glad to get it.

Tuesday night Grandpa and Grandma invited me to supper and after supper we all went to here Elmensdorfs [2] lecture on the Art Galliers in Europe [.] He told us when all the pictures were painted and showed us the exact picture on canvass and told us much more and I enjoyed it very much. That night I stayed at Grandpas, and went to school in the morning.

Father has writen two or three letters.

We are all well and happy.

With much love/ Harold Crane

The gap of four years before the next letter marks the beginning of Harold's sometimes happy and at other times difficult adolescence. His room in his grandparent Harts' home was the scene of some of his happier moments. Taking up the entire third story in one of the house's twin towers—a room he remembered more than

[1] Eva Tanguay (1878–1947), the vaudeville singer and actress.

[2] "Grandpa and Grandma" were Harold's paternal grandparents, who had moved to Cleveland from Garrettsville in 1910 and owned for a short while an apartment building at 2033 Cornell Road. Later, in 1913, they bought a house across the street from the Harts. Crane probably refers to Dwight Lathrop Elmendorf (1859–1929), a popular lecturer of the period.

CLARENCE A. CRANE
WARREN, OHIO

Cleveland O

Nov. 5, 1910.

My dear Mother-

      I have been going to write you for a long ti me but I have
been so busy with my home work that I have not had time.

    This afternoon we all went to the Hipp. and I never saw a better show
Eva Tangua was the princepul feature of the show. She was even better than
I thought she would be. She had seven new gowns and they were beautiful
just the kind I like.

    I got your letter and we were glad to get it.

    Tuesday night Grandpa and Grandma invited me to supper and after supper
we all went to here Elmensdorfs lecture on the Art Galliers in Europe
He told us when all the pictures were painted and showed us the exact
picture on canmass and told us much more and I enjoyed it very much.
That night I stayed at Grandpas, and went to school in the morning.

    Fathershas writen two or three letters.

    We are all well and happy.

        With much love

Harold Crane.

Letter of November 5, 1910,
from Harold Crane to Grace Hart Crane

a decade later as his "sanctum de la tour" [1]—it offered him the privacy he needed for reading and writing poetry. Judging from the books of his library that are still preserved, his reading during this period included the poetry of Shelley, Lionel Johnson, Coleridge, and Swinburne, Wilde's *Lady Windermere's Fan,* and Poe's *Tales of Mystery and Imagination.* Crane's poetry from this time certainly reflects the romantic elements of these writers. One poem, "The Moth That God Made Blind," a work that truly can be termed juvenilia, depicts the poet as a blind moth born in the light of "Arabian moons" who, because of his blindness, can fly to the sun and be gripped in its "octopus arms." Another unpublished sonnet of this period begins: "Ere Elfish night shall sift another day." "C—33," Crane's first published poem, which appeared in the September 23, 1915, issue of *Bruno's Weekly,* took its title from Oscar Wilde's cell number in Reading Gaol; in it Crane describes the incarcerated author as one who has "woven rose-vines / About the empty night."

In 1914 Harold was enrolled in Cleveland's East High School, which his parents hoped would give him the preparation he needed to enter college. Never a systematic worker, Crane earned marks that were always on the borderline, yet he did excel in subjects that he liked, especially English. Part of the reason for his low grades must be attributed to frequent absences from school brought about by extended travels with his mother to Chicago and to the Harts' vacation home on the Isle of Pines, fifty miles southwest of Cuba. East High School and the neighborhood where his grandparents lived introduced Crane to the three closest companions of his youth: Kenneth Hurd, George Bryan, and William Wright. Of the three, Wright remained his lifelong friend.

Yet not all the memories Harold had of this time were happy ones. Clinton Hart's health deteriorated steadily through 1912, and he died early in the following year. Grace and Clarence argued often, so that both felt the need for more frequent and lengthy trips to mitigate the pressures on their married life in Cleveland. In January and February, 1914, Mrs. Crane stayed on the Isle of Pines with her mother; that summer she traveled through the East with

---

[1] Crane wrote this on the face of a picture postcard of the house that he sent to Gorham Munson on August 6, 1925.

her son, stopping for extended visits with friends in Boston and Rye Beach, New York. In January, 1915, Harold and his parents embarked on another trip to the Isle of Pines. Upon their arrival, C.A. grew anxious over Harold's absence from school and his own absence from business. After an emotional quarrel over the date of their return, Clarence headed home alone to Cleveland. Once away from his wife and son, C.A. began a steady barrage of letters— sometimes three a day—to the island, begging his wife's forgiveness ("I'm forever sorry and in the future we will go and come to- gether") and imploring her to "come home as soon as you can." [2] The tension of that winter had left its mark on Harold, who, as he later told William Wright, had twice attempted suicide at this time —once by slashing his wrists and once by taking his mother's ver- onal powders. After the second attempt Grace decided to embark for Cleveland. With the return of mother and son at the end of February, the Cranes' marital problems were settled once again, but only temporarily.

C.A. wrote the letter immediately following to his son while he was en route to Cleveland. The others, written in early 1916, are from Harold to his grandmother Hart, who was spending the win- ter on the island.

From Clarence Arthur Crane

Jacksonville, Florida
[January 24, 1915?]

ALS, 1 p.
LETTERHEAD: Hotel Seminole, Jacksonville, Florida

Dear Harold:—[1]

I guess you must have thot that dad behaved badly. Last year we lost mother for six weeks but you were both with me & this year I

---

[2] Quoted by John Unterecker from Clarence Crane's letter of January 24, 1915, to his wife. See *Voyager: A Life of Hart Crane* (New York: Farrar, Straus, and Giroux, 1969), pp. 35–36.

---

[1] Clarence included this letter with one that he wrote to his wife.

lose you both & she seems to think you won't be home for so long that I'm fearful dad is going to be all busted up.

I'm hoping that you'll both realize that I'm worth saving and come back a good deal sooner than April 1st. Tonight I start north and Thursday will be in my office. I shall appreciate more than ever before in my life your letters so try and write me by Every boat. Life wouldn't be worth but very little without you both and it's worth something to have your father feel that way isn't it?

Take care of yourselves and come back to me as soon as you *can* [.]

With love / Papa

To Elizabeth Belden Hart

Cleveland Ohio

Jan 7, 1915 [1]

ALS, 3 pp.

My dear Grandma

Well the date above will tell you the story. I am so lonesome now as both Father and Mother have been gone two days now. Perhaps this lonsomeness will wear off in a little while as it usually does you know.

I rec'd your good long letter and thought it was fine—so interesting and I am hoping for some more.

Of coarse a long letter every other day would be fine but they only come once a month so I would really rather have a short one every-other day.

But now you won't have to write so much for Father or rather Mother will write to me. Of coarse that doesn't mean I want you to stop.

Well I suppose they are in St. Augusytine or Jacksonville today. Father is selling goods on the way down so as to make the trip pay and of coarse Mother is enjoying the hotels and resorts. Ill bet there will be a wagging of tongues when you meet them.

[1] Misdated. Actually 1916.

They seem to have thought it best for me to stay in school *this* winter anyway as I am not getting along very well and I would have to be pretty good to get along down on the island.

A week ago last Sat and Sunday we were down to see Zell and Helen [2] and I guess they'll come down if Zell feels well enough although she was feeling pretty bad when we were there.

Sam is going to go to a military school in the south and of coarse that means that he must leave his mother as his father is paying for it. It seems too bad for he was a promising chap once and now he is getting worse and worse all the time. I presume his mother will be broken hearted over it. She has had to go to scrubbing floors and dish washing for a living while he wont lift his finger. Well now I must close for it is getting late and my studies may suffer.

Your Grandson/ Harold

To Elizabeth Belden Hart

[Cleveland]
Jan. 26, 1916.

ALS, 2 pp.

My dear Grandmother:

Examination time is *on* now and I am kept completely occupied in the preparation for them. We had *English* today and Latin and Geometry are due tomorrow. They are my hoodooes and so I am not a little worried tonight about the out come. I am invited over to G. Cranes for supper tonight as Aunt Bess [1] is to be there on about a day's visit so Dora [2] can go out early. As you already know, father and mother are in New York and I am running things alone now. The store was doing surprisingly well today when I was there owing perhaps to the balmy weather (almost summer) which we are

---

[2] Helen Hart, the daughter of Zell and Frank Hart, later married Griswold Hurlbert. She now lives in Warren, Ohio, and publishes the Warren *Tribune*.

---

[1] Aunt Bess: Mrs. N. B. Madden, Clarence Crane's sister, who lived in Garrettsville.

[2] Dora: a woman who worked as a maid for the Harts.

having. Alice [3] has been *very sick* and in response to my gift of
some roses she sent me a beautiful note as soon as she was able to
sit up. Your letters would augur a fairly favorable winter and good
conditions on the island. So you rest as much as you can and enjoy
the care-free feelings while you can whirl around with the Wilcoxs [4]
in the machine. It is fine that you have found a group of such sympathetic thinkers and be sure and carry the *science* as far as you
can.[5] I know of few better places to get a foothold in the faith than
in the quiet and beauty of the island.

Mother left feeling fine for New York and suppose, tho busy, she
is enjoying a splendid time. They will be back Sat. morn. With the
exception of a little sore throat I have felt fine myself lately. I think
it is unnecessary to go to Mr. Ely.[6] My writing has suffered neglect
lately due to study for examinations, but I will soon resume it with
vehemence as I am intensely, grippingly interested in a new ballad
I am writing of six hundred lines.[7] I have resolved to become a
good student even if I have to sit up all night to become one. You
will undoubtly wink when you read this state declaration so often
made but this time it is in earnest.

Yours affectionately—/ HAROLD CRANE

To Elizabeth Belden Hart

Cleveland Ohio
Feb. 10, 1916.

ALS, 2 pp.

My dear Grandmother—
    I have just returned from the store and got so car sick on the way

---

[3] Possibly Alice Calhoun, a friend of Crane's, who later starred in silent films;
possibly his aunt, Alice Crane.
    [4] Walter Wilcox was the caretaker of Mrs. Hart's property on the Isle of
Pines.
    [5] Harold is referring to his family's interest in Christian Science.
    [6] Daniel M. Ely, a Christian Science practitioner, whose office was in Cleve-
land.
    [7] Possibly "The Moth That God Made Blind" is a fragment of this six-
hundred-line ballad. See *Voyager,* p. 42.

home, I havn't recovered yet. I am sorry you think I am neglecting you, as indeed I have, but, if you knew how busy I have been you would readily appreciate it. However there is no passing of a day without my thoughts at some time reverting to you and I am glad to say they always picture you as happy as your good letters indicate; at least there is no other thought ever flowing through the lines.— Mother is well and down at her store post.

You see, I am now a Junior (capital) in high-school and I feel quite elated at having so passed my examinations. The present too, is more encouraging as fine marks have been in the great majority since my promotion.[1]

We had a good laugh over your last "squirting" letter, and I suppose it (the bathroom apparati) is by this time completely installed.

I'll bet you were glad to be rid of that musty, fusty old preacher! Let him seranade the Andersons a while with his talk. It is strange, in view of the fact that last winter I defended the desirability of northern winters to the expense of much discomfiture from other arguers, that the whole illusion has melted away and I have often this winter thought of the South with longing—yes, even Florida. My blood, I guess, has been thiner or digestion poorer. Some of these days have cut me thru and thru so that I have for the most part of the season, been exquisitely uncomfortable, "Once south has spoilt me" so they say.

Dora has been working down in the store kitchen for the past few days, as Penelope[2] had to attend her brother-in-law's funeral in Chicago, and she has literally bubbled over all the time for her excitement and love of the work. It is surely lonely for me here, eating alone and seldom seeing any one but in the darkness of morning or night. If you were here it would be so different, but I am consoled amply by knowing of your comfort and welfare where you now are. I have been working hard lately at my writing but find it doubly hard with the task of conjoining it to my school work. They are so shallow over there at school I am more moved to disdain than anything else. Popularity is not my aim though it were easy to win it

[1] See the account of Crane's high school years, including his academic record, in *Voyager*, pp. 27–29.
[2] Penelope: a woman who worked for the Crane company.

by laughing when they do at nothing and always making a general ass of one'self. There are about two out of the twelve hundred I would care to have as friends.

Alice and I are become better acquainted and I like her better always. Now write *me* occaisonally a note too, and give my love to Ethel, Bruce and Laura Bell. Supper is ready so goodby—

                                        With much love—/ Harold Crane

To Elizabeth Belden Hart

                                                        Cleveland O
                                                    Feb. 13, Sun. '16

ALS, 1 p.

My dear Grandmother:

We have just unpacked Mother's new Tiffany lamp and placed it in front of the smaller parlor window. It is indeed a beauty and the room looks one-hundred dollars the better for it.

Last night I went to the Hipp. with Bill Wright, (you remember him) and saw one of the best shows ever.[1] I didn't get home until unusually late and then read awhile, so I am a little nervous today. Someone sang a Hawaian melody that sounded so much like a native's song as he goes by the bungalow at night that [I] thought immeadiatly of you and wished to be there beside that calm southern sea.

I suppose you will soon take a first splash in your new bathroom's tub! I know how good one feels after it on those delightfully cool mornings. Well, my letters are short as life as a student is rather dull as far as events are concerned, but I presume you would prefer the often-shorts to the scarce-longs; so good-bye, with a heart full of love for you—/ Harold Crane.

[1] At the Hippodrome on February 12, 1916, Crane saw Sam Chip and Mary Marble in "The Clock Shop." The other acts included Bronson & Baldwin with "pickings from singing and dancing land"; Mullen & Coogan in "Old Nonsense"; Vera Sabra in "Fantasies of the Dance"; and singing by Burnham & Irwin.

By the fall of 1916, Grace and Clarence's quarrels were not only frequent but often public. In November they enlisted the aid of John J. Sullivan, a lawyer and family friend, to file a divorce petition in the county court. At the end of December, Harold, then seventeen years old, left Cleveland to pursue a career as a poet in New York City.

Before his arrival in New York, Crane had met only two people who were engaged in literary activity: Elbert Hubbard, the popular philosopher, and Mrs. William Vaughn Moody, widow of the Chicago poet. When Crane visited Hubbard's Roycrofters Colony at East Aurora, New York, in 1915, he was disillusioned with the commercial nature of the operation. Most members of the group worked in the Roycroft Press, which printed, bound, and distributed elegant editions of Hubbard's writings. More important to Harold was his friendship with Mrs. Moody, which ironically began through that lady's association with the Crane Chocolate Company. In an effort to understand his son's desire to become a poet, Clarence Crane sought advice from Mrs. Moody, whose Chicago catering business was a steady customer for Mr. Crane's confectioneries. Advising him to encourage Harold, she arranged to meet C.A.'s son while on a business trip to Cleveland in the winter of 1915. Judging from her letters to Harold, Mrs. Moody not only criticized his poetry and stressed the need for revision and hard work ("love of your work, and work, will give you your full voice") [1] but also introduced him to the literary world by reporting on the activities of other writers, including Rabindranath Tagore, Padraic Colum, Vachel Lindsay, and Carl Sandburg. Later, she saw Harold in New York and introduced him to artists and writers whom she knew there. In his letters to her, Crane expressed a desire to leave Cleveland and the chaos of his family life so that he might concentrate on his poetry. His parents' final separation in 1916 offered him the opportunity to do just that.

[1] Quoted by John Unterecker from Mrs. Moody's letter of July 2, 1916. See *Voyager*, p. 42.

Grace and Clarence were disturbed by their son's desire to live in New York, yet they consented on the condition that he continue the preparations for college ostensibly begun at East High School. Though Harold would essentially be "alone" in a strange city, his parents had alerted several family friends to his arrival. The young poet could visit the Crane company's New York office on East 33d Street, which was managed by Miss Hazel Hasham, a good friend of both C.A. and Grace. Far more important was the artist Carl Schmitt, who had recently established a studio at 308 East 15th Street. Harold, who had known Schmitt when the artist lived in Warren (where he was assisted financially by Crane's aunt Zell Hart Deming), looked forward to seeing him again in New York. It was at Schmitt's studio that Crane arrived fresh from Cleveland shortly before New Year's, 1917, and it was with his help that the poet located a room several blocks away at 139 East 15th Street. Almost immediately Schmitt became a major influence on the young poet, for it was through his conversations with the artist that Crane began to develop his first conscious artistic theory: that art lies between good and evil, beauty and ugliness, and grows from the tension created by these opposing forces. As the following letters to his parents show, Harold's relationship with Schmitt cooled after a month; yet the artist was Crane's most important tutor at this time.

His other tutors, first a M. Tardy and later a Mme Eugénie Lebègue, who Harold maintained in letters to his parents were preparing him for college, were of little importance from the start. The poet's preparations were halfhearted and made only to allay the fears of his parents. The four hours a week devoted at the beginning to tutoring soon dropped to two; six months after his arrival he stopped the lessons altogether. While he spoke in his letters of studying for the entrance examinations at Columbia, the garrulous poet spent most of his time cultivating new friends, exploring the city, attending concerts and plays, engaging Schmitt in long aesthetic discussions, and writing poetry. His efforts to attain a formal education were never serious.

Harold himself looked up several people in New York with whom he had corresponded before his arrival. They were the editors of little magazines that had published his poetry: Guido Bruno, of *Bruno's Weekly,* which had published "C—33" in September, 1915; and Joseph Kling, editor of *The Pagan,* which had published "October-November" in its November, 1916, issue.

In the weeks that followed his arrival Harold met several other people important to his early development. Charles Brooks, the successful, Yale-educated essayist and short-story writer from Cleveland, who had been acquainted with Crane's parents there, maintained an apartment in New York. Brooks and his wife, Minerva, soon became useful to Crane by offering him entry into a circle of literary and literate men and women. No doubt Clarence and Grace were happy about their son's acquaintance, for this popular author was to them the quintessence of all that a successful writer should be— witty, urbane, and financially successful. Mrs. Moody arranged for Harold to meet Padraic Colum and his wife, Mary. Writing of Crane in her book *Life and the Dream,* Mary Colum characterized him as one who knew "the difference between the art of literature and the trade of writing." To her, Harold seemed a "raw western boy . . . a gangling, semiliterate youth of about seventeen. . . . He would come round to see us about twice a week and talk about poetry, never getting over his excitement at how much we seemed to know about it." [2] Crane's conversations with the Colums ranged over the world of publishing, the work of other writers living in New York and Dublin, Irish literature, the French Symbolists, and, at times, his relations with his parents.

While Harold was making new friendships and experiencing the freedom of New York, his parents were waiting for their divorce to become final. Clarence, having moved from the Hart house in November, was living in the Cleveland Athletic Club and devoting most of his energy to the confectionery business. Grace attempted through extensive travels to mitigate her unhappiness and to recover from a recent operation. Traveling had always seemed the best way for her to escape the tensions of her life. Now she embarked on an almost interminable journey, covering many thousands of miles, to resorts, to friends, and to relatives. First she went

[2] Mary Colum, *Life and the Dream* (New York: Doubleday, 1947), pp. 256–57.

(with her maid, Molly Abrogast) to Chicago and then to her friends Blanche and Frank Ross in nearby Oak Park, Illinois. The Ross family had known the Harts well since the time Grace's father had worked for the Sykes Roofing Company.

From Grace Hart Crane

[Cleveland]
[December 30, 1916?]
Saturday 7 P.M

ALS, 3 pp.

My dear Harold:—

I was so glad to receive your wire about yesterday noon & needless to say you have been almost constantly in my thoughts ever since you left.

You will be surprised perhaps to know that Molly & I leave tonight for Chicago— We will stop at Hotel Congress for a few, days until I feel stronger & then I will go to the Ross's & Molly come back— I shall think of you especially on New Years Eve in the big City. I shall be in Chicago & grandma & your father here— What strange positions fate places us in—

Geo. Skeel [1] has just called up & I have given him your address at your fathers office on 33rd st— Said he would write you soon— Bob also called yesterday & was much disappointed.

Give my love to Carl & here are my most earnest wishes for the happiest year you have yet had— Loads of love from/ mother.

My best wishes to Miss Hasham—
Write me often

531 East Ave North
Oak Park, Ill—
c/o Frank Ross—

Don't neglect your grandmother Hart.—Remember she is *all alone.*

---

[1] George Skeel, a classmate of Crane's at East High School. Crane corresponded with Skeel for a short while after his arrival in New York.

To Clarence Arthur Crane

308 E 15 St. N.Y.C.[1]
Dec. 31, 1916

TLS, 2 pp.

My dear Father,

I have just been out for a long ride up Fifth Ave. on an omnibus. It is very cold but clear, and the marble facades of the marvelous mansions shone like crystal in the sun. Carl has been very good to me, giving hours of time to me, advising, help [ing] me get a room, etc. The room I have now is a bit too small, so after my week is up, I shall seek out another place near here, for I like the neighborhood. The houses are so different here, that it seems most interesting, for a while at least, to live in one.

It is a great shock, but a good tonic, to come down here as I have and view the countless multitudes. It seems sometimes almost as though you had lost yourself, and were trying vainly to find somewhere in this sea of humanity, your lost identity.

Today, and the remainder of the week, I shall devote to serious efforts in my writing. If you will help me in the necessities, I think that within six months I shall be fairly able to stand on my own feet. Work is much easier here where I can concentrate. My full love to you, dear father. Write me often and soon./ Harold

To Grace Hart Crane and Elizabeth Belden Hart

308 E. 15th St. N.Y.C.
Jan. 2, 1917.

ALS, 3 pp.

Dear Mother and Grandma:—

Harold Thomas [1] of Warren, who has been down here about a

---

[1] 308 East 15th Street was the address of Carl Schmitt's studio where Crane received his mail. He lived several blocks away at 139 East 15th Street.

---

[1] Harold Thomas had known Crane in Warren. A few years after this, Thomas went to Pittsburgh, where he remained until his death.

year, I guess, spent the evening with Carl and I. Of course, I didn't remember him from *my* Warren days, but he did me, and also, incidently I like him "muchly". Carl and I dine around the corner nearly every evening on a sumptuous meal (no fooling) for 50¢. I never found anything like it in Cleveland for the money: it includes soup, entree, roast, desert & demitasse.

What splendid times I am having wandering about town, and meeting entirely interesting people.

Really, as I expected, I am right in the swing. Tomorrow I call on the noted irish poet & dramatist, Padraic Colum. There I shall meet Frank Harris,[2] editor of "Pearsons," and friend-biographer of Osc[a]r Wilde. Mr. Blum [3] will conduct this.

Within a few weeks I expect to be printed in the colums of the "New York Evening Sun".[4] Fine, isn't it.

Well I havn't seen anybody as fine as you, Mother, and probably wont. But I am meeting humanity here; all kinds of it; and it is absorbing. Last night I saw Warfield in "The Music Master.["] [5] It was tear-moving.

Carl is a more wonderful man than you have any idea. A tremendous thinker!

You are in Chicago, as I suppose from your letter today—rec'd. How I do long for your ultimate, complete happiness! You are a queen, and you shall have it too. Often I have come accross the most charming, odd apartments in my walks and I like to think of you entirely happy in one of them, happy with me and Grandma, in a few clean rooms.

Life is fine here. One can leave the gorgeousness of Fifth Ave., and in a few minutes buy olive-oil-soaked, Italien ripe olives, and long French bread and things you never heard of, in little shops in the foreign sections, near which I am living.

Good night, for now, and write/ your affectionate son,/ Harold—

---

[2] Frank Harris edited *Pearson's Magazine* in New York from 1916 to 1922.
[3] Jerome Blum (1884–1956), the American artist.
[4] Crane's work was never published in the New York *Evening Sun*.
[5] David Warfield was playing in Charles Klein's *The Music Master* at the Knickerbocker Theatre.

From Grace Hart Crane

Chicago
Jan 3—1916 [1]

ALS, 5 pp.
LETTERHEAD: Congress Hotel and Annex, Chicago

My dear Harold:—

You will never know how happy your letters which came to me today, made me. Molly & I arrived here Sunday noon, & grandma had *as usual* neglected to write me a word—or send any kind of message—altho I have had Molly write her & had wired her twice. Consequently I was very unhappy not having heard from any one— Your letters were a joy & I am so glad you are there & happy.

Have just had a conversation with Mrs Moody over phone & given her your address. You will very probably hear from her soon. Tagore [2] has been ill & I imagine she has had plenty on her mind. She is being urged by them to go to California with them & on account of the meeting being called off for which she was going to New York you may not see her just now. She will probably write you about it. She hopes to run in to see me here at the hotel tomorrow noon.

I find I can stand very little but getting away from home was the only thing for me now—

I find visiting uses me up—so I am just taking things to suit my strength here. Molly is a treasure—

Today Stella [3] gave a luncheon at the Blackstone for her oldest son who is in the Cornell Glee Club which sings here tonight. It was a very beautiful affair & I was able to go & enjoy it. The guests

---

[1] Misdated. Actually 1917.

[2] On an introduction from Mrs. William Vaughn Moody, Crane met Rabindranath Tagore briefly when the Indian poet and novelist visited Cleveland in 1916.

[3] Mrs. Stella Jannotta, a friend of the Rosses from Chicago. Her oldest son was Alfred Vernon Jannotta, who was then a senior at Cornell. Jannotta served in both world wars, won the Navy Cross and the Silver Star for gallantry, and was promoted to the rank of admiral.

were made up of [4] the young boys & girls & a few older folks in which class I suppose I belong.

Yes you will love New York any way for a while & I believe always & during the coming year I will try to arrange my plans so that I can come there & have a little home, even if a modest one & you can be happy & so shall I. But remember I shall expect by next fall that you will be ready to prepare for college. You never will be sorry. It will be time well spent & you will never regret it.

Now I will change my dress for dinner & then go to the Glee Club concert with the Ross's & Janottas. You & I are both very fortunate in having some fine friends & the best of all is that they chose us rather than our having to seek them.

Keep your body & mind clean & you will get there I'm sure. Write me here until I wire you not to & remember me most kindly to Carl. Write me often.

From Your Dearest / Grace.

From Clarence Arthur Crane

[Cleveland]
January 3rd, 1916.[1]

TLC, 1 p.

Mr. Harold Crane
308 E. 15th Street
New York, N.Y.

My dear Harold:

Ervin and Mildred [2] are leaving Lima tomorrow night, and will be in New York Friday morning. I think they will be at the office the greater part of a week and I want you to see Ervin and talk with him all you can, conveniently.

I had a letter from Molly today saying that Grace had been out

---

[4] The word "of" is repeated in the text.

[1] Misdated. Actually 1917.
[2] Erwin and Mildred Shoot of Cleveland. Mr. Shoot was the chief chocolate maker in Mr. Crane's company.

to Frank's [3] and was feeling fairly comfortable, but hadn't as yet made up her mind to go out there for any permanent stay.

There is nothing new here, for during Ervin's absence, I shall be in Cleveland all of the time. I sent your telegrams and letter on to Chicago, but they will be a day late in getting to her, because I sent them to Blanche.[4]

With much love,

To Clarence Arthur Crane

308 E. 15 St. N.Y.C.
Jan. 5, 1917

TLS, 2 pp.

My dear father;—

Your letter informing me of the arrival of Mildred and Erwin, has just come; and I shall go up town this afternoon to see them. It does me a great deal of good to hear from you often, and I hope you will continue to write me as often as you have lately done. While I am not home-sick, I yet am far from comfortable without letters, and often, from you.

Nearly every evening since my advent, has been spent in the companionship of Carl. Last night we unpacked some furniture of his which had arrived from his home, and afterward talked until twelve, or after, behind our pipes. He has some very splendid ideas about artistic, and phsychic balance, analysis, etc. I realize more entirely every day, that I am preparing for a fine life: that I have powers, which, if correctly balanced, will enable me to mount to extraordinary latitudes. There is constantly an inward struggle, but the time to worry is only when ther is no inward debate, and consequently there is smooth sliding to the devil. There is only one harmony, that is the equelibrium maintained by two opposite forces, equally strong. When I perceive one emotion growing overpowering to a fact, or statement of reason, than the only manly, worthy, sensi-

---

[3] Frank Ross.
[4] Blanche Ross.

ble thing to do, is to build up the logical side, and attain balance, and in art,—formal expression.

I intend this week to begin my studying,—Latin, German, and philosophy, right here in my room. They will balance my emotional nature, and lead me to more exact expression.

I have had only one letter from Mother, so far, but I hear from Grandma, this morning, that she is in Chicago and fee [l]ing much better.

Hazel has been fine to me, tho I haven't seen her often, as she has been out nearly every time I have been into the office. Miss Bohn, tho, is a dandy, and I have enjoyed talking to her. She has a very sweet way, sincere, and earnest way.

I do most of my bathing and dumping over at Carl's, as these rooming-house privys, and bath-tubs are frightful. Sometime later I expect to be able to afford a small bath-room of my own. Bedbugs, too, have been an awful trial; but never you fear, I am having some fine experiences. In spite of all, tho, I insist on a fair amount of bodily cleanliness for health. Bun-shop food has really made me quite magnificent and fat.

Love always from sonny,/ Harold

To Grace Hart Crane

308 E. 15 St. N.Y.C.
Jan. 5, 1917

TLS, 1 p.

My dear Mother;

Today has been both rainy and busy, that is, "busy" in the most pleasant sense of the word. This afternoon I made a call on Padraic Colum, whom I mentioned to you before. We shall be great friends, I think, and he has asked me to call again on next Monday afternoon. In the conversation I found that he is a great friend of Mrs. Moody, so that added a great interest in our acquaintanceship. Also I was much pleased, on mentioning her name, to hear him quote some lines of my verse, which she had evidently shown him, and which he seemed to think excellent.

Carl and I dine together nearly every night. Then afterward spend the evening in esthetic talk. I bathe over at his room, as the bath-rooms in the boarding-house are a nightmare, they are so filthy. Today I went over to see Jerome Blum, and stayed for tea with his wife and a cock-eyed lady, who was evedently a friend of Mrs. Blum, and whose sole expression of admiration for any of his pictures was, "this has feeling". Carl said no wonder: every cock-eyed person feels every time he sees; therin is the pain.

Write me often, and send as much love as I am sending you./ Harold

From Grace Hart Crane

CHICAGO ILLS
JAN 6 [1917?]

TELEGRAM

MOLLIE AND I RETURNING TO CLEVELAND TONIGHT IN ORDER THAT GRANDMOTHER AND I MAY LEAVE FOR PALMBEACH TO ATTEND SKIFF GOLDEN WEDDING [1] ON JANY TWENTY THIRD. HAD FINE CALL FROM MRS MOODY TODAY YOU WILL SEE HER SOON FEELING BETTER AND HAPPY AS POSSIBLE LOVE./ GRACE

To Elizabeth Belden Hart

139 E 15 St, N.Y.C.
Jan. 7, 1917

TLS, 2 pp.

Dear Grandma;

Yes, please do send my magazines on to me, as I have a year-subscription to them which is as yet only about half finished.

---

[1] This was the wedding anniversary of Mary Frances and William Vernon Skiff, whose son, Frank Vernon Skiff, of Chicago, owned the Jewel Tea Company with his brother-in-law Frank Ross. Frank Skiff had an estate at Palm Beach, Florida.

Mr Sullivan [1] wrote me a splendid letter, which I read this morning along with yours. Also one from Alice Calhoun, and one from Father. My friends have all been so very considerate in writing me, that I can not appreciate it enough.

Yesterday Mother's night-letter reached me, and I want to tell you how much I am happy, that you both are going to Florida to enjoy the Skiff's and Ross's company.

Miss Hashem entertained me along with The Shoots yesterday with a long ride all over the city in her machine, and afterwards with a dinner in her apartments. Mrs. Shoot will be over to call on you and Mother as soon as she returns, as I asked her to do, and she will tell you all about me.

Things are proggressing splendidly; I am striking up a real friendship with Padraic Colum, who is really enthusiastic about my work, and whose wife is a dear, red-haired, cultured Irish-woman. Also, there is Alfred Kreymborg, and William Carlos Williams who accepted my work,[2] to see yet, so you see that by the time you arrive in New York, I shall have quite a bunch of splendid people for you to meet.

I dont know whether I told you in the last letter or not, but my intention is to go right on studying and working at my poetry, and next autumn to enter in for a special course at Columbia. At this age there is no necessity to drudge, when so much awaits me in the future. I live cheaply, and furthermore wish to do so. You know my demands are not much anyway.

Zell comes tomorrow, and I shall devote a few days to her, as Carl is at present, very busy on some potboiling.

We have some marvelous talks, and are a mutual benifit to each other. As you must see, everything is optimistic.

Love to you, Mother, and Molly, who is one of the few.

Sonny,/ Harold

[1] John J. Sullivan, the Cranes' lawyer.
[2] Alfred Kreymborg, the founder of the little magazine *Others,* and William Carlos Williams, one of the magazine's editors, had provisionally accepted several poems. However, these were never published.

Mrs. Crane went to Florida with the Rosses (as well as the Jannottas). In the meantime Harold became so caught up with his frenetic life in New York that he neglected to write his parents as frequently as they wished. Perhaps one reason for not corresponding was his minor disagreement with Carl Schmitt. Continually bothered by his young friend, who would often spend the entire day at his studio, the artist resorted to locking the door and pretending to be out. When Harold learned of Schmitt's action he was deeply hurt, and afterward his ties with Schmitt were never as strong as they had been during the first two weeks of 1917.

From Clarence Arthur Crane

[Cleveland]
January 17, 1917.

TLC, 1 p.

My dear Harold:

Father hasn't had a communication from you for two weeks. At that time you wrote me you were changing your room, so I didn't want to send any letters to your former address.

Don't you think it is about time to write me a letter and tell me what you are accomplishing, and how you are getting along?

There is nothing new here, and I presume that mother writes you frequently.

With much love, I am

Mr. Harold Crane,
#18 W. 33rd Street,
New York, N.Y.

From Grace Hart Crane

CLEVELAND O
1917 JAN 17 AM

TELEGRAM

YOUR LETTER TO GRANDMOTHER RECEIVED TODAY AM TOO
BUSY TO WRITE BUT AM HAPPY TO KNOW YOU ARE HAPPY HAD
A NICE CALL IRWIN AND MILDRED [1] LEAVING HERE THE NIGHT
OF THE NINETEENTH ADDRESS US HOTEL ROYAL PONCRANNA [2]
LOVE / GRACE.

From Grace Hart Crane

[Cleveland]
Friday—Jan—19—'17

ALS, 5 pp.

Dearest:—

Our trunks have just gone & the house & we look just as we always do after preparations for leaving for the south— I am about
dead & so is grandmother but I am so thankful we a[re] leaving
Molly to close up the house—

Your father is going away somewhere soon from what he said to
me over the phone & soon you will be almost a real orphan. The
old home looks lonesome enough now & I am anxious to arrange
my affairs to go east to live with you or near where you will be
going to school. You must not give up the college plan for a minute. You know I shall never give in on that for I firmly believe you
will regret it having passed it up, if you do—

So much to be done has nearly finished me—but when I get on
the train I shall know as before I can do no more & shall settle
down to rest. Harold perhaps it will be a satisfaction to you [to]
know that I am really happy & that my dear son has with his own

---

[1] Erwin and Mildred Shoot.
[2] Actually the Royal Poinciana, a large Flagler hotel at Palm Beach.

courage & philosophy done almost all there was to do to bring me to that state of mind.

You in my trouble, have been able to pay me for all the care & anxiety I have had for you since you came to me nearly eighteen years ago— I am expecting great things of you & when we see each other again we can talk over our plans which look very beautiful to me now.

I am asking you to send me your love every day as I shall you— Write me often at the Royal Poinciana. I shall think of you on the night of the 23rd when the three Jannotta boys from Cornell & Verna & Mildred Ross [1] are there & shall be saying to myself— How much I wish you all could see *my* boy— If we dance my partner will not be there—but I shall dance & be happy thinking of how rich I am in having you—

Love by the bushel / from / Grace—

From Clarence Arthur Crane

[Cleveland]
January 20th, 1917.

TLC, 3 pp.

My dear son Harold:

Your letter of yesterday comes in on the last mail this afternoon.

It is a peculiar one to answer, for you are supersensitive, and have not construed my previous letters in any such light as I intended them. In asking me how I was pleased with your progress, do you realize that for over two weeks I did not receive a single communication from you, nor have you indicated to me in any way or manner that you had made any progress, or come to any conclusions. How was I to comment on something which I knew nothing about? You may have written these things to your mother, but I have not had access to the letters, and if Zell has come and gone I have heard nothing from her; so you see I am absolutely in the dark as to what you [r] intentions or accomplishments have been.

[1] The daughters of Frank and Blanche Ross.

When you left here it was your avowed intention to get something to do in New York, preferably on a magazine, and I told you to take plenty of time in doing that, and it would not matter if it took several weeks. From this letter today I should judge that you did not intend to do anything of that kind, but was going to study your regular school books, and live in New York.

Zell wrote me that she wanted you to room with Carl, and wanted me to pay for a studio so that he could afford to give up half of his room to you. I declined to answer this, and am glad now that I did not give her an answer, for you tell me that you do not want to live with Carl.

The conditions at home, I quite agree with you, have been anything but condusive to good work or peace of mind, and it is all right for you to stay in New York for a while, and get an experience there, but I do not think it is the right place for you to stay until next fall, provided you are not employed. This arrangement will do for a while, but if you are simply going to study your text books, there are certainly better places for you to do [1] [this] than in the metropolis, and I have never heard of any one going there to remain and for that purpose.

You do not have to make plans for your maintenance or come to any understandings after you have obtained the age of 20. If you had followed my desires, you would plan on a splendid college career, the better to prepare yourself for what I think you are perhaps best adapted to. I scarcely [know] how you can gain the result desired unless you do have that college education.

My present suggestion to you is that you remain on in New York for a few weeks longer, until you have digested some of the things which you wish to, and then crystalize on something which will employ your time from then up until about July 1st.

How would you like to go to Culvert [2] or some military school this summer, where you would get a liberal amount of outdoor exercise, as well as some book work, and perhaps prepare yourself to enter college or some preparatory school this fall?

I have no other interest in life than to see you map out your ca-

[1] The word "do" is repeated twice in the text.
[2] Culver Military Academy, Culver, Indiana.

reer along good and consistent lines, and I am hoping to be of great benefit in aiding you to bring about this condition of affairs, but you must not expect your father to sense your ideas without being told what they are.

The store and its tribulations are going to keep me here in Cleveland until about the 20th of February, with perhaps a side trip or two to Chicago and Kansas City, then after things have assumed a normal basis, I hope to go out West and make myself useful in visiting the trade, and incidentally get a vacation out of it myself. I have no intention of coming to New York, and if I am going away for a protracted time, and you want my advise on anything, I will have you come on here about the 15th of February, and we can talk things over.

I do not want you to imagine that you read between the lines of my letters any dissatisfaction, for I will express openly anything which I want you to know or feel. Your going to New York was your own idea, and it came at a time when I did not want to make myself prominent in the matter of giving you advice. I felt that for you to get away for a little while was really the best thing, and as New York was your choice, it was satisfactory to me.

I do not mean to convey the idea that I think you extravagant. I only think that you should have a certain allowance, and should live within that. I haven't told you how much it should be but I did ask you how much you thought it should be. If you were working for a stated salary, you would expect to live within that salary, and so long as I am living and fairly prosperous, you can have an allowance which will be adequate for your needs.

I am sorry to learn that you are growing tired of Carl. You know I never talked with him more than five minutes myself. I only know what conditions he has to contend with, and these conditions are, I should judge, about the same as most artists and writers have to combat. He has to make a living, and live within his income.

Now Harold, suppose you sit down and write me just what you hope to accomplish by being in New York, what you are accomplishing, and if you have any idea how long you want to stay there, —under present circumstances, etc., then I will get a much better idea of your views and perhaps can write you more intelligently.

I am enclosing herewith my check for $25.00 which I know you will need by the time it reached you, and I do not want you to doubt your father's sincerity, or his undying interest in your present and future wellfare.

Lovingly,

From Grace Hart Crane

PALM BEACH FLO
JANY 22 [1917?]

TELEGRAM

MOTHER AND I ARRIVED HERE THIS MORNING WAS SO DISAPPOINTED NOT TO FIND A LETTER FROM YOU HERE DO WRITE ME SOON I AM THINKING OF THE LAST TIME YOU AND I WERE HERE HOPE YOU ARE WELL AND HAPPY WEATHER HERE JUST LIKE SUMMER LOVE / GRACE

[Below the message Crane wrote in pencil the following figures, which were probably his expenses for the week:]

        $ 2
          5
        2.50
        2.50
        1.25
        1.50
        1.25
        1.75
         .50
        4.00
        4.00
         .50
        ─────
       $28.00

       30.000

To Grace Hart Crane and Elizabeth Belden Hart

139 E. 15th St. N.Y.C.
Jan. 26, 1917

TLS, 2 pp.

Dear Mother and Grandma:—

Your communications, so far, have ended with the telegram dated
the twenty-second. I am sorry that letter did not reach you on your
arrival, I thought it would. I have not been too busy to write, but
thought you might be tiring a little of the continual state of exuber-
ance I am in, and all the letters seem alike. Today I have been over
at Carl's studio, for the most part, chaperoning a girl who is sitting
as a model for him, and I havent been able to accomplish much of
anything. Molly's smock left the day before yesterday, and I sent it
c/o of Crane's Store. That was right, wasn't it?

Earl Biggers, [1] the author of "Seven Keys to Bald Pate" was in for
some grub, and I was shocked nearly off my feet by the quietness
and un-worldliness of his behaviour. He is a fine fellow however. I
hear only pessimistic lines from Father, and hear from Erwin [2] (via,
rather) that he is very unwell. The travel that he is planning, will
straighten him out into better shape. We all needed to get away
awhile.

I wouldn't be at all surprised to see Sullivan [3] drop in any day,
for his letters intimate such. He will be darn welcome, I can assure
you, and promise you also that we shall have some fine times. You
heard, I suppose, that I sent him a choice volume of Irish songs
auto graphed by one of the principle literary figures in America
today, Padraic Colum. I have invited Colum and his wife to dine
with me tomorrow night at Gonfarones, an Italien eating-place,
where the table d'hote costs only 60 cents per plate, and where the
food is fine. Colum says I should have a volume of verse out in two

[1] Earl Derr Biggers (1884–1933), the novelist and author of the Charlie Chan
detective stories. *Seven Keys to Baldpate* had been published in New York in
1913. Biggers was from Warren, Ohio, and was a friend of Carl Schmitt's.
[2] Erwin Shoot.
[3] John J. Sullivan, the Cranes' lawyer.

years without any difficulty, and has offered to write a preface for it also. He has seen, as I said before, all my work,—nearly all, and admires it.

Every day I do my studying, and read a good bit also. The room I have been occupying has been too dark, and I shall change lodgings as soon as is possible. Friends of Carl have asked me out to dinners several times, and I have enjoyed as much of social life as I have ever cared for. When you move here, there is a fine bunch of friends waiting for you. O this is the place to live, at least for nine months of the year.

I want you to know that I do not forget you, and anticipate a fine little, cosy home, with you both sitting there enjoying life next winter. I would give much to have you with me for supper tonight, and I know you feel the same. I cant possibly write all I am thinking in one letter, so will have to let some of it season until the next letter.

Love,— Harold

From Clarence Arthur Crane

[Cleveland]
January 29th, 1917.

TLC, 2 pp.

My dear Harold:

Your letter came this morning, and I was quite disappointed that I did not hear from you Sunday. When you know a letter should reach me Sunday, always send it to the Club, and put on a special delivery.

This last one seems in a better tone, and I am glad to hear you say what you do about Carl. He is struggling for an existence and I would think you were very foolish not to make every effort to like him and especially appreciate his position. You are often a victim of moods, and sometimes they lead us to depths that are hard to understand when they have passed away.

I seem to be afflicted with a very severe cold this morning, and after a few letters are dictated I am going back to the Club and spend most of the time in my room.

Yesterday we had much to do. The down town store looks like a mess of ruins. We worked there all day yesterday with a gang of men getting out the floral equipment, and I question if any one will be able to eat there with pleasure for a few days at least. When you come home you will find the store very much changed. Perhaps it won't be any more beautiful but we are getting rid of a condition which has cost me several thousand dollars this year. Even more than I care to mention. If the store continues to lose from now on, we will be able to know exactly where the trouble lies, and perhaps correct it.

Business in the factory has been fairly good, although we never looked for much in January or February, for people are tired of sweets at Christmas.

You haven't written me about your expenses. I sent you a check for $25.00 last week. Now you must get this matter settled so that I can know of what you are in need of, and then you can live within your allowance and not have much to think of in that particular.

I am still in Cleveland and cannot as yet set any date for my leaving, and when I do go, it will not be for an extended trip, for there seems to be so many things here which I want to give my personal attention.

Just now we are having a regular blizzard. Every one has colds, and I haven't escaped. For some reason or other I could not cease coughing last night and did not close my eyes until after three o'clock.

Now write me some good long letters, and tell me what you are doing, and do not be unmindful of the fact that Carl is unquestionable sacrificing much of his time and concentration to be company and of service to you. I do not know him personally, but I know that both your mother and Zell think that he is an A-1 fellow.

With much love, I am / Yours / Father.

From Grace Hart Crane

Palm Beach, Fla.
Jan 30—1917

ALS, 11 pp.
LETTERHEAD: Hotel Royal Poinciana, Palm Beach, Florida

My dear Harold:—

I have never done any letter writing under such disadvantages as here— It is almost impossible to snatch a monent to write to any one—so much to see hear & do and one feels extravagant to miss any of the attractions that are here when it costs so much to stay at the hotel which provides them.

Today we went in the Skiff launch up Lake Worth to the oyster beds and ate fresh raw oysters together with our picnic lunch which we had brought with us. In order to do this we missed our morning dip in the ocean which is the biggest attraction here to me. Every morning we go in at eleven & such fun— It recalls our stay at Rye Beach [1] only I have had as yet no trouble with my toe. I have a jersey suit & a black satin hat lined with orange— I wish you might see me my dear, for I have some very pretty sport clothes & this is the place where one has to have them. Do you remember the beautiful ride to the Garden of Eden? We are *very* fortunate to be here with the Skiff's, as they do a lot for us. Last night was the annual hotel Cake Walk given in the dining room after dinner by the real "coons". All of the swells were there & two orchestra's playing. How I did wish that you could have seen those darkies parade & dance back and forth down through that long room. They were GREAT & I could hardly restrain myself from getting up & joining them. They *loved* it!! Everynight there is a dance in the ballroom—& an afternoon tea dansant at 5 oclock in Cocoanut Grove which is the lovliest spot imaginable. When the Jannotta boys were here we went to all the dances & I had my turn with each one of them. How I did wish for you. They are fine boys & I am sure you would like them. Two of them are at Cornell & I gave Vernon the oldest one your

[1] Harold and his mother had stayed with family friends at Rye Beach, New York, in the summer of 1914.

address so that he might look you up when he goes to New York, which may be soon. This June he graduates.

Grandma has been ill most of the time since arriving. First with a severe cold & afterwards with a bilious attack. These kept her in bed some days & made it hard & confining for me. The truth of the matter is we were both about dead from overwork & worry when we arrived. I am just beginning to feel a little bit natural.

Florida resorts, & especially Palm Beach are simply packed with tourists this winter. I made a two weeks reservation here thinking if I liked it I could stay as long as I wished. But they just laughed at me & all I have been able to do is to get an extention of one week which brings it up to Feb 18th. So you may see me in New York soon after that—unless I am called back to Cleveland, or something unforseen turns up.

I might consider going to the Isle of Pines but grandmother is not well enough for me to leave behind or take with me. She has failed a great deal lately but still insists that she is in the ring. It has not yet been decided what she will do when she leaves here— She may go back to Cleveland & stay with Mrs Kirk, & she may go to Winter Haven where Marthena Evans is.[2] It is very hard for her to decide.

Stella Jannotta is much interested in you. I have read her your two letters, & you know she is a great student of literature & philosophy. She may come to New York with me from here. She has asked me to tell you to read Shopenhauer's Essay on "Style" which she thinks is in his book of Essays.

Your letters show much improvement in diction & style & I congratulate you. I am anxious to know more of what you are doing & HOW you are working—hoping that your study of German & Latin is being done under conditions that will count as credits for you next fall when you enter college— I trust you are going about that in a systematic way so that your winter will have counted for a place for you in school— There are many questions I should like to ask you but will not now— Only tell me all about yourself when you write again which I trust will be soon & often.

[2] Mrs. Frank Martin Kirk and Marthena Evans were friends of Mrs. Hart's from Cleveland.

Carl wrote me a fine letter which I did enjoy & appreciate. Will answer before long. How he would enjoy this scenery— Some day if we still own the home on the Isle of Pines we will invite him down to paint, & you can do some writing.

Had my first letter from Molly today and she mentioned having received the Smock, liking it & said it was a good fit.

Your father sent me your letter to him. I thought it was a fine one & remember always to write him just as good ones. Who knows but what our separation is as much of a tragedy to him as to me. We have both suffered much & perhaps have some sorrow yet to overcome. You have not yet told me where he was going. Several have mentioned he was going to travel but I do not know whether for business or pleasure.

On my way down here I lost my wrist watch— Wasn't that a shame. I missed it after leaving the train at Jacksonville & I could not have lost anything that I am more conscious of than that. I wrote your father about it because the porter on our train said he knew him & I thought he might find it in my berth & turn it in, but your father said he had not received it nor any word concerning it.

I notice what you say about expecting Mr Sullivan in New York soon. Hope he will be there & you will have a good time. In fact I know you will— Have not heard from him since I left but expect that he is working on my case & may hear any day when to appear in Cleveland.[3] Would you like to have me come to New York for a week or two before returning to Cleveland? Now I must stop & write Molly & John [4] & maybe a few others—

Yours with deepest love—/ Grace—

Love to Carl—

[3] This is a reference to the Cranes' divorce, which was being arranged by John J. Sullivan.
[4] Probably John Lloyd, a handyman who worked for Mrs. Crane.

To Grace Hart Crane

308 E. 15th St. N.Y.C
Feb. 1, 1917

TLS, 1 p.

My dear Mother;—

Grandmother's good letter came yesterday, and I am glad to find my expectations fulfilled, that you are having a fine time. Alfred Jannotta, I forgot to mention in my last letter, called, and found me out. Of this I am very sorry, as I have wanted to meet him for a long time.

Next week I shall change my room. I don't know now just where it will be: but I do know that I am tired of filthy closets, poor light, and the coldness of the present room I have.

David Page and Harold Thomas [1] of Warren have become good friends of mine. They at present are working in a Wall Street brokerage firm for the wages of nine dollars per week. Page seems to man [age] to really hobnob with the Astors, and Whitneys etc. on that wage, so you see what a lot you can do in New York on a little (?) They are both serving their apprenticeships now on Wall Street, but expect in time to be more in the partnership section.

Mrs. Moody gave a fine dinner, and I can't tell you how many distinguished people were there. Then there was music in the evening up at Mr. Moody's old apartment on Washington Square, and Mr. Colum read from his last book. Mrs. Moody left hurriedly, as usual, yestserday morning.

Well good-bye for now,/ Harold

---

[1] David Paige, now deceased, later became a partner in the Paige and Burns insurance agency in Warren. For Harold Thomas, see letter of January 2, 1917.

From Clarence Arthur Crane

[Cleveland]
February 2nd, 1917.

TL, fragment

Mr. Harold Crane,
139 E. 15th Street,
New York, N.Y.

My dear Harold:

I am sending this out to you special delivery so that you will have a letter over Sunday. Your mother wrote me yesterday that she had received only one letter from you since she arrived at Palm Beach, and you must be careful to write her often and she misses you and I know has much to contend with in the matter of her own trials and tribulations. I would arrange to write her at least twice a week always, and make her feel that you are just as interested in her as you always have been, and are not unmindful of the fact that she is going through one of the hardest trials of her life.

You haven't answered any of my questions yet, and as long as you have no stated occupation, it seems to me that you could let me know what you are doing, who you are meeting, and instead of inquiring if I am satisfied with your progress, tell me what your progress really is.

I had a talk with Zell a few days ago and she would like to have you come to Warren and work on the Tribune any time you see fit. She thinks it much better for you to do that than to be in New York without occupation. You can think this over, and if you think you would be gaining anything in the newspaper world by doing this, you might try it.

Your mother's letter yesterday tells me she is going to New York from Palm Beach to see you. It is just about as near that way home, and I hope she will do it, then perhaps you and she can come to an understanding.

From Grace Hart Crane

Palm Beach, Fla.
Feb 4—1917.

ALS, 8 pp.
LETTERHEAD: Hotel Royal Poinciana, Palm Beach, Florida

My dear Harold:—

Have just returned from a long walk and am now going to answer your last letter which was truely short but sweet. I do not
blame you for not writing me long letters when Mrs Moody is there
but I do expect to hear all about it when I see you. For I am coming to New York before very long and then we can talk a lot of
things over. Stella Jannotta may come with me and stay a few days
before she goes to Ithaca to see her boys. Grandma will leave us at
Washington and go on to Cleveland and get Molly to help her
open up the house. Our plans have changed many times since we
left home and I feel now very uncertain as to just when we will
leave here. The War News this morning has stirred everyone up
and as this is the most fashionable resort & consequently many
moneyed people here, there is much excitement & concern. I feel as
if I were out of touch with everything & everybody here and would
be happier to be somewhere where it would be possible for me to
get home over night if necessary—

For the past three days we have had the most terrible weather—
so cold that all the shrubery froze & the only place that one could
be really comfortable was in bed. It came right in the heighth of
the season when the richest were arriving from New York & the big
cities & on top of that the War situation so that there has been
plenty to make one feel subdued— They tell me that 40% of Wall
Street stocks was manipulated from here, so that shows who's here.

You and I will have to have some serious talks about our plans for
the future when I see you. For it is my earnest desire now to arrange things in Cleveland so that by next fall at the farthest I may
join you in New York. In the midst of your enjoyment & entheu-
siasm of your new enviroment, I don't want you to be entirely un-

mindful that you have a duty to me as well as I have toward you. After nineteen years of married life I am obliged to admit that it spells *"Failure"* for your father and me. For him it does not mean *all* because his business has been his profession, but for me it means all but you, for marriage has been my profession. Most of the time I am optimistic about my future because it lies with you I *hope,* but once in a while I must confess I loose hold of myself and let me tell you my dear boy that those hours are real agony. Not that I wish to return to your father nor do I regret the step I have taken, but rebellion, resentment, malice etc for the manner in which I have been treated, come forth for me to fight back, about every so often, no matter how hard I try to keep them out of my consciousness. Being physically weak makes it the harder for me to fight these moods. Health is such a wonderful thing & in that I am most bankrupt. So I am asking you to write me often Harold because your letters even though short are a stimulus to me, & surely you love me enough to do what you can to help me fight my way back to peace, happiness & health—

Your father's provision for me has been very small everything considered.[1] Every one says that but he refuses to do more & so if he is content to send me away after nearly twenty years of service, I say Amen— I will manage some way—& if I can only get strong I can

---

[1] The Cranes agreed to the following divorce settlement: "the husband shall and will pay to the wife the sum of Twenty Thousand Four Hundred Dollars ($20,400.00) cash, as follows: the sum of Twenty Four Hundred dollars ($2,400) in installments of Two Hundred Dollars ($200) each, payable on the 1st day of each month of the year 1917, commencing January 1, 1917, and ending December 31st, 1917, inclusive. The sum of Three Thousand Six Hundred Dollars ($3,600) in installments of Three Hundred Dollars ($300) each, payable on the 1st day of each month of the year 1918, commencing January 1st, 1918, and ending December 31st, 1918, inclusive. The sum of Four Thousand Eight Hundred Dollars, ($4,800.00) in installments of Four Hundred Dollars ($400.00) each, payable on the 1st day of each month of the year 1919, commencing January 1st, 1919, and ending December 31st, 1919, inclusive. The sum of Four Thousand Eight Hundred Dollars ($4,800.00) in installments of Four Hundred Dollars ($400.00) each, payable on the 1st day of each month of the year 1920, commencing January 1st, 1920, and ending December 31st, 1920, inclusive. The sum of Four Thousand Eight Hundred ($4,800.00) in installments of Four Hundred Dollars, ($400.00) each, payable on the 1st day of each month of the year 1921, commencing January 1st, 1921, and ending December 31st, 1921, inclusive, making in all, as aforesaid, the sum of Twenty Thousand Four Hundred Dollars ($20,400.00). In addition to the foregoing, the said husband shall maintain, support,

work & he is welcome to his money & all it may bring him. For awhile I shall have to spend money & take life easy—for the effects of my operation & all that followed, are manifesting themselves now more & more.

Now no more of this—only one thing more— Do not allow yourself to become & egotist & undmindful of others— But just remember that true happiness is largely due to service & no matter how rich your day may have been in opportunities, it is not entirely complete unless you have done or thought of some one else— Please write me often—you have no idea how much you help me in so doing— We are planning to leave here the thirteenth stop a few days in Washington and then I am coming to see you & I want you to be glad to see me. It has been so long since anyone has been *glad* to see me—

Love to Carl always—

As Ever / Devotedly / Grace—

Mrs. Crane's plans changed from those she had outlined in her letter of February 4. On February 17 she returned directly to Cleveland to see John J. Sullivan about the divorce proceedings, a Dr. Lyttle about her recent operation, and the bankers at the Guardian Trust Company about the Hart property on the Isle of Pines and any problems that might arise in connection with the political unrest in Cuba. Cuba and the island were often in a state of turmoil, this time because of a rebellion over Cuban government frauds. Grace had good cause for concern, as the island's political status had been uncertain since the Spanish-American War. Though it was agreed in 1904 that the United States should cede the Isle of Pines to Cuba, special interest groups were successful in delaying

---

and clothe their said son Harold Crane, until he is of age, whether said son shall reside with his mother during the years of his minority or any part thereof, or elsewhere and shall give to said son the priveleges of a full college education and pay all legitimate and necessary expenses therefor, and during any time in the minority of the said son that he shall be or reside with his said mother, the board and lodging expenses of said son, shall be paid to said mother in behalf of said boy."

ratification of the treaty until 1925. As a result, neither government exercised any absolute control over the territory. While she was attending to these matters and recovering from a severe cold, Grace planned for a reunion with her son in New York.

Meanwhile, Clarence had embarked on a business and vacation trip to California. From mid-February until late March, Harold and his father probably did not correspond.

To Grace Hart Crane

54 W. 10 St. N.Y.C.[1]
Feb. 19, 1917

TLS, 2 pp.

My dear, dear Mother;—

I am supposing that this will find you at home by several days, and hoping that you will not remain there very long, but come and see your anxious son as soon as you can.

Last night I took dinner with Harold Thomas and Carl in an Italien restaurant where you have to speak Italien to get anything at all to eat. They cook everything in olive-oil so that one has a good cathartic with his meal besides a splendid gratification of the palate. And this morning, it being Sunday, I took a long ride on an omnibus out into the Bronx and back, and saw all the fashion on Fifth Ave. When you see the display of wealth and beauty here, it will make you crawl. It is the most gorgeous city imaginable, besides being at present the richest and most active place in the world. The swarms of humanity of all classes inspire the most diverse of feelings; envy, hate, admiration and repulsion. But truly it is *the* place to live.

---

[1] This date is suspect. In the sixth paragraph Harold writes that he will attend the private opening of the exhibition of William Merritt Chase's paintings on the following day. The show opened on February 19 at the Metropolitan Museum; therefore Harold very likely wrote this letter on February 18.

Am so anxious to have you settle here, and I know you will be happy.

I am very sorry that I didn't get the chance to see Mr. Sullivan when he was here. He probably did not have the time to search me out, but secretly, I don't think he expended any extra effort.

The Rosses must have been very kind to you and Grandma, and someday I hope to thank them in some degree at least. People here have surely treated me splendidly; Mrs. Moody, Carl, the Colum's, and last but not least, the Lords,[2] people you have yet to meet in order to become fully convinced.

I wish above all other things that you could be here this week, for there are s[e]veral Big things that I have been invited to. The enitial exhibition of the choicest of Chase's pictures is to be privately (by invitation) opened tomorrow afternoon from four until six. The greatest painters of the day will attend. Carl having given me his invitation, I am going to take Mr. Colum and perhaps his wife. Then Mr. Colum has given me a ticket to the reading by Vachel Lindsay of his own poems at the Princess Theater. Also, on Thursday, I shall attend the meeting of the Poetry Society of America, which is quite exclusive. By the way, Mr. Colum intends to suggest me for membership.[3]

But then, when you do come, there will be hosts of other things to do, as no one in New York is ever without some new place to go, or some event to witness. If you want a quiet time that can be easily had too; and I am not making any definite plans for you, as I want you to be unencumbered by any engagements during your stay. It will be enough to me to talk quietly with you, and have you with me. I am inquiring about schools etc. and we can also discuss that definitly when you arrive. N.Y. is overflowing, so let me reserve rooms for you ahead.

Loads of love to you and Grandma, who has been very kind in her writing, and whom I hope to see soon.—/ Harold

[2] The Lords were the parents of Gertrude Lord, who later married Carl Schmitt.

[3] According to the late Gustav Davidson, executive secretary of the Poetry Society of America, Crane never belonged to the society.

From Grace Hart Crane

1709—E—115 St—
Cleveland, Ohio
Feb—19—1917.

ALS, 7 pp.

My dear Harold:—

By the above address you will see I am once more back in the old home. Grandmother and I arrived Saturday morning three hours late, after a tedious tiresome journey and found Molly (bless her heart!) at the station to meet us. She is the only beau we have now & first plays the part of cook & housekeeper, & next that of escort. I came home a few days before I had intendend because of the news of the Cuban uprising and wanted to see the Guardian people in regards to any difficulties which might develop on the Isle of Pines. I have not been down to see them yet but will tomorrow if I am able, having developed a very severe cold. This annoys me very much because it is principally in my nose & I have had to use the hankerchief so frequently that said nose is as red as a ripe tomatoe.

It was very disappointing to me and I am sure to you to have the knowledge that Mr Sullivan was in New York the other day and missed seeing you. He told me about it over the phone when I got home & said he was in N.Y. only a few hours, very busy—but made a strenuous attempt to see you but did not succeed. He left here on a half hours notice, & had to be back the following morning to try an important case— He will probably drop in upon you sometime when you least expect it, for I observe he has little time to plan trips & just leaves on a moments notice. I have some things to consult him about also Dr Lyttle as I am having trouble with the place where I was operated upon & he is fearful of an adhesion. I have suffered a good deal of discomfort & he wishes to make an examination. If every thing is all right, after I get a little rested I am coming on to New York for a while—and it may be that Zell may come to—altho' you know she is at all times an uncertain quantity. She is coming up to Cleveland some day this week and we are going to talk over our plans. I shall ask you in time when I decide to come

to New York to secure a good room for me a [t] some good hotel—
as I must be absolutely comfortable & have a large part of my
mornings undisturbed for a while. I am very uneasy & cannot
promise you how long I will stay—but if I find I am happy there
may make you quite a visit and you & I have many things to discuss
and some to settle. You have written me so little about *yourself* that
I can hardly realize I have a boy—

Molly had the house all warm & clean & it really seems restful &
good to be back—altho we were wonderfully blessed with friends &
entertainment while at Palm Beach. It seems very lonely here without you, and it isn't home anymore. There is no news I can write
you as I have seen no one yet— Your father is in California so I've
been told—you probably know— I hope you will not advise Miss
Hasham or any of the Crane employees of my intended visit to New
York—as I would prefer the priveledge of going & coming without
being watched—just as your father does. Kindly regard this request
—seriously Harold—as I have grown very tired of having every
body in the family knowing just when I was to disappear or appear.

You did not tell me much about Mrs Moody's visit— I suppose
you had a few wonderful times in her society. I am reading Chitra,[1]
which is dedicated to her. Speaking of books—I will bring your
music & the books you wrote John [2] about when I come— I hope
you find your new room quite comfortable, clean and satisfactory in
every way. Is there any way one can reach you there by phone—
Write me about this in your next letter which I hope will follow
this very soon—

Very Devotedly Your Mother / Grace—

[1] *Chitra* (New York: Macmillan, 1914), a one-act play by Rabindranath Tagore.
[2] Probably John Lloyd.

To Grace Hart Crane

54 W. 10 St. N.Y.C.
(Phone: Stuyvesant 5155)
Feb. 22, 1917

ALS, 2 pp.

My dear Mother:—

Your good letter I have just read, and it cheered me up a good
deal. You know, I am working hard and see very few people and
even now haven't had more than a half-hour's talk with anyone for
over a week. My work, though, is coming along finely, and I shall
be published both in "Others"—and again in the "Pagan" this next
month.[1] Yesterday was a day of tremendous work. I turned out in
some ways, the finest piece of work yet, beside writing a shorter
poem also.

Mother, you do not appreciate how much I love you. I can tell
by your letters that there exists a slight undercurrent of doubt, and
I do not want it there. If you could know how I long to see you
perhaps that might make some difference.

Now everything is in truth going splendidly, only I get terribly
lonesome often when I am through working. A man *must* wag his
tongue a little, or he'll lose his voice. Hurry, so that we can both
wag!/ Harold

From Grace Hart Crane

[Cleveland]
Monday A.M.
Feb. 26—1917

ALS, 4 pp.

Dear Harold:—

Yours of the 23rd received this morning and I hasten to reply.

---

[1] Crane probably is referring to his poem "The Hive," which was published
in *The Pagan*, I (March, 1917), 36. None of his poems were ever published in
Others.

I have been terribly ill with grippe & tonsilitis for a week— Today I am up, dressed and hope to soon be on my way to The Guardian Trust Co to see them about some important business which brought me home & then was too ill to attend to. Things pile up so fast and everything seems mountainous.

Now I am planning to leave here this coming Saturday night so as to be with you in New York Sunday morning, and I want both you and Carl to meet me at the station if you can. In the meantime don't delay at all in making a reservation for me at the Waldorf Astoria for single room, *with bath*. It need not be a large room but must be quiet. I want a hotel for awhile, a week at least and feel most at home at the Waldorf— It would be a terrible thing for me to arrive in New York & not have a place to stay— Mr Sullivan says he couldn't get a room when he was there, & you must attend to this immediately and get some thing by which I can claim my reservation— They can wire me at my expense. I want to hear from you about this as soon as possible. Will bring with me the things you mentioned in todays letter and am looking forward to a fine time with you & your friends. I must warn you however that I have grown very thin and look like a girl until you get a good look at my face. We will have so much to talk about—so many plans to make!

Molly wishes me to tell you that she is much pleased with the smock and is going to write you very soon. You see our coming home so soon really kept her busy opening & shutting up the house — She is on the jump every minute all day and my being down sick with tonsilitis hasn't helped any—

Will write you again & wire you exact time & train on which to expect me. Will look that up today as travel is so great I may not get a berth if I delay—

With much love—/ from/ Grace—

Keep the news of my arrival to yourself & Carl— Will explain when I see you.[1]

---

[1] Grace suspected that Clarence had hired a private detective to follow her. See *Voyager*, p. 70, and Mrs. Crane's letter of March 26.

❦

On March 4, Mrs. Crane arrived in New York for a three-week stay at the Waldorf Astoria Hotel. Harold had arranged a steady round of entertainment for his mother that, in addition to shopping excursions, evenings at the theater, and visits to museums, included dinners with Schmitt, the Brookses, and the Colums. Perhaps in an effort to take her mind off the divorce proceedings, Grace developed an interest in eurythmics and Rhythmical Physical Culture. Her teacher, Mrs. Florence Fleming Noyes, stressed that harmonious and expressive body movements led to mental well-being. One of Harold's friends described these dances and the costumes the dancers wore as "short chiffon sort of Greek costumes . . . one's hair was worn loose . . . and one went into a sort of trance." [1]

Grace enjoyed her son's company as well as the city. Soon she was making serious plans to live permanently in New York with Mrs. Hart and Harold. In the meantime Harold was learning that entertaining his mother could be costly—it was not long before he had spent all his funds. Unable to wire his father for more money (as his mother insisted her presence in New York remain a secret), Harold resorted to borrowing cash from the Crane company. When C.A. learned of his son's expenses—in two weeks he had borrowed $168.00—he sent a telegram demanding Harold's return to Ohio. Though this message is lost, it was sharp enough to precipitate Mrs. Crane's hasty return to Cleveland. Harold, however, decided to stay in the East and wrote this reply to his father.

To Clarence Arthur Crane

54 West 10 St., N.Y.C.
March 23, 1917

TLS, 2 pp.

My dear Father:—

I have been very negligent for not writing you for so long, but

[1] Quoted from Mrs. Claire Spencer Evans's undated letter to John Unterecker.

you know Mother has been here, and we have been so very busy that there has been no time spent here in my room at all. Your telegram has just come telling me to be home in a week, but I really must stay now, for I have begun tutoring for the summer course at Columbia, and there is no time to waste now in preparation. I shall have to cram day and night to attain the examinations at all, and so you see it is impossible to return just now.

I sincerely want to get something done now in some direction and I realize it is time to go about it. This tutoring is the only way to begin, leaving off in school as I did, and assured of approval in your eyes I have begun. I do hope it will be satisfactory to you. The catalog of the summer course will be issued soon and then I shall send it to you so you can see all about it.

We are having beautiful weather here now, and the city is very pleasant in the spring sunshine. Poor Orsa [1] must be having a terrible battle, and I may suppose that it is over, one way or the other, by this time. But I am sure it must have been a happy duty after all, to have been by him as an old friend, and to have helped in some manner to ease him.

Carl is the same old boy, with interesting talk, which by the way, I fear I shall have to deny myself for the next few months to study continuously. He is surely one of the best friends in the world.

I hope that in spite of all your worries, your western trip may have helped you a little, for the fact that we have see[n] a place after our own heart is often a consolation when we are away from it, however the present may be.

Hazel Hassam [2] is as anxious as I am to have you come here and I certainly hope you can manage it soon. I shall write you often now, and please answer me soon, wont you?

Much love from sonny,/ Harold

[1] Orsa Beardsley, a cousin of Clarence Crane's.
[2] Hazel Hasham.

From Grace Hart Crane

[Cleveland] [1]
[March 26, 1917?]
Monday—A.M.

ALS, 8 pp.

Dear Harold:—

Knowing how hard it is for me to write letters these days I hope you will forgive me for what might appear neglect or forgetfullness of you. Certainly you must know that would be impossible. I arrived home on time getting off at 105th St. and coming over here right away in a taxi.

I did not see Mr Sullivan right away—but when I did I had a very satisfactory talk with him. The laws for Ohio are not the same as New York so New Yorkers are hardly capable of giving advice as to what to do.[2] Of this one thing be assured & that is Mr Sullivan is *your friend* and *admirer* and any advice coming from him you may rely upon. He is glad you did not come home with me, but thinks you have done the right thing in getting started upon your college work & seems to have every confidence that you will reach your goal. He admires your pluck & determination to succeed— I know you will not disappoint us and now pitch into your work and don't bother about my side of the question, for I will work out my future the best I can & we will all be happy "by & by." Under no consideration give up your work, but get your living expenses down where you can show what your money goes for— If you are without money let me know & I will see what can be done. Please refrain from talking [about] our personal matters with any one— I feel sure Everything will come out all right—

Your father may be home any day this week, if he arrived in Chicago yesterday as his wire would indicate,—and it would seem quite

___

[1] John Unterecker suggests that references to Grace's return to Cleveland and to "Physical Culture" indicate that this letter was written on the last Monday in March.

[2] Crane had sought legal advice in New York about his parents' divorce, specifically about his father's financial responsibility for his maintenance.

natural that he would wish to see his attorney Mr S——[3] soon
afterwards— I have told Mr S—— your situation exactly & I feel
quite sure you can trust your case in his hands.

The weather is beautiful here today & every one in this neighborhood is house cleaning. I was so glad you had not returned with
me when I got off the train the other morning. The town looked so
empty & dead & I knew your heart would have gone into the
depths.

Saturday night your S.D. [4] came about midnight & I did love you
for thinking of me— Your letter told me of many good things & I
was impressed very strongly with the thought that you are a child
of fortune after all, to be thrown so easily into the society of the
people that you wish to know & who are working along your line.

I was delighted that you were with the Brook's, also Mr Colum &
when we are back in New York again together we will have quite a
little colony of friends.

Grandma Hart & Mollie have listened eagerly to all I have had
to tell them about you & what we did.

I told them about my few lessons in *"Physical Culture"* and they
think it is the thing—

John Lloyd was out awhile yesterday afternoon— He was much
surprised to find me here. Looked very wistful when I talked about
what you & Carl were doing, and had many questions to ask about
you. He thinks a very great deal about you & wishes you were back
here. When I told him you would probably never be back here to
live he looked more wistful. He says you owe him a letter. I told
him how fine Carl was and that he must answer his letter— He said
he would this week. Dear Carl!! How glad I am you have him. It
has meant so much to you to have such a friend and neither of you
can possibly understand what it has meant to me. I shall hope that
the future holds many good times for us three.

I have not been out of the house since I came but shall get out
today—

You know that I hated like the ——— to leave you boys the
other night—but I was glad you were left behind & I remembered

---

[3] John J. Sullivan, who was attorney for both Grace and Clarence Crane.
[4] The Cranes' abbreviation for "Special Delivery."

your smile—which told me much— You are a brave soul my boy &
that fact will carry you to success— It is fine to have attained brav-
ery so early in life—

Much love—from/ Grace

From Clarence Arthur Crane

[Cleveland]
March 29th, 1917.

TLC, 2 pp.

My dear Harold:

Your letter reached me at Hotel Sherman.[1] I would not have expected you to bother writing me as long as your mother was there,
but I am rather surprised that you have taken the matter into your
own hands in reference to you [r] future schooling. It is not as I
would have wished it. I have talked with a great many people who
ought to have more knowledge than I have from an educational
standpoint, and I have yet to find one who has agreed with the
course that has been outlined in the matter of a boy of 17 years of
age living a practically free life in New York City, and tutoring for
Columbia college. It really is the most unusual case I have ever
heard of. If you can do it, and accomplish good work, you will surprise me. But I am willing to be surprised.

Then again I want to know what the expense of it is to be, for I
have that to pay. In other words, my dear boy, if I am to be in
every sense a father to you, as I want to be, I want you to take me
into your confidences. You must consult me in all these matters.
Send me an itemized statement of your accounts and realize that at
all times I have your best interests at heart.

Hazel has become hopelessly confused in the matter of advancing
you money. I could not understand why you should have gone to
her for $168.00. You mailed me the itemization of what your ex-
penses were, and you must come to me for everything that you have.
Our company is an incorporated one. I am not the only stock-

---

[1] The Hotel Sherman, Chicago.

holder, and the accounts settled in New York have to be reported to this office in regular form. I am sending her a check to cover this amount, and as you have now had considerable money, let me know what your expenditures are, and how much I should send you regularly.

I have returned home to an accumulation of many matters after an absence of several weeks, so for a few days I shall be in doubt as to my movements. It may be that I will come down to New York. But whether I come or not, I want you to know that your father thinks of you every hour of his life and is vitally interested that your career shall be one of consequence and credit to us all.

To that end, I shall always give you my best support, and I want your full confidence.

Sincerely,

Mr. Harold Crane,
50 West 10th Street,
New York, N.Y.

After three months in New York, Harold did have some evidence to present to his parents which he hoped would convince them of his success. The March issue of *The Pagan* published his poem "The Hive."

From Grace Hart Crane

[Cleveland]
Thursday—Mch—29—1917.

ALS, 9 pp.

Dear Harold:—

The Crock of Gold [1] has been proving such a delight and also the continuing of the rhythmical Physical Culture which I discovered

---

[1] *The Crock of Gold,* the prose fantasy by James Stephens (1882–1950), which was published in 1912.

in New York that you have been neglected in my letter writing—
but not in thought. How could that be when you are writing me
such good letters, and the world such poems [.] To be serious Harold, I was so proud at seeing you appear in the Pagan which arrived
yesterday, that I straightway turned on the Victrola & expressed my
delight in the most original dance you have yet to see. The only
trouble was that my bedroom being small & very full I had some
difficulty & was obliged to restrain my feelings more than I would
have had there been more space. Your grandmother is always my
most interested spectator and once yesterday in my effort to get on
the other side of the room avoiding both bed & bureau in my flight
she looked a bit frightened. But she was soon herself again and
tried some of the fancy steps herself. Last night before retiring we
both played catapillar & spring flowers [2] etc. Mother informed me
this morning that part of her bunion left in the night—so I think
she is a very apt pupil [.] We cant be poets but we are doing our
best to be nimble & keep up with the latest ideas.

Your last letter which told of your arrangments with your tutor [3]
came yesterday afternoon. I sincerely hope you will not be interrupted any more in your attempt to get an education— I shall do
my best to keep your road smooth in this direction from now on.
You did not tell me where your money is coming from. *Please* do
remember to do this when you write next.

People look too fat & slow & sleepy here for me, and my heart
and desires are with you back there. I wonder how it ever looked
good to me— So you may count on my being at least a neighbor of
yours just as soon as I am free to do so. Just how or when that freedom is to come to me is yet a trifle indefinite.

Am glad you are going to see Nancy & Albert. They will be your
good friends I trust, and one needs plenty of those.

Here I left you & a whole day has passed without my finishing
this. In the meantime Grandma's secret plans for celebrating my
birthday were unintentionally made known to me & so I know that
Zell Helen & our two selves are to go to the Colonial tonight to see

[2] These were eurythmic exercises.
[3] M. Tardy.

Faversham [4] in Bernard Shaw's "Getting Married." They say he considers it his best play & Mrs Baker [5] has seen it and thinks it *great*. Zell & Helen will remain over night & spend Sunday with us. Am looking forward to seeing them— Havn't seen Helen since that day she came to the hospital.

Mrs Baker called me over there for a little chat last night & I took over the copy of your poem. She was very very complementary & said she was going to get one to show her sister Mrs Wolf— who by the way has a very remarkable young son of twenty one who has just been made assistant professor at Harvard. [6]

Mrs Baker is strong for Harold Crane. By the way, writing that name brings to mind this question— In signing your name to your contributions & later to your books do you intend to ignore your mother's side of the house entirely. That was the only thing I criticized about it. It seems to me that Hart or at least H. should come in some where— I understand that the Cranes say you get all your literary talent from them—uncle Fred for instance being the example they point to. If you feel that way leave "Hart" out—but if not, now is the time to fix it right. How would "Hart Crane" be. No partiality there— You see I am already jealous, which is a sure sign I believe in your success. If your father should come to see you try & get him to go to Gramarcy Park & look at some studio apartments that will do for you & me. He will get a beter idea of the rents. Everyone I talk to that understands the conditions says that down town is the place to live rather than out— I think it would not be at all bad for you to send a marked copy of your Pagan to Arthur & Ella Crane— [7] Of course you have to your father. It would please them and that is almost always the thing to do.

I am told your father is in town— You do not tell me where your funds are coming from and that is legally very important for me to know *just* now.

This is a dandy day & I feel fine—better than lately— Hope you

---

[4] William Faversham (1868–1940) played the part of the Bishop of Chelsea in Shaw's comedy.

[5] Mrs. Sarah Baker, a friend of Grace's.

[6] Robert Wolf, who later married the poet Genevieve Taggard.

[7] Clarence Crane's parents.

will send me a lot of love tomorrow. Tell Carl I will write him soon—and I still think & talk a great deal about him—

Devotedly / Grace—

To Grace Hart Crane

54 W. 10 St. N.Y.C.

April 3, 1917

ALS, 2 pp.

My dear Mother:—

Carl has just come over with Grandmother's letter. My board costs at least $11.00 per week

room————————————————6.00
Laundry————————————1.50

And the clothing, I can't say. I repeat again after my letter Sunday that I am not denied money by Father any more. At least the office gives it to me, and he sent a check of twenty-five two weeks ago.

But why all this list business? Isn't he supposed to pay what is reasonable until I am twenty-one without any such business as this? Grandma hasn't made it very plain in her letter what you want this for. Don't make any stipulation about what I am to be paid if you don't have to.

You haven't written me anything about the case and I am in a sea of uncertainty. Grandma writes it is soon to come off. That is all I know. I want you well provided for. Has your aggreement been altered any for the better?

Let me know all about the case now, as soon as you know. And if you absolutely need me, I can come home for a few days, though not without some expense, as you know.

Much love and confidence, / your steadfast son, / Harold

Grace, of course, wanted to know if Clarence was paying all that he should for his son's maintenance. As she had decided to live

with Harold in New York, she was worried about her own expenses
as well. In the months ahead she would become more concerned
with financial matters, because she was faced with the prospect of
living on a limited income and for the first time in her life had to
manage her own affairs. There is some evidence to suggest that
both she and Clarence had hoped to effect a reconciliation before
the divorce became final. As the date drew near (the divorce was
granted on April 19), C.A. grew increasingly friendly toward Grace.
In the second week of April, Harold returned to Cleveland for a
few days to collect some of his belongings and to help his mother
and grandmother pack for New York. While there he spoke with
his father about the war that was then ravaging Europe and the
possibility of his entering the army; no doubt both father and son
spoke as well about the likelihood of a reunited family.

From Clarence Arthur Crane

[Cleveland]
April 16th, 1917.

TLC, 2 pp.

My dear Harold:
    Your very short little letter of April 13th reaches me this morn-
ing.
    Now I want you to get over all this disturbance in your mind.
The war need cause no such turmoil as you indicate. If the time
comes when our country needs us, why we will both go. I would
make a very poor marcher, but some one has got to drive automo-
biles and I can do that.
    I talked with mother once yesterday, and again this morning. I
think that she will gradually emerge from her present troubles now
that they are all over, and I am going to try to put life and attention in my business which has never before been in evidence.
    I want you to study hard, and accomplish all that you set out to
do. To finish something is the greatest thing in the world, provided
you finish it well and to your own satisfaction. If your forte is along

literary lines, I am willing to lend you my support that you will accomplish what will give you the greatest pleasure. I know how devoid of pleasure my work would be here if I could not inject into it some of the things which I like, even though my tastes may be quite plebeian.

By the terms of the contract, you are turned over to your mother in the matter of custody; but that need make no difference, and I do not intend that it shall. We are both centered upon you, and your success will be our happiness. If mother keeps up her present friendliness for me, I think we will both have performed a miracle in that we have come out of our troubles willing to forget and forgive, and nothing would please me better than the opportunity of not only doing for her, but going to see her as frequently as she might ever wish it.

As soon as Ervin [1] comes home and mother is in New York, I am coming down to show you both a good time and for a few days at least you will get away from the boarding house hash.

                                    With much love, I am

Mr. Harold Crane
54 W. 10th Street,
New York, N.Y.

When Mrs. Crane arrived in New York with her mother on May 1, she and Harold spent two weeks looking for a suitable apartment, finally finding one at 44 Gramercy Park. Feeling that her daughter and grandson were comfortably settled, Mrs. Hart returned to Cleveland; however, soon after she left, Grace grew increasingly despondent over her divorce from C.A. and her pressing financial problems. Her son became fearful of the consequences of his mother's nervous condition, and, when his father hinted he might join them in New York, Harold implored him to do just that.

[1] Erwin Shoot.

To Clarence Arthur Crane

54 West 10th St., N.Y.C.
May 5, 1917

TLS, 1 p.

My dear Father:—

We certainly have had bum weather since Mother arrived. This was on last Tuesday, and it has rained ever since.

I am sorry not to have answered you before this, but there has been a great deal to do, and there is the studying to be done besides, you know.

How is business? The war seems to put the blink on ever[y]thing in the confectionary line, but you will have to suffer no worse than the rest. They are all getting out patriotic packages now, and you had better do the same. Pictures of Lincoln and Washington seem to be on all the boxes here, and they are tying them with red-white-and-blue ribbons. If the candymakers are to live at all now, they have GOT to be patriotic.

We hope to find some place to live soon, and believe me it is some job to find anything at all decent just now.

Love from sonny,/ Harold

To Clarence Arthur Crane

44 Gramercy Square, N.Y.C.
May 15, 1917

TLS, 1 p.

My dear Father:—

My neglect in answering you was occasioned by our moving into this apartment, and you can conceive how many things there were to be done. It is a comfortable place, and I think that when Mother gets used to New York, she will settle down to enjoy it. It is subletted for the summer, and of course, furnished. There are two rooms, a bath, and a kitchenette.

Grandma is still here with us, and I hope will remain until Mother gets to feeling better. Hazel is around occaisionally, and took them out for a ride yesterday. The weather is clearing up lately, making the city more pleasant for them than when they first arrived.

I do wish you would hurry and come. There are so many things I want to discuss with you, which cannot be satisfactorily done in letters. I have to accept much money from Mother for expenses, and she really cant afford it at all. Mother and I must eat together now, and I cannot econemize now on food so much as before.

The festivities of the Foreign Commission [1] during last week were very interesting, and I got opportunities to see a good deal. The city was very beautiful.

Much love,/ Harold

[*On the obverse of the page the following figures appear. They are explained in the next letter.*]

$$\begin{array}{r} 140 \\ 12 \\ \hline 280 \\ 140 \\ \hline 1680 \end{array}$$

From Clarence Arthur Crane

[Cleveland]
May 16th, 1917

TLC, 2 pp.

Mr. Harold Crane,
44 Gramercy Park,
New York, N.Y.

My dear Harold:

The wire from your mother received at the Club after closing time at the stores last night, is, I believe, pretty well explained by

[1] The "Foreign Commission" Harold speaks of was the visit of Arthur Balfour, British Secretary of State for Foreign Affairs, and Joseph Joffre, Marshal of France, to win United States support for the war effort.

your letter this morning, and also one from Hazel bearing on the same subject.

I promptly wired your mother that I was sending her a special delivery and wrote her at some length regarding matters which I inferred she desired to confer upon.

Mr. Sullivan has just gone over the letters, one and all, and has asked me not to send it. His advice as a friend of both parties is what it has been from the beginning; that there is nothing gained by continued communications between your mother and myself. The court has settled it and not until the contract now in existence shall have been broken is there any cause whatever for further communication.

Mr. Sullivan's thoughts were for all concerned, and as he represents the advice which we seek and pay for, we are very foolish not to adhere to it.

I gained from your letter that it is money matters which you wish to talk over, and I can say in a few words all that I could say if I came to New York, which is out of the question until my own business matters permit.

When you were here, I told you I would pay a portion of the rent if it could provide a home for you with your mother, and I told her at the last conference that we had I would pay half of the rent up to $80.00. This I am willing to do. Instead of taking $9.00 a week for your board, you utilize your whole $25.00 for your expenses and I will on the first of each month send you $40.00 to apply on the rent of the flat.

This is your allowance for the time being. Whether it is ever increased or decreased depends entirely upon conditions under which your father has to submit. If you are conversant with what I am paying mother, what I have returned in interest, etc., and the monthly drain upon me, together with my own expenses, you will believe me when I say that it is in excess of my income, and I have had to borrow for it.

I want you to make progress for what I am allowing you now represents $1680.00 a year—much more than anyone in my employ outside of Ervin and Miss Hasham, and it is yours for the development of your education and under such conditions as I have never known before. My two years at Allegheny College did not represent that this does in one year, and I am perfectly willing that you may have the experience, only I want you to know that your father is doing it because of his affection for you and not because any Court would grant you such an allowance under such conditions as exist. I am hoping that wartime conditions will not strand me, although we are dealing in very high class luxuries.

I am quite certain that this answers the questions that your mother wished answered, for I know of nothing else between us to be discussed other than your welfare.

With much love, I am / Your father,

The events of the summer and fall of 1917 were somewhat complicated for all members of the Crane family. Against his lawyer's advice, Clarence began to correspond with his former wife. Soon the letters became most cordial, hinting that there might be a reconciliation: "if out of all this curtain fire of trouble, we can emerge, seeing the best in each other and blinded to the mistakes and hasty utterances, I shall have much satisfaction and confidence that perhaps life is really worth living." [1] By the middle of July, Harold and his mother were once again in Cleveland where preparations were being made for a remarriage. But on the eve of this second union C.A. quarreled with Grace about their son's wish to live in New York. On the last day of July Harold returned to New York, leaving his grandmother to care for her daughter, who had suffered a severe nervous collapse.

To Clarence Arthur Crane

44 Gramercy Park, N.Y.C.
June 5, 1917

TL, fragment

My dear Father:—

I hear you are back from the West now, and so I can reach you all right.

---

[1] Clarence Arthur Crane to Grace Hart Crane, July 10, 1917. Quoted in *Voyager*, p. 79.

I am very busy now in preparations for the examinations for Columbia in about two weeks. Algebra is all I am to be examined in this time, but next autumn there will be several subjects. However, as soon as one passes an examination, the credit is given him for the same, and as soon as he has passed examinations on enough subjects to give him fifteen units, he can enter the college. Just what college-life during the next few years is to be, is very indefinite. Some have already been practically left empty, as Dartmouth, and there are large contingents going both from Yale and from Harvard. But I expect to go right ahead, and prepare myself, not allowing uncertainties to effect me at all. During the summer my expenses for tutoring may be changed, I don't yet know, but, of course there will be plenty of time later to write about that.

Zell blew in this morning, and informs us that she is stopping at the Martha Washington Hotel with her mother, and has already been there a day. We shall enjoy going around with her a great deal during the three weeks she intends staying. She looks better every time I see her, and even younger.

To Clarence Arthur Crane

44 Gramercy Pk. N.Y.C.
June 5, 1917 [1]

TLS, 2 pp.

My dear Father:—

I envy you your visit with Maxfield Parrish.[2] You didn't tell me much about him in the letter, but I suppose you are reserving that for the first good visit we shall have, and I hope that will be soon too. The Seiberling place must be fine.[3] I came within one of getting to it myself last winter when Korner and Wood[4] sent me to Akron on a special trip for the family, but I was met by their chauf-

---

[1] Hart very likely wrote this letter on July 5, 1917.

[2] Clarence commissioned Maxfield Parrish, the artist, to design a box cover for his candies.

[3] Hart is referring to the estate of the Seiberling family in Akron.

[4] Hart worked briefly at the Korner and Wood store, which sold reproductions of paintings at the time.

feur and had only the opportunity to wait around the station two hours and then ride back home.

I finally had to go to a doctor about my rose fever and some lung or palate trouble (I don't know yet which it was) and of course did not get away from him without undergoing some sort of operation. He slyly reached in and cut my palate so that it was sore all day, which may have later helped in alleviating an incessant cough I had, but which is better now. I never before had such a cold, and blow and sneeze all through these fine warm summer days. But in every other item of health I seem to hit a high mark. Mr. Sullivan, who was here last week said he thought I was looking finely, and I am submitting a little photo I had taken the other night on Broadway, and hope to hear your opinion on the subject in the next letter.

Also, there was an article in last Sunday's "Sun" which I have been planning to send you. It is written by your old associate, E. T. Bedford.[5] I think it will interest you.

Thank you very much for your generous allowance for my suit. I shall get it tomorrow. One really cant get along very well with one suit for every day including Sundays.

The Lord's have asked me up to their country place in Connecticut for this week end, and promise me a game of tennes and much lung-room. I shall surely be glad to see a bit of country.

I am very much interested in my study of French. Someday you may be surprised at having a marquise for a son.

Now I am awaiting your long letter promised in the last you wrote, but it will have to be pretty darn good to beat that last. I shall be mighty glad to see the Harts and Mother will too.

Goodbye for now, much love,—/ Harold

[5] E. T. Bedford (1849–1931), the president of the Corn Products Refining Company to whom Clarence Crane sold his maple syrup cannery.

From Clarence Arthur Crane

[Cleveland]
August 1st, 1917.

TLC, 1 p.

My dear Boy:

This morning you woke up in New York, and by this time you are back in your chosen haunts, bag and baggage, after a visit at home.

You know I recall, and always will remember the pleasure I had in coming back after my first few experiences at Meadville. Father used to talk expenses to me and a few other things that were not just to my liking, but just the same, home-coming is a good thing —even dogs wag their tail when they get in sight of the old farm house.

This visit has meant much to me. You are the only treasure I have on God's green earth, and whatever has or ever does happen, I want you to know that your father's love for you is equal to any emergence.

Do the work that is before you, with the sincerity which will bring the very best results. It isn't at all necessary that you should achieve great financial success, but it is necessary that your own peace of mind should never be disturbed, and the building of character is the only thing that will possibly insure it.

Your mother called me up this morning, and seems to have spent a very comfortable night, and is in a good frame of mind. My visits to the house will be much less frequent now that you are away, but I hope I have impressed you with the fact that I wish every good thing in the world for her.

                    With my love, I am/ Your father,

Mr. Harold Crane,
#44 Gramercy Park,
New York, N.Y.

To Clarence Arthur Crane

44 Gramercy Pk. N.Y.C.

August 8, 1917

TLS, 2 pp.

My dear Father:—

I am very, very sorry that things are going so badly with Mother. I guess there is nothing for her to do but to get back here as soon as is possible and try to re-instate herself in poise and health. I look for her this week. At least I see no re[a]son why she should linger longer. But I have received no word from her and am uncertain as to much of the true s[t]ate of affairs with her. I only hope you are avoiding any meetings as much as possible, for as I said, it is now too early,—she is not yet established well enough to endure the strain w[h]ich you know any contact causes.

The picture is to go this morning.[1] Its name is "Olga", and I am sure you will like her very well. Carl is thinking of returning to Warren and Youngstown for a month to fulfil some portrait contracts, but you have pulled him out of a very serious difficulty. He is a little bashful about sending you his doggerel on so slight an acquaintance so maybe I can get it and send it later. I hope that when he comes west you may be able to spend a day together. I assure you an entertaining time.

I have been diabolically nervous ever since that shock out at the house, but Sunday Carl, Potapovitch [2] and I went out to long beach, and lying in the sun did me some good. If you could shake responsibilities like this for a week or so, it would work inestimable good upon you. You cannot worry on such a beautiful beach with the sound of waves in your ears. We all get to thinking that our heads are really our bodies, and most of the time go floating around with only our brain conscious, forgetting that our bodies have requirements also.

---

[1] C.A. had bought a small picture from Carl Schmitt.

[2] Stanislaw and Anna Portapovitch, who were introduced to Crane by Carl Schmitt. Portapovitch was a dancer who worked at Healy's restaurant on Broadway at 145th Street.

I feel so near to you now that I do hope that nothing can ever again break the foundation of sincerity that has been established beneath our relations. Never has anyone been kinder than you were when I was last home. I want you to know that I appreciate it, and also your two fine letters.

Much love,—/ Hart Crane

The signature of the preceding letter is significant, for it is the first time in correspondence with his parents that the name "Hart Crane" appears, and ironically it is one of the few times that the poet used the name "Hart" in letters to his father. To the Crane side of the family he remained "Harold," while for his mother's side he became "Hart."

Less than two weeks after Hart wrote this letter, Mrs. Crane again sought a reconciliation with her former husband. This time she was rebuffed by a sharp reply: "Forget C.A. Crane does or ever did *live*. Get busy with things that make for your happiness. There is a sunny side to every *street*. You're due to cross *over*." [1] Several days after receiving this note Grace arrived in New York with her mother. Still acutely depressed by the events of the preceding two months, she was "confined to her bed" through most of September.

To Clarence Arthur Crane

[New York City]
Sept. 18, '17

ALS, 4 pp.

My dear Father:—

Your good letter rec'd yesterday. From what Hazel says I presume this will find you back in Cleveland, and busy looking over what has happened while you have been away. I haven't written more be-

[1] Clarence Arthur Crane to Grace Hart Crane, August 21, 1917. Quoted in *Voyager*, p. 82.

cause, as you can readily perceive, I haven't known your address most of the time, but once again you may expect regular letters.

This one thing though, I am going to ask of you. If, when you write me, you are thinking of Mother in a distasteful way, please conceal it, remaining silent on the subject. And if, in thinking of her, one kind thought should occur (as I know it does) express it. You remember that when I last was home, I said that I "was through."— That was possible with me for but one hour. My heart is still as responsive to both your loves, and more so, than ever. I have seen more tears than I ever expected in this world, and I have shed them through others' eyes, to say nothing of my own sorrow. And now, when I hear nothing but forgiveness, tenderness, mercy, and love from one side, how can [I] bear resentment and caustic words coming from the other without great pain? Happiness may some time come to me, I am sure it will. But please, my dear Father, do not make the present too hard,—too painful for one whose fatal weakness is to love two unfortunate people, by writing barbed words.

I don't know how long we three shall dwell in purgatory. We may rise above, or sink below, but either way it may be, the third shall and must follow the others, and I leave myself in your hands.

Write soon, I do hope you come to New York.

Affectionately,/ Harold

Hart's letters of August 8 and September 18 show his attempts to maintain affection for both sides of the family—perhaps in the hope of a remarriage. C.A.'s reply to the last letter is lost, but it must have been harsh. When Grace read it she became enraged and replied with an equally strong letter to her former husband. Characterizing Clarence's letter as "the hardest blow you have ever dealt him," she responded: "I will not tell you . . . how *earnestly* Harold has hoped that he might see his father and mother once more happy together. . . . I think he would have been the happiest boy in America if he could have been the means of bringing his father and mother once more into harmonious relationship." [1] Because of his father's reply, Hart sided with his mother almost entirely.

In the last week of September the lease expired on the apartment at Gramercy Park. Grace and Mrs. Hart returned to Cleveland, where they devoted considerable energy to redecorating the house on 115th Street. Hart moved into a rooming house at 25 East 11th Street run by Mrs. Frances Walton. It was there that the poet met Mme Eugénie Lebègue, his second French tutor, whose interest in continental literature soon became more important to Hart than her knowledge of the French language. Their tutorials usually consisted of discussions of modern French writers.

Mrs. Walton and her young boarder grew to be good friends. Having a few acquaintances in the motion picture industry, she encouraged Hart to write movie scenarios; he tried this, but had no success.

To Grace Hart Crane

[New York City]
Friday—Sept. 28, '17

ALS, 5 pp.

My dear sweet Mother:—

I have just read your letter and find it hard to express my rage and disgust at what you say concerning C. A. Crane's conduct. "Forget him," is all I can say. He is too low for consideration. I am only quietly waiting,—stifling my feelings in the realization that I might as well get as much money as possible out of him. Why be scrupulous in one's dealings with unscrupulous people, any way?

I breakfasted an hour ago with the Brooks'. Mrs Brooks had attempted to call on you at the Waldorf two days ago, and was not surprised when I told her of your absence. They ended by inviting me to a *home* dinner tonight at six-thirty, which I shall of course accept.

[1] Quoted from a rough draft of a letter dated September 23 that Grace Crane wrote to her former husband. See also *Voyager*, pp. 83–87.

Maxwell Bodenheim [1] called the other evening, complimented my poetry excessively, and has taken several pieces to the editor of the "Seven Arts," [2] a personal friend of his.

Bodenheim is at the top of American poetry today, and he says that after four years of absolute obscurity, he succeeding in getting publication only through the adverse channels of flattery, friendships and "pull." It is all a strange business. Editors are generally disappointed writers who stifle any genius or originality as soon as it is found. They seldom even trouble to read over the manuscript of a "new man". Bodenheim is a first-class critic though, and I am proud to have his admiration and encouragement. As soon as "Others" begins again this winter, he says I shall have an organ for all of my melodies, as he is one of the editors.[3] Success seems imminent now more than ever. I am very encouraged, poetically, at least.

This ought to reach for Sunday. It is more considerably than has reached C.A. for I don't intend him to hear much about me in the future. You have all my love, and if I *am* a little reckless, you shall find in the end, some wisdom. Forget all the past and leave C.A. to that bastard, T——.[4] You have lived too long in a house of shadows, ignoring the pulse and vivacity of life around you, and it is time to forget. Your letter sounded good, and I am so glad to hear of your work in the house. It will be looking finely when I come home for Christmas.

Give my love to Molly and dear Grandma. Of course I am ·well—/ Hart

[1] Maxwell Bodenheim (1893–1954), the American poet and novelist.

[2] *Seven Arts*, a little magazine edited by James Oppenheim that was published monthly from November, 1916, to October, 1917.

[3] Bodenheim's title was that of associate editor.

[4] Both Hart and Grace seem at this time to have been convinced that C.A.'s mind was systematically being "poisoned" against them by an employee of the Crane company. See *Voyager*, p. 86.

From Grace Hart Crane

[Cleveland]
[September 28, 1917?] [1]
Friday night 8:30—

ALS, 6 pp.

Dear Hart:—

If I didn't love you very much, & know that you would be expecting this I would not attempt a letter tonight as I am so very tired. We have been cleaning & moving furniture about all day & tonight I have the prettiest room I ever have had and am writing you in bed, in your four poster, which we have brot down from upstairs. Also your chiffonier & mothers bureau are keeping it company & things look very grand indeed. We also have a beautiful new hall & stair carpet which was laid today. Monday the paper hangers are coming to repaper what used to be Clarence Cranes room & which will soon look quite changed & ready for guests— We have plans to turn the back bed room into a little library & reading room, using book cases & grandpa's desk—your students lamp etc. I think the house will look quite good to you when you return & some of the old landmarks & unpleasant reminders removed— We have all new plumbing & new bowls—I forgot to add & now the water works fine. I have just had a good bath & tested it.

I was so glad to receive your letter today—To know you were happy—studying some and had been accepted by The Little Review.[2] I have great hopes for you & in a short time I shall pull myself together I believe & surprise you. Action & mental occupation is what I need now & I am getting it. If I have much time to think it is not good for me—& I always get my thoughts centered upon your father— My love for him is not the kind to leave when bid-

---

[1] Statements about the paperhanger in Grace's letter of October 3 suggest that she wrote this one on September 28.

[2] Margaret Anderson had accepted "In Shadow" for the December, 1917, issue of *The Little Review*. See Vol. IV, No. 8, p. 50.

den, but unless he can feel different & treat me as I feel I should be treated I never wish to see him again.

After the house is straightened around I may come to New York for a while— & do the Opera with you & go to Miss Noyes[.] [3] Just now I think I am happier here than in New York & I am of great help to grandma. I have made regular oppointments with Mrs McTague [4] for facial & if I can arrange shall take swimming lessons — The weather has been beautiful & Cleveland looks good— Saw Miss McMyler [5] down town yesterday & she inquired about you. Every one thinks you are preparing for college so don't disappoint them & most of all me. Saw Mrs Shultz yesterday & she said that Joseph had just entered Dartmouth. Get in any way even if you don't finish. It is coming to you.

Am glad your landlady is taking such an interest in you[.] I like her & feel comfortable about your home. I get a little homesick for New York but I had nothing to do & no home which was largely responsible for my getting so blue.

Give my love to Hazel & tell her I shall write her soon. Also that I have a new moleskin muff to match my cape & every body thinks I look quite fit—as she always says— I think of you so much & live with you in my thoughts a great deal— Be sure to write me often & if things do not go right—

Give my love to the Brooks & tell them I will see them later— Don't forget to pay them $3.50.

Goodbye & don't ever forget to love me & do as you know I would have you— Love/ Grace

[3] Mrs. Florence Fleming Noyes, who had given Mrs. Crane lessons in Rhythmical Physical Culture during her March visit with her son in New York.

[4] Mrs. Agnes McTague, a dermatologist in Cleveland.

[5] Miss McMyler, a teacher at East High School.

To Grace Hart Crane

[New York City]
[Postmarked October 1, 1917]
Monday evening

ALS, 1 pp.

My dear Mother:—

Perhaps, if my last letter arrived on Saturday as it should certainly have done, you will forgive the lack of a "Sunday Special" from me. That day I spent with Anna and Stan.[1] We ferried to Staten Island and back, had dinner, and then I took Anna to the Strand, as Stan is dancing every evening from six until two at Healy's Restaurant. (100 dollars per week). Surely, you will say, he *has* earned it. What a diabolical proffession! And yet he likes it. I suppose that the occaissional opportunity for expression is the scant reward.

O if you knew how much I am learning! The realization of true freedom is slowly coming to me, and with it a sense of poise which is of inestimable value. My life, however it shall continue, shall have expression and form. Believe me when I tell you that I am fearless that I am determined on a valorous future and something of a realization of life. The smallness of hitherto large things, and the largness of hitherto small things is dawning. I am beginning to see the hope of standing entirely alone and to fathom Ibsen's statement that translated is, "The strongest man in the world is he who stands entirely alone." [2]

I have now let M. Tardy go as he could only tutor me at the inconvenient hour of seven P.M. and have arranged with a French teacher here in the house who teaches at the Scudder School, to give me lessons at the same price and at convenient hours.[3]

The news of the repairs pleases me, Especially in this, that you are to be more comfortable. Your facials too, sound encouraging.

Now about my books. Please do send them. They might just as

---

[1] Stanislaw and Anna Portapovitch.
[2] Quoted from *An Enemy of the People*, Act V.
[3] Mme Eugénie Lebègue.

well be here, and needless to say, I need them. It wont cost too much, I am sure, to send them.

As to father, I am thinking almost nothing at all about him. I have ceased to respect him, and dislike is dominent anyway. Please forget about him, and master yourself as decidedly as you once did. Someday, all the remaining Crane's will creep around and disappear. Their opinions as to myself are not of the least consequence to me, and I would prefer to have them as ignorant as possible as to my conditions, life, intentions and whereabouts. You and Grandma are the only ones who matter a snap of the finger. No, I am not malicious nor "blue" as this might possibly deceive you into thinking. I have never felt as encouraged, as free or as clean. Think of me often as such or not at all, for I hope you will understand me.

Goodbye for now, dear Mother. Love to Grandma. / Hart.

To Grace Hart Crane

[New York City]
[Postmarked October 3, 1917]
Wednesday afternoon—

ALS, 3 pp.

My own dear Mother:

There is not much to tell you except that I am about to begin a novel. The plot is already thick in my head and tonight the first chapter will be written off,—at least in rough draft. It is a story whose setting is to be Havana and the Isle of Pines. Walter Wilcox [1] is to be the hero, and the heroine a N.Y. society maiden who is attending the races in Havana. More of this will doubtless bore you, now at least, so enough!

Grandma writes that you are succeeding beautifully. As soon as you found some active interests I knew you would improve in outlook and distinguish between a disgusting personality and the world in general.

[1] Walter Wilcox was the caretaker of Mrs. Hart's property on the Isle of Pines. See Harold's letter of January 26, 1916, to his grandmother.

These delightful autumn days, filled with cool sunshine, make me feel fine. I am alone a good deal of the time and am glad of it. My work will always demand solitude to a great extent in creative effort. Your son is improving every day, so don't worry one moment about me. Thank Grandma for me for those good letters of hers.

your affectionate/ Hart

no word yet from 208 St. Clair.[2]

From Grace Hart Crane

Wednesday—Oct 3—1917—
1709—E—115 St.
Cleveland, O.

ALS, 16 pp.

Dear Hart:—

Your S.D. was very good and very welcome altho' a little late for Sunday—Next week you must try to remember in time to get me one for Sunday, for they are fully as welcome here as they are in New York.

This is Molly's afternoon out, and grandma is down town so that leaves me entirely alone. I suppose I would be out too, were it not for the fact that I have one of the very worst colds I have ever had —in fact more like the grippe and for several days I've been utterly miserable and in the house, which always makes me uneasy and cross. Up until last night the weather has been wonderful and I have resented not being able to get out in the warm October sunshine.

The paper hanger this morning finished papering in the room that your father used to occupy—and tomorrow Molly is going to clean it thoroughly and it will look quite changed with the different furniture and rug. You will be delighted with the looks of the old home when you come back for Christmas and I hope everything will be conducive to a happy Christmas for us all. But most especially your Grandma Hart. She is such a brave soul, her interest in

[2] The address of the Crane Chocolate Company in Cleveland.

life and what she has left of a family never lagging for one instant. She is as keen about the looks of the house as you would expect her to be over her first home, and her principal interest in it is to have it please you and me.

While I miss New York and you, and find situations very trying here sometimes, I am not yet sorry that I returned. My battle must be fought out right here—and when it is really won, I can better judge whether to stay here or go somewhere else. One thing seems very good and that is a good respectable home, with comforts and plenty of room—and in taking care of my share of it I am kept busy & have less time to think of unpleasant things. I shall soon seek some kind of public work to do. Mrs Baker [1] returned from New York and Atlantic City yesterday and in a few days I shall again get in touch with her. She can likely find me a work to do as she has more than she can attend to.

Grandma is not well— She has those numb spells and they are not desirable at any stage in life—much less at seventy eight. On top of all her other trouble, a letter from Walter Wilcox came today telling us of the most terrible hurricane that the Island has ever experienced, and our place, with the exception of the house alone, is in total ruin. The house is some damaged and was almost blown off the foundation— Many families are destitute— No boats have been heard from—and the only way of leaving the Island is by a freighter which they hope will be sent from Havana soon. Can you imagine how discouraged & heart sick Grandma & I feel. So much money sunk in that place, and now no hope of ever getting a cent out of it. Walter is utterly discouraged & disgusted and will leave for the north as soon as we write him what to do about our house. Of course it must have a tenant until we can dispose of it, but grandma and I both feel we shall put no more money in that proposition. There is little likehood of either of us going down there this winter. I do not want to see it, for Walter writes that all trees vines shrubs, etc are laid flat on the ground. He said it had never looked so nice and he was so very proud of it. He writes that he is utterly discouraged and wants to come North by the first boat. So we must decide upon some plan for him to pursue concerning the

[1] Mrs. Sarah Baker, a friend of Grace's.

house and let him know as soon as possible. This is all very discouraging in a financial way to me, as I had thought that by getting the place in good shape we might be able to sell it perhaps this winter even at a sacrifice— It looks now that one couldn't give it away. Please do not repeat this news to anyone, even your father, for it doesn't help a bit and is bound to harm— I do not want your father to know what misfortunes seem to beset me— I presume you can fully understand my feelings in that direction. I do not know whether you have written him or not since I left—but if not you must— You can & should write him a courteous letter giving him your address & some idea of what you are doing. As long as you receive & accept his support you must do that at least & I beg of you not to be foolish & cut off your nose to spite your face. I appreciate more than I can say your loyalty to me and it comforts me in many a lonely hour. But you would only be pleasing him & placing yourself in a position which might prove to be very difficult—by antagonizing your father at this time. Your are entitled to his support— *Take it!* Only remember that you have a certain duty towards him also. My affairs need never again be mentioned between you—Far better not. You know now what he is capable of being with one whom he professed before every one, to love better than life. It is horrible to think such natures exist & we have to cope with them— but they do & you *know* it, so be *wise*—and don't allow your feelings to cheat you out of what is *rightfully* yours. All this can be accomplished without being a hypocrite either.

So far as I am concerned, I must *forget* him— It will not be easy —but it must be accomplished one way or another and that is my first task. I want to accomplish it without either hate revenge or malice, so that he may some day look back upon himself with condemnation, & upon me with admiration. No matter what misfortune may be mine, I want to always remain true to my ideals— That is about all there is left for me—

Now it is getting nearly dinner time, and I must close this. No bills or mail has come from N.Y.C. yet— Give Hazel my best regards if you see her— Also the Brook's. They are so good to you. Have you paid them for our dinner? You must, else you will have placed me in an embarrassing position— Also I hope some time to

receive thro' you from your father his part of the last month's rent
& also the amount I spent for your Clothes. As I have nothing
whatever to say to him it is up to you to inform him of what he
does not know.

I forgot to tell you that Hazel Kirk's [2] wedding occurs the latter
part of this month and Grandma & I are both invited to the church
& the reception & dance following at the Union Club. From what I
hear it is to be a wonderful affair and we are planning to go.

Mollie is well also John [3] who has not yet been called to War.
Harry Vaughn [4] left last night & Alice & Fred Crane are heartbroken.

Fifteen Hundred boys left this morning and as many more go
Friday— There's plenty of War doings here now—

My most devoted love is yours and your are always my dearest
sweetheart—

As Always—/ Grace—

My best regards to Mrs Walton. If you or she can get me a job in
the Movies, just wire me & I'll be there the next morning— [5] Write
often, or I shall be miserable.

To Grace Hart Crane

[New York City]
October 5, 1917

ALS, 2 pp.

My dear Mother:—

I dined with the Brookses again last night and took a French lesson afterward. I wish you would please send me my copy of "Char-
denal's Complete French Course" as soon as you can. If you don't

---

[2] Hazel Kirk, daughter of Netta and Frank Martin Kirk, was married to Captain Tyler Waterman Carlisle on October 22, 1917.

[3] Mollie Abrogast, Mrs. Crane's maid, and John Lloyd, the handyman who
worked at Mrs. Hart's house.

[4] Harry Vaughn worked for N. B. Madden, the husband of Clarence Crane's
sister Bess, at the Burroughs Adding Machine Company.

[5] Crane's landlady, Mrs. Walton, had had some experience in the movies. At
this time she helped him with his scenarios.

find it lying about, it doubtless is packed with some of my other books and can be sent right along with them.

Yesterday witnessed the great red-cross parade on Fifth which took three hours to exhaust itself. I am still working hard on my novel's plot.

Sometime today, I expect to hear from you, and may be I can get a special delivery to you on Sunday.

Love to all/ Hart.

To Grace Hart Crane

[New York City]
Saturday Oct. 6, 1917

ALS, 6 pp.

My dear Mother:—

The Isle of Pines trouble, I think, should be finished with this last fatality. I wouldn't invest another cent in the grove, and would only expend enough to keep the house from falling down. Surely, this is all you intend to do isn't it? Grandma can ill afford to spend any of her money for repairs on that investment. About the only thing to do is to regard the amount it was worth as thrown in the sea, and face around and forget it. Thank the Lord, not *all* of Grandma's money was invested *there*.

I am writing to C.A. today and I shall mention the rent overdue and your expenditure on my clothes. They, the clothes, have meant a great deal to me. I feel quite comfortable now when I go out.

Isn't it really astonishing how C.A. has managed to keep away from New York. Erwin is ruining him, I guess. Hazel says that all the buyers here are furious about the twenty-five cent raise on the price of his candy. That is too bad about Aunt Alma.[1] She was deserving of much better treatment. Tell me about her, and what she finds to do.

---

[1] "Aunt" Alma, the wife of Elton P. Crane (a cousin of Clarence's), worked for a short time as a hostess in a tearoom that C.A. ran in Cleveland. After Mr. Crane dismissed her, she worked in the Burrows Book Store.

George Bryan [2] called on me this morning on his way to school in N.J. He will probably spend some week-ends with me during the winter, which will make it pleasant.

My novel about the Isle of Pines has been somewhat blown to pieces by that blasting letter of yours. However I am busy thinking up plots for Smart Set stories.[3] You see, I want to make my literary work bring me in a living by the time I reach twenty-five and one cannot begin too soon.

Grandma writes that you are terribly upset about people not coming to call on you. Now this forgetfulness, Mother, is all it is. Half of them doubtless are ignorant of your return from New York, so try and look them up and inform them of the fact.

George said he saw you and you looked very stunning. You can't expect people to coming flocking in as soon as you get in the house anyway.

Doesn't Mr. Ely [4] help you any more? I wish you would really understand Science, because you would cease this useless suffering immeadiately. Now do cheer up, you have a good home to live in, plenty of money, and a son who loves you to death,

                                                    your/ Hart

To Grace Hart Crane

                                        [New York City]
                                        Monday, Oct 8, '17

ALS, 4 pp.

My dear Mother:—

I do hope that you got my S.D. on Sunday as I intended. You see, I have acquired some specially sized paper for your daily letters, and quite distinctive, don't you think? [1]

---

[2] George Bryan, Crane's friend from Cleveland, attended Carlton Academy in Summit, New Jersey.

[3] There is no record of Crane ever having sent a story to this magazine.

[4] Daniel M. Ely, the Christian Science practitioner who had treated the Crane family. See Harold's letter of January 26, 1916, to his mother.

---

[1] This was a single sheet of gray writing paper that measured 9 x 5½ inches. The present letter is the only extant letter written on this paper.

I take my second French lesson this evening, and there remains only a few hours in which to get it, so I cant write long. I like the Madame very much. She is training me more extensively in the grammatical points than M. Tardy did. And also does she know all about the artistic and literary side of Parisian life, her husband being quite a prominent painter there. She tells me considerable about the Awards too.

Mrs. Walton and I are working out movie scenarios. She has had considerable experience and is of great help to me.

Now I feel obliged in honour to tell you that the Brooks have *not* been paid for that dinner yet. After you left town, I found that I had spent entirely too much of that week's allowance on the last meal at the Waldorf and on tips and taxi-fare. I have had to borrow on the next week's allowance every week since, and as 25 dollars is *just* enough to exist on, you see, I haven't felt it possible once to repay them. They have also *treated* me several times since and I feel that it cannot go on any longer. If you can send four dollars in your next letter it will clear that snag out for good.

Mr. Kennedy [2] sent me a note last week and asked me to call on him at his Bway. office. I shall do this very soon. Now cheer up, my blessed virtuous Mother. You'll never know how much I have admired you. Can't you see that C.A. is not your equal?

Love and kisses / Hart.

To Grace Hart Crane

[New York City]
Tuesday—Oct 9, 1917

ALS, 2 pp.

My dear Mother:—

It is cold and pouring rain today. I have just returned from the library and barely escaped ruining my beautiful felt hat in the rain.

Parades,—parades,—parades: I am so tired of them. All the firemen in town, undaunted by the rain, insist on parading up Fifth

---

[2] Mr. Kennedy was a friend of Mrs. Hart's.

Ave. and blockading traffic so that one can't get either a bus or reach the subway. There have been nurse parades, and dog-parades and cat-parades and all to that eternally rapturous and boresome melody "Over There." I must confess that these days I am thankful to be *in* most of the time.

I wrote C.A. yesterday about my financial condition, and ought to hear from him soon. Please hurry with my books. I need them.

Affectionately, your son,—/ Hart.

From Clarence Arthur Crane

[Cleveland]
October Tenth
Nineteen Seventeen

TLC, 3 pp.

Mr. Harold Crane
25 East 11th Street
New York City

My dear Harold:—

Your letter of October 8 was duly received. It is the first one that you have written me for three weeks, so I can easily understand that I am not to receive communications from you frequently.

It is a hard letter for me to answer for many reasons. Our visit in the summer seemed to be very satisfactory so far as you and I were concerned. I thought we had established a very good basis and pleased me very much. It has not endured the test of time, apparently, but perhaps you will see things in a different light later on, at least in so far as they pertain to you, personally.

Your father wants to do everything for his only boy that he should do. It will not matter to me that one or two opinions should be against my own in any decisions which I may come to with reference to your welfare. There are certain standards which are considered good by men who have made a success of life, and they are not influenced materially by sentiment.

I am coming to New York before long, and when I do, we will go over our matters very carefully and consider them from the standpoint of what it is best for me to do under existing conditions and what it is best for you to receive under your conditions. I am not going to dwell upon the matter extensively now. I am just going to give you a few things to think about, and we will talk them over at close range.

You contradict yourself in your letter. You say I owe your mother $51 for your winter's coat and suit, and on the last page you tell me that you haven't a single winter's suit, and are in debt $7 on your next week's allowance, etc. You must have meant that you did not have your suit and coat until after your mother purchased it, for I know you went back to New York splendidly equipped for the balance of the summer.

You are doing an unheard of thing, and have for almost a year; —living in New York and simply studying,—having a good allowance sent you each week without regard to your qualifying in any way for you to make a part of your living in any way yourself. For instance, you have taken a room and are paying $11 a week for it. That is on the basis of $47 a month, and the quarters of your father, who is forty-two years old,—with his life well spent—only exceeds your apartment cost by $3 a month. I would always be glad to have you so live that the environment was conducive to your intellectual growth, but I do not believe in letting you go on in this way indefinitely without some thought as to where the money is coming from and whether or not it is the right course to pursue.

I set your allowance at $25 per week. This I will continue, and will also, at intervals, take great pleasure in providing you with suitable clothing as I have done in the past, but if you are only devoting $2 a week to tutoring, you must have a large amount of time on your hands. I think it would be well for you to seek some employment for, say, half the time each day. Surely, if you study all of the forenoon and a portion of each evening, you are accomplishing a great deal. That would give you some revenue and more than the revenue, it would give you independence, which you must absolutely crave, to the extent of buying a few things without asking father for the money. This is your youth; it is the time in which you are laying the foundation for your life, and life is work and nothing but work.

I appreciate what you say with reference to living cost in New York and it is very true. The same applies here. I have never been able to understand why it was necessary for you to be in New York to accomplish what you are doing, but I am not averse to your following this scheme out for a little while until we mutually determine upon a better course. I do not want you to have the idea that your father is making an unlimited amount of money.

Whenever the world condition gets in its present shape, each and every one of us must bear his full share of it. Our profits have been cut very materially since we had to purchase a new supply of goods last spring. Our advances have cared for some of it, but a long way from all of it. On top of that, we are called upon, this year, to turn over to the Government in one lump sum, on June 1st next, in our case a percentage of better than fifty percent of our profits. This is going to be a hardship of which we do not even know, as yet, how we are going to meet.

I do not desire to take these things up with your mother, nor do I desire you to quote me. You are approaching maturity; we ought to talk together as two business men,—face our issues, and arrive at what is best for you. I do not want you to get the idea that I am facing hardship, I only want you to know that your thought and purpose must be earnestly along the lines of good useful citizenship, and that you are now forming habits which are going to be a powerful influence in a very few years.

My younger life was not one of privation, but it surely it was not one of "easy-going". If there is any one thing that I can thank my father for, it was the willingness on his part to let me know the value of money and to get a taste of how it was acquired. When you were a baby in arms, I moved to Warren with less money than I give you every four months, and with a full responsibility of a family. It has always meant that there was earnest work for me at every sunrise. I have now reached an age when I think more seriously than ever before. I have gone through experiences which tell me every day that "life is earnest".

I want you to appreciate that the condition of affairs today is not easy, neither to endure nor to compass. No one can tell what is going to happen. It all depends on the duration of the war and the condition that it leaves us in at the end of it.

You may think from this letter that your father is in low spirits this morning, but I am not. There is just as much "game" in me as ever, but I frankly confess that I am no prophet, and we are only living from day to day, making as good a guess as we are capable of, as to what is going to happen. I can carry my burden very nicely so far as the burden itself is concerned, but I would like the satisfaction of the knowledge that my efforts for others, and for you more than any one else, are fully appreciated and understood.

The obligation which I have with your mother the next year, under the conditions, will represent more than fifty percent of my income, and we must all have a care as to the future.

Write me, now, about the suit and coat, for if you really have it and your mother has paid for it, I want to send you a check to cover.

Very truly yours,

From Grace Hart Crane

[Cleveland]
Thursday 8 P.M.
Oct 11—1917

ALS, 8 pp.

My dear Hart:—

When grandma & I returned a few moments ago from town where we went this morning, I found two letters from you in the box. Molly and John went out today, so we had our dinner on our way home at McNally Doyle's— And there we found Miss Butler [1] behind the counter. She has just accepted a position with them and I should think in a short time would feel quite at home and prove quite an acquisition to them. This has been such a busy day—in

---

[1] Miss Butler formerly worked for Clarence Crane. McNally Doyle's was a confectionery store in Cleveland.

fact all are—because we have upset the house so and must get things back in shape. Today we selected new electric fixtures for dining room & front hall. I know this will be good news to you. I also bought a new library table—and we have new lineoleom on entire kitchen hall & pantry. This time it [is] the right color and makes the place so much more cheerful.

Sunday & Monday I unpacked about 12 or 15 barrells of dishes of ours that were packed in Warren when we left there, & after saving out what we need we are going to have a sale I think to get them out of the way. The old house is beginning to show the work I have put on it and at Xmas I am sure you will be glad we have done what we have.

Zell was up the other day and I have invited her, Nannie,[2] Griswold & Helen here for Xmas, and she has accepted. So when you come home we will have some fun. I shall probably be with you for Thanksgiving and I hope Mrs Walton can give me a room for several weeks, but I do not want Hazel to know of my plans, so don't mention me to her. I have not seen your father at all only once at the store when he did not see me. He told Alice Crane that he had a lot of new help coming from the West—and Aunt Alma was asked to leave immediately, after having given her three weeks notice. To put it mildly, his actions are very strange & unfair—but I am trying to forget—

Hazel Kirks' wedding is to be the evening of the twentieth and I am doing all I can to be extremely fit—for the occasion— I tried on my last years evening gowns last night and find the white and gold to be the choice. I am improving in looks every day—and Mrs McTague's facial are getting in their work—

Dear boy I miss you *so much* I hardly know how to stand it. Saw Mr Sullivan today and he inquired about you. He said he had been trying to get to New York every day—asked for your address and phone number, which I gave. He thought you had improved so much—

Grandma & I had to get a wedding present for Hazel Kirk, which we did today. One doz. beautiful desert plates—Dolton ware.

With one or two days of rain we have had fine weather ever since I returned. I am able to wear my new fur cape with good effect

[2] Nannie was Zell Hart Deming's mother.

apparently— You do not mail your S.D. letters early enough on Saturday for me to get them on Sunday. Try to do better. Zell tells me that Gertrude & Carl [3] are in Warren, but not married—and that Gertrude is only on a visit & will return and leave Carl to his painting. Zell thinks they never *will* be married. Griswold has not been called yet but may be any day— I want to get down there very soon now. There are so many things I want to do but as yet can't find the time. This house must be gotten in shape so that it will look well if we should entertain over night any of the guests for the Kirk wedding—which we have offered to do.

There are other things I should write but havn't the time now[.] Will run down to the mail box with this now.

My best & quantities of love goes with this to you. Let me know what my chances are for a room with Mrs Walton. Remember me to the Brook's.

As Ever/ Your Devoted Mother Grace—

From Grace Hart Crane

CLEVELAND O
1917 OCT 21 AM

TELEGRAM

HOUSE FULL OF COMPANY UNTIL AFTER THE WEDDING NO TIME TO WRITE YOU FOR SUNDAY ALL YOUR LETTERS RECEIVED AND WILL ANSWER SOON HOPE YOU ARE FEELING BETTER ALL WELL AND SEND MUCH LOVE / GRACE

To Grace Hart Crane and Elizabeth Belden Hart

[New York City]
Oct 26, 1917

ALS, 5 pp.

My dear Mother and Grandma:—

Yesterday afternoon Elizabeth Gardiner gave me two complimen-

[3] Carl Schmitt and his fiancée Gertrude Lord.

taries to a concirt at Aeolion Hall, and this enabled me to take Mr. Brooks and return at least one of the many favors he has bestowed on me.[1] We enjoyed it very much, afterward meeting Mrs. Brooks and dining at Gonfarones. Their apartment is quite charming with lots of colour in draperies furniture etc. which Mrs. Brooks is fond of. I nearly laughed myself ill during the evening and then returned and wrote a poem.

Dont write, Mother, if it makes you nervous. I can readily understand how that might be, for I myself have often felt so about it. Especially letters.

Your stories about the house surely sound inspiring. It must be quite beautiful around there now. I always felt that with a few modern accessories the house would be very liveable.

Now if I knew exactly when you want to come to New York, I could make some arrangements for rooms, but you understand it might be quite confusing otherwise, surely. I think that I can undoubtedly find a room very near me here at any time, but in making a reservation a certain exactness is necessary. My room is quite lovely and whenever we want to have a few people in, it can be done here. I have lately discovered that I can have an open fire in the grate, any time I want it. When Carl returns, I may be able to procure a few of his pictures and that will add much.

Mother, when you arrive, I hope you will take up the Noyes dancing [2] and enter the movies. You will find it fun I am sure, and I shall help you too. I am really getting a reputation for poetry and can find space now in at least two magazines for most of my better work. But let me know when you are coming for I am anxious to see you. We shall have no more melancholia around now. I am sure I shall never let you succumb to that again. I think you will enjoy meeting my French teacher. Then too, it might be a good idea for you to take it up yourself. The freedom from responsibility which you will have on your future visits here will make it seem very comfortable for you, I am sure.

Now I cannot see how C.A. is going to send my books without

[1] Crane and Brooks heard a recital given by the French soprano Gabrielle Gills.
[2] Hart refers again to Mrs. Florence Fleming Noyes, who had given Mrs. Crane lessons in Rhythmical Physical Culture.

having to communicate with you, and so, wont you send them and let me pay you later. If you fail to do so soon, I shall have to purchase several which I already own, and that would be especially foolish. Any way, it wont cost so terribly much.

Write soon if you feel like it and remember that I am always faithful to your love. Mrs. Brooks told me last night to send you her love in my next letter.

Affectionately, / Hart.

This letter is a terrible jumble, but please excuse it.

From Grace Hart Crane

Cleveland—Ohio—
Oct—26—1917.

ALS, 6 pp.

My dear Hart:—

This evening I intended to write you a long letter telling you all the news—but grandma and I got to talking & the time passed until it is now after ten— So I will not write all I had expected to — I want this to go S.D. tomorrow and I want it to tell you I love you more than any thing in the world. I received your good letter this morning with enclosure of poetry which I have read twice but not enough to feel that I can give you an intelligent opinion on it yet. I am so happy to know you are meeting people who are giving you favorable comment, and feel sure you will win eventually if you keep your head—which I have reason to think you will.

The Kirk wedding was a very grand affair and your grandmother & I went attired in our best, our very best. I believe I am not saying too much when I say that you would have been pleased with us both— We had a good time everyone was nice & I had a few dances & saw quite a number of old friends— We stayed until twelve oclock— Next week I want to get my teeth fixed— Would have done so before but have had such a terrible cold I would have been unfit to work on. We had so much company too—- Clara Dunham stayed two nights, Mrs Wilcox the same & Helen Hurlburt

one. We have fixed up the house so nicely you will enjoy your
Xmas visit I am sure—

I want to come to New York very soon, say in at least two weeks
& stay until Xmas— I am so anxious to get a room near you—
Hasn't Mrs Walton any possibility in vacancies? I find I miss you
very much and I just must be near you for a time at least— I do
not wish you to mention that I am contemplating coming to anyone only Mrs Walton— I realize I must have a reservation some
where at this time of year—else I will have to bunk with you. So
make some inquiries around there & see what you can do—

Grandma is quite well— John does not yet know whether he is
really going to War or not—& Molly is knitting. In fact evry one
but myself.

I would write oftener—but I have been so busy & when I had
the time I was too nervous. Tomorrow I am going to town to buy a
Liberty Bond or two— We may go to Warren for over Sunday—

I think the Brooks' are just fine to you Harold. Please do not neglect to show your appreciation. Alice & Fred [1] have just returned
from New York where they told me they tried to get in touch with
you and failed. You spoke some time ago about your father saying
he was coming to New York soon— Has he been yet and if not
when he does come please do send me a wire as I should not want
to be there when he is—or run in to him— Besides there are reasons why I should like to know when he is there.

> Goodnight, & my best love—/ from/ Grace. (over)

On second thought I do not mind your mentioning in your next
letter to your father that I am planning to spend Thanksgiving
with you, as it will keep him off the ground that particular day,
which we must plan to be festive in some way.

[1] Possibly Hart's aunt Alice Crane and his great-uncle Frederic Crane.

To Grace Hart Crane

[New York City]
[October 31, 1917?]
Wednesday—

ALS, 2 pp.

Ma chére et charmante mére:—

Yesterday it poured rain all day and I remained sheltered, studying French. But November is less evident now, and the sun is out
again. I suppose that you are all right although I have had no letter
since Sunday. Mrs. Walton went off to the movies this morning,
which makes me think again that it would be aggreeable for you to
enter them when you arrive. After I mail this, I am going up to the
"Little Review" office & have a talk with Margaret Anderson, (and
perhaps dispose of a poem).

I suppose you have seen Hazel,[1] but maybe not though after all.
She was thru on vivid business difficulties, and may not have had
time.

My love to all,/ fondly,/ Hart.

I hasten to add that I have changed my mind somewhat about the
room. I shall take one temporarily here in the same house, and you
can have mine. This will be very convenient, you see. Please hurry
and tell me *when* you are coming for reservation.

From Grace Hart Crane

[Cleveland]
[November 1, 1917?]
Thursday A.M.—

ALS, 4 pp.

Dear Hart:—

Your letter written Tuesday came this morning and bless your
dear heart I am so sorry not to have returned to New York with

---

[1] Hazel Hasham.

Hazel— The reason was that I was not able to hurry up & get my things together. You know I have not been well for sometime, & therefore undecided about what to do & when to do it—but Hazel left here Monday saying she would make reservations at the Nassau Hotel, Long Beach—& let me know. I have not yet heard from her —but am expecting to get a letter today. Grandma's letter which you must have received by this time will explain our plans—but I think it will be Saturday or Sunday night before I can leave here. Everything hinders— The laundress disappointed us this week & Molly is doing the washing alone— Grandma has quite a good deal to attend to and that leaves me with my own things & some house-work to attend to—& it is hard to get reservations on trains going east just now too. But will wire you just as soon as I know something— The weather has been something terrible here and I shall be *so glad* to get back to you & Old New York once more. That seems like home to me, now.

Was so glad to learn of your meeting Mdm. Petrova [1]—and con-gratulate you upon being [2] able to meet most any one you wish— You were certainly born under the star of Luck—

The Warren Tribune of recent date announces the engagement of Mr Carl Schmidt to Gertrude Lord—of New York. I *never was so surprised*.

We will have to get busy & hunt for an apartment *soon*— Have Mrs Grosse clean things up & be sure to meet me at the train when I wire you we are coming. Lots of love from us both/ from / Grace—

[1] Mme Olga Petrova, the actress, in a letter to the editor, remembered meeting Crane at the home of theatrical producer Edyth Totten.
[2] The word "being" is repeated in the text.

From Grace Hart Crane

1709 E—115 St.
Cleveland, O.
Nov. 2—1917.

ALS, 8 pp.

My dear Hart:—

This is Friday night and I am dead tired and totally unable to account for the time and how I have spent it. Sunday morning Grandma and I went to Warren & stayed until Monday night, seeing & visiting with a lot of people. Since then I don't know where the time has gone. I have been going to the dentist for one thing and am still—

Miss Hasham came out for a short call one evening while here, of which she will no doubt tell you about.

Mr Sullivan came out last night and I had a good talk with him. Of course the sugar proposition [1] has caused me a good deal of anxiety and then your letters containing what they did have made me wonder just where we were at— But today things have straightened out beautifully and I am very happy & not at all worried for the present. Your letter telling me of your intention of taking another room at Mrs Waltons has been a great relief to me—both because I did not want you to leave there & because it opens a possibility of our being together in the location which we so much desire.

Think as kindly of your father as you can—write him as often as you feel you should, and above all say nothing to anybody—against him. It looks now as though he and I were perfectly able to live without the society of each other, and I am getting a better grip upon myself— You won't have such a droopy mother to manage when I come back to you, I feel quite sure, & there are good times & plenty to eat in store for us. I think when we get together many difficulties can be straightened out and we can have some jolly good times. I intend going to Miss Noyes school, for *one* thing. All your trials can be turned into valuable results in your line of work if

[1] There were reports in newspapers at this time of Cuban rebels destroying the sugar crop.

you will only look at it that way. *Human* nature & *Human* experience are with us constantly and we do not have to go far away to study them. Keep out of debt as much as *possible* and if you owe your landlady anything I will attend to that as soon as I come, which will probably be a week for Sunday morning. I have a lot to do this coming week which I want to relieve mother of. I am going to Mr Ely & he is helping me wonderfully. Go slow on treating your friends this week— You know that debts worry me and I want you to keep out of them as much as possible. If the Brook's ask you to dine with them I would want you to accept because they are wholesome people & have your best interest at heart. When I come we can do something for them.

Now dear boy keep a level head as you most always have, and try to be charitable a[nd] fair to your father— Altho' he is fast passing out of my life, I want always to give him credit when credit is due, & I find hating any one or resentment are very disastrous things to ones health & in fact to one's whole life. I will not go further into this matter until I see you.

Grandma & in fact we are all quite well once more— The house will be a joy to you when you return for Christmas, & we will try to have a happy one—

I did not see Carl when in Warren— But Helen & Griswold have a charming home, & they make one feel that marriage can be a wonderfully successful adventure, sometimes.

I shall have much to tell you when I return & I want you to be happy thinking of the good times in store for us. Don't let your nature be embittered by anything you hear or see, but always know there is a sane way out of every difficulty.

This is all for tonight as I am so very tired I want to take a bath and go to bed early—

My best love to my dear Hart from/ Grace—

P.S. I forgot to say that we are going to entertain at dinner Sunday night The Kirks & The Collvers.—

Grace went to New York shortly before Thanksgiving, 1917. For an account of the disastrous events that occurred there we must rely almost entirely on Philip Horton's biography of Crane, since nearly all records of this period are lost. Upon her arrival, Mrs. Crane told Horton nearly twenty years later, Hart was taken "seriously ill" with "obscure nervous disorders." Grace called C.A., asking him to help, but, according to Horton's account, "Mr. Crane replied flatly that he would not come to New York even if his son were dying." [1] With this rebuff Mrs. Crane succumbed to her own poor nervous condition and was confined to her bed. In the meantime Hart had recovered enough to be seriously concerned for his mother's health, and he wired his aunt Zell in Warren, who came East to restore—temporarily at least—a semblance of order in the lives of her sister-in-law and nephew. By Christmas, Hart and his mother had returned to Cleveland. Once again Clarence renewed his affectionate gestures, this time making Hart and Grace "guests of honor" at a New Year's party. Remembering all too well the troubles of the previous summer and fall, Hart threatened to break with both parents if their relations became more cordial.

Grace and her son returned to New York in January, 1918; unaffected by his son's feelings, C.A. pressed his quest through correspondence and handsome boxes of Mary Garden Chocolates. In February another crisis developed. This time Clarence said he would withhold his son's allowance if he did not have evidence that Hart was employed. Thinking that her son's employment would bring her closer to her former husband, Grace urged Hart to take a job with the Crane company. Another bitter argument followed, and again the poet threatened to break with both parents. The quarrel was serious enough to drive Grace back to her bed in a state of nervous collapse. This time Mrs. Florence Spencer, a former Clevelander, friend of the Brookses, and a Christian Science practitioner, effected Grace's recovery. Grace was well enough to return to Cleveland for Easter. Mrs. Spencer and her daughter, Claire, who soon became Hart's good friends, persuaded the poet to take a temporary position at Brentano's bookstore, thus assuring him his allowance.

Mrs. Crane sent the following telegram to her son after she had returned to Cleveland.

[1] Quoted from Philip Horton, *Hart Crane: The Life of an American Poet* (New York: Viking, 1957), p. 54.

From Grace Hart Crane

1918 MAR 30 PM 11 31

S CLEVELAND O

TELEGRAM

I AM SENDING YOU MY LOVE AND EASTER GREETINGS WITH ALL
THAT THE TERM MEANS AM FEELING BETTER AND HOPE YOU
ARE WELL AND YOUR PLANS WORKING OUT TO PLEASE YOU/
GRACE

Another emotional crisis for Mrs. Crane took place in early
May. She learned that Clarence, whose attentions toward her had
diminished in the late spring, was planning to marry Frances Kelley, a young woman who worked in the Kansas City branch of the
Crane company. More than ever before, Mrs. Crane felt she needed
her son. She urged him to return to East 115th Street, promising a
car, good food, and a comfortable lodging. One letter reminded
him of the war and advised him to work in one of Cleveland's defense plants.

Life was not going well for Hart in New York. Though he had
recently been appointed associate editor of *The Pagan,* the position
did not provide him with an income; as a consequence he was continually short of funds. By June, 1918, Crane was unable to resist
any longer. He returned home to take a job in a munitions plant.

From Grace Hart Crane

[Cleveland]

Friday 5 P.M.—

April 8, '18

ALS, 3 pp.

My deart Hart:

For two days snow flurries have spoiled my chances for a drive to
Akron with Miss McMyler & her mother in their car. So now it is

postponed until someday next week— Tomorrow we four have luncheon at the Hollenden [1] & afterwards go to the Colonial to see The Gypsy Trail,[2] which as you know has been in New York all winter & was written by a Cleveland man. Tomorrow night I am going to become a member of The [3] little playhouse Co—which has a mission something like the Greenwich Theater in New York— Your book store man of The Taylor Arcade is a member and I shall hope to meet & talk with him— [4]

Next Wednesday night I am going to hear Joseph Hiepth [5] the violinist at Grays Armory. Mrs Baker is going with me.

Further than that I have no definite plans—only I find that there are a lot of things both in business & household ways for me to attend to before I can feel right in returning to New York. In the meantime—want you to know that I have certainly appreciated your good letters & assurances of affection— That I miss your comrardship very much but hope you will write often & let me know what you are doing & your plans— Please know that I always love you & feel that you will before long find your right place & an opportunity to express yourself to your satisfaction. Give my love to dear Mdm LeBegue & tell her I appreciated her Easter & birthday card. Remember me to Stan—& tell him I went to the Blue Bird [6] purposely to see him but they reeled the films so fast that he was not like most of the others given a fair chance to be appreciated.

I hope you are still fond of the Spencers[.] I do not see how you can avoid being so—and I miss them even though I have known them so short a time. Give them my love and tell Mrs Spencer her letters have been most helpful—

Please do not worry about me one minute but just know that I am always alright—I have my problems to work out and I am doing them in the best way I know, I hope you will always remember to keep me informed as to your work etc— Grandma sends

---

[1] The Hollenden Hotel in Cleveland.

[2] *The Gypsy Trail*, a comedy written by Robert Housum from Cleveland.

[3] The word "The" is repeated in the text.

[4] Richard Laukhuff, whose excellent bookstore located in Cleveland's Taylor Arcade had an extensive collection of British, American, and European literature, as well as numerous little magazines. See *Voyager*, pp. 47–48.

[5] Jascha Heifetz gave a special performance on April 17, 1918.

[6] Stanislaw Portapovitch had a small dancing part in the silent film version of Maurice Maeterlinck's *The Blue Bird*.

much love along with mine— Always Devotedly Your Mother—
/ Grace.

From Grace Hart Crane

Saegertown, Pa.
[Late April or early May, 1918?]
Tuesday

ALS, 3 pp.
LETTERHEAD: Ye Olde Inn, Saegertown, Pa.

My dear Hart:—
You would know it is Spring down here— [1] Have just returned
from a long walk in the sunshine which has appeared in full glory
after a shower—
Mrs Baker and I return home tomorrow after a few pleasant days
here. I see much to remind me of you and my early life here—once
you may remember you fell in the river close by here & were fished
out by a Jap—I am sure if you were here now a wonderful poem
would be the result. Maybe you & I can come here together sometime in a machine. I am thinking of buying a "chummy Roadster,["]
& if you decide to spend your vacation in Cleveland this summer I
will see that you learn to drive it—
What would you think of coming to Cleveland for the summer,
taking a job somewhere & motor for diversion. I do not write you
often my dear boy but my love goes out to you constantly. Shall
hope to find a letter from you when I return home tomorrow.
Give my love to Mrs Spenser & Mdm Le Begue—

Devotedly/ Your Mother/ Grace.

[1] Mrs. Crane was on a short visit to Saegertown, Pennsylvania.

From Grace Hart Crane

[Cleveland]
[Early May, 1918?]

ALS, 4 pp.

My dear Son:—

Your letters including enclosures from your father were here when I returned from Saegertown— Now I am going to make this *suggestion,* notice I do not command—

There is a good home awaiting you here & food that you have forgotten how good it tastes. There are also plenty of jobs if you want them & a warm welcome for you if you should decide to spend the summer here instead of hot New York—

I am thinking very strongly of buying a car, & as I wrote you from Saegertown you may learn to drive it.

The War now is a real issue & there is no dodging one's duty towards helping in one way or another. I think I have found where I can be active & not deppressed— Whether you are in N.Y. or here, The Government demands that all young men 18 or over be occupied in some way— Don't you think that during the summer it would be a good change to come back here & get a job of some kind & have the use of an auto on Sundays— You have within your grasp the privildge of making me very happy by having you with me for a while during a time which may be very trying & hard for me to bear— You have often said you considered it a privildge to live— Then thank your father & mother for that and repay them for their desires for your happiness & welfare by doing something for them— It may be that your father has selected a wonderful woman for his second wife—or at least one who will make him happy— I am not going to say that I am glad that he is to be married so soon—because I had thought that someday with the necessary separation & time to view things more broadly we might all three again be happily reunited— But it doesn't look that way now[.] However you have no quarrel with your father over that anymore than if I should take the same step.

So please write him a good letter to that effect very soon— I know he does care for you & you for him. Then if you see nothing more tempting accept my suggestion & return here to the best bed & meals & the most devoted hearts await you. Wire me your decision when you have made it. This plan is only for the summer you know—

I was delighted to know you had stopped smoking—no wonder you feel better. My best love to the Sensors. Molly says if you come home bring a Pomer[a]nian dog with you— You cant buy them here. My what a summer with dog, flees, gasoline, & poetry!!

If you decide to come you can likely store your desk, book case & Object D'rt at your fathers office—bringing such books as you may need here back with you in your little trunk—

Love from us all—

Devotedly Your/ Mother Grace—

From Elizabeth Belden Hart

[Cleveland]
May 16—1918
10—AM—

ALS, 3 pp.

Dear Harold:

The Pagan [1] has just arrived—and as Mother is trying to be ready for her driving lesson—(The man is due here now.) and she is not ready— She is so anxious for you to know she will write you as soon as she has time to read it more thoroughly— She glanced it over & tears of joy & pride came into her eyes—to see that her boy is going to realize some of the things he has long been laboring for — She is very happy over it. She is busy every minute— Yesterday the McMylers took us on a long drive, in the country & had ordered a very sumptuous luncheon for us— We drove over 100 miles — She also took a riding lesson at the Armory with Gertrude [2] and in the evening she went to the Play House, a company she has

---

[1] *The Pagan*, Vol. III (April–May, 1918), published Crane's "Carrier Letter" and "Postscript," p. 20, as well as his essay "The Case Against Nietzsche," p. 34.

[2] Possibly Gertrude Lord, Carl Schmitt's fiancée.

May 16 – 1918
10 – AM –

Dear Harold;

The Pagan has just arrived –
and as Mother is trying to be ready for
her driving lesson – (The man is due here
now.) and she is not ready – She is so
anxious for you to know she will write
you as soon as she has time to read it
more thoroughly – She glanced it over &
tears of joy came into her eyes – to see
that her boy is going to realize some
of the things he has long been laboring
for – She is very happy over it – She is
busy every minute – Yesterday the McMylers
took us on a long drive, in the country
& had ordered a very sumptuous luncheon
for us – We drove over 100 miles – She also –

First page of letter of May 16, 1918,
from Elizabeth Belden Hart to Hart Crane

joined—and they are working on a play—called the Marionette [3] which is to be called off—in June—& this takes three evenings practice a week—so you see she is getting very busy—which is her only salvation— She loves her car which is doing the work that nothing else could have— We expect to drive to Warren Sunday if the weather permits— They say her car is the handsomest in Cleve —& they wanted to show it in the Window— It is very plain but elegant & nobby— I am now ready to go to town but listened to Mothers importunities to write you— Excuse my long letter—there is much more to tell you—that would please you I am sure but am trying to abbreviate—

Every body is lovely to Mother and are trying to plan things for her pleasure [.]

So don't worry— She is thinking lovely things of her boy if she does not write—and feels sure of his final success—

As Ever / Grandmother

Recd Mrs. Spencers letter [.] She has taken a new practitioner here —[4] and everything is coming on beautifully—and one of us will write soon [.] She was so bad for a time [.] She had to have some one right here [.] Much love to her—from Mother & myself [.] She will try to write her soon [.]

From Grace Hart Crane

1918 MAY 19 PM 10 45
CLEVELAND O

TELEGRAM

BUSY DAYS FOR ME HAVE NOT FORGOTTEN TO LOVE YOU GRIS-WOLD JUST ARRIVED AND WILL PROBABLY SEE ZELL AND HELEN HERE OR WARREN TOMORROW MAY DRIVE NEW CAR TO WARREN NOTHING CERTAIN THESE DAYS FEELING FINE MUCH TO WRITE YOU SOON BURGLARS AGAIN/ MOTHER.

[3] Possibly *The Marionettes*, a four-act comedy by Pierre Wolff.
[4] These sentences refer to Grace Crane, not Mrs. Spencer.

Clarence Crane's marriage to Frances Kelley was set for July, and as the date drew near, Grace became more and more tense. This time she resorted to travel to ease her nerves. Mrs. Hart, Grace, and Charles, their chauffeur, set out on July 4 for a tour of New York and New England in Mrs. Crane's new roadster that she had affectionately named "Diana." Just two weeks after their departure, Hart left his job at the munitions plant; the rest of the summer was spent looking halfheartedly for other work.

The following five letters from Mrs. Hart and Mrs. Crane were written while they were on their motor tour.

From Elizabeth Belden Hart

9-30 AM—
New York, July 15 1918

ALS, 6 pp.
LETTERHEAD: The Waldorf Astoria

My Dear Hart.

Mother and I have just returned from breakfast at the McAlpin restaurant— A splendid meal for 65 cts. and excellent service.[1] While she is having a shampoo and her feet doctored I will talk to you a while. The day is bright and bids fair to be *hot*, which makes me feel weak in my pedals— We have so much to do—and so many plans—it is hard to know which way to go first but thus far —Mother seems to be quite equal to it. Our meeting so many we know has kept her mind busy—and I think she is getting along beautifully—and improving very rapidly the last three days—

We had a wonderful day yesterday. Left W. Point yesterday morning—after a very quiet nights rest, at a private boarding house just out of the military grounds— We got up early & had breakfast at 7-30—in order to take the Ferry—then we travelled south along

---

[1] The restaurant was located in the McAlpin Hotel at Broadway and 34th Street.

the Hudson all the way—striking Tarrytown for dinner—a lovely wayside Inn—you know there are so many in the Suburbs of NY. Then we succeeded in getting admission to Pocantico Hills [2]—of which we will tell you when we get home— Oh its beyond description—then we came on down via. Riverside drive—and reached here just as a big storm came up— You should see how beautifully Charles drives, but his eyes were in every direction and he made no mistakes. He is out and cleaning up the car, and getting it shining for this PM. He just *loves* that car. We had a delightful evening with the Colvers—and a Mrs. Clinger from Cleveland—whom I know, also Mrs. Spencer called—and she seemed so delighted to meet us again— Clare had the keys to the Photo gallery or studio,[3] and had to be there to open it for a party at such a time and could not come with her Mother—but we will see her today— Mrs. Spencer had so much to ask about you—and tell how she loves you. She certainly is a very charming woman. Mother misses you at every turn, and feels badly that you are not with us—but feels very proud of you for being so brave—to stick to your work and says you shall have a tour back this Fall if all goes well— Mollie writes you are doing fine and making the work much easier by your thoughtfulness. We expect Hazel in some time today —perhaps to lunch with us— She leaves for her vacation Wed. up in Maine— The Colvers leave at 1.PM today.

We have done the country so thoroughly thus far that we shall take a different route home—but what way has not been yet decided on— If Mother keeps up and improves right along—I shall try to keep her out as long as I can—or the money holds out. It might as well or better be spent in this way as Dr Bills— The war has changed conditions every where—and nothing seems the same here or any other place. I think of you very very often, and hope you are not unhappy—or at least are resting more quietly—since our departure—for it was anything but restful there. Once in a

[2] The name of John D. Rockefeller's estate at Tarrytown. The grounds were open to the public several days each week.

[3] The photography studio and gallery referred to, located at 1 Fifth Avenue, was owned by Nancy Shostac, a friend of Claire Spencer's. Mrs. Crane had her picture taken there in the dancing costume that she wore when she practiced eurythmics with Mrs. Noyes.

while Mother says, Oh how I wish I were at home—but it soon passes away—and lately she has not said so— I feel so comfortable to know you have Mollie to take care of you and look after things—in general— It is a great relief to me—

I presume you got your telegram last night & probably so late it may have alarmed you—but Mother had so much to look after when we first arrived it was impossible to wire sooner[.] Now I cannot tell you just where to write us[.] Possibly it might reach us here if you write immediately[.] Now I have sent one of my long letters again but I am killing time while waiting for Mother.

Oceans of love from Grandmother & all

Mothers letters would be much more interesting—but she has so much else to see to— I will try to releive her in this way—

[*Written sideways at the top of page five:*] Mother feels badly not to find her white oxfords in. She has no white shoes at all with her[.]

From Grace Hart Crane

New York,
July 19 1918

ALS, 3 pp.
LETTERHEAD: The Waldorf Astoria

My dear Hart:—

You see we are still here and will be until tomorrow or Sunday night. So many places to go & people to see here that we have been literally stuck. Have seen most of our old friends, including a visit to Ida Skiffs [1] wonderful home, a trip up to Mrs Noyes summer school and two trips to camp Merrit [2] where we found Helen & Griswold. Oh I have so much to tell you, you will be so interested to hear about. Have seen the Spensors several times & Stan once for an evening on the roof garden here which has been done over very beautifully this year— Today mother & I are resting and trying to get our plans made for our route home. Carl is still at camp

[1] Ida Skiff was the wife of Frank Vernon Skiff.
[2] Camp Merritt, an army camp, was located near Tenafly, New Jersey.

Gordon [3] where he is to enter a school for war artists & which will likely mean a commision later on— Charlie is simply amazed beyond words & says he doesn't know himself— Think he will never forget this trip— Today he is taking in the trip on boat around Manhattan Island— Pat Spenser [4] may be in Cleveland most any time on a furlough before going across— He will be with the Wintons, so keep your eyes & ears open for him & invite him out. We may not take the New England way home as I am getting very tired of motoring—but even so we have had a most wonderful trip & you will be amazed at all we have seen & done when I tell you.

Helen & Griswold have taken a little house and are intending to stay there for awhile—say two or three months— Gooz [5] looks very fine in his officers uniform & we had a lot of attention & some kodaks taken with the different men— There are 40,000 men [in] camp & while wonderfully cared for & etc, the most pathetic sights I have ever seen— About 5000 embark from there for over seas every day. I saw some leaving for boats yesterday & I nearly fainted. Be thankful that you are *permitted* to work in an ammunition factory these days. Must stop now [.]

> Much love from/ Your Mother Grace.

From Grace Hart Crane

> New York
> July 21—1918
> Sunday 10:30 AM

ALS, 3 pp.
LETTERHEAD: The Waldorf Astoria

Dearest:—

Have just wired you and now will drop a line to tell you that we are celebrating your birthday here by inviting Mdm Le. Begue &

---

[3] Camp Gordon, another army camp, was located near Atlanta, Georgia.

[4] Pat Spencer was the son of Mrs. Spencer. While in Cleveland he stayed with his aunt and uncle, Mr. and Mrs. Alexander Winton.

[5] "Gooz" was the nickname for Griswold Hurlbert.

Mrs Walton for luncheon at 1:30. The day is very hot & we are going to church in the car—

Gooz & Helen dined with us here last night— Gooz in his full dress uniform & looking corking—also Helen— We afterwards went to the Spensors for a short call & met Mrs Spensor & Clare. They had just received a line from Pat saying he had spent last Saturday & Sunday in Cleveland with his relatives—so you must have missed him. His next furlough will be here and then over seas— The city is full of all kinds of soldiers—& they are being sent across in large numbers now—

Must stop—

Much love/ from/ Mother.

We will likely leave here Tuesday for Boston etc—

From Grace Hart Crane

[New York City]
July 21—1918

POSTCARD

Dear Hart:—

We three have spent the afternoon together and ended up at 25—E—11 St. and am writing this on Mrs Walton's table. We all send our love & congratulations & have thought of you often. Charlie & Diana are out in front— [1]

Grace Crane—
Frances Walton.
Eugénie Lebègue

[1] "Diana" was the name that Mrs. Crane gave to her car.

From Grace Hart Crane

Manchester-in-the-Mountains, Vermont

Sunday, 6 P.M.

Aug 4—1918.

ALS, 2 pp.

LETTERHEAD: Equinox House

My dear Hart:—

After a ride of 175 miles through the White & Green mountains we landed here about an hour ago— It looks like rain but I am hoping it will not so that we can go to Lenox Mass. tomorrow and through the Berkshires. Then from there we will start home as fast as we can via Rochester, Niagara Falls, Buffalo and home. This place and Bretton Woods are full of Golfers— One can hardly move for golfsticks & the conversation is principally about that game. Give me horse back riding and swimming—

Tell Molly to expect an express package for me from Bretton Woods & to please open & take care of it— We have been gone a month today and seen so much it seems as tho' it must be twice as long. You will look very good to me. Hope you will be as glad to see me—

Love to all at home and if you need any advice go to Mr Sullivan.

Devotedly Your/ Mother—

Grace was considerably upset to learn on her return to Cleveland in mid-August that Hart had not been working. Prodded by his mother, Crane went one morning to enlist in the Army, only to learn that on that very day the government had decided to refuse all minors for military service. After the Armistice of November 11, 1918, the poet took a job with the Cleveland *Plain Dealer;* but life in Cleveland without his circle of New York friends was boring— and living at 115th Street was often explosive. By early 1919, Hart decided that the East would be preferable. Toward the end of February, after having secured the guarantee of a small allowance from his father, Hart left for New York.

When Crane arrived there on February 21, 1919, he learned that veterans, who were returning daily from Europe, made accommodations as well as jobs difficult to find. As he could not stay permanently at Mrs. Walton's rooming house (something both he and his mother counted upon), he took a small room on West 76th Street. A few weeks later he moved to a small apartment at 307 West 70th Street, which he shared with a new acquaintance, Alexander Baltzly. Many of his old friends, including the Colums, the Brookses, and Claire Spencer (recently married to Harrison Smith, the editor and publisher), soon issued invitations to dine. Joseph Kling introduced him to a new associate editor of *The Pagan*, Gorham B. Munson. Crane and Munson—one returning to New York and the other a recent arrival—found that they held many views in common about life and literature.

Partly to allay his mother's fears about his living in strange surroundings rather than at Mrs. Walton's, and partly because he believed it was having a beneficial effect on her constitution, Hart included frequent references to Christian Science in his letters to Cleveland. Often he reported on conversations he had had with Mrs. Brooks and Mrs. Spencer, both of whom believed deeply in the religion, and he hinted at times that Science had caused his own personality to change for the better. But, if we can believe a letter Crane wrote to William Wright on May 2, 1919, he was not as serious about his beliefs as he wished his mother to think:

"No:—at present I am not a Christian Scientist. I try to make my Mother think so because she seems to depend on that hypocrisy as an additional support for her own faith in it. So,—mum's the word to her. If it weren't very evident how very much good it has done her I should not persist in such conduct —lying to both Lord and Devil is no pleasure,—but as I frankly was very much interested in Christian Science at the time of my exit from home, I have not made any distinct denial of it to her since, and for the aforementioned reasons. However, Bill, I have unbounded faith in its efficacy. Not that a normal optimism will not accomplish the same wonders,—it is a psychological attitude which will prevail over almost anything, but as a religion, there is where I balk." [1]

By early March, however, the hypocrisy had gone too far. Crane was distressed to learn that he was being treated by his mother's practitioner, Dr. Ely, and asked her to have the treatments discontinued. References to Christian Science are not as frequent after this.

At first Hart hoped to support himself on the earnings accrued from his movie scenarios, which he was still sending (with Mrs. Walton's encouragement) to several studios; however, all were rejected. In mid-March, when he began looking for a full-time job, he found little work available. At the same time that he was searching for employment, Hart had to depend upon irregular funding from his father. Instead of having her former husband send his son a weekly check for twenty-five dollars, as he had agreed to do, Grace insisted that Hart submit a statement of expenses twice a month, which she forwarded to their lawyer, John J. Sullivan, who in turn forwarded it to Clarence. C.A. would then write a check, send it to Sullivan, who forwarded it to Mrs. Crane—eventually Hart received his allowance. As these letters show, such a complicated and irregular system of payment gave Hart great anxiety and left him with little financial security.

To Grace Hart Crane

25 East 11 St. New York,
Feb. 24,[1]
Saturday evening 10:30

ALS, 4 pp.

Dear Mother:—

I have just returned from a dinner and evening with Mrs. Spen-

[1] Quoted from Brom Weber, ed., *The Letters of Hart Crane* (Berkeley and Los Angeles: University of California Press, 1965), p. 16.

[1] Misdated. Actually February 22, 1919.

cer. After the dishes were cleared away we sat before the wood-fire and talked Science, and I played the piano while she washed the dishes. She tells me some astounding stories about the numerous demonstrations she has made. Pat.[2] is very deep in it too, it seems, and has been twice saved in very dangerous falls from over 500 feet which would otherwise have meant instant death. It is convincing enough testimony that he is the only one living of the ten instructors chosen for the position at the time of his appointment. I am to help Mrs. Spencer move some things from her rooms over into Claire's apartment next Tuesday afternoon. Mrs. Brooks has evaded all my efforts at a meeting today, but I hope to get to go to church with her tomorrow morning. Mrs. Spencer says that Mr. Brooks will arrive from Florida tomorrow, so I shall have the opportunity of seeing him too.

What I wrote you about remaining here at Mrs. Waltons was wrong, I find. There is no probable vacancy among the other rooms of the house in sight, and, while I would be willing to put up with the one I now have, small as it is, the noise of a typewriter through the thin partitions that divide the rooms would be highly resented by the other tenants. I have [been] looking all day for a room in this section, but so far, not one can be found. They are all filled with army and navy men, with enthusiastic relatives, and there simply is not a nook or cranny to be had. Tomorrow I shall spend in following newspaper ads. to the various land ladies in question. Meanwhile I ought to consider myself lucky to be able to live here for $1 a day.

Saw Eugenie [3] this morning for a few minutes. Happy as usual. Inquires about you, etc. I shall see her again tomorrow.

Also went in to see Joe Kling today. The magazine has grown and I'm pleased to say, there is much to support the hope of immediate further improvement. Kling was remarkably glad to see me, and I guess we'll go to the opera every night next week (Chicago Co) which sounds good.

I do certainly hope to get settled by next Tuesday, get my machine, and begin work.

The city is ablaze with life, even in this rainy weather. The ave-

[2] Pat Spencer was an instructor in the Royal Canadian Air Force.
[3] Mme Eugénie Lebègue, Hart's former French tutor.

nues sparkle and money seems to just roll in the gutters. I am looking on it all with different, keener happier eyes than ever before. In
a way it is just like coming the first time, as I seem now to have
been looking at different things before. Of course the truth is, I am
looking at things (the same things) *differently*.

Please send my mail via Spencers. I shall not be here after Tuesday.

My love in deluges,/ Hart

Love to Grandma!

To Grace Hart Crane

[New York City]
Sunday evening
Feb. 23, '18 [1]

ALS, 1 p.

Dear Mother:—

I must have walked, in all, 20 miles today. I never dreamt that I
would experience such difficulties in finding a room, but at last one
has been found at 119 West 76th St. $7 per week, a large closet, an-
other with running water, and the room faces the south and front
and is of good size. Other details will develope after a few days. Indeed I am fortunate to get anything at all. I move in tomorrow
morning, so address my mail there until further notice.

Supped with Mr. & Mrs. Kreymborg and have just returned from
an evening with the Brooks'. I wanted to go to church this morning
but simply had to devote every moment to the quest of a room. I
dine Tues. noon with Mr. Brooks at the Yale Club. Will write
again and more tomorrow.

Love, as ever,/ Hart

[1] Misdated. Actually 1919.

To Grace Hart Crane

[New York City]
Wednesday, Feb. 25, '19 [1]

TLS, 1 p.

Dear Mother:—

Your letter yesterday was a real pleasure. You certainly must be used to my abscence by this time. At any rate, you can have no "fault to complain" about my writing you often.

Yesterday I helped Mrs. Spencer move some of Claire's things from her rooms to the bridal suite on Madison Ave. Their new place is decorated quite lavishly, and will be a wonderful place for them to live in. We shall probably go to church together tonight. This afternoon I have asked her to go to the bank with me to identify me in cashing the draft.

I was much pleased by that letter from the editor of "The Modern School",[2] and hope you will send me the file of his magazine that he promises to send under seperate cover. I am going to send my moving picture scenario around to some other companies instead of waiting to hear from those people until the story has become stale in interest. In this morning's "Times" there is a report of just such an impending strike in the Hog Island shipyards as I had included in the story.[3]

I had a wonderful lunch and talk with Mr. Brooks yesterday at the Yale Club. I certainly have been on the go ever since arriving, but I expect to begin to refuse invitations for a few days now,—get my typewriter,—and get a little business done. The Browns [4] will be here in a week and I expect some excitement then. I wrote Mrs. Brown yesterday and thanked her for her remuneration. All the Cranes have been attended to with postal cards, and, added to that,

---

[1] Misdated. Actually February 26, 1919.

[2] *The Modern School*, published between 1912 and 1922, was edited at this time by Carl Zigrosser.

[3] The Hog Island Shipyards were located in what is now a part of the Philadelphia Airport. None of Crane's movie scenarios have survived.

[4] The Browns were friends of Mrs. Crane's from Cleveland.

the due attention to several friends, you see I have been busy writing.

Love to Grandma, too.—/ Hart

(over)

[*Written on the back of the page in ink:*] I enclose pictures [5] of Claire and "Hal" which you are to return at an early date. They were taken on the "weddin day" up near Hartford.

To Grace Hart Crane and Elizabeth Belden Hart

[New York City]
Feb. 26th, '19 [1]

TLS, 1 p.

Dear Mother and Grandma:—

There isn't much to tell you today, but I am writing because I know you would miss your Saturday letter.

Last evening I was dined at Mrs. Spencer's with a charming young lady, and we three went to the village theatre afterward. The play was a rollicking farce,[2] written by the same man who wrote that funny story we all read a few weeks ago in the Saturday Evening Post, Sinclair Lewis, who is, by the way, Hal Smith's best friend. I enclose the program. Mrs. Brown must see it when she comes.

I stayed in all day yesterday waiting for the typewriter I have rented to come. It hasn't arrived yet, so I guess I'll have to telephone and give them a calling down. This, that I am writing on, is worn out, it is all I can do to get out even a letter like this on it.

I shall enclose a list of last week's expenses in Monday's letter. They have been somewhat irregular as naturally would follow under the circumstances, but I shall be able to plan better this next

---

[5] Mrs. Claire Spencer Evans told the editor that she was unable to find these pictures in her collection.

[1] Misdated. Actually February 27, 1919.

[2] The play Crane saw was Sinclair Lewis's *Hobohemia*, which was playing at the Greenwich Village Theatre. However, no Lewis story appeared in the *Saturday Evening Post* around this time.

week. In Science, too close a sense of limitation must not be admitted. I am trying to keep all channels open for the entry of everything good that there is, and fear must not close them. I have had some fine Scientific talks with Mrs. Spencer, and discover how very deep she is immersed in the study of it.

I do hope that my machine will come today so that I can begin to get out a few scenario's that I have thought of. I heard also from Bob, George, and Zucker today.[3] How did you like Mr. Darling?[4] Don't be too shy, that is, if you like him. I hope you won't continue to miss me with all the lovely friends and invitations you are having. You know, it's only an erroneous "claim" that demands my presence.

With love to you both, and Molly and John,—

Your/ Hart

To Grace Hart Crane

[New York City]
119 West 76th St.,
March 7th, '19

TLS, 3 pp.

Dear Mother:—

The landlady has committed enough atrocities since writing you last to fill a book, and I have found another room [w]hich I expect to move into some time next week. In all truth she is quite insane. Mr. Brooks called me up three times the other day, and each time he asked for me was he told that there was no such person as Mr. Crane living here. Finally one of the roomers came to the rescue and took down his name and number, so that when I got in I was duly informed. Then in other ways she has been unbearable, coming up to my room several times, and vaguely pointing to some unseen object and inquiring, "Is that your's". At other times she has

---

[3] "Bob" cannot be identified; "George" is George Bryan; and "Zucker" is Roger Zucker. George Bryan and Roger Zucker were friends of Crane's from Cleveland.

[4] Very likely Hart is coyly referring to someone who was courting his mother.

come up and announced in a hushed voice, "It's down there". That would be all one could get out of her as to what was "down there"; —letter, caller, or delivery man, and several times it has been nothing at all. This morning the final offence was committed when she sent a *carpenter* into my room at an unearthly hour to fix the plumbing under the wash basin. She had evidently told him that the window needed fixing, or something to that effect, as he first went there to see what was the matter. Yesterday I got into conference with two other fellows on my floor and they both have had enough of it, and intend to get out next week also. It has been very funny and very unpleasant, and I regret having to incur the expense of moving again. However, the room I have secured is better than the one I have;—on the first floor, front, and much roomier. One of the fellows in the house here,[1] a Harvard man and lieutenant just out of service, has roomed there before and swears to the complete sanity and integrity of the little Irish woman that runs the place. All these little trials have to be accepted in true sportsmanlike fashion, in fact one might as well take them that way, or else get out of town.

I went with the Browns to the boat yesterday morning, the details of which I suppose Mrs. Brown has told you by this time. I never dreamed that Mrs. Brown would be so fearful of her husband's safety as her actions at the time indicated. They are very, very devoted to one another without a doubt.

I had dinner with Mr. Brooks at the apartment last evening. Mrs. Brooks returned from Philadelphia at about eight o'clock, having been down there w[i]th Mrs. Noyes to assist in some class of dancing and an entertainment. I am not sure, of course, but I feel quite certain that Mrs. Brooks is afflicted with consumption against which she is doubtless putting up a strenuous Scientific fight.[2] I have noticed an incessant little cough that she has had on both my meetings with her since I arrived in town. She is quite thin, too, and without much colour. It must be due to a change of disposition within myself, but I find the Brooks's much more cordial and ag-

[1] Alexander Baltzly.
[2] Crane was right. Mrs. Brooks had tuberculosis.

greeable. That I, myself, am largely responsible is borne out by what Mrs. Spencer told me the other day. She said that Mr. Brooks had remarked about the astounding change in my manner and disposition, and said that I was now quite a delightful personality. I should blush to tell this on myself were it not such an interesting testimony to the influence of Science.

Claire and "Hal" will be back probably about the last of this month. They are in Florida at present. Yes, Hal is a fine fellow, at least Mr. Brooks, who has met him several times, attests. Everywhere Claire is mentioned some tribute is paid to her, and everyone seems to think that the two make an ideal couple.

I received the returned scenario with the letter, day before yesterday. While waiting for it, I sent out several copies to other producers from whom I haven't heard as yet, but it may get placed after all.

I hope you were not offended at my reply to your very generous and thoughtful suggestion about my laundry. I only think it rather elaborate for me to be sending a few ordinary clothes over three hundred miles each week to be cleaned. Then too,—you can see for yourself that it would be at best a little undependable. I should have to send some things to the laundry anyway, and there would be a lot of details to bother me as to where was which, and when would it come.

I am sending an itemized account of my expenses for the last two weeks ending tonight. I think it would be wise to make it a monthly arrangement of payment, though, and not bother Sullivan with too frequent duties about such details. But here it is, and I am sure you know what you want to do with it, and my whole thought is to be as pleasant and dutious to you in this matter as possible. I shall need some money now as soon as you can send it, as this second moving will demand a little extra from what I had planned would last me until about the middle of next week. I'll be mighty glad to be able to contribute to my own maintainence as soon as I can get started, but as Mrs. Spencer says, I shouldn't feel at all wrong about accepting this which is certainly my due.

Your loving boy, / Hart

P.S. My new address will be 307 W. 70th St.

Against any violence on the part of the landlady here, please send your next letter to that address.

[*The expense account enclosed in the letter of March 7, 1919:*]

New York City

119 West 76th St.,

March 7th, '19

The following is a list of my living expenses during the period of two weeks, extending from February 21st to March 7th, '19.

$14.00   room rent
$21.75   board
$ 4.65   car-fare
$ 3.00   clothes-pressing
$ 4.00   typewriter rent (per month)
$ 2.00   purchase of collars
$ 1.50   stationary
$ 2.23   laundry
$ 1.50   postage stamps
$ .30   shoe-shines
$ .20   telephone calls
$ 1.50   baggage transfer
$56.63   total expenses

Harold Hart Crane

To Grace Hart Crane

[New York City]

TLS, 1 p.

Dear Mother:—

Just a word to let you know that I am busy casting about for a postion somewhere. I have several ideas suggested by friends as to where to find jobs as an ad-writer etc., and am investigating the matter. I may make a call on Mr. Kennedy, the friend of Grand-mother's, if two or three other projects do not turn out well. He runs a trade-journal, you know. Zell writes me that she is to be here for two weeks next month, and if I am [not] settled by that time, I am positive that she will be able to get me in somewhere.[1] You have no conception of the difficulties here in finding work of any description just now. Every day a couple of troupe-ships dumps a few thousand more unemployed men in the town, and there really is danger of a general panic and much poverty as a result unless the government takes a hand to assist in the matter. I know you are not worrying about me. As it happens, I am very fortunately situated in comparison with the rest. I wrote Mr. Ely yesterday, and so that is off my conscience. I would prefer that you discontinued his treatment of me, as I fell quite able to stand on my own feet and demonstrate the truth without assistance from without. I shall probably not move from here for some time. I have decided to make a demonstration over the landlady, and already have noticed an improvement. Love to you and Grandma by the bushel./ HART

Tuesday, March 11th, '19

To Grace Hart Crane

[New York City]
307 West 70th Street
March 21st, '19

TLS, 4 pp.

Dear Mother:—

I enclose a list of my expenses for the past two weeks. A new draft ought to be sent me this next week, as you see from the figures. If you cannot make the arrangements about identification that I suggested in my last letter and to which you replied, I will do my best to get the money somehow or other anyway. You seem to think

---

[1] Hart's Aunt Zell, who published the Warren *Tribune*, had offered to use her numerous connections to get her nephew a position on a New York newspaper.

that I made no effort to establish my identity along the line that
you repeated in your last, but I most assuredly did. I went to Mrs.
Spencer's bank in company with her, (I refer to the cashing of the
draft which I brought here with me), and the check was cashed
only after she had sub-indorsed it herself. The bank was willing to
cash the check under such conditions as a favor personally granted
to Mrs. Spencer, but informed me that it would under no conditions consent to regularly fulfill my checks unless so endorsed, etc.
as there was no evident reason to them why I could not just as well
take the check to the bank it was written on and thus avoid their
unnecessary handling it. I dislike hawling Mrs. Spencer into the
matter every time I want some money, and I think that if it is quite
convenient to the Guardian [1] to do as the Guaranty Trust insists regarding the red tape identification, it would be the best way, after
all, and once done, all trouble in the future would be assuredly
eliminated. I'm sure you'll see how it is with this data.

Your good work on Bessie's "claim" sounded very good indeed.[2]
Also it was fine for me to know that you are enjoying your friends
now so much. I myself certainly am being warmly received in several places. I dined with Hal and Claire last night at the first dinner given in their new apartment, only two others, both "males,"
being guests. It was lots of fun to assist Claire as butler,—cutting
bread, (which for once I did properly as all aggreed,) and pouring
the wine,—(yes, we had a little). Claire cooks better than the average newly-wed: her first adventures in that line of endeavor began
sometime back, as you know. Hal is, I find, one of the kind that improves with acquaintance. He is writing a novel now,[3]—something
about sea life, and we intend to read some of it when I come up for
Sunday evening tea. Mrs. Spencer is presently in Boston, having
been called their suddenly on account of Mrs. Brooks' illness, which
has prevented their return to New York this week as I had expected. Mrs. Spencer leaves us in the dark as to all the details of her
patient's claims, so I, or Claire either haven't much idea of what the
cause of Mrs. Brooks illness is. You will doubtless recall my mention

[1] The Guardian Trust Company of Cleveland, Mrs. Crane's bank.
[2] Possibly this refers to Hart's "Aunt Bess" Madden; however, Mrs. Madden
could not recall what the "claim" was.
[3] Harrison Smith never published this novel.

of something in regard to it which I included in my last letter to you. It may be that,—I don't know. I was Mrs. Gardiner's [4] guest for dinner at the Pen and Brush Club on Wednesday evening, and this afternoon took tea with Ridgely Torrence and his wife,[5] who were extremely gracious to me. I haven't succeeded in getting a job as yet, but am still looking. Hal thinks that I am very foolish in trying to get myself locked up, as he calls it, in any such way, and recommends my writing for all I am worth, serving my apprenticeship, as it were, and thinks that a year's work and effort under the present advantageous conditions of my situation would result in my ultimately earning more money by stories, etc. than the drudgery in publishing houses, and on magazine's employ, etc. would ever promise. If I don't find something soon, I shall, I imagine, be rather forced into this course. But so it goes. I hope you will not be ruffled or impatient, I am feeling better than I have for years, better every day, in fact, and such symptoms are surely promising enough.

Aside from a few very petty and altogether negligible personal peculiarities, which are really not peculiarities at all, but merely happen to rub me a little bit the wrong way, I like my companion roomer very much. He is very much a man of the world (in the finer sense, I mean) and his conversation is extremely stimulating to me, especially as he has a wide knowledge of literature and art, and a thorough appreciation of music. Our quarters are quite capacious and we have fitted it up splendourously with some very beautiful pictures w[h]ich we secured very cheaply. It is doing me considerable good to be more in the company of someone completely outside of any knowledge of me or my family. You can see yourself how this would be, and I must say that I am in wondrous luck to have found such an extremely suitable person.

Love to you and Grandma by the bushel-full,/ Hart

[*The expense account enclosed in the letter of March 21, 1919:*]

The following is a list of my complete living expenses covering the two-weeks period extending from March 7th, '19, to March 21st, '19.

[4] Elizabeth Gardiner.
[5] Frederic Ridgely Torrence (1875–1950), the poet and playwright. At this time he was married to Olivia Howard Dunbar.

$14.00	room rent
24.50	board
3.00	laundry
1.50	suit-cleaning and pressing
2.35	car-fare
.25	telephone
.68	postage
.35	tooth brush
$46.63	sum total

(signed)/ *Harold Hart Crane*

March 22, '19

To Grace Hart Crane

March 26th '19
307 West 70th St.
N.Y.C.

ALS, 3 pp.

Dear Mother:—

I've just been down and cashed your checks. I think that my
identity is established there now, although they told me they intended to write themselves to the Guardian about it. The point is,
—I got the cash, and I don't think you or I will be likely to be
troubled about it so much again.

At the recommendation of Colum, I am going to interview the
publishing house of Boni and Liveright tomorrow in the effort to
secure a job as proofreader etc. with them. I have been around to
several Sunday Feature Syndicates today but have found nothing
there. I hope you aren't worrying,—for you must realize that one
cannot continue looking and looking as I am doing without finding
something in time. I have some interesting news for you. I phoned
up Alice Calhoun [1] last night and find that she is starring in a

---

[1] Crane's friend from Cleveland. See his letter of January 26, 1916. She began
her film career with the Vitagraph Company. Later she went to Hollywood and
worked for Warner Brothers.

newly organized moving-picture production company here.— She is now engaged in her first big picture, and is very busy, she tells me. How about writing a movie-story for her? It looks as though there might be a chance for some of my work to get an attentive reading after all. She can't see me this week, but we are going to have a visit soon and I imagine it will be interesting. Alice certainly is pretty enough for success in the movies, and young enough (only 18) to develope a good deal of dramatic talent.

A telephone conversation is rather a slight thing to offer judgement from, but I was rather impressed with a decided improvement in Alice, both in manner and character. Bryan's [2] letter arrived this morning. I think he is certainly a sincere well-wisher of mine. I hope to get into some sort of position in time to write him about it when I do write, because it "makes more to say", as it were. I'll write again in time for a Sunday delivery. The days are amazingly beautiful and the night's superb. Last night I took a long walk up Riverside Drive which is just around the corner from my room, and the Hudson was beautiful with the millions of tiny lights on the opposite shore. Your letters are genuine treats to me, so don't fail to continue with them, will you?— Love to you all.

from/ Hart.

To Grace Hart Crane

[New York City]
307 West 70th Street,
March 29th, '19

TLS, 1 p.

My dear Mother:—
I have been troubled considerably the last two days with a claim of sore-throat and hard cold in the head. The weather is certainly disaggreeable enough just now to warrant staying indoors, there being a terrific blizzard of snow which has continued for twenty-four hours.

---

[2] George Bryan, Crane's friend from Cleveland.

My friend and room-mate [1] left for his home at Hudson, Mass. yesterday morning to remain with his parents until about next Wednesday. So, to pass the day not too uncomfortably, I think I will call up Eugenie,[2] whom I haven't seen for some time, and invite her to go to a movie with me, that is, tomorrow.

The Boni and Liveright matter that I wrote about has not eventuated yet as I have not so far succeeded in getting in touch with the proper man. I took dinner last night with a fellow who knows all the people on the Evening Post, and I may utilize him for a position there. I take dinner with Mrs. Gardiner tonight, and perhaps Stan and Anna may join us.[3] Your letter has not arrived as yet, but I am expecting it before bed-time. Hope you are having a real good time now all the time, not saying "no" to anything good that comes down the line. I got your pictures put into the lovliest little frame yesterday that I ever saw., and as a result the landlady went into ecstacy no. 2 about you[r] beauty. If it's as cold in Cleveland as it is here, I fancy you as sitting about the little fire in the living-room quite close and snug.

Love to Grandma too,—/ Hart

At the beginning of April, Margaret Anderson and Jane Heap, the editors of *The Little Review,* offered Crane a part-time job—on a commission basis—as advertising manager of the magazine. Hart confidently wrote his mother that *The Little Review* only needed someone with initiative in the advertising department to transform it into a financially successful periodical. But after several months during which he had sold only two advertisements, one for Mary Garden Chocolates and another which read "Stanislaw Portapovitch—Maître de Danse," Crane's visions of a large income had faded considerably.

By early May, in an effort both to save money and to be closer to his friends, Hart moved to several small rooms that Harrison Smith

---

[1] Alexander Baltzly.
[2] Mme Eugénie Lebègue.
[3] Stanislaw and Anna Portapovitch.

kept as an office at 24 West 16th Street. The rooms were directly
over the headquarters of *The Little Review.*

To Grace Hart Crane

307 West 70th Street,
New York City
April 2nd, '19
Telephone: Columbus 2037

TLS, 3 pp.

My dearest Mother:—

Your letter just came. Evidently you had not received my telegram before writing it:— I wanted you to be assured that I had not
forgotten the date.[1]

Yes, you do seem to be qyuite occupied with various engagements, pleasant and painful, as in the case of the dentistry, although
I am very glad to hear of your having that duty performed as you
have needed work and attention expended on your teeth for a long
while back. I think you are holding the wrong and un-Scientific
thought concerning me and my attitude toward Science. The fact
that I do not talk and write about it continually is no sort of testimony that I am not as much interested as ever in it. You know that
I am not and probably never will be one of those who make the
matter a complete obcession, reducing every subject and thought
and description to the technical language of the textbooks. I have
met a number of Scientists who by such proceedure managed not
only to bore me and others quite dreadfully, but also to leave one
with the impression that they were scared to death about everything
and found it necessary to maintain a continual combat against
every aspect and manifestation of life in general. Perhaps it may
serve as sufficient testimony to the efficacy of right thought, etc. that
I am finding far less problems and fears that demand denial. I certainly have not felt quite so well or quite so clear-headed for several
years, and that is, or ought to be enough to reassure you and alter-

[1] Grace's birthday fell on April 1.

ate your somewhat morbidly anxious fears for me which have
leaked into your last few letters. I again beg you to relax from such
fears, etc. which seem to have you in their power enough to prompt
you to such seemingly strenuous conflicts of resistance and denials.
Your letters seem to be prompted by some fear (I mean certain references in them) that seems to me entirely un-Scientific. Please do
not mistake me and beomce [become] hurt or offended. I only feel
that you have not overcome, not quite, what might be called "the
fear of fear" which is an ultimate Scientific triumph.

It is very nice to think of Mrs. Zucker's [2] calling on me. I certainly hope that she does it. My room-mate is due to return from
Mass. today. I guess I told you that we get along very well and have
many tastes in common.

I am considering a plan which might work out very well. The editors of The Little Review have offered to let me take over the advertising and subscription department of the magazine on a commission basis. If once started up well along this line, the w[o]rk
would prove to be reasonably remunerative for me,—affording me
at least as much per week even from the start, as I got working in
the Plain Dealer office. To a certain extent I would be my own boss
with unrestricted initiative freedom to develope my department systematically and along my own lines. I am just about ready to assent
to the proposition for the summer months anyway. Three months
trial would be quite justified, and the work interests me. There is
no reason why The Little Review could not be developed into as
paying a periodical as The New Republic, The Nation, or The
Dial. All it has lacked from its inception has been someone with
business initiative ability to develope the advertising and subscription departments of the magazine. I am going to talk the matter
over again with the editors, however, before deceiding definitely.
One good thing about it will be the advantage it will give me of association with influential people who have to do with The Little
Review and also a certain amount of personal freedom to develope
my own talents along with the other work.

Will you do something for me? I wish you would send me via
parcel post these volumes which [you] will find up in my room on

---

[2] Mrs. Zucker from Cleveland was the mother of Hart's friend Roger Zucker.

front shelves:—"Lustra, poems" by Ezra Pound,[3] "Complete Poetical Works of Swinburne", and the "Portrait of the Artist as a Young Man", by James Joyce.

I am glad to hear of your connection with the Playhouse. It ought to afford you many a good time to get in touch with the crowd that supports it, in my mind, the most interesting set in Cleveland. I dined with Kreymborg one night, as I guess I wrote you, and he said that he had been especially invited to stay with Mr. O'Neil [4] when in town. I was glad to hear this because I anticipated the season of house-cleaning in which he would have found you at present had he accepted our invitation. I understand that he is having great successes in Chicago and throughout the middle west. He is a member of poets' lecture bureau recently started here and to which belong our most distinguished 'moderns'. I may join and lecture myself,—you never can tell.

Haven't been to see Hazel [5] yet, in spite of your report of what she said about my conduct. I don't think I shall go, either, unless conditions alter my reasons which prevent such, and which you know,—deceidely. Please send my new check by next Monday, as my expenses have been slightly heavier lately than the preceeding weeks were. As soon as time enough has elapsed to warrant a report on C.A.'s response to our present arrangement of allowance, I hope you will let me know about it. It seems to me that you ought to have received recompense for your first month's advancement to me by this time. I was glad to hear that his conduct toward you on the street, etc. had suffered a change for the better. I hope that in addition his courtesy will have been not only a superficial compromise, but, better, a voluntary expression from deeper, (under the skin,) and will extend to the more fundamental obligations of a contract faithfully fulfilled.

I certainly hope that it will warm up a bit for a few hours at least. I have been rarely colder than during the last few days. The sun is out now, however, and the papers predict 'fair and warmer' for tomorrow. It will interest you to know that I met by accident

[3] Crane's copy of *Lustra* is now owned by Norman Holmes Pearson.
[4] Eugene O'Neill.
[5] Hazel Hasham, who ran the New York office of the Crane Chocolate Company.

M. Tardy, the bookseller and my old tutor in the subway on the way to a meeting of the Poetry Society a few evenings ago. He inquired very anxiously about you, and was glad to know that you were quite well again.

That man, Charley Bubb,[6] is going to make you a call if ever he gets any time, so he informs me in his last letter. He has been very kind in presenting Colum with some of his de luxe books in answer to an order I gave him for them, but for which he refuses to accept payment. William Wright is in Cleveland now, and if you would like to warm up a little with remembrances of last summer, you could probably reach him with a dinner invitation at the home of Wheeler Lovell, which is somewhere on East 84th, 85th or thereabouts. The phone-book would locate it exactly.

I have told you all the gossip, etc. that I could think of at the moment, and only hope that I'll have something interesting enough to supply matter for your Sunday letter. Please discount misspelled words, etc., this machine is at times quite balky and at others quite exuberant.

Lovingly, your son,/ Hart

Thank you for your letter, Grandma,—I'll write you personally quite soon

To Grace Hart Crane

[New York City]
Saturday, April 5th, '19

TLS, 1 p.

Dear Mother:—

I enclose my expense account for the last two weeks.[1]

I expect to take up the 'Little Review' proposition beginning

---

[6] The Reverend Charles C. Bubb of Cleveland operated the Church Head Press, which published limited editions of poetry. In November, 1918, Crane submitted "Echoes," "Exile," "Love and a Lamp," "Meditation," "Medusa," "Naiad of Memory," and "To Earth" to the press for publication. The letter from Mr. Bubb which Crane refers to and which is published in part in *The Letters*, pp. 11–12, is in the Columbia University collection.

---

[1] This expense account is lost.

next Monday. Otherwise there is nothing new to report except perhaps, that I enjoyed myself 'muchly' at dinner with Claire and Hal
last Wednesday evening, and am invited there again for dinner tonight.

Mrs. Zucker hasn't looked me up as yet, but I am still hoping
that she will.

Love in abundance to you and Grandma.

your offspring,/ Hart

To Grace Hart Crane

[New York City]
April 12, '19

TLS, 1 p.

Dear Mother:—

I have just finished breakfast following the reading of your letter
which came about 7:30. I am glad to know of your increasing interests and activities in the Woman's Club. Your acquaintance must be
growing considerably too. Keep up the good work!

Claire and Hal come into my letters so often of late that I am beginning to fear boring you, but as long as they are responsible for
so much of my pleasure I shall have to include them anyway. The
circus Tuesday night was a great success. Then I was there to dinner Wednesday also. And last night there was quite a gathering.
Chas. and Minerva, Jessie, Mrs. Mc Bride of Cleveland, and a relative of Hal's, Mrs. Clarke of Hartford,[1] and myself were all the
guests of Hal and Claire, and of the Brooks' afterward at the theatre, after which we all adjourned to a cabaret and drank beer and
ate cheese dreams. Mrs. Mc Bride seemed to take a great liking to
me, and mentioned her acquaintance with you.

Mrs. Zucker will make you a call, I think, when she returns
which will probably be tonight. I took her to lunch at "Puss In
Boots" on Thursday and expect to see her a moment this afternoon
before my engagement with Mme. Lebegue whom I am escort to a

[1] Charles and Minerva Brooks; Jessie Winton, a cousin of Claire Spencer's;
Mrs. Clarke, a cousin of Harrison Smith's.

tea a[t] Mlle. de Villeneuve's apartments. Again I am the guest of Hal and Claire at a musicale in the evening. You see I am busy enough.

Yesterday, the first entire day devoted to the advertising work, I found to be rather discouraging. I didn't succeed in landing a single ad. However, it is largely luck in attacking the right kind of people at the right moment, and I am not thinking of giving up the work for a good while yet.

I have had to buy a brief-case and a new hat this week, and so the fifty you sent last Monday will hardly carry me for the usual two weeks. I wish you would kindly send me an extra $25 Monday, if possible. You haven't told me a thing about whether you have succeeded in collecting anything yet, and I wish you would. Hope you haven't forgotten my request about those books in the letter before last. A letter from William [2] yesterday informed me of his expectation of going to Columbia next year. I think he will call you up on his way home via Cleveland, he is at present visiting in Springfi[e]ld, O.

The house must be looking fine with all the attention you have recently given it. I would like to have a good long look in upon you.

Devotedly and affectionately yours, / Hart

To Grace Hart Crane

[New York City]
Thursday morn.
April 17, 19

TLS, 1 p.

Dear Mother:—

Many thanks for the check. If I am [to] follow out your suggestion regarding the opening of a savings account here, I think you had better have another $50 here for me next Monday in order that I may be able to keep a $25 deposit in the bank. Nothing less

[2] William Wright.

would be admissable, as you are aware, and I shall need a good twenty-five between now and Monday to repay a few borrowings that have been temporarily necessary.

I am busy with projects for The Little Review,—got my first ad the other day, etc. I will write you further Sat. and until then, Addio, (which in Italian, "Good-bye".)

Love to you all, / Hart

Your lovely ties have just arrived this moment. Bless your dear heart:—they are admirably beautiful. By the way,—how did my poem in The Modern School [1] strike you? I was sorry that the editor was unable to find a suitable illustration for it, but think it looks fairly well anyway. Guess I haven't told you that Lola Ridge [2] wrote me the other day that she wants two of my poems for "Others".

To Grace Hart Crane

[New York City]
[April 20, 1919?]
Easter, '19

TLS, 1 p.

Dear Mother:—

Were I in Cleveland today you should have flowers instead of this poor letter, but as it is I'm afraid I haven't anything better to offer than lots of love and optimism, which, even so, can't be amiss. I shall celebrate the day by wearing one of the splendid neckties you sent me, and maybe write a poem.

I must tell you that I have a subordinate.[1] A man turned up at the Little Review office last Wednesday and wanted a job getting ads. And having had several years experience, he is proving a wonder. I have charge of the whole department and get a commission

[1] "To Potapovitch" [*sic*] was published in *The Modern School*, VI (March, 1919), 80.
[2] Lola Ridge was an associate editor of *Others* at this time.

---

[1] The name of Hart's subordinate is lost.

on whatever he does in addition to my own efforts, so you see things are about to happen. We expect to hawl in several year contracts next week of no less than $480. each. We are after about all the great establishments on Fifth Ave., and I am learning a few things in going about.

It will be tiresome for me to continue telling you about Hal and Claire, but I dine with them quite often. Stan and Anna no longer interest me very much. They are quite incommunicable and smug, having settled into married life and a flat. I haven't been to see them for nearly a month. Isn't it about time for Mr. Brown to be returning, and am I not to expect a word from Mrs. Brown [2] upon her arrival here in town? I got a pleasant booklet from Bubb the other day by way of Easter greeting, which reminds me that I have been so occupied with plans as to have neglected a good opportunity of remembering my friends this holiday with a card. I am hoping that you will not think I have neglected you. Still, I know you won't think so, and rest, assured.

Please give my best to Molly and John and "Diana", and my blessed, magnificent Grandma!

Love from/ Hart

To Grace Hart Crane

24 West 16th St.,
New York City
May 3, '19

TLS, 2 pp.

My dear Mother:—

You were a dear to send us such a fine box of candy, and very right also in saying that New York hasn't any candy as good as Cleveland. I gave it to Hal and Claire yesterday as soon as it arrived, and shall probably have a taste of it myself tonight when I go to their place for dinner.

[2] The Browns were friends of Mrs. Crane's from Cleveland. See Hart's letters of February 25, 1919, and March 7, 1919, to his mother.

Zell is leaving this afternoon for home. I saw her yesterday afternoon and we had a fine time walking about buying clothes for
Gooz and Tom Deming,[1] I being the clothes-model in each case. I
know she has written you, as I mailed the letter myself. I don't remember whether I wrote you of it or not, but we also went to see
Phillip Moeller's "Moliere" at the Liberty Theatre last Saturday
night.[2] Moeller is the same author who wrote "Mme. Sand", and his
second play is almost as good.

Bill Wright wrote me that he had a very pleasant talk with you
when he was in Cleveland, and says that he intends to come to Columbia next year. By the way, I hope you weren't down town the
other day at the time of the rioting.[3] If you were, you must have
been severely frightened. The newspaper accounts of the affair
sound very exciting, and I had no idea that the I.W.W. and the
Bolshevici had such a following in my home town. Compared with
Cleveland, New York is behind the times.

I have been up to see Hazel Hasham this morning. Zell told me
that when she met her Hazel had expressed a very cordial attitude,
so I thought that perhaps it was getting about time that I paid her
some attention. She was extremely gracious and I intend to drop in
again soon. She said that she had never seen such a change in her
life as she noticed in you when she was last in Cleveland, and said
you looked like a girl of sixteen.

I am sorry not to have been able to write you more this last two
weeks, but they have been filled with so many plans and then the
last few days the magazine has been in preparation for press so that
there has hardly been a moment. The advertising man about whom
I wrote you has gone on a spree or else left us completely, and that
has kept me stirred up the last two days. I intend to carry the thing
along just the same though, even though it will be a little slower.
The advertising business is a very good one, and I might just as
well learn it as any other. As I said, if I can manage to fill up the

[1] Tom Deming, William Deming's brother, was an editor of the Warren *Tribune*.

[2] Phillip Moeller (1880–1958), the playwright and director, probably known
best for his direction of Eugene O'Neill's *Strange Interlude*. Moeller was a
founder and director of the Theatre Guild.

[3] Socialists rioted in Cleveland on May Day.

allowable space in the Little Review, thirty two pages, I can get $4,000 per year on commissions. Anyway, nothing else in the way of a job is to be found at this crowded hour, so I might as well try out my capacities.

I suppose Diana has her new spring suit by this time and that you are gallavanting about the boulevards in style. Beautiful days are with us at last, and I am sure that this letter finds you with a blue sky overhead.

Love from your/ Hart

P.S. I haven't been able to locate Rae. The Prince George is not the place, and there isn't any hotel at the corner of Broadway and 19th Street.

To Grace Hart Crane

[New York City]
Tues. May 6th [1919?]

ALS, 1 p.

Dear Mother:—

Everything is going along finely. Am busy working at the ads most of the time etc. I may send some sox home to be mended any day so be prepared for something astounding. If you haven't already sent my fortnightly check, wish you [would] do so at once as you know I don't like to borrow even with the surety of repaying at once. Why doesn't Grandma indulge me with a letter now & then? She shouldn't need urging, as she ought to know how much I like her letters.

Love and kisses from/ Hart

To Grace Hart Crane

24 West 16th St.,
New York City
Decoration Day, '19

TLS, 2 pp.

My dear Mother:—

I received your letter with check enclosed night-before-last, and hasten to thank you for them. Your letter was filled with the customary complaints about my not writing oftener. Now I admit that the last two weeks have been poorer in letters from me than usual, but you seem never to have realized, Mother, that there is absolutely nothing to fill up the three-or-four-letter-a-week program which I have been trying to conduct,—even were my days filled with tremendous action. A couple of letters a week will contain all the news worth telling, and whether you have appreciated that fact or not, the truth remains.

I see you are displeased at my having changed rooms, but I would like to ask you what you would have done faced with a like situation at the time I was. I felt indeed very fortunate to have located so successful a bargain as the two rooms here on the top floor of 24 West 16th St., for ten dollars per month. It only costs me that because Hal Smith uses one of the rooms as a study separate from his apartment to come for his writing, and so I have the use of his room as well as my bedroom. When I told Hal and Claire of my predicament, Claire rushed to the cupboard and the result was that a bed was bought for me and temporary bedding loaned. Hal also sent over other furnishings etc. which [h]as made the place livable and even comfortable for me. I see no reason for returning now to a rooming house, and shall probably remain here for sometime to come. I asked for the rugs because they would be simply an additional comfort, but if it's too much trouble for you to send them, or against your principles, it's all right with me to do without them.

What I wrote you about sending money still holds good. I have cashed the checks you sent as there is no use in my being foolish about such matters when I have only fifteen cents in my pocket and a very empty stomach. I do ask you for more, however. I am very much against your sending me money from your personal allowance. It seems to me that it would not be very much trouble to go down and see Sullivan for a half and hour for a few days and get sufficient results from the enactment of a perfectly just and practical contract so that I would not be due to hear within a few years the accusation of having made you economize and scrimp your own pleasures for my assistance during this trying time when I am making every possible effort to get started in something. You know, Mother, I have not yet forgotten your twitting me last summer at my not paying my board expenses when I was at home, and I don't welcome your generosity quite so much now on the possibility of a recurrence of such words at some future time. I don't want to fling accusations etc. at anybody, but I think it's time you realized that for the last eight years my youth has been a rather bloody battle-ground for your's and father's sex life and troubles. With a smoother current around me I would now be well along in some college taking probably some course of study which would enable me upon leaving to light upon far more readily than otherwise, some decent sort of employment. Do you realize that it's hard for me to find any work at all better than some manual lobor, or literary work, which, as you understand, is not a very paying pursuit? My present job in connection with The Little Review possibly offers me an opportunity for experience in the advertising world, which is a good field for money,—but it's the hardest thing in the world to get worked up, especially with my complete inexperience in the work. I am looking for something else now every day,—anything that comes along,—with the intention of one way or another, establishing my independence from all outside assistance. In the meantime I am carrying on with this job, and should it give enough promise, will continue in it. I have found out recently what it is to be like a beggar in the streets, and also what good friends one occasionally runs accross in this tangle of a world. For some time after your letter I was determined not to write rather than compromise with hypocrisy or hurt your feelings. If this letter has wounded you, then I am ready to beg your pardon in apology with the understanding that I write no more, for I have discovered that the only way to be true to others in the long run, is to be true to one's self.

Your son,—/ Hart

As is apparent from these letters, lack of commissions from his job forced Hart to rely heavily on Claire Spencer and her husband, Harrison Smith, for meals and small loans. In July the Smiths invited the poet to accompany them to their summer cottage at Brookhaven, Long Island. By this time Hart was so discouraged by his failure to sell advertisements that he readily accepted the invitation.

To Grace Hart Crane

[New York City]
July 10. '19

ALS, 8 pp.

My dear Mother:—

Your nice letter arrived this morning just a few minutes before the books, and I must thank you much for them and the check enclosed in the letter, which I have certainly sufficient use for as I need a haircut badly and a new set of razor blades besides being much in debt to Hal for the this last weeks meals. It has been rather humiliating to have to come to one person for absolutely everything, rent, food, and minute sundries and rather than do it I have several times gone for long periods without food. But Hal and Claire have been wonderfully thoughtful and I haven't yet had to ask,— evidences seemed to be enough and better than words. At last now, things seem to have lightened a little. I leave with them tomorrow for Brookhaven, Long Island, where Hal has rented a beautiful establishment for the rest of the summer. I am going along as their guest, although Hal lightened any embarrassment I might have felt at receiving such endless munificence at their hands by suggest[ing] an office for me as handy man about the place,—gardner, chauffeur, etc. My duties will be light, however, as they are taking the Japenese cook along too, and so I am anticipating some idyllic days of sailing, bathing, romping and reading. The place they have taken is simply superb. I was out with them last Sat. and Sun. when they rented it and so have already seen it. The owners, (now in California) were evidently art lovers, for the place bears ample proof of it. I never heard the term "farmstead" before, but it is better than it sounds, I assure you. An old, immense barn has been changed into a most romantic and ample house, with the living room extending in the center to the roof, and a gallery around the second floor containing about eight bedrooms that on one side look down into the living room below, and on the other have a view of the country around. There is also a library (all ready stocked) and servants quarters with private bath on the side. A lovely orchard of peach and apple trees and a rose garden surround the house which is quite a distance from the road and its unpleasant traffic of continual machines. I will write you more of the place later, but you can already see something of its charms. I shall be with them there at least a month, and perhaps will remain until the end of September. I may never again have such an opportunity and as the city offers me at this time nothing better than a machine shop job, I don't feel that the time is wasted. Work will be easier to find next fall, without doubt, and meanwhile I see no reason for denying myself this pleasure. Pat will join us there within a week [1] or two and I'm sure I shall enjoy him as I liked him so much at our first and only meeting. If you can afford to send me another check for $25. in about two weeks from now I shall feel a little more comfortable out there and less beggerly. Why do things look so dark for you now, as you mention in your letter? Can it be that you are not recieving your alimony as due? If you are getting it, I should think it would [2] be enough to keep you quite comfortable, and even save some of it. I have been trying to assist you in that all I could, and during the last two months I don't feel that I have called heavily upon your

[1] Claire Spencer could not remember if her brother had visited them that summer.
[2] The word "would" is repeated in the text.

funds. I have done all I could to locate work that I respect, but
haven't been successful thus far. George Bryan wrote me from Denver where he is working for the Thos. Cusack Advertising Co. (his
father's firm) that he would see that I was placed in the employ of
their huge establishment here, I have been waiting and hoping on
that now for the past four weeks, but I guess he has decided to drop
it in spite of all his promises, as I haven't heard from him in answer
to my acceptance yet. I have been to advertising agencies, and publishers but, as I said, in vain so far. I can always find work in the
machine shop and shipyard but cannot help avoiding them as a last
resort, as this would merely suffice to keep breath in the body and
get me nowhere in particular. I made no requests for assistance
from C.A. in regard to the Columbia summer course which began
day before yesterday. In answer to his letter which announced his
intention and *promise* to take an advertisement in the Little Review, I thanked him and told him that his payment would help me
in taking a course in business advertising which I was hoping to
take at Columbia this summer. That was all there was said about it.
He didn't mention the matter in his next (and last) letter and has
not even paid for the advertisement which he said he would do as
long as I was associated with the magazine and he has heard nothing to the contrary, I am positive. Of course all my friends think his
treatment of me is disgraceful and unaccountable. My own opinion
is hardly less reserved, as you know, but I try my best to turn my
thoughts to other channels as much as possible. It is only when
hunger and humiliation are upon me that suddenly I feel outraged.
I wouldn't care to have you take the Columbia matter with Sullivan
as, you see, I didn't ask him directly at all. As regards any work
there next fall, I must think it over during the next two weeks and
make some inquiries. I do not know certainly that I would be allowed to take the same things in the same way as I might have
done this summer. I don't know why C.A. hasn't answered my last
letter of a month ago. It was certainly cordial, pleasant and without
a single feature that I can imagine anyone objecting to. Meanwhile
no check for the ad. comes either. I suppose he had a quarrel with
his wife and as a reaction felt kindly enough disposed toward me to
write his first cordial letter in three years. I won't take him so seri-

ously after this. I have written almost a book. My clothes must be packed today and off, so— Godbye with lots of love. I don't feel a bit downhearted today with the prospect of such pleasant weeks before me, and hope this rather definite letter doesn't leave too bad a taste in your mouth. Write me soon, addressed to

H.C

c/o O. H. Smith,

Brookhaven, L.I.

P.S.—A letter from George has just arrived which reinforces his promise in regard to the Cusack matter. I think there is a good chance for me there next fall. George owns a Ford and is planning to tour cross country next month and bring back to Denver his blushing bride (not married yet,—but *expects* to. His poor family!!

At Brookhaven, Hart felt even more acutely than he had in New York his dependence upon the Smiths, and soon his hosts' endless munificence became a source of irritation for all. "Our fights were quite often," [1] Claire Spencer Evans remembered forty years later, and usually they would end only after Hart had packed his bags and threatened to leave for the city. When his father wrote toward the end of July with an offer to introduce him to the Rheinthal and Newman Company, a New York firm that supplied C.A. with Maxfield Parrish prints he used on the boxes of Mary Garden Chocolates, Hart gladly accepted. After an interview on July 29, Hart took a job with the firm as a shipping clerk; he began work in mid-August.

Clarence Crane had not corresponded with his son very frequently since his marriage to Frances Kelley, and as the following letter shows, Grace had reservations about Hart's accepting help of any sort from his father.

[1] Quoted from an interview with the editor in July, 1969.

To Grace Hart Crane

Brookhaven, L.I.
July 30th, '19

TLS, 3 pp.

My dear Mother:—

Your letter dated the 28th has just come, and in answer, I of course will not need to repeat the contents of yesterday's note. At best I think your words are a little unkind and very inconsiderate. I will not attempt again to reckon with your misunderstanding, etc. of the part you and I together, and as individuals, have played in relation to C.A. You either have a very poor memory, or are very confused when you think you have a right to accuse me of either a wrong or a right attitude toward him,—an unfriendly or unfriendly one,—after the continually opposite statements and accusations you have made to me for the last four years yourself. At one time you recommended a course of diplomacy toward a veritable devil, and five minutes later a blow in the face and scorn of any relationship whatever. And now you suggest a wiley and conniving attitude toward a character which you claim as fundamentally good. With such inconsistences in memory I fail to see how you have adequate reasons for 'accusing' me of a 'wrong' attitude toward him, whatever position I might have taken. It has all been very hard, I know. Probably the truth consists more moderately in the estimate of him as a person of as many good inclinanations as bad ones. Your feelings as a woman lover were bound to be dangerous in diverting you from an impersonal justice, and, however much I may have been blinded by my own relationship with him, I cannot deny having been influenced by your sufferings and outcries. There are reasons for acts and prejudices which cannot always be justified at the turn of the moment, but look hard enough, and substantial roots will be found.

I returned to Brookhaven last night after a very satisfactory interview with Mr. Reinthal, of the firm of Reinthal and Newman, which handles the Parrish prints. I shall begin work there in the order department early in September,[1] until which time I'll be out here with Hal and Claire. My note of yesterday was expressive enough of the satisfaction I am feeling about the matter without repetition here. Everything is pointing toward very friendly relations with C.A. in the future, which good turn is greatly due to the interest of the New York office. People change in their attitude either from enlightment of the understanding or change of impulse. In the case of father toward me I think a revival of interest was seconded by a more adequate understanding of my motives, interests, character and position which the office supplied. Also, a certain pride, (now that his wealth begins to assume rather large dimensions) in the position of his only son, was equally responsible. Again, yesterday's note supplies you with conjectural details regarding the possibilities for the future, to spoil which, as you see, will only demand more floundering about of a kind which has confused greatly the course of the last year or two. I am not building many air castles, as I have learned too much already for that,—but it is hopeful, at least, with present relationships prevailing.

Of course you will understand that the advertising project is off under present situation. However, don't think that I fail to be grateful for your interest, and that you always retain my affection and love.

Best regards to Grandma, too,—/ Hart

Even though his job with Rheinthal and Newman was not interesting, it was a source of steady income and security for Hart. His spirits were bolstered by the publication of some of his work. He reviewed Sherwood Anderson's *Winesburg, Ohio* for *The Pagan,* saying, "America should read this book on her knees," and he published in the November, 1919, issue of *The Modernist* three of his early poems: "North Labrador," "Legende," and "Interior." But, as with so many of the jobs Crane held, he found the work at

[1] Hart planned to begin working in September. However, after a quarrel with Claire and Hal Smith in mid-August he returned to New York and took his position at Rheinthal and Newman.

Rheinthal and Newman boring; by the end of October he had decided to quit. The dreams the poet had had when he first arrived in
New York of earning easy money from writing movie scenarios and
advertisements were now dim; the payments of his allowance were
still irregular. When the weather grew colder, he was driven from
his poorly heated rooms on West 16th Street to the Hotel Albert on
East 10th; prospects for winter were not good. Again it was Clarence Crane who helped his son by suggesting two possible positions:
one with Hart's uncle Fred Crane at the Burroughs Company, and
the other with the Crane Chocolate Company. On November 6,
1919, Hart returned to Cleveland to work for his father.

To Grace Hart Crane

[New York City]
Monday, Sept. 22nd '19

ALS, 4 pp.

Dear Mother:—

Well,—I am feeling better, and I cannot but feel it is only justice to you that your check rec'd last Fri. is partly responsible. It
helped me by relieving my worries about the long over-due rent,
and also enabled me to feel at ease with "the boys" [1] who arrived
last Sat.—Roger on Friday. I was called on the phone as soon as he
arrived and plans were made at once for the next two days. We
went to "Chu Chin Chow" [2] Sat. night and they were all aglow with
the beauty of the theater and the performance. William, in spite of
an heroic attempt at boredom was confessedly impressed, and Roger
has been gasping "My God" at everything since his arrival. My admiration is inclining away from William, I find. You were, I fear,
sadly near the right, when you told me what you thought of his last
visit. I don't know whether his nervous breakdown and its causes
were responsible or not, but I don't recollect ever before encounter-

---

[1] William Wright and Roger Zucker. Wright was attending Columbia College
at this time.
[2] The Oriental fantasy by Oscar Asche.

ing such an example of conceit,—and conceit unmingled with any aggressiveness or animation which often make it interesting, even charming. "Bump on a log" seems to express him about as well as anything I know of. He may be under the effect of a bad cold, which he is having, or some other temporary affliction,—but I can't think of anyone less interesting than he is at present. I only hope that I will be forced to change my opinion soon, as I have always liked him, and hope to find more in him. He really has changed considerably. Perhaps though Columbian interests and activities will take him away from himself, and then he will revive,—I hope so. Roger is enthusiastic and excited as a young calf, and that is always refreshing. If he would only leave off his incessant sophomoric obsession of talking "naughtily" about ladies etc. I could like him more. Anyway, I took them to Churchills after the show, and we ended up merrily with beer and sandwiches and cabaret music.

I have been "on the job" since last Fri. morn. and feel enough better now to expect this work to run clearly complete. I have Thurs. as a holiday on account of the Jewish religion, and will enjoy it more than the rest of the my brother employees on account of being priviledged to eat. Pat[3] probably arrived from England today, and I expect from what Hal said yesterday to be invited to dine with him this week. His father had just died a day before his leaving, and I am informed that the gent leaves an annuity of $5,000 (a year) for each of the children. This indirectly assures Jessie of plenty of money in the future and they are all glad. Hal brought some pieces of furniture in from the West Englewood bungalow yesterday,[4] and I find that the mirror looks very handsome over the little mantleplace here in the room, with the fire screen employed pretentiously below. I am (it is tacitly understood) the only tenant of the rooms now, so that rent falls entirely upon me now. It is only $5.00 per week, however, and that is cheaper than practically *anything* I could find in any rooming house. I find that since the bedbugs left, and the cooler weather begins, it is much more comfortable here, and don't look forward to the winter here with anything but

[3] Pat Spencer, Claire Spencer's brother.
[4] Hal Smith and his wife, Claire, had a small cottage in West Englewood, New Jersey.

pleasant anticipations. I find that I am valued as an aggreeable and reliable tenant, and that makes me still more comfortable. Yes,— you were right,—John [5] did succeed in making a bad-mood worse, —and now that he has left, I see that his ignorance and conversation were a great annoyance. I rec'd. a pleasant letter from C.A. today (Frisco) dating his arrival in Cleveland for next Monday. He had been to Guy Bates Post's performance of "The Masquerader," [6] and if you remember the play, you see how his mood was broadened for the moment, as I can easily detect in the tenor of the letter. He speaks of going into the publishing business (perhaps with M. Parrish) and also the soft drink business. As his business is now well beyond the million mark, he says he [is] planning on the second. His plans sound stupendous, and certainly command much admiration. I can honestly flatter him in many ways. This is all for tonight— I'm tired and want to do a few other letters yet, and read some. Bob writes that he is expecting to work here next summer and perhaps stay with me,—which might be aggreeable. Will send you my poems Wed.

Much Love from Hart.—

Do wish you would send me the old dining room rug (third floor) to stop my bed from singing and knocking so much on this bare floor.

To Grace Hart Crane

[New York City]
Hotel Albert
Oct. 31st, '19

TLS, 2 pp.

My dear Mother:—
    Thank you for your fine appreciation of my poems which came this morning. It is good to know that you like them, and that your

---

[5] Probably John Lloyd.
[6] *The Masqueraders* by Henry Arthur Jones. Guy Bates Post had several roles in the play.

interest in me extends even to my efforts in that line of work which is not generally of much interest to you.

Father did not come, as expected, and probably will not come for some time. I was somewhat disappointed, and the results of his absence have kept me busy enough during the last couple of days. A letter from him yesterday explained his reasons,—having too many things on hand at home, etc.,—which I can readily understand. He made the suggestion that I should come to Cleveland and work for Fred Crane and the Burroughs Adding Machine Co. This I may do,—you may see me home within a week. But if I can find something here better than what I have been doing at Rheinthal and Newman's, I would prefer avoiding working for someone for whom I have so little liking as Fred Crane. He wants me to sell adding machines, and I do not think I am fitted for salesmanship at all. However,—if I do not succeed in getting in with the Habicht Braun people [1] here, whom I mentioned in my last letter, I shall probably attempt this in spite of my present feelings. I have simply taken in my own hands to do what father wrote me he intended doing when he came to New York, and I am sure that should it work out right, he would be as pleased as myself. I wrote you the advantages of the position relative to father's business, and I cannot help but think that it would be a far better and more direct thing to do than the adding machine proposition. I am to dine with the Habichts tonight and will know afterward what the prospects are. I'll let you know at once what I have decided to do.

I have just sent a bundle of sheets and a bundle of magazines, for which I have no room here, to you. There may be a few more things coming on from time to time. I have quit work for Rheinthal and Newman, as it was impossible for me to accomplish anything in the way of looking around for new prospects after spending the entire business day there. Mr. Rheinthal has been very decent, and I am going over tomorrow morning to have a pleasant talk with him. But my working there has certainly been to no advantage beyond that of a purely diplomatic nature. Three months

---

[1] Habicht-Braun was an import-export company with which Hart hoped to get a job. He had met Hermann Habicht, an executive in the company, and his wife, the poet Charmion von Wiegand, through Alexander Baltzly.

of tiresome and unprofitable work. Any child could do it that had sufficient muscular strength, and toward the last the insult that it branded on my intelligence grew rather painful. Whatever I do now I am sure will be much better. I want a job where I can have a chance to use my brains a little. They have become very heavy and rusty lately.

Mrs. C.A. leaves for Cleveland tonight, I understand. I have not seen [her] here at all, for which I am rather sorry. I have been so rushed that there wasn't any time. I hear that she has asked about me several times, and no doubt, would have been glad to have met me.

I would like to see you soon. Maybe I shall. We ought to spend Thanksgiving together somehow or other. That makes me think— Roger's mother [2] is here this week on account of an eye operation that he is undergoing. Nothing severe or dangerous, however. Bill [3] spent last Sunday with me. College has done him much good, and he is quite changed since his arrival. Claire and Hal had me up to dine with them last Tuesday evening. Claire looks as though nothing whatever were about to happen.[4] Oddly enough, she is much pleasanter than she was in the early stages last summer.

I hope that you are well and contented. Sorry that I haven't written you more this week, but you see how its been. Zell is in town but I haven't succeeded in locating her yet.

Much love from / Hart

In the eighteen months that he worked for his father—from November, 1919, to April, 1921—Hart held a series of jobs that always began with great promise but ended without significant promotion. After a short visit with his mother and grandmother in Cleveland, he moved to Akron to sell Mary Garden Chocolates in a drugstore, but as Clarence had not advertised his product well enough, business was slow. The few Christmas shoppers who did

[2] Mrs. Zucker.
[3] William Wright.
[4] Claire Spencer was expecting her first child, Harrison Venture Smith.

come to Hart's counter usually found him reading a little magazine or a book of poetry. Though Akron, Ohio, was a typical Midwestern city devoted to commerce and industry, Hart managed to make several friends and had one serious homosexual love affair. This affair, which he characterized as "the most intense and satisfactory one of my whole life," [1] lasted from December, 1919, through April, 1920. Hart also met Harry Candee, who, like him, was living temporarily in Akron. In Candee, Crane found a person who shared his interest in literature and who had a great knowledge of European culture. With Candee, Crane shared some of his happiest moments —moments he recorded in his poem "Porphyro in Akron." Crane met another exiled artist, Hervey W. Minns, whose photography had been praised in Europe, but who was virtually unknown in the United States. It was through Hart's efforts that *The Little Review* published two of Minns's photographs together with Crane's "Note on Minns" in its September–December, 1920, issue.

At the beginning of January, 1920, Hart returned to Cleveland to work in his father's factory. For a time he was happy, and the prospects of his success in the business were considerable. As his mother and grandmother were spending the winter on the Isle of Pines, he enjoyed the freedom and privacy of an apartment on Euclid Avenue. But in early March, when they returned, Hart was forced back into the constrictive atmosphere of 115th Street. At the end of a quiet summer, C.A. offered his son a chance to open up a new sales market for his chocolates in Washington, D.C., which Hart, who was happy to leave both sides of his family and the staid atmosphere of Cleveland, accepted immediately. However, through no fault of his own, Crane's Washington trip was a complete failure— for all of the sample chocolates that arrived from Cleveland showed the effects of the September heat. On October 15, Hart resumed work at his father's factory.

Through the autumn of 1920, the working days at the factory gradually were lengthened to keep pace with the Christmas rush, and as this happened, Hart grew more tired and despondent. The

[1] See Crane's letter to Gorham B. Munson of December 27, 1919; published in *The Letters*, p. 27.

only relief he had that winter was when Grace and her mother took another trip to the Isle of Pines; the trip began on January 1 and lasted several months. In the meantime, Hart's relations with C.A. again became strained, for he felt that he was getting nowhere in his job and was not receiving the pay he deserved. Finally, on April 20, 1921, father and son confronted each other in the basement of a restaurant Clarence operated on Euclid Avenue. C.A. reprimanded his son for his poor work; Hart refused to apologize, and after Clarence had made a humiliating remark about Grace, Hart announced that he was through and stormed out. He did not communicate with his father for two years.

Freedom from C.A. and the consequent respite from work brought a severe financial crisis as well. As Crane came to realize that he was solely dependent on his mother, he became more and more restless; but the postwar depression had begun—there simply was no work to be found. During this period Crane spent most of his free time with the friends he had made in Cleveland. All were interested in the arts: Sam Loveman, who later lived with Hart in Brooklyn; Richard Laukhuff, who operated a bookstore in Cleveland; William Lescaze, the architect; William Sommer, the artist; and, later, the artist Richard Rychtarik and his wife, Charlotte. At first, because of his despondency, Hart's writing suffered; but by September, 1921, he was working hard on "Chaplinesque" and what eventually became the first part of "Voyages": "The Bottom of the Sea Is Cruel." Hart realized that he had to have a skill in order to find work, so he enrolled in an advertising course at Western Reserve. His effort paid off, for in early January, 1922, he got a job writing copy for the Cleveland advertising firm of Corday and Gross.

For the most part, 1922 was a year of mental and poetic growth; indeed, it was one of the happiest years of his life. He read and re-read Donne, Marlowe, Webster, Vaughan, Blake, Jonson, Pound, Eliot, Joyce, and Wallace Stevens—to name but a few. Harry Candee introduced him to P. D. Ouspensky's *Tertium Organum,* which along with William James's *Varieties of Religious Experience* led Crane to the notion of a higher and timeless level of the mind that only the true visionary could attain. In May, he began one of his finest poems, "For the Marriage of Faustus and Helen," which he worked on until February of the next year.

Hart was even fortunate enough to enjoy another brief respite from his mother, who, since her alimony had stopped shortly before, spent September and October in New York City looking for work. While she was there Hart wrote the following letter to her.

To Grace Hart Crane

Cleveland, Ohio
[Postmarked October 7, 1922]
Saturday

ALS, 2 pp.
LETTERHEAD: H. HART CRANE/1709 E. 115TH STREET/CLEVELAND, OHIO

Dear Grace: [1]

Just a line to put with Grandma's— Heard from Harry Candee yesterday—just landed from Europe. I have telegraphed him at a *likely* address to phone you, which he will do, of course, if he gets the telegraph in time. Hope you had a good time with the Munsons. Am anxious to hear *all* about things. Have a good time right up to the last minute. Chuck your thoughts about anything so drab as work—and laugh with 'em all!

I'm glad everyone has treated you with such affection. Give all *eligibles* my regards.

Love/ Hart

Grandma has been chipper and quite unruffled!

When Mrs. Crane returned to Cleveland, her relations with Hart deteriorated once again. This time it was Hart's predilection

---

[1] Grace was staying at the Waldorf Astoria Hotel in New York.

for alcohol that caused the break. The poet, who began drinking on his first trip to New York in 1917, was consuming as much bootleg alcohol as his limited finances would permit. Upset by his drinking, Grace decided in early December not to allow any liquor in her home—a decision which so upset Hart that he moved into a hotel for several days. This episode was soon forgotten, and Crane returned to his mother's house for Christmas. But in March, 1923, a crisis of a different sort occurred. Crane had been successful in his job with Corday and Gross, but resigned to take a position with Stanley Patno, who ran a direct mail advertising service. Though Hart did well in his new position, the firm did not have enough business; in early March he was dismissed. Discouraged by his dismissal and tired of Cleveland—and worried that friends would think he had failed once again—Crane went to New York at the end of the month to search for another job.

To avoid any embarrassment, Hart, Grace, and Mrs. Hart told friends and relatives that he was going on a business trip to New York and did not know when he would return. Expecting it would be only a short while before he found a new position, Crane had arranged to stay with Gorham Munson and his wife, Elizabeth, until he had the promise of an income. Yet, as so often before, his search for employment was long and frustrating; Hart was forced to live with the Munsons for two months.

As the next seven letters show, Grace and her mother sent words of encouragement, advice, family news—even of their bird, Clip— and information about his paternal grandparents, whose house on 115th Street had been sold for an apartment building. At the same time, Mrs. Crane often expressed the hope that her son would abandon his New York venture and return to live with her.

Wishing to continue in advertising, Hart applied in mid-April for a position with the J. Walter Thompson agency. Though initially receptive to his application and his samples of advertising copy, the personnel manager at Thompson's kept deferring a decision on hiring him. As the weeks wore on, Hart's position became increasingly difficult. He did not want to return to Cleveland, yet he had used nearly all his money and felt embarrassed at having overstayed his welcome at the Munsons, who had to keep post-

poning the arrival of another house guest, the poet and novelist
Jean Toomer.

From Elizabeth Belden Hart

Cleveland, Ohio

3—29—'23

AL, 3 pp.
LETTERHEAD: MRS. ELIZABETH B. HART/ 1709 EAST 115TH STREET/
CLEVELAND/ OHIO

My Dear Hart:

Your very interesting letter of Monday, was thoroughly enjoyed
at the breakfast table this morning—and made us very happy to
note the changed state of mind it reflected all through.

We feel sure of your ultimate success—when supported by such
favorable conditions— It only needs a little time and perseverance
to prove the good that is in store for you—

Mother wished me to write you a line to go out today, so that
you may know we are both well and gradually overcoming the terrible loneliness we felt after you left— Mother won't go near your
room yet, but Margarett [1] was here yesterday and put up clean
curtains—and remarked about how nice and clean you left it—

Helens interests has been a good thing to take her mind off
herself— She has gone to take Zell to train and we have had a bid
from the nurse that we may go over this evening and view the little
blue eyed—brown haired Miss who has come into our family
circle [.] [2] Mother was into see Helen just a few moments, but she
had hardly come out from the influence of her twilight sleep to
know what she was saying—she said "Aunt Grace: its a *real nice
baby*. I didnt think it would amount to much, *but it does*. it has
got "fine toes", and *"everything"*."

We have had lots of fun over it. She hardly knew what she was
saying—but another remark she made, (excuse me for telling it) she

---

[1] "Margarett" worked as a maid for Mrs. Crane and Mrs. Hart.
[2] Mrs. Hurlbert had given birth to a daughter, Zell.

said Mother it seems very strange they can't determine the "sex."
She was a little hazy—see? Every thing is about as when you left—
very cold—and not enough gas to even heat water to wash dishes
—but paper says warmer soon— I hope so for Easter will not be
very pleasant, if this continues. Griswold comes up tomorrow and
will stop with us while here over Sunday— Becky [3] called up this
morning—and invited Mother to a dinner party Sunday Eve—
Very sweet of her to remember her birthday— I appreciate it very
much. She wishes to be remembered to you— We are carrying out
our plans we made before you left in regard to your business trip
etc. so no one questions us— Remember me kindly to Gorham—
and also his wife for I know she is nice. Mother has praised her so
much— I need not tell you how much Grandma thinks of and
loves you—you know it [4] Write often, it makes us happy to hear
from you. Devotedly—

From Grace Hart Crane

Cleveland, Ohio
[March 30, 1923?]
11:30 P.M. Good Friday.

ALS, 8 pp.
LETTERHEAD: MRS. GRACE HART CRANE/ 1709 EAST 115TH. STREET/
CLEVELAND/ OHIO

Dear Hart:—

  Griswold is spending the night with us & says if I have this letter
ready for him when he leaves for town in the morning he will mail
it. I want you to have the news up to date from home on Easter.
    We have the house all clean & orderly for Sunday—clean curtains
at every window & glass shining. The weather will have to moderate considerably or there will be more fur coats & gulashes than
anything else in the parade. It has been terribly cold for several
days & everyone is sick & tired of it.

[3] A friend of Mrs. Crane's who is mentioned several times in the following letters.
[4] The final word of the sentence is illegible.

Griswold has come up to be with Helen over Sunday & will sleep here & eat some of his meals with us. On Sunday noon we are to be his guests at luncheon at The Sovreighn, and in the evening I am invited to dine with "Florence & M.J".[1] & other invited guests. So you see my birthday will not be so dull after all. Mother & I will probably go to church in the morning.

Binet called up today for your address to forward to Willy who must be in New York.[2]

I had a nice little visit with Charlotte[3] today & she tells me that Chas. Harris[4] will be there also for a few days. So I can imagine what a lot of fun you are going to have being with your old friends. She tells me that Richard will also be in N.Y. the first of May.

I wouldn't want you to know how lonely I am without you, or how much I miss you nights, and mornings. No one to bring me a cup of coffee—and no victrola & tramping over head,—just deathly still and deadly dull—I HATE it!!

Glenn[5] & I had a rumpus, and he has neither been out or called up until today. I have let him alone and I really tho't it was all over—but evidently not entirely. I asked him about the dinner last night and he said if it didn't have more to offer soon, he would have to drop out. Sam read from something, & Ted Robeson recited some of his stuff. Glenn says that the only person in the club that is congenial is Baldwin.[6]

Last night while I was at the hospital calling on Helen, Harold Thomas came in.[7] He tho't he might give you the benefit of his experience with New York Advertizing Agencies if you would not consider it a bore—& I asked him to write you c/o of Gorham.

[1] Florence was possibly Mrs. Florence Spencer. M.J., another friend of Grace's, was Mrs. M. Jessie Barker of Cleveland.

[2] Jean Binet, the pianist, whom Crane met in Cleveland. Willie is William Lescaze.

[3] Mrs. Richard Rychtarik.

[4] Charles Harris, whom Hart had met at Richard Laukhuff's bookstore in Cleveland. An engineer by profession, Harris had a wide knowledge of literature and occasionally wrote poetry.

[5] Glenn Whistler, who at this time was courting Mrs. Crane.

[6] These sentences probably refer to the Warren Society of Cleveland. Sam Loveman, Ted Robinson, and Charles Baldwin, all writers, were part of Crane's circle of friends in Cleveland.

[7] Harold Thomas was Hart's acquaintance from Warren, Ohio. See Crane's letter of January 2, 1917, to his mother and grandmother.

Helen's baby is the sweetest most perfect little darling you could ever wish to see. She is just a perfect little doll & I am clear carried away with her. You would be too if you were to see her. Helen is getting along all right and I go to see her twice a day when Gooz or Zell are not in town.

Clip misses you I feel certain. He does not sing as much & especially from six to eight—the time you were around.

Your letter of Tuesday was a wonderful one, & I just hope you will keep your resolution to work persistantly to get a job—and not lose any of your determination to secure that first of all, regardless of social pleasures. But it seems now, as if every one of your most interesting men friends are in or are going to soon be in N.Y. — Well have a good time but remember what you are there for. That is all the advise I am offering this time. I shall hope to receive my S.D. on Sunday, & I know that you will be thinking of me—

Your grandmother Crane is improving—at least that seems to be the case. No other news to report from that locality.

My love to Gorham & E——and you know what a lot I am sending you—

Devotedly / Grace—

Nancy will probably go down on Monday night.[8] She stops at the Vanderbilt.

From Grace Hart Crane

[Cleveland]
Tuesday A.M.
April 24—1923

ALS, 8 pp.

My dear Hart:—

Last week was so strenuous and so crowded with things to do etc that I could not find one moment to write you even a note. I was sorry too, because I believe you look forward to hearing from home.

---

[8] Probably Nancy Sommers, a friend of Grace's who was a buyer for the Halle Brothers department store.

Blanche came Tuesday morning and so did Verna [1]— Verna stayed at M. A. Bradley's but was here for a few hours every day, & when she wasn't visiting with us she was ordering a taxi to take her to some luncheon or dinner, or sending telegrams to her fiancé in Chicago—who came on to attend the wedding. Our household was in a constant state of irregularities and you know how hard that is on grandma—to say nothing of myself. I was pulled forty ways at once—and while Blanche did everything she could to make it easy for us, she is a difficult person to have in ones house at such a time. We went to some of the pre nuptial festivities and ended up with the wedding Saturday night at the Church of the Covenant, & reception at Wade Park Manor. It was all very grand, & if I could talk to you I would love to give you the details—many of which were very grand, and beautiful. We had Verna's young man here at the house to dress & go with us to the wedding, & after the thing was all over they came back here about 2 o'clock in the morning, changed their clothes & took the 2:40 A.M. train for Boston. Verna had been away from school a week & had to be back for 8 oclock class on Monday morning. As the wedding party was largely composed of Harvard students & girls from the east, the Drake[s] had a special car attached to the Boston train for their convenience.

So you see we were up practically all Saturday night, & Sunday found me with a bad headache & pretty nearly all in.

Sunday afternoon mother & I took Blanche to Regnauty for dinner & Blanche thought she never had eaten such food before. She went home Sunday night at 11:15 and Glenn came out & went with me to the Union Depot to see her off.

I hope she had a good time. We were busy doing something every minute, but with no help I could not make any parties. We took most of our dinners out at McNally's or the Cleveland or Womens City Club—and went to Keiths Palace,[2] & all the best movies. One afternoon I invited M J & Becky and Sara for tea, & she enjoyed them very much. I thought Becky very charming &

---

[1] In this letter Grace writes about the marriage of Josephine Chisholm Drake to Edwin Clapp Lincoln that took place on April 21. Verna Ross was one of the bride's attendants. Blanche Ross, Verna's mother, was a friend of Grace's.

[2] B. F. Keith's Palace Theatre featured "SUPREME VAUDEVILLE TWICE DAILY AND SUNDAY."

M.J. delightful. I was invited to the Drakes for tea one afternoon to view the wedding gifts. Such gorgeous things I never before had seen in such quantities. Just imagine solid gold knives, forks, spoons with beautiful green jade handles. Those from the Drakes of hotel Drake, Chicago—Desert plates from the Frank Rockefellers that were $600.00 a dozen. It looked to me as if half of Seltzers store were there. Thirty five dozen beautiful service plates, gorgeous tea services priceless antiques of various kinds— It was a joy to look upon them.

Verna is a sweet pretty girl—but a perfect type of the steriotype college society girl—with the regulation clothes, phrases etc. Her Education has been thorough & perfectly regular. I don't believe she has ever questioned anything she has ever read about art or literature. She is a dear sweet girl—you can't help but love her. She is practically engaged to this young Charles Stiger of Oak Park who is attending Harvard, and they had a wonderful time together here at the wedding. She asked many questions about you and said she was greatly disappointed at not seeing you. She had counted on it.

Yesterday I attended a meeting of the executive committee of the Warren Society of Cleveland—which has its meeting this year on May 8th, the birthday of Judge Hutchins.[3] We met at Anna Wilsons, she having returned from a winter in California only Saturday night. We decided upon the Wade Park Manor this year—and it is to be in the form of a dinner dance. I shall be very forlorn without you. In fact I am all of the time— I miss you terribly—but I am to be happy if you can get located in New York in the advertizing business. You have no idea how happy I shall be when I know you are really settled, or how much interested I am in your success. Are you answering the Ad's in the paper— & why not put one in for yourself?

It has been too cold to do any house cleaning yet but we must wade in very soon.

I dropped in on Sam[4] one afternoon about a week ago. He was very nice— & said he missed you more & more. Glenn said last

[3] John C. Hutchins (1840–1932), a prominent lawyer and judge from Cleveland. Hutchins was born in Warren, Ohio, and was a member of the Warren Society of Cleveland.
[4] Samuel Loveman.

night that Sam was very depressed & much discouraged because he wasn't getting anywhere.

Glenn bought a second hand Cadillac roa[d]ster yesterday— & it is to be over hauled, & painted in the next two weeks— He was quite over come with the prospect last night, & we selected the color of paint etc. He depends upon me for advice about a lot of things. I think it is going to be a broadening experience for him to have a machine—and now that he is going to run for Judge next fall—he just must have one.

Preparations for moving are going on over across the street, but I think their troubles have only begun. Mrs Crane does not gain very fast—and today she is down in bed again, Bess is there helping & the doctor also. Francis is very *scarce*— I don't think she has taken her out more than twice— So far as I know they do not know of your being away, & I shall not volunteer any information—until I have to.

Jim told me that C.A. & Francis are considering buying a Packard coupe— It will certainly be a very acceptable change to me, to have them off of the street.

Zell will be in New York very soon now, if she is not already. Her Associated Press convention meets there on the 29th I think. She stops at the Waldorf—so be sure to get in touch with her— She may be able to do you some good— & any way will want to see you. If you don't find her drop her a line & leave it in her room box, telling her your address & how she can reach you.

Helen and Gooz & nurse & baby all left here in their machine for Warren last Wednesday afternoon, & I have not heard from them since.

We all have invitations for the wedding of Justine Gilder— occuring Sat. the 28th. We do not intend to be there but must send something of course.

Well this is all of the news I think of just now—and it has made a long letter. I gave "Clip" your love. Since the bright days have come, he sings almost without stopping— Remember you are to write often—whether your news is good or not—

Love from us all from/ Grace.

[*Written on the back of page 8*:] There are some quite bulky packages of magazines here from Europe for you. Do you wish me to send those to you & how can I?/ GHC.

From Grace Hart Crane

Cleveland, Ohio
May 4th 1923—

ALS, 7 pp.

LETTERHEAD: MRS. GRACE HART CRANE/ 1709 EAST 115TH. STREET/
CLEVELAND/ OHIO

My dear boy:—

If you were here you would go into ecstacies over the cherry tree in our yard. It *is a* thing of beauty—and from the third floor rear window as you look down into it you feel as if you were in fairyland. I feel as if I should advertize it as being on exhibition to the public.

How could you have missed Richard? He must have been terribly disappointed—as he asked me several times at the station if he thought you would surely be there.

Well no doubt you have seen him long before this and everything is explained.

Poor Charlotte. She is very lonely & hasn't had a letter from Richard yet— He sent her a night wire yesterday, but she wishes to get more particulars. I have called her every day & tried to cheer her the best I knew how.

When Richard returns, I shall have them over.

Just now we are in up to our eyes in house cleaning. There's so much to be done all at once, I hardly know where to begin. The Crane mansion across the street, is almost a thing of the past. The wreckers have been busy for nearly three days & the house is roofless, doorless, windowless & nearly sideless. They make an awful lot of dirt & muss, & you would think you were in the factory district, the way things look at present in our immediate vicinity.

The family moved out early Wednesday morning, & right in the midst of the muss, they brought out your grandmother Crane, & took her in C.A.'s car over to the apartment. She certainly was a pathetic sight, so weak she could scarcely walk, & weeping as though her heart would break. She felt very badly to leave this house—for I think she has cared the most for this place of all the homes she has had. I don't believe she will ever be happy where they are—but she is too much of an invalid now to [have] anything to say about where she is to live.

Francis has been down in bed again—nervous breakdown so I hear.

Well anyway we are as free from the sight or sound of them now as if we lived in another town.

Tonight mother & I are going to have dinner with Sara in her new apartment. I have been there & it is charming. I wish we were moved & located as attractively.

I think about you almost constantly, and am hoping hourly that you will get some thing to do. How are you managing at Gorhams —and your money—is there any left. Oh Hart dear, if you could only know how a mother's heart and mind are constantly with her boy.

If you don't succeed in getting a job pretty soon, I think you would better come back & see what you can do here. You know you have a home here, & plenty to eat while you are looking. It worries me to have you accept so much from Elizabeth & Gorham.

I had a short note from Zell—said she had seen you & was sending you around to some friends of hers. Shall expect to see her at the Warren Banquet on Tuesday evening.

Sam calls me quite often & is always very much interested in talking or hearing about you. Nancy Sommers expects to go to New York Sunday or Monday night.

Saturday 3 P.M.

Stopped here to wait for to days mail. It bro't me yours & Richards postal—am glad you finally met. Working hard to finish the cleaning down stairs for Sunday. Old house looks pretty good— Write often. All my love— Grace

From Grace Hart Crane

Cleveland, Ohio
[May 12, 1923?] [1]
Saturday P.M.

ALS, 5 pp.
LETTERHEAD: MRS. GRACE HART CRANE/ 1709 EAST 115TH. STREET/
CLEVELAND/ OHIO

Dearest boy:—

I am going down to market and will try to get this in the 105th
P.O. so you will get it Sunday.

I received your letter Thursday night upon my return from town,
and you may be sure I was glad to receive it. You do not write half
often enough to suit me.

Our W.S. of Cleveland banquet was most enjoyable—good food
music & dancing & no speech-making. I missed you very much & we
would have had some good dances together—however I did not
lack for partners[.] Zell came up & stayed overnight with us, and I
devoted the next day to her.

Yesterday Helen, Griswold, the nurse & baby drove up to see the
doctor, and stopped here for lunch. Everyone was looking fine &
happy—including the baby. She is the prettiest little thing & has
such lovely clothes— Well that busted up the day for us, & we did
not get any housecleaning done as we had expected.

Last night Sara & I had our regular night at the movies, & she
told me that M.J. & Florence have invited her to motor with them
to Philadelphia to attend Jimmy Wolf's [2] wedding which comes off
on May 17th. I believe they are leaving here Monday noon.

Zell tells me she is sending you some more introductory letters
which may secure you something to do, even if not exactly what
you most desire. I do think you should take some job & work while

[1] The description of the Warren Society banquet, which Grace said in her letter of May 4 would be held "next Tuesday" (May 8), suggests that this letter
was written on the following Saturday, May 12.

[2] Jimmy Wolf was the son of one of Mrs. Crane's Cleveland friends. See Grace's
letter of Thursday, March 29, 1917.

you wait— It is easy enough to resign [.] I certainly hope you can land some thing in the advertizing line & while I am not worrying as I once would, I can't help but be anxious for you to get located & get to earning something again.

Things here at home & our friends are all about the same as when you were here. Let us hear more often from you. You are perfectly right about looking up you [r] friends there or from here as long as you are so unsettled—

My best love & all of it / Grace.

From Grace Hart Crane

Cleveland, Ohio
[May, 1923?] [1]
Thursday 2 P.M.

ALS, 8 pp.

LETTERHEAD: MRS. GRACE HART CRANE / 1709 EAST 115TH. STREET / CLEVELAND / OHIO

My dear Hart:—

Needless to say we—(*especially* I—) were mighty glad to receive your letter written Sunday afternoon, & were much amused over your bathroom escapade with Elizabeth.

Margaret & I have just been raising H—— with housecleaning for the past few days— I wish you could see the third floor—it is a delight to look at & model of order & cleanliness. It all opens up together & looks like a little apartment. How I wish you & Gorham & Elizabeth had it down in New York— It is no use to us, & means many hours of hard work for me to keep it in order— Today Margaret is here cleaning bathroom & hall woodwork. I hope next week will finish the housecleaning.

Katherine and Phil called late Sunday afternoon— They were out looking for apartments in this neighborhood,— At present they have two rooms in the New Amsterdam.

---

[1] The date of this letter is uncertain. Grace writes that the Crane house has been torn down; therefore she wrote the letter after May 4. She also says that Glenn's car is not finished, so she wrote it before May 18 when they went for a drive. Therefore she wrote this letter either on Thursday, May 10 or on May 17.

Nancy, Edna[2] & Glenn were also out for the evening—so you can imagine something of the noise & see grandmother fleeing to her apartment on the second floor. Edna thinks there is a job for her in New York very soon—so you will probably see her before long, if you remain. Glenn is still pegging away at the Law, & living in a one room & bath apartment in the Haddam—which I think is awful! His car is not finished yet but will be very soon. I think he is going to be pretty timid about driving it.

The Crane House across the way is a thing of memory only—torn down & hauled away. Excavation has begun for the new apartment and the street is full of Fords—Chevey express wagons & carts hauling away the dirt. It is going to be a dirty noisy summer for the Hurds[3] & us, & I am fearful that our porch pleasure will be much interfered with.

The weather has been so cold that as yet I have not been out at all to work in the yard. The "drapsnaggons" are up, also the larkspur. The white lilac bush is quite full of bloom—

I have not seen Richard or Charlotte since his visit to New York. The housecleaning has left me too tired to undertake any entertaining, even of the simplest sort. Will do so very soon, however.

I cannot imagine how you are getting money to buy food or pay car fare by this time. I *do* wish you would take *any* job to meet expenses until you get one you want. If Zell hasn't sent you those letters yet—it is because she is waiting for you to write when you want them. At least mother says that she told her that you were to write for them when you were ready. Better let her know if she hasn't sent them by this time.

Put an advertizement in the Times & perhaps The Monitor— I feel sure you will get something. I am trying not to worry about you—but my dear I certainly will feel happier & much relieved when you get something to do to meet expenses—

You do not mention Clare or Harry Candee— How are Gorham and Elizabeth getting along?

I must rush this to the front porch to catch the postman—so will say goodbye—for this time—with *all* my love./ Grace—

---

[2] Mrs. Edna Moore, a friend of Grace's.

[3] The Hurds were Mrs. Crane's and Mrs. Hart's neighbors. Their son Kenneth had been a close friend of Hart's when the poet attended East High School.

Last night about 12:30 I felt impelled to get up & go to the dining
room & see if dear little "Clip" were all right. When I switched on
the light, I saw a mouse just running down the standard from the
cage— I found that he had been inside the cage. Well you bet I
just took bird cage & bird right up stairs with me & hung him in
the spare room on side light where no mouse could get at him. I
couldn't stand it to have any thing happen to Clip— He is sweeter
every day—

Tell me if my S.D.'s have been failing to reach you on Sunday. If
so I must mail them earlier.

From Grace Hart Crane

Cleveland, Ohio
May 22—'23
Tuesday A.M.

ALS, 7 pp.
LETTERHEAD: MRS. GRACE HART CRANE/ 1709 EAST 115TH. STREET/
CLEVELAND/ OHIO

Dearest—

I don't want another Day to pass without my getting off a few
lines to you. I have been so busy cleaning house and driving Glenns
new roa[d]ster that I have neglected you. He got his car Friday & we
went for a ride that night & also Saturday afternoon & evening. You
know it is a second hand one—& he was anxious to see how well
the engine worked. We found there were some things to be done,
like burn carbon—etc—but all together he was very much pleased
with his bargain, & it is a beautiful paint job & really looks like a
bran new car.

We decided Saturday that we would drive to Warren & see Zell
on Sunday—so we called her up & she asked us to have dinner with
her.

There is a swell road from here to Warren & we just flew. I drove
both ways & must say for real sport for two a roadster is the thing.

We arrived at Zell's front door at exactly one o'clock & she had a
dandy dinner for us— Her house has all been redecorated inside up

stairs & down & new shades & matting & carpet in the library. She has a fine maid who is an excellent cook & housekeeper. Helen came in for dinner with us—Griswold eating with his folks— Helen's motherhood is making her *beautiful*[.] She was lovely to look at Sunday. After dinner we all went out to her house, saw the baby —which is a darling, & then down to Tribune office, which was of great interest to Glenn. He has *great* admiration for Zell & warmed into courtesy & attention of which you would never believe him capable.

We started home at 5:15 & got caught in the darndest thunder storm & down pour you ever saw. Some of the time it was too bad to see a foot ahead & we just sat still—but we got along allright & arrived home about eight.

Yesterday Margaret was here & we cleaned the pantry—All day long washing dishes & grandmother didn't want to part with even an odd plate or cup— We have enough dishes for three families.

I told Zell you would like to have the letters now, & she said she would write them this week—that she was waiting for you to say whether you wanted them as you said you would in New York—

I heartily approve of your free lance work—& especially that merchantile type—because I believe you should learn low brow advertizing as well as high brow. I think versatility is a big thing in your business.

The weather continues cold & gloomy—it is very depressing & grandma is full of aches—which, I believe would disappear with warmer weather.

Zell is giving a luncheon at the Union Club at 1 o'clock on Saturday to ten of her Cleveland friends who used to live in Warren. I have been doing the inviting & arranging—

Here comes the postman

Goodbye/ Grace

Finally, at the end of May, Crane was offered a job paying $35.00 a week in the Thompson agency's statistical department which he quickly accepted. Looking forward to the time when he would be no longer dependent on Grace, the Munsons, or anyone

else, he moved into the Hotel Albert for three days and then sublet
a room at 45 Grove Street. It was from the Hotel Albert that Hart
sent the news of his new position to his mother and grandmother.

To Grace Hart Crane and Elizabeth Belden Hart

[New York City]
[May 25, 1923?] [1]
Friday evening

ALS, 8 pp.

Dear Grace and Grandma:

All week I've been trying to get a chance to write you, and you
will neven understand *all* the complications that have prevented me
—simply because they are beyond description.

I got hired by J. Walter Thompson Tuesday morning at the
same time that the other job with the trade journal, "Machinery"
broke through also. It was a matter of choosing the better one,—
which wasn't hard to do. This agency is either the first or second
largest in the world and provides a maximum of opportunities.
They liked my copy from the first, and so much so that they have
practically made a place for me in the dept. of statistics and investigation until they need me in my real field. I work in a beautiful
building on Madison Ave near where the Noyes school used to be,
and just a block from 5*th* Ave. Thompson occupies four whole
floors of the building and you get a fine series of views from the
windows. They have started me in at 35.00, but most of their copy
writers get 75.00 to 100.00 a week. I think I have, all considered,
made a big jump in the last 2 months, though it would astonish
you to know the many sleepless nights and dreary days it has cost
me. I haven't talked about *that* and I won't begin to now when
things are on the mend, but suffice it to say that it is very hard living with two people who don't know anything about housekeeping
in a tiny apartment,—and then to have them both get sick and ne-

---

[1] Statements in Mrs. Crane's letter of May 26 suggest that Hart wrote this
letter on May 25.

cessitate your moving around from one place to another, clothes here, there and everywhere and not knowing where the next meal was coming from.

I don't know what I should have done had it not been for Slater Brown who has done all kinds of gracious things for me. Given me money, the key to his room and slept on the floor (insisted on it) that I might be comfortable. I'm not feeling anything but love and gratitude toward Gorham, but had it not been for Brown I should certainly have given up long before my job. Gorham and Liza live on the edge of things all the time, and so—I could accept only so much and no more from them when my funds gave out.

As Gorham is entertaining a writer from the South [2] at present I am staying again with Brown until the first of the month when my pay comes and I can afford a room. About 2 weeks ago I asked Bill Sommer if he could pay me the $20.00 I invested for him in the photos (you know how long ago that was) and after all this time he comes back with a letter containing $5.00! That's thoughtfulness for you. The only pictures he has ever sold have been sold through my efforts, and their total returns alone amount to nearly $100.00. I'm through trying to help such people out. If I hadn't been damned tough I couldn't have got through this ordeal without sickness, but I guess I've pulled through very well. I nearly died for awhile with hemmoroids and extreme constipation, but have finally found a very satisfactory cure for that. Now that it's all over I feel free to tell you some of my past troubles, and mainly by way of assurance that I've done my best all the time to keep you free from worries (they wouldn't have done any good, after all) and write as often as I could.

It's very fine, I think, that I should have accomplished all I have recently instead of waisting for two more years in Cleveland. My samples wouldn't have proved any more effective in convincing a N.Y. agency then than they have been lately, and I am where its best for me to be in every sense now—just so much sooner!

Today was lovely on the Ave. I enjoy my walks at lunch hour when every body is out and the streets just blaze with life and

---

[2] Jean Toomer.

colour. N.Y. has never been so gay before—it certainly is the only place to live in this country.

This has been a very sloppy letter, rushed off at a great rate and full of unpleasant details. I just felt like getting rid of some confidences inasmuch as they are so much on my mind that I can't settle down to write a gayer letter until relieved of them. You can imagine how busy I am—working all day, and bustling around for food and lodging until bed time. The details of the decent toilette, alone, under such erratic circumstances, take a lot of extra time. But it's all going to be cleared up now very soon, and I'll settle back to a steady gait, plenty of sleep and more peace and quiet.

I *must* get to bed. Write me soon, and mention as casually as you wish that I'm connected with J. Walter Thompson. *To those who know* it is a very flattering connection.

Good night!/ Hart

Write me at 4 Grove until further notice

For a while everything went well. Initially Hart was enthusiastic about his work, and a month and a half after he began he proudly wrote his mother of his promotion to the copy department. While unemployed, Crane had found it impossible to concentrate on his poetry, especially his new work, *The Bridge,* the idea for which he had conceived shortly after finishing "For the Marriage of Faustus and Helen." Now that he had settled into a comfortable room and a secure job, he worked assiduously on the "Atlantis" section as well as the entire structure of the poem. This was a time of expansion for Crane, a time to meet people. His most important new acquaintances were William Slater Brown and Susan Jenkins, and the author Waldo Frank. It was Frank who had helped Hart get a job by writing a letter to a friend at J. Walter Thompson. Brown and Jenkins, who were later married, took a great interest in Hart and he in turn found them both to be good companions. Crane met others, including E. E. Cummings, Eugene O'Neill, Kenneth Burke, the sculptor Gaston Lachaise, Lachaise's stepson, the painter Edward Nagle, the photographer Alfred Stieglitz, and the Munsons' new house guest, Jean Toomer.

From Grace Hart Crane

Cleveland, Ohio
Saturday A.M.
May 26—1923.

ALS, 6 pp.
LETTERHEAD: MRS. GRACE HART CRANE/1709 EAST 115TH. STREET/
CLEVELAND/OHIO

My dear Hart:

I have been expecting a few lines from [you] thro' the mail relative to your new position, but as none has come,[1] I assume that you have been too much engrossed in your new job to find time to write, & so I will send you the news up to date from here—which isn't much. It is hardly necessary for me to say we were delighted to receive the news which your telegram conveyed, & I shall be equally glad to know more about it etc.

This is the day of Zell ['s] luncheon at the Union Club. It is a warm beautiful day & I feel as if I had been born again after this long gloomy cold winter & spring.

The yards around here look beautifully green & fairy like. Margaret and another woman are washing the porches & their furniture & by night the swing, chairs awnings rugs etc will be in their old places once more & you can picture us sitting there evenings & every spare minute we can.

The housecleaning has dragged & been unusually strenuous this year & I am *completely fagged.* I need a week off to lay around & read & rest—

The building across the way is both very noisey & dirty & when it is finished I don't think it will enhance the value of our property any. But if you are to remain in New York, we certainly should get

---

[1] Hart had probably sent his mother a telegram announcing his appointment at the J. Walter Thompson Agency.

into a smaller home, & there is no point to keeping up this big house.

Zell may stay over until tomorrow—but not longer. Her long talked of suit comes off for sure next week.

Glenn is here almost every night. His roadster makes him very happy & he likes to stop here & talk about it.

The other night when looking at some of your book[s] in your room with Glenn, I picked up one of those small Shakespear volume[s] & out fell a $20. bill. What do you want me to do with it? I can send it registered or my check for that amount, or keep it to pay on some of your bills here. Let me know what to do.

If I do not receive a letter or some word from you today I certainly will expect a S.D. tomorrow.—

I get terribly hungry to see you dear, & I do not see how I am going to get along this summer without you. There is no one I love so much as you—you know don't you?

Devotedly Yours, / Grace.

From Elizabeth Belden Hart

[Cleveland]
Sunday 4, PM—
May 27—23

ALS, 4 pp.

My Dear Hart:

My thoughts are upon and with you so much to day, that it seems to me I must have a little chat with you—and tell you how much we (*I*) miss you, especially when I am alone— When I knew you were up in your room even tho' I didn't see you, I knew you were there.

I miss you *very very* much dear, and now that I know you have decided to stay in New York—I wonder if I will ever see you again.

Your room looks so pretty now, that it is all dolled up—but it lacks something that no one can supply but you.

Your S.D. came yesterday PM. Mother was not at home—so I did not open it until she came. Zell had her party at the U. Club yesterday so Mother was there.

When she read it I saw the tears come to her eyes—and we said you were mighty brave to go through what you have and not give up—and we feel mighty proud of our Hart.

I am glad Mother did not know all this—until it was over, for she felt badly enough as it was and I had hard work to cheer her up many times. I told her I knew you would win out give you time enough—and now while I know everything is not as you wish it, but you have made big progress—and it seems now as if you were with a firm that will recognize your worth and will advance you as fast as work improves— You now have a chance to reach out and up—as the time permits.

I think you have had wonderful friends. Gorham certainly has been very kind to divide room with you—and while it has been hard for you—they too have labored under some sacrifices— I do not want to write a long letter, but just to tell you how grateful we feel for all that has come to you through friends— I do not think much of Bill Summers appreciation of your kindness to him but all are not of his stripe—

Mother sent you an S.D. before yours came. Glen was here for dinner to day and they are off for a drive in his car— It is very snappy and good looking.

We finished our house cleaning. Yesterday Margarett brought a woman & they cleaned the two porches—so every thing looks fine to day [.] Awnings up chairs and swing up and it looks lovely— I am wondering how you are putting in the day—but you have no lack of places to go in N. York.

Now dear Hart, I want you [to] take good care of yourself— Health is a great assett and you must try not to take things too strenuous— I can have some idea of the anxious days and nights you must have put in—but I *knew* you would get something good eventually, and I stuck to that thought. When you get a room and a bath, and live as you have been used to you will be very happy in your work—

Every body is going along in the same old way here. Nothing

new. We never see any more of our old friends across the way—but we are not mourning at all—

Now good bye dear with my best love which you always have— / Grandma

[*Written on the side of the first page:*] rather late, but I guess I'll send them.

[*Written on the side of the second page:*] Don't scold at this long letter—

To Grace Hart Crane and Elizabeth Belden Hart

[New York City]
45 Grove Street
June 1st '23

ALS, 4 pp.

Grace, dear, and Grandma:

The above will be my address from now on.[1] I just moved in today and am about as happy "as they make 'em". I have a fine large room, just repainted in grey and white with running water and right next to a bath. The room is well furnished, but it is *not* a rooming house. I was in luck all around this time to have such friends. It seems that one of Slater Brown's friends who recently sailed for Europe left all his furniture here, and it comes all gratis as far as the rent is concerned. Its on the second floor and cool and quiet, and I can hire a man to come in and keep it clean for .50 a week. As for the rent,—it's only 30.00 a month! If you knew what is being asked here for miserably small and inconvenient places you would understand how fortunate I am. It seems wonderful at last to settle down, stretch my legs, and have a place to call "home".

I saw Mrs. Walton last week and she wanted $800 a week for one of those tiny rooms on the top floor, smaller even than the one Mme. Lebegue used to have! Gorham pays 6500 a month for his tiny two-room apartment etc. I was worried greatly for awhile at the

[1] Crane rented Louis Kantor's room while Kantor, a newspaper reporter, was in Europe.

prospect of having to spend all my money for just rental. But now I'm fixed up very economically as well as comfortably. I may change my mind before long, but I don't need my trunk yet. I'd rather not have the huge bulk of it to face me all the time. And, besides, I don't know of much that it would need to bring me. I'd like that bed-spread, but you can send that in a box by mail. Otherwise I'm completely fixed up here, bedding and all.

I got paid yesterday and now am able to "carry on" without outside help. It will be some time before I can catch up on some of my debts to my friends, but that will come out all right. My friends have been everything to me, and sometime I'll get time to tell you the chain of their cooperation that landed me my present fine connection. Waldo Frank gave me a letter of introduction, and then interviews started. Of course my own samples were what really convinced them, but everything in this country depends on a *little* bit of *personality influence* no matter what your qualities. What finally wound up *this* job was a word or so from Miss Alys Gregory,[2] who likes my poetry & is a critic (also formerly worked [as] a writer for Thompson) so you see my artistic friendships have proved to be worth something even in the business field.

I'm tired, need to go to bed. Job goes fine. Write me *here* from now on.

Love,/ Hart

To Elizabeth Belden Hart

[New York City]
[Postmarked June 5, 1923]

POSTCARD [1]

Dear Grandma: I like my room better all the time. My friends clubbed together and got me a Victor and records—so imagine my

---

[2] Alyse Gregory briefly mentions Crane in her autobiography, *The Day Is Gone* (New York: Dutton, 1948), p. 187. At this time Miss Gregory was managing editor of *The Dial*.

[1] On the obverse of the postcard was a picture of the Cathedral of St. John the Divine.

bliss! I hope this hot spell isn't too strong for you, it's bad here, but I don't mind. I'll go swimming soon. Love,/ Hart

To Grace Hart Crane

[New York City]
Sunday, June 10th '23
45 Grove Street

ALS, 8 pp.

Dear Grace:

This is really the first moment this week I have had to write you. There is always someone who wants you to dine with him and then it is quite usually difficult to get away before bedtime. I have been getting to sleep more, however, and today, after a regular home cooked dinner with Brown & his lady (who is a fine cook) I feel "as usual" for Sunday. Really, I'm having the finest time in my life. There's no use trying to describe the people I go round with. Not that there are so many—there could easily be, but I'm always cutting down on all but the few I like the most. Last night marketing with Sue and Bill Brown, down in the Italian section (where every one looks so happy!) was a perfect circus. We carried pots and pans, spinach, asparagus etc. etc. from place to place—only buying one kind of thing in each store—jostling with the crowds etc. I've never been with young people I enjoyed so much, and they, of course, have had real lives. Then there is Kenneth Burke up at the Dial office, Matty Josephson (who has suddenly been moved to value me highly), Edward Nagle, Gaston Lachaise, Malcolm Cowley—but what's the use going on with so many mere names. You can see how much fun I am having—and all the more because I have a job and a totally different world to live in half the time. Did I write you that I am getting quite a reputation with my "Faustus & Helen" poem? Although it is only now being printed in Florence,[1] those

[1] Part II of "For the Marriage of Faustus and Helen" was published in *Broom*, IV (January, 1923), 131–32. A version much different from the one in *White Buildings* was published in *Secession*, VII (Winter, 1924), 1–4. This is the version that Crane is referring to here. The complicated publishing history of

critics and writers who have seen it are acclaiming me with real gusto. Waldo Frank asked me to luncheon with him recently and said I was the greatest contemporary American poet with that piece alone. And John Cowper Powys, whose "Suspended Judgement" and "Visions & Revisions" you have read,[2] is very enthusiastic. Since I got presented with my Victrola I [am] all ready to start again on "The Bridge". Waldo Frank is very anxious for me to have that finished, as he intends to take me up to his publisher, (Boni & Liveright) and have me published in volume form. But, of course, such things *can't* be rushed as he understands.

I have not seen or heard from Miss Spencer since I made her my initial bow. She spoke of finding me something but evidently didn't sprain herself in the attempt. That's alright, however. There was little reason why she should have. I didn't *ask* her, anyway. I shan't see her again, as she is your friend and we have nothing special in common any way. Waldo Frank, Alys Gregory & others used some influence in getting me my job with *J. Walter Thompson* (get the name right this time!) but I never would have got it if my samples and conversation had not convinced them. I begin to see N.Y. very much more intimately since I've been working. It makes living here far more pleasant than ever before. Such color and style (on men, too) I've never seen before—no two alike. That's what is so interesting—the perfect freedom of wearing what you want to, walking the gait you like (I have a much less hurried gait than you're familiar with) and nobody bothering you.

I don't know many at the office yet. It's too immense and I'm confined to a highly specializing dept. but I've already been invited out to tea by the personnel secretary. They employ a lot of real writers as copy writers at Thompson's and have an entirely different feeling about art & business than you encounter any place west of N.Y. In fact its a feather in your cap if you know a little more than you're "supposed to" here. I think I've gained immeasureably by

---

this poem is covered in *Voyager*, pp. 312–14. See also Frederick J. Hoffman, Charles Allen, and Carolyn F. Ulrich, *The Little Magazine* (Princeton: Princeton University Press, 1946), pp. 93–99.

[2] The English author John Cowper Powys (1872–1963) wrote *Visions and Revisions* (New York: G. A. Shaw, 1915) and *Suspended Judgements* (New York: G. A. Shaw, 1916), two books of essays and criticism.

coming here now instead of dragging along in Cleveland month after month.

Willy [3] bounced into the office the other day and quite surprised me. I expect to see him some evening this week and hear more of his plans. He is staying with some friends at Rye, (N.Y.) at present. Charlotte lives just around the corner from me. I found her card in the mail box this morning saying that she was back from her visit to her mother in Rayland, Ohio, where she has been for three weeks or so. She is more cheerful here than I've ever seen her before. Is making good money & has plenty of company. I didn't know anything about Binet's operation.[4] He'll probably settle in Paris, however, if Bloch stays on in Cleveland. Frank cannot understand why I didn't know Bloch [5] in Cleveland and is going to introduce us soon when Bloch comes here for a month's vacation.

You asked about Mrs. Walton. She looks as uncanny as ever, and more severe as she gets older. Mme Lebegue is almost a mystery. But Mrs. Walton knows she went back to France two summers ago and never came back, and *thinks* she is staying with her husband again from a hint on a postal card she sent.

The Smiths move out on Long Island tomorrow for the summer. The Habicht's whom I have had time for only one visit with, will probably also go soon. I look forward to a swim or two at Long Beach soon. I haven't had a touch of rose fever—that is great to escape and alone would be reason enough for my living here.

I'm glad to hear about the C.A. trouble. I think we are to be envied as compared to *that* family. I want to congratulate you on your gift from J. Taylor, Esq! [6] I can see you speeding around in a perfect frenzy of excitement and elation. Willy mentioned your great kindness in driving him to the station and your pulchritude & style as well.

God, but what a long letter, but you *would* have it!

Love to Grandma / Hart

---

[3] William Lescaze.

[4] Jean Binet, the pianist. See Grace Crane's letter of March 30, 1923, to her son.

[5] Ernest Bloch (1880–1959), the Swiss-born composer, was the director of the Cleveland Institute of Music from 1920 to 1925.

[6] A person who courted Mrs. Crane briefly.

To Grace Hart Crane

[New York City]
[June 18, 1923?]

TL, 1 p.

Grace dear:

I'm sorry not to have been able to write you Saturday or yesterday, but it was impossible then—as now. Between my friends here and those in Cleveland, I was kept hustling every moment. Don't mention anything about it to the Rychtariks, but I have been put to endless troubles the last two days getting some passport troubles fixed up for that friend of their's, Weinberger. Even now it is not fixed up, and I should never be put to so much worry and trouble for anyone but Richard and Charlotte. They sent me special deliveries and implored, and so there is nothing to do but oblige as much as possible. Consequently you will have to wait a couple of days for your letter, in the meantime remembering that everything is alright, and that I'm doing my best in correspondence all the time.

Give my dearest love to Grandma, and tell her that she must not work too hard.

Love,

Monday morning, before breakfast

To Grace Hart Crane

June 18" '23
45 Grove St. N.Y.C.

ALS, 8 pp.

Grace dear:

This is probably a bit unexpected after my hasty excuse note of this morning, but you see I never put off writing you a moment when the time is granted me for doing so. Convenient and complete as my room has been from the first, you know me well enough to understand how I would just naturally spend hours in changing things around and in "making it my own". That was one of the reasons why Willy found it so charming—there are Lescazes, Sommers and Rychtariks on the walls, besides a very large oil painting by Edward Nagle, two of whose drawings you may have seen in the last *Dial* if you opened it. New York is always dusty, too, and in summer when your windows are open it involves a lot of sweeping and dusty cleaning. All the same, I would much prefer to incur these extra labors than have them otherwise dispensed with by a disaggreable landlady. As it is I am much a law unto myself.

I'm glad I missed the Shriners national picnic. You know how much I approve of such bovine celebrations and general back-slappings! It was interesting to hear about the Belden girls,[1] who, after all, will doubtless satisfy themselves and their imaginations better in Canton or some such place, than in New York. They really might gain as much or more money for themselves, however, right here in N.Y. (in the end) if it weren't for their aspirations toward some sedate profession like the law. But they will never take a breath or eat a chocolate nut sundae until they can do it on the veranda of the White House!

I have been seeing a little of Charlotte Neely since she got back from visiting her mother. I find she makes a very genial addition to my friends here, and doesn't grumble or sigh so much as she did in Cleveland. In fact, none of my friends would like her if she did.

I really can't understand *why* the Crane's should have called on you (from such a distance!) unless from an unsupportable accumulation of curiosity. If they did it from any other motives, I certainly feel sorry for them as snubbed people, doubly-snubbed! I'm not at all worried about C.A's manipulation of any tricks with me down here. He knows better, I'm sure, than to risk making himself very foolish, and would be afraid on other grounds anyway. I hope you impressed them with my "luck". Of course,—I *really* don't care anything about it, except they realize that they won't see me sweating any more in Cleveland. For no matter how things go here, I feel

---

[1] The Belden girls were distant cousins of Crane's on his mother's side.

definitely settled, with more and more opportunities in view as I get further into my own professional field and have the opportunities to see them. You mustn't mind my absence, but realize that I'm only 8 hours riding distant, and *eventually* your next-bedroom neighbor! You really must feel a lot happier yourself just knowing that everything is so salutary. O, I almost forgot to tell you something interesting. I very casually dropped my old "boss", Patno, a post card last week telling him that I missed seeing him on his projected "visit" here early in April, and mentioned where I was working also. Back came a two-page letter (as I knew it would, on account of the name of J. Walter Thompson & *possible* future business with them through Hart Crane). The letter *indirectly* stated, also, the *real* truth as to why I was asked to leave when Patno stated that *no one* had been hired in my place and that *he* was doing all the writing. You see, it simply came down to this: that they didn't get as much business as they expected to have when they urged me away from Corday & Gross, and all this left Patno comparatively unoccupied—at least he felt he would rather do *my* work as well as his own (inasmuch as his time permitted it) and put in his own pocket the extra 50.00 per week that I was getting. Naturally, these circumstances were unforeseen when I was hired, but it would have chagrinned him too much or implicated his honesty too deeply to really have admitted them to me at all. You get the truth eventually (usually!) and from his letter I can see it all quite clearly—just from that one statement. Of course my copy was *fine,* or the director of Thompson's wouldn't have fallen so quickly for my samples. My Cleveland exit, you see, was a real turn of fortune, enforced by the merry wheel of fame and fortune!

I'm all ready for my trunk now, and hope you will send with Nancy [2] on her next trip. Please include following items PARTICU-LARLY:

1. bathing suit
2. Indian bed cover
3. 2 old pillow cases

---

[2] Probably Nancy Sommers, a friend of Grace's, who made frequent trips to New York in connection with her work for the Halle Brothers department store.

3. white linen pants

4. my last year's straw hat

5. 2 or 3 old saucers or such for pipe ashes.

The rest you will find already in the trunk. *Do not* send my dress clothes or fine dressing gown!

Regards to Clip, too.

Love, / Hart

[*Written sideways on the last page:*] tennis racket, case and balls, too, *please!*

As his friends left the city for the coolness of the country, Hart's enthusiastic and expansive mood ended. Gradually he became more frustrated with his work, which he found to be enervating and neither as financially nor as spiritually rewarding as he had first expected it would be. The summer heat, and the noise and dirt that came with it, made him more irritable. Bill Sommer's tardy payment for the reproduction of some paintings was only the first of several annoyances. The Rychtariks were remiss too in sending a box of books he had requested. His mother was not forwarding his mail to him quickly enough and she had never sent on his trunk. Momentary improvements in the weather, a weekend visit in mid-July to Rye Beach as the guest of William Lescaze, and a promotion to the copy department at J. Walter Thompson (with no increase in salary) had no lasting effect on his mood.

Perhaps the most troubling note of all was his mother's discussion of the possibility of selling the house, which she had hinted at in her letter of May 26. Mrs. Crane wanted to be closer to her son, something Hart had referred to in his letter of June 18 when he wrote: "I'm only 8 hours riding distant, and *eventually* your next-bedroom neighbor!" Remembering the eighteen months he had spent at 115th Street, Hart eschewed any suggestions that he might join his mother in Cleveland, or that she might join him in New York.

To Grace Hart Crane

[New York City]
45 Grove Street
Sunday, June 23 '23

ALS, 3 pp.

Dear Grace:

I certainly am effected by what you say about selling the house. Not sentimentally at all,—but that I feel you are making a great mistake by such an action. You don't like to have me tell you such opinions, and you, of course, are not bound to respect them by any connection with me. I am thinking, however, purely of yourself and my suggestions are dictated in that light alone.

When I saw Zell here some weeks ago, we got into conversation regarding certain real estate matters of her's, and when I brought up the idea of your selling the house she agreed with me that it would be much better to rent it and still retain your hold on a solid piece of ground. For even supposing the up keep of the house did take quite a bit from its rental dividend—regardless of this you would have enough left over to cover your rent in an apartment— which, in itself is a much higher dividends than you would be likely to get from the value of the house invested in anything else. *And* in the *end* you could always have the house to do what you pleased with. Just wait, if you do insist on selling your best financial steadier, and see your apartment absorb like a sponge, month after month, the sale price of the house,—with always a little more gone, and nothing coming in, you have time enough, or you will have it (living in a flat) to devote a few hours a week to the matter of keeping up the house under rental. I'm telling you out of heart that I pray you consider a little what I say and *don't* always do the (what *appears* to be) *easiest thing*. You know I'm strongly in favor of your moving into an apartment, and have felt that way for a long time. But please do not sell your best bet just for a moments whim or quick relief. You know how fast money goes when its loose,—and a drawing account at the bank is damned loose!

The week has provided me with little news to interest you. It has been hot and almost cold by fits, and very strenuous on one's nervous system. I'm awfully sorry to hear that Grandma has been so effected and wish something could be done. You needn't worry about my room. It's very decent and comfortable. The only thing I'm lacking is a rug. But that's just as well for summer any way. Please send me my bathing suit parcel post if the truck can't move pretty soon. I'm dying for a swim, and can't afford to buy a new suit this year.

Love from / Hart

To Grace Hart Crane

New York City
Tuesday, June 26th, [1923?]

TLS, 1 p.
LETTERHEAD: J. Walter Thompson Company

Dear Grace:

The special, VERY SPECIAL purpose of this is to remind you to forward my letter mail to me AT ONCE. There may be serious consequences involved, especially in the event that I have already forfeited my insurance policy, if they have notified me very back that a payment is due. I really don't see why it is so difficult for you just to scribble my present address on what mail comes to me and leave it for the postman to attend to instead of risking its loss around the house with old papers, etc. For I know how easily letters have escaped me several times that way even when I've been on the spot. Don't bother about magazines, or any second class mail,—but I've been expecting for weeks to see what may be there, and apparently you aren't very worried about it.

It is too hot and stifling here to sleep (even though my room is exceptionally cool) or do anything beyond the barest duties. I spose you are going through the same furnace. A PARTING WORD IS: PLEASE DON'T KEEP ON FORGETTING! / HART

To Grace Hart Crane

[New York City]
Monday evening
July 2nd '23

ALS, 6 pp.

Grace, dear:

I'm sending this "special" so you will have something from me on the famous Fourth. I've been trying for several days to get something to you, but with my head simply bursting with the "Bridge" poem which has been coming out simply by leaps and bounds, with the laundry to travel for, the suit to be pressed, the room to be dusted up and cleaned and friends coming around to invite me out to eat every evening—all this added to my duties and time at the office has made it impossible. My correspondence all 'round is dropping off, and must continue if I keep on at my present rate of writing—for it is very hard, extremely painful to tie your mind down to anything as personal as a letter when you have the drive of a hundred horse power steed propelling your brain in other directions.[1] And when I have finished with my (above) list of excuses,—I have also somehow told you in broad out line about all the news there is. You'll have to excuse me if I dilate a little more on my writing these days,—if only because I am doing things of universal consequence, and better work than I have ever done before. This "Bridge" poem is still in fragments but you should hear the comments that have come out about it from the intimates to whom I have shown it! I am enclosing a letter from Waldo Frank which you will please remail back to me in your next letter. It shows what present day America's greatest novelist thinks of me and my work, and measures pretty fairly with what Gorham and Jean Toomer also think,—the only others who have seen any of the "Bridge". I am, you see, in just the proper environment now to put forth all my leaves, my work at the office is pleasant and promising, there is the

---

[1] Hart was writing the "Atlantis" section of *The Bridge* at this time.

freedom and exhilaration of the streets, and the stimulation of good friends and conversation.

The head of the statistical department at J. Walter Thompson told me last week that he had spoken to the Treasurer, Mr. Clarke, about promoting me to the copy department whenever the right time came,— That while they could use me very well in the statistical department for some time etc, but that I had proved my abilities there and that there was no reason to hold me back. There has been no change as yet, but it all means that I am progressing, and that when there is an opening higher up for me I shall get it. This company, its offices, personel and methods are certainly clean and courteous. There is no one person or two or three, even, who are evidently "running things." Of course someone, The President, *does*. But you never see any "personalities" storming around, nor fretting, nor bossing nor complaining. And there's no atmosphere of *fear* around.[2] The wheels all move as smooth as glass, the sun streams in the windows onto the heavily carpeted floors, and very simply, everyone seems to be doing what he is supposed to do without any fuss or rush.

I haven't see[n] Willy [3] for two weeks. But last Friday came a note from Rye inviting me conjointly with his friends there, the Fords, to come out there and stay over the Fourth. I have sent regrets, mainly because I feel I am getting off easily to have so little Rose Fever this year, and don't want to excite it any by courting temptation. I have just had dinner with Gorham, Liza and Toomer in their apartment and left promptly to write this to you.

I'm glad [to] hear that you have sent the bathing suit, etc. as I don't want to miss *all* the bathing this year, and it's so easy to, if you aren't insistent. We've been *much* cooler here for some days now. I hope there has been the same general relief in Cleveland. I would like to see you,—get very hungry to every so often. Probably I'll be home for Thanksgiving or Xmas. Perhaps before, if they send me West on any investigating.

Richard & Charlotte are very pleased at some news I sent them last week. The Dial has taken 3 of Richard's pictures for reproduc-

---

[2] Hart possibly had his father in mind when he wrote this.
[3] William Lescaze.

tion and bought one to keep.[4] Bill Sommer's name is on the newsstands here this week—the pictures in it that I paid for reproducing and for which Bill got a check.[5] I have asked him in three special letters to pay me what those reproductions cost because I needed the money. He sent me $5. (one quarter of my investment) and never replied again. Next week all his pictures which I have shown and "talked up"—go back to him,—to stay, so far as I am concerned. I have really been astonished that anyone of his talent could be so leather skinned!

I hope you find a good tenant for the house soon. You probably will as the neighborhood is so desirable. Remember my advice, and *don't* sell it. It's good sense, and *you know it*. Forgive my slowness, and remember that I always love you.

Your/ Hart

I'm *going* to write to Grandma soon.

[*Written at the bottom corner of the page:*] *Don't forget that letter from Frank!*

[*The enclosed letter from Waldo Frank is printed below:*]

DEAR HART

I am not going to be so rash as to say anything in detail about The Bridge, until it is done. Suffice, that it impresses me as a body amazingly simple, fecund and grandiose, to flesh the spirit that I know not only you possess but are able very wonderfully to articulate . . . vid. Helen and Faust. I have not begun to tell you what that poem is to me: I find it difficult to put such words into a casual letter. You understand, I trust. You are tremendously important, and you are a great deal in my thoughts and very deeply in my heart. Good luck . . . and à bientot.

yours/ Waldo

---

[4] Two of Rychtarik's pictures, a drawing and a linoleum cut, were printed in *The Dial*, Vol. LXXV (September, 1923), facing p. 246.

[5] *The Dial* printed two of Sommer's drawings. See Vol. LXXV (July, 1923), facing p. 12.

To Grace Hart Crane

[New York City]
45 Grove Street
July 8" '23

ALS, 3 pp.

Grace, dear:

Next Sunday I shall be out at Rye and probably in the water (or *on* it) at this time. Willy (and his hosts there,) have invited me out for the week-end and I shall return direct from there to the office Monday morning. Friday evening was quite pleasant, the first really long and intimate talk I've had with Willy since before he left for Europe last fall. He stayed all night, because he was so glad to see my old bed-spread, so he said. The bathing suit and letters were very thankfully received also, and you are a *dear* to have got all my clothes together in such fine shape as you stated in your last letter. You wont worry about sending it, I hope, before Nancy's [1] next trip —provided she comes within six weeks. I was sorry to hear about her loss, and I wish you to convey my sympathies to her as soon as she returns.

After a late breakfast with Gorham I have just finished quite a thorough cleaning of my room. It is a brilliant and cool day—air filled with sungold like champagne. The breeze sifts through my two windows while I sit between them making the usual Sunday effort to catch up on my belated correspondence. I get letters from Charles Harris and Sam [2] and the Rychtaricks regularly. Poor Sam keeps mentioning his hopes of coming here in the autumn, but I honestly hope he doesn't—he simply wouldn't mix with anyone I know.

His kind of complaints and sighs aren't at all fashionable, and I'm afraid he'd be driven to as solitary a corner here as he is in Cleveland.

I've just re-read your letter to be sure I answer any questions therein. You'll possibly find my trunk key (tagged and labelled) in-

[1] Nancy Sommers.
[2] Samuel Loveman.

side the tiny *left* drawer (near the pigeonholes) in my desk. I'm not sure that I didn't give you the key to put away yourself before I left, but if I didn't you'll find it *there*. I have a key to it *here with me*, so you don't need to send the other along at all,—and you probably won't need to even lock it up, as the trunk is open there any how. About the things to be sent—I think I partially packed it my self before leaving—but there was so much space left that I'll leave it to your own exquisite judgement to add anything aside from dress clothing which you think would make me gleeful. An old pillow wouldn't be bad, my album of photographs, if not there already, my pen tray, *old heavy* bathrobe, tennis shoes, etc. It's up to you, Lady!

Give Grandma every consideration. (I wish I could do something!) I'm very happy these days but I'd be happier if I could tighten my arms around you both a "little oftener."

Love/ Hart

Just re-address my mail & put it back on the porch!

To Grace Hart Crane

RYE [New York]
Sunday Morning
July 14th, 23

TLS, 2 pp.

Grace dear—

Here I am with Willy's friends [1]—about ten of us here altogether. I slept with the smooth deep sleep of the guilty after sailing on the Sound all yesterday afternoon in the Ford's two-master, about the same size boat as you remember eating lobster on one weekend when we visited Ned. I may be wrong, but I think his place is somewhere not far from here across the Sound.[2] We took our dinner along, having cocktails, chicken, sandwiches, ice cream etc. I

[1] Hart was a guest of Mr. and Mrs. Simeon Ford. Their children who are mentioned in this letter are Ellsworth and Hobart Ford and Miss Lauren Ford.

[2] Hart very possibly is referring to the trip he and his mother took to Rye in the summer of 1914.

nearly burst—my appetite was so stimulated after my swim, salt air, etc. And today—starting about an hour from now, we shall be on the water again for hours and hours. Nothing suits me better, as you know, and you would die to see Willy commandeering his host around as though he owned the boat.

I wish you could see the room I have been sleeping in. There is an alcove in it—like the forecastle of a boat—that looks right out over the water, leat[h]er cushions around, seats etc. The room, like the rest of the house, is immense. Red walls, turkey carpets and black carved furniture. Curtained bed with fancy drapings etc. The family is easy going. I have seen my senior hostess, old Mrs. Ford, only about three minutes, and old Mr Ford is always back and forth on his way to clubs and business. I have only shaken hands with him. As for the younger set—there is Miss Ford, who is the real cause for Willy's stay here, I surmise. She paints, draws, etc and Willy is both a thorough help to her in that way and also particularly good company for her. As you know, he is also designing a new town house for the family in very original style. The two younger brothers are delightfully easy company, sailing, playing the harmonica, painting, etc. To economise on detail—they are the kind of people we both like. I think it was tremendously nice of them all to have Willy invite me out here this way without even having met me.

I was delighted to hear about Nancy's trip and getting my trunk. I shall have a note at the Vanderbilt for Nancy on Tuesday morning, probably containing an invitation out to eat with me. There is no particular news for you. My work at Thompson's goes on smoothly and very pleasantly—I never worked for such a fine organization. Yesterday came a letter from Harry Candee. He and his mother have taken an old farm house built in the 18th century, near Windsor Castle, and does not intend leaving England until Sept, thence to China again. I do hope that Grandma is feeling better by this time. Somehow I am very confident that her present troubles are quite temporary, and that in a few weeks she will be thoroughly recovered. But I think there is every reason for your getting a maid to help you both, and you know that I have had that idea in my head for more than a year past. That, to my mind, is a far more important requirement for you both than Diana, at least under recent circumstances. I haven't any doubt that you can rent the house, especially furnished. You have so much extra furniture that you would still have enough left over for a small apartment and you would not be paying storage on the amount you couldn't use yourself, if you took that plan of procedure. These are just suggestions on my part, however. You may know that I am thinking of you anyway.

Someone is calling, so this is all for now. Tell Grandma that this is just as much her letter as it is yours, and you both have my deepest love!/ Hart

Grace probably enclosed the following short note with Hart's trunk, which arrived several days before his birthday.

From Grace Hart Crane and Elizabeth Belden Hart

Cleveland, Ohio

ALS, 1 p.
LETTERHEAD: MRS. ELIZABETH B. HART/ 1709 EAST 115TH. STREET/ CLEVELAND/ OHIO

A very happy Birthday
from
Mother and Grandma—
Oceans of love and
good wishes go with it.

July 15—1923

To Elizabeth Belden Hart

[New York City]
Thursday, July 19th, '23

TLS, 2 pp.

My dear Grandmother:

Both you and Mother have my most spontaneous enthusiasm and gratitude for your most appropriate (and needed!) gifts. There was so much love expressed in that trunkfull that in taking things out, seeing familiar objects, putting them around my room, etc. I had one of the pleasantest evenings I have had for months. There was not an extra or useless thing in it, and you don't know how much is added to my satisfaction and ease by all your thoughfulness. The socks are superb, the shirts just right in every way, and you sent me the first fresh ties that I have had for many months, for I've bought no clothing since I came down here. The famous 21st will be spent quietly but "richly and luxuriously" thanks to you dear ladies.

You don't know how glad I was to hear in the letter that Nancy brought that you are up and around again. I am sure there will be no return of your troubles if you keep to your diet and do not do too many things. Is it terribly warm in Cleveland? It is here during the middle and late parts of the day, but by bed-time its always cool enough to sleep in my room, and the early mornings riding up Fifth to work are very dewy, bright and pleasant. I tried to get Nancy to take luncheon with me Tuesday, but she was somehow or other too busy or tied up elsewhere. I was sorry not to have seen her, but shall make another attempt on another of her visits if you or Mother will inform me in time to get in touch with her.

I still think with great fondness about my hours at Rye. It did me a world of good, rested me and all that. The sweet clean air of woods and water is better than anything else I know of. I may be invited out there again, but am certainly going out to Darien Connecticut a week from next Saturday to spend two days with Waldo Frank. His invitation just came this morning[.]

Mother need not worry about sending me anything else for awhile, so I won't bother her with the details she asked for about bedding, stove, etc. I can use what came in the trunk very well, but for the present I really don't need anything more.

When you feel just like it, dear, I hope you'll write me another one of your fine letters. You know I am very fond of them. I'm slow in answering you, in particular person,—but you always share in what I write to mother, and, as you also know—

in my deepest love . . . ./ Your/ Hart

PS I have just opened up the envelope again to tell you some good news. Mr. Clark just a moment ago called me into his office and tells me that I am to be promoted to the COPY Dept this coming week, to remain there for at least three months. Isn't that fine news! It means very likely an advance in salary, also.

To Grace Hart Crane

[New York City]
45 Grove St
Sunday, July 22nd, '23

TLS, 1 p.

Grace dear:

There isn't much to tell you since my last letter except that it is very very hot, that Munson and his wife have left for two weeks in the Catskills with the Reverend's family,[1] that my good friend, Slater Brown has also betaken him to the cooling hills, and that everyone I know is also out of town—which makes my time quite concentrated on myself. I don't miss them quite so much today as I did yesterday. One's birthday ought to be celebrated somehow. I still am elated, however, about your fine gifts and the things you sent in my trunk. I've used the "Darling" wash-board already on some handkerchiefs and socks.

There is one good justification for this letter, however, and that is to tell you on Tuesday evening I shall board a train for the west to be gone for about a week or ten days. It will probably be for Chicago and the territory around there. I shall also probably stop off at

[1] Munson's father, a minister, lived in Ellenville, New York.

Buffalo and Rochester on the way back. It is investigation work for the U.S. Gutta Percha Company, of Providence, one of Thompson's clients, of course. I am to interview paint dealers (a hundred or so) and find out necessary information for the next campaign on "Barreled Sunlight", a new kind of white paint that they manufacture. After I get back I shall probably have some of the copywriting to do. It ought to be very pleasant work if the weather cools a little, anyway it will be very good experience for me. I'm awfully sorry that I cannot give you any kind of schedule and I probably wont be able to even later on. Hotels, etc, are a question of the moment, anyway, so it wouldn't do you much good, that is, just to know what town I was in on a certain day, even though I could tell you.

I suggest, however, if you need me badly to send your wire direct to J. Walter Thompson, 244 Madison Ave. Address it personally to "Miss Stocking" (who knows me) telling her what you want her to wire me at whatever place she knows me to be. I shall, of course, write you something en route, but that correspondence will be somewhat one-sided from necessity. I made an attempt to get sent to Cleveland, but couldn't be too urgent about it. Such good luck *might* turn up sometime, though, and that would be GREAT, wouldn't it!

Here's hoping you both are well and happy!

With love,/ Hart

To Grace Hart Crane

[New York City]
Friday, Aug. 11" '23

ALS, 2 pp.

Dear Grace:

Your letter came while I was busy cleaning out my room this morning. It has occupied most of the day—just getting things out again, (or back in place) and now once more the place looks natural. It seemed very good to get back to New York. I was in Chicago only two days but don't think I should ever care very much for the place. It might be better in winter, I suppose, but even then it wouldn't have the sparkling simplicity of New York. I thought I would be melted to nothing before I got away. There was a good deal of steaming rain and I found it hard to find my way around. The Blackstone is not at all the place to stay if you are on business. I felt very uncomfortable and out of place. Posey, who was there before me didn't like it either. The La Salle is the place to go, I guess. My day in Buffalo was cool and pleasant. Yesterday I was very cordially greeted at the office and I guess my work has been entirely satisfactory. I shall probably start in working at copywriting next week, at least that is the plan. Most everyone is still away, but Gorham and Brown will return early next week, and Sue [1] has already asked me over to her place for a home-cooked dinner Monday evening.

The news about Arthur E. [2] was quite surprizing. He'll probably live to be a hundred now. I'm rather glad I went over to see him, nevertheless. I didn't get time, naturally to call up or see anyone while in Chicago, so I still have Verna's [3] little gold lip-stick case. I'll devise some way of getting it to her soon.

Love to you both!/ Hart

To Grace Hart Crane and Elizabeth Belden Hart

[New York City]

TLS, 1 p.

Dear Grace and Grandma:

There really isn't much to write about except to mention that I have been in the copy department all week, am more satisfied with this work, of course, and things look stimulating enough as regards the immediate future here. Aside from that there has been a few evenings with Gorham and Liza, back from the country again. I came near a collapse near the middle of the week—the trip, hot weather, etc certainly tested me and worries keep me from much

[1] Susan Jenkins.
[2] Hart's paternal grandfather, who had been ill.
[3] Verna Ross.

sleep—as things are. NY is bad in the summer anyway—takes all the vitality you have to give and gives you back nothing to build with or repair. I hope things are going better now. I'll write maybe during next week—but worry about correspondence is a burden sometimes when I have so much new work to think about. You'll understand me, I hope, in any case. I enjoyed your letter, Grandma, and it wasn't too long. You write extraordinarily well!

My best love to you both/ Hart

Saturday, August 18th, 23

Hart's irritability reached its zenith that summer when he accused a good friend of having stolen his copy of *Ulysses*. The accusation was very likely incorrect; however, the friendship cooled considerably because of it.

To Grace Hart Crane

45 Grove Street,
New York
Aug. 24th, '23

TLS, 3 pp.

Dear Grace:

Probably Glenn has already told you about what I wrote to Sam concerning ———— since I came back to town, but there may be some point in assuring you of a grain of the truth that a rough summary will provide. The man, I am convinced, is not only a crook, but a little unbalanced! He took "Ulysses" all right! Early in the first week after I got back from my trip he came down to the office to go out to lunch with me. I waited until we got to the table before I gave him any hint of my dissatisfaction. Then I told him that I was very much peeved and provoked that he should have come out to the house and borrowed my book without either my knowledge or permission.

He got quite excited and red at this—and then proceded to tell
me that he had not even been up to my room— fancy that! I then
reminded him that he had told me all about going up to my room
before I had gone west, the reason he had given being to see the
Sommer picture, etc. He then accepted that rather tacitly, especially
when I brought up your own statement that he had been up to the
room and mentioned borrowing "Ullyses" on that very occasion.
Then what do you 'spose he said? ! He said that he would look in
his trunk and see if [he] could locate it anywhere! If that was not a
perfect admission I'd like to know what is. But I didn't accuse him
of anything further at the time—and haven't since—hoping that he
would possible be able to get hold of the book and return it to me
somehow, if he got frightened enough. However, I have a letter all
written to him. It will be sent just as soon as I get time to type it
out: probably this week-end. There's nothing doubtful about what
I say in it either. I'm only sorry that no action can be taken against
him. We are both out of the state where the theft occured—and the
book has been banned by the mails, anyway, so I wouldn't get
much favor in the courts on that account. ——— had the brass to
come here the other day (this makes me think him almost nutty)
and instead of having himself announced at the outer reception
room—comes ranging around among the people in the office, inquiring for me, and then comes up and stands and chats at my desk
without the least concern! AND—what do you suppose he wants of
me. He has heard that Mr. Fleischmannn, the yeast man, is going
to have a house re-modelled, and won't I somehow get in touch
with him, or get the word flashed to him somehow that ——— is a
clever young architect and is ready to do it up in fine shape for
him!! Just think of such an idiotic project—to say nothing of assuming that I would care to risk my standing around here for such
a project! Then he keeps asking me out to the Ford's with a kind of
desperate insistence, as though he thought I caould be recompensed
for his defaulting by satisfying some "social aspirations". He certainly is terrible, silly as well.

I feel one hundred percent better since I got back to copy work.
I'm up on the fourteenth floor now with a wojderful view out over
the Murray Hill section and the East River right off the edge of my

desk. I'm far from being dissatisfied, as you suggested. The plain fact was, and still is—that New York takes such a lot from you that you have to save all you can of yourself or you simply give out. I need a good bed, but it will be a long time before I can get one unless you feel like shipping that little brass bed on the third floor down here to me sometime. That would be fine, and could serve me always here, but you'll probably think it out of the question to send it.

It doesn't make much difference how early you go to bed if you can't get to sleep—you know that. And that has been the state of things with me for some time here. However, I'm really feeling all right. It [is] just tiredness—and worry that you are very, very unhappy—what to do—etc.

I don't know what is wrong with Charlotte and Richard. They haven't sent my books to me on the date they said they would, nor have I had a word from them since Cleveland. If they are going to get upset and offended about something that I don't even guess having said to injure them—then, they, like a whole lot of other people who go around just aching to cut the their own heads off, will have to do it. Perhaps they've just been very busy, though, it's certainly too early yet to make any definite assumptions.

Everyone is out of town over this week end. Have seen much of Gorham and Liza since they got back from the Catskills, but they have cleared out for a visit to Kenn[e]th Burke over in New Jersey, today.[1] It's too cool to go swimming Sunday—and so I suppose I've had my one and only swim this year already. I have not had a single sneeze yet—so my hay fever is going to be a lot milder than ever before.

I am writing a letter to Edward Sommer, Bill's son, to come out to the house and get the pictures which I left already done up on the third floor, so he'll introduce himself some day. Had a l mg [long] letter from Minns[2] this morning in response to the first I have written him since last Jan. He is still living in his world of ideas and sentiments—and is a very touching old fellow.

Love to you both,/ from/ Hart

[1] Burke lived in Andover, New Jersey.
[2] Hervey W. Minns, the photographer.

From Elizabeth Belden Hart

[Cleveland]
[September 2, 1923?] [1]

ALS, 5 pp.

My Dear Grandson

Mother has gone to church. I sat down to read but found I could not keep awake so must busy myself about something even tho' it be mischief—

My first thought was I'll send a little message of love and best wishes to our boy feeling sure he will be glad to hear from home & Grandma—

I have thought of you very often since reading your last letter. I thought I could read between the lines, you weren't up to your standard in good cheer— I know its because you were all tired out, so many callers, and the weather too has & is so hot, that *every body* is complaining of being so tired. I never experienced such a summer [.] But we will soon have our glorious Autumn days—which will put new life into us all. I am quite myself again. Mother seems to be well and much more cheerful and contented. I fear you were made unhappy by a false impression you may have gotten from what she told you. That is why I explained to you the situation, but I followed your advise and we get along fine ever since.

I shall never see her want as long as I have anything to share with her— She is all I've got to depend on, and I need her & she needs me. I am going to stay right where we are. We cant better ourselves—and we will be far happier under our own roof than wandering from one place to another paying rent and nothing to show for it when through [.]

We are agreed on this, and now I am going to order my coal for this winter [.] The more I hear & see of our friends who are trying

[1] Though this letter is undated, several things indicate when it was written. At the end of the letter Mrs. Hart refers to the person who Crane thought had stolen his copy of *Ulysses*, and she says that they will not sell the house. In his letter of September 8, Hart writes that he is happy to learn of their decision. His grandmother quite possibly wrote this letter while Grace was at church on Sunday, September 2, 1923.

the apartment living, the more I am convinced we better let well enough alone. Don't you think the same?

I had a long & very interesting letter from Blanche [2] to day—Telling of the improvements they are putting on their home—also of how she did enjoy her visit with us. She seemed so glad you were so well located, and sorry they could not have seen you while in Chicago—

Verna is not going back to school this fall—but Mildred *is*.[3] Verna is taking a course in House decorating at the Chicago Art School— I think she (Blanche) will invite Mother to visit her in Oct. after they get through with their house improvements.

I presume Grace has told you all the news there is to tell—so I will not write much more least I repeat some of it. Helen seemed to enjoy her stay in N. York—and seemed very much pleased with your room, said it was just such a one as she would like were she to live there. She wound up by saying the last thing Zell said we were to spend Christmas at #8. S. Elm St.[4] Helen has improved a 100 per cent both in looks, actions, and every way since her baby came.

Don't let the trouble with ———— make you unhappy. He is to be pitied. Be charitable and do him no harm—you won't be any happier for it.

Don't worry about us or anything else. You can't do yourself justice, or your work if you do— Everybody is all right here and I want to know you are. A heart full of love to you Dear Hart

Devotedly / *Grand Ma*

write when [you] feel like it.

[2] Blanche Ross.
[3] Verna and Mildred Ross.
[4] Zell Hart Deming's address in Warren.

To Grace Hart Crane and Elizabeth Belden Hart

[New York City]
45 Grove Street,
Saturday, Sept. 8th, '23

TLS, 2 pp.

Dear Grace and Grandma;

Both of your last letters have been so sweet and gratifying that I am very grateful. I am glad to think of you as located for the winter, putting in coal, and assured of the comforts that I know you ought to have. They have raised the rent on Gorham and Liza,— and they have been trying to locate a new place at a more reasonable figure, but they may not move at all—so discouraging is the search. That's one of the banes of New York—one is on a moving cloud here most of the time, for, either the house you live in is being torn down for an ap[a]rtment, or else the landlord is gauging you constantly for the last cent. I never want to have any of us without some property of our own—land and building—whether we live in it or not, but just so that "we have it" and are not entirely su[b]ject to the whims of fortune. If I ever get any money, I know that I shall attend to that investment before I travel or anything else. You've got to have an anchorage somewhere if you are ever to have any repose of mind.

Of this latter-mentioned article—I can't say I have had much recently. Of all the abominable snakes I ever heard of ———[1] is the worst. I got a letter on Wednesday from the young Miss Ford whose family he is staying with at Rye. He had evidently feared my exposure of him to them—and to ward it off he took the pains to tell her that I was a venomous person, upset by the heat in the City, and trying to torture him for mere pleasure. She recommended a dose of pills, a swim, etc. as a means of clearing up my head—and otherwise insulted me. The next morning comes a letter from ——— himself—in which he denies that his letter constituted a confession at all, said that the money was sent merely out of consid-

[1] Another reference to the person who Crane thought had stolen his copy of *Ulysses*.

eration for my loss, etc, and other kinds of weak trashy statements. I shall not reply to him, but I wrote Miss Ford that if she had any interest in the truth or cared to alleviate her own responsibilities in imposing such opinions on me—she might come into town someday next week and take lunch with me. I mentioned that I hadn't the time to write out the extensive evidence that I had, but that I should be glad to discuss them with her vive voce. The whole matter made me ill the next day—but the worst now is over, whether I ever get anything out of ———— or not. I shall not press the claim further than the telling of the story to Miss Ford—it isn't worth it. There is absolutely no doubt about the confession in the letter, however, and I am keeping it well out of reach in my trunk.

Charles Harris was here for dinner and the evening with me yesterday. He is going to spend a week in the country, and then return to Cleveland when he has promised to look you up. He's a nice boy and very considerate,—I was glad, however, that he didn't make me an extended visit this time. By the end of a summer in New York everybody is at the limit of endurance; there is no place to rest, get away from the constant noise and vibrations of trucks, etc, and there's a kind of insidious impurity in the air that seems to seep from sweaty walls and subways. Next year I shall have at least a month in the open country or by the sea—I haven't had a real vacation now for several years, you know. The time spent in idleness when out of a job was always a worse strain than the hardest kind of labor, so that hasn't counted for much with me.

Waldo Frank has invited me to take dinner with him tomorrow night. He is in town for a month before going to France and Spain where he says he can find a little rest. I see much of Gorham and Liza—they are restful to me and always kind. I don't think I should care to stay in New York long if they weren't here.

I have been writing some trade paper ads for O'Sullivan's heels this last week. They will keep switching me around to a lot of varied accounts until a particular need developes for me on a definite account, I 'spose. There certainly is nothing to complain of at the office—I get the utmost interest, consideration and cooperation. I only wish they would raise my salary a little, for it's positively nerve-racking to have to figure so closely as I do all the time just to make ends meet decently. I have[n]'t been to any shows or bought myself a dud either,—when I have to get a new suit I shall either have to prompt them to a little more generosity or look around for a higher salary. You know how far twenty-five went in Cleveland when I was staying at home! Well, thirty-five here is even less, and I am under more pressing demands.

I wish you would mention it as soon as anyone calls for those pictures of Sommer's. I wrote his son to call for them, and I want to know when he comes. I am sending back all his things which I have here when I get time to go to the post office. The Rychtariks were much pleased at the way the reproductions of Richards things came out in the Dial. Charlotte wrote me a lovely letter that came this morning. Well,—I've said nothing at all, but I've been trying to rush this so you would get it before Monday. But I guess you won't, after all. Anyhow, I'm doing my best, and please don't worry about me. Charlotte Neely was married to someone I haven't met this afternoon, and I'm glad she's fixed up at last. I always felt sort of responsible for her—at least unpleasantly sympathetic.

Love,/ Hart

To Grace Hart Crane

New York City
Friday, Sept. 14th, [1923?]

TLS, 1 p.
LETTERHEAD: J. Walter Thompson Company

Dear Grace:

I am writing this little bit right now because I may not get time to write a bit more before too late to get to you on Sunday. Edward Nagle is coming down from Woodstock where he and Slater Brown are settled for the winter, and plans to stay with me. He is such a lively person that I'm sure my time will be scarce!

My hay fever was very severe the first part of this week, but has died down a little the past two days. Altogether it will not possibly

be as bad as it was last year in Cleveland, but I am always su[b]ject
to slight "flurries", I guess.

I am very, very busy here at the office. New responsibilities are
developing every day, it's mostly very interesting to me, however. I
am not so tired out as last week—the cooler days are really superb
here. Gorham and Liza arn't going to move, after all. Gorham has
got an advance from his publisher on his next book, and is feeling
great about it. They asked to be remembered to you in my next letter.

How do you like this paper for a change?!¹ It's what they write
the copy on here. Well, the crowd is coming back from lunch, so I
must leave you. All kinds of love, dear. A kiss for Grandma,
too!/ hart

To Grace Hart Crane

[New York City]
[September 14, 1923?]
Friday

ALS, 2 pp.

Dear Grace:

I forgot to mention in my letter that I shall soon need the two
blankets (black & grey) which you'll locate on the 3rd floor. The
bedding has been sufficient up to these last few cold nights. I think
you had better send along that tailor-made black suit of mine very
soon, too, as my other clothes are getting worn looking. Your cards
from Tiffany's have probably arrived by this time.¹ I had them send
the plate along. Thompson's is such a dressy place that one has to
keep a different pace here than in Cleveland.

Your letter yesterday was full of good sense & cheer. I'm all right

---

¹ This was a single sheet of advertising copy paper from the Editorial Department of J. Walter Thompson.

---

¹ Mrs. Crane had ordered calling cards from Tiffany's.

now,—and am letting the ———— [2] case drop. If I hear anything more from them I'll send you & Glenn the whole correspondence. In fact, I shall probably do so anyway for the fun of it.

Harry Candee is back! I found him waiting in my hallway when I came home last night. Looks well and leaves soon for Great Barrington, Mass. This is all for now as I'm busy at the office.

Remember me to Glenn,

Love / Hart

Though still maintaining a valiant front for his mother and grandmother that all was going well at Thompson's, Crane had grown increasingly despondent over the summer. Except for a burst of enthusiasm on his part in May and June, his poetic accomplishment had been meager. Then, too, many of his friends were absent. Slater Brown and Edward Nagle had announced their intention to stay in the country for the winter. Gorham Munson developed tuberculosis, which meant he had to leave the city. And Waldo Frank separated from his wife, Margaret Naumberg, and prepared to spend the winter in Europe.

All of these events contributed to Hart's malaise. His salary was still $35.00 a week. "I have been getting so little that I am kept down to the bare necessities of life all the time," [1] he complained to Charlotte Rychtarik in a letter of September 23 that contained a request for a $15.00 loan. It was his poor salary, the enervating life of New York, and his dearth of friends that prompted him to think of leaving the city.

[2] Another reference to the person suspected by Crane of stealing his copy of *Ulysses*.

[1] Quoted from *The Letters*, p. 147.

To Grace Hart Crane

[New York City]
45 Grove St.
Friday—Sept. 21 '23

ALS, 5 pp.

Grace dear:

Your letter has just come with the enclosure from Binet. Both this and the one that came last Sunday were bracing and made me easy about you to some extent. You are very good to be so considerate. This is the first letter I have written to anyone this week. I'm sorry not to have written you before, but once a week is about as often as you must plan on hearing from me.

I have been rather expecting a ring from C.A. all week, but have decided that he has passed me by this time. It's just as well that I didn't know when he is around anyway, as the knowledge carries with it a number of tremulous forebodings which are better explained in the science of psychoanalysis than in common language.

After a very cool spell here it has suddenly become very warm and stifling—especially today which has tired everybody out. My hay fever has been very persistent and so you must not expect me to be very enthusiastic about anything. Beyond all this my friends are in such trouble that my sympathies are full engaged in a somewhat heavy direction.

Gorham went to see a doctor last Saturday about a cough which has persisted so long that he got worried. The diagnosis revealed that he is not yet effected—but that he is at any moment and on the slightest provocation *threatened* with tuberculosis. He left the next day for the country and a diet, and is now with Jean Toomer at Ellenville, N.Y. He comes back on the 29th for a few days, and then plans to go back to the open country for a large part of the winter. Poor Liza has been worried and almost heartbroken. I saw her tonight in tears at the added complication that they must move out before another week and she has found no place to move to. The landlady has already signed up some others for the Munson apartment! With her husband away and herself tied down to school job and all that—could anything be worse? Don't come to N Y. until you have enough money to face the terrific rental situation that seems to get worse and worse here. I don't know what on earth Liza is going to do—& only know that I'm powerless to do anything whatever myself to help her. As for Gorham he has worked too much, fought too hard with the stupidity of the critics and the press and not taken enough exercise. He has simply strained himself with the tremendous developement he has been going through this last year. He will come out, all right by getting away from the crashing hubub and fever of this city.

Waldo Frank and his wife have separated. I have heard each of their stories seperately and there are no sides to take. One simply agrees quietly with the other that there were certain spiritual issues which should have been solved I gather, but which they finally gave up as impossible. They are very sane and wise (on very good terms still) but I [think] Waldo is in a very disordered state of mind (for him and for the time being, certain possibilities in his future work seem to be seriously threatened. Life is doing hard things to almost everyone I know, and as I grow older and more sensitive to such things it seems to be growing harder on me. All the same it is quite glorious in its chaos of mixed joy & pain!

Thursday afternoon I had tea with Harry, his mother and in-laws. Mrs. Candee has just written a book on Indo-China.[1] I still like Harry very much, but he naturally doesn't mean so much to me here as he did in Cleveland. *He* hasn't developed— I have gone a long way in certain spiritual adventures since I first met him. I shall always love him because he is certainly worthy of much love, —but he isn't able to go so far with me in some intensities of life as he was a few years ago.

I am working under almost perfect conditions at the office. And, I'm learning a great deal. I think everyone I have met has liked me. The only drawback is the Salary. I shall broach the subject quite soon now. I don't know what I should have done without your dear

[1] Helen Churchill Candee was the author of *Angkor the Magnificent, the Wonder City of Ancient Cambodia* (New York: Frederick A. Stokes, 1924).

5 dollars in the letter. But I don't want you to send any more. You need it all yourself. Give my love and kisses to dear Grandma. I love you both *so much.*/ Hart

From Elizabeth Belden Hart

[Cleveland]
Sunday Eve
Sept 23—23

ALS, 4 pp.

My Dear Hart:

I have been thinking of you so much since reading your S.D. received this AM and after coming to my room have concluded to write you before retiring.

Glen was here to dinner, then went away but is here this eve. He is gathering in his petitions he sent out for Judgeship.[1]

It requires 2500 names to allow him to be a candidate. His acquaintance is so limited, and so many in the race I think his chances very uncertain, but he will get some advertising which may do him some good in the future. He is so blue all the time its enough to kill one to be in the atmosphere.

When I see what a struggle some are passing through these days, in trying to get something to do, I certainly feel very grateful that you landed the position you have and my prayer is that you will be able to hold it. It means a lot to be connected with such an institution. We are often asked how you ever got in there, if I have a chance to tell them, I look very wise and say you know Hart is very persevering, and has a wonderful personality, so it was mostly through his own efforts, and some of his work he had been doing that they saw he had done that he was accepted, and they seem very much pleased—and he finds them exceptionally fine people to work for. It makes some of the folks a little envious.

Mr Sullivan spent the evening here last week. He asked very in-

---

[1] Glenn Whistler ran unsuccessfully for a judgeship in Cayuga County.

terestedly about you and seemed surprised & pleased you had such a fine position. He knows them well, or of them.

Just remember when you are lonely and discouraged, and your way seems hedged with difficulties, just remember there are many many others in even worse condition, and (of course that don't make it any easier for you) but be resolved not to yield to any thing that will cause you to lose your health or determination to win out, but stick to it at all hazards and you will soon see the clouds part, and these troubles will vanish, then victory will crown your efforts. Truly the warfare with ones self is glorious. Health is your greatest asset. Without it all efforts are vain.

We are indeed very, very sorry, to learn of Gorhams condition. I am quite sure one thing that has brought this upon him, is the way they have lived, *Underfed*. I think if he gets where he gets good wholesome food, he will come out all right, but it will have to come soon. It is enough to kill any one the way they lived— Don't allow yourself to worry too much over your inability to help them. I know just how your heart goes out after their interests. They were so kind to you, but it would take more than what one person could do to put them where they could be comfortable[.] Gorham should not have applied himself so strenuously, and should have exercised & gone out more—but I think he will soon pick up now that he finds his mistake— I hope Elizabeth will finally see her way out of her trouble—tell her to keep up good courage all will be all right soon— I would think his father could help them temporarily at least. Don't worry. *You can't afford to,* you have too much at stake to allow anything to interfere with your work. I think I would not ask for a raise—you know how easy it would be for them to say there are others who would come at that price, besides I think they would appreciate the pleasure of volunteering the raise themselves, then you would know they appreciated your work. Wait a while longer any way, and I will try to help you out if you can't wait for the raise[.] You haven't been there very long yet, and they are testing you out to see how much you are worth to them, as some one said the other day, that there was some one on the waiting list always, so it was not a matter of sentiment with such a large concern that it was up to whoever get[s] it, to be *efficient*[.]

Mother is going to send your blankets and suit this week. Margarett has got back now & will wash them.

Will you forgive this long letter but I have put in an otherwise lonely evening— Hope you are feeling better tonight. I know you will miss Gorham & Elizabeth, and some of your other friends but you will make new friends, who will take their place—and you are in the mean time broadening your acquaintance and growing in business acquaintance which means much to you in the future.

Goodnight with love/ Grandmother.

P.S. On reflection I think you know best whether to ask for a raise of salary—but if you do—be *very sure* you do not convey the impression you are going to leave if you *dont* get it.

To Grace Hart Crane and Elizabeth Belden Hart

[New York City]
Saturday, Sept. 29th, '23

TLS, 1 p.

Dearest Grace and Grandma:

I have received so much from you both this week that I really don't know where to begin to offer thanks. The first thing was a most thoughtful and lovely letter from Mrs. E. B. Hart. Her admonitions and cheer were both appreciated and beneficial. Then, Lo and behold! the comforter cameth, along with extra and scrumptious "undies" and Gracey's kind letter! Well, it is nice to think that I have two such people as yourselves with quite a bit of thought about me. "I'm worth it though" says I, as I drew myself under the rosebuds on the comforter last night,— "Thinks I, "there's nawthin like makin your wants known." I think, however, that for the present I shall have enough bedding if you send *just one* of those blankets,—preferably the black one, as there is no place to put any extra thing in my room now.

Gorham came back day before yesterday to help Lisa out with the moving. They have found no place yet, but Gorham has been to see a lawyer and served a notice on their landlady which will prevent any one else from moving in until they are able to find a place to go to. Lisa will now probably take a small place, maybe a simple room, as Gorham leaves in a week or ten days for the woods again. I am not a bit worried about him if he will take the pains to give himself a little exercise and avoid too much smoking. I think he has been frightened enough now to guard himself a little. I have had a great deal to do this week in keeping up Waldo Frank's mental state to anything like normal equilibrium. This sounds silly enough, as he has really not definitely come to me for any relief or counsel, etc. I mean that I have seen him so dangerlusly upset by his present marital relations and money problems that it has made me feel a responsibility to[w]ards him which has caused me considerable personal confusion, as well. It will be a good thing for him when he takes the boat to Europe. New York is hard on him, because he feels so much personal antipathy to him and his work from a lot of stupid editors and colyumists around.

I have had a great deal of work at the office—with some new work this week on a kind of travelling bag, Naugahydes. Everything is going along all right, and, as describing any of my work would involve rather lengthy explanations, there isn't much use telling more. O, yes,—I've meant to tell you for some time that I am working at the next desk to a woman who knows Zell, Mrs. Upton,[1] and a lot of my friends down here. Francis Maule,[2] who used to be the wife of Edwin Bjorkman, the tran[s]lator of Ibsen. She was one of the first to take up suffrage work in New York, and she came out to help out in an Ohio campaign once. Bobbed grey hair, rather slender and very pleasant. She was the one they first set me to working with on the "Sloan's Liniment" and "Pine Tar Honey" accounts.

I am planning a late sleep tomorrow morning, and a restful day. If I get plenty of sleep I am always OK. I have been getting caught up some the last few nights and when the people in my neighborhood stop fighting all night and the cats stop yelling a little more

---

[1] Harriet Taylor Upton (1855–1945), of Warren, Ohio, was treasurer of the National Women's Suffragist Association for twenty-five years and the first woman member of the Republican National Committee.

[2] Frances Maule (1879–1966) was married to Edwin Bjorkman from 1906 to 1918. She edited *The Independent Woman*, a publication of the National Federation of Business and Professional Women's Clubs.

there won't be much trouble. Don't worry about me, I'm working hard, but don't think I'm hurting myself much yet.

                    Love in bunches to you both,/ Hart

To Grace Hart Crane and Elizabeth Belden Hart

                              [New York City]
                    [Postmarked October 3, 1923]

ALS, 1 p.

My dears:

Just a line or so. I've just come back from the first play since I came to N.Y. A pleasant evening all by myself.

Gorham has been in town helping Lisa move. They are already installed in a very pleasant place with a bathroom like those in the Blackstone! G. looks much better and leaves on Sat. next for the woods again.

Your comforter arrived in time to keep me warm and happy during the recent cold spell. My whole attitude toward N.Y. changes with this improved weather. I can sleep better, too, because people keep their windows down (at least until they go to bed and I don't hear so much Dago yelling. Nor cats either!

I hope you are enjoying some nice rides these days. The country must be gorgeous as usual.

Did I tell you that I made a drawing of Waldo Frank that everyone is talking about? [1] It will be reproduced soon. Had a card from Arthur E.[2] today. Very chipper & cordial.

                              Love,/ Hart

[*Written on the side of the page:*] I'll write you more later, of course. Tell me if the cards from Tiffany's came. They should have —long ago.

---

[1] The sketch of Frank was printed as the frontispiece of *S4N*, Vol. IV (Fall, 1923).

[2] Hart's paternal grandfather.

To Grace Hart Crane

Friday, Oct. 5″ '23
New York

ALS, 4 pp.

Grace, dear:

I had just got my pajamas on last night when there was a rap on the door. I opened and in walked Waldo Frank—behind him came a most pleasant looking twinkling little man in a black derby—"Let me introduce you to Mr. Charles Chaplin",—said Waldo, and I was smiling into one of the most beautiful faces I ever expect to see. Well!— I was quickly urged out of my nightclothes and the three of us walked arm in arm over to where Waldo is staying at 77 Irving place (near Grammercy) [.] All the way we were trailed by enthusiastic youngsters. People seem to spot Charlie in the darkness. He is so very gracious that he never discourages anything but rude advances.

At five o'clock this morning, Charlie was letting me out of his taxi before my humble abode. "It's been so nice", he said in that soft crisp voice of his modulated with an accent that is something like Padraic Colum in it[s] correctness. Then he, blinking and sleepy, was swung around and was probably soon in his bed up at the Ritz.

I cant begin to tell you what an evening night and *morning* it was. Just the three of us—and Charlie has known Waldo quite a while— They've been in Paris together and have a few mutual friend[s].

Among other things Charlie told us his plans (and the story of it) for his next great film. He has a five acre studio all his own now in Berkley, and is here in New York at present to see that the first film he has produced in it gets over profitably. *He* doesn't act in it. But he wrote story, directed and produced it entirely himself. It's running now for just a week or so more at the "Lyric" Theatre to box prices. Then it will be released all over the country. "A Woman of Paris" it's called. I havent seen it yet.

Our talk was very intimate—Charlie told us the complete Pola

Negri [1] story—which "romance" is now ended. And there were other things about his life, his hopes and spiritual desires which were very fine & interesting. He has been through so much, is very lonely (says Hollywood hasn't a dozen people he enjoys talking to or who understand his work) and yet is so radiant and healthy, wistful, gay and *young*. He is 35, but half his head is already grey. You cannot imagine a more perfect and natural gentleman. But I can't go on more now. Stories (marvellous ones he knows!) told with such subtle mimicry that you rolled on the floor. Such graceful wit, too—O that man has a mind. We (just Charlie & I) are to have dinner together some night next week. He remembered my poem very well & is very interested in my work. [2]

There's nothing else worth telling you about since my last letter. I am very happy in the intense clarity of spirit that a man like Chaplin gives one if he is honest enough to receive it. I have that spiritual honesty, Grace, and its what makes me dear to the only people I care about. Love/ Hart

From Elizabeth Belden Hart

[Cleveland]
Thurs—2 PM
10—11—'23

ALS, 8 pp.

My Dear Hart.

Mother was unexpectedly called down town. I know she will be glad to have me write you a line in her stead, for she has said many times, *I must* get a letter off to Hart and tell him how delighted I am to know of the wonderful opportunities you have of meeting so many celebrities and especially fine it was you had of meeting Charlie Chaplin in such an intimate & friendly way— I hope all of these acquaintances may in the future prove to be of value to you as well

---

[1] At this time it was rumored that Pola Negri, the star of German films who had been brought to Hollywood, was engaged to Chaplin.

[2] Hart refers to his poem "Chaplinesque."

as a pleasure. You are certainly widening your circle far more than you could ever do here.

The weather is glorious here now, and I wish I might use up every hour out of doors while it lasts. I feel sorry that Mother has so little come into her life to cheer or happify her— She does miss you so much—you will never know, or how your letters cheer her— Don't deprive her of them, promptly—no matter who else falls short. You should see how she brightens up after getting a letter from you— It makes it much easier for me to get along— She has no one to come to see her but———[1] & he is so *poor* that we have to do all the entertaining, and that she tires of—but as she says its better than not to have any one to hang on to. She has squelshed Jim W. I guess—he has not made any particular effort to extricate himself, altho' he has made many promises what he was going to do and *when*—& she has forbidden his coming time & time without number until he has a right to come[.] I am glad she has taken the stand. I think she has offended him now as he understands what she means.

I do want to take a trip to Warren, Canton & G-ville [2] before it gets cold—but when the day is right, there is some thing on hand to prevent. I want to see Hart so much too. We miss you more than you can guess. I want Mother to get out of this town. She will never meet any one here that will benefit her any. Too many of the Ex's around—& so it was with you— Every body seems to think you have done the right thing in going to N. York, and I hope it will prove out so— Cleveland is all right for those who are already established here and have made their little pile—but not for the young beginners— Sam [3] was wild when Mother told him of your meeting Charlie. We are so glad to hear that Gorham is better, and Lisa is settled again— Give them our best wishes for all the good that can come to them [.] If he can only take warning to be more careful of health & exercise more in out door life and eat nourishing food—

[1] The name omitted here and "Jim W." in the following sentence refer to two of Grace's suitors.
[2] Garrettsville, Ohio, where Hart was born.
[3] Samuel Loveman.

Helen, Nannie, Inez, the maid arrived yesterday forenoon & spent the day here & certainly little Zell Petite is the cutest & best natured child I ever saw[.] [4] She never even whimpered once while here—has a smile for every one who speaks to her. We had several callers to see her & she held her little hands to go to every one who spoke to her.

Mr Kennedy—A Mr Brown Helen used to know, who has just been abroad[,] Glen, Becky—Sarah—etc— We had a grand good time but we were very tired when they were gone. Oh yes Nannie came too. They left between five and six— Then Ford————[5] came in the evening to see Mother, he has just returned from a long trip through Cal.—and the Coast.

He would like to go with Mother, she says she never could stand the family— He bro't her a lovely #5 box of Candy—but don't give me away on telling what little news there is—even if it is not interesting to you. I must talk about something you know.

If I thought it would do Mother any good to take a little trip to N. York—or make her any happier to have a little visit with you I would be glad to make it possible for her to go—but if she did not meet anyone she knew, I don't see the use[.] Do you ever meet Ned— [6] If he knew she were coming he would invite you both the weekend—or come in to the city and take her around some— She would only stay a few days—at most but this is all my planning, please not worry about her. She is all right only at times get[s] very lonely & discouraged. Don't hint that I have said anything when you write.

Don't fail to write Mother for Sunday & a card middle of week   Please—

Much love from/ Grandma

another long letter I cannot help it.

[4] Helen Hart Hurlbert; "Nannie" was her grandmother; "Zell Petite" is Helen Hart Hurlbert's daughter.

[5] A reference to another of Mrs. Crane's suitors.

[6] "Ned" was a friend of Mrs. Crane's who lived at Rye, New York. See Hart's letter of July 14, 1923, to his mother.

To Grace Hart Crane and Elizabeth Belden Hart

New York
45 Grove Street,
Oct. 12th, '23

TLS, 2 pp.

Dear Grace and Grandma:

This is a holiday: consequently I have had a late snooze and am left to read and write and do as I will for the rest of the time. It has been a very busy week. I have not seen Chaplin as I expected to, he has been under the weather up at the Ritz with too much champagne, parties and a bad cold. But Jean Toomer, Margaret Naumburg and Waldo Frank have been very much in evidence, and to the extent of a very fine home-cooked chicken dinner one evening at Margaret's which almost left me gasping—I ate so much. Toomer and I are great friends. I want to send you a copy soon of his book of short stories and a play which has just come out.[1] It may interest you to read the inscription which he placed in the copy of this book which he recently gave me:—

For Hart,
instrument of the highest beauty, whose art,
four-conscinal, rich in symbols and ecstasy,
is great—
whose touch, deep and warm, is a sheer illuminant
with love

Jean   New York
24th Sept 23

I want you to meet Jean sometime. I can't begin to tell you my impressions of him now, but the biographical introduction to one of his review[s] in the Dial last month is amusing in a certain sense: —"Jean Toomer, who is of negro extraction, is the grandson of P.B.S. Pinchback, the governor of Louisiana during the reconstruction. He was born in Washington, D.C. in 1894, and has travelled extensively throughout America. He studied at the University of

---

[1] Crane is referring to *Cane* (New York: Boni & Liveright, 1923).

Wisconsin, New York University and the College of the City of New York, and later taught in the University of Chicago." etc. Jean is only partly negro, looks more like an indian in color. In feature he is sharp and graceful.

Gorham and Liza were satisfactorily moved before G returned to the country last Monday. He was evidently better, even from his short stay before, but he intends, I think, to remain away for most of the winter. At least I hope so. We have all been very much implicated (entirely on the spiritual plane) with the present crisis in Frank's life, precipitated by the separation that has evolved between him and Margaret. It is a long story, very deep and interesting, which I shall speak more about when we get together. Waldo has never faced certain spiritual issues in his life—and now we all realize that he must either do so squarely and firmly, or else curtail his future development to a disastrous extent.

Since the weather cooled I have felt almost a new being. Having had the gas turned on in my radiator and tried it out several times, I am now confident that I shall be able to keep quite warm during the winter. Two friends of mine have offered me the use of their tubs and faucets whenever I want a hot bath, which I shall avail myself of, providing I cannot succeed in persuading the landlady to instal a hot water heater here. I do not think I shall have to buy any more clothes before spring what with the suit you are sending and what I have on hand to use. This certainly is fortunate, as my present salary at Thompson's just suffices for rent and food, really nothing more. I am waiting until the end of this month, the sixth month, to inquire about the possibilities of a raise. If I find that I am stalled off, I shall quietly investigate for a position elsewhere. I hear from all sides that Thompson's are famous for their low salaries anyway. A few people get vast amounts, and the rest are left to compensate each other with so called "cultured" environment. I have been working very hard this week on a stiff sort of proposition. So far they have given me only tough little nubbins to handle —jobs that didn't pay them anything and could best be turned over to a cheap man,—these little left-overs are, however, very often the most uninspiring and difficult things to handle.

I hope that your efforts for Glenn are going to have strong results. Please give him my heartiest salutations and good wishes when you meet him next. I think of you a great deal, and you must not be lonely. We are all going on in the regular course of things toward a higher consciousness of life and what it means. We have no reason or right to suppose that it should be predominantly happy—seen completely, from end to end, however, I think it is a great happiness. We must keep on over-riding the details of pettiness and small emotions that dwarf it to keep on seeing it that way, and that can't be done without a real conscious effort and vision. We know each other too well to let physical separations mar very much. Christmas is not far away now, either, and then I shall see you for several days.

I meant to thank you for the five dollars before this, it enabled me to pay the advance deposit on my gas. You ask me if there is anything else I need in the way of clothing. Only a few soft collars, size 15 "Ideflex" brand, style "Montebrook". Don't bother much about them though,— I think I can manage that alright.

Remember that I am all right, and please don't worry any more. I have grown more in this last year than I can account for yet. I think we all have, and that's what matters. Love from/ your/ Hart

P.S.—If you ever want to write Gorham or Lisa—their new city address is *144 West 11th Street.* Give "Clip" a kiss for me.

The hints in Mrs. Hart's letters about her daughter's condition and the advisability of "a little trip" were too great for Hart to ignore. He realized that his mother was suffering in Cleveland, and what was worse, that nothing could be done for her. "If you think a minute about my grandmother's age," he wrote Charlotte Rychtarik toward the end of July, "you will realize from that alone that my Mother could not possibly leave her to come here or anywhere else. . . . You must never think I am not doing all I can to make my Mother's life as bright as possible, even though I do not always succeed." [1]

Working for the Thompson agency, too, left him with little time to write poetry. In a short letter to Alfred Stieglitz, written on August 11, Crane apologized for not writing previously. "My mind is like dough," he wrote, "and *The Bridge* is far away." [2]

Thwarted in his efforts to secure a raise in salary, Hart decided to leave his job and spend the winter on the Isle of Pines. There he felt he could at last devote his energy to *The Bridge*.

To Grace Hart Crane and Elizabeth Belden Hart

[New York City]
45 Grove St
Oct. 20th,'23

TLS, 2 pp.

Dear Grace and Grandma:

I'm sorry that this letter will not reach you on Sunday (it is now Saturday evening) but I haven't had the necessary time before. I've been feeling so altogether rotten lately that my energies are about reduced to their minimum. In fact I am seriously considering going to the Isle of Pines this winter for a thorough rest and recuperation from the strain of the last five years. This is no sudden idea in my head,—it is something I have reconsidered many times for several months, and always with the growing conviction that it is the thing to do. I think that in weighing the numerous reasons you will agree with me quite thoroughly.

In the first place—my state of nerves and insomnia here due to the mad rush of things and the noise nights around the place I am obliged to live, makes it imperative that I get away before I have a real breakdown. I feel that this is certain to happen before the win-

---

[1] Quoted from Crane's letter of July 21, 1923, published in *The Letters*, p. 140.

[2] Quoted from *The Letters*, p. 142.

ter is over unless I get some relief. And, as there seems to be no prospect of a raise in my salary at the office I cannot afford necessities here that make life bearable and sufficient to keep me in a state of health.

And then, besides all this, the Island needs some personal attention from someone in this family. You, neither of you, are able to go, and if you were, it would cost you three or four times as much as I will need to live there. (My expenses would be just the boat fare and after that about 5 dollars a week for board with the Simpsons.) [1] I need absolutely no more clothes or equipment in any way than I presently have, so that needn't be bothered about. I would have a chance to breathe in some clean air, swim and use my body a little freely. I could live very simply and constructively— and really make it pay besides by seeing the lay of the land, how things are being cared for, what marketing opportunities are developing in the way of cooperative fruit markets, etc.

I think this and other letters of mine have said enough about living conditions in New York as it has now become—to make it plain that you will never want to settle here. I have never accented these points in any particular relation to you—but I am more and more certain that you will never want to *live* here. Rents are terrific, food very high and unless you have unlimited funds you have to content your self with trying to keep clean in a dinky stuffy apartment without a porch or any of the outdoor privileges that go with the poorest shanty. I think we have been not fools, but fooling ourselves, to have worried so about selling the island place. That is the best place to live I know of,—the place where you will be far happier than ever tied up in an overcrowded city—paying out every month more money than your food would cost you for a year on the Island. Besides,—that grove is going to pay, and *pay well* sometime. It will pay you well enough to afford a month's change in New York every year. And that's enough! I have learned that from plentiful experience.

After the winter I can come back here to New York and get plenty of jobs that will pay more than what I have now. I can come

___

[1] The Simpsons were the caretakers of Mrs. Hart's home on the island.

back with a fund of health and energy that simply couldn't be gained here even if I weren't working at all. I think I deserve this much assistance not only as a son—but as [a] man who has done his best to cope with all situations that have come up, and I have been faced with some hard ones. This isn't a dodge—it's a sane precaution, and if you really care for me in right sort of way you will give it your approval, I'm sure.

Please don't think that I'm flat on my back or anything like that —by what I've said. I have been at the office every day and doing my regular work. It's the steady and growing strain of it all that I feel—without relief or rest, and I don't want to disregard too many red signals—at least with the obvious means we have of checking danger of this seriousness. I don't want you to waste a lot of money by coming down here in the belief that I need bedside attention, I only want you to know the facts as they are. If I went I should certainly spend a week with you beforehand. But, of course, I'll never consider living in Cleveland again permanently—no matter what happens.

Write me soon what you think of my suggestions. I think we should certainly not let that island property slip away. It's a clean home with beautiful surroundings and sunshine with quiet and tranquillity—compared to this metropolitan living with its fret and fever—its a paradise.

Much love, from/ Hart

To Grace Hart Crane and Elizabeth Belden Hart

[New York City]
Wednesday,
Oct. 24 '23

ALS, 2 pp.

Dear Grace and Grandma:

The company has just given me six weeks to two months leave of absence for the Island trip. They want me to come back after that time and resume the same work as I am doing now and were very pleasant about it when I told them that it was a matter of business for the family—that no one had been down there for over two years, etc. I shall consequently be finished and free to go a week from Today. And as soon as I can get my accomodation, passport, etc. I want to get started. It will take at least 3 weeks to get these matters attended to. I shall go second class—or as cheaply as possible. I shall have to borrow some money, of course, unless you feel that you want to help your son out a little on this matter. Two hundred dollars will be enough, and if you dont feel you can raise that amount I shall borrow it at 6 per cent. But if I have to do this I shan't be able to afford a trip to Cleveland to see you. Please let me know what you intend to do, and write the Simpson's that I am coming.

                                 Hastily—with love/ Hart

In a letter that is now lost Mrs. Crane replied to Hart's plan with a "contribution" of money, but she told him the house on the island was for sale, making it impossible for him to stay the winter there. Crane then decided to accept a long-standing invitation from Bill Brown and Edward Nagle to visit them in Woodstock. On November 2, he went to stay with Eugene O'Neill at Ridgefield, Connecticut, for several days, and then on to Woodstock.

To Grace Hart Crane

                                 [New York City]
                                 Friday, Oct. 26th, '23

TLS, 1 p.

Dear Grace:
    I am not going to the Island, but I expect to go up state to Woodstock for 6 weeks, leaving late next week. Have been invited to stay with Nagle and Brown in a house they have taken there for the winter. Please arrange to send me $15.00 per week while I am there. That will buy the necessary food, etc. When I get my rest and come back to town I expect to try some other kind of literary

work, maybe with a publishing house, before accepting Thompson's offer again. They pay so damned little and expect so much—that I might do better another place.

At any rate I am going to have some time in the country and in the open air. Just now I am very exhausted, as I have said. Thank you for inviting me back to Cleveland, but you know there are too many people to talk to there and, after all, it's city life too. My present plan is much cheaper and better. The Island would have been best of all, but feeling that it was for sale and might move out from under my feet any moment I certainly should not enjoy it there now. I am very very sorry that you are selling it. Don't let yourself get taken in on any fake deal of exchange by this Cleveland man.

I'll write you more very shortly. Thank you for the contribution.

Love,/ Hart

On the same day he wrote to his mother proposing his trip to the Isle of Pines, Hart sent a short and probably curt note to his father. Though Hart's letter is missing, Mr. Crane's reply survives.

From Clarence Arthur Crane

Cleveland, Ohio
October 27th, 1923

TLS, 2 pp.
LETTERHEAD: CRANE'S CHOCOLATES/ CLARENCE A. CRANE/
CLEVELAND, OHIO

Mr. Harold Crane
45 Grove Street.,
New York City, N.Y.

My dear Harold:
Your letter of October 20th came as a surprise. I really did not count on hearing from you, and would have been very glad if you had told me more of yourself, your work, and your prospects.

To be free in action—sound of health—youth and its big opportunities in New York must look wonderful to you. It offers a comparison with my bum start in little old Garret[t]sville and the days that I spent there thinking of the things I really liked to do. My vision has always been dwarfed by my poor conception of the opportunities in the outside world at a time when I should have struck out for bigger and better things. So I count that I have poorly played the game and wasted many of my inherent talents. I could soliloquise for hours along this line but it is past history and amounts to nothing now.

It seems very strange to be in New York for a few days and not even know your address or the man you work for. I thought of it many times, but I have learned to know and come to feel that if that is the way you wish it, it *must* be alright with me.

Your letter doesn't ring true of affection—rather it emphasizes the fear that I have always held, that you feel yourself humbled if you suggest a warm affection for your father—a sort of condition where you feel that I should come to you rather than you come to me. If that is the case, just let me say that it is so different than I have ever felt for my own father that I cannot underst[a]nd it, and therefore do not act as you might perhaps wish me to.

It is now almost three years since you left my store with strange words and strong determination to never again be associated with me. In those years no word has come to me that you have felt differently, no change of attitude on meeting, and no favors asked or given. As I recall, Frances on the only occasions presented did her utmost to make you feel comfortable, and I felt that she was doing her part one hundred per cent.

So Harold, as you have asked me, I will call you up when next in New York, but I am not unmindful of the fact that for all this time you have maintained a very dignified silence and that no later than a few weeks ago you were in Cleveland for several days and made no effort to get in touch with me. Your father will never ask for recognition from you. For many years I did my best by you and probably you will have to have children of your own before you appreciate or share just the same feelings that I entertain.

No doubt you and every child suffers from conditions such as happen, but I have never known a reason why you should have turned on your father or felt the way you have. In this same office you came to me one day, asked me to destroy the disgusting letter which you had written me, and told me that your determination was in the future to do quite differently.

Whenever you get around to have real affection for me, I think it will be better expressed than in a letter such as you have written—a six line challenge after a silence of years. I have always had faith in you, believed that you had sterling qualities, a good mind, and good morals. I am always pleased and have a pride in your accomplishments, and happy to hear of good fortune attending you.

This is not the only case of its kind in the wide world, and if you have a real desire to mend it now, you will find me in the same receptive mood that I have been all of this time, but don't expect your grey-haired father to "jump through the hoop." Do your full share and I will try to do mine. Write me when you have time, and believe me, always your father, / C A Crane

To Grace Hart Crane and Elizabeth Belden Hart

[New York City]
Thursday, Nov. 1st, '23
45 Grove Street

TLS, 2 pp.

Dear Grace and Grandma:

The weather's change to almost cold makes me feel that my trip and visit to the country is going to be stimulating and invigorating. I have succeeded in getting someone to take my room for the month I am away—thus preserving some place for me to return to in December and clearing the cost of some of my rent. Tomorrow afternoon I leave, stopping off for a couple of days at Ridgefield, Conn. as the guest of Eugene O'Neil (the author of Anne Christie, Emporer Jones, Beyond the Horizen, etc) I met O'Neil at some friends last week end when he was in town. He likes my poetry very much and invited me to come to stay with him. He has a regular estate, I am told,—an establishment that is quite complete, and breakfast for guests is never served out of bed. If everything goes right they are to drive me up to Woodstock on Sunday,—about three hours through beautiful hills and foliage. My address from then on will be *Woodstock, N.Y. care-of Slater Brown*.

You must not fool yourselves that I was fired at all. If that were so I shouldn't hesitate to admit it, but my run-down state and a certain distaste it developed for advertising work in general simply made it impossible to go indefinitely there without at least a temporary relief. I have been very cordially invited to call around there again when I "get home from the Island". In the meantime, Hal Smith has promised me a position with Harcourt Brace and Co, the publishing house in which he is a partner, if anything comes up.

I am depending on you to help me some, as I said in my last letter. I think you will agree that a thoroughly out-of-doors life for a month is not only a sensible thing for me, but really due me after all the time I have denied myself such a natural privilege. If you don't understand such a rightful desire on my part, then I can only say that your vision is warped. It was fine of you to ask me home, but I know you will realize that the atmosphere of Cleveland is anything but conducive to rest *for me*. The amount to which I am asking you to help me will not exceed the carfare to and from Cleveland—at most. Brown is poor and can only offer me the hospitality of the house he has taken,—any extra board he is unable to provide, so I am anxious to do my part and be decent about not stretching his hospitality unreasonably. So please send me fifteen dollars in cash or check at Woodstock sometime next week. Even if you have to pinch a little bit, I think that the things I am trying to do deserve a few sacrifices. I make as many as I can myself, and still keep sound and living,—and I hope you will [be] faithful enough —whether you see my complete ends or not—to lend me some assistance.

I hope you are both well and happy. Don't worry about me. I know damned well what I'm doing. I'll write you as soon as I get to Woodstock.

Love,/ hart

The nearly two months spent at Woodstock in the company of Bill Brown and Edward Nagle were ones of great happiness for Hart. No longer in the oppressive environment of New York, no longer prostituting his mind for the Thompson agency, Hart found that Nagle and Brown provided the ambience he had longed for while in the city. The three proved to be good companions and excellent conversationalists whose ideas about art and life complemented each other. They soon discovered that the owner of the house, an eccentric inventor named Rector, had left a large cask of elderberry wine in the cellar, which they often served to their neighbors and frequent guests Gaston Lachaise and William Fisher. Though there was much carousing and much conversation, Crane found the time to revise his poetry and write some of his best letters to Cleveland.

Throughout this period Hart was sent checks intermittently by his mother, father, and grandmother. However, Mrs. Crane's financial situation was not secure, and to make matters worse there were no "prospects in sight"—the delicate phrase Mrs. Hart used to speak of her daughter's chances for remarriage. For by this time Grace realized that only a husband—and a wealthy one—could save her from the financial morass into which she was sliding. Feeling the pressures of a diminished income, she took a job as a saleslady at the Josephine Shop, a small gift shop operated by an acquaintance of the family. The position, which Hart described to Gorham Munson in a letter written shortly before Christmas as "helping a friend of hers in a very de luxe antique and what-not establishment," [1] left her at the end of each day without the energy to speak to her mother or write letters to her son. "She has not personally written me for a month now. All reports and symptoms come from my grandmother," [2] Hart wrote to Munson. Though Crane was somewhat irritated by his mother's silence, his own letters to Cleveland reveal an ebulliency seldom matched in the correspondence.

[1] Quoted from Crane's letter of December 20, 1923, published in *The Letters*, p. 162.
[2] *The Letters*, p. 162.

To Grace Hart Crane and Elizabeth Belden Hart

Thursday
Woodstock, Nov. 8th, '23

TLS, 1 p.

Dear Mother and Grandmother:

Felling trees and piecing them up for warmth is a new sport to me, but I have taken to it with something like a real enthusiasm. This is my fourth day here in the mountains, but already I feel like a new person. My muscles are swelling and blood simply glowing. It is quite cold, even snowed today and the top of the nearest mountain is hooded white.

Slater Brown and Nagle make wonderful people to live with. I told you how fond I was of B when I was home last summer. I am made to feel not at all a guest, as to a large extent I am not, of course, but they want me to stay all winter here with them now. I may and I may not, depending on how I find I can manage to earn enough money by poems and articles. Certainly I should like to become a giant again in health, as I naturally am. And I have never had an outing like this before in my life.

We do all our own cooking. Brown has developed a surprising faculty for supplying tempting and enormous meals. You have no idea what an appetite is developed with wood chopping, sawing, and much walking in the brisk air. I have a heavy army shirt of wool and cordoroy trousers. I got all this along with some woolen socks for surprisingly little in an army and navy store in New York before I came out here. It was a good thing, now, that you sent that heavy underwear of mine in the trunk when you sent it.

The house we are living in is, of c[o]urse, already furnished by a family that lives here only in the summer. There are four bedrooms, a bath, dining room, large studio with a huge open fireplace where we burn our logs, and kitchen provided with an oil stove. There's just enough furniture and not too much, simple and in pleasant taste. The town is about two miles away. Walking in for our provisions is very pleasant—over rolling land, set in a valley by low mountains on all sides around. We are quite set away from everybody—no people passing to speak of and in a quietness that is a tonic after the endless noise and reverberation of New York which you feel there even in your sleep.

I certainly am hoping that nothing serious has happened to prevent you from writing me. I have been expecting a letter from you for several days now, and have thought that maybe the Nov. election and Glenn's participation therein has been delaying you. Please do write me soon.

ever your affectionate/ hart

To Elizabeth Belden Hart

Sunday
Nov. 10th. '23
Woodstock, N.Y.

TLS, 1 p.

Dear Grandma:

Before I got your letter mailed your check came, but as I was at the postoffice at the time, there was no chance to open up the letter and include my thanks to you. I was sorry that the letter contained no words from either of you, but I suppose you were in a rush of some sort and maybe the election excitement had not yet subsided enough. I am going to assume at least that you are all well, or you would have said something[.]

It is a rainy day, but the last two days have been superb. We climbed up halfway on one of the mountains near here one afternoon. You could see for miles around, the same as the postcard that I sent you shows. I am getting myself hardened up—not wearing too much clothing and keeping meanwhile in motion a good deal. As I may stay here all winter I think it is a good way to avoid the possibility of later colds. At all odds it is certainly much better than stuffy offices, they are the worst things in the world for one. I remember last winter was quite miserable with all the colds I had.

I suppose Zell and Helen have been in the City and gone by this time. Sam has lost his job again,[1] and writes me very touchingly. Eglin has taken a partner and pushed him out. Have you seen the Rychtarik's lately? Charlotte says she is studying music (piano) under Beryl Rubenstein.[2] Richard LeGalliene,[3] the poet, is living just half a mile away from us, and Gaston Lachaise and Mme. arrived last evening to spend the winter in a house they have taken for the winter here. We are going to have a great celebration on Thanksgiving. John Dos Passos (author of Three Soldiers) and some other folks are coming out from N.Y.

I'll write more very soon. Much love,/ hart

To Grace Hart Crane

[Woodstock, New York]
[Postmarked November 19, 1923]
Monday

TLS, 1 p.

Grace, Dear:

Brown is waiting to start for the postoffice directly and I have only time to send thanks for your letter and Grandma's kind check. I also want to mention that the idea of the fruit cake is splendid if it doesn't cost you too much trouble. My confreres here have both applauded it heartily. There will be 12 to feed at the dinner.[1] If you still want to send it to us, better start operations right away, as there are only about ten days left.

I'll write you more tomorrow. Feeling simply superb, and do hope that you are better.

with love, as always/ your hart

[1] At this time Loveman had a job in a bookstore.

[2] Beryl Rubenstein (1898–1952) was head of the piano faculty and later dean of the Cleveland Institute of Music.

[3] Richard Le Gallienne (1886–1947), the English poet and essayist, and father of Eva Le Gallienne, the actress.

---

[1] Mrs. Crane had suggested that she send a fruitcake to Woodstock for the Thanksgiving celebration.

It was the atmosphere of Woodstock and the freedom from the constrictions of New York that made Hart decide to spend Christmas with Brown and Nagle rather than with his mother and grandmother—a decision he delicately announced in this letter to Cleveland.

To Grace Hart Crane and Elizabeth Belden Hart

Woodstock, N.Y.
Nov. 21st, '23

TLS, 2 pp.

Dear Grace and Grandma:

After a triplet of very cold days that [1] threatened snow it has warmed up a little again. There is a fine blue haze over the woods and mountains and it would be hard to wish for more delightful weather. By inuring myself to the cold I demand much less clothing than I would were I less active. After you have carried 150 pounds of log on your shoulder and sawed about a quarter of a cord your system steams up with abundant heat. I certainly am beginning to gain a lot of muscle here and nervous equipoise. And in view of the very salutary results I am going to remain here until January first. That will be long enough to have re-established me in better shape than I have ever been in before. What I have gained now might be too easily lost should I return to town next week. Of course I shall not be home for Christmas, but you will be jolly enough at Zell's without me this time. The trip back to Cleveland would entail a great deal of expense anyway.

I fried some apples this noon for lunch in the fat left over from some pork sausage. I have been rather surprised how I have remembered some of the ways you cook things without my ever having been conscious when I was home as to just what was done, etc. Did I tell you, also, that I made some whizz of a gravey for dinner one

---

[1] The word "that" is repeated in the text.

night that everybody praised? We are going to have an enormous turkey for Thanksgiving, and roast it over the fire in the big fireplace. We have a barrel of cider, and two barrels of fine northern spy apples that Mme. Lachaise sent us from Maine when she and Lachaise were leaving. Last night we had Gorham and his host, Fischer, who live about half a mile through the woods from here, in to dinner. I never ate so much in my life, great quantities of ham, baked potatoes, and the sweetest beets ever cooked. The weather and the exercise breed tremendous appetites.

I was very much surprised to hear that Arthur E. had so recovered as to start out quite alone to the sunny west. I guess they (of the rest of the family) were damned glad to get rid of him for awhile. Poor Ella! [2] Her old age is certainly confused and fuddled.

Wouldn't it be easier and better to rent the house furnished and let that pay for a comfortable apartment for you and some of your expenses than to sell it outright? I am not trying to "run affairs", especially as you have never taken me into any of the family financial discussions [(]that I have an interest in) but only want to suggest what seems to me the better way. If you part with both the Isle of Pines place and 1709, I think you will feel pretty much on the high seas, while perhaps a little more effort in another direction less drastic would prove much better in the end.

Did I tell you that I had word from Elizabeth Smith,[3] who is in New York for a job? I directed her to a friend of mine who is occupied in editing a cheap magazine, a very nice woman who knows the ropes very well. She has just written me that she gave Elizabeth several letters of introduction to other editors, but I have not yet heard from E as to how things are coming. I shall be glad to let Glenn know if I run across anything in New York later that I think

[2] Arthur and Ella Crane, Hart's paternal grandparents.
[3] A cousin of Hart's on his mother's side. Hart sent her to Susan Jenkins, who edited *Telling Tales*, saying: "A young female cousin of mine from Canton, Ohio, has just arrived in N.Y. to find a job. She has worked on a newspaper, and may still be a virgin, for all I know. (Still, she has been to Smith!) I thought you might not mind talking to her a few minutes and have suggested that she calls at your office some day soon. I hope you won't mind giving her a little advice of some kind or other—all advice from you is good. . . . Elizabeth Smith is the girl's name. . . ." See Susan Jenkins Brown, *Robber Rocks* (Middletown, Conn.: Wesleyan University Press, 1969), p. 17.

would interest him as a working proposition. Just now I am hoping
to hear from Hal that there is an opening for me in his firm. But
I'm not worrying much about anything, it would negate all that I
am out here for if I did so. I may take a job on a boat for awhile
when I go back if I can't keep from starving otherwise. I certainly
am hoping to get my first book together and published before many
months, as that would provide me with enough literary prestige,
without any doubt, to make a wider market for my writings and literary services.

It's time to go lumbering again, and I've bored you long enough
with this anyway, I guess, so adieu for now.

affectionately,/ Hart

From Grace Hart Crane

Cleveland, Ohio
[Postmarked November 27, 1923]
Monday Evening

ALS, 3 pp.
LETTERHEAD: MRS. GRACE HART CRANE/ 1709 EAST 115 ST./
CLEVELAND, OHIO

Dear Hart:—

Just a line before I turn in—to tell you that I have sent the fruit
cake I promised by parcel post last Saturday, & you must be sure to
inquire about it at the Post Office. I am too busy to bake cakes
these days, as I have a job & go to work at 8 & come home at six. I
had McNally's [1] send this. I hope you will all have a wonderful
Thanksgiving up there in the woods & mountains. If you have a little wine to spare, pour it on the fruit cake a day before, and keep it
well wrapped in a cloth & put it in a box.

I have no plans for that day, excepting a late sleep in the
morning—which is the most desirable thing I can get these days of
being on my feet all day.

Grandma feels pretty well, and does not complain about being

[1] The McNally Doyle confectionery store in Cleveland.

left alone. I have to turn in now or I will not be on time in the morning.

My job is just a modestly paid one until Christmas, but I tho't that I would better take it.

Cut your cake very thin & have a sharp knife— Wish I were to be there to help make the dinner a success.

Lovingly / Grace.

To Grace Hart Crane

[Woodstock, New York]
Tuesday Nov 27, '23

TLS, 1 p.

Dear Grace:

Day before yesterday came a welcome card of announcement from McNally's—and this afternoon a still more welcome parcel. We opened it only so far, being convinced from the beauty of the lacy mat and ribbon that the contents were too choice and tempting even to be sniffed at until the proper time on the Day of Thanks. Then your lovely gift will be delivered to the table as the piece de resistance after the turkey. I guess I told you that we are going to roast that on a special contrivance in the big fireplace in the studio. That room has already been decorated with fragrant pine boughs that we brought today from the woods. There is a balcony all along one side that opens into bedrooms. That has been well hung with green, as well as the banisters of the stairway that leads down. There will be only eight of us, but we are going to eat in the studio in order to have the most room possible to spread out in, the regular dining room being best for four or five at table. Dinner does not begin until three—ending with wine and cider—and midnight bells as far as time goes, I guess. We shall have a good time if the three from New York (Dos Passos and two others) arrive here tomorrow as expected. You may be sure that not only I, but Brown and Nagle are very grateful for your thought and kindness with the cake. And you may be sure that I shall be thinking of you much around the board at home, and hoping that your guests and you both are merrily engaged.

It has not been as cold here yet as I had expected. However, a few flakes of snow are liable to start down at any time and I shall welcome them. The mountains around here are so beautiful in their various aspects and under the different skies that everyday brings— I haven't been here long eno[u]gh yet to ignore them from habit, and doubt if I ever should be indifferent to their presence. For one thing, teyey [they] are not too picturesque in the obvious way so that they stand up and shriek for your attention all the time. They are very much an easy and careless part of a natural landscape.

I have been having a great time for the last two hours making apple sauce—a tremendous quantity of it, and without knowing how much of water, suger, cinnamon or anything to put into it. Finally ended up by getting sore at Brown who kept on making suggestions until I got aggravated enough to tell him where to go, leaving him to make or spoil the batch as he can judge. Nagel's great vice is super-neatness, always whirling around with a broom or wash pail: and you know I am prety bad on that score myself! But we really get al[o]ng remarkably well. I am very very fond of Brown. How do you make dumpl[i]ngs, and a few other simple dishes, stews, baked beans, etc.? We have about a dozen things that we make very well, but are without a cook book. I thought you or grandma might write a few directions.

This typewritrer is so bad I can't go further now. My best love to you both

as always—/ Hart

To Elizabeth Belden Hart

Dec. 5th, '23
Woodstock, N.Y.

TLS, 3 pp.

My dear Grandma:

Your interest in my culinary triumphs is certainly very much appreciated. I've been waiting quite a while for the moment to tell you about the Thanksgiving dinner, etc. and have just about got adjusted again, the house in order and our simple program restored although the last guest left on Monday. Altogether, the party and every detail of the festivities was quite a success. Some things were very funny and some were a little aggravating. I think I did most of the cooking when it came right down to the last moment, as both my confreres were so occupied with their lady friends and rather daffy that they went around like dizzy roosters, and keeping the rest of the company entertained and out of the kitchen was some job, too.

The people we bought the turkey from had already cleaned it and plucked it, and had promised to make the stuffing. But at the last moment they went back on the stuffing, and so it was left to me entirely. You should have seen me going at it, sewing it up tight afterward and everything! Everyone said the stuffing was great, and I liked it myself. I rubbed the outside all over with salt and butter, and then the ten pound bird was put into a wonderful roasting machine that Lachaise brought out from New York which he got in the French bazaar. You put the bird on a long spit which had a crank and catches. One side of the cage was entirely open and that was turned toward the fire in the big studio. I never ate more luscious turkey that this process produced. You must have seen one of these roasting devices because similar ones have been used in New England for many many years. It's a large, fat oval shape and looks a little like a big tin pig on its legs. We kept turning the bird around inside until it was a rich brown and thoroughly done. The meal began with potato and onion soup made by Nagel. Then turkey with mashed potatoes, cranberry sauce, squash and gravey. Celery too. Then I made some fine lettuce salad with onions and peppers and french dressing. Dessert was composed of pumpkin pie and mince pie and the marvellous fruit cake. We had cider in abundance, Marsala wine and red wine as well as some fine cherry cordial. Nuts, raisins, etc. Quite a dinner, you see. And everyone went wild about the cake. We had all the walls hung with candles as well as the table. Sat down at five and didn't get up to dance until eight. I danced fat Mme Lachaise around until we both fell almost exhausted. Then there was a girl who could match me on

my Russian dance and we did that together at a great rate. I forgot
to mention that we had a Victrola, of course, which Lachaise
bought in Kingston just the day before. Lots of jazz records, etc.
Most of the guests had left by the following evening, but we have
spent most of the time since in getting things straightened around
again and catching up on our supply of wood.

While I had a wonderfully good time, I am hoping that we have
no more company for the rest of this month. It's too much work
and is distracting. I want things as quiet and restful as possible, and
guests are always interfering with more personal pursuits. I was very
much surprised, of course, to hear about Grace's job. Who is Josephine? and where is the establishment, what sort, etc.?[1] I am glad
that she has got into some kind of action other than housework,
and I hope that it will not seem too strenuous for either of you. I
keep thinking that an apartment would be so much better for you
both. Rent out the house and let that pay your expenses in a
smaller place. But maybe you can't get up the steam to move.

It is raining steadily today, and you can't even see the mountains
through the overhanging mists. I like this country here more and
more. In all kinds of weather it has unique beauties and I shall be
sorry to leave it in January, which I must do, of course, as I must
find some kind of work again. Your check was very welcome. I had
begun to think that much embarrassment was due to come to me if
I couldn't meet the modest demands of my board here, especially
since both Brown and Nagle have just enough for themselves and
no more, regardless of their generosity. Fifteen dollars a week is
cheaper than I have ever been able to live before, but they pay the
rent and fuel, etc. and would have to do[2] so to the same extent
whether I were here or not, so I am in very lucky to share only in
the cost of the groceries and meat.

I see you won't give me the chance to try out the dumplings! Perhaps it's just as well. I've been kidded a great deal about the apple
sauce, or rather my 'temper' about it, as it has all been eaten up
with avidity by all of us. Recipes or no recipes, I hope you will
write me another such a good letter as the last one, Grandma, and
soon! I'm not flattering you when I say you are superb. I hope that

[1] A reference to the Josephine Shop where Grace was working.
[2] The word "do" is repeated in the text.

Grace will feel like writing me a longer letter than the last one soon. My love and deepest thanks to you both.

as ever,/ Hart

To Grace Hart Crane

[Woodstock, New York]
Monday
Nov. 10th, '23 [1]

TLS, 1 p.

Dear Grace:

I guess you cannot have had any more rain that we have had here. But rain and clouds are less depressing, I think, in the country than they are in the city for some reason or other. I have done the usual amount of walking and errand running into town, but we have had to suspend our usual wood cutting.

About last Friday, I guess it was, I climbed the mountain at whose base we live here, Mt Overlook, height 2,500 feet, and never enjoyed any day's work more in my life. It was quite clear and about noon when I got to the top, and I could see clear across the Hudson valley and miles up and down the river. It only takes about an hour and a half to walk up if you go along briskly. On the very top is a house and the ruins of a rather nice hotel that burned down only this last summer. The caretaker of the property lives in the house attending to a cow, two horses and chickens in a barn ne[a]rby. It is all quite charming, and I should like to live there myeself. [2]

I have been hoping for a letter from you, and have about decided that working effects you worse than it does me even when it comes

<hr>

[1] Misdated. The date should be Monday, December 10, 1923. In another letter of December 10 Crane wrote to Gorham Munson: "Last Friday I climbed the mountain (Overlook). . . ." See *The Letters*, p. 161.

[2] In his letter to Munson, Hart gave more details about the possibility of becoming caretaker at Mt. Overlook: "I am seriously thinking of taking the place myself at pay of 40 bucks per month and all expenses gratis. It would be a hard winter, perhaps a terrific experience, but I should like to keep away from the city and its scattered prostitutions for awhile . . ." (*The Letters*, p. 161). Hart's plan never materialized.

to letters. Grandma seems to think that I was very negligent but my letter after Thanksgiving bore its own explanations in regard to that, so I won't bother you by repetitions. I'll try to write you every other day or so—postcards may have to do as a rule, as there isn't much happening nor much to tell about. I haven't been ill or half-ill a moment since I came here, so don't worry about me a moment.

Wish I could give you a good hug and kiss!

your / hart

It appears that shortly after his arrival at Woodstock, Hart again corresponded with his father. Though none of the poet's letters to his father from this period have survived, several of Mr. Crane's replies have.

From Clarence Arthur Crane

Cleveland, Ohio
December 10th, 1923.

TLS, 1 p.
LETTERHEAD: CRANE'S CHOCOLATES / CLARENCE A. CRANE /
            CLEVELAND, OHIO

Mr. Harold Crane,
Woodstock, N.Y.

My dear Harold:

I have intended for several days to answer your letter of November 13th, but your father seems to be a very busy man, particularly at this season of the year.

Your letter was much more gratifying to me than any one you have written for a long time, and I hope that when you do come to Cleveland you will come to see me and talk it all over. I haven't been in New York and won't get there now until sometime after the first of the year. We are moving from our present factory in January and February and are also changing two stores at that identical time, consequently my every minute is taken up and Christmas is here with its usual difficulties.

As you probably know, father Crane is in California and seems to be enjoying himself and regretting that he didn't sooner in life find out that the Golden West really existed.

No doubt you have all the news from your mother and there is nothing of real consequence in my life except to work out my problems as they appear.

I don't quite understand your fresh air impulse, but I haven't any doubt but what you have analysed it and found out that it is the proper thing. If you live in the woods and still carry on your work, you have solved the problem much better than most of us.

This is a hurried letter because I have very little to write you and think perhaps we had better postpone any analysis of conditions until we can talk it over. Write me when you have time and I will try and give you a more satisfactory answer when I am not so pressed for time and my head is not so full of pending obligations.

Sincerely your father,/ C A.

To Grace Hart Crane

Woodstock, NY
Dec. 14th, '23
Friday—

TLS, 2 pp.

Grace dear:

A little flurry of snow this morning—and now the sun has come out to melt it quickly. Certainly this is a relief after yesterday and the day before—which were so warm that we began to have spring fever, stiff joints and colds threatening. For once you get used to cold weather, the lowering of the temperature is unpleasant at best.

I've been sawing a lot and working hard. There is someone here for tea almost every day. Generally Mme. Lachaise and Mr Fisher, an art critic and friend of Gorham's that lives near here. Gorham, by the way, has gone to Croton-on-Hudson for another month after seeing the doctor in New York. He has been gaining steadily—over 15 pounds last month—but the doctor wants to insure complete recovery by all the extra time she can make him serve.

I have just come back from the village whither one of us has to go at least once a day to get the mail, milk, and groceries. It is so fine to walk through the quiet woods and meadows quite alone by oneself and watch the clouds floating over the edge of the mountains like white chariots in the sunshine! There isn't any more beautiful country in this continent than right here. Sometime it would be fine for you to come here for the summer and live in one of the modest houses, costing very little, and you could dress as you damned pleased, read and sleep and take long walks on level or hilly land, as you chose. I have never looked so well in my life as I do now, and I'm strong as an ox with the fine exercise I have been having. I think city life is a fake and a delusion, and I'm certainly going to see to it that I see more of this sort of country in the future.— Only three hours from New York, too.

I had a letter from the O'Neil's this morning, enclosing a photograph taken of me the day I was visiting them in Ridgefield. But this letter must be rushed off so fast and there is so much to be done today that I'll have to postpone sending it until my next to you. Time flies even faster out here than it seems to in the city—I don't quite know why except that I am always so happily busy.

I haven't heard from you in quite a long time, now, and I hope you'll not be too tired to write me soon. How does the job go? I don't even know what sort of work you are doing yet—nor where you are engaged.

My best love to you both—/ hart

By Christmas week Hart had decided to return to New York shortly after the new year. His letter informing his mother of this decision attempts to explain the reason for his interlude in Woodstock and to make her understand his need to write poetry.

To Grace Hart Crane

Woodstock, NY
Dec. 21st, '23

TLS, 2 pp.

Dear Grace:

If it's as warm in Cleveland as it is around here—people must be hunting around to find Christmas, and Santa Claus must be still in Alaska waiting for more proper signs. I have just come back from town and all in a sweat with a few packages of provisions. The lilac bush beside the house has begun to sprout several times, and there is an epidemic of butterflies around Toronto, so the paper says. You don't like winter, so I suppose you are in comparative comfort so far. If you are using coal in the furnace it will make it easy to care for, which is good.

Grandma says that you are very much exhausted and too tired to go down to Zell's for the day. I'm sorry, because I think it would do you good in the end despite the extra effort involved. We are, all of us, in something of a strained state this Christmas but I don't think we need to be so much wrought up about it as you and Grandma apparently are. After all, Christmas is only one day in the year— and as a special day, I don't get half so excited about it (and haven't for some years) as I used to. It's too bad that we can't all be together, but that can't be helped. It wouldn't have made any difference so far as I could see, had I remained at Thompson's during all this time—so far as money side [of] it goes. I was just keeping things going as it was, and had nothing left over for travelling expense, and had I remained I might have incured much more expense by this time by being flat on my back. I think you take my little rest and vacation a bit too strenuously. I'm going back to NY on the second or third of January (if I can get the carfare) and after that I won't ask for any more money. I don't know what I'm going to do, but I can probably wash dishes or work on the docks or something to keep skin and bone together. I shall keep my old room at 45 Grove Street (which is as cheap as any that can be found anywhere) as long as I can bamboozle the landlady. After that I'll have to depend on my good coat, or the kindness of friends. I've been able to store up a sufficient reserve of physical and nervous force while out here in the country to last me quite awhile, I think. I am not at all discouraged about anything, and I think that if you and Grandma will use your natural wits at a little better planning —you'll be able to get along fairly comfortably without working so hard. One can live happily on very little, I have found, if the mind and spirit have some definite objective in view. I expect I'll always have to drudge for my living, and I'm quite willing to always do it, but I am no more fooling myself that the mental bondage and spiritual bondage of the more remunerative sorts of work is worth the sacrifices inevitably involved. If I can't continue to create the sort of poetry that is my intensest and deepest component in life—then it all means very little to me, and then I might as well tie myself up to some smug ambition and "success" (the common idol that every Tom Dick and Harry is bowing to everywhere [)]. But so far, as you know, I only grow more and more convinced that what I naturally have to give the world in my own terms—is worth giving, and I'll go through a number of ordeals yet to pursue a natural course. I'm telling you all this now, dear, because I don't want you to suffer any more than inevitable from misunderstandings—for once we see a thing clearly usually nine tenths of our confusion and apprehension is removed. Surely you and I have no quarrels, and I think you understand me well enough to know that I want to save you as much suffering from Life's obstacles as can be done without hypocrisy, silliness or sentimentality. You may have to take me on faith for some things, because I don't know whether it is possible for all people to understand certain ardours that I have, and perhaps there is no special reason why you, as my mother, should understand that side of me any better than most people. As I have said, I am perfectly willing to be misunderstood, but I don't want to put up any subterfuges before *your* understanding of me if I can help it. You have often spoken to me about how you lamented the fact that you didn't follow certain convictions that you had when you were my age because it wasn't easy enough; and I know what strong obstacles were put in your way. I, too, have had to fight a great deal just to *be myself* and *know myself* at all, and I think I have been doing and am doing a great deal in following out certain natural and in-

nate directions in myself. By Jove—I don't know of much else that
is worth the having in our lives. Look around you and see the numbers and numbers of so-called "successful" people, successful in the
worldly sense of the word. I wonder how many of them are happy
in the sense that you and I know what real happiness means! I'm
glad we aren't so dumb as all that, even though we do have to suffer a great deal. Suffering is a real purification, and the worst thing
I have always had to say against Christian Science is that it willfully
avoided suffering, without a certain measure of which any true happiness cannot be fully realized.

If you will even partially see these facts as I see them it will make
me very happy—and we can be much closer and more "together"
that way than merely just living in the same house and seeing each
other every day would ever bring about alone. I have been thinking
much about you and about dear Grandma—and I shall have you
with me much on Christmas day. We'll be dancing a little, and are
invited around to a couple of celebrations at other houses here, but
there will be no such pretensious preparations as for Thanksgiving
and no extra guests here. I really hope there will be a little snow
both here and in Cleveland. It adds to things.

I am hoping that you will find time and will have the inclination
to write me soon. It has been over a month now since your last. I
want to thank Grandma for her check—and do, both of you,—have
a little fun. I'm sure your friends must mean something to you, and
they will not all forget you.

Love,/ Hart

From Grace Hart Crane

[Cleveland]
Saturday A.M—
Dec 22—1923

AL, 8 pp.

Dear Hart:—

As usual I am in a terrible rush. My being at work and away
from home every day, has found me late in getting off what few lit-

tle Christmas gifts I have been able to grab—and this morning finds your grandmother in an almost state of collapse because things are still undone & cards unmailed. These four weeks I have been working have been very hard on us both— Grandmother has been a brick—never given up a minute—but she [is] about all in now, & realizes that she could not take care of this house without me. My job ends next Monday night—I have worked for a very small amount just to see what might develop[.] But the organization is too young and inharmonious for me to either hope or desire a place with them. I will write you more about that later.

Mother & I shall spend our Christmas day alone at 1709—E 115 St. Zell expected us to join the family party at her house on that day, but neither of us felt we would be equal to a night & day of it down there. Nothing is so tiresome to me as a visiting debauch and as I shall work right up to Monday night, I do not want to get up the next day until I am good & ready.

I certainly am lonely & forlorn without you, and wish you were to be with us for the holidays— I had expected you on Christmas ever since you left us last March. I do not think you should be away from us so long at a time— You will see a big change in your grandmother, & I feel you should be with her as often as you possibly can, & do all the nice things you can to make her happy. Her stay is short now, and I realize more each day what a superior wonderful woman she is.

T. J. Keenan [1] called Long Distance from Girard P.a. last night, and said he was coming up tomorrow (Sunday) to see me, before he goes to the Isle of Pines. You know he has just returned from three [months] all over Europe. Well that means he will be here for dinner & perhaps over night, & needless to tell you that makes lots of work for us—& mother is so keyed up & nervous she is about crazy.

I am sending you a little package today & I can only hope you will get it on Christmas day. I have not been down town to do one

---

[1] Thomas J. Keenan (1859–1927), publisher and editor of the Pittsburgh *Press*. In addition to being one of the largest property owners in Pittsburgh at the time, Keenan had a large estate on the Isle of Pines and operated the Isle of Pines Steamship Company. As president of the island's American Association, Keenan had been instrumental in preventing the United States Senate from ratifying the Isle of Pines treaty of 1899.

bit of shopping—as the Josephine Shop is at 7218 Euclid. The collars are some I bo't you right after you asked me too weeks ago before you went to Woodstock. I did not send them because I tho't you would not need them there.

I hope you are going back to town right after Christmas & get started to work again by the first of the year. You probably will feel much more like it since you have had this chance to recuperate in the open air. If you don't do that, I hope you will come back to us, & get some thing here. It is a shame for us to be separated, anyway. Mother told you about losing dear little Clip. I feel just terribly about it, & can't get used to doing without him. He was the bravest, loving spirit up to the very last minute, & I shall never forget him nor the lesson he taught me.

The two checks enclosed are our Christmas—& I thought you could use the money in helping you get back to town again. I wish it were more— Let me hear from you & how you spent Christmas. I shall be thinking of you all the day. Love from us both.

To Grace Hart Crane and Elizabeth Belden Hart

> Woodstock
> Dec. 30th '23

TLS, 2 pp.

Dear Grace and Grandma:

A good fall of snow at last! and the country here has not been so fine before since I came. There have been so many teas and parties around here and such an urgency for wood during the last few days that I haven't had a moment to write you before this and to thank you for remembering me. I almost thought that I was not going to hear from you at all, but the day after Christmas along came your letter in the purse in the box, etc. and I was somewhat dismayed to get so much affection and kindness from you when I can do so little in return for it all. The checks will help me tide over some in New York when I get back there next Wednesday. The purse (I hope!)

will be useful as well as the calender, and it was nice of you to have r[e]membered my collars.

Zell sent me a little check, also the Rychtariks. Mme Lachaise gave me a harmonica, Nagle a pipe, and Brown a horn and an embroidery set! Card from Bren from Chicago, Lucy Hartzell, Verna Ross and a few others, also. We had a fine Christmas tree which we went up on the mountain and chopped down ourselves. The Lachaises brought all kinds of toys and silvery bubbles, etc. with real candles first ignited on the Eve of Xmas when we roasted a chicken before the fire and danced and drank wine and cider. Another big dinner next day at the boarding house where the Lachaises are staying and the best and liv[e]liest dance I ever went to at the home of a Miss Rixcson who lives here and who has quite a case on me. I'm the acknowledged crack dancer everywhere now, and was even in danger for a while, of having to pose quite nude for Lachaise—which would have been rather tiresome I imagine. For the next three evenings are scheduled dinners and dances (until New Years) and I expect to keep quite limbered up.

I was washing clothes all morning and my hands feel like doughnuts on this machine. Certainly have become a jack and mistress of all trades and domestic sciences out here!

Here's hoping things are going easier now at 1709 and that you had a jolly day after all. How did you get along with Keenan?

With much love and gratitude,/ as always—/ Hart

I'll try to write more very very soon, but there's so much to do every day!

On his return to New York Hart immediately began searching for employment, tracking down several leads he had received from friends and making an appointment with the personnel manager at J. Walter Thompson. Shortly after his arrival, his father offered him a position as a salesman for the Crane company. Hart graciously declined (though the terms he used to describe the offer to his mother were most ungracious), a gesture that helped improve re-

lations with C.A. considerably. When Clarence Crane went to New
York in February, he made a point of meeting with his son.

To Grace Hart Crane

[New York City]
45 Grove St.
Jan 4th '24

ALS, 3 pp.

Grace dear:
    Your letter forwarded by Brown from Woodstock has just come.
I'm awfully sorry that my letter written to you last Sat. didn't reach
you sooner. If you haven't got it before this it is because Nagle forgot to mail it. I gave it to him last Sat. and he should have put it
directly in the box. Perhaps its impossible to trust anyone for such
matters, and I only hope the accident hasn't caused you too much
worry.
    I got the package, checks, purse and all—and there is no use
trying to tell you how pleased I was and grateful.
    I won't go into other details of our Christmas until I hear from
you as to whether my letter finally reached you after all, as it contained an account fairly complete. New years brought forth another
series of parties and a grand dance with every sort of drinks known.
Since then I've been in a mad rush, of course. Came back here day
before yesterday (Wednesday) and have been arranging my room,
collecting things and hauling them in and out. The first of next
week I'll begin chasing around for work and I don't think it will be
as hard now as it was last spring. One never can tell, however.
    Gorham is still out at Croton, but all my other friends are here
now—there are too many people to talk to almost.
    Critical attacks are being made on my "group" by a number of
magazines and it's rather exciting.[1]

[1] Crane is referring to the quarrel between Gorham Munson and Matthew Josephson, which began in the fall of 1923 and continued until the summer of
1924. Malcolm Cowley gives a good account of the events in *Exile's Return*
(New York: Viking, 1951), pp. 171–205.

Im now due out to dine with Lisa and Jean Toomer so—more later.

My love to you both/ as always/ Hart

To Grace Hart Crane and Elizabeth Belden Hart

[New York City]
[January 6, 1924?]
Sunday

ALS, 1 p.

Dear Grace & Grandma:
I've been washing socks and writing letters and don't want to leave you out. Florence Spencer dropped me a card yesterday and I'm to have a talk with her about some retail job tomorrow morning. Also—I have another appointment with the editor of "Machinery".
I hope you're both alright— Please write me soon— I expected a *special* today and nothing has come.

Love,/ Hart

From Clarence Arthur Crane

Cleveland, Ohio
January 7, 1924.

TLS, 2 pp.
LETTERHEAD: CRANE CHOCOLATE COMPANY

My dear Harold,
As days go on I do not see an opportunity to come down to New York. We have so many changes going on here, and with the annual meeting of The Crane Chocolate Company next Saturday, there is little lik[e]lihood of my getting away.
Yesterday I called up your mother and had a chat with her regarding the subject of which I had intended to tell you of when we had an opportunity to talk.

We have outgrown our present quarters, not only in the matter of space, which for three years has been so il [l]-arranged that it was impossible to manufacture at a reasonable cost, and now the advancing rent in this part of town makes it quite prohibitive for a chocolate factory. We have taken over the Narwold plant and will move from this location between now and April 1.

Our floor space will be double what it is here, and the rent considerably higher, but our added floor space and better facilities are intended to modify the increased cost. It is, however, incumbent upon us to do a lot more business than we have previously done, and I have a sales plan formulated in my own mind, which, I believe, will be effective. This new sales proposition calls for someone to visit the trade in many different states, presenting the proposition whereby the cost of selling may be reverted to the benefit of the customer. I do not know how successful this will prove to be, but I know of no reason why it should not be a real help under conditions that exist.

You have never indicated that you wanted to come back into the Crane Chocolate Company. In talking with your mother, she did not feel that she could offer any real advice or suggestions. I do not want to try to make you over into something which does not appeal to you, for now as never before our business must show progress and profit, and it is only by my association with people who are genuinely interested in accomplishing this that the desired results will be obtained.

I just seem to have the feeling that if you are ever to take up this work, that now is the time to do it, and if you feel that you have something else in prospect or in mind that is better for you, I strongly advise you to turn a deaf ear to this and go on with your work, whatever it may be. In other words, in later life I do not want you to feel that if your father had not been in the candy business that you might have developed into a real advertising success.

This position which I outlined will pay a small living salary to start with, but if you are successful you can, I believe, get a real hold in this organization and ultimately make it of splendid consequence, so I invite you to tell me what your plans and your chances are, and if you can do so, tell me just what your feelings are in reference to making an effort to associate yourself with this business.

Ultimately it must be guided by someone other than myself. The retail division is well administered to, but the wholesale will ultimately offer a great opportunity to the right party. A gentleman in Boston, with whom I am on intimate terms, has tried for several years to get me to make him a proposition to come into this organization, but up to this time I have not wanted to make any affiliations which would be permanent, and if you are ever to be associated with me, the road job and the ability to sell merchandise is in my opinion the first and greatest requisite to the permanency of the business.

Write me just how you feel, and if you would like to come into the organization and spend two or three years in direct constructive work upon the road, then I feel you would be set to be of great service to me here.

Affectionately,/ Your father/ *C A C*

Mr. Harold Crane,
45 Grove Street,
New York City, N.Y.

To Grace Hart Crane

[New York City]
[January 7, 1924?] [1]
Monday 2PM

TLS, 1 p.

Dear Grace:

Your strange telegram came last night and I'm writing merely to thank you and to say that I haven't seen or heard of C A so far. Of course I'm still expecting to today or early tomorrow. I take it that he phoned you to say that he was leaving Cleveland Sunday night, etc. or something like that.

[1] C.A. had phoned Grace and outlined to her his proposition to offer Hart a job as salesman. She immediately sent Hart a telegram which told him to expect a letter or a visit from his father.

Four interviews this morning, and I am going out for two more this afternoon.

hastily / hart

To Grace Hart Crane

[New York City]
45 Grove St.
Jan 9" '24

ALS, 6 pp.

Grace, dear:—

Eugene O'Neill and his wife have unexpectedly been here with me all evening—so I've not the time to write you that I expected. But I do want you to know that your fine letter of explanation came—and also the letter from C.A. this morning. First of all I want to thank you for your splendid wisdom in every detail—both in what you said to me and in what you said to C.A. Your good judgement in all this is the fruit of much unselfish love for me and you don't know how much I appreciate it! And it gives me an added zest in living, dear, that you should manifest such careful understanding of me and my relationship to you and my (natural) father. Now further—regardless of certain tender feelings which I do (and always shall) entertain toward you and being near you—nevertheless I'm turning down the offer of the Crane Chocolate Co. It was written to me just as you outlined it to me, but there are a number of things involved against it, and decidedly. First, I see through every sentence of the letter a stiff and after-all unyielding disposition to reduce me to a mere tool. (I am therein even promised in hints the direction of the wholesale side of the business!) I see through all the words, my dear! Not yet are things ripe; but on the other hand, I am not going to destroy the bloom of the fruit. I shall reject this offer in a most tactful way. If my father really has an affection for me he will not resent my explanation that I value my career as a writer more than anything else in my personal life and he *may* understand that from diverse other explanations that such a position as he offers now is incompatible with those interests (even though in the end it might offer me more money).

I shall ceremoniously thank him (I could not be more "ceremonious" than his calculating letter, threatening me with this as the last business offer he will make me, if I don't accept it at once!) No, dear, if I starve I don't get led into such a false and artificial life as he would guide me into with that letter! But, as I said, I shall not offend him. There is no object in that. I am no mere cog in one of his machines and I shall answer more cleverly than to be included in such a category. And so, again, I want to thank you for your good sense—to have left the thing entirely to me and to have kept us both pure from misinterpretations on his part!

Did I tell you that Miss Spencer put me in touch with "Deans" (the Bon Voyage Box people) on Fifth Ave. who want a new manager for their 5" Ave. store? I had a talk with Dean the other day— and he seemed a bit interested in me. But I have heard nothing yet. Today I had a fine talk with B. W. Huebsch, the publisher, who is going to do what he can for me. Meanwhile I need 15.00 more to pay my rent for this month. Can Grandma do anything about it?

Love to you both/ Hart

To Grace Hart Crane and Elizabeth Belden Hart

[New York City]
Nov. 12" '24 [1]
45 Grove St.

ALS, 2 pp.

Grace, dear and Grandma:

I have been late in writing you (that is as a Sunday letter) because I have been so rushed in chasing around to find work, and there have been ads to answer—and it all takes time.

So far I have not had any decisions offered me,—pro or con— and I am rather up in the air—and with less than $2.00 left for next week's food.

[1] Both the address and the reference to his father's offer suggest that Hart wrote this letter on Saturday, January 12, 1924.

I have written father, as my last letter indicated, that I would not be doing fairly either by him or myself to accept the position.

If I don't get located here in some work during the next two weeks or some assistance you may next hear from me in Australia for all I know. Goodbye for now, dears— I enclose a picture taken out at O'Neil's place last November.[2]

Love, as always,/ Hart

From Grace Hart Crane

Cleveland, Ohio
[January 12, 1924?] [1]
Saturday 1:30 PM

ALS, 4 pp.
LETTERHEAD: MRS. GRACE HART CRANE/ 1709 EAST 115 ST./
CLEVELAND, OHIO

Hart dear:—

Your letter came yesterday afternoon while I was up at Becky's for luncheon.

Well, your decision was what I expected it to be—if I had had to make a prediction.

It may hurt your fathers pride and make him wrathy, but he will get over it, and I only hope that your decision was made entirely free from any desire to punish him or get even with the past.

I my self do not see how you could succeed in pleasing him & still hope to succeed in your chosen line—so if you have been honest with yourself & him, I am sure you have decided right.

Now keep your mind free from hate, malice or any unpleasant reflection in his direction & you will find success of your own in due time. Above all keep clean mentally, no matter what the other fellow does. I realize that necessity for myself more & more, & sometime when I have more time, I will tell you how hate & revenge for

---

[2] The photograph, which may be one of several in the Columbia collection of Crane materials, is no longer filed with the letter.

---

[1] Grace very possibly was replying to her son's letter of January 9, 1924.

JAN 12, 1924.

MRS. GRACE HART CRANE
1709 EAST 115 ST.
CLEVELAND, OHIO

Saturday 1:30 P.M.

Hart dear :—

Your letter came yester-
day afternoon while I was up
at Becky's for luncheon.
Well your decision was what
I expected it to be— if I had had
to make a prediction.
It may hurt your fathers pride
& make him wrathy, but he
will get-over it, and I only hope
that-your decision was made
entirely free from any desire
to punish him or get even
with the past.
I my self do not see how you

First page of letter of January 12, 1924,
from Grace Hart Crane to Hart Crane

past injustice is causing ———² to utterly fail in everything he does
& with every friendship he makes— He is a pathetic example & if
he doesn't wake up pretty soon I think he is coming to utter ruin.

I want you to keep in touch with your father from time to time,
even if his reply to your letter riles you. Forget it, & congratulate
yourself on having a vision which carries you beyond such trifles.

He is liable to call me up when he gets your letter, & then he
may not. Any way I am ready for him if I can know you have been
tactful & kind—& I no longer fear any thing he may do or say.
Someday he is going to understand & appreciate you very much
more than he seems to now. I think you will soon succeed in getting a job, & please do this to please me. Do not keep late hours, or
have too much company— When are you going to write if you do
not have some time & quiet to yourself? And if you don't write, how
are you going to get anywhere towards your goal? I am going to
town now so will say goodbye— If you should ever decide you
wanted the aid of a C.S. there is a wonder they say by the name of
Tweedy—200 W 72nd & Broadway—Phone Endicott 8229—

Devotedly Grace

[*Written at the top of page one:*] Remember you have a right to
ask for help in getting a position as well as cure for ills—

From Grace Hart Crane

Cleveland, Ohio
Monday Evening
Jan 14—1924

ALS, 6 pp.
LETTERHEAD: MRS. GRACE HART CRANE/1709 EAST 115 ST./
CLEVELAND, OHIO

Dear Hart:—

Grandma and I have just finished our supper—which consisted
of chicken & dumplings that were intended for yesterday— I tho't
to have Charlotte & Richard over for dinner last night, also Sam,

² Grace refers to one of her suitors.

but they had a previous invitation and so I am going to have them some night this week [.]

Your letter written Saturday late, arrived this morning—& the picture enclosed is a darling— As long as I cannot have you, I suppose this will have to substitute. If I could have the negative I should like to have it enlarged— Probably you could get it for me—

Your letter denotes a sort of panicky state of mind—because of your reduced funds & no success in landing a job— As I sent you a check in S.D. of Saturday—no doubt you have enough to eat by this time, & I am enclosing another little help in this. Now Hart dear, you must not be particular about the job you get just *now* being just what you want or paying you as much as you think it should; *Take the first thing you can get* & be constantly on the look out for something better. You can always resign & I think you ought to get *something* if only at selling books.

Pull every string you can get a hold off— See Luella Belden at once— [1] She might be able to help you land something. I think Elizabeth Smith is there, & if so she is working— Try an ad in the N. Y. Times (for which I will pay) [.] Try to get some advertizing work with some one, or on the side. Some of the big Department Stores might be able to use you in their advertizing dept— Don't become discouraged—just keep going after something night & day til you land it. Try some of these agencies I enclose—may be they can get you just what you want—and above all don't become *discouraged*— Grandma & I will try to send you enough for your needs, & if at the end of two or three weeks you haven't anything, then I want you to come home & you can write here—& get a job too.

Bill Wright is in town & looking for a job— He called me on the phone a few days ago & wished to know if he might come out & call some evening— Also asked all about you.

It is very cold out, but since starting to use the coal, we are warm as toast all over. I am feeling rested since I quit my job & very much better.

I am watching with great interest the action of Congress when

[1] A cousin of Hart's on his mother's side.

the Isle of Pines matter comes up before the Senate. We are fighting hard to defeat the treaty which would turn it over to Cuba— instead of letting [it] come under U.S. ownership where it belong[s] by the Treaty of Paris. I have been writing Mrs Upton,[2] & some of the women from the Isle of Pines who are now in Washington on the matter. It will mean a big difference in the valuation of our property down there & besides it is known by a few that one of the biggest gold mines in the world has been discovered there. But we do not want to advertize the fact to the Cubans at the present time.

I must stop now but will enclose Luella's house address & her present business is directly across the street from 26 Broadway— Roominghouse

Home address—418 W. 118 St. Apt. 62 Telephone Morningside 6656.

I think she will know where Elizabeth Smith is & I would not be surprised to find her with the American Hispanic Society[.]

I want you to write me often—

Love from us both/ from/ Ma—

To Grace Hart Crane

[New York City]
[January 15, 1924?]
Monday night

TLS, 1 p.

Grace dear:

Enclosed is a copy of the letter I wrote CA. I think you will agree with me that it is tactful and sincere. The mention and explanation of what I told you is, as you see, adjusted to match your statement of my J Walter Thompson relationship over the phone to him. Please return the copy to me with your next letter, I want to keep it on file of course.

[2] Harriet Taylor Upton, a member of the Republican National Committee. See Hart's letter of September 29, 1923.

Thanks for your fine understanding letter on Sunday, it did me a lot of good to see that you really feel with me so much. No job yet, but I have some prospects started. I'm so grateful to Grandma for her check.

Hastily,/ hart

[*Crane's letter to his father is printed below:*]

45 Grove Street,
New York City,
January 12th, '24

My dear Father:

Your letter has been on the table for longer than I had expected. I had wanted to answer it more promptly in view of your real consideration in offering me such a favorable opportunity in your business, but I've been so altogether occupied since I came back from Woodstock in looking around here for a new position, interviewing people and answering advertisements, that there has been only the evenings—when there was either someone in to call, or I was too tired to write you as I wanted.

By all this you will probably have guessed that I don't find it practical to accept your offer, kind as it is, and beyond all that I must also add in justice to us both that it would also not be honest of me to do so, either. I realize that in order to be understood in both the above reasons it is necessary that I at least attempt to explain myself in more detail than I may have gone into with you ever before, and as that is rather an unwieldy process within the limits of a letter I may only touch on a few points about myself and try to make them clear, leaving the rest to some later date when you may care to look me up in New York, provided I am here at your next visit. In what follows, father, I hope that you will take my word for it that there is no defense of my personal pride involved against any of the misunderstandings that we may have had in the past. I have come to desire to talk to you as a son ought to be able to talk to his father, that is, in a pure relationship, without prejudices or worldly issues interfering on either side, That was the basis of my first letter to you in three years—that I wrote a little over

two months ago, and I hope it may be the basis of your interpreta-
tion of what I am writing you now. I, at least, am doing the most
honest thing I know to do in whatever I have said to you and in
whatever I may say to you since that time. That's a pledge from the
very bottom of my heart.

In your letter you carefully advise me to turn a deaf ear to your
offer if I find my advertising work so absorbing, pleasant and profitable that I might in later time regret a transfer into so widely diver-
gent an enterprise as your business. You were perfectly right in pre-
supposing that I had a considerable interest in this sort of work, for
in less than three years I had got into the largest agency in the
world and was to all outward appearances very much engrossed in
carrying myself through to a highly paid and rather distinguished
position.

But if there had been any chance to tell you before I should have
stated to you I had no interest in advertising beyond the readiest
means of earning my bread and butter, and that as such an occupation came nearest to my natural abilities as a writer I chose it as the
quickest and easiest make-shift known to me. Perhaps, in view of
this, it will be easier for you to see why I left my position at J Walter Thompson's at the last of October, unwise as such an action
would be understood from the usual point of view, I went to the
country because I had not had a vacation for several years, was
rather worn with the strain of working at high speed as one does in
such high geared agencies, and above all because I wanted the precious time to do some real thinking and writing, the most important things to me in my life. The director of the copy department
asked me to see him when I came back to New York, but he has
not returned yet from out of town and I don't know whether or not
I shall return there. I told Grace that they had asked me to return
definitely because I didn't want here to worry about me: she has
enough worries as it is. But so much for that. . . .

I think, though, from the above, that you will now see why I
would not regard it as honest to accept your proposition, offered as
it was in such frankness and good will. I don't want to use you as a
makeshift when my principle ambition and life lies completely outside of business. I always have given the people I worked for my

wages worth of service, but it would be a very different sort of thing to come to one's father and simply feign an interest in fulfilling a confidence when one's mind and guts aren't driving in that direction at all. I hope you credit me with genuine sincerity as well as the appreciation of your best motives in this statement.

You will perhaps be righteously a little bewildered at all these statements about my enthusiasm about my writing and my devotion to that career in life. It is true that I have to date very little to show as actual accomplishment in this field, but it is true on the other hand that I have had very very little time left over after the day's work to give to it and I may have just as little time in the wide future still to give to it, too. Be all this as it may, I have come to recognize that I am satisfied and spiritually healthy only when I am fulfilling myself in that direction. It is my natural one, and you will possibly admit that if it had been artificial or acquired, or a mere youthful whim it would have been cast off some time ago in favor of more profitable occupations from the standpoint of monetary returns. For I have been through some pretty trying situations, and, indeed, I am in just such a one again at the moment, with less than two dollars in my pocket and not definitely located in any sort of a job.

However, I shall doubtless be able to turn my hand to something very humble and temporary as I have done before. I have many friends, some of whom will lend me small sums until I can repay them—and some sort of job always turns up sooner or later. What pleases me is that so many distinguished people have liked my poems (seen in magazines and mss.) and feel that I am making a real contribution to American literature. There is Eugene O'Neill, dramatist and author of "Anne Christie", "Emperor Jones", "The Hairy Ape", etc., Waldo Frank, probably the most distinguished contemporary novelist, and others like Alfred Stieglitz, Gaston Lachaise, the sculptor who did the famous Rockefeller tomb at Tarrytown and the stone frescoes in the Telephone Building, and Charlie Chaplin who is a very well read and cultured man in "real life". I wish you could meet some of my friends, who are not the kind of "Greenwich Villagers" that you may have been thinking they were. If I am able to keep on in my present developement, strenuous as it is, you may live to see the name "Crane" stand for something where literature is talked about, not only in New York but in London and abroad.

You are a very busy man these days as I well appreciate from the details in your letter, and I have perhaps bored you with these explanations about myself, your sympathies engaged as they are—so much in other activities, and your mind filled with a thousand and one details and obligations which clamour to be fulfilled. Nevertheless, as I've said before, I couldn't see any other way than to frankly tell you about myself and my interests so as not to leave any accidental afterthought in your mind that I had any "personal" reasons for not working in the Crane Company. And in closing I would like to just ask you to think some time,—try to imagine working for the pure love of simply making something beautiful,—something that maybe can't be sold or used to help sell anything else, but that is simply a communication between man and man, a bond of understanding and human enlightment—which is what a real work of art is. If you do that, then maybe you will see why I am not so foolish after all to have followed what seems sometimes only a faint star. I only ask to leave behind me something that the future may find valuable, and it takes a bit of sacrifice sometimes in order to give the thing that you know is in yourself and worth giving. I shall make every sacrifice toward that end.

Affectionately, your son

P.S. When you next write better address me care of G. B. Munson, 144 West 11th Street. I may not be able to hold on to this room longer than the end of Jan./ HC

From Clarence Arthur Crane

Cleveland, Ohio
January 15, 1924

TLS, 2 pp.
LETTERHEAD: CRANE CHOCOLATE COMPANY

Mr. Harold Crane,
45 Grove Street,
New York City.

My dear Harold,

This morning I have your letter, and have read it with a great deal of interest. On account of growing responsibilities which have come to me, I have felt it necessary at this time to determine whether or not you wanted to follow a commercial life. If you did, there was and always will be an opening for you here.

Your letter made a deep impression upon your father, for I realized profoundly that you are determined to follow out a life work which is quite different from what has been mapped out for me. I am not telling you your work is wrong; your letter convinces me that your decision is right, and if followed with the clear, honest purpose that is indicated, I feel very certain that you will at least be satisfied with the results you propose to obtain.

Through the mistake of wartime inflation, a rather cumbersome estimate of some things pertaining to our business, we haven't been able in the past three years, to get our institution over on the credit side of the ledger, but with the two changes which we are now making, I feel that we will emerge from our unsatisfactory state within a period of a few months, and that things will soon be better than they are.

There is such a thing as one branc[h] of a family digressing from the usual channel and upholding the intellectual reputation. I rather feel this morning that your choice is not an unwise one, and that you will be able to make a mark along more satisfactory lines than your father.

Anyway, I shall endeavor to be helpful, and to that end am enclosing you a check which will come in handy, and I want you to feel that this is not given in any spirit that you would not like.

I do not come to New York often. You must not think anything of that, for it is quite impossible for me to leave home unless all matters here are running smoothly, which is not the case at present.

As soon as you can, I want you to go up to our New York office, located at 6 East 39th Street, and introduce yourself to Mr. T. H. McClure. Mr. McClure is handling all of the territory east of Altoona. He has had some splendid experience in advertising, and is one of the most resourceful and capable young men ever associated with me. He was out here and spent two days with us last week, and I have asked him to look you up, which I am sure he will do, but better still, go in and see him.

In conclusion, Harold, let me say that I thoroughly appreciate, in every detail, your splendid letter, and you and I can turn over a new leaf in our lives so far as they concern each other. I will endeavor to keep my attitude altruistic, as well as fatherly. There is much more in this world than money, and while I perhaps may have the reputation of considering that element as quite essential, it is not for the love of money that I have ever worked. I do like accomplishment, and I have recognized the fact that my nature continually urges me on in that direction, just the same as yours urges you on in another.

I don't want your present financial status to keep you from having good food and lodging. I think it is only foolish tradition that tells us that all authors write better if they are starving. So long as you are a man in effort and good morals, you are entitled to "he" food, and your father will endeavor to be helpful.

It is quite impossible for me to write you a good letter, for I am interrupted here at the office so many times, but when I do come to New York we will have a good visit and try and establish ourselves on a good foundation where small things do not interfere with a perfect understanding.

Affectionately,/ Your father/ C.A.

From Grace Hart Crane

Cleveland, Ohio
[January 18, 1924?] [1]
Friday 10 P.M—

ALS, 6 pp.
LETTERHEAD: MRS. GRACE HART CRANE/1709 EAST 115 ST./
CLEVELAND, OHIO

Dear Hart:——

Grandma has retired to her apartment slightly peeved at me because I demanded that she *cease* talking about the house being too hot— I know she is peeved by the way she brings down her heels as she walks about above in her stockings—*very emphatic*— but I rather her displeasure would work off that way than conversing at me & I intend remaining here in the living room until I have written you your weekend S.D. If I have it ready for the postman in the morning, I do not have to take it to the postoffice myself—

First of all, I want to tell you how wonderfully fine and kind & honest & sincere I thought your letter to your father (of which you sent me a copy [)], was— It was truly a masterpiece of its kind, & I don't see how he could ever misunderstand you, or depreciate your ambitions again. Surely that ought to break down any unpleasant feelings or past grievences, & open the way for a more satisfying relationship between you two, than has existed for many years. It is bound to make him think. I am *very very* proud of the way in which you presented yourself dear boy—

Sam, Richard & Charlotte [2] are to be with me for Sunday night supper—& of course most of our conversation will center around you. Of course I shall not mention anything that has transpired between you & C.A. because I really think better results come from discussing ones intimate affairs with as few people as possible. I firmly believe that just as "too many cooks spoil the broth" so do

---

[1] References to the letter that Hart wrote to his father suggest that Grace's letter was written on Friday, January 18.

[2] Sam Loveman; Richard and Charlotte Rychtarik.

too many minds interfer with the successful solution of one's problems.

I am providing escallaped oysters & broiled bacon [,] tomatoe aspic salad, hot rolls, celery, preserves, pickles, coffee cake & canned plums, for our meal—which is set for seven o'clock.

Sam is a very busy fellow, between his job which keeps him about three nights a week, and his Theater Workshop duties for the remaining nights, I found it difficult to find a time when he could come out here— He calls me up quite often, & Christmas day came out and called, I really appreciated it very much and also his genuine admiration for you. He says he misses you *terribly!*

Katherine Goetelle has taken a position of Society Editor on the Times Commercial, so Sam says, I never see her— [3]

The Collvers [4] & their "Around the World" party are in New York now & sail tomorrow (Saturday) on "The Resolute" for a five months sail.

There is just the faintest possibility that I may get a trip to New York for a few days, perhaps the last of next week— A friend of mine who is contemplating starting a new shop for sport clothes & hats etc. may be able to pursuade her boss to let me go to New York with her to buy her first bill of goods. I have said I would go for my expenses—so if I should send you a telegram that I was coming you may know why. But I do not believe there is any chance that I will get the offer.

Well I must turn out the lights & go to bed.

I hope this finds you well & in good spirits— If not a job, some good prospects. Keep me informed about *everything,* and always know that you have my love, my sympathy in what you wish to accomplish & my sincere faith in your ability—

Devotedly / Grace—

[3] Kathryn Goetelle, often called in this correspondence by her maiden name, Kathryn Kenney, was a friend of Crane's from Cleveland. She later wrote a column for the Cleveland *Times Commercial.*

[4] William B. and Pauline Colver, of Cleveland and Chicago. A lawyer and newspaper editor, Mr. Colver served as chairman of the Federal Trade Commission from 1918 to 1919.

To Grace Hart Crane and Elizabeth Belden Hart

[New York City]
[Postmarked January 19, 1924]
Friday night

TLS, 1 p.

Grace dear and Grandma:

I don't want you two to be without some word from me over
Sunday—so (especially since I have such goods news to tell) here's
an inkling of my present situation. Yesterday morning came the
finest letter from CA that I have ever had. To put it briefly, he has
finally come around not only to accept my interests in writing as
genuine, but he actually commends them and says that he wants to
help me some in the future. How quick he may reverse his opinions, is, of course, not to be conjectured, but I am glad that I wrote
him the letter I did containing such a thorough explanation of myself, and his reply seems a sincere and cordial document—including
a check which, along with your recent generosity, helps me out a
great deal just now. He didn't seem to resent my refusal of his offer
at all. Altogether, I've felt unusually jolly for the last 36 hrs. . . .

I finally got around to take Elizabeth Smith [1] out to dine tonight
and we've been together all evening. She's been working up in
Macy's book department, you know. It just happened that at the
next table was a warm friend of mine, Susan Jenkins, to whom I
had sent Elizabeth to look for work when she first came to town in
Nov. (Sue edits a magazine) Sue had nothing to offer then, but she
had just heard this evening from one of her contributors that he
needed a secretary, and wouldn't Elizabeth care to accept her recommendation. Well, Liza nearly whooped with joy, and we went
up to the man's house forthwith, closed the deal, and Liza thinks
she'll be much happier thus at $25.00 per week than her book store
job had provided, at 18. She's an awfully nice girl and I hope to see
her as often as time permits.

Last night at Hal's for dinner. Chas Brooks in town, but I shall

---

[1] Hart's cousin. See the poet's letter of November 21, 1923.

happily not see him, he bores the Smiths and they aren't behind-hand in announcing it. Gorham was invited to lecture at a very spiffy Yale literary club today—all about Waldo Frank, Burke, Cummings[,] Cowley and me,—the younger writers, in fact. I hope the curtain went up all right and that he spoke loud enough to be heard above a saucer! He's back in town now for the rest of the winter unless he has a hint of a relapse, but I guess he won't.

I'm being considered in four or five good offices for copywriting. I expect to hear something final from them all on the same day and be uncertain which to grab. No use describing them as yet, but they are as pleasing propositions as I have heard of possible to myself and my present experience. Meanwhile I make a few calls every day at chance sources. This is a poor letter, but it is quite late and you say to get to bed early. I'm afraid, dears, it's too late now (tonight) to observe your very kind and sensible orders, but the nearest approximation now is a quick "GoodNight", Love/ Hart

Hart's quest for employment temporarily succeeded when the Pratt and Lindsay advertising firm hired him for $50.00 a week. He announced the new job in a short note to his mother.

To Grace Hart Crane

> [New York City]
> [January 21, 1924?]
> *Monday*

ALS, 1 p.

Dear Grace:
Begin a new job (ad. writing) next Monday—hired today 15.00 per week more than Thompson's paid.
I'm due out to dine—hence more later.

Love to grandma/ Hart

To Grace Hart Crane and Elizabeth Belden Hart

[New York City]
Jan 24—'24
45 Grove St

TLS, 1 p.

Dear Grace and Grandma:

My slight note was reassuring enough, I presume, to stave off any misapprehensions about my present state—even though I haven't written you as promptly as I had expected. Tomorrow I go up to see my boss preparatory to beginning work on Monday. It may be simpler at Pratt and Lindsey's than it was at Thompsons because it's a much smaller company and I shall have many less people to take orders from and to please: so far as I know yet Mr Pratt is the sole authority, and he decides things quickly. It only took him five minutes of talking with me and looking at my samples to make up his mind. I spoke up for my salary and got it without quibbling. Pratt is one of those racehorses, at least in manners, but with the added money I'm to get there 'll be more instigation to please than Thompson's offered.

Just a day after I met Pratt along came a note from B W Huebsch, who evidently had some proposition to talk to me about. It only said to phone him, which I did today, and we're to have lunch together on Saturday just for the personal pleasure. I told you, I guess, that I find him one of the smartest men in New York —and he certainly is the most cultured publisher here. I am thinking of submitting my book to him when it is ready, in preference to Gorham's publisher who is pretty commercial and pettyfogging.

To give you many details of my activities and contacts since I got back to the country would take four or five pages. I was prety blue for awhile and poor, as you know, but that didn't prevent my plunging into a lot of varied company, meeting new people and revisiting the old, dining here and there and enjoying free tickets to modern concerts, plays and exhibitions of modern painters, etc. New York is abristle with its first acceptance of European art and artists this year. It's become fashionable for the high hatted uptowners now to buy Matisse's paintings, Picasso, and all the other cubists, and there's a great amount of "patronizing" going on. And talk, talk, talk!!! My visiting list has reached its limits. I'll be glad to quietly come home evenings and work when I get into the treadmill again. I know about the most interesting and vital people in New York, but there isn't time to take advantage of all that constantly. Someday when we get together you will be astonished at the flow of anecdotes and amusing trifles that'll just naturally begin to rise out of me, but which can't be written about.

I was so glad to hear about the plans for the Loveman-Richtarik dinner. Sam wrote me a letter about two weeks ago, but I haven't had time to answer him yet, and don't know when I will. There is simply *too much* to tell him of interest, and that's the way it is with Waldo Frank. A card arriving today from the Sahara desert reminds me that I haven't answered his letter from Paris which came when I was out at Woodstock, and that was over a month ago! I'm still expecting the possibility of a telegram from you announcing your arrival for the week-end, but don't worry too much if you have failed to make it. I might make a flying trip myself not so long away./ hart

To Grace Hart Crane and Elizabeth Belden Hart

[New York City]
Tuesday
Jan 29th, '24

TLS, 2 pp.

Grace dear and Grandma:

I enjoyed both your letters so much, and its too bad that I can't do anything at present but gasp back a few salient details about my job and how things are going.

I started in yesterday morning, and have been working like a tiger since then, of course. So far I like boss and office very much. There is only one other copywriter besides myself, and he is an old friend of Gorham's. The two stenogs and office boy are the only otherwises. I, personally and alone, occupy the nicest niche I ever sat in—15 stories up, and the corner of the building with windows, of course, on two angles. Perfect privacy and quiet and a desk and chair that are quite massive and comfortable. Ever[y] hour or so the office boy comes in inquires if I want anything, otherwise I press a neat button on the corner on the desk and service is immeadiate.

I always get mixed up in some strange topic. This time it is a book on cheese, how happy it makes you and how good it is for tissues stomach, and bowels, etc. A large importing house wants it, and I've been having to write it in no time. I hope to finish it tonight. Life certainly is amusing. I've been quite happy up there the last two days.

Late last week I called on CA's representative here, as he had asked me to do, and found quarters about as large as the old ones on 33rd st, and a very cordial reception. They're about to move up to 42nd stree[t],—way over east beyond the Grand Central—also, he said, planning to open district offi[c]es in Phila and Boston. I was presented with a Crane boxed fruit cake and invited to call for more candy whenever wanted. Your advice about CA and money was just in line with my intentions. I'm glad to let things ride this easy for even a long, long time—so much has already been accomplished, and I doubt if I'd feel very easy right now about accepting anything like an allowance from so fickle a source. I'm very pleasantly disposed, however, as you know.

I don't believe that I told you about my second interview with B W Huebsch, the publisher. It was at his request, and when I got there and found what I wanted I fairly whooped. His office isn't ready for it yet, but he said that he had been wishing that in time I might enter his employ as a kind of personal assistant to him and his responsibilities. The combination of my advertising and literary jud[g]ement, he said, was rather rarely found, and he thought I would be able to read manuscripts, attend to certain details of printing, and superintend the publicity where certain others would be too limited for that range.

I felt considerably complimented, especially after so brief an acquaintance with him. As you [know]—that sort of work is what I have been looking for for years in New York.

Well, inasmuch as I told him that I was at least temporarily bound to work at this agency, I would have to postpone his offer at least a few weeks. But he wants me to take lunch with him a couple of weeks from now and let him know how I like my present work, and discuss the prospects with us both as they stand then. Right now, I am only interested in making as good as I can at this job, and I'm not going to let that prospect, alluring as it is, absorb me much. However, it's fine to have it to occasionaly ponder, and, of course, something may develope.

I had loaned my room during the last few days to Elizabeth Smith and the writer she was working for. Last night when I came in she was almost in tears,—said he had just paid and fired her, and that he couldn't stand the room. Well,—Eliza was a little foolish in not finding herself a separate room away from the club sorority, Smith Girls Home, or whatever it is—so that she could have carried on his work under pleasanter conditions. I know that in time I should have had to ask [her] to seek other arrangements because— after all, on Sat afternoons, I would have felt the lack of a place to go and work. She's out of the Macy book store possibilities, too, now —and running all over town for something else today. It's too bad, but I did my best,—even to the extent of putting down money for a phone installation (which she said was necessary) when I don't have any use for it myself. She'll find something, though, I'm sure.

Your notes on Sam and the Rychtariks were pathetic. Everyone almost who writes me from Cleveland seems to be so unhappy. I have ceased writing to Katherine—her Christmas card was the only reply to my last letter: and Chas Harris stopped because I told him —as he asked me to, what I thought about one of his sketches. Sommer so says Sam, goes from worse to worse, and so on. It's all too bad, and it's too bad too that you both don't see the wisdom of renting that chilly house and living more snugly and cheaply next winter in a steam heated apartment. But I won't dig on that any more now.

If I get paid in time I want to send you the fare to the opera and Mary Garden, but I haven't found out yet when I get the check,—

weekly, or bi-monthly as at Thompsons. Well, so long, dears, and good luck in reading this hasty jumble. I'll try to do better later in the week.

your affectionate/ Hart

From Grace Hart Crane

[Cleveland]

Saturday 2 P.M.

Feb. 2—1924.

ALS, 6 pp.

My dear Hart:—

We were both very much satisfied with your last letter, and it is very gratifying to know things with you are going along as nicely as they are now.

It would do your heart good to see how much grandmother gets out of your letters. She carries them around in her apron pockets, & puts them on her bed table so she can read them after she is fixed for the night. I have many a smile to myself that she doesn't notice.

It seems to me that nothing could be more to your liking or advantage in the rather near future than an association with Mr Huebsch such as you described— The work ought to bring you into the environment & experience that you would want, and has a number of desirable possibilities. But I agree with you— Let it work out, & in the meantime be as much interested in doing your present job its full justice as you are capable. It may lead you in to just as satisfactory work as the other, & anyway do your best while you are at it.

I am sorry Elizabeth had such a disappointment. You will do all you can to help her land another job—I know. Why doesn't she try copywriting— Perhaps Florence Spencer can help her to something.

There is really no news of interest with which to make this letter the least bit alive. I have been working very hard with Margaret for two days at a semi winter housecleaning, including clean curtains[,] windows etc. It certainly means hard work to keep ahead of the work.

Father Crane made us a long call the other morning & told us much about his California trip— He is now planning to return in May for a month, accompanied by Ella. Frank Ross writes that he & Blanche & Verna, are planning a West Indian Cruise, & next summer hope to go to Norway, Sweden, Iceland [,] Ireland etc—for about two months. Much the same trip as Zell took. I suppose Zell is somewhere near Alec Moore, our Embassador to Spain—who is now on a visit to this country.[1] It is thought by some that there is a serious side to their friendship. I certainly wish she would marry him, & invite me to visit her at Madrid.

Did you know that Ernest Block was soon to be in New York at some musical affair where all of his compositions are to be played— [2] Wouldn't you like to see him?

Edna St. Vincent Millay is to give a reading of her poems at the Statler on next Friday evening— I see by the list of patrons [and] patronesses that [it] is to be quite a high brow affair. I may go. I want to keep in training, so that my behavior will be correct, when you become the rage & tour the country giving readings & selections.

Well I must be on my way to market—

Grandmother sends all her love & so do I.

Devotedly / Grace.

To Grace Hart Crane

[New York City]
Sunday
Feb 3rd, '24

TLS, 2 pp.

Grace, dear:

I had meant to have a special delivery for you and Grandma today, but the time I usually get for such writing was taken up this week, and yesterday afternoon I had a long talk with CA up at the

[1] Alexander Pollock Moore was ambassador to Spain from 1923 to 1925.

[2] Ernest Bloch, the composer. Crane did not attend Bloch's performances in New York that winter. See his letter to Charlotte and Richard Rychtarik, March 5, 1924, in *The Letters*, pp. 177–78.

Waldorf. He phoned me at my office yesterday morning and asked for that time. He had been here since the morning before, but had been so tied up with engagements, he said, that there had not been time even to phone me before. Frances was also along, but I didn't have to see her. They are returning home tonight.

We talked from 3 until five—and in the end it was very satisfactory. He began in the usual arbitrary way of inquisition into my attitude toward business life, etc. just as though there had been no exchange of letters and recent understandings on that subject, and did his best to frighten me into compromises. I parried these thrusts very politely, although it was very hard many times not to jump up and begin declaiming. However, I realized this time that my ordinary language about such topics is simply beyond his comprehension, so I quietly kept on doing my best to explain myself in terms that he would understand and not resent any more than possible. He finally ended by accepting me quite docilely as I am: in fact there was nothing else to do, especially as I did not so much as hint that there was anything I hoped he would do for me—or was every planning that he would do for me.

Then he talked to me, as usual about his own affairs, and finally came around to asking my advise on a new product of his, its proper naming, and the best way to advertise it. He is going to send me data on the subject, and wants me to write some ads for him about it! You see, from this alone (and I have also other grounds to judge by) that he really respects me. He inquired in detail about you and Grandma and seems to have the right sort of intere[s]t in you. He also came around to aggree that I was quite exemplary of both sides of my family in not being made of any putty—knowing what I want to do, and sticking it out despite adversities. At parting he spoke of his anticipations of more extended contact with me on his next visit here, urged me to write him often, and thrust a greenback in my pocket. So that's that!

The work at the office goes smoothly enough to reassure me somewhat. My copy on the cheese book went over without any changes whatever, and that makes one write the next job a whole lot faster and imaginatively. Your own dear special has just come, and I'm awfully glad to know that things are alright and that my letters are worth something to you in spite of the haste they always have to be written in.

Tonight is the opening of a new play at the Provincetown Theater and I am invited to attend with Sue, who is the wife of James Light, the stage director.[1] Through Light and O'Neill I know the whole crowd over there now, and it is very interesting to watch this most progressive theater in America in the details of its productions,—going behind scenes, watching rehersals, etc. I have changed my opinions, or rather prejudices, about Clare Eames since meeting her there and watching her work in two recent productions. She isn't at all stiff or pompous,—and as an artist she is very flexible and exact. O'Neill, by the way, recently told a mutual friend of our's that he thinks me the most important writer of all in the group of younger men with whom I am generally classed.

Last night I was invited to witness some astonishing dances and psychic feats performed by a group of pupils belonging to the now famous mystic monastary founded by Gurdieff near Versailles, (Paris,) that is giving some private demonstrations of their training methods in New York now.[2] You have to receive a written invitation, and after that there is no charge. I can't possibly begin to describe the elaborate theories and plan of this institution, nor go into the details of this single demonstration, but it was very, very interesting—and things were done by amateurs which would stump the Russian ballet, I'm sure. Georgette LeBlanc, former wife of

---

[1] Light directed the revival of Anna Cora Mowatt's *Fashion; or, Life in New York*. The cast included Clare Eames, Stanley Howlett, Helen Freeman, Walter Abel, Mary Blair, and Charles Ellis.

[2] Susan Jenkins Brown remembered: "Early in February of 1924, Hart took me to a 'demonstration' at the Neighborhood Playhouse on the Lower East Side, given by pupil-disciples of G. I. Gurdjieff, himself a disciple or a colleague of P. D. Ouspensky, the Russian philosopher and author of *Tertium Organum*. . . . Hart and I were irreverent but well-behaved, even at the sight of Mr. Gurdjieff visible from our sixth-row seats standing in the wings dressed in a costume resembling that of a lion-tamer. . . . Startlingly prominent in the well-filled auditorium were Margaret Anderson . . . and her companion, Georgette LeBlanc, former wife of Maurice Maeterlinck—because they stood, side by side, in the third row with their backs to the stage most of the evening, facing the audience. . . . Georgette was got up in a peculiar, exotic style, especially as to make-up, which she had used to emphasize, rather than conceal, departures from the facial smoothness of youth. . . . Hart was so convulsed that he had to duck his head." Quoted from *Robber Rocks*, p. 25.

Maeterlinck, was seated right next to me (she brought them over here, or was instrumental in it, I think) with Margaret Anderson, whom I haven't seen since she got back from Paris in November. Georgette had on the gold wig which the enclosed picture will show you,[3] and was certainly the most extraordinary looking person I've ever seen; beautiful, but in a rather hideous way.

If I can scrape up any of the recent newspaper notes on the dances of these people I'll send them on to you. These certainly are busy days!

Love, / Hart

From Grace Hart Crane

[Cleveland]
Tuesday—
Feb 5—1924

ALS, 8 pp.

Dear Hart:—

Your interesting letter of Sunday came a few moments ago, and grandmother and I have had much pleasure and satisfaction in reading it. It contains interesting news, & I feel that you are happy, and must feel much satisfaction in the way things are adjusting themselves with your father & yourself— It also seems to me that the interesting group of which you apparantly are one, must not only stimulate & keep you from becoming bored, but must make you feel that you have reason to expect you will arrive yourself, one of these days.

It would appear that you handled your father very tactfully during your last interview and though he protested he was finally won over and acknowledged that you evidently knew what you wanted. I thoroughly believe that more & more he is going to regard your opinion worth while along the matters he asked you about—and after a while the old unpleasantness & strain will all be ironed out.

Tomorrow morning at 8:10 I go to Garrettsville to attend Rollin

---

[3] This enclosure is lost.

Belden's funeral at 1 o'clock.[1] Mattie phoned us last night that he died very suddenly Sunday, of heart failure. He & Cora have been living in Detroit for a number of years. The funeral will be at aunt Margarets & burial at Farmington. Poor Mattie, with aunt Margaret ill & to care for, & then this to go thro' with.

I did not tell Grandma last night[,] she cannot stand such news as she once could. Anyones death who is at all near to her, seems to almost prostrate her.

She has decided not to go down with me— It is a hard trip for her even under the best of conditions. I am afraid this experience will shorten aunt Margarets time.

Sunday night I had for supper Nancy, Mary (Nancy's sister) Edna & Glenn.[2] You know the crowd & also where Edna is there is plenty of noise. She has recently returned from a months business trip to New York—& her recital of her experiences, together with her new bobbed & dyed & permantly waved hair, furnished plenty of zest for the occasion. Glenn altho the only male present, seemed perfectly at ease, and just purred around all evening.

I was much interested in reading a recent article in The Monitor, describing the exhibitions & exhibitors in the recent display of Modern Art at the New York Galleries—and from what I read I judged it was those which you recently attended & wrote me about.[3] It mentioned Maurer, Davis at Meyhe's, & Living Art, Demuth, Marin[,] La Chaise & Robinson at The Montross Galleries. It also spoke of Alfred Steiglitz & said Sherwood Anderson had written an enthusiastic introduction to one of the catalogues.

There was a very handsome picture of Madam Le Blanc in a recent Sunday Plain Dealer—mentioning that she was considering entering the movies. I am always glad to get any thing pertaining to

[1] Rollin Belden was Elizabeth Belden Hart's brother. Margaret was Mrs. Hart's sister, and Mattie was Rollin Belden's daughter.

[2] Grace's friends, Nancy Sommers, Edna Moore, and Glenn Whistler.

[3] Mrs. Crane had read an article by Ralph Flint entitled "More Modernism in New York" in the Christian Science Monitor, February 2, 1924, p. 11, which reported exhibits of the works of Albert H. Maurer, Arthur B. Davis, and Paul Klee. Sherwood Anderson and Alfred Stieglitz had written appreciative notes in the Maurer catalogue. Much of the article was devoted to an exhibition at the Montross Galleries of works by Braque, Bonnard, Matisse, Signac, Picasso, Demuth, Marvin, Lachaise, and Robinson.

the new artists & art before the New York critics, & besides I must keep posted if I am to eventually find myself the parent of a celebrity! So don't grow discouraged in your efforts in bringing up mother. I may surprise you.

All my love—/ from/ Grace.

From Grace Hart Crane

[Cleveland]
[February 9, 1924?] [1]
Saturday 9. A.M.

ALS, 3 pp.

Hart dear:—

I do not want you to miss getting your S.D. from me—even if there is no news at all as is the case today. It is a lovely sunny winter day. This is Mrs Kirks birthday & we are invited to Hazel Carliles for luncheon to celebrate the occasion.[2] Grandmother is anticipating a good time with her old cronies & I am going to enjoy seeing Hazels new adopted baby girl for the first time.

I went to Garrettsville Wednesday to attend Rollins funeral— It was very dramatic with poor aunt Margaret propped up in bed in the next room, & her family around her during the services. Mother did not go— I felt it would be too much for her—as she seems not to be very well—& cannot stand those strains as she used to.

I shall look for a letter from you tomorrow—

Zell is in New York, probably at the Waldorf—better call her up — I think she wants you to as Helen has written for your address—

Loads of love/ from/ Grace—

[1] The reference to Rollin Belden's funeral suggests that Grace wrote this letter on the following Saturday, February 9, 1924.

[2] Netta Kirk was a friend of both Mrs. Hart and Mrs. Crane. Hazel Carlisle was Mrs. Kirk's daughter. See Grace Crane's letter of October 3, 1917.

To Grace Hart Crane and Elizabeth Belden Hart

[New York City]
Saturday—Feb. 9, '24

ALS, 1 p.

Grace dear, and Grandma:

There is so little to write that I wouldn't waste the stamp if I
didnt know that at least an envelope is expected from me around
Sundays.

I enjoyed your letter of last Tuesday but was awfully sorry to
hear about the decease. You have probably been engrossed in the affair most all the week. As far as I'm concerned, there has been little
but steady plugging at my job. I hope to get to bed early tonight
and sleep until 10 tomorrow when I'm invited to breakfast with
Gorham & Lisa at their place along with Jean Toomer.

I never heard how that heavy black-grey suit of mine came out
after repairs, cleaning, etc. Could you send it on—before things
begin to warm up?

Sorry not to be more exciting today. I didn't have time to see Zell
who was at the hotel when CA. was here.

Love,/ Hart

Finding that the advertising firm of Pratt and Lindsay had
overextended itself, the personnel director dismissed Hart after two
weeks of employment. Thus began a "terrifically hard period" [1] for
Crane when everything conceivable went wrong. First, B. W.
Huebsch turned him down for a position in his publishing house.
Then the personnel director at J. Walter Thompson missed several
appointments for an interview that Hart had arranged. Possibilities
of employment with other publishers and advertisers never materialized.

As his meagre funds diminished, Hart found it increasingly diffi-

[1] Quoted from Hart's letter of April 15, 1924, to Charlotte Rychtarik, in the
Columbia collection.

cult to find a place to live. The return of Louis Kantor, from whom the poet had leased the room at 45 Grove Street, necessitated his moving to Waldo Frank's former landlord's house at 15 Van Nest Place; when his credit ran out there, he sought refuge in James Light's apartment at 30 Jones Street.

Hart was at this time entirely without funds from his parents and was left, as he wrote to Charlotte Rychtarik, "simply on the hands of friends." [2] Grace and Mrs. Hart could not support him with a regular check and suggested he return to Cleveland. Though his father initially sent him some money, C.A. was taken up with his wife's steadily declining health; Hart's letters to him often went unanswered. Had it not been for Susan Jenkins, Eugene O'Neill, and Malcolm Cowley, the poet's problems would have been greater. Jenkins provided meals, O'Neill had the poet stay with him in Connecticut, and it was Cowley who secured Hart a position as a copywriter at Sweet's Catalogue Service. The new job began in the week of April 10.

To Grace Hart Crane

[New York City]
45 Grove Street,
Feb 13th, '24

TLS, 1 p.

Dear Grace:

There's a pack of troubles to listen to shortly so don't mind too much.

In the first place, I have been sick with the grippe for three days, but am getting better. In the second place I lost my job on Monday last—because, plainly, the man who had employed me had overestimated the volume of his business. I had heard that he was prone to extravagences of such sort from one of the other men in the firm before I took the job, but I took the chance. He couldn't say a thing against my work or copy as an excuse, but he had to invent some

[2] Letter of April 15, 1924.

fantastic pretenses that I saw through right away as grounds; it was a dirty deal, and the only hope I have is that Huebsch is still considering me for the position there, which, if it eventuates, will certainly be better than anything I have ever had yet. To make matters worse, just a moment ago I got a letter from the man from whom I have been renting this room and its furniture. He is coming back to take possession again on the first of March! I have only fifty dollars on me in the meantime, and my 30 dollars rent for this remaining month on the room has not been paid.

So, you see how matters stand. I am going to try some feature articles for the newspapers while I am looking for another job, but I have not yet got paid for them yet, nor even made connections, nor written them. *I shall do my best.* Right after this letter I am going to write CA and ask for a *loan* or a hundred dollars to carry me over. If he can't do that at 6% interest I think he is rather careless, to say the least. Otherwise I shall fare as best I may among my friends. They have been so kind, and they so respect my genius that probably you need not worry about anything serious happening to me. I feel quite indomitable. I shall not return to Cleveland to live permanently, at any rate, until I am such a wreck that I might as well go there as anywhere else. I am so sorry about all this, because I had been planning on saving the first sixty dollars possible to save and returning for a week end to see you and dear Grandma. You don't know how I have longed to see you! But we must wait. It may be long or a short time still before that is possible. There are opportunities for quick and plentiful money in the newspaper field if I am lucky.

Meanwhile, there is the enclosed insurance payment to think about. I can't spare a cent now. If I should ever be killed by accident, on the other hand, it means 4,000.00 dollars to you. I've been paying all I could on it so far, and it rests with you and Grandma at the moment, as to whether or not it is to be carried on. Pay, as directed, at the Hanna Bldg. Offices, if you like.

Thanks for your dear Valentine. I'm your's too./ Hart

To Grace Hart Crane and Elizabeth Belden Hart

Ridgefield, Connecticut
[Postmarked February 19, 1924]
Monday

TLS, 1 p.
LETTERHEAD: BROOK FARM/ RIDGEFIELD, CONNECTICUT

Dear Grace and Grandma:

Eugene O'Neill took me out here last Sat. and I'm having a great feed and time for a few days. Probably will get back to New York tomorrow or Wednesday.

I hope I'll get you a longer letter tomorrow, but we have to drive into town to mail it. etc. Anyhow. this will tell you where I am. etc. until I get back.

love.—/ Hart

From Clarence Arthur Crane

Cleveland, Ohio
February 21, 1924

TLS, 2 pp.
LETTERHEAD: CRANE CHOCOLATE COMPANY

Mr. Harold Crane,
45 Grove Street,
New York City.

My dear Harold:

Your letter of February 14 did not come to my attention until last night. I have not been feeling at all well of late and went out of town for a few days, returning only yesterday. With your kind permission I will write you in a few days more fully.

I can't quite make up my mind, Harold, where you and I stand. It would be easier for me to determine this if you had not injected one paragraph in your letter, and just because it annoys me I am going to repeat it to you. You say, "And there have been other complications which may afford you the pleasure of vindictiveness against my ideas and standards," etc. Does it ever occur to you that I could get any possible pleasure out of assuming that attitude towards you or your work?

I do not agree with what you are doing, but that is really none of my business. I wanted you to accomplish something along worthwhile commercial lines, but you failed to respond to the call. You seem to be perfectly satisfied to be poor, financially, and yet you require money the same as every other human being. You do not require very much, and you have not made any unreasonable demands, but I can't seem to make up my mind that you are going to, in the end, arrive at any accomplishment which will keep body and soul together, unless you take a real interest in your advertising work.

We could not get any results here unless the people who worked for us were interested in what they were doing, and when you told me in New York that you had no interest in what you were doing I felt as though the way was going to be very hard for for you.

If your writing could only be a side line, a sort of pleasure to be taken up in the evening, an ideal to be followed as an avocation rather than a vocation; if you would only think of it just as men play golf, then I would see things differently.

Anyway I will write you again in a few days.

Affectionately,/ *Father*

To Grace Hart Crane

[New York City]
45 Grove Street
Saturday
Feb. 23rd, '24

TL, 1 p.

Dear Grace:

Your two fine letters were here waiting for me when I got back from Ridgefield Thursday. It's too bad that so many things had to hit you and Grandma at once. I can't say much about this—nor anything else right now.

CA hasn't answered my letter at all as yet, and I don't know what on earth I am going to do. I'm glad you are taking my attitude and present predicament so very sensibly, and also to know that you would care to have me come back to Cleveland for awhile in case I have to. Huebsch has practically given up the idea of taking me on, and he wouldn't be ready to start me in for several weeks, anyway, during which time I can't guess how I should live. There is another job possible with the Crowell Publishing Co. but I haven't enough money left now to wait for that. Life is hard to keep going without some slight sum or capital to draw on in emergencies!

I enclose a reminder just received on my insurance,—as, in your recent extreme busy-ness, you may have overlooked the former notice.[1] If I send back any books or other packages soon "collect" I hope you will receive them. As soon as I get some "light" I'll let you know.

Love,

To Grace Hart Crane and Elizabeth Belden Hart

[New York City]
[February 26, 1924?] [1]
Tuesday

TLS, 1 p.

Dear Grace and Grandma:

You both are so wonderfully kind and sensible—that you don't know the full extent of my gratitude! I am writing at the earliest opportunity to say that CA wrote me a really sincere and fine letter, explaining that he had been out of town when my letter came, and enclosing at least half the amount I had asked him for as a loan. It

[1] Hart enclosed a premium notice from the Equitable Life Assurance Society. The bill was for $9.32.

[1] The references to the Huebsch letter of February 25, 1924, and to his father's of February 21 suggest that Hart wrote this on Tuesday, February 26, 1924.

came yesterday, but I have been rushed to death looking for a place to move to, and even now haven't found what I want. But at least I have the wherewithal now to *get* it when I do find it, and that relieves me more than I can tell you.

I still have my cold which seems to have developed into a chronic cough, bronchitis, or something. I thought for several days that I should have come back to Cleveland, but I am determined to stay now, despite this attack of homesickness. I have a terrible fear of the reaction I would have to Cleveland,—after I had been there a month or so! And, also, somehow I feel that at the present stage of my renewed relations with CA it is better that I be not too close to him! He has gone far enough to say that even though he does disagree with me on my chosen career, etc. that it is none of his business, and he doesn't make any of the old stipulations on my conduct, location, etc. etc. that he used to. It marks a real advance, I think, either in his spirit or in his diplomacy (I am not sure which it is, so far).

Huebsch wrote me this morning the enclosed note, having told me last week that he would be likely to take on a personal friend of his in preference to myself. It's alright all around, I guess. Meanwhile, unkwon [unknown] to be [me], the Thomas Crowell Co has been considering my samples with interest and wants to see me soon. Now that I have enough to "move me" I feel tremendously better. And I can get on the chase again in a few days. I was "done" so dirty on that last job that, truly, I was quite upset in every way.

I'll write you very soon. Saturday is the last date for moving. Write me here until then,—later, care Munson, 144 West 11th St. unless I get word to you before.

Gratefully and affectionately, as always,/ Hart

[*Written in ink on the side of the page:*] You are right: please don't ever approach CA on my account unless I especially ask you.

[*Huebsch's letter to Crane is printed below:*]

25 2 24

Dear Mr. Crane,

I have about decided to try it out with the other man (E. T. Booth), because of certain aspects of his experience which I think will be particularly valuable to my needs. My only regret at getting one good man is that I have to pass another by.

Thanks for your time and good nature. It is not impossible that we may someday work together if you should still be willing.

Cord [i] ally yours/ B W Huebsch

To Grace Hart Crane and Elizabeth Belden Hart

Mar 1st, '24
15 Van Nest Place
NYC

TLS, 1 p.

Dear Grace and Grandma:

I really have been quite lucky in finding so comfortable a room as this,—the one that Waldo Frank used for awhile before embarking for Europe. At last a comfortable and good sized bed, too! And a fine bathroom in the house with hot water, etc. etc. My two days and nights here have rested me considerably, and it is nice not to have to make up the bed, sweep and dust. Of course, eventually I'll pay less and have an unfurnished place, but this is better for now. I can settle things more simply and get around to look for work quicker.

I'm really not far from my old place at Grove St.—just about four blocks up, but moving was ardurous none-the-less. Suitcase after suitcase of books, then pictures, knicknacks, pillows, victrola, and then the grand voyage with that frightfully large trunk of mine that is too big to even get up the stairs here! Thank God—its over with for awhile!

I guess I told you that I had tried to get in touch with Mr Leffingwell at J Walter Thompsons, pursuant of his suggesttion when I left there last October. Each time he was out,—but the other day he invited me to take lunch with him on next Tuesday, so, you see, there may be something there again. It shows, at least, that they had no fundamental dissatisfaction with me there when I left, supposedly for the West Indies. I have not been able to see the man at the Crowell Publishing Co as yet, but Monday will see me inter-vi[e]wed and we'll see what comes of that.

Gorham has just been in. He is writing much these days, and the Dial recently took an important and long essay of his on the critical methods of Van Wyke Brooks (who got the Dial prize this year).[1] G's next book isn't far away—at the present rate of his writing now. It is fine that Lisa is willing to support him thus until his standing is sufficient to enable him to "put over " his critical tenets on a wider audience than the editors of our magazines seem at present willing to grant him. Waldo Frank sends me postals from the Sahara desert and Spain. Stieglitz has a new photograph exhibition opening Monday at the Anderson Galleries, along with some paint-ings by his wife, Georgia O'Keefe. There is much excitement about the new play by O'Neil at the Provincetown Playhouse about a negro who marries a white woman.[2] He has been threatened by the KU Klux and the woman who is to take the leading part gets frightfully insulting letters from anonymous maniacs all over the country.

I'm feeling quite well, cold is disappearing, and my spirits have been much braced by the fine way you are taking things and the kindness of CA (about which I wrote you). Write me soon and lots.

Your grateful and affectionate son,/ Hart

[1] Van Wyck Brooks received the Dial Award in 1924 for his contribution to American literature. Though *The Dial* published other articles by Munson, it did not publish his article on Brooks.

[2] *All God's Chillun Got Wings*, directed by James Light, opened at the Prov-incetown Playhouse on May 15, 1924. When rehearsals began in March, O'Neill, his family, and Light, as well as the leading actor and actress, Paul Robeson and Mary Blair, received numerous threats.

To Grace Hart Crane and Elizabeth Belden Hart

[New York City]
[1924?]
15 VanNest Place,
March 8th (Saturday)

TLS, 2 pp.

Dear Grace and Grandma:

From what I have been reading in THE WORLD you must have been having a great time lugging water jars over to Wade Park spring![1] And I'm sure you have been in a rage, at the persistent carelessness and folly of Cleveland's municipal administration of it's water supply. One wonders why that important detail is never drastically amended: every year there is some new outrage—excused as an unforeseen accident.

It has been like spring here. The weather veering from bright skies into showers. The wind blew a little snow this morning, but not a handful, and now there is brilliant sunlight, the wind continuing in almost a gale. It is always so pleasant to here you mention spring in your letters: the note is so genuine. And while I like winter, too, and don't respond as entirely to that season as you do, I sympathise with you much. It always makes me hope that we shall have a place in the country some time where I can come and go, and bring friends occasionally that will charm you, while you can have endless days and weeks for quiet reading and gardening. That beats life in the city all to pieces!

Since lunch I have been around to the printer with Gorham to see about the new number SECESSION containing my Faustus and Helen poem complete.[2] I guess it will at last be out on Monday, and I shall then send you a copy right away. I think I'll send one to Mrs. Brown also as well as to my other friends in Cleveland. Do you

[1] On March 6 it was discovered that the Cleveland city water supply had been tainted with phenol and was unfit to drink. Residents were forced to get their water from the spring in Wade Park.

[2] The publication history of "For the Marriage of Faustus and Helen" is somewhat complicated. Part II was published in *Broom*, 4 (January, 1923). Two editors of *Secession*, Kenneth Burke and Gorham Munson, accepted the entire

ever see her any more? And how about Sara Baker, MJ and the rest? I would like to look up Jimmy Wolff sometime if you will send me his address. As I remember it was on Charles Street, the very street I now am living on (one side of it between two blocks is called VanNest Pl).

I am paying ten dollars a week for this room, cheaper than what it used to cost me at Mrs Walton's, and much cheerier and pleasanter. As such places go nowadays, I have a bargain, and I am very anxious to keep hold of the room even if I have to cut down on meals and other things. I do wish I might have my heavy black suit sent to me now while it is still cool enough to wear it comfortably. I would rather save the light suit I am now wearing out fast—for the summer. Will you remember to send it to me sometime next week, please? I think you said that it was quite ready.

My dear, you know I can't tell you much more about CA's letters than I have been doing without retyping them or forwarding them on for you to return. I am telling you all there is in them that is definite enough to matter, and while I have thought of sending them to you to read successively as they came,—something has made me feel that while there might be no harm in it nor real injustice, at the same time and in the sum of things, I think it a little confusing, somehow not quite right. I can't put it into better words, but perhaps you will feel what I mean, and not misunderstand and think me obtuse or ungrateful, or unfeeling toward you. You see, it's just because this present relationship between himself and myself was started on such an entirely fresh basis, without any more elements of the past entering into it than could be helped. And also, because, really I don't yet have much idea as to how he really feels about me. He is a long time answering my letters, and I now haven't heard from him for over two weeks and don't know when I'm going to. I don't feel that there is anything at present between us but a fragile thread of feeling and communication: perhaps there

poem for publication in the September, 1923, issue; however, John Brooks Wheelwright, who was in charge of printing the magazine, decided to use only Parts I and III on the theory that Part II had already appeared. Wheelwright's decision precipitated a bitter quarrel among the editors. It was not until the winter, 1924, issue of *Secession* that a complete version of the poem appeared.

never will be anything more. At any rate we can speak on the street without getting upset about it.

The people up at the Crowell Publishing Company have been moving and changing there offices around, so a decision about myself has been delayed until next week. My luncheon engagement with the man at Thompsons was called off finally on account of a conference he was involved in at the time: we expect to lunch together sometime next week. I have been around to other places, but have struck nothing as yet. Still I am not discouraged; I don't think I ever get discouraged any more in that black-as-night way that I used to. Please don't worry about me too much, and things will take care of themselves alright within a few weeks. I shall soon need more money but if CA won't complete the amount of loan which I asked him for, then I'll borrow it from someone else.

The news about Zell's plans is very interesting; I hope that it goes through. Wouldn't it be great for you to be coming in town together for dinner with me on some summer evening! Whenever you hear about Zell's coming to NY be sure to let me know, as I would like to see her whenever possible.

My love to you both!/ Hart

To Grace Hart Crane

15 Van Nest Place,
New York City
March 15th, '24

TLS, 2 pp.

Dear Grace:

Of course I was glad to get your letter eventually, and be relieved of the possibility that something disastrous had happened to either you or Grandma to keep you from writing. And yesterday came your note about the suit, which I'll be awfully glad to get as soon as the rails can carry it here.

Just now I haven't a cent,—that's literally true, and must ask O'Neill for a loan this afternoon. My rent for the last week has not been paid, and I've given the landlady a box of Mary Gardens to appease her for the time being. None of my calls this last week have turned up anything particularly promising, and if Mr Leffingwell, of J Walter Thompson's, doesn't meet me for lunch on Monday as he has promised I think I'll go up an[d] scalp him this time.

On my visit to CA's new office and store room on E 42nd St day before yesterday I was told that shortly after his visit to NY (when I saw him) he had had a "nervous breakdown". He wrote me in the one letter which I've had from him since then that he had just returned from out of town and had missed my letter when it first arrived—on that account. On further inquiries at the office, I found that he has been back in Cleveland for sometime, so I guess he has had plenty of time to read my two letters sent to him since then,— the last one written last Sunday, and appealing for the little loan. But no word comes back, either of help or denial, and I guess he is not so interested in me as to care one mite what happens. He may be trying to draw be [me] back to Cleveland by these tactics, but he's a long way from the right method, I can only say!

I am in a strange state: feeling very well (everyone keeps saying, "how well you look!") and yet not knowing what is going to happen next. Yet I know that there is a limit to the uncertain trend of my existence as it is now, and I'll have to drive a truck, stevedore, or dig ditches if my profession can't afford me some relief pretty soon. Is it any wonder that I don't write you oftener than once a week when there is so little pleasant to tell?! At least, you, in Cleveland (however much you may dislike that place) are sure of a place to sleep next week,—which is much more than I am sure of!

About my poem:—there wasn't any other place to publish it but in "Secession".[1] The main pity of that is, that I didn't get any money for it. Gorham had to pay for the entire issue himself. But if you look over the rest of the contents you will see that I am in very good company,—there is nothing in the issue which is not both dignified and creative. My work is in advance of the times, and I'll probably have to wait for a good while before getting my dues. At present—only writers, themselves, and a few advanced intelligences

[1] Hart is referring to the publication of "For the Marriage of Faustus and Helen."

understand me. That has been true of many others in the past. But I am proud of my admirers.

Keep on writing me here—at least until you hear further from me. If I have to pile out I can still come around for mail for a few days. I'm sorry I cannot be more interesting in this letter, but what's the use, when the present state of things overbalances anything pleasant or entertaining I might have to tell.

My love to you both,/ Hart

To Grace Hart Crane

[New York City]
15 Vannest Place,
March 23'24—Sunday

TLS, 2 pp.

Dear Grace:

I expect to be beheaded very neatly in your next letter for this failure to page you with the usual Sunday special delivery. However, the whirl during the last three days has been too much for me to write you anything but the merest note, and I've kept on postponing even that in favor of a lengthier pause. Before anything else I want to thank you for the fine long letter you wrote, its assistance and thoughtfulness and its unwavering confidence in me—the last-named most of all! And the suit came, too,—and seems to look better than ever on me.

Your advice about self-reliance, etc. is, of course, quite right. But there are times when everyone I know has had to ask for a little help. This has been one of those times with me:—otherwise you would not have known by this time quite where even to write me. I went over an[d] saw O'Neill, but finally didn't ask him for any loan whatever. Instead, almost right out of the sky the next day came a cash gift from a friend of mine who was managing editor of the Dial when my first poem was accepted there,[1] and who simply had heard from others that I was in a predicament. Consequently,

---

[1] Stewart Mitchell (1892–1957), managing editor of *The Dial*, 1919–20.

my rent is now paid for two weeks more, and I can keep on feeding a few more days. I've been invited out for dinner considerably, and have accepted more generally than I should if I had a job—for the obvious reason that free meals are a considerable help. The Habichts last Sunday evening, Claire and Hal on Friday night, and I generally eat with Gorham and Lisa one night a week, if not oftener. Then there are numerous other friends of mine about whom it is usel[e]ss to mention much as they are too unfamiliar to you. I certainly am developing some interesting and perhaps valuable connections here as time goes on, and my natural manners seem to induce a certain amount of popularity and comment. How strange it seems to me sometimes to be gradually meeting and talking with all the names that I used to wonder over years ago,—and to find how, in most cases, I am valued as an individual—for the attributes most natural to myself! It does give me more confidence than I ever thought I should have.

"Well,—and what about the job?"—I can hear you asking, quite naturally. And I can only answer,—"Well, I don't know—yet". I have been up to see some people who advertised in the paper last Sunday, and they are considering me—as they sit in their offices up on top of the Flatiron Building. Mr Leffingwell (curse him!) of Thompsons baulked me again. I shall not attempt another interview,—there, I mean. This is (for the next six weeks) the dull season for all advertising work, but I am pretty sure to land something within the next two weeks. Malcolm Cowley, the poet, who works at one of them says that there are about to be two vacancies —and I'm sure to get a bid at one of them within the next month. So things are. I don't see any use at present on planning to return to Cleveland (much as I should love to see you!) I have a revived confidence in humanity lately, and things are going to come very beautifully for me—and not after so very long, I think. The great thing is to Live and NOt Hate. (Christian Science, in part, I think; and a very important doctrine of belief. Perhaps the most important.[)]

I hope that CA will realize just a little bit of this truth before it is too late for him to think of anything at all,—even his business! But we are really so far apart, I'm afraid, that I have few ways of knowing whatever he does think about practically anything. I shall keep on doing my best to NOT DENY him anything of myself which he can see as worth realizing (which means *possessing,* also) meanwhile not depending on him either in thought or deed for anything whatever. He has not answered my letter yet. And despite what you say about his probable need for quiet and recuperation, he must be reading his mail all the time. The trouble is that he might much prefer me off the scene anyway,—and it's just possible that such a thought was behind his urging me when he was last here to go to the Isle of Pines (not a bad idea, I think, myself), but I realize your feelings on the subject. His probalems are many, and I think he may realize in time that they are more than strictly those concerned with his business, however much and fast they multiply. What I love to think about is the way YOU have come through! And myself! It's a great game. We may realize that we are always losing, but it means a lot to realize that; also, all the while you are losing you are also gaining! And I think we both understand what that means.

Tell Grandma that I hope to hear directly from her whenever she can get around to write me. She is famous in NY already,—for her vitality and temperament! Gosh! I hope you both come down here this summer for a visit to Zell's place.

Write me soon, and forgive my tardiness!

devotedly,/ Hart

To Grace Hart Crane

[New York City]
Saturday
March 29th,'24

TLS, 1 p.

Dear Grace:

Your sweet letter came this morning, and I'm only sorry I can't answer it as it deserves. But there's nothing to say. The "sparrows" are all I can see at present to feed me during next week, but, of course, nothing to worry about much. I'm thinking of taking some kind of boat job on a West Indian cruiser,—United Fruit, Munson line or some such. I'll try and write again early in the week when something may have developed.

my best love to your both,/ hart

To Grace Hart Crane

[New York City]
30 Jones Street,
c/o James Light, Esq
April 3rd, '24

TLS, 2 pp.

Grace, dear—

I got all my stuff moved over here yesterday: my landlady being expeditiously "settled", I'm camping here with Sue and Jim who have made me feel quite welcome. I don't know what to say yet in answer to your last letter, but I certainly want you to know that I am duly appreciative for all the kindness it contained. I would appreciate having the carfare to return to Cleveland,—but right now I'm afraid I should use it for other things—once I had it in hand, —so you see, you had better not send it until I am more resolved on pulling up anchor here. Of course I've been simply a case of friendly charity for about a month now, but somehow I feel I am worth a slight investment and so far don't feel that I have been so gross an imposition as many other cases that I hear about. In other words,—the poorer I get—the prouder I get, in a certain sense,—a reaction to the damnably unjust mechanics of business everywhere prevalent. But, of course, there's a limit to my expectations—and I *might* come home after two weeks more or so. But I can say nothing definitely, absolutely nothing. Don't worry about me any more than you can help: it's not so bad to miss a few meals, and there are one or two people in New York that I can't make up my mind to leave without trying a little longer. Besides,—when you got me back again I wouldn't be so thrilling, nor such good company as anticipated after a few weeks—however much we long to see each other. As I remember things I'm a pretty unwieldy person around the house; isn't that so?

I just had lunch with Luella Belden down in the Wall Street section. She wanted to be remember[ed] to both you and Grandma. Lillian [1] expects to be in Canton starting her law practice during the summer, she says. And their mother has been far from well since her fall last fall.

CA's silence can mean only one thing to me now—an absolute denial and confession of complete indifference—if not enmity. I don't mind about the money,—but he has not even written me any kind of words,—and right on top of the most evidence of cordiality that he has ever put on paper to me! Well, so it goes. . . . He is the strangest animal I ever heard of.

Of course I can't understand why you want to go out to California when you have such a perfectly lovely place in the West Indies, —all your own, with certain traditions and associations, and with (after all) as pleasant a group of people as you will run into in Cal. to associate with. And for me to be struggling around here in dirty NY when money is actually being paid out of the estate to *hire* strangers to live in such a delightful place as the Island—is one of those jokes of fate that make words seem futile! But everything in my family on both sides seems always to have been quite "balled up", and that's one reason why I begin to feel no use in worrying about responsibilities toward such a waste of time, energy and emotion—to say nothing of money. I'll probably end up quite a bum,—but I [2] shall try to keep enough at a distance so that you won't feel too compromised. There are two or three oportunities in sight for me now,—and I'll let you know as soon as possible if anything matures. In the meantine, take this letter with a grain of salt: I've a bad headache at this moment and am rather overwrought nervously. In some ways I am very happy, however,—and so please take that for what it is worth to you, and keep on smiling.

My love to dear Grandma, too—/ Hart

---

[1] Lillian Belden, a cousin of Hart's and sister of Louella.
[2] The word "I" is repeated in the text.

To Grace Hart Crane and Elizabeth Belden Hart

[New York City]
30 Jones Street
Friday—April 3rd, '24 [1]

TLS, 2 pp.

Dear Grace and Grandma:

I know you will be glad to know that I have just acquired a good connection,—starting in work early next week for Sweet's Catalogue Service (the job I mentioned a while back and in reference to Malcolm Cowley, my friend and brother poet who has been working there). I get less than the last job to start with, but I think there is a good opportunity there for me to work up to more in time. It's catalogue selling rather than the human interest sort of copy which I have always written before, and it involves less hypocrisy and more scientific knowledge—all of which pleases me provided I am able to grasp the necessary details fast enough. I feel quite encouraged, however, and feel certain that I'll be given a decent trial. (Did I tell you that I have since learned that I was hired in the last place entirely on the momentary whim of the president, and that as soon as the secretary and treasurer found out about my presence he raised a hell of a row, all of which resulted in my dismissal. There wasn't enough work to have done to have kept me busy there anyway. I am told that nobody has been hired since then in my place, and there is no intention of such, etc.)

Recently I've had long and interesting letters from Sam, Charlotte, and Kathryn Goettel (the latter working now on the Commercial, musical criticism, drama, movies and social). The Rychtariks leave for NY on the 28th,—and I hope you see them before they leave. Charlotte writes in a rather hectic state of mind, and seems very sorry not to have had the time to come out and see you recently.

We've been having a great blizzard here most of the week, but today it is warm and promising again. I hope that your Sunday is

---

[1] April 3 fell on a Thursday in 1924.

light and merry now,—especially since you have the assurance that I have acquired some work again. . . . . . You don't know how glad I am!

I probably won't be able to move away from my hosts here for about two weeks—when I'll have some money. So keep on address-ing me here, *care of Mr James Light.*

I wa[s] dreadfully sorry that I was able to send you nothing on your birthday—not even a telegram! But I did think of that date before your letter including mention of it did arrive. So if that knowledge is worth anything to you—you'll know that I think more than I sometimes give evidence of doing. We'll all make up for lost time some of these days!

Love, as always,/ Hart

Hart had reasons other than his new employment to be "glad"; over the spring he had developed with Emil Opffer the deep-est love he had ever felt, and soon he was writing to Waldo Frank that this love had reached the level where the "flesh became trans-formed" and "where a purity of joy is reached."[1] Opffer and his family offered Hart an ambience he needed so badly: Emil was a merchant seaman, his brother, Ivan, was an artist, and his father, Emil senior, was the editor of the Danish weekly *Nordlyset.* By April 13, shortly after he began at Sweet's, Hart moved to the Hotel Albert for several days and then to 110 Columbia Heights in Brook-lyn in the building where the Opffers had rooms. Hart was pleased to discover he was living in the same building (and later in the same room) from which Washington Roebling had directed the construction of the Brooklyn Bridge half a century earlier, following the death of his father, John Roebling, the designer of the bridge. Crane's new job, his attachment to Emil, as well as his room with its excellent view of the bridge, the Statue of Liberty, and the Man-hattan skyline, helped to release a new wave of creative energy.

Crane was glad as well for his friendship with Susan Jenkins,

[1] Quoted from Crane's letter to Waldo Frank, April 21, 1924; published in *The Letters,* p. 181.

Malcolm Cowley, Kenneth Burke, and James Light. Often they would gather in John Squarcialupi's restaurant on Waverly Place to spend the evening talking and drinking. Perhaps Malcolm Cowley in his poem about those evenings, "The Flower and the Leaf," captures best Hart's mood at this time:

> And this man, who has spent his day
> wrestling with words, to make them mean
> impossibly more than words convey,
> now pours them out like a machine
> for coining metaphors. He stalks
> between the tables. His brown eyes
> gleam like a leopard's as he talks
> with effortless brilliance, then grow smaller
> and veiled, the eyes of a caged fox.

The words of poems Hart wrestled with over the summer and into the autumn were those of Parts II, III, and IV of "Voyages" and "Lachrymae Christi" (a poem he had written more than a year before and was now revising to include in the volume he hoped to have published), and the "Harbor Dawn" section of *The Bridge*.

To Grace Hart Crane

New York City
Sunday, April 13th, '24

TLS, 2 pp.
LETTERHEAD: Hotel Albert, Eleventh Street & University Place, New York

Grace, dear;

This letter heading must look familiar enough to you! I'm here for a couple of days until I can find a room. Simply had to get away from the pleasant but fatiguing social life where I was staying as a guest, but, of course I could not accomplish that until my first pay day.

The work at Sweet's is quite difficult, and very detailed and exacting, at least until one gets on to it thoroughly. My friend Cowley, has been very nice to me in explaining the customs of the place, and what I have turned in so far has not been severely criticised. The first week is the hardest, and that is over with, although I am frightfully tired.

Today has been very warm and sunny, and I imagine it has been likewise in Cleveland much to your added happiness. I got a fine letter from Waldo Frank the other day (he is in Spain now) and am enclosing it for you to read and return to me directly, please. I think it will give you some satisfaction to read what this man thinks about me, who is hailed in Europe today as our greatest novelist.

You will excuse me, I hope, if I break off rather briefly tonight, with the promise of a better letter to you in the week. I really am quite exhausted. You haven't written me much about yourself and grandma lately, and I certainly hope you will this week.

my love as always to you both!/ Hart

Keep on writing me at Jones Street until I get a steady address. I may move over to a wonderful section of Brooklyn facing the East River, Brooklyn Bridge and the NY skyline—later on. It would be cool and quiet for the summer, quite reasonable, and marvellously beautiful from the window.

[*Frank's letter to Crane is printed below:*]
Morgan Harjes Co
Place Vendome
Paris

Madrid
Mar. 28, 24

Dear Hart

How glad I was to have your letter a day or two ago, even tho it contains the bad news about your job. Surely, your mother and grandmother will see to it that these interims are not a hardship for you! It would be a disgrace if too much of your energy had to go through the channels of physical discomfort.

I have just come through a month of intense writing: and it has left me depleted even more than usual, for I was only superfic[i]ally rested when I began. This makes difficult writing to you the letter I wish to write to you. But perhaps my message, however

clumsy, will be better than silence just now, my friend: so I'll
chance my ina[de]quate co[n]dition. You are a man of genius. Of
this I have not the slightest doubt. This means that your personal
life is involved as an expression of a universal, of a divine force,
more immediately, more intensely, more consciously, above all more
articulately than is the usual case of men. This means, moreover, inevitable dislocations in your living in the personal human plane.
What you speak of as the strange illogic which has led you, and as
the miracles of progress, point merely to this: that you are moving
in a design which rational life does not contain and can therefore
not measure or judge. So you are right, dear Hart, when you feel
that whatever vagaries you may have gone through (I do not know
of any, but I'll assume them), I shall understand, for I have my eye
on your inner principle. But the question is more complicated than
that. Our human existence is essential in the sense of a tool: we cannot articulate God, as we are called to, without a well functioning
personal body, any more than we could write a poem with a punk
pen or typewriter. Therefore, you must look to the job of getting
your body, personal as it is, attuned to this cosmic urgency to whose
expression you devote its energy and its life. For otherwise, it will
fight you, fight your expression .. hinder you like a pen which at
the crucial moment ceases to put down your words. [*Written at the
side of the page with an arrow pointing to this place in the paragraph:* This comparison is bad, of course, because the life of the
body *enters* the expression, & the pen does not. All the more reason
why it must be in good shape.] That is why, my friend, you will
study more as time goes on, the problem of conserving your physical and emotional forces. But you cannot solve that problem con-
ventionally. That is where criticism of you now is wrong. You must
experiment and discover the own logic of your adjustment, which
will most surely be unlike any other logic in the world because of
the law that Revelation is one, but all of its forms are unique. . . . .

Everything you say about the new novel pleases me.[1] When I first
wrote it I remarked that it had one less dimension than my other
books. There is no harm in this. I realise now that I am going back
temporarily to expository prose (this novel, and Spain), because I

---

[1] Frank is referring to his novel *Chalk Face* (New York: Boni & Liveright,
1924).

am recasting my rhythms. When I return to the novel, you will see that my masses have become slower, vaster, more approximate in their details to the ultimate immobility which they mean to express. I am delighted however that you and Gorham find good in To Life. (What do you think of calling it simply The Story of John Mark). Every one who has read it so far, thinks it an achievement. But I am convinced it is secondary, even as you and Gorham say......

The man in Paris who must see your Marriage of F and H is *Valery Larbaud,* 71 rue du Cardinal LeMoine, Paris. I have spoken to him of you, but had nothing of yours to show him. He knows ten times more about Am. letters than Gide. When I introduced him to Cummings and Gorham and Jean, I regretted having nothing of yours to back up all I said to him about you. Send him Secession.

ever my love, friend,/ Waldo

[*Written at the top of the letter:*] I like the idea of your being in my room. I hope you stay. Give Mrs and Mr Bollini my kind regards. They are good folk. But dont drink too many highballs—with Mr B......

From Grace Hart Crane

Cleveland, Ohio
[April 17, 1924?][1]
Thursday, P.M.

ALS, 6 pp.
LETTERHEAD: MRS. GRACE HART CRANE/ 1709 EAST 115 ST./
CLEVELAND, OHIO

My dear Hart:—

After a long hard days cleaning with Margaret, I am very tired and my letter will probably show it—but I want you to have a letter for Easter—so here goes.

[1] The references to the Hotel Albert and Easter (which fell on April 20 that year) suggest that Grace wrote this letter on April 17, 1924.

When I saw Hotel Albert on the envelope of your last letter, I knew you were again either in transit or in flight, for that is the place you always light to get your breath. It was a great relief to know that you were all right etc. & right here my dear I wish you to realize that you treat me very badly indeed when you let almost two weeks go by without sending me even so much as a postal. It isn't fair at all to me Hart, & you should always write me much oftener than that—if only a note or a post card—& even if there is no news, or things are all wrong— The last line I had from you stated that you were at the Lights, and had secured a job— Then dead silence for two weeks—and I began to imagine everything—your job fallen thro, or you were sick, blue[,] discouraged—everything which you were not—as I now know. Now I won't *have* such neglect & I won't love you at all any more if you ever repeat this indifference. Its the only responsibility you have toward me—and I think you should not overlook it.

I read with much interest & surprise, the letter of Waldo Frank's and was delighted to discover that his concept of life was so spiritual. You have always disliked to have me even mention the word "God"— It seem[s] to rub you the wrong way—irritate[.] And here I see Frank speaking of Him most confidently & familiarly to you & I see that he refers to him as, "inner principle" "Revelation" & Spiritual Force. You must or ought to know that that is the God I believe in & that C.S. teaches, & we are his idea's, or as Frank puts it, "Revelation is one, but all of its forms are unique. ["] We each have our own separate individuality, & place in the Universe. His reference to "cosmic urgency" is something you would do well to think about. In fact most of his letter has to do with what seems to me a *very loving* effort to direct your thought to see the great importance of controling your physical body & emotional forces, so that there will be nothing to restrict, obstruct, or defeat your purpose. Latterly I have felt that unless you could resist the temptation to spend so much time with your interesting & no doubt fascinating associates, you were not going to accomplish anything either at your job—or your writing, & for that reason I had thought you had better come back here where life outside of your work would be less interesting & you could have more time to write. Your salary goes further here

& I still think you would be better off here—but I would not urge —no[r] want you to come back to please me, against your judgement.

I never want you to plan to go to the Island or give it another thought— It is too absurd to consider, & if your father advised you to go & thought I should go it was only because he wished to remove us as far as possible from where he would be likely to see any duty to us, for himself. If you knew the troubles & complications that are constantly confronting me with that property, you would want to stay as far away as possible—that is the way I feel, & I don't propose to sink the few remaining dollars that we have, & bury my life down there.

I shall hope to know very soon that you are in your own room again, & that you are comfortable & happy again.

If you go to Brooklyn, won't you find that it consumes too much time in going back & forth, to be practical. Why don't you go out near the Columbia University or College, where there is good air & some tennis courts handy for the summer?

Just as soon as you can I want you to come home for over Sunday — You could probably get Monday off so that you could have two days here— I will pay your fare one way— Come while the apple blossoms & lilacs are out.

Zell will arrive at the Waldorf either Sunday or Monday morning for the Press convention which will last one week.[2]

Make an effort to see her, & she will expect it & wants to see you.

Nancy Sommers is also to be in N.Y. over Easter until Tuesday night at the Vanderbilt. How I wish I could afford to go down for a few days vacation—I really need it very much.

Grandmother & I will probably go to Church Easter morning & for a ride in the afternoon. In the evening I am expecting to go see Duse—[3] Zell sent me her pass—but I do not know what seats it will draw.

If you received a package we sent you the first of the week, you

[2] Zell Deming was attending the annual Associated Press convention that was held in New York from April 22 through April 24.

[3] Eleonora Duse (1859–1924), the Italian actress. Grace never saw her, for Duse became ill in Pittsburgh and died on April 21.

will have new ties & new socks for Easter. I sent them c/o James Light.

I shall hope to hear from you *very soon.*

All my love—/ Grace

To Grace Hart Crane and Elizabeth Belden Hart

[April 20, 1924?] [1]
110 Columbia Heights
Brooklyn, NY

TLS, 2 pp.

Dear Grace and Grandma:

As I said in my wire, your gifts were an almost overwhelming surprise and certainly both a necessity and a delight. In each case the selection was perfectly to my taste, so I need not envy the haberdasher's windows so much for awhile as I have been lately.

It is, as usual, hard to believe that this is Easter. It has been raining and shining, and raining *while* shining ever since I woke up this morning. I had intended to attend mass at St. Patricks (the Fifth Avenue structure, very beautiful, which you will remember) but a drinking bout with some Danish friends of mine last night proved to much for an early rising. Emil Oppfer, an old man but very distinguished as an editor and anarchist, and whose two sons, Ivan and Emil, jr. I am very fond of, dines at a certain Italian restaurant on West Housten St every evening, and it was there that the party was heldM. .[2] In fact he is the same old fellow whose room I am to have in this same house when he moves out at some indefinite date, but soon. I have a small room in the front now, which is quite clean and comfortable. But when I get his present room on the back of this same floor, I shall have the finest view in all America. Just imagine looking out your window directly on the East River with nothing intervening between your view of the

---

[1] Since Crane mentions Easter in the second paragraph, he probably wrote this letter on April 20.

[2] This "M" occurs three times in this letter and once in his April 24 letter.

statue of Liberty, way down the harbour, and the marvelous beauty of Brooklyn Bridge close above you on your right! All of the great new skyscrapers of lower Manhattan are marshalled directly accross from you, and there is a constant stream of tugs, liners, sail boats, etc in procession before you on the river! It's really a magnificent place to live. This section of Brookyn is very old, but all the houses are in splendid condition and have not been invaded by for-eignersM. . . It's quieter than 115th Street, by a good deal and that's saying a lot for any locality near one's business in NY. In fact I can ride to Times Square, under the river and all and without changing cars on the subway in twenty minutes. This is the finest place to write in the world, and it will be well for me to be re-moved just as much as I am here from my friends over in Manhat-tan. I'll be able to do more reading and writing.

You'll be glad to know that everything is going along in excellent style up at my office. As I said, the work is very exacting, but I am catching up on some of the special requirements necessary which I lacked somewhat at first. You cannot easily imagine how difficult it has been moving here and there, for such a long time without any money. There will be a burden of debts to carry I don't know how long now, but good sleep and a place that you feel is your own help a lot in alleviating. I'm glad I shall not feel that I am extravagent about the rent hereM. . . What I pay here is about the lowest on record,—six dollars a week. The Back room will cost 2 more, but that will be very reasonable.

I'm awfully anxious to hear all about you both. Our correspond-ence on both sides have been curtailed a good deal of late, and I hope you realize that it has been quite unavoidable on my own part. In about ten days the Rychtariks will arrive, at least so I un-derstand. Wouldn't you care to ask them out to the house some eve-ning before they leave, or at least make a call on them? I have con-jectures that they will probably not return to Cleveland at all *to live* when they get back from Europe, but I may be wrong about that. At least Charlotte wrote me a very spirited letter in which she announced plans of storming the city here for work for Richard on their return from abroad. The dear lady has the usual expectations of recognition which are liable to cause her a great deal of pain before shes through, I imagine. It takes months and years of steady effort to get any sort of artistic recognition in New York,—at least for the kind of work that Richard does. But, of course, this is the place they should be, and I have always thought it unwise for them to spend so much money on this trip when it might well suffice to start them out on their board and keep here where they so much want to be. But do phone them, whatever happends. . . They think a great deal of you, and it would be too bad to have them leave town without some little fuss being made.

Be sure to return the letter from Waldo in your next to me. I think it contained some splendid praise and understanding. I keep thinking about a visit to you these days, but I guess it's a long way off yet. But sometime before next Oct. we'll have to get together. I'll get a few days vacation on pay if this job continues.

With much thanks and love,/ Hart

To Grace Hart Crane

110 Columbia Heights
Brooklyn, NY
April 24th [1924?]

TLS, 1 p.

Dear Grace:

Just a word to show you that I am doing my best after the high dudgeon you gave me in your special of last week!

I called up Zell and Helen at the Waldorf day before yesterday, and while I have not been able to see Zell on account of her preoccupations and rush with purely official matters, I had dinner last evening alone with Helen, later going to see the movies with her.

Helen expects to stay over until sometime next week, and will be the guest of Dorothea Evans [1] for awhile. She wants me to beau them around a little, which I'll be glad to do provided I'm not too tired. Just now a few days of early spring heat in the stuffiness of

[1] Dorothea Lewis, a friend of Helen Hurlbert's from Meriden, Connecticut.

the office and under considerable eye-strain have made me feel rather fagged. But there is nothing serious pending.

I was sorry to hear about Dr Hurd's death, and I wrote a note to Kenn[e]th [2] at once after reading your letter. There's no more news at present, but I'll try to get you a special delivery on Sunday. That means, of course, devoting my afternoon to the matter, generally, and if something comes up, as it generally does, you mustn't always mind. I do the best I can.

Lots of love, Hart

Hart was surprised when C.A. called him in New York on April 26, because it was the first communication he had had with his father since Mr. Crane's letter of February 21. Still preoccupied with his wife's illness, Clarence was quite enigmatic during the visit with his son.

To Grace Hart Crane and Elizabeth Belden Hart

New York
Monday, April 28" '24

ALS, 1 p.

Dear Grace & Grandma:

—Not a moment over the week-end to write you. I'm awfully tired and need sleep. CA. here and around with me until midnight Sat. and Helen & Dorothea last night and again tonight.

I see CA. again this afternoon before train leaves. He has been very pleasant, indeed, this time, and I'm still at a loss to explain things. But more about that later.— I must rush out to lunch now.

Love,/ Hart

[2] Kenneth Hurd, Hart's childhood friend from Cleveland.

To Grace Hart Crane

[Brooklyn, New York]
110 Columbia Heights
Sunday afternoon,
May 4th, '24

TLS, 2 pp.

Dear Grace:

The hectic pitch and pace of the last ten days has left me about flat, to say the least. You have no idea what it means to put in the hours of social service that I have been compelled to lately and keep up my efforts at the office to say nothing of the travelling back and forth miles and miles between times on the subway. But thank God I think I have at least a full week ahead of me now without one engagement. I may have to spend an evening with Helen and Dorothea again (they were after me for this afternoon and evening, but I managed to escape) but they'll not succeed in keeping me out until dawn, as happened once before. Dor[o]thea seems to have taken a great fancy to me, but I have neither the money nor the time to fulfil her ideas of entertainment. She's a nice girl, but has the conventional attitudes about gallantry, and as she has nothing whatever to do in the world but look about for people to entertain her pleasantly, I guess she'll find a more suitable escort than myself without much trouble, if, in fact, she has not, probably, already. Please don't mention any of my attitude to Helen when you see her, because I wouldn't want her to think that her visit had caused me any strain whatever. Of course it wouldn't have, ordinarily,—it was simply the fact that so much had been taken out of me beforehand and also at the same time she was here CA, the Rychtariks, and several others were equally importunate.

Even now I don't seem to be able to relaxM. . But I've wanted to get this letter off to you as soon as possible, and somehow yesterday afternoon I HAD to flop down on the bed and sleep. I'll try to tell about CA's visit first. . . . . . Of course I had no idea that he was coming. The first I knew was his voice on the phone last Saturday morning, inviting me to have lunch with him at the Commodore,

and later go to a matinee. We did both, later having dinner together and going to another show in the evening. My understanding of him, I must say, is quite as vague as ever. He made no effort
to explain his long silence, nor did I question him directly on the
motives involved. He was however, more companionable than I
seem so far to remember at any time in the past. Told stories,
talked about his business, enthused about NY as a splendid candy
market and spent a good deal of time talking about the splendor of
the S[c]hrafft's establishments which he had been inspecting with
the gen. mgr. He seems to be trying to sell out his chocolate business, but the man he wanted to sell to didn't have enough money to
interest him, it seems, and I have my doubts about his having
wanted to sell out at all anyway. He says he can't make money on
either candy nor food in Cleveland at the prices that the people insist on there, and cited the enormous differences in prices between
his places and S[c]hrafft's, etc. insisting that people in NY were
willing to pay for good things, whereas people in the west made a
great rumpus over nothing. I'm sure I don't know what he means
by all this talk about his continual loss of money. But he has always
talked that way, and whether he makes or loses, I like to think, is
much the same to me. We had dinner together before he left on
Monday evening, and he mentioned pleasantly as I put him on the
train that we had had "quite a reunion". It will probably take a
number of years to convince me one way or the other on that
matter—after the way I have seen things turn out in the past. I suggested his phoning you next morning when he got in town. Did he
do so? He seemed to react well enough to the suggestion. Frances
was not along, of course.

I missed connections with Charlotte and Richard the first day
they were here, so I didn't see them until luncheon on Thursday.
Then we had a grand blow-out Friday night, with Gorham and Sue
Jenkins along. After dinner we all went over to Sue's place and
danced until after midnight. Richard showed his pictures to Jimmie
Light, and there may be a chance, I think, for R to make a place
here for himself in theatrical work when he comes back. Charlotte,
as ever, however, seems to be the central spirit in that family. I enjoyed her very much. She was simply giddy with love of NY and

doesn't see how she can ever live anywhere else again. We didn't get as much time to talk about you as I had wanted, there being others along, but Charlotte is very, very sympathetic to your viewpoint and very fond of you, so whenever it was possible we managed to draw aside a little for snatch words. In seven weeks I suppose I'll be seeing them again, which time certainly is not as long a visit as I expected they would take.

Your sweet letter of last Th[u]rsday made me so want to peep in on you! That bright clean room on the third floor would mean a pleasant rest for me. I hope the weekend that I am destined to spend with you is not too far away! I'm well liked at the office, I think, and there is every reason to feel that I am as permanent a fixture there as I may care to be. The work is very exacting of the eyes, however, and a time may come when I can switch to something else in the same field but with less strain on me. However, everything is OK except that, and plenty of sleep and rest for awhile now may alter that somewhat.

William Wright is supposedly still in Cleveland and in advertising work. He wrote me—just a line asking me to write—when I was moving from Grove Street, but the letter and his address got lost and I never wrote finally. Kathryn Kenney must know where he is because in her last letter to me of about a month ago she said "Who is Bill Wright, and Why?" She enclosed clippings of her theatrical and movie critiques which she has been doing for the Commercial, also. But I haven't had time to answer her yet.

I'm sorry to have been so late this week with you, but you must understand how it has been!

Lots of love to dear Grandma, too—

your/ Hart

To Grace Hart Crane and Elizabeth Belden Hart

[Brooklyn, New York]
110 Columbia Heights
May 11th, '24

TLS, 2 pp.

Dear Grace and Grandma:

I am told that this section of Brooklyn around here (Brooklyn Heights) is very much like London. Certainly it is very quiet and charming, with its many old houses and all a little different, and with occasional trees jutting up an early green through the pavements. I have just come back from breakfast and saw some tulips dotting the edge of one of the several beautiful garden patches that edge the embankment that leads down to the river. It certainly is refreshing to live in such a neighborhood, and even though I should not succeed in acquiring a room that actually commands the harbor view I think I shall always want to live in this section anyway. Mr Oppfer, who has such a back room in this house, has invited me to use his room whenever he is out, and the other evening the view from his window was one never to be forgotten. Everytime one looks at the harbor and the NY skyline across the river it is quite different, and the range of atmospheric effects is endless. But at twilight on a foggy evening, such as it was at this time, it is beyond description. Gradually the lights in the enormously tall buildings begin to flicker through the mist. There was a great cloud enveloping the top of the Woolworth tower, while below, in the river, were streaming reflections of myriad lights, continually being crossed by the twinkling mast and deck lights of little tugs scudding along, freight rafts, and occasional liners starting outward. Look far to your left toward Staten Island and there is the statue of Liberty, with that remarkable lamp of hers that makes her seen for miles. And up at the right Brooklyn Bridge, the most superb piece of construction in the modern world, I'm sure, with strings of light crossing it like glowing worms as the Ls and surface cars pass each other going and coming. It is particularly fine to feel the greatest city in the world from enough distance, as I do here, to see its larger proportions. When you are actually in it you are often too distracted to realize its better and more imposing aspects. Yes, this location is the best one on all counts for me. For the first time in many weeks I am beginning to further elaborate my plans for my Bridge poem. Since the publication of my Faustus and Helen poem I have had considerable satisfaction in the respect accorded me, not yet in print, but verbally from my confreres in writing, etc. Gorham has made the astounding assertion that that poem was the greatest poem written in America since Walt Whitman! Malcolm Cowley has invited me to contribute about a dozen poems to an anthology that he is planning to bring out through a regular publisher, and I am inclined to assent, as the other contributors are quite able writers and it will be some time before my Bridge poem is completed and I bring out my efforts in individual book form.[1]

This week has been quieter than the last, I'm more than glad to say. I had a terrible and ominous cold for several days but that has cleared up now, and as there have been no more people from the west to entertain no others to see off on transatlantic liners, I feel considerably relieved. Helen and Dorothea had me out for dinner and the evening last Wednesday before Helen left, Thursday morning, and I only hope I successfully preserved the camouflage of my genuine boredoom. A continuous round of puns and tittering really strains me more than some more difficult exercises. I enjoy Helen very much when we are alone together, but her friends allow one less control of the conversation, and in spite of all their good intentions one is glad to get away.

Before the day is over I hope to get a special from you, or at least some word tomorrow. You both have at least a little time more than I do for writing, and you should practice better what you preach than go ten days without sending me a word. I'm not complaining: nor should you, for all that, against me. But you must allow me to murmur back at you whenever I get the chance, just because you are ready to do it yourself. I do hope you are both alright, and shall begin to worry if I don't hear from you soon.

Work goes steadily on at the office. There is little to report excepting that I am living as economically as possible in order to pay

[1] This anthology was never published.

back some rather overdue bills and obligations. It's a long drawn out matter that has just begun, but with an even regularity I can gradually relieve myself. Sometime in the next six weeks I am pretty sure to make you a Sat-Sunday visit, but I can't be more definite than that at present.

Much love, as always, your / Hart

To Grace Hart Crane

[Brooklyn, New York]
[May 13, 1924?] [1]
Tuesday

TLS, 1 p.

Dear Grace:

This little personal write-up of O'Neill I discovered in Sunday's TIMES. Inasmuch as it was written by a friend of mine about another friend of mine, and as it says a number of very interesting things about Gene, I'm sending it to you to read. Please hold on to it, and RETURN it to me soon, won't you! [2]

[1] As the enclosure Hart included with this letter is from the New York *Times* of Sunday, May 11, 1924, Crane probably wrote the letter on the following Tuesday, May 13.

[2] Hart enclosed a long article entitled "O'NEILL DEFENDS HIS PLAY" that appeared in the New York *Times* on May 11, 1924. Written by an acquaintance, Louis Kantor (from whom Hart had rented a room on Grove Street in 1924), the article describes at length the controversy over the production of *All God's Chillun Got Wings*. O'Neill defended his choice of subject matter and his casting of Paul Robeson as Jim Harris: "'I chose Robeson,' he said, 'because I thought he could play Jim Harris better than any one else. And what's been said about having a white actor for the part is beside the point. I don't believe it follows that a white actor could play the part of Jim any better than Mr. Robeson just because he is a white actor, any more than a black actor couldn't do Othello just because he isn't white.'" O'Neill ended his statement with a discussion of what he perceived the dramatist's role to be: "'The dramatist does not present life, but interprets it within the limitations of his vision,' he said. 'Else he's no better than a camera, plus a dictograph. The dramatist works just as Beethoven did, employing every sound in existence, molding tones, giving them color, new meaning, thus creating music. . . . I don't think it is the aim of the dramatist to be true to life, but to be true to himself, to his vision, which may be of life treated as a fairy tale, or as a dream. Conceive of life as a huge mass of clay and the dramatist scooping up some of it, creating certain forms with his imagination and art, and then calling in his fellows and saying to them, Here you are as godlike beings.'"

Your last letter, arriving Sunday afternoon (after I had written you) was very encouraging and cheering to me. I'm just starting the day, so addios, for now. . . . . .

love, / Hart

P.S. Those two dogs, "Finn" & "Mat Burke", are out at Ridgefield.[3] I was almost presented with "Matty" the last time I was out there. The picture of Gene is very fine in the original—taken on the roof of his home last summer in Provincetown.

"All God's Chillun" opens this Thursday night. I've been invited by Gene to attend. Forgot to tell you that I dined with Robeson, the negro actor, and his wife, at Sue's & Jimmie's last Sat. evening. Robeson is one of the most superb sort of people. Very black, a deep resonance to his voice and actor eyes. Phi Beta Kappa, half-back on Walter Camps all-star eleven,[4] and a very fine mind and nature.

From Elizabeth Belden Hart

1709. E. 115th—Cleveland
May 15th, 1924

ALS, 4 pp.

My very Dear Hart

When Mother left this afternoon to do some errands down town she made me promise to send you a few lines so you would get it Sunday—

Now her gain will be your loss—but that you will have to shoulder and be satisfied for once at least.

I am no good at writing any more, especially when I address such illustrious stars of the literary world. I feel my mental inefficiency, so you will excuse the lack.

We have been working very hard of late trying to get the house cleaning done—so it will be passably clean for the Summer [.] We have firmly decided not to winter here again. This past winter has

---

[3] O'Neill's dogs were referred to in the *Times* article.
[4] In 1918, Paul Robeson, who attended Rutgers, was named an all-American football player by the sports writer Walter Camp.

been a very lonely hard one, and we hope to sell before late Fall, so we are not doing any more than we can help.

Mother is on the Cleveland, Warren committee [1] for the Banquet set for tomorrow eve at Wade Park Manor—so she is & has been very busy looking after that. Zell comes up tomorrow noon & wants us to meet her at train— She will stay until Saturday or Sunday Eve— We expect about 125. & perhaps more[.] Mother has a new gown to wear and so has your Grandmother, the first new toggery this season[.] Zell is going to speak—with several others, just briefly—as there is to be dancing—for the younger set. Saturday we are all invited for lunch at the Alcazar with the Wilsons— [2] Now I think I have given you all the news of interest. I want to tell you how much good your letters do Mother. She is very homesick to see you and when she has gone about so long, a letter is a wonderful bracer—even if its but a few lines— We enjoyed reading your description of the beautiful view you have from your room— I hope it will prove more restful, and conducive to your comfort than where you were before— We thought of you while Helen and her friend were there, and Charlotte and others who take much of your time & strength, but these conditions come to us all—and we have to make the best of it, but they all have their recompense in some way or other— It must be grand to live where you can see so much of this great world. It is so staid & lonely here for Mother[.] nothing or no one to go out with her—I feel very sorry for her many times. she misses your companionship more than you will ever know. Hope you can come to see us sometime soon— Now I must stop & get supper[.] She will be here soon— How I would like to look on your dear face tonight[.] Oceans of love from Grandma

[1] The Warren Society of Cleveland.   [2] Alcazar Hotel, Cleveland Heights.

From Grace Hart Crane

[Cleveland]
Thursday—
May 22—1924.

ALS, 8 pp.

Dear Hart:—

Today has been so very beautiful it just hurt to remain quiet &
contemplate. I felt like clapping my hands & jumping up and
down, singing, running or flying. I've thought about you too every
minute & in fact I have almost constantly since your letter to grandmother the other day, in which you begin to make some definite
plans for coming to Cleveland, in the near future. *Why of course* I
meant what I said about buying your return ticket—I have the
money all saved up & in my bureau drawer[.] Your old room is
spotless with a gay quilt on the bed just waiting for your coming—
and I have decided that if you can make a satisfactory arrangement
with the Sweet Catalogue Service Co. about being away from work
one day, it would be a splendid idea for you to come here for over
Decoration Day. You would likely have that day a holiday any way
—& would probably only work half a day on Saturday—Decoration
day, comes on Friday May 30 one week from tomorrow[.] You
could leave N.Y. Thursday night & have Friday Saturday & Sunday
with us, arriving back in N.Y. on Monday morning. Let me know
right soon what you think of this plan— It is such a lovely time to
come now while everything is fresh and green— I am sure you
would enjoy the beauty of the season out here—and oh I am just
starved for a sight of you. Now I do not see any thing to prevent
your coming, providing it meets with your firm's approval, which is
the first thing of course. We don't want any thing to jepordize your
job—they are too hard to get.

Grandma wrote you that we have been terribly busy with cleaning house, getting the yard straightened, awnings & screens up—&
entertaining Zell & Taylor for over the Warren Banquet.[1] It certainly kept me stepping every minute. Zell stayed over into next day

[1] Probably Jay P. Taylor, a lawyer from Warren.

& so did Taylor. That meant that I had to be dancing attendance upon Zell every minute. You know how she is. She can think of somewhere for you to take her in the automobile every minute she is here. I finally finished after ten on Saturday night after taking her to the 55th St Station, accompanied by Taylor who rode over there & back as far as 115th St. where he took the car for the Statler. Oh Hart I was that tired I was nearly insane—constant conversation for twenty four hours—just think of it! By the time I reached the house, Grandma was ready to start all over again. She had had an hour alone and was rested for a new start. I just could have killed her— I went to bed & slammed my door, instead.

I wanted to tell you that the article you sent me from "The Times" about O'Neil was very interesting, & I want to read it again —before I return it. I showed it to Zell—& read extracts from some of your letters, which she seemed very much interested in.

She made a very nice little speech at the banquet [,] looked very handsome in her skin tight beaded gown from Paris, Spanish shawl from Madrid—& two strands of pearls. I had a new gown too—very inexpensive but *effective*— Black chiffon with *big red roses* on it, & combined with black lace. It was a *jolly* little frock & that was what I wanted— I've been sombre so long that I had to deck out & if I could have found a solid red one I should have bo't it. We had good music & I danced a lot— We missed Sullivan— He was sick in bed, but Mrs S. & Mary came— [2] Henry Gordon, formerly Maitre d'Hotel at the Statler, (that good looking Austrian, do you remember him?) is now at the Manor & he did his best to please me with his share of the party, the dinner was unusually good.

I haven't had a line from Charlotte yet. It may be she became seasick before she got to my letter, & it was never written. I'll hear from her before long, I'm sure. I haven't seen Sam or heard from him for an age. May be he is too crushed by the criticism of his latest literary effort to have any desire to see me.[3] The criticism was in the N.Y. Post recently— I did not see it—but Glenn did—

Blanche Ross & Ida Skiff are at the Hotel Astor N.Y. in order to

[2] The lawyer John J. Sullivan. Mary was Sullivan's daughter.
[3] Grace refers to *A Round-Table in Poictesme: A Symposium* (Cleveland: Pergamon Publishing Co., 1924), a collection of essays on James Branch Cabell, edited by Don Bregenzer and Samuel Loveman.

be near father Skiff, who is in some near by hospital for a serious operation on his eyes for cataract. I think it would be very nice for you to call her on the phone. You remember how nice Frank Ross was to you & me one time when we stopped off in Chicago.

Well I've written a long letter & I am going to help get dinner now. I wish you [were] here—but when you do come we are going to give you a feeding up that you will remember. Broiled steak—mushrooms, chicken, asparagus, strawberry shortcake—shrimp salad & everything!

I hope my plan will meet with your approval and work out right — If so, I won't have to wait very much longer to see you.

Devotedly/ Grace.

Be sure to bring your mustache along—(It will match my bobbed hair—) but prepare to shave it off the next day if I don't like it.

To Grace Hart Crane

New York,
May 24", '24

ALS, 1 p.

Dear Grace:

There is a tiny chance that I might get to see you over Decoration Day—arriving, if at all, on the morning of the 30". But don't let it effect your plans. I may not have the money, nor get the extra time on Saturday morning. If my friend, Emil Opffer, can afford me the loan when he gets back from his boat job to S. America next Monday, it will help *some*.

There's no news except good weather at last! and steady work at the office. I'm going to have lunch with Gorham today and then walk home across Bkl'yn Bridge. I'm hoping to hear from you tomorrow.

Love as always,/ Hart

From Elizabeth Belden Hart

[Cleveland]
May 25—1924

ALS, 3 pp.

My Dear Harold:—

This is Sunday P.M. as you see by date, and I am going to mail
you a line to go out tonight to tell you to make your plans to be
with us on Decoration day as you spoke of in your letter (altho') I
have not yet read it, but heard Mother say just as I was clearing up
dinner dishes, that the Postman had bro't your S.D. and as she read
it hurriedly, says Hart says he may be able to get away to spend
decoration day with us—which by the way you have Mothers S.D.
by this [time] asking you to come, providing you could do so without in any way jeopardizing your position, as you have had such a
serious time to secure one— Now you know best about this, but we
are very anxious to see you—and so that you may not be in doubt
about the wherewith to come—or spend any anxious moments
about trying to borrow it, I will send you the price of your ticket
when you inform me when it will be I will have your check there in
time. Now Dear we will be SO glad to see your dear face again—
and I hope nothing will interfere with your doing so. When you
read Mothers letter you will see how she has planned and how anxious she is, as well as my self included but if in your good judgement you think it not best, we will be patient hoping it wont be
long— Glenn [1] was here to dinner today & Mother got it alone
while I went to church with Sarah— We are usually well—house
cleaning about done and ready to receive you & want you to come
while it is so beautiful, and green in this neighborhood, especially
— Mother has gone out for a drive & I am writing this while she
knows it not, but I wanted you to know what you could depend on
so there need be no delay in making your plans— I will leave the
rest I want to say until you come—but my love is always with & for
you my Dear Boy

As ever Grandma

[1] Glenn Whistler.

[*Written in the margin of the last page:*] I got your sweet letter [.] Thank you so much.

To Grace Hart Crane and Elizabeth Belden Hart

[New York City]
Saturday
June 7th '24

TLS, 1 p.

Dear Grace and Grandma:

A week of very mad rushing. Hardly time to even reminisce about my pleasant whirl in Cleveland with you all. But it *was* fine, and I'll never forget how lovely you both were.

Emil and Sue have gone up to Woodstock to see Brown over this week end. Do you remember the anecdote I told you about Sue's excuse about not going there once before?! Allen Tate arrives either today or tomorrow and I must rush around to find him a room. I'll be busy entertaining him somewhat next week—at least until he gets introduced around a little.

This is writing on office time. I had to get you a special for Sunday, but you can understand why it must be so brief. I'm feeling in fine shape, and hope your hospitality to me didn't prove to have been at all exhausting.

You'll both hear something from me before the end of next week. I've made a note of it and tacked it on my desk.

Much love,/ Hart

To Grace Hart Crane and Elizabeth Belden Hart

[Brooklyn, New York]
110 Columbia Hts
Friday—June 13th '24

TLS, 1 p.

Dear Grace and Grandma:

I haven't wondered much at not hearing from you for so long.

It's mostly due, I suppose, to the convention.[1] But I am wondering who is at the house, and if you got your seat, etc.

Harriet Taylor Upton's [2] picture has been steadily seen in NY papers and it seems her national prominence has never been so evident before. No doubt you have seen her and Zell quite recently in Cleveland. Have you heard from Ned yet? [3]

I have been quite busy at the office (the rush season is beginning now) and I have also been guiding Allen Tate about a little. Found him a room quite near me on this same St. and he seems to be already attached to NY. He has been taken up rather enthusiastically by Sue; we all like him, in fact.

I have been having an un[p]leasant time with my uric acid trouble, so bad that I finally went to the doctor about it. For the last two days I have been on a milk and water diet and deprived of coffee. Consequently I have a chronic headache and am in a bad mood.

Sorry I couldn't be more attentive on your birthday, Grandma, but the usual rush of things simply limited me to the telegram.[4]

Now one or the other of you write me very soon, please.

Love, from / Hart

Hart's short letter of June 13 was answered by his mother with a sharp reply, which unfortunately is lost. (Many of Mrs. Crane's and Mrs. Hart's letters of this period are missing; the great number that survive are testament to just how many letters flowed from Cleveland in 1924.) But the summer had begun for Crane, typically a period of stress for the poet. The heat and his hay fever

[1] The Republican Party held its presidential convention in Cleveland, June 9–14, 1924. Both Mrs. Crane and Mrs. Hart attended.

[2] Treasurer of the National Women's Suffragist Association and a member of the Republican National Committee. See Hart's letter of September 29, 1923, to his mother and grandmother.

[3] A friend of Mrs. Crane's from Rye, New York. See Hart's letter of July 14, 1923, to his mother.

[4] Thinking that his grandmother's birthday was on June 11 (actually it was on July 11). Hart had sent a congratulatory telegram. See his letter of July 10, 1924.

troubled him, and urethritis—brought about by increased drinking —added to his discomfort. When his mother learned in her son's letter of June 19 just how serious his condition was, she phoned C.A., who promptly wrote a letter of advice.

To Grace Hart Crane

[Brooklyn, New York]
110 Columbia Hts
June 19" '24

ALS, 3 pp.

Dear Grace:

The "wind-up" of your last letter was far from gratifying and I am sorry that anything so common as my usual lack of time for writing should have given you the impression of indifference or ingratitude on my part. Now—lest I get no other seconds before Sunday in which to write you, I'm going to get this off—for tomorrow evening I'll be tied up with a kind of picnic to Coney Island that the office is giving and there won't be a moment before midnight for myself. .

I'm awfully glad you got your seat to the convention and that Grandma got her chance to go with you as she did. All the excitement is just beginning afresh here,—but one gets no particularly rushed or crowded feeling going about one's usual work. N.Y. is too big, I guess. I wish I could be more interested in politics, but I guess it takes a different kind of mind than mine and a different education. You, however, seem stimulated very much by the spectacle and it makes me almost wish that you would become active in some work of that sort.

As for myself this last week— I've been most unhappy. My uric acid resulted in urethritis which has been very painful and nerve wracking. A steady diet of butter milk has finally relieved me, however, and I am going to continue it for some time yet. I'm looking better now than when you saw me in Cleveland but get neuralgic immediately as soon as I deviate the slightest from my diet. I was in a perfect panic for several days, fearing I had a venereal disease but a complete examination of my body and urine disproved any trace of that. I know now, however, just how one is parylized with fear at any such suspicion. Believe me, it's awful!

The whistles are tooting midnight, and as this is the latest I've been up for a week now, I'd better turn in. Don't let my news alarm you. I'm practically mended already—am working every day at the office, etc. I certainly do realize better than before that I must be careful.

Love to you both,/ Hart

From Clarence Arthur Crane

[Cleveland]
June 23, 1924

TLC, 1 p.

Mr. Harold Crane,
110 Columbia Heights
Brooklyn, N.Y.

My dear Harold,

Your mother called me up this afternoon and told me that you are really suffering with an attack of uric acid. I thought when you were in Cleveland you must have some difficulty along those lines, but she told me that you are now under the care of a doctor and are really much annoyed with it.

I think perhaps, if I may be permitted to offer a suggestion, that you should be more careful with your diet. You feel that anyone who offers you real advice is out of order and that you have a very good understanding of your own problems, but just the same it might be well to theorize a little on some of these things and see if you will not make better by the elimination of a few of your natural inclinations.

Having fought uric acid conditions all my life, as you perhaps will remember, I found it necessary to give up coffee when I was about your age, and since then I have never gone back to it. Licquor is one of the most foolish things, but I do not believe you are foolish enough to indulge in that.

You should cut out all meats, and live as much as possible on milk. For years it has been my custom to take a bottle of Alkalithia about every two weeks. There is a bottle standing right in front of me now. By watching my diet and adhering to some of the simple rules, I can completely overcome the acute trouble which I used to suffer from, and I think that you can do the same.

If you are going to a doctor as your mother says, no doubt he has given you just about the same instructions, for it [is] a well known fact that uric acid conditions are all brought about by excessive smoking, meat, and coffee drinking, and that they are best corrected by a milk diet.

There isn't any news that I can write you of. Everything is about the same here, and your mother's voice sounded as though she was feeling good, only worried about you.

I hope to hear shortly that you are better.

Affectionately,/ Your father,

To Grace Hart Crane

[Brooklyn, New York]
110 Columbia Hts
Sunday, June 29th, '24

TLS, 1 p.

Dear Grace:

A bright day and windy, but hot! I have taken (or tried to take) a snooze on a pier near here, walked, eaten and come home, only to partially undress and write poetry. But none of these ordinary pleasures has eventuated in much comfort or satisfaction. Anyway, it can be called a quiet day, and what dissipation there was to it wasn't against my present precautions for improved health. And I am feeling much better, by the way.

I should have written you before, but there was a dinner and evening engagement on Friday—and yesterday as soon as I escaped from the office I made for Long Beach where I had a good swim. Allen Tate had to be seen off on the train in the evening, etc. so now please don't blame me!

CA responded very promptly to your phone call, explaining that you had called him up about advising me, and prescribing to me the usual measures and diet for uric acid with first rate avidity, attempting, however, a certain reluctant and slighted tone which makes his letter very amusing to anyone who knows him as well as we do. Hay fever and uric acid are at least two subjects that we can have in common, and if I were only constantly racked by one or the other of these diseases I'm sure we might have a much more ample correspondence. As it happened, I had just sent him a post card which must have crossed his letter on the way, and which contained a slight reference to my trouble. IT also contained about everything else I have been able to think up to say to him since my Cleveland visit,—so now that I have to answer his letter in some sort of equal physical measure I'm at a loss to know what "all" to fill it with. In a way, it's funny.

The things you say about Zell's preoccupation with her business confirm certain fears about her life which I have had for a long time. Successful people don't by any means have to become dull, but most of them do in the USA in this century. Zell has a good heart, however, and that goes a long ways—at least it often surprises one. It was especially good to hear about Glenn's recent encouragements and really funny to hear about Edna's fall from such Olympian heights as she boasted of when I last saw her.[1] I hope she isn't completely deflated, though, as that would provoke incessant tears, I'm sure.

My hours this week at the office are two days short. I'll probably go swimming on the Fourth and maybe again Saturday. You know how I love the beach, and such hours will be my only vacation this summer. Love to you both./ Hart

[1] Edna Moore, a friend of Mrs. Crane's.

To Grace Hart Crane

[Brooklyn, New York]
July 4th, '24
110 Columbia Hts

TLS, 1 p.

Dear Grace:

This has been one of the coolest Fourths that I can remember, but your letter of today leads me to think it has been much cooler in Cleveland than anything we have had here. I certainly am glad that you and Grandma or Glenn didn't happen to be riding around Ellyria last week at the time of the tornado.[1] The papers here have been featuring photographs of the ruins all week, and I've never seen more evidence of complete destruction than they revealed.

The Rychtariks arrived three days ago on the Leviathan and I have been busy the last two evenings entertaining them. They're awful dumbbells about keeping engagements, and I could give them a good scolding right now for not showing up at all or letting me know the trouble that prevented them from attending FASHION. I took them last night to see ALL GODS CHILLUN' GOT WINGS and they were very much pleased with the theatre, meeting Jimmy Light again, as well as Sue and the woman who plays the part of the white woman, Mary Blair. The theatre simply presented me not only with last night's seats, but those tonight for FASHION. I thought it was very nice of my friends there. If I had not already seen FASHION twice I should be more put out about such behavior tonight, but it isn't pleasant to stand around waiting for people anyway, and I really wanted Richard to see the fine settings and costumes of this play. I didn't even use my own seat, finally, but came home and have been reading. I spose they lost their way or something, but why don't people take a taxi when they get lost and not go flopping all over the place!

Charlotte and Richard are looking better than I've ever seen them. They spent quite a time in Paris, and are simply mad about

---

[1] On June 28, 1924, a tornado destroyed much of Lorain and Elyria, Ohio. The death toll was over one hundred.

living here in New York as soon as they can get a connection. Charlotte is sorry not to have written you, but I can well understand, as
she said, that there was no time to write anyone on such a trip. I
think they intend to leave for Cleveland on Sunday, but I'm not
sure. They'll look you up very soon, I'm sure.

I had intended to go to Long Beach today, but there were too
many people to see around here, and now I'm hoping it won't rain
tomorrow so I can go then. Did I tell you that Gorham and Liza
are planning to leave for two months in Woodstock early next
week? I'll soon be having to devote some of my evenings to over-
time work at the office, as the catalogue (2250 pages!) is soon to go
to press.

Perhaps I'll send this via the new aerial mail. At any rate it will
carry the same weight of love to you,—one way as another!

Lots to you both—/ HART

Crane addressed the following letter to Mrs. Hart on the eve
of her eighty-fifth birthday, remembering his mistake of the previous month. For his own twenty-fifth birthday, which took place
ten days after his grandmother's, Hart received a dressing gown and
pajamas from Cleveland. He alludes to these gifts in his letter of
July 22 and that postmarked July 28.

To Elizabeth Belden Hart

[Brooklyn, New York]
110 Columbia Heights
July 10th, '24

TLS, 1 p.

Dear Grandma:

In order to balance the scales of Time properly in deference to
your date of birth I really should wait until August 11th to greet
you now—for one can hardly have a birthday *every* month, and I

certainly was early enough in greeting you once before—I refer to my June telegram. But it's nice to be exactly on time once in awhile,—and this time, if I may trust the airship that is supposed to carry this letter to you—I shall be. Of course I should like to be much more personal and have the airship bring myself along, with a posy in my buttonhole and a bouquet of roses for your own sweet self. I will make a wish, however, that you'll have enough more birthdays for that to be not only possible, but plausible. Then I shall drop down on you out of a perfectly clear sky, guiding my parachute so as to land right on the front porch. You will then serve me with fresh doughnuts and coffee and all will be merry!

I have been very much pleased to notice in recent letters from Grace that you have been feeling quite well, at least there has been no mention of anything to the contrary. I have said it many times, but I must keep on repeating that I think you remarkable in this and many other ways,—your animation, interest and courage have been so unflagging through many trials that we have gone through together,—and how many more, too, when one stops to think that my years are so small a share in your's! I'm awfully proud of you, as you know already. I'm very undemonstrative at times, but I think you know me well enough [to] believe in my constant affection and admiration for you. I only wish I could be with you more, but after all, you and I have had many more months and even years together than are usually granted the first and third generations. And our intimacy and comradeship have been unusual;—you've always been such a good sport.

There isn't very much news to write this week as yet. I'll try to get a letter to Grace by Sunday, however. Meanwhile I have been very glad to hear such rather pleasant news as her letter brought today—simply that my last letter pleased her, that it's not too hot (although it probably is NOW), that she may get off to Buffalo for a little trip with Zell, etc. I hope that you won't celebrate your birthday with too much strenuosity, upsetting tables, breaking chandeliers, or scuffing the floor with high kicking. Above all, don't drink too much, that Jamaica Rum, you know, always does go to one's head in hot weather!

Your devoted grandson,/ Hart

[*Mrs. Crane wrote the following note in the margin:*] The first paragraph refers to a lettergram he sent June 11th thinking that was her birthday. Kindly return this— Hastily G. H. C.

From Elizabeth Belden Hart

Cleveland
July 11, 1924

ALS, 6 pp.
LETTERHEAD: 1709 East One hundred and fifteenth Street/ Cleveland

My Dear Hart:

Once more am I reminded that another mile stone has been reached, and here I will pause and rest. The journey has at times seemed weary, and beset with many trials and obstacles that were at the time hard to surmount, but by pressing forward, determined to win I have found that the greatest enemy I have to battle with is fear— I find I have been unnecessarily "detouring"—and thereby frequently lost the beaten trail but with firmness and perseverence —have always been able to come out in to the open—and gather up my *pack* and go on, so today finds me well & happy. The sun shines, the birds are singing, (*all for me*). My friends are so lovely to remember that I am still here, by sending flowers[,] candy— Telegrams—and many congratulations over the phone—etc, until I begin to feel I am on a *par* with the Presidents family— Now I intended to send you a special Delivery for Sunday a good long message—but if I write at all I must do it now, as I am told I am to receive many calls this P M, so I must put on my best, and look my "sweetest," and so will have to save my message in part for the next time.

Just as I left this, your S.D. came. Oh how sweet it is to have such a dear Grandson—: Your wonderful compliments, and still *dearer* to me is the knowledge that I still hold a place in your affections and admiration. Yes you are right, we have had intimate comradeship, quite beyond the usual. You are as dear to me as my own— and ever will be—

Mother says hurry up and send this in a box of cherries we are sending you by parcel Post.

There is also many thanks for your kind remembrance of me on this my birthday—and also the one of June 11*th*. These cherries are off the old home trees. Hope you will enjoy them

Love from Mother and me, as always/ Grandma

To Grace Hart Crane and Elizabeth Belden Hart

[Brooklyn, New York]
110 Columbia Hts
July 22nd, '24

TLS, 1 p.

Dearest Grace and Grandma:

I have been trying to write you for over three days. Now, I feel very neglectful indeed, especially after your two fine letters of last Sunday and the lovely gifts which arrived this morning. I hardly know how to explain myself nor to adequately thank you for so much love and attention. I know that I scarcely deserve it all, but certainly that makes it all the more pleasant. I am wearing the new dressing gown this minute. The handkerchiefs and case of Grandfather's are lovely to have and to use—as are also the socks and tie. The deep wine color of the silk handkerchief is one of the rarest shades I've ever seen, and I'm wondering if that wasn't also a possession of Grandfather's; one doesn't see such shades very often.

Altogether, my 25th birthday was quite happily passed. Emil Oppfer, whom I've mentioned to you before, and who is staying with me since he came back from his last trip to the West Indies, spread the news around and before I knew it a dinner had been arranged. Sue gave me a necktie and brought her husband, James Light, and Slater Brown, who arrived in town last Saturday for a week, was also along. There was much white and excellent wine and general hilarity. Emil even hired a taxi for transportation and I was re-christened "child of the earthquake".

Aside from all this there is very little to report. Work at the office

becomes more and more hectic, and I'll be very glad when the extra
strain of my hay fever relaxes. It isn't as bad as it always is in Cleveland, but enough to be very irritating to say the least. You will notice the two photographs enclosed [1] and wonder where on earth they
were taken. My expression is amusing enough, I think, even though
it isn't a very good picture. To explain, Emil and I spent most of
last Sunday afternoon cooling off on the roof of the house here, and
looking out over the river. There is just one little piece of the panorama in the ph[o]to herewith—looking to the right and toward
Brooklyn Bridge. The Wall Street section is directly opposite, and
the whole bay to the left. I include a snap of Emil, also, who looks
cooler than I do (in a sweater of his which I liked so much that I
had to have myself taken in it). Emil, by the way, is a very lovely
person, and I know you would like him very much. He will probably start working on The Leviathan (bound for England) next Saturday, but will stay with me always while he is in New York.

I hope that the trip to Buffalo with Zell was a real diversion.
Being on a boat is wonderful—and I can't tell you how I am
tempted to jump some boat for Europe or South America and get
away from the stuffy confines of an office and office work for awhile.
I think I might really save more money that way than this, and
really consider taking a boat job with Emile for awhile before many
months. I hope you approve.

My thanks again for all your love, and remember I love and
think of you both very constantly, even if I seem to be slow in writing.

                    your sonny—"grand" and otherwise/ Hart

[1] These photographs are no longer filed with the letter.

To Grace Hart Crane

[New York City] [1]
[Postmarked July 28, 1924]
Monday Noon

TLS, 1 p.

Dear Grace:

It's certainly too bad that I didn't get the chance to write you before this. The office has been moving to another building, however, and I had to help out with some of the rough work Saturday afternoon, although I was ready to keel over any moment, so dizzy and incapacitated was I with several rough days of hay fever, A strange disease, indeed,—so completely enervating and hard on one's temper. Then, yesterday afternoon, just as I was sitting down to write you, some friends called and took me away to dinner and the evening—so that's that.

We are now on 40th Street, 21 stories up where it is much cooler, and directly below the main office of the Dodge Publishing Co., parent concern of Sweet's.[2] I look out directly on the Times Building and the Astor Roof. The other place was low, dusty and hot, and I look forward to easier conditions here for my personal afflications—both in the eyes and nose.

I was awfully glad to hear that your trip to Buffalo turned out so pleasantly. If you can get Zell away from her business *long enough* I imagine she changes her mind toward different topics than presses and circulation. So you saw Dorothea and Helen. I don't know whether or not I mentioned it, but Dorothea sent me a card from Mackinac in which she invites me to come up to her summer place in the mountains during August. I have been waiting until she got back to her NY address before thanking her and declining. I, of course, couldn't think of it, regardless of my wishes, because I don't get any vacation this year and week ends are too short for so much travelling back and forth.

[1] Crane probably wrote this during his lunch hour at Sweet's Catalogue Service.
[2] The new address was 119 West 40th Street.

You please me very much by liking the snapshot I sent you, and it's good to know that you appreciate other expressions on pictures than the insistent smile so generally demanded. There were two others of myself in that batch, but they didn't turn out as well as the one I sent, but whenever I do have one taken that I think you would like, depend upon it—I'll send it to you.

You are about the only people I get time to write any more. It's amazing how little time one gets. When I can rob a bank or something like that I may once again get a chance to write some poetry. Badly as I feel about it sometimes, however, I must say in all good conceit that the literature of our country is missing considerably more than myself in the facts that deny me the chance to concentrate on that side of myself—which is my main justification for living. It's a barbarous age indeed, or else I have too much timidity to throw the glove completely in its face and live on air.

Never any words from CA—since he wrote at your request. I promptly and cheerfully answered. A strange animal. Well, I'm happier than I've ever been before in some ways,—and no one should ever expect complete happiness.

Thank you so much for the dressing gown and pajamas!

love from   HART

To Grace Hart Crane and Elizabeth Belden Hart

[New York City] [1]
110 Columbia Hts.
August 1st, '24

TLS, 2 pp.

Dear Grace and Grandma:

I'm sitting up in the office, waiting for 6 o'clock to arrive before starting out to dine with Elizabeth Smith at her little flat which she is sharing with some other girl up on West 55th Street. She was very nice indeed to have asked me, as I have unintentionally neglected to give her the slightest attention for several months now. Did I tell

---

[1] Hart wrote this letter and the next one at his office.

you that we did manage to have lunch together several weeks ago, and that she is working in the statistical dept. of some huge paper manufacturing company? It will be amusing and very pleasant to eat some of her home brews and stews, I'm sure. Inadvertently it saves me the price of a meal, too, and at a time when every penny counts. Food is, after all, the big item here. And I get awfully tired of trying to find handy and cheap places continually, and then to pick over the menu (generally a card on the wall) to find what I can afford to eat. So it is a pleasure to eat at somebody's table once in awhile.

Have you heard from the Rychtariks yet? If not, it's about as strange as their conduct while here and the letter of explanation that Charlotte finally sent several weeks later. I am getting rather bored by them, I think. They are nice enough, but so impossible in the extent of their ambitions,—or so it seems to me now. And whenever they get together the little "scenes" begin to develope and one is obliged to violate the interesting and vital course of the conversation to make up and keep an adjustment between them.

Kathryn Kenney must have seen you recently, as a letter came from her this morning in which she lamented not seeing me when I made the Decoration Day trip. K is not so very happy, nor are they prosperous, according to the letter, yet there is still evidence of a lot of K's temperament there, and I hope there always will be. I was awfully sorry to get the news through your letter that Sam [2] had lost his job again. And that mere mention is all I have heard so far about it. Will you write me what more you know? I'll write him more lengthily than a recent postcard whenever I get the time and wits, but in the meantime do your best to inform me.

Helen phoned me the other evening and wanted to get me to break an engagement and come right out and entertain her and Dorothea. Of course I didn't and Helen seemed rather peeved, in a pleasant "tone", however. The next night she was scheduled to leave for home, and I made a great effort to join the two girls for dinner. However, being about broke I had to rush to Brooklyn after work in order to borrow some funds from Emil. The subway broke down and delayed me so, however, that I both failed

[2] Sam Loveman.

to get there in time and to even get the girls on the wire. They were probably sore, but at any rate life is so darned much easier, I think, for them, that they need a *little* seasoning now and then. The whole business certainly did put me out a lot. And one gets awfully tired during these hot days and the extreme rush now at the office. I was [3] so darned tired when I got home that I didn't try to catch them at the train gate as I might have done under better circumstances. I've just written Helen and Dorothea separate explanations.

The pajamas came, and of course they will be very useful. I have got to have a suit sometime soon, but how I'm to get it is beyond my imagination. I owe the doctor money, friends, bookstores, one restaurant, etc. etc. All these together don't amount to over a hundred dollars, but they have been mostly long standing, and require at least as immeadiate consideration as my suit, even though I get into rags. Well, I don't mind, only I don't want you to get the idea that I have such a salary as permits me but the barest necessities, and practically permits no margin for either saving or back payments. My insurance premium notice came the other [day] —for $9.35—to be paid by the first of August, and I don't know yet how I can get enough together to pay it before the end of August—at which time even the special extension period for payment will have been exhausted.

All this is very tiresome to you, I know. And, the funny part of it is, I doubt if I'd be mentioning any of these matters at all if it weren't that you require at least a large hunk of news from me every week, and to tell you the truth, there isn't very much other news to tell you other than these petty worries that are continually in my mind. If my letters are drab, it's because most of my thoughts are occupied with such drab speculations. I've sat fifteen minutes, straight, sometimes, trying to think of some pleasant item to tell you. But if I let these little matters leak through once in while, don't worry about them particularly, because, as a matter of fact, they have been pending for a long, long time—during and over much more pleasant correspondence, and there's nothing left to them at the moment to especially startle one. One goes on living in

---

[3] The word "was" is repeated in the text.

another half of one's self that is a little more imaginative, after all, no matter what happens to the other half.

I hope to hear that Grandma is more rested in your Sunday letter (which, by the way, is awfully good to get), and that you both are using the car, getting out a little and cooling off.

A great deal of my love—/ Hart

To Grace Hart Crane and Elizabeth Belden Hart

[New York City]
110 Columbia Hts
Aug. 12" '24

ALS, 2 pp.

Dear Grace & Grandma—

I hope you got the postcard—it was all I could muster up for the time being. Three more hellishly hot days since and at 4 this morning it began to rain. I hope it pours for days—as I have been having queer feelings in my head from lack of sleep, swelling spells and all the nervous tremors that go with such a state of disorder. You may be glad to be in a place where you can have some privacy, go riding in the country and take your time about things. If you were once to pile into a steaming, rushing mob in the subway where the stinks of millions accumulate from day to day—you'd see how I feel about the next day's work after a sleepless night. And when one goes to one's room afterward, believe me, it isn't to write letters! There isn't much you can do in N.Y. in the summer but work & complain. I seem to be doing both, I guess.

I'm sure you have been having a very busy time with so much entertaining. And that's probably why I haven't heard from you for ten days.

Don't make the extra effort to write me any oftener than you just feel like it. I'll understand, because I know myself how hard it is.

I'm at the office now and have just had lunch. It's about time for some of the girls to come around with some snapshots of themselves in bathing suits.

I don't know what CA.'s doing these days as I never hear from him. And I'm not going to try to keep up a one-legged correspondence. I think of him entirely too much however,—as a poisonous and unnatural person—whom it puzzles me to feel any attitude whatever toward, because from all angles he is so baffling. If he would lose all his money and feel himself disgraced I might come to have some feeling for him better than hatred. But now—I can only think of him in profane terms. But enough of this! I'm in a trap that will probably confine me the rest of my life, so I might as well laugh at such a world as my imagination qualifies me for.

When people like Gorham & Waldo Frank ask me why I don't write more, it fairly makes me rage. They—with money supplied them and their time all their own!

But there's no use in my going on like this when I know it will displease you. You *will* have *letters* though!

Love from / Hart

To Grace Hart Crane and Elizabeth Belden Hart

[Brooklyn, New York]
Sunday
Aug 17th—24

TLS, 1 p.

Dear Grace and Grandma:

I have just written Kathryn Goettel and two or three other letters that were long-standing obligations with the result that it is already evening and one begins to think about the next day's work. As I still owe the Rychtarik's a letter it reminds me to ask you if you haven't yet seen them since they returned from Europe. If you haven't, or they have made no efforts in your direction, I shall be rather offended at them; as a matter of fact, I am anyway. But please let me know if they hav:t [haven't] even phoned.

The last few days have been cool enough to allow me a slight recuperation from the mood in which I last wrote to you. I also admit feeling better, due to a long talk I had the other evening with Waldo Frank, just back from abroad, on the present situation and hopes for the artist in America, etc. In order to make some money, Frank has signed up for a literary lecture tour beginning next March, which will take him through the middle west and to Cleveland. He is planning on calling on CA for a little persuasive exercise in arousing CA's interest in me. I told him that I certainly wanted him to meet you, whatever else he did while there, and that he is planning on. You, I'm sure, will give him a readier welcome than the chocolate maggot.

Frank has been showing some of my work to several of the finest writers in France (most all of whom read English very well) and says there will even be a little audience there for my first book (when it comes out!). But that will be years from now, at my present rate. Even so it's not so bad. Conrad and Anderson did not begin to write until they were over thirty-five. And Frank seems to think that I have written a few classics already. I can allow my best, and that only, whatever happens; there are too many others writing trash and near-trash these days for me to envy them.

I hope you both well recovered from your deluge of company, and that there are no other taxes of that kind in immediate prospect. I should be glad to know in a little detail what the Heerens had to say about present conditions on the Island.[1] Do matters look brighter or "worser", and why?

It's *you* who've been neglecting the mail-box lately, so write me soon and "sooner".

Lots of love to you both,/ Hart

To Grace Hart Crane

[New York City]
[Postmarked August 20, 1924]
noon hour Wednesday

TLS, 1 p.

Dear Grace:

I've meant to ask you to do this long ago, but always forgot around the time of writing. Will you please send me a little (very

---

[1] This is a reference to the political situation on the Isle of Pines.

tiny) pearl which is loose in the bottom of the little indian basket on my bureau upstairs? It worked loose from the stick-pin of Grandfather's that I have, and if you will put it into a little separate envelope inside your next letter to me, I can then have it cemented back on the pin, below the amythyst, as you will remember. I had meant to attend to this little matter when I was home last, but forgot it.

There is practically no news. I may move sometime within the next month as the room in back of the house where I am, and which I have been hoping to get hold of for so long, is being split in two ugly little corners, and the front room which I have been using all along is depressing during dark weather, and really not large enough. It will be in the same neighborhood, however, as there as [are] plenty of attractive houses nearby.

I hope this cool weather continues. It's rainy here today, but I prefer it so much to the usual torridity!

How is everything? Remember me to Ralph and Mart [1] once in awhile.

Love to you both—/ Hart

As these letters show, Hart had a good deal to fret about over the summer of 1924, and he lost no chance to do so. Frank and Munson wished he would write to them more frequently. His cousin Helen and her friend Dorothea Lewis encroached on his time. His father's intermittent letters necessitated a "one-legged correspondence." The financial pressures in Cleveland, Hart realized, would soon require the sale of the house. And, something Hart does not mention in his letters home, Emil Opffer's long absences aboard ships and his short periods of time in Brooklyn meant that Hart was often alone. But one thing was taking place in Cleveland that mitigated his irritation in New York: Mrs. Crane had a suitor. In confidential letters to her grandson—written whenever Grace was out—Mrs. Hart told of her daughter's courtship with Charles Cur-

---

[1] Ralph and Margaret, who worked for Mrs. Crane and Mrs. Hart.

tis. Finally, in his letter of September 4, Hart hinted about Grace's suitor. Realizing that his well-being and his mother's were inextricably bound, Hart encouraged the romance as openly as he could. Grace reported many details of the courtship—including such events as a trip to Canton, Ohio, to introduce her beau to her cousins the Freases and the Smiths; her son enthusiastically commented on all reports.

To Grace Hart Crane and Elizabeth Belden Hart

[Brooklyn, New York]
Sept. 4" '24

ALS, 4 pp.

Dear Grace and Grandma—

I poise a handkerchief in my left hand about as steadily as I hold this pen in my right—and if page looks distracted and erratic you will please realize that it is hard to do two things at once—sneezing, alone, is an engrossing occupation. The recent change to cooler weather (it has really been chilly) was so sudden that I somehow picked up a sore throat as well. But that is getting better today.

Grandmother's charming letter of last Sunday tells me that Gracie is having a few attentions paid her these days,—and I was certainly made gay and glad to hear of the pleasant "doings." "Gracie" must write me some of the details very soon,—if, indeed, she is ever intending to write me again. When you say that you are really in love, then I'll forgive you all kinds and lengths of silence. But meanwhile I'm sometimes left to blame myself—which is deserved, I know—for being so remiss. Yet I am awfully busy at the office—and even had to work Labor Day.

Tuesday night I had dinner with Zell—who had been here over Sunday and was leaving the next night. Through some mistake on the telephone service I didn't get in touch with her until after work, Tues. When I met her she was all for dining a la Italien—so I took her to one of my favorites—and we had one cocktail after

another. "What! Zell drinking cocktails!" you say. "Yes"—and I was
very much her guest, too. Altogether we had the best time with
each other that I remember. And I greatly look forward to her next
visit here. Zell is very much worried, however, and though she did
not make me swear to tell no one, I'm sure she doesn't want anyone
but us to know the present cause of her fears. So be very careful!

She had just got word through a reliable source that the big
Scripps people are meditating the establishment of one of their
newspaper enterprizes right in Warren—and just after she had paid
so much to buy out "The Chronicle." [1] With such a perfect trust as
they are to face and fight I don't wonder she is concerned. If they
carry out their intentions I fear our Zell will either have to sell out
at some sacrifice, or dedicate herself to an unrelenting and long battle and exceeding uncertainties. It's too bad, I think, and I only
hope that the news was unfounded.

I want more letters from you, Grandma, and you, Grace,

Hope you are both cool and cosy—

With love,/ Hart

To Grace Hart Crane and Elizabeth Belden Hart

[Brooklyn, New York]
Sunday morning—
Sept. 14th, '24

TLS, 2 pp.

Dear Grace and Grandma:

I have just come back from a breakfast with Sam, and he has left
to spend the rest of the day with the widow of Edgar Saltus [1]
(whom you must have heard him talk about enough to identify). I
have been greeted so far mostly by his coat tails, so occupied has
Sambo been with numerous friends of his here ever since arriving;
Miss Sonia Green and her piping-voiced husband, Howard Love-

[1] The Warren *Tribune*, of which Zell was publisher, took over the Warren
Chronicle in 1924.

[1] Edgar Saltus (1855–1921), the American novelist. His wife was Marie Giles.

craft, (the man who visited Sam in Cleveland one summer when Galpin was also there) [2] kept Sam traipsing around the slums and wharf streets until four this morning looking for Colonial specimens of architecture, and until Sam tells me he groaned with fatigue and begged for the subway! Well, Sam may have been improved before he left Cleveland, but skating around here has made him as hectic again as I ever remember him, and I think he is making the usual mistake of people visiting NY, attempting too much, getting prematurely exhausted, and then railing against the place and wanting to get back home. This last alternative is really what I am expecting him to do, although he has not yet finally decided. But he does think that NY is too swift for him—and perhaps it is, I don't know. Sam is so often in an unsettled state of mind, however, that it is hard to know in what direction to urge him. I have been able to offer him a temporary room on the same floor with me, at the back, —the same room, in fact, that I have been hoping to acquire for myself sometime. As Mr. Opffer, the father of Emil, who has been at the hospital for an operation, succumbed and died, the room is unoccupied until taken over sometime soon by Ivan, Emil's brother, who says he expects to take it for himself. So Sam has had a [t] least several days lodging free, and a room that is most beautifully located. He is to see some hotel man tomorrow about an advertising job, and that may determine whether he remains here or returns to Cleveland. So far, his most coherent and welcome conversation has been about you, Grace, and several matters that you seemed to think were inadviseable to put on paper to me.

But why you have been so cautious, or sweetly shy, I'm at a loss to understand, because I certainly would never be timorous about writing you any news about myself, however intimate, and feeling quite sure enough that you would not be apt to quote it either far or near—just from the very facts of our relationship. However, I don't want you to think that I in the least minded hearing such delightful news quite orally from dear old Sam: good news is too welcome, only too welcome, however it comes. And now I want you— or rather want to reassure you about something that I have

[2] Howard Phillips Lovecraft (1890–1937), the horror-story writer. Sonia Green was his first wife. Alfred Galpin was an acquaintance of Crane's from Cleveland.

intended to write for some time, and in which you must believe my fullest and most intense sincerity is voiced.

When grandma wrote me awhile ago about Mr. Curtis and his devotion to you—describing as she did, such a human and very loveable person, I was exceedingly happy. But when—later in the course of the letter she mentioned that you felt that no alliance was worth anything that "broke" our relationship—that made me very worried and sad. I have spoken to you about this attitude of your's before, and you should not persist in assuming what I feel is a somewhat biased and un-natural attitude toward it. I also feel that you are unduly influenced by what Zell has to say on such subjects, and you should know that she is a very different type of personality than you and is in a very different relationship to life. The same differences—you should be aware of in whatever opinions you hear from other people on the same subject. [(] And remember that people —sometimes no matter how much they like you—are quite ready to sacrifice your personal happiness to prove or falsely prove their own merely personal theories, etc.) What I want to repeat to you again —and with emphasise—is that I, first, have an incessant desire for your happiness. Second, that I feel you are naturally most happy— or would be, given the proper opportunity—as a married woman. And thirdly, that I have perfect faith in your ability to select a man that loves you enough, and who has spirit and goodness enough to not only make you happy,—but to please *me* by his companion-ship. And you must remember, that *whoever you chose and no mat-ter what the circumstances might be, no such element could ever ef-fect our mutual relationship* unless you positively willed it,—which doesn't seem likely by the undue circumspection you feel about the matter.

You must remember, dear, that nothing would make me happier than your marriage—regardless of such matters as money. And for God's sake don't marry—or least *seek* to marry a mere moneybag. It has always hurt me to hear you jest about such matters. A few ma-terial limitations are not so much to the heart that is fed and the mind that is kept glowing happily with a real companionship. That's what I want to caution you now,—and I must speak plainly before it is too late, because you have made as many mistakes in your life as the average, and I don't want you to persist in what is a very sentimental attitude, I fear, regarding my reactions to your natural inclinations. As the years go on I am quite apt to be away for long periods, for I admit that the freedom of my imagination is the most precious thing that life holds for me,—and the only reason I can see for living. That you should be lonely anywhere during those times is a pain to me everytime I contemplate the future; you have already had a full share of pain, and you must accept—learn to identify and accept—the sweet, now, from the bitter. And that you are able to do that if you follow your trained insti[n]cts—I have not the slightest doubt. I'm not urging you to do anything you don't want to; you, I hope, will see that clearly enough. I only want you to know that life seems to be offering you some of its ripeness now, and that if you will stop trying to reconcile a whole lot of opposing and often very superficial judgements—and recall some of the uninjured emotions of your youth which have revived, very purely in your heart, I know—you will better decide *your happinesss* and *mine* than if you allow a clutter of complex fears and unrelated ideas to determine your judgement. I shall always love you just the same, whatever you do; and you know that. I can't help but say that I shall respect you even more as a woman, however, if you learn to see your relationship to life in a clear and coherent way; and you are doing that, I must say, with more grace and rectitude every day.

Do not, please, hesitate to write me your feelings after this. You should not fear—and you should trust to my understanding at least as much as to anyone I know.

My everlasting love,—/ your Hart

From Elizabeth Belden Hart

[Cleveland]
Sunday Eve
8. P.M. 9—14, 24

ALS, 4 pp.

My Dear Hart—

I fancy you and Sam are having a good visit to day. You will have much to talk over since you last met.

I have no particular news to write, so you must not expect much —but there comes times when I get so hungry to see you that the only way I can satisfy that desire is to write you— Father Crane has just left. We did not know he had come home, Bessie said he was to stay until the 20*th* [.] [1] He looked quite well and said he had gained three lbs. & had paid $125. per lb. He brot over the Garrettsvill[e] Journal to read a letter to Grace that he wrote to them while away, but as she was not here he asked if he might read it to me— It was very flowery— Quite a long letter.

Mother and Mr Curtis had just left for a drive & later have dinner at Hotel Cleveland— Nothing *too good* for Mother these days — Quite a change for her for which I am very glad— He certainly knows how to court the "Ladies"

We have had a very busy week. Bessie Smith [2] came up one week last Saturday to bring Elizabeth to the Clinic Hospital to be operated on for Goitre—and she stayed with us when she was not with her— All the other relatives have been up to see her in the meantime and of course were back & forth with us— Today William & Bessie & Edith [3] came for her, and took her home—

She went through it very successfully and recovered quickly— Will return to N.Y. in a few days— They are all happy over results —but it has been a very confusing time for us—so disturbing with our work—

We still are waiting to know if the house will be sold— Don't

---

[1] Arthur Crane was staying with his daughter Bess Crane Madden.

[2] Bessie Smith, a cousin of Grace's, and the mother of Elizabeth Smith.

[3] William Smith, the father of Elizabeth; Edith was her sister.

know what provisions to make for Winter [.] I feel every moment of delay means less in price— The street down to Euclid is getting filled up with very unsightly things. Gasoline stations, Garages etc. How are you getting along— Is your hay fever abating any? It certainly has been cold enough to check it. Rec'd a paper from Chicago with Verna Ross picture, announcing her engagement. Did you get my letter containing the pearl you wrote for— So very small. I wrapped it up in tissue paper—and hope you did not lose it out without opening it— I hope my dear boy you will soon be over your trouble and be normal again. We think of you a great deal & love you still more

Lovingly Grandma—

Write *me* soon—*sooner*—*soonest*

To Grace Hart Crane

110 Columbia Hts
Brooklyn, NY
Tuesday—9—23—24

TLS, 2 pp.

Dear Grace:

I allowed myself the luxury of three roses last Sunday, and I intend to make it as much a habit as my more persistent taste for "smokes" and wine will allow me—so pleasant have they made the room these last three days. . . But you are already aware of how much flowers effect me. And I am feeling better gradually as the cool days increase and the sneezing and nervous fever attending it begin to subside. You ask me about my summer, and I feel like answering that I am glad you feel that you have known little about it, for summer in a place like New York (and especially when you are rushed with work as I have been) is provocative of little but groans and sarcasms. Now it's over and "Sweet's Architectural Catalogue" is ready for press. I may be layed off, because of this latter fact, because there is very little to do there for the three months following the grand climax of the publication of that monstrous volume; but whatever happens it wouldn't be as bad as the stifling days and nights and the strain of working with your head as raw as beefsteak. Of course I had always some solace from my happy times with friends, and I had a little swimming at Long Beach and one week-end visit to the country, but you know about that already. O'Neil has been at his place in Provincetown, Mass. all summer, so I have not seen him as you thought. My happiest times have been with Emil, and I am looking forward to his return again from another South American trip next week. He is so much more to me than anyone I have ever met that I miss him terribly during these eight-week trips he takes for bread and butter. He doesn't know his father has died during his absence, so it will be a considerable shock to him on landing.

The news about Mr. O'Brien's offer is welcome in the sense that it promises you and Grandma a relief in smaller and easier quarters, but I can scarcely imagine the old house as a foreign property, perhaps no more standing.[1] It's so deep in my consciousness and so much the frame of the past. When it comes to my things, please chuck what books are in the glass-doored bookcase (never mind the others) in the drawers of my desk, the only article of furniture which I should like to keep. If you can't keep that you might box the books and mss and send them on to me here. There are photos, clippings, letters, etc. in the desk which I should like to try to hold on to. I have gotten so used to never being sure of next week's rent, however, that I feel like never accumulating an extra sheet of paper because it's painful for me to think of giving up things that have become a sort of part of me. I should rise above such feelings, I know, but haven't been able to thus far.

Sam is still here, and sleeping in the back room. His catarh improved. What his present plans are—I don't know, as I have scarcely had a word with him since last Friday night. He doesn't evidently think about spending much time with me. He has really had enough opportunity, and even broken engagements on the spur of the moment. It is all right with me, because I realize that Sam touches life at very few points where I do, and this even comes into our abstract discussions of literature, quite naturally, of course, be-

[1] Crane refers to an offer Grace received to buy the house.

cause I see literature as very closely related to life,—its essence, in fact. But for Sam, all art is a refuge *away* from life, and as long as he scorns or fears life (as he does) he is with [h]eld from just so much of the deeper content and value of books, pictures and music. He sometimes talks about them in terms as naive as an auctioneer would use. Yet he is instinctively so fine and generous that I will always love and pity him, however much my admiration is curtailed. I don't think he will remain in New York much longer. He is really bound to his family more than we've ever realized, although I have thought of that a good deal. He must have the assurance of his mother's attendance and he fancies that the "quiet" of Cleveland is a more normal environment for him. Well, if he feels that way, it's so. Feeling, his own feeling, is the only scale to use in such a matter, and I shall not urge him to stay here aginst his will—which couldn't be done anyway.

I have only written three short poems all summer, although I have had four previous ones published: two in the Little Review and two in "1924", a magazine published in Woodstock. These have brought me the usual amount of select applause, but no money.[2] I have sent a recent work to the Dial, from which I hope to God I get twenty dollars because I'm in bad need of a new suit—and that would help. Becky must have mis-read the "Times" if she saw any reference to me or a book of mine in it. I am being urged frequently to publish a volume, and I think I would have no trouble in finding a friendly publisher, but so far I have been withheld by my own desire to complete a long poem I am working on,—you have heard me speak of "The Bridge" poem—before gathering my things together. I need one good sized slice in the basket, and "The Bridge" I expect to fulfil that part. But a long poem like that needs unbroken time and extensive concentration, and my present routine of life permits me only fragments. (There are days when I simply have to "sit on myself" at my desk to shut out rhythms and melodies that belong to that poem and have never been written because I have succeeded only too well during the course of the day's

[2] "Possessions" and "Recitative" were published in *The Little Review*, X (Spring, 1924), 18–19; "Interludium" was published in *1924*, I (July, 1924), 2. Crane did not publish any other poems in *1924*.

work in excluding and stifling such a train of thoughts.) And then there are periods again when the whole world couldn't shut out the plans and beauties of that work—and I get a little of it on paper. It has been that way lately. And that makes me happy.

I note your reference to young Curtis, and hope he looks me up.[3] I think it had better be that way 'round than for me to be perhaps unduly aggressive. You don't know how it has pleased me to hear about your pleasant times together. It has really given your letters a new spice and charm, as I've already mentioned. You will have as merry a winter season as Time ever gave you, I'm sure!

An awful lot of love to Grandma, too!/ Hart

From Grace Hart Crane and Elizabeth Belden Hart

[Cleveland]
Monday Oct 6—1924.

ALS, 9 pp.

Dearest Hart:—

Mother and I are sitting here alone in the living room tonight—quite an unusual thing for us recently—but both very willing & satisfied as yesterday & day before's visiting has left us quite fatigued. She spent Saturday night & Sunday with Mrs Kirk while Mr Curtis & I were in Canton. We left here Saturday afternoon about two and had a beautiful ride, thro' the country arriving at Bess Smith's front porch about 4:30 where she served tea before we dressed & set out for Brookside Country Club for dinner & dancing. Their dinner party consisted of Geo. Frease & wife,[1] Bess & William, Chas. & myself— We met some very nice people and I had a wonderful time dancing all fine dancers— We came home about 12:45 had another bite to eat & then went to bed— Sunday, which was a simply gorgeous mellow day, began with late breakfast followed by a won-

---

[3] Kent Curtis (1891–   ), a popular novelist who wrote *The Blushing Camel* (New York: Appleton, 1927) and *The Tired Captains* (New York: Appleton, 1928).

---

[1] George and Jessie Frease and Hurxthal Frease, mentioned below, were cousins of Grace's.

derful drive around to some country estates, luncheon at the Congress Lake Country Club as the guests of Geo & Jessie Frease. Later to some wonderful homes on the other side of the lake—Chas & Geo. going in swimming, then back to Bess's where about twelve extra came in for supper—including Hurxstal Frease & his wife. He asked particularly about you, & wished to be remembered. About 8:30 we started for home & arrived here at 10:30. So much society & senseless conversation had just about finished me, & I tumbled into bed groaning. However we had a wonderful time & I did enjoy seeing all my relatives whom I haven't seen for a long time. There was a girl at the dance who asked particularly about you. She used to play with you and Joe [2] on those tragic visits you used to make to Canton. So you see you occasionally make a lastly impression on the girls—You actually would have enjoyed the country's beauty & wonderful air & I thought of you a great deal of the time, as I *always* do.

You probably have received my last long letter mailed here Thursday evening & sent by air mail— We were very glad to receive your little postal this morning—telling of your change of room—good health etc.

I am glad Sam has a job & is going to try out New York. Don't be too critical of him—poor fellow he has a difficult nature, & he has to work things out in his own way—as we all do— This is an awful wrench for him, & he is no doubt suffering a great deal in getting adjusted to everything at once.

Mr O'Brien has backed out of his offer for the house—which leaves us looking forward to another winter in the old home. Well things might be worse and by spring we may make a sale that is a better one.

I am going to bed now and a full quota of sleep—for a change.

Loads of Love—Grace

My dear boy—: I see mother has left a space for me to fill out— providing I can find anything to put into it, that will be of interest to you now that she has told you all there is to tell, but I can tell you how much Grandma thinks of & loves her absent Grand Son,

---

[2] Probably Joseph Frease, a cousin of Hart's.

and how glad I was to read your little note or card this morning—. Which was so cheery, it sent a thrill of gratitude through our hearts to hear that you were feeling well again—after your hard summer & also that you have at last got the room you have wanted so much— and that your work is not so strenuous.

The last few days here have been gorgeous—I feel it is positively cruel for any one to have to stay in doors— Mother seems to have had a wonderful time in Canton, so much fuss and attention shown She & Mr Curtis— Not a moment was wasted. They certainly know how to entertain—I was so glad she could go.

Lillian [3] has come to Cleveland for good now, to get some position preparatory to getting established in her chosen profession— She has several things in view—and seems to take quite well— She is taking a night course to prepare for her final examination. I feel sure of her success—

If we have to remain another winter in the old home—we have much ahead of us to do—no house cleaning done—coal not in, etc, but may be its for the best—any way its home to me—I love it for its associations— I only wish I were ten years younger and I were'nt getting so lazy. I really don't like to work any more. Isn't that too bad?

Well—I'm getting too sleepy to write intelligably, so I know you will excuse me won't you dear—

Write us just as often as you can its such a joy to hear from you when we can't see you—as Mother remarked after getting one of your letters—it gives me more of a thrill to get a letter from *"my boy"* than from any lover I ever had. I thought that was a pretty nice compliment to you so I send it on—so you may think of it and give her that pleasure *"very often"*—and I shall share it also. Be of good courage—your success is almost in sight— We all have to struggle for the things that are worth having in this life—but the battle with ourselves is grand; when we have over come [,] but good night—I wish I could have your goodnight kiss as in times gone by—

Lovingly/ Grandma

[3] Lillian Belden.

Dear Hart,

The enclosed snapshots were taken in our back yard the day Helen, Zell, Mrs. Smith and the baby were here. I think they are excellent. Especially of grandmother Hart.[4]

Hart began a week's vacation from Sweet's on October 14. Most of the time he spent in his new room with its view of the Manhattan skyline, the harbor, and, of course, the Brooklyn Bridge.

To Grace Hart Crane and Elizabeth Belden Hart

> [Brooklyn, New York]
> 110 Columbia Hts.
> Oct. 14"—24

ALS, 3 pp.

Dear Grace and Grandma:

Magnificent days,—the last week and today also. I am glad to be free from the office during this week—as I hope to take long walks, write, sleep late and read, and perhaps take a few days with Brown in Woodstock. (He is still living there on the slope of a mountain.) Yesterday, tho a holiday, I spent at the office by special request as there was some final work on the catalogue to be finished up. You may be interested to know that my detention there seems to be quite certainly assured and I'm on very good terms with the entire organization. I'm accordingly, looking forward to many more months there, and a raise in salary within 2 months. I certainly deserve it, and my clothes are now causing me real concern. There comes a stage in repairs when almost daily attention is needed— and that, in itself, can consume considerable funds.

I'm enormously happy in this back room. Ever since moving in I've slept better. And it's fixed up almost as charmingly as my old room at home. It's only about one third as large, yet there is the

---

[4] This note was written by Grace. The enclosures are lost.

view, which compensates for lack of inside spaciousness, and room enough for me to pace back and forth plentifully while a poem or idea is brewing. At first I thought I should keep the old front room, too, but the first week's expensive rent proved ridiculous for one of my means.

Sam, as I wrote before, has been working in a bookstore. For nearly two weeks I didn't see him at all. Then last Saturday I called on him at his shop and invited him over for Sunday evening. He brought that queer Lovecraft person with him, so we had no particularly intimate conversation. Just as well, of course, as I am sure they would have been the same disparagements of everything and almost everybody, as usual. He isn't getting along any better with his boss here than he did with Eglin [1] in Cleveland, and despite my reminding him of this and other examples of the past he still feels himself the eternal martyr and longs for his bed at home, his mending and home-washed laundry and home cooked food. I've stopped caring what he does until he has more interesting complaints to offer against life than such childishness. He may decide to go back at any time. I don't know. Meanwhile, instead of hiring himself a decent room here where he could have rest and solitude when he craves it,—he continues to stay in one room on a noisy street with George Kirk [2] and some other book peddler.

Harry Candee and his mother are back from another long trip in Italy and England. Harry said (I've only talked with him over the phone so far) that he lost my address here and had written me a letter addressed to 1709. If it has come yet please remember to forward it. They have gone to Maine for ten days after which Mrs. Candee is to undergo an operation. It may be 2 or 3 weeks before I see Harry, then.

One of the first things I had planned to mention in this letter are the recent snaps. I was very much delighted, and especially, Grandma, to have some really good pictures of you! They are very endearing and characteristic. Zell also sent me a series which in-

[1] A bookseller in Cleveland for whom Loveman had worked. See Hart's letter of November 10, 1923.
[2] A bookseller from Cleveland.

cluded a wonderful picture of "Nanny" [3] in one of them. "Nanny" is certainly one of the oddest looking of the human species that I have ever seen. She looks always like a fragile female satyr, if there could be such a thing. Since our last so successful and merry meeting, Zell and I have reopened our correspondence. Yesterday she wrote me that she was leaving for Europe on the 22nd, etc. and would see me here a few days beforehand. Helen is also coming along. But you know all such matters already, no doubt.

Your recountal of the Canton social excursion was delightful, in fact all your letters lately are filled with the kind of charm that emanates from a gain in happiness and a victory over stubborn and harsh memories. You don't know how happy it makes me! You seem to become more and more your essential self. It takes someone's real affection to do that for you—to permit the conditions, at any rate, for such a rejuvenation of the spirit—and you know how much I have been hoping that you would let nothing come in your way to keep you from responding completely to your happiness. I know you are quite in love, so you need not bother to spoil it all by keeping on saying that you are afraid that you are "going to." Most women never know when they are really in love anyway—but you can't fool me any longer about yourself, Madame, because I'm too delighted to be able to encourage you in this happy direction.

O I must tell you that Gorham has suddenly fallen on a very remunerative job. It's a joke—his work, I mean,—but it pays to be the managing editor of a magazine that circulates to 160,000 every month. You have probably see[n] "Psychology" on the racks in drug and book stores.[4] He started in only last week. His new income combined with Lisa's ought to make their living almost luxurious.

Emil left last Saturday for another long trip to S. America and back. His father's death and the shock of first knowing about it at the pier almost transformed him all the while he was here. It was something of a strain on me, also, to be with such an unhappy man and to be able to do so little.

[3] "Nannie" was Zell Hart Deming's mother.
[4] Munson edited *Psychology* from 1924 to 1926.

I am going to look [up] Elizabeth Smith very soon. Have meant to do it for some time, but Sue, Gorham and others take up so much of the little time I have. It's been a pleasure to write you like this,—for once in the daylight and without the sense of rushing so.

Love,/ Hart

From Grace Hart Crane

[Cleveland]
Wednesday Evening—
Oct. 15—[1924?]

ALS, 5 pp.

Dearest Hart:

When I returned from town this afternoon I found your very charming letter—which was really one of the most delightful ones we have ever received. It was full of relaxtion & geniality which no doubt was due to your absence from the office—and the knowledge that the next few days were *all yours.*

Your reference to my being in love & it being so tracable in my recent letters, certainly makes me smile. Purely imagination on your part my dear, *purely imagination.* I've written you just as cheerfully many times before, altho I may not have been able to recite so many pleasant experiences or attentions as have been mine in the last two months. Yes I think I am in love or something, & I do not want to be—it is slavery. But Chas. is so thoughtful and considerate of me—that I just feel myself slipping slipping slipping. Maybe my wise, sophisticated son can offer me the proper advice for the situation. Please do answer my "S.O.S."

Last Sunday was the most wonderful day—& mother & I got an early start for Warren, arriving there about eleven thirty and having luncheon at Zells. Later we called at Uncle Lo's who is in a very critical condition, in many ways much like your grandfather Hart's last days. They do not expect he will recover from this attack and so we shall not be surprised to hear almost any day, of his death. Later we called at Helen & Griswolds and had a good play with the baby. She certainly is a prize—but her perpetual motion & activities do not permit you to do much loving. She just flies from one thing to another—never still a moment, & chuckles out loud most of the time. We started home in time to get the wonderful picture of the autumn hills in the rays of the setting sun. It was rare beauty which you only see for a few days every year—and I felt greedy to get all of it I could.

Zell has planned a very interesting trip, and you will likely hear all about it when you see her. She is planning to be gone until about the fifteenth of January.

It was good to hear of Gorhams good fortune— I am an admirer of his and Liza's you know—& I feel that such earnestness as theirs, should and will win them suitable compensations. Remember me most affectionately to both of them. I often think of them.

It is needless to say that your comment upon your own position with your firm, is most gratifying and I am both cheered & assured by it. It makes me so happy to think of you in a room that you enjoy as much as your present one— It is the one spot that is absolutely all yours—to be yourself & to think in, & I just know how *much* that means to you.

I have been very much shocked & depressed this week over the tragic misfortune which has come to Ada Stevens. I think you will recall whom I mean— She was on her way to a dinner party last Saturday evening in a machine with four others, when an intoxicated driver from the opposite direction rammed into their car, & wrecking it & pretty nearly everyone in it. Ada was on the front seat with the driver—a Dr Curtis—She was thrown through the car & her skull fractured in two places—& one of her eyes so badly injured that the doctors predict the loss of it's sight, possibly both. These besides body bruises from head to foot. They were on the West Side—in Edgewater park when it occured—so that they took her to a hospital on West Franklin Ave. I drove over to see her today—& I just feel broken hearted over her condition. It is pitiful beyond words. You know her husband died just a year ago & left her bankrupt. Since then she has given up her lovely home, gone into a flat & has been working hard every day to support herself & keep her adopted daughter—(about 15 yrs) in school. Her good looks were about all that she had left—& now she may be scarred for life, & blind! I'd much rather she wouldn't live than to have any such recovery. Life is certainly *hard, impossible* to understand at times.

So glad you liked the snap shots—but I knew you *would*. It is such a good likeness of grandmother—and she was determined not to be snapped.

My Chas. is sojourning in Chicago this week—so I am having more time to myself in which to do many things which have been neglected. He will be back Friday.

I want you to plan on Christmas at home with us this year. Never again do I want to be deprived of you on that day—when you are no farther away than New York. You must come home more often if for no other reason than to look me over & tell me in what respect I am falling behind. I need your criticism & suggestion both for my physical appearance & mental status. I value your opinions along these lines—more than all the rest put together—& I *mean* just that. I need your criticism for I am horribly afraid I am getting behind.

The hour is late, & I must go to bed— I am very tired besides—

I am inclosing Harry Candee's letter. Did you know that Charlotte Neally was going to have a baby—

With all my love,/ Devotedly/ Grace

P.S. If you have any duplicates of the snap shots I sent you—send them to me, as I am minus those like I sent you.

Hart replied to his mother's "S.O.S." by confirming his intention to return to Cleveland for the Christmas holidays, promising a celebration of what he hoped would be his mother's engagement to Charles Curtis.

To Grace Hart Crane and Elizabeth Belden Hart

[Brooklyn, New York]
110 Columbia Hts
Tuesday—
Oct. 21st, '24

TLS, 2 pp.

Dear Grace and Grandma:

The last day of my vacation, and somehow the best! So cold and sharp it is, you might think it time for turkey. You know how keenly brilliant the atmosphere around these parts can be—frequently in any season. On such days one gets an even better edge to this glorious light here by the harbor. The water so very blue, the foam and steam from the tugs so dazzlingly white! I like the liners best that are painted white—with red and black funnels like those United Fruit boats across the river, standing at rest. And you should see the lovely plumes of steam that issue from the enormous heights of the skyscrapers across the way. I've been toasting my feet at an electric stove, a kind of radio heater that I have in my room, and glancing first at the bay, then with another kind of satisfaction at my shelves of books and writing table,—for a long time unable to think of anything but a kind of keen sensual bliss, that is in itself something like action—it contains so much excitement and pleasure.

After breakfast I called up Zell and Helen. They arrived yesterday but I was too occupied with other things to look them up that early. I see them at the Waldorf at four this afternoon. Which reminds me that I have already posted a steamer letter, or rather, poem, to Zell, which she won't glimpse, I hope, until she starts down the bay. She had written me, asking for a poem in this connection, and knowing how hard such "occasional" pieces are for me to write, I worried considerably. But it's not so bad for a piece of pure invention. I enclose it here for your amusement,—the only thing lacking is the photo of myself looking out my window here, of which I haven't a copy now to send you.[1]

---

[1] A copy of this photograph very likely appears in *Voyager*, facing p. 358.

On going up to "headquarters" the other day for ch[o]colates for my friends, I learned that CA had been here during September,— just how long I didn't ask. Which shows that I'm to expect the complete "go-by" from him in the future. He must be mortified about something—too much so to show his head. I'll send him a Christmas card once a year, and bless his soul! Which reminds me that I certainly do hope to join you at Christmas,—it will be high time, and we'll celebrate. I shall bring two quarts of something good from the metropolis and you'll BOTH have to break ALL THE RULES! I also want Mr. Curtis to join us during part of it. I'm sure to like him, and we'll tching-tching your health.

Give Margaret and Ralph [2] my regards when you think of it.

Love, as always—/ Hart

WITH A PHOTOGRAPH
TO ZELL, NOW BOUND FOR SPAIN

From Brooklyn Heights one sees the bay:
And, anchored at my window sill,
I've often sat and watched all day
The boats stream by against the shrill
Manhatten skyline,—endlessly
Their mastheads filing out to sea.

And just so, as you see me here
(Though kodaked somewhat out of focus,
My eyes have still the proper locus)
I'm flashing greetings to your pier,
Your ship, your auto-bus in France—
All things on which you glide or prance
Down into sunny Spain, dear Zell.
Good berths, good food and wine as well!

I hope to know these wishes a true
Forecasting. Let me hear from you.
Enclose some petals from a wall
Of roses in Castile, or maybe garden stall;
While I'll be waiting at this old address,
Dear Aunt, God-mother, Editress!

[2] Ralph and Margaret worked for Mrs. Crane and Mrs. Hart.

To Grace Hart Crane and Elizabeth Belden Hart

[Brooklyn, New York]
110 Columbia Hts.
Oct. 25"—'24' Saturday

ALS, 2 pp.

Dear Grace and Elizabeth B:—

One might say justly that this "Season" has begun here. At least this last week convinced me of it as much as I'll ever care to be, Everybody is getting back to N.Y. from summer vacations, trips abroad and where-not; the new plays are starting up everywhere; orchestras and divas tuning up—and unless one holds on to his head mightly—it's liable to take complete flight and leave you some kind of applauding machine, handshaking automation or what not.

I saw Zell on Tuesday, after writing you. Pacing around her room at the Waldorf, folding nightgowns, hanging coats, fuming about passports and packages which had failed to be delivered, Zell looked tired, and we didn't have much of a meeting. I nearly sank with mortification when she informed me casually that she was not even going near *Spain* and had not intended to from the outset of her plans. How did you ever get so bawled up on her plans as to write me about that as you did? I finally explained the joke of my verses to her on that score, as I thought she would enjoy them all the better, maybe, when she found them in her stateroom.

Helen stayed over with Dorothea until this evening. They had me out to dinner Thursday evening, and last evening both of them called on me here. Allan Gordon brought them over. Helen went quite as wild as anyone when she saw the view. She said she would tell you all about her "approval" when she sees you. Yesterday afternoon after work I had coffee with Josephson and Burton Rascoe,[1] a celebrated critic (though a bad egg), lunched today with Gorham and Edwin Seaver, editor of "1924" magazine,[2] and later had tea as

[1] Burton Rascoe (1892–1957), the author of the popular newspaper column "Bookman's Daybook," and editor of the book review supplement of the New York *Herald Tribune*.
[2] Edwin Seaver (1900–   ), the critic, who was one of the founders of *1924*.

Stewartt Mitchell's guest at the Brevoort. Monday night I'm invited out to theatre and dinner by Waldo Frank—and so you see why it's evident that the "Season" has begun. As usual I'm spending as much time as possible in my room first because it's attractive, second, because I like a *little* loneliness, and perhaps mostly, because I want to get some reading and writing done.

Last Sunday morning I took some more pictures of my Quarters and environs. What "turned out" I'm sending you.[3] Two of them showing the harbor and skyline across I found could be made into a partial panorama with a little glue. This is just about one half of the picture from my window as I look out every morning. You've already seen a part of the other magnificent half looking to the right, toward the Bridge. Then, I'm sending one view (with the roses on the window ledge) just as you see out through the glass— directly across. Isn't it refreshing to wake up and find a brilliant white steamer cleanly "parked" so near you—and from all sorts of spicy countries? The other picture shows a corner of my room. Writing table at the right—your gay dressing gown installed as you see. Don't lose track of these photos as I want to keep them always. I think I have been remarkably successful with such a tiny kodak.

I'm dead tired tonight (do you blame me!) and so shall turn in early.

Haven't seen Sambo [4] for about two weeks. He promised to call last Sunday but didn't. Well, well "not at all", as Charlotte used to say.

fare-thee-well, my dears!

I'm expecting to hear from youse tomorrow./ Hart

[3] Several of these pictures are in the Columbia University collection. See also the photographs in *Voyager*, facing p. 358.
[4] Sam Loveman.

From Grace Hart Crane

[Cleveland]
Friday 5 P.M.
Oct. 31—1924.

ALS, 7 pp.

Dearest Hart:—

Another week has passed & that makes two, since you last heard from home. Certainly you must be thinking that something unusual has happened—but not so—just rushed from morning til night trying to do all of the things that come along this time of year, like house cleaning, business, looking over ones clothes & trying to determine what you have to have & where to get it the cheapest. I havn't gotten very far in this last particular, & I am nearly frantic sometimes trying to make myself presentable. L—— B—— is to come at five tonight to stay all night and maybe tomorrow & Sunday. Of course I am delighted?—I think I wrote you before that she resigned her position in Washington some weeks ago & came here to seek one & to attend the classes which prepare her for the Ohio Bar examination in December. Well we did not ask her to stay with us— I thought that as long as she had other relatives here she should stay with them— She is an *awful bore,* & nearly drives me insane—besides she smells & I can't endure that you know. But I think it looks as if we would have to for a few days—

One of the things which has taken a great deal of my time is my visits to Ada Stevens who is in the hospital on the West Side. I wrote you about her accident I'm sure. She has been a pitiful object —& I have gone clear over there on an average of three times a week to try to cheer her up & take her food etc. She is coming through much better than anyone ever dreamed—& may be taken home tomorrow, altho' so far hasn't been allowed to raise her head one inch from the pillow on account of the compound fracture of the skull[.] She has lost the sight of one eye—but will not be nearly so badly scarred as we thought at first. While we are speaking of the sick, & hospitals etc. I will get the rest of such news across to you so that you may know which friends of yours are being cut up & losing some of their organs. A wire from Frank Ross from Battle Creek today states that "Blanche successfully underwent a serious operation this morning & was resting comfortably." I knew she was there but did not know that she was going to undergo an operation. Yesterday I received a long letter from Bess Smith in which she tells of Eleanor's [1] being in the Canton Hospital for an appendicitis. Operated upon on Tuesday—seemed it was a hurry up case. Bess also said that Elizabeth was back at the Smith College Club (something must have gone wrong with the Mehans) and wasn't feeling very well—very nervous & somewhat homesick or depressed. She wants you to go to see her.

Well that is about all of the health report, excepting that I myself spent two days in bed this week as the result of a vicious attack of acute indigestion which struck me in the night—Sunday—& I really thought my time had come. It was more like ptomaine. Mr. Heller's [2] work fixed me up by six that morning & I have been going very slow on food ever since.

Your little kodaks were so interesting I must congratulate you on having such a wonderful view from your window. I should think you never would be lonely with such an interesting ever changing scene streatched out before you & I love to think of you there on Sunday morning's when you do not have to hurry away and leave it. I can see you just as plainly as tho' I were there—pipe in your mouth, dressing gown on—strolling back & forth in your room, gazing & thinking on many many things.

Your letters have recently reflected such an improved happier—stronger more hopeful even gayer state of mind, that I am very happy in thinking you are getting more enjoyment greater satisfaction out of life than a few months back. You certainly have written me some wonderful letters—letters that show your growth your soul more clearly to me than ever before. I know you are making progress I am bursting with pride to be the mother of such a dear boy. Sometimes I think that the knowledge that I am having someone good & thoughtful to me, makes you happy. It ought to—but goodness knows I've waited a long time for the right sort of consideration.

[1] Eleanor Smith, a cousin of Mrs. Crane's.
[2] Mr. Heller, a Christian Science practitioner in Cleveland.

I am counting the days until Christmas & nothing must be allowed to keep you away from me on that day. Yes we will all drink out of the bottle you bring along—and we will have as gay & happy a Christmas as we've ever known & probably the most so of all.

I do not know just what your opinion of Mr Curtis will be—but Hart he has a wonderfully gentle nature, big heart & great tolerance—most unselfish & is devotedly in love with me. He is a thorough bred—altho' a little bit oldfashioned in his type. Loves life & beauty [,] music & art—& all of the best things that life has to offer— He plays poker—dances—swims—is 64 & the figure of a youth. He is prepared to like you & is only worrying about whether you will like him or not.

I think his son Kent will be here for Christmas unless he decides suddenly to go to Europe again. He is now at the Allerton Hotel— #45, E. 55th St. I think—& I do wish you would break the ice & call him up. He is collaborating with some fellow who is writing a light or comic opera—I do not know how "literary" he is or in what class to place him—but I don't believe he is any fool—& I wish you would try to get in touch with him—for a lunch or something. If you *should, be cautious* about revealing the extent of his fathers regard for me—as I think he is not as well informed on that subject as you are.

Your poem to Zell on her departure was very clever & you needn't care it it did refer to Spain. I knew she wasn't going *directly* there but she told me that she was expecting to touch Spain on her return.

It must be wonderful to be in New York these marvelous days— I have thought about it so often of late—and I feel sure you enjoy it fully as much as anyone could. It has so much to give to a person like you, & you would never be satisfied very long back here, or any where any less attractive.

Hart I have nothing to say concerning your father's action in failing to see you in New York. He isn't like any other human being I ever knew, & certainly a failure as a parent. Probably Frances was with him, & he didn't receive much encouragement in any interest in you. I never have felt that she wanted any thing but indifference from C.A. toward you & while I don't excuse him a particle on the account I am not blind to her part in the affair. I think I never will believe him again—let him talk on—but forget anything & everything he has to say. The moment he has left you—it is as though he hadn't said it. I haven't seen him since July—& I hope the day will come when his name will have no power to move me one way or the other. I believe you are getting there—& the sooner the better.

Tomorrow Chas. has to drive to Akron on business & I am going along. We will have lunch at the Portage and I shall go into that Drugstore where you used to slave for C.A. & I shall think of you, *everywhere*. It makes me weep when I think of it, and the struggles you went through those days. I am sure there can never be anything half as bitter again.

It is getting late & I must go to bed. Since starting this, I've stopped for dinner, done the dishes, talked politics with Lillian & grandmother (who is just bursting with campaign news) & have come up stairs for the night.

Write me more good letters soon, & believe me when I say I just "love you to death."

Devotedly/ Grace.

P.S. I am planning a luncheon for Wednesday—Mrs Wilson, Mary Kent, Mrs Reed, Mrs Collver, Mrs Barnes and Mrs Kenny. So I have a lot to do before then.

Iris Brown was married very suddenly last Monday morning to a Mr Lheiber, of Wade Park Manor, and they are honeymooning at the West Chester Biltmore. He is a Yale graduate of 1920 Columbia post graduate. He must be awfully smart!!!!!

To Grace Hart Crane and Elizabeth Belden Hart

[Brooklyn, New York]
Sunday Nov. 9—24
110 Columbia Heights

TLS, 1 p.

Dear Grace and Grandma:—

I was long enough hearing from you, and, I guess, have been long enough answering. No revenge and tit-for-tat intended, however. I've been just too rushed to even brush my teeth!

Last Saturday the Munsons and I went over into the New Jersey hills to visit Kenneth Burke and family. His farmstead, wife and kids made us welcome—including a collie dog and tom cat who sleep, eat and play together. We consumed six quarts of fine home made blackberry wine in the evening and then all went out and made the roads and hillsides resound with songs and merriment. I sat down in the wrong place once, and in the darkness whacked my head against a tree—which I felt the next morning. But our hilarity was worth remembering. Sunday afternoon we had to taxi several miles through the country to catch a train in time to bring us back to town for dinner with Waldo Frank. Afterwards a lecture by R. A. Orage,[1] former editor of the "New Age" (London) and now returned from Avon-Fountainbleau, France. Jean Toomer has also just returned from there and there was much to talk over.

Monday Allan Tate arrived from Washington to take a job that Sue has been good enough to recommend him for in her office and at the same time I had to greet Wilbur Underwood [2] who had been here about a week, then, but whom I had not met thus far, Harry,[3] who just got back, you'll remember has left again for a winter in

[1] Alfred Richard Orage (1873–1934) edited from 1907 to 1922 the *New Age*, a predominantly socialist weekly review of politics, literature, and art. A follower of P. D. Ouspensky and George Gurdjieff, Orage lectured on the year that he had spent at the Gurdjieff Institute, Le Prieure, at Fontainebleau.

[2] Wilbur Underwood, a poet whom Hart had met when he was working for his father in Washington in 1920. Underwood had a minor position in the State Department.

[3] Harry Candee.

England—so suddenly that I didn't get round to see him at all. Provincetown Theatre for some O'Neill one-act sea-plays on Wednesday night,[4] dinner with Sue on Thursday, and last night a wild jubilee with Tate and some of Wilbur's friends—so you see how it goes. I have not had a moment to follow your suggestion about young Curtis, nor to see Elizabeth Smith, which I feel rather badly about.

Sam is still staying with George Kirk and they both made me a call on Friday evening. Sam misses his telephone conflabs with you very much, and mentioned that he wanted to write you soon. He is apparently in the very pink of good health. I guess he will remain here indefinitely, after all.

Zell has already sent me a note expressing her pleasure and admiration at the "bon voyage" poem, which reminds me that I have had a singularly pleasant Sunday—all alone in my room and writing some verses for "The Bridge". I'm feeling very cheerful these days and am glad to know from you that you are able to think of me in such complimentary terms. If I can manage to get my request for a raise in salary fulfilled I'll be able to get a new suit soon and that will relieve my spirits considerably.

I'm glad you have and liked so much the pictures I sent of my room and environs. Grandma, dear—*you* must write me a letter soon! You know I expect one now, every so often. I'll try and write more leisurely next time. Just now I *must* get back to my poem!

Love, / HART

4 Hart saw *S.S. Glencairn* at the Provincetown Theatre. This title was given to four plays in the **Glencairn cycle**: *Moon of the Caribbees, Bound East for Cardiff, In the Zone,* and *The Long Voyage Home.*

From Grace Hart Crane

[Cleveland]
Thursday, 8:30 P.M.
Nov 14 '25 [1924?] [1]

ALS, 7 pp.

My dear Hart:—

I have just been looking at the little kodaks you sent me a short time ago—and especially the one with the roses which seems to say that you were very close just a few feet back—and I just feel almost like weeping because I can't reach out & touch you, see you or really hear your voice. Sometimes I just revolt with every fibre of my being when I allow myself to think about how separated we have become. I never dreamed when you left here over one year & a half ago, that I should see you only twice in that time. Really sometimes I find myself startled at the thought that I have a son—over twenty five—living entirely independently of me in every way. Well I do hope you will not disappoint me at Christmas, & while we won't be so attractive around here as we once were, we will enjoy one another. Christmas comes on Thursday—so you can get away no later than Wednesday night, & perhaps sooner—& remain with us until Sunday night at least. Do you think Sam will be home for Christmas? I can think of only a very few whom you will be interested in seeing back here— We will try to go to Warren & see the baby—if you would care to—

I had a letter from Zell written in board S. S. Paris enroute to France—& she spoke very flatteringly of you & your work—so that I think your poem made a hit even tho it *did* refer to *Spain*.

Tuesday night I went with Mr Curtis to dine at his daughters and her husband—"the Burgins". We had an excellent dinner & a very pleasant evening. She seems to be much more closely in touch with Kent Curtis than does his father—remarking that that day she had had a cable from him announcing his arrival in London. He intends to return after Christmas, & if he hasn't sold his yaght, &

---

[1] The reference to Zell and the poem that Hart wrote for her suggests that Grace wrote this letter in 1924.

sail to Florida in it. I do not see how he can ever expect to arrive at any literary fame unless he settles down for awhile. I do not think I am going to like him, as from what I have heard them say about him & his ways has made me think him to be an intellectual snob & egotist, two things I *despise*. But I shall wit[h]hold my criticism until I have met him—and even at the very best I know he is not *one half* as *fine* as you. This is no jest, I am serious about it. You do not know how much I love your big, broad outlook, and your ability to appreciate the real & worth while, whenever & in whom ever they appear. I can see that your understanding is growing deeper & more comprehensive all the time, & it is going to be invaluable to you in your writing, & in you[r] contact with people & life in general.

I told you Sam would calm down after he had been in New York awhile. To Sam's kind New York frightens, & it is apt to take some time to get any repose. I miss Sam too—with his telephone visits & rehearsal of his difficulties but I am glad he made the break from his family— You must tell him I miss him.

Saturday night is the first of Mrs Slaghts' dancing parties at the Manor—& Chas. has invited me to attend all six of them. I suppose they will be very smart affairs. Your old friend & boss, Amsden [2] & wife are going I am told. They are very good friends of Chas.['] daughter & husband, the Burgins. They play poker together.

Frank Ross writes that Blanche continues to improve. I must write her again tomorrow.

Good night my dear—

With all my love/ devotedly/ Grace—

Do go to see Elizabeth Smith. She is feeling sort of discouraged & would welcome you, I am sure.

Did you receive my last long letter sent by air mail which should have reached you on Sunday evening Special Delivery?

[2] Amsden, with Stanley Patno, operated the direct mail advertising firm in Cleveland where Crane had worked from August, 1922, to March, 1923.

To Grace Hart Crane

[Brooklyn, New York]
Sunday evening
Nov. 16"—24
Columbia Hts.

ALS, 2 pp.

Dear Grace—

Another very active week. Luncheon with someone different every day,—and nearly always someone to take up the evening. But I have been so interested in several incompleted poems that I've sat up very late working on them, and so by the advent of Saturday felt pretty tuckered out. There's no stopping for rest, however, when one is the "current" of creation, so to speak, and so I've spent all of today at one or two stubborn lines. My work is becoming known for its formal perfection and hard glowing polish, but most of those qualities, I'm afraid, are due to a great deal of labor and patience on my part. Besides working on parts of my "Bridge" I'm engaged in writing a series of six sea poems called "Voyages" (they are also love poems) and one of these you will soon see published in "1924", [1] a magazine published at Woodstock and which I think I told you about heretofore.

It darkened before five today and the wind's onslaught across the bay turns up white-caps in the river's mouth. The gulls are chilly looking creatures—constantly wheeling around in search of food here in the river as they do hundreds of miles out at sea in the wakes of liners. The radiator sizzles in the room here and it is warm enough for anyone's comfort, even your's. I feel as though I were well arranged for a winter of rich work, reading and excitement—there simply isn't half time enough (that's my main complaint) for all that is offered. And the weeks go by so fast! It will soon be sneezing season again before I know it.

O'Neil has a new play at the Greenwich Village Theatre—a tragedy called "Desire Under the Elms" which I'll see sometime this

---

[1] No part of "Voyages" was published in *1924*. Parts I–IV were published in *The Little Review*, XII (Spring–Summer, 1926), 13–15.

week. He and Agnes [2] were in town for the premiere and I called on them at their rooms in the Lafayette one evening. They have gone back to their place at Ridgefield for a few days and then are going to Bermuda—perhaps to remain all winter. I'm reminded every now and then that I might have sent you interesting clippings and articles about O'Neil and his work in papers and magazines, and I intend to do better in the future and send some of them to you. I think you'ld be interested. Rheinhardt [3] is staging his "Hairy Ape" in Berlin this winter, and dozens of performances of his other plays are being produced in Vienna, Paris, Copenhagen, Budapesth, Munich etc. He seems to have Europe in applause more than America. That is true of Waldo Frank's work in France, also, where he has been much translated and more seriously considered, far more so, than here at home. The American public is still strangely unprepared for its men of higher talents, while Europe looks more and more to America for the renascence of a creative spirit.

Your letter came last night—was tucked under my door when I came in at one o'clock. Its tenderness and affection were welcome adjuncts to a good long sleep. I thought of you, too, just "turning in"—very likely—after the dance you mentioned, and I was very happy to think of your having had a lyric evening, dancing as you so enjoy doing. I'd like to see the Amsdens and the Patnos myself. They were a little unfair to me,—but good sports too, in a way and unusually merry bosses. I still like to think of those five o'clock booze parties we had in the office and how giddily I sometimes came home for dinner. You were very charming and sensible about it all, too, and I thank my stars that while you are naturally an inbred Puritan you also know and appreciate the harmless gambols of an exuberant nature like my own. It all goes to promise that we shall have many mery times together later sometime when we're a little closer geographically.

My—but how the wind is blowing. Rain, too, on the window now! There was a wonderful fog for about 18 hours last week. One couldn't even see the garden close behind the house—to say noth-

---

[2] Agnes Boulton, Eugene O'Neill's first wife.
[3] Max Reinhardt (1873–1943), the Austrian actor, author, producer, and director.

ing of the piers. All night long there were distant tinklings, buoy bells and siren warnings from river craft. It was like wakening into a dreamland in the early dawn—one wondered where one was with only a milky light in the window and that vague music from a hidden world. Next morning while I dressed it was clear and glittering as usual. Like champagne, or a cold bath to look it. Such a world!

Love, as always, your/ Hart

From Grace Hart Crane

[Cleveland]
[November 18, 1924?] [1]
Tuesday A.M.

ALS, 4 pp.

My dear Hart

Yesterday I went into Halle's & had Mr McWaters help me select a suit for you [.] I sent it from the store and it will probably arrive at 110 Columbia Hghts. before this does. Now if you do not like it, or it is not a good fit, so that a tailor there could not fix it with slight expense—return it to me, right away—parcel post, *insured.* I rather think it will be all right. Grandma & I were going to give it to you for Christmas but think you need it to come home in & before—so have taken the risk of sending it to you.

I do hope it pleases in every way—but if not return it & I will try again if you give me instructions.

Have you had to buy a new overcoat this year? I hope you get your raise in salary. I am expecting a letter from you this morning. Margaret is here today— The weather is cold but sunny.

I had a *wonderful* time last Saturday night—& did not get home until 4 in the morning—

Helen & Griswold were up the other day— I ran across them

---

[1] In the following letter of November 20, Hart thanks his mother for the suit which she had sent him. Therefore, Mrs. Crane probably wrote this letter on November 18, 1924.

down town. Helen says you are looking very well—& seem happy. I asked her if you kept your mustache trimmed—& she said *no*—now Hart get busy with the scissors & trim it—you look so much better when you do. She also says you are in love— I will address you in that connection when you come home. You havn't been very confidential with me in that respect— I do not care how much you are in love, just so you do not *marry*— You know that would end your writing career and other ambitions. *So keep your head.* Love is a *sickness.*

Let me know right away about the suit—

Devotedly Yours/ Grace

Let me know as soon as possible when you will get here for Xmas, & how long you can stay.

To Grace Hart Crane and Elizabeth Belden Hart

New York City
Thursday morning
Nov. 20th, '24

TLS, 1 p.
LETTERHEAD: SWEET'S CATALOGUE SERVICE

Dear Grace and Grandma:

Nothing could have been more timely than your gift of the suit. It came last night; I have tried it on—and the tailor around the corner will have it ready for service in a few days. Everything fits that is already sewed up—and the cut and cloth of it are very pleasing indeed.

You don't know how much I appreciate it all. I was feeling rather hopeless about collecting enough for both a new suit and the carfare home—by a few week's savings. Well, it simply couldn't have been done, and I should have had to appear much as the prodigal, returning in woeful tatters. You see, your idea of sending my Christmas to me in advance was a very good one.

As far as coats are concerned—my purchase at Halle's two years ago is still in excellent shape. I had it re-lined this fall, thoroughly cleaned and pressed, and now the red cross stripes and cut seem to be more in style than ever. Don't you dare buy me anything more, now, for sentimental or other reasons. I feel undeserving enough of such wholesale gifts as you have already lavished. My raise, so far, is not forthcoming, so I may not be able to bring much to Cleveland but me and myself, but we'll have a jolly time, won't we!

I can't tell you yet how long I'll be able to get away, but I certainly won't be able to arrive before Christmas morning. I don't want to ask for extra time just now while there still is a chance of my getting a raise. It's simply a matter of not turning in too many requests at once.

I've got to get to work now. Thank you both again!

Love,/ Hart

To Grace Hart Crane and Elizabeth Belden Hart

[Brooklyn, New York]
[November 24, 1924?] [1]
Monday morning—

TLS, 1 p.

Dear Grace and Grandma:

Just a word . . . Yesterday was too occupied for me to get anything to you. Engagements both for luncheon and dinner. Tonight I am going to see O'Neill's great new play, "Desire under the Elms".

The suit is finished and on me now. Sue admires it, which, if you knew her better, would confirm our own judgement in a final way.

It is foggy and altogether disaggreeable, but I happen to be feeling very well and gay.

I'll write you more before next Sunday. Meanwhile, my apologies and fondest love. You have Zell's itinerary. Please let me know where to get her a letter for Christmas./ HART

[1] Crane's reference to *Desire under the Elms* in his letter of November 26 makes it clear that he wrote this letter on November 24.

To Grace Hart Crane and Elizabeth Belden Hart

[Brooklyn, New York]
110 Columbia Hts
Nov. 26th, '24

TLS, 1 p.

Dear Grace and Grandma:

I am writing rather early—for me—but it may be just as well, as I don't expect to have another moment in which to do so again before Sunday. Emil is back from the sea for ten days, and I have other engagements,—one, on Saturday night, which may be of special interest to you.

Paul Rosenfeld,[1] the critic, of whom, as you know, I am not especially fond, has just called up and invited me to a sort of reception he is going to give on Sat. evening for Jean Catel,[2] a French critic formerly on the staff of the Mercure de France. When Rosenfeld gives this sort of party—whatever you may feel about it—you at least know that everybody (spelled with a capital E) in modern American painting, letters and art generally—will be there. Well, I'm not only invited, but am urged to give a reading before them all from my poems. Alfred Kreymborg and Miss Marianne Moore will also read from their poems. So far I have declined to read anything—as I am no vocalist, and I certainly fear the stage fright. But on the other hand, I probably shall essay a poem or so, if I'm feeling at all assured at the time, as I hate to be known as too shy a wall flower to speak to even such a "picked" audience as that will be. While I lack almost no assurance on the value of my poems, taken generally, I admit that I am considerably flattered at this invitation occuring, as it does, before I have published a single volume. (The other two have been known for years). And so, pray with me that the tongue be less stubborn than usual in conveying my intentions from the written page.

Night before last I witnessed the most astonishing play ever

[1] Paul Rosenfeld (1890–1946), the American music and art critic.
[2] Catel, who had recently arrived from France, often wrote reviews of French literature for *Poetry* and the *Saturday Review of Literature*.

written by an American—O'Neill's tragedy, "Desire Under the Elms". And the acting was very fortunate, too. Knowing many of the actors at the Provincetown Theatre really adds to the pleasure I have in their performances. The city does yield one more interesting intimacies as time goes on. This winter promises to add more than ever. One gets tired of the swim at times, however, and it is good to have as restful a retreat as I have here by the river and upper harbor.

Saw Sam and George Kirk at dinner last night. They have taken to Italian restaurants with great zest, and Sam becomes more and more cosmopolitanized. He never fails to ask when and what I last heard from you. Maybe he will come home for Christmas, too, but I fear that he will be kidnapped by his family if he does, and not return here again. He says they are all complaining at his absence.

I hope you are both happy and in some state of thanksgiving.

my love to you—as always,/ Hart

To Grace Hart Crane

[Brooklyn, New York]
110 Columbia Hts
Sunday morning
Nov. 30th, '24

TLS, 1 p.

Dear Grace:

When I look back on the last 48 hours I must think myself lucky to be able to sit up to the table and write you at all. As it is, I feel both a little giddy with pleasure—and otherwise on the edge of a spell of grippe. But I seem to have an amazing amount of energy, and with regularity and quiet for a few days I think I'll pull through all right. My reading last night at the Rosenfeld party was a considerable success. The wonder is that I was able to attend.

On Friday night I am quite certain that I suffered at least a mild attack of the real ptomaine poisening from something I ate at dinner. I started to walk home after dinner, and before I got half way I began to swell up and burn like fire. Just the usual and bad-enough case of the hives, I thought at first. I finally managed to get to my bed, but was deathly sick besides. My pulse was pumping so that at the sink, as I was drinking some bicarbonate of soda, I lost my sight and hearing in a kind of rushing and smothering of the blood, and would have fainted had I tried to stand up any longer. Later on, when the case had apparently subsided and I was lying rigidly still in bed, it began all over again. It was perfectly maddening, and I never slept a wink all night. All this convinces me that my malady was something more than urticaria, and that I had eaten something positively poisenous. I was able to evacuate in both directions during the night, however, and somehow managed to go up to the office yesterday morning, retiring back to bed again as soon as work was over and not getting up until it was time to go to Rosenfeld's. In the meantime I had refrained from practically all food and taken a great deal of alkalithia and milk of magnesia, hot bath, etc. I was still very weak when I got to the party, but as whiskey and soda was served I quickly revived, and everyone thought I was a picture of health.

I'm very glad to have made the effort, after all, for I have reason now to feel more assured than ever in regard to my poetry. The crowd was representative as I had expected, delightfully informal, and proved very receptive. I had met at least half of them before,— Steiglitz, Georgia O'Keefe,[1] Seligman,[2] Jean Toomer, Paul Strand and his wife,[3] Alfred Kreymborg, Marianne Moore, Van Wyck Brooks, Edmund Wilson and Mary Blair,[4] Lewis Mumford, etc. etc. There was music by Copeland, a modern composer, and after that the readings by Miss Moore, myself, Kremborg and Jean Catel (who read a long poem in French by Paul Valery) occupied the rest of the time until one-thirty when the crowd broke up. I began by reading three of my shorter poems: "Chaplinesque", "Sunday Morning Apples" (the poem to Bill Sommer which seems to be talked about everywhere since it was printed last summer in "1924") and thirdly, a new poem which has not been printed, called "Para-

[1] Georgia O'Keeffe was the wife of Alfred Stieglitz.
[2] Jacques Seligmann, who owned an art gallery in New York.
[3] Paul Strand, the photographer.
[4] At this time Mary Blair was married to Edmund Wilson.

phrase". As I was urged to read "Faustus and Helen" I finally did so. Kreymborg came to me afterward and said that it was magnificent and even the conservative Van Wyck Brooks clapped his hands, so Toomer told me. I certainly read more deliberately and distinctly than I ever thought I should be able to, and I find I have already been recognized with the applause of the most discriminating.

No more today in the way of writing. I shall look out the window or read until bedtime.

Hope I hear from you soon. Love to Grandma—/ Hart.

To Grace Hart Crane

[New York City]
[December 15, 1924?] [1]
Monday morning
at the office

TLS, 1 p.

Dear Grace:

I'M SORRY, but there has been no chance to write you over the week-end—constantly filled with engagements. Nor is there now, as you can understand. Hence, a few short hand answers to your questions.

I have not seen the Miracle,[2] but may not, for all I know, have time to see it in Cleveland if I have to take the train back that evening. Get my dress shirts ready. They are on the third floor in the dresser. I'll have everything else with me necessary.

I was practically ill all last week, but kept at the office. Now I feel quite recovered.

Sam doesn't yet know whether he's going or coming, so I can't tell you his plans.

Apologies and love,—/ HART

[1] As Crane mentions details about his trip to Cleveland for the Christmas holiday, he very possibly wrote this letter on Monday, December 15, 1924.

[2] *The Miracle* was a popular play of the time that was created and staged by Max Reinhardt.

To Grace Hart Crane and Elizabeth Belden Hart

[Brooklyn, New York]
[December 18, 1924?] [1]
Thursday

ALS, 2 pp.

Dear Grace and Grandma:

Am feeling much better today—although the constant changes of weather constitute a threatening element yet.

Sam is moving—I think to Columbia Hts. but don't know the number yet.

Better send what you want to give him to me and I'll deliver it or forward it.

I'll have to leave Cleveland on Friday night train and work Sat. afternoon to make up lost time.

More later,/ Hart

From Christmas, through the New Year's holiday, and well into the first two months of 1925, Hart's frenetic social life left him little time to concentrate on his writing. Crane gradually became more open with his mother and grandmother about his drinking habits, no longer trying to conceal from them the extent of his alcoholic consumption. Certainly Grace had known that Hart enjoyed drinking, for his enjoyment sometimes had precipitated quarrels when he was living in Cleveland. Then he had consumed his liquor quietly in his tower room; now he spoke of his consumption quite freely.

[1] Hart's references to Sam Loveman and to his Christmas plans suggest that he wrote this on the final Thursday before Christmas.

To Grace Hart Crane and Elizabeth Belden Hart

[Brooklyn, New York]
Sunday morning
Jan. 4th, '25

TLS, 1 p.

Dear Grace and Grandma:

I might say that this is the first "day of rest" that I've had since I came back,—but fortunately that doesn't mean that I am all fagged out by any means. I've managed to get some regular sleeping hours, have curtailed my liquor rations (since New Year's eve) and am feeling as well as anyone could ever ask. Just came back from a luscious breakfast (I make a practice of a regular meal on Sunday mornings because I sleep so late and also walk a good distance to the restaurant) and have bought some gay mar[i]golds and narcissi from the funny little florist woman nearby who has a regular case on me, or rather has an amusing way of flattering one. She's a sight, alright! Bumpy body, pocked face, mussy hair and a voice that simply barks at you it is so raucous. I can't be seen passing her place without her glimpsing me, and signaling. When I enter she jumps at me with such phrases as—"Well my handsome Good Looking again!, How's my big boy?; Ain't he a dandy!", etc., etc, etc. I generally get enough from her to make my room gay on a quarter, and indeed, today, with my Christmas decorations still up and the snow-light coming in from the roofs of the piers below me—it is festive. Allen Tate, Sue and Brown are coming over for tea this afternoon, so I won't be the only one to look past the little flying swan still dangling in the window.

Tuesday night as I sat alone in my room I pictured you at the "Miracle". You must tell me how you liked it, and what you did on New Year's eve. Our party at Squachaloupi's [1] (what a name!) was a delight. I was sent out to get some more Victrola needles about midnight, and before I got back the whistles began to blow. Even though it was in an uncrowded neighborhood—people began

[1] John Squarcialupi's restaurant.

throwing their arms around each other, dancing and singing. Whereat I went into such an ecstasy as only that moment of all the year affords me. I hugged my companion and started singing Gregorian chants or something of my own version approaching them, and I hope in good Latin. O New York is the place to celebrate New Year's! There is such spirit in everyone, such cordiality! Your telegram came next morning before I was up (I didn't retire until 6) and I trust you got my answer on my way to breakfast. I am very happy these days and the more so because I trust you are.

Friday night I had a very pleasant dinner and evening with Waldo Frank. Dorothea was very lovely to ask me to dinner on New Year's afternoon, but I was wise (knowing how much I would want solitude and rest about that time) in excusing myself on another pretext, and I have invited her out to dinner some evening next week. On Satu[r]day night I am taking Waldo to the Stravinsky concert (if he comes to Cleveland you must hear him conduct his own works. He is the greatest composer living today). And the rest of the week is already dotted with all sorts of occasions.

I enclose the trunk key, which I at last found in my little ivory box. Let me know when Nancy [2] is coming next.

Love to you both, and remember me to Charles. / Hart

To Grace Hart Crane

> [Brooklyn, New York]
> 110 Columbia Hts.
> Jan. 11" '25
> (Sunday morning)

ALS, 2 pp.

Dear Grace:

Your S.D. has just come. I've been sort of waiting for it before writing because I expected it would contain news about the trunk, Sam, etc. which would be important to acknowledge. (You asked me about the last *Air Mail* letter: It did not arrive at least until

[2] Nancy Sommers.

after ten o'clock last Sunday night as I didn't get it until I noticed it on the hall table on my way to work Monday.) From your letter I'll expect to get my trunk tomorrow—will get in touch with Sam as soon as possible, etc. Let me thank you for your loving interest (and Grandma's, too) in attending to the details. The cake and the tin box shall be quickly "omployed", I assure you.

Before it slips my mind I must join your laughter over the clipping about Mrs. Miller who seems to have gone quite mad, hasn't she! [1]

Ive been interrupted since the last paragraph by a long call from Jean Toomer, and as I re-read the first of this letter I begin to think that there isn't much use in trying to be consecutive, but let the merry-go-round keep whirling. That's what this last week has been, at any rate, and I'm hoping for a little respite as soon as possible. In the meantime, don't blame me for writing like a bird cage on a spree.

Thursday night I took Dorothea to dinner and to see "Desire Under the Elms." Last night Waldo and I heard Stravinsky conduct his works at Carnegie Hall. He is coming to Cleveland, I understand, and I hope you won't miss him. His work is novel, but he is already a classic and you should hear him as much as though old man Wagner were in his shoes.

Glad you enjoyed Charlot's Revue.[2] It's something I missed, actually, but heard much quoted from—.

Your visit with Becky reminds me that I still have the same advice as her's to offer you, and I'm expecting to go to church at least once in *1925* though I haven't been near for 3 years.

It was also good to hear such news about CA. *But* I beg you, for the sake of all of us, not to let conjectures or opinions of any nature from that direction occupy very much of your thought. I'm not cynical nor stubborn, but I can't be concerned very much nowadays about either his favor or disfavor. I'll do as you say—but I hate to think of you as worrying about it—one way or another—guessing

[1] Hart probably is referring to a negative review of Alice Duer Miller's *A Priceless Pearl* that appeared in the Cleveland *Plain Dealer* on Saturday, January 3, 1925.

[2] Hart refers to *André Charlot's English Revue,* which was presented at the Hanna Theater in Cleveland.

this or hoping that, you get what I mean, I'm sure. For haven't we been through enough of it. I'll be cordial—and that's enough for now, anyway. And for lord's sake don't complicate you[r] life and happiness right now—*or ever again* with conjectures as to his intentions.

It's late and I'm tired. Give Grandma a kiss for me please—

Love as always—/ Hart

To Grace Hart Crane

[New York City]
[January 27, 1925?]
Tuesday morning

TLS, 1 p.

Dear Grace:

Read this editorial from the *World,* today. What are you hearing or reading about the I of Pines?

Love—/ Hart

[*The editorial from the January 27, 1925, edition of the New York* World *is printed below. The editorial presents a good account of the problems surrounding the ratification of the Isle of Pines Treaty.*]

AN INJUSTICE TWENTY YEARS OLD

When the treaty with Spain was signed at Paris in 1898 there was nothing to indicate that the United States intended to lay claims to the Isle of Pines. No Administration since then has pretended that the island passed to the ownership of the United States.

It was an Article II. of the treaty with Spain—"Spain cedes to the United States the Island of Porto Rico and other islands now under Spanish sovereignty in the West Indies and the Island of Guam in the Marianas or Ladrones"—that a loophole was found for certain American interests to assert that the Isle of Pines had become American territory.

If it was a part of Cuba the United States was barred by the

Teller resolution from annexing it. For Congress in 1898 by that resolution expressly disclaimed any intention of exercising "sovereignty, jurisdiction or control over said island [of Cuba] except for its pacification," and pledged the United States as soon as its object was accomplished, "to leave the government and control of the island [of Cuba] to its people."

It was entirely as an after thought that the plea for American sovereignty was made by American residents. Development companies had been organized in this country to buy land in the island and had resold it in small parcels to American purchasers on the representation that the Isle of Pines had become American territory. They never had anything to go on, except possibly the offhand statement of an obscure Assistant Secretary of War name Meiklejohn, who without consulting Secretary Root, once wrote that the Isle of Pines had become American territory.

When it came time for the United States to prepare for the evacuation of Cuba by the military forces under Gen. Wood and for the establishment of their own Government by the people of the island, Congress attached to the Army Appropriation Bill of March 2, 1901, the Platt amendment. This was designed to provide for a quasi-protectorate over Cuba by the United States and intervention in certain contingencies. To the amendment as drawn by Secretary of War Root Congress attached two new provisions. The first was, "That the Isle of Pines shall be omitted from the proposed constitutional boundaries of Cuba, the title thereto being left to future adjustment by treaty." By the second, Cuba was required to sell or lease to the United States "lands necessary for coaling and naval stations at certain specified points, to be agreed upon with the President of the United States." The two conditions were balanced one against the other.

Cuba promptly did its part by leasing to the United States land and water for naval and coaling stations at Guantanamo and Rahia Honda. The United States has never got beyond the point of negotiating a treaty relinquishing "in favor of Cuba all claim of title to the Isle of Pines."

There were two treaties. Both declared that "this relinquish-
ment on the part of the United States of claim of title to the
said Isle of Pines is in consideration of the grants of coaling stations in the Island of Cuba heretofore made to the United
States of America by the Republic of Cuba." For twenty years
the United States has had and used its naval and coaling stations in Cuba. For twenty years the Isle of Pines treaty has lain
neglected in the United States Senate, where today the Chairman of the Committee on Foreign Relations urges that it be rejected.

The good faith, the honesty, the honor of the United States
are clearly at stake. The Senate cannot longer withhold action
on the treaty or reject it without heaping disgrace upon the
United States Senate and imputing bad faith to this Nation. It
cannot deny Cuba its plain right in its property without con-
victing the United States on its own confession of robbery and
oppression.

To Grace Hart Crane

[Brooklyn, New York]
110 Columbia Hts
January 29th, '25

TLS, 2 pp.

Dearest Grace:

I trust that you got my night lettergram in time to prevent any
undue worries about me. I had intended writing that very evening
but an invitation to see a theatre program that I was quite interested in finally forestalled me, and I took the readiest means at
hand to assure you. The last ten days have been as lively as all my
nights and days since the holiday season, but now I am rebelling,
and for some time expect to spend the majority of my evenings in
my room reading and writing. There is only one more engagement
this week, and that I feel I must attend—a dance on Saturday eve-

ning at Dorothea's—evening clothes, and all, as I imagine they will be expected.

Just phoned Dorothea and also talked to Helen who arrived yesterday and expects to remain until a week from Saturday or so—by which time Zell will have returned from France. Speaking of phoning reminds me that I tried to get in touch with CA's office here the other day and got no answer. Later I went around and found the door locked, and from all I could see, most of the office furniture removed. I'm wondering if he has changed his agent here, merely moved quarters, or what. And I've sort of [been] expecting to get a phone ring from the old chocolate king, himself, at any hour—as such circumstances might readily bring him here for a few days. But I have yet to be informed of any details on the subject whatever. I've been delayed in writing him since Christmas, and so cannot expect to hear otherwise from Cleveland, I suppose. It's so hard to know what to write him about that I keep procrastinating indefinitely.

Sam came up to Times Square for lunch with me today. It's the second time, only, that I have talked to him since he visited with you, and the first encounter was merely accidental, a chat on the subway going to work one morning after I had run into him in front of 110 here. I must say that he seems glad to get back, and especially glad to get back to this neighborhood. His room near here (also overlooking the river) seems to have been the final factor in deciding him to remain, although, with all my enthusiasm for this section, I think other considerations should have been sufficient, regardless. He said that he had never seen you looking so "radiant" —and by the way, I think that is a good term for you myself. So eveidently the fatigue and slight illness that you mentioned feeling at that time had not been evident in your appearance or mood. It's amusing how Sam has finally got all his circle, including Kirk and Lovecraft, located over here now, right nearby. I really think he's as happy as he ever will be, and he wants to be a little miserable, you know. He tells me his book (on Saltus) is now on the press and that he's sick to death of it all already.

I must tell you that the fruit cake did not last nearly as long as I expected it would. My own appetite to say nothing of my friends' appreciations made short work of it. But it lasted for two teas during which times there was all but incense offered up to my dear Grandmother on account of her splendid dexterity and taste in compounding such a treat. The box, as you suggested, has been retained for storing my bread. Everything else in the trunk, as I wrote, arrived in good condition and it's a pleasure to have so much of my old home here with me.—Wish you'ld come along once in awhile!

Will you please give my very best to Charles whom I think pleasantly of many times. I haven't got around to write him—nor any one else as yet. Have you heard from the Rychtariks? Why not call them up—via the Sherwin Williams Co. (Ad. department, where R works?),

I want to write Grandma next time. Lots of love—/ Hart

[*At the end of his letter Hart included a short handwritten note describing the solar eclipse he had seen from his office on January 24, 1925:*]

The eclipse was splendid. I saw it from a fire escape (21 flight[s] above Bryant Park and the Library at 42nd St.) and the queer green light that spread over everything—the total darkness and stars at the moment of totality—the mad crowds in the subways on the way to see it—etc. made a great impression, I must say I didn't think it would "amount" to so much.

The enclosed rather humorous card [1] was presented to me recently by Sue in appreciation of my own famous exploits in the same dance. Tell Sara Baker that she must practice with Guy Livingston—for a perfect round of such dances when I next return.

[1] This card, probably given to Hart by Susan Jenkins Light, is no longer filed with Crane's letter in the Columbia collection.

To Grace Hart Crane

[New York City]
Sweet's
noon-hour,
Feb. 10th, '25

TLS, 1 p.

Dear Grace:—

I suppose you've been reading about the great unprecedented fog here, which still more-or-less continues. Well, it's just been hell for me over at Columbia Heights. I haven't had 6 hours of solid sleep for three nights, what with the bedlam of bells, grunts, whistles, screams and groan of all the river and harbor bouys, which have kept up an incessant grinding program as noiseome as the midnight passing into new year. Just like the mouth of hell, not being able to see six feet from the window and yet hearing all that weird jargon constantly. It does no good to go to bed early under such circumstances, yet I'm forced to do so, just because I'm too tired to do anything else. I hope tonight will be somewhat better.

I didn't see Zell at all when she was hear, as you possibly know by this time. I phoned her hotel several times, and left messages for her to phone me at the office, but never got a reply. I was busy with another engagement Saturday afternoon and evening, and, as I understood she was to leave for the west that evening, I haven't made any further efforts. Gooz finally came, too, I understand. If Zell wants to get miffed at my "neglect" she'll have too—I couldn't do any better.

Friday night I went up to a party at Dorothea's—and I haven't been the same since. Imagine making anything fit to put in one's stomach out of two quarts of heavy cream, a dozen eggs and a bottle of Johnny Walker whisky! It was the richest and most disaggreeable egg gnog I have ever had, and it tasted just like ivory soup [soap] melted down in a wash tub. Saturday and Sunday I spent as quietly as possible—that is, as previous engagements would permit me—and I must say that I am far from desiring any excitement further this week or next.

I may be invited to a trip to Denmark, Norway and Sweden (perhaps including Paris) very soon—all expenses paid. But it is too uncertain yet to give you the details. I might be gone anywhere from 8 months to a year, and I certainly think I'd be a considerable fool not to take the opportunity. Emil Opffer will probably come into about 2 thousand dollars soon, and that is what he proposes to do with it. It is certainly magnificent of him to ask me to share this bounty with him, don't you think so?

I'm hoping to hear from you today or tomorrow. Please give my best to Charles, which reminds me that I do not share your trepidations concerning him which you expressed in your last letter. I don't think you ought to let such minor doubts annihilate the affection and devotion that he has proffered you so beautifully. I'm really planning on your marriage this spring, and I think you will be foolish to delay it until later.

Love, as always to you both—/ Hart

By February, 1925, Hart had decided to gather his completed poems into a book, which meant extensive revision of his most recent work, "Voyages" and "Lachrymae Christi." Samuel Jacobs, an admirer of Crane's writing and owner of the Polytype Press in Greenwich Village, offered to publish the poems in a small private edition. Hart initially accepted the offer. However, Jacobs progressed so slowly on the volume that Crane decided to withdraw the manuscript and submit it to a commercial publisher. Sending it first to Horace Liveright, then to Thomas Seltzer, and then to Harcourt, Brace brought no immediate success. It was only after Eugene O'Neill and Waldo Frank praised Crane's writing that Horace Liveright agreed to publish the volume through his firm Boni and Liveright.

To Grace Hart Crane and Elizabeth Belden Hart

[Brooklyn, New York]
[February 23, 1925?] [1]
Monday

TLS, 1 p.

Dear Grace and Grandma:

It being the birthday of our country's father and a legal day, I'm not obliged to be at the office. But it doesn't mean that I haven't been mightily busy. In fact, for the last three days I have been working very hard to finish up a series of poems for my book (if the printer ever gets around to take it seriously) and they are about done. There are two more to be finished—and then I'll feel better, even if the book is a year in getting printed. You know one makes up one's mind that certain things go well together—make a book, in fact—and you don't feel satisfied until you have brought all the pieces to a uniform standard of excellence. I have revised a good many poems, and had to complete others that were half finished, and it all takes a great deal of work. This sounds as though there were going to be a great number of poems in the book, which, however, isn't exactly so. But the book will at least afford me some credit in the world, if not at once, at least later on.

Right now I am beginning to wonder what has happened at 1709. No word for two weeks. Can't you get me a line or so this week? The valentine was very sweet. I couldn't find anything half so clever to send you.

There are again more foggy nights on the harbor here. Papers report that a whole flock of liners are stalled outside the bay, afraid to come in at all, as there have been one or two real collisions lately.

You remember that I wrote you about not being able to unravel the Crane Chocolate Co. office headquarters mystery here: well, I later find that CA has had them moved or caused them to move

---

[1] Though Crane indicates that he is writing this letter on Washington's birthday, February 22 fell on a Sunday in 1925; he wrote this letter on the following day, which was a legal holiday.

into a little cubicle office on Madison Ave., where there is no storage room. Goods consigned direct to customers from Cleveland etc.
so that puts me a little out on free candy—unless I want to make
special requests to headquarters in Cleveland,—which I do not feel
like doing, at all. CA said something about his dissatisfaction with
the agent here when I was home at Christmas, and I suppose that
this change is one of the results of it.

Dorothea called up the other day to give me two tickets to a theatre which she could not use, and incidently mentioned that her
mother had enjoyed you both extremely. I guess Mrs. Valleau is
back here by this time.[2]

There isn't much other news that would interest you. I have been
feeling fairly well, and no better. But I have been taking better care
of myself and think I'm on the mend. The office goes on as always
and I seem to be in good standing.

Please remember me to Charles. Had breakfast yesterday with
Sam, who always asks about you both.

Love, as always, from your/ Hart

Throughout the first six months of 1925, both Hart and
Grace faced the crisis of having to plan for their future. Tired of
the routine of his job with Sweet's Catalogue Service, dissatisfied
with his low salary, and fearful of the effect the job was having on
his nerves, Crane decided to resign. At first he and Emil considered
traveling to Scandinavia with the funds from Emil's share of his father's estate, but they abandoned this plan when receipt of the
money was delayed because of legal problems. Hart next thought of
working on a boat; however, the publication of his book, he decided, demanded that he remain in New York. To complicate matters, he received two tempting offers of employment. The first was
from Corday and Gross, the advertising firm in Cleveland that Hart
had worked for briefly; the second was from his father, who had visited him when in New York on business. While he was considering

[2] Mrs. George Valleau, the future mother-in-law of Dorothea Lewis, from
Warren, Ohio.

these offers, his friends the Lachaises invited him to visit them in Maine, and Bill Brown invited Hart to stay with him in Patterson, New York.

Just as Hart was without direction in New York, so was his mother in Cleveland. She had delayed her impending marriage to Charles Curtis until he completed several financial ventures he was engaged in. Then, also, the two properties that Mrs. Hart owned were in jeopardy. More than ever before, Mrs. Crane and her mother realized the enormous expense of maintaining their house in Cleveland, and by spring they put it up for sale. Passage of the Isle of Pines Treaty by the United States Senate in March, 1925, put the island under Cuban control—something American interests had so successfully resisted in the past. Finally, both Mrs. Hart and her daughter suffered from a bad case of flu during the spring. All these problems are reflected in the following letters.

To Grace Hart Crane

> [New York City]
> Sweet's Catalogue
> noon hour,
> March 10th, '25

TLS, 2 pp.

Dear Grace:

It takes this night work at the office to make me continually sulky, and with two more nights of it again this week in prospect, don't blame me if I'm not exactly gay. I would have written you on Sunday had I been in a better mood. I certainly resent going around and around feeling as though my legs as well as nerves would give out at any moment. I dread to think fot ehsummer [1] and all that it means—and it's not so far away. I have pretty definitely made up my mind to take a job on a boat for S. America during that season, at any rate, and avoid the otherwise exhausted state of mind and body that the city, heat and my hay fever always

---

[1] Crane probably meant "of the summer."

cause. But more of that later. The trip to Norway possibly may not come through at all as there has been some difficulty in settling the estate of Emil's father, and things are at present very much tied up.

I wish there were a little more news. I have been seeing practically nobody that you know excepting Sam, who had breakfast with [me] last Sunday. He is just as unhappy as usual, spends a good deal of time working evenings for his boss, who he says 'rides him'. But that all sounds just as always— In Cleveland, Eglin or some other person was always making Sam a victim. He thinks constantly of getting back to the peace and quiet of Cleveland, and says that he has a chance to get back on his former advertising job again there this summer if he chooses.

Waldo Frank and Jean Toomer came over to Brooklyn last week to have dinner with me, and I'm having lunch with Jean again tomorrow. Gorham, of course, I don't see at all, nor hear much about. I understand that he regrets his awkwardness in dealing with me as he did, etc. But his change of personality which had long preceded this particular situation at which I took offence, had already changed my feelings about him considerably, and I strangely enough, don't miss seeing him half as much as I had once thought I would under such circumstances. Of course, I'm really his friend, as I know he is mine, but it may do us good to separate a little while. Many of his ways and opinions had begun to bore me a great deal, and that feeling may have been mutual, so far as I know.

I haven't seen or heard from Dorothea for over two weeks, but I told her that I was very busy when we last talked. Friday evening I am going to attend a special performance of the Stravinsky Ballet, "Petrouchtka", to be given at the Metropolitain. Adolph Bohm will lead the dancing, and there is to be special scenery by Soudekine. Emil gets passes to such things, but we generally have to stand up. Saturday afternoon I hope to get around to see a special exhibit of paints and photographs that Stieglitz has assembled at the Anderson Galleries. And SUNDAY I hope to spend in bed,—at least the way I feel right now. But of course I won't!

I'm still working on a few fragments necessary to clear up for my book. . . . . But I haven't been able to get in touch with my printer for weeks now . . . Owing to his engagements and mine. Most everything is just like pulling teeth, isn't it?

Well, I'm hpong [hoping] you'll write me soon, so's I'll have something besides local matters to think about. I'm getting a little bored with myself, I guess that's about all that ails.

Please give Charles my very best felicitations.

My love, as always, to you both—/ Hart

From Grace Hart Crane

[Cleveland]
Saturday 2 P.M.
Mch 21—1925

ALS, 9 pp.

Dearest Hart in all the world:—

Yes sir! that is what you are to me and always will be.

I am just ready to go to market & will stop to write you a few lines for Sunday—& mail it S.D. at 105th St. Post Office.

Your last letter was certainly very gloomy & it made us feel badly. Now you must not allow yourself to indulge in any such moods— It is not pleasant to work nights & days too—but it won't be a steady thing, & every one I know is doing things that they positively hate. Few escape & even for those few there comes a time. Just remember you are young & strong & have no obligations or responsibilities to any one but yourself—

Yes we were terribly sorry that the Isle of Pines Treaty was not defeated—but not surprised. I am glad they settled it this year instead of holding it over until next December— At least we can know better what to do. We are anxiously awaiting the arrival of the next "Isle of Pines Appial" which will probably tell how the news was received & perhaps give us some idea what the Americans are planning to do.

If you have an opportunity to get a position as Ship's writer, or something like Emil has had on a boat going to South America, I have no objections to your doing it. I certainly feel it would be a wonderful experience for you & you can afford to do a little adventuring in the next five years. I do not know what financial arrangement they make in such a position— You told me once but I have grown hazy about it. It seems to me it was $60.00 per month & board & room—& transportation. Write me more about it.

Of course you know I cannot be counted in for financing you in even a very small degree—as grandmother & I certainly are having our own share of financial troubles—which are greater than you even dream of. But I am trying to keep our troubles to ourselves & be game.

Chas is coming to dinner tonight— He took grandmother & me to hear Schuman Heink [1] at the Masonic Hall last night. It was her twenty fifth jubilee with Mrs Hughes [2] and she had a magnificent audience to greet her. She is 64 & sang like a woman of 40. Such a spirit, & outlook upon life, as she has— She certainly is a wonder.

Thursday night Chas. took me to a dinner dance at Manor—& we had a very peppy time— It was like a New Years eve celebration—favor, confetti, & cotillions led by Miss Flinn— [3] Solo dancing by some Broadway barefooted darling—who wore almost nothing but a short lace flounce—

Grandmother wrote you how under the weather I have been feeling. I've had three terribly hard colds this winter that have nearly finished me & listen to this—I have lost *twenty* pounds, I am just perfect now as far as weight goes—but I must admit I don't feel very energetic.

Don't worry about my turning Chas down— I am thoroughly convinced he is the nicest man I've ever known—but we can't live on bird seed—& as soon as he can see his plans work out encouragingly, we will not wait very long. You know he is building a house to sell & a great deal depends upon how soon he sells it & for how much profit—

There are many things I would love to tell you and talk to you about, but I must hurry on. Please make a big effort to look at life more cheerfully & try to see some things that you have to be happy about. Don't indulge in the blues—

Next week I will write you again. I seem to have a very little

[1] Ernestine Schumann-Heink (1861–1936), the Austrian-born contralto.

[2] Adella Prentiss Hughes (1869–1950), a concert and orchestral manager from Cleveland, who helped found the Cleveland Orchestra.

[3] Eleanor T. Flynn, who ran a dancing school in Cleveland. Hart attended her school when he was a boy.

time for anything but housework when I am not going about with Chas. In cleaning house the other day, the beautiful cameo that you gave me & which for four years I have tho't stollen, came to light *very mysteriously.* I was almost overcome with joy at the sight of it —& I know you will be glad to know that I have it again. I will tell you more of the circumstances some other time.

Give my love to Sam—& tell him to behave himself & stop pining for Cleveland— He would be very much dissatisfied if he were back— He ought to *know* that.

Loads of love—/ Devotedly/ Grace—

To Grace Hart Crane

[New York City]
March 24, '25
noon hour

ALS, 1 p.
LETTERHEAD: SWEET'S CATALOGUE / NEW YORK

Dear Grace—

So glad to get your good letter. It was a tonic,—and I'm feeling better—and somewhat rested.

Little details in regard to my book, etc. are keeping me busy. Last night had intended to write you, but some people came in and remained until too late.

Meanwhile my love and thanks for your consideration and affection.

Hope grandma is top-notch!/ Hart

To Grace Hart Crane and Elizabeth Belden Hart

[New York City]
Sweet's
Saturday noon—
3/28/25

TLS, 1 p.

Dear Grace and Grandma:

An altogether quiet week, enforced partly by a bad cold and partly by a resolution to remain as quiet and alone as possible— away from distractions and all activities at the office.

I have also been in a state of rush regarding the completion of a few remaining lines and corrections on poems to be included in my book, which the printer is beginning to set in type. This little man, Jacobs, by name, certainly is devoted to the cause of literature in going ahead as he is—paying for the cost of the paper and binding as well as dedicating his time and strength—free of charge—to the details of typography, setting, etc. For he is well enough convinced that he will, on no account reap any more remuneration from the book than I will. Poetry of my kind, is not popular enough nowadays, you know, to sell.

Nevertheless, I am somewhat stimulated by the fact of the book being actually now in progress. Get[t]ing that wad of my past work into permanent collection and out of the way, so to speak, is an hygienic benefit. Then—I shall feel myself all ready to begin the honest-to-goodness efforts on my long Bridge poem.

I guess I told you, Grace, how charming and cheering your last letter was to me. And I'm sorry I haven't more details or events to offer you this time.—but the above explains. I think of you both a great deal, no matter how little evidence of it all you get.

Rode to work along with Sam this morning on the subway. He always asks about you. We have regular Sunday morning breakfasts together.

Love again and again,/ hastily,—/ Hart

To Grace Hart Crane and Elizabeth Belden Hart

[New York City]
Monday
3/13/25 [1]

ALS, 3 pp.

Dear Grace and Grandma—

I don't know how to tell you what a pleasure it was to be so well remembered at Easter. The only one to share the delicacies, so far, has been Sam—but it's just as well—as I would like to make them last as long as possible. We spent a good part of yesterday together —having breakfast, a long walk after which he retired for a nap and then came over to my room at tea time. The socks and cravat have not arrived yet although I may find them waiting for me on the table when I get home tonight. I hope you had a pleasant day —and if it was as fine weather as we had here you must surely have had a spin through the country.

I have been able to lift my head with a little more calm and cheer since a week of almost sanatarium regime—going to bed early and what is better, sleeping soundly again. I have been letting the dreams of voyages etc. subside for awhile under the illusion (for illusion I suspect it to be) that my book may appear by next fall and that [it] is advisable for me to stick around and correct proofs etc. My printer is proving to be even slower than I expected, and I am at present trying to put the book into the hands of a regular publisher. Waldo Frank is going to do what he can to influence Boni & Liveright, his publishers, to make the investment. But all this is a little late to bring them now, as I understand—so that it may be this time next year before the book actually comes out. You see the publishers all know that such poetry is a dead financial loss to them its audience being extremely limited, but they never the less bring out (I mean a few of them do) a certain amount of such work when they think it flatters their literary judgement before the public and proves them to be more interested in literature than in the so-called

[1] The references to Easter, which fell on April 12, 1925, indicate that this letter was written on April 13 rather than March 13.

"best-sellers". However, the radio and cross-word puzzles and other such baby-rattles for the great American public have so badly cut into book sales this last year that most publishers have felt it seriously—and shy at such philanthropic interests as good poetry. This is the only reason that Waldo has to doubt the acceptance of Hart Crane's poems by his publisher,—but he is going to attempt the improbable, anyway, and let me know within 10 days or so.

Someone was telling me about reading that the paper had left the Island and that settlers were pulling up by the wholesale. Have you got any such news as yet. It all sounds perfectly plausible to me. But a few Americans less on the Island would certainly not spoil it for me, and we're all fed up on papers anyhow.

For heaven's sake let us not donate the place to charity—better let it rot and keep the land. To own a grass plot even that far away gives one a relieved feeling and the island isn't half bad in so many ways that other places are unliveable.

I've been writing this at the noon hour at the office and have already overrun the time. Will dovetail a little more later on. By the way, how is the canary bird? The word "dovetail" made me remember him for the first time since our introduction at Christmas.

My love and deepest thanks to both your dear and thoughtful souls—/ Hart

To Grace Hart Crane and Elizabeth Belden Hart

[New York City]
SWEET'S
Tuesday—
April 21st, '25

TLS, 2 pp.

Dear Grace and Grandma:

It has seemed somewhat irregular not to have heard from you sometime during the week-end, but I guess I have no right to talk. Even thought of getting up early this morning and writing you, but I guess this noon hour at the office will do just as well—and I won't have to rub my eyes over the paper. The last ten days have been pretty busy—and I can see where I had better plan on another respite from friends and celebrations unless I want to be uncomfortably on the edge of things. There certainly was much rum and running about during last Sat. and Sunday!

You probably know that Zell is here. I got a call from her last Thursday morning to come along to dinner with her that evening and later go to the theatre. I had thought she said something about "che-ild" being along with her at the phone conversation, and expected to see Helen, of course, just returned from Mexico. But my ears were at fault. Imagine my surprise when I found Carl sitting at the table with her.[1] I certainly was glad to see him again, more than I had thought I would be. He was as always, looked and acted exactly the same as we remember him. He hadn't heard anything whatever about me, I later found, and thought that I was possibly still in Cleveland working for C.A. After the theatre we walked down to 14th St. together and then parted affectionately. He was leaving next evening for Silvermine.[2] Says that he only comes in town for a couple of days every three months. He has at present a commission from some church in Mamaroneck, N.J.[3] for fresco painting, which probably means some kind of contemporary relief for him. He asked in detail about you both, and plans to see me as soon as he next comes to town.

When it comes around to Zell, I must say that she seems to grow mellower and more jovial, generous and pleasant as time goes on. And of all my relatives she is about the only pride or satisfaction I have beyond the present occupants of 1709. Helen, of course, counts to. . . . . I haven't been able to see her since last Thursday evening, but I hope to again before she leaves—later on this week. You know how busy she always is when attending these conventions.

The socks and tie arrived last Monday, and represent your usual flawless choice. The jelly has not escaped being sampled even though I haven't yet spread it on anything. And the fruit cake is by

[1] Carl Schmitt.
[2] Silvermine, the village included in Norwalk, Connecticut, which served as an artists' colony and was where Schmitt lived.
[3] Crane no doubt meant Mamaroneck, New York.

no means devoured, either. I've been out so much that now I still have an opportunity to enjoy it all with some kind of blow-out, which may transpire this week. However, I'm invited out to Staten Island to visit the Cowley's at their new house taken for the summer as soon as work stops next Saturday, so the tea may be further delayed.

Waldo Frank has been elected editor of a new magazine well backed by the Garland Foundation,[4] so I may have a little more chance to publish that way as soon as it gets started. So far, however, I haven't heard from him about the outcome of his interview with Boni and Liveright regarding my book, and am becoming a little impatient. Until that book is published I'm afraid I shall feel a bit tied to the ground—and I want to get it out of the way as soon as possible. But enough of that now. I've got to close—as work is beginning again.

Hope to hear from you today or tomorrow.

Love, as always,—/ Hart

To Grace Hart Crane and Elizabeth Belden Hart

[Brooklyn, New York]
110 Columbia Hts
Sunday afternoon—
May 2nd, '25

TLS, 2 pp.

Dear Grace and Grandma:

This has been a very busy week, although practically nothing of any importance has been effected. The usual jambourees and dinner parties with my friends have kept me out late, and I felt that the telegram sent you this morning was only justice in preventing any undue worries on your part.

I am enjoying a quieter afternoon than I had expected, due to the happy failure of some people to call whom I had invited for tea.

---

[4] Crane probably means the money that Charles Garland gave to the American Fund for Public Service. The foundation supported numerous magazines.

I have received so many courtesies at one time and other from Gaston Lachaise and his Madame that I invited them along with Slater Brown and Sue. But each of the parties finally phoned and called it off for various reasons. The Lachaises are soon to leave for their country place near Bath, Maine, and have been nice enough to urge me to an extended visit with them this summer if I can possibly do so. Just a mile from the ocean—and a wonderful beach set in a cove of rocks topped by pines! How I would love to go—and I really may decide to. As I have been mentioning, the summer at the office and the extra night work required looms up before me as almost unthinkable. I have asked for a raise—but it has not been settled as yet. I think I impressed it upon the boss, however, that if it isn't forthcoming I have other plans. I inquired again yesterday, but have been put off until Tuesday. Well, we'll see. I have got into such a rut of repititious, feeling, thought and dissatisfaction with myself that it seems the only salvation to break away for awhile into some change of work and environment. I am still considering a trial of ocean. Even if it's not at all ideal it may jog me up a bit. I really need more air and exercise at my time of life, and after four years or more of this sedantary office routine you can hardly blame me. Sam would take over my room and things while I'm gone. All in all, though, I've repressed my instincts so much that I can't seem to make up my mind with any decision about anything.

Sam's new job as an advertising writer seems to please him a good deal, but he feels terribly shaky about the details of printing, engraving etc. that constantly crop up. I have tried to encourage him by telling him that after all the time I have spent at such work I'm still very ignorant but so far have not found that a fatal handicap. He is working for some special beauty culture agency and has to get excited about cold creams, lotions, etc. all of which is "comical" to say the least, in relation to Sam's own rosy beak and shining cheeks. His office is in the same block as mine, and the coincidence of our intimacy in both living and working quarters is remarkable. He has gone to Philadelphia this week-end to attend to some details about his Saltus book which has been greatly deferred in publication and will not come out until next spring.[1]

[1] This book was never published.

I have not yet heard what Thomas Seltzer, the publisher, thinks about my book, but I ought to before another week. When I told Waldo Frank about submitting there he became somewhat excited, said that he had wanted to bring it to his own publisher, Boni and Liveright, and made me promise to turn over the mss to him immeadiately if Seltzer didn't take it. As you perhaps remember, Waldo had originally intended to take the book to Liveright, but told me some weeks ago that Liveright was not in the proper mood to be talked to at the time, etc., etc. Well I got little satisfaction from waiting around indefinitely—so decided to start the book on its rounds. It takes long enough to find a publisher, as a rule, without depending on the moods of any one of them. Even now, if the book were accepted today, it would probably be next spring before it could actually appear. I'm figuring that publication in book form will give me at least enough prestige to get a little money for my magazine contributions. Besides this, I have begun to feel rather silly, being introduced everywhere as a poet and yet having so little collected evidence of the occupation. There won't be any explosions of praise when the book appears, but it will make me feel a little more solid on my feet.

I certainly hope that you both are having no relapses into recent illnesses. You certainly had a fearful time and I began to see your countenance, Grace, as almost spectral—that is, from the loss of weight which you described. I was so glad to get Grandmother's sweet letter telling me that there had been a general recovery. I can picture you as a little tired today from rigors of entertaining and the Warrenite celebration Friday. That society seems to show no abatement—and I imagine it is growing a little in membership every year. I should like to have talked with Helen and Gooz about their Mexican trip. I suppose they have stayed up over Sunday.

I'll try to have a letter for you by next Sunday. In the meantime be good to yourselves and take things lightly.

                                    Your affectionate che-ild!/ Hart

To Grace Hart Crane and Elizabeth Belden Hart

[New York City]
Sweet's office
Thursday noon
May 7th, '25

TLS, 2 pp.

Dear Grace and Grandma:

The photos of the cherry tree in bloom were a joy to have and keep. I liked especially the one with yourself, Grace, standing underneath. The attitude and expression you took were gracious and lovely. The tree and the entire yard, for all that, have a great place in my memories, and now that the place is liable to be sold at any time I'm especially glad to have the pictures.

By this time I hope and pray that you are both fully recovered from your attacks of grippe and indigestion and nerves. The recent weather has been pretty decent here, and as far as myself is concerned, great improvements have been made. I'm feeling even better than at Christmas when I was in Cleveland, and guess my color shows it. Diet and general caution have put me in fine shape along with some slight medicine the doctor gave me. It certainly makes a big difference in one's mental reactions and attitude, as you said in your letter, Grace.

Last Monday I had luncheon with Bill Freeman,[1] and with the result of some statements that may interest you. We talked about everything else under the sun *but* business during the meal, but before we left the table Freeman abruptly introduced the proposition which I had faintly expected. He asked me if I ever expected to go back to Cleveland to live, and I replied that at present I had no wish to do so, but that such a thing was by no means improbable if, for certain reasons I should sometime feel obligated to. Then he went on to say that The Corday and Gross Company needed someone of my type in their copy department very badly, and that they would be glad to connect with me in case I cared to go back. He

[1] Crane had worked for William Freeman at the Corday and Gross advertising firm in 1922.

further mentioned that I was the one "brilliant" copywriter they had ever had there, that the company had fully realized, long since, that they made a great mistake in letting me be lured away without raising my salary, etc. etc. Well! I must say it was a satisfaction to be so spoken of. I was glad to know, too, that such an opportunity will always be at least plausibly open to me in case I am ever again located in Cleveland for any length of time. I suggested to Freeman that I might still do some writing for the company on a free-lance basis, here, if they cared to commit some special job to me now and then, and from his answer I judge that the possibilities on that score are not exceedingly remote. I would certainly like to make a little extra cash on the side, as you know how pared down my present salary keeps me.

I went in and made application for a raise again the other day, this time with the expressed desire of knowing definitely within a week, as I said "the decision will effect my future plans." Which is no threat merely, but a fact. I think I will get the raise, but if I don't—it's me for the sea during these summer months, and a change from office routine for awhile. It ['s] going to be hot enough without working nights at the office here, the way we shall undoubtedly be forced to, at a bare living sum! If I can't be paid enough with all the time and effort here at the office to save at least $5.00 a week, then I might as well, for all I can see, be seeing a bit of the world while I'm young enough. Two more years of this routine here will kill my imaginattion anyway, but I'd rather stay around here awhile now until my book is published and out of the way.

About that book, by the way— The printer finally gave up publishing it because he became too occupied with some new business project he went into. He wants to dedicate his services at setting it up in type, however, to any publisher, free of charge, who decides to take the book. I have accordingly sent it out to the firm of Thomas Selzer, Inc. When I hear from them—that is, if they don't take it—I'll send it around to another, and another. But Waldo Frank will probably place the book with his publishers, Boni and Liveright, as he is very much interested and wants them to have the book for reasons of reputation, etc.

On the whole I think it's better that the printer acted as he did, as it will mean much more recognition from the general public to have the insignia of a regular and recognized publisher on the volume than it would to have just a printer's sign. That would suggest to the general public, whether true or not, that I had paid to have the book brought out myself, which makes a bad impression on reviewers, and puts me in an unpleasant position. That's one thing I would never do,—at least with a first book. It's enough to put good food on the table, without having to rub people's noses in the plate who don't want to eat!

Sam is still undecided about coming back. He will not know until Saturday when he hears about some advertising job which is pending here for him. If he fails in acquiring that, he says he intends to go back at once.

I am glad that Charles is so kind to you, and that you are having the good time I can appreciate your having in selecting the details of trimming, etc for the house he is building. He probably won't have any trouble in disposing of it at a considerable profit.

Please pardon the abominable spelling, typing and wording of this letter, written in a dreadful hurry between working hours. I want to call you up some night, after twelve, long distance. You know you can do it for about 90 cents. Write me your phone number, and tell me what evening to do it next week, when you'll be in, etc. Plan to be in from eleven onward, as the special rate may begin at that time, I'm not sure. Sam has been doing that quite often, he says, and I think it would be fun for us to try it once, at least. You can hear very plainly, he says.

Loadfuls of love to you both,/ Hart

At the end of May, 1925, Hart accepted Bill Brown's invitation to stay with him over the summer at his "isolated, unmodernized, pre-Revolution farmhouse" in Patterson, New York.[1] He left

---

[1] Quoted from *Robber Rocks*, p. 29. The house, which had a postal address at Patterson, New York, was situated on the Connecticut state line.

his room in the care of Emil Opffer and arrived at Brown's about June 6.

Meanwhile, Mrs. Crane decided to attend the wedding of Verna Ross in Oak Park, Illinois. Alone in Cleveland, Mrs. Hart had the opportunity to write to her grandson about her daughter's nervous condition.

To Grace Hart Crane

[New York City]
Sweet's Office
Thursday,
May 28th, '25

TLS, 1 p.

Dear Grace:

I was going to write you between work and dinner engagement this evening, but Hurchstahl [1] Frease just called my up from the Commodore, and wants me to drop in there immeadiately after work. So here is a jot or so on the office time.

I gave notice to the boss as soon as I found out definitely that I was not going to get a raise. The time is set for a week from this Saturday. You know my feelings and reasons well enough from former letters, so it's not necessary for me to repeat them now. Later on in the summer I may take a boat job on the South American or West Indian Routes, but at present I have been very lucky in being invited out to a lovely farm near here, (Brewster, N.Y.) [2] to spend a month or so. Brown has just bought it, and has urged me to come out and help him plant the garden, etc. And this is just what I have been needing, exercise, open air, and relaxation from the tension of the desk (which had become very threatening to my health and nervous stability, I can assure you). This invitation came subsequent to my resignation at Sweet's—so don't think that I have been seduced by a tempting prospect of any kind. I was ready for ANYTHING after

[1] Hurxthal Frease, Hart's cousin.
[2] Brewster is one of the larger towns near Patterson.

the prolonged tension and confinement here for the last year, and whatever happens I shall not regret having left the office.

Emil Opffer has or rather will take my room over at Columbia Heights, and I have reserved it for myself again after October, as it's such a good room I don't want to loose my hold on it if possible. Write me here up to June 6th, when I leave for the country, and I shall write you much more in a few days. You certainly haven't been very generous, yourself, with correspondence lately. I hope you are both very well. C.A. looked me up here recently and offered me a job which I was all ready to take. Whereupon he became so pettily dictatorial that I withdrew quickly. In some ways it was all very funny, and I'll write more about it later. We parted on friendly enough terms, I guess.

Sam is home, as I suppose you know.

Sorry to rush so. . . Love,/ Hart

From Elizabeth Belden Hart

[Cleveland]
[June 2, 1925?] [1]
Tuesday 12–30—May 2 '25

ALS, 9 pp.

My Dearest Grandchild;

This is a very busy day with me—but I must stop and rest a bit, so while I sit in the [2] old red rocker in my bay window and look out on the beautiful view all around this corner. I can but wish you were here to see how beautiful it is just *now*. The foliage is fully out, and never will be lovelier this year—

It is like sitting in a grove but I must not spend too much time on this, for I have other things of more importance to say— When you called up last night— We were trying to find a place cool enough to get a wink of sleep— I was on the lounge & Mother had

---

[1] The reference to the phone conversation (which Hart mentions in his letter of June 4) suggests that Mrs. Hart wrote this letter on June 2, 1925.

[2] The word "the" is repeated in the text.

just got stretched out in her room to see how she could stand it when the phone rang— (about 11–30)—(Chas had not been gone long—) It rang & then for a long time not a sound from any one— so we thought it a mistake, but shortly our doubts were dispelled [.] Mother was quite excited so much she wanted to say—and she said your voice was as clear and natural as if you had been down town [.] I am so glad you called her—for while it was not fully satisfying I think on the whole it has done Grace good to get in sound of your voice. She is not well at all [,] has no appetite, seems losing flesh all the time & no strength. She has not fully recovered from that poisening and then twice attacked with the Flue—which has & is yet quite prevalent here— We have had a pretty hard time pulling out of it. Your Grandmother however never gave up to go to bed—& I took care of Grace—all through both attacks. Each time in bed two or three days—but fortunately no one visited us, except Chas, and I got along very well—but I have to smile sometimes when Mother is talking over the phone and making excuses—for some remissness. She says she was so busy doing the work taking care of Mother, but I say nothing. She never even had the opportunity of bring [ing] a meal up to me & she had hers served in bed for two or three days each time—bless her heart I was so glad I was able to do it, Chas would come up evenings and stay a while which always proved a tonic [.] Now she is down town today trying on a dress she is having made over for her trip to Chicago [.] She thinks she doesn't feel well enough to go—but I wouldn't have her miss it for anything [.] She is receiving invitations every day now to some of the parties that come before the wedding & yesterday a card from Blanch [3] saying she must not fail to come—and be there the 9th— so I am doing my best to help her off— She must get away—for a change and such a chance as this must not be turned down but she thinks she will be back in time today to write you but I know better so I will send you this, and you will understand if she don't. I wont tell her I have written until I have to & you need not mention what I write. Lillian [4] will stay with me nights while she is gone— after seeing Sam yesterday we have been crazy to see you & have

[3] Blanche Ross, Mrs. Crane's friend from Chicago.
[4] Lillian Belden, Hart's cousin.

you come home as he said he thought you might and was going to write you to do so & so was Mother, but after talking with you last night and thinking the matter over, much as we want to see you— we think your decision sensible. If we had anything to offer you that would be bettering you[r] condition during hay fever—we would insist on your coming but last nights heat & today does not warrant very much of an inducement for benefit— You would not be any better off—than where you are—and it would cost you so much to come—that if you will be more comfortable up in Maine —I say go there & come here later[.] I would be so overjoyed to send you the money to come with, but my dear boy I know you know that I haven't got it & I don't know just now where I am to get it for Grace to go with—but I know or *believe* when the time comes, some channel will be opened to provide a way[.] I want to see you oh more than I can begin to express—I love you as my own & I believe you are loyal to me— We three are all that is left & we must stick by each other. I think Grace will get you a line before you leave— This is hard to read—but you will excuse dear wont you[.] I will enclose the wedding invitation the Rosses sent us to forward to you[.] Oceans of love/ from Grandma Hart

To Grace Hart Crane and Elizabeth Belden Hart

110 Columbia Hts.
Brooklyn, N.Y.
June 4" 25

ALS, 5 pp.

Dear Grace and Grandma:

Practically everything is packed up. There has been a real turmoil, too, I can tell you. The frightful and sudden heat of the last 3 days brought on a fearful attack of uric acid trouble—headaches, bladder trouble and urethritis. No sleep for three nights and I have been dieting on butter milk and crackers. Besides trying to complete all arrangements by Saturday and still give some time to the office, I have had 3 engagements with the dentist. I thought one tooth had an abscess and had to have an X-ray taken to find out that it hadn't. There is one more trial with a filling tomorrow and then I'll be through. I'm about done out, however, and a feather could knock me over. Furthermore all these exigencies have about used up all the money I had saved up, little enough!

But I'm sure the change and exercise will do me up and its better to be a pauper with health than a near-pauper and a perfect wreck here in the city. My present feelings and state of being pretty well prove that in advance.

Emil Opffer is going to sublet my room until October. Brown doesn't yet know where he is going to locate his post box, so I'll have to wait until next week to write you that. Emil will forward my mail from here, however, when any comes here. I am hoping to hear from you by tomorrow.

I did enjoy that talk with you over the wires to Cleveland! Your voice is so much better than ink and paper.

Have a good time in Chicago, and, by the way, why don't you explain my case to the Ross's—that is—if any opportunity appears. They give thousands to charities every year—and boast about being patrons of art. Why don't they help some artist who is trying to live —and still get something done? A small allowance for me six months of the year would mean almost nothing to them—and it would keep me alive and productive in some cheap place in the country. You might mention Frank's and O'Neill's and Anderson's admiration for my work,—and that I have a book about to be published.

They won't be hard to convince on C.A.'s neglect of me, as they have had their own evidence of that side of him.

Everyone thinks it a crime the way I have been treated. I'd be glad to work six or eight months of the year if I could have the remaining time for my natural creative activity. Please see what you can do about this.

I hope Grandma is not too overborne by this torridity.

Love to you both/ Hart

From Elizabeth Belden Hart

[Cleveland]
Friday June 12 [1925?]
2 PM—

ALS, 7 pp.

My Dear Hart

I am writing this not knowing whether it will find you or not, but I want you to know that we are thinking of & loving our boy all the time and hoping you are improving since getting out of city life—

We felt *awful bad* to learn you were having such a terrible time right through that hot wave—many died from the effects of it here in Ohio & I kept watch of the papers to see if it was as bad in NY. No doubt your trouble was largely due to its effects— If it had not weakened when it did here I fear the consequences would have been very serious with me, and also Mother, for she is not well any way—and it told on her seriously. Not any sleep during that week — She looked awful— It was terrible here nights, we wandered over the house & porch to find a breath of fresh air. You know how it is in this house—in hot weather—but the night before she left she about gave up going—but fortunately it changed in the night, and she got a few hours sleep & in the morning she felt & looked more like her self— She left here Tuesday morning on the Lake Shore at 8. oclock Thinking it would be better to get there at night and have a little rest for the following days festivities, as there was to be a "trousseau" party at Blanches[.] Ross met her at train, 5. PM—and they went flying to Oak Park. When she arrived Blanche met her & informed her she had just 45 minutes to dress for a large dinner party on the N. Side— She said what to do she didnt know. She was tired & dirty from traveling all day but fortunately her trunk was there and she rallied enough to be on their way all right. She says that every moment up to the 20th is taken so I can't see how there will be anything left of them—or where she will benefit from the change unless it be to get away from the "humdrum" life here— I am hoping it will change the outlook, or help her to forget it for a while at least. She hasn't been out of town for so long. It has really got on her nerves & mine to. It is warming up again today—but hope it won't be as hot as before[.]

Lillian stays with me nights, and to make or give me a little more to do than I have had— Louella [1] is here too. She came on for her vacation, & will be here until Saturday. So you see my cares are none the less—but if Grace only is happy—I shall feel well repaid for her trip— Now Hart, I hope you will keep well—and your vacation will be beneficial along that line[.] I guess you thought my last letter was a rambling thing—I had only a few moments before mail left, and I found after I sent it that I had left out the most important part of it and am wondering whether you got any sense out of it at all— Mother says in her line that I rec'd today, Dont forget to write Hart.

I know she wont have one moments time to write from now on —I will direct this to your room & may be it will be sent on—Now please write Grandma a few lines & tell me just how you are and if you have a comfortable place to stay, and are happy[.] Cheer up: Your future will soon be brighter I'm sure & remember I love you the same as Mother does—I think the reason she is in the shape she is is because she is so homesick to see you & to help you but she hasn't a cent to help herself—and I am trying to do all I can for her but it is mighty little & that wont be long—but there is always a way out someway—and I am going to know that if we live right, we are not going to suffer—

Be a good boy dear and write me soon all about your dear self
                    Love by the bushell   Grandma

Harold I think you will be disgusted with this scrawl—sometime I will may be have time to write you a decent letter

[1] Louella Belden, sister of Lillian.

From Elizabeth Belden Hart

[Cleveland]
June 15. 25
Monday 11 A M—

ALS, 8 pp.

While I am trying to cool off a bit I am going to scratch a few lines to our boy out on the farm— I know he will be glad to be in touch with home once in a while.

When I came down stairs yesterday morning, I found on the front door knob a notice that I would find a *Special* in the letter box— I was quite surprised to find it was from Mother instead of Hart, but I was none the less pleased— It contained a very elaborate description of what she was having the pleasure of participating in. She wishes me to forward it on to you so I am going to slip in a line also— [1] Write her as soon as you can, (Her address is # 531 *E. Ave. North, Oak Park Ill.*) Now I need add nothing more on that subject as her letters explains how she is spending her time, and further that I am happy that she can be there for she would miss much that will never come her way again, & I do hope she will come back feeling more cheerful mentally & better physically—

I am getting along fine with so much to do I find no time to be lonesome—in fact it is a treat to be alone, and not have anyone to find fault with me. I know I can't do as I have in years past, but so I get there what matters it just how its done, or whether its according to *"Hoyle"*[.]

I put in from 12 to 15 hrs every day—and thats more than the majority of much younger people do—

Lillian & Louella left Sat. morn for Hiram commencement.[2] Lillian will be back tonight, Louella goes to Canton to spend the balance of her vacation in Canton with her Mother. I had Ralph sleep on the front porch nights while they were away—so I felt I was as well protected as if I had a big *"watch dog,"* and I wasnt

[1] Mrs. Hart enclosed her daughter's letter which described in elaborate detail all of the extensive preparations for Verna Ross's marriage.

[2] Hiram College in Hiram, Ohio.

bothered with getting breakfast for any one but myself— It would
have been far easier for me to have done that way while she was
away but Mother wasnt satisfied for me to be alone—so I have had
two besides myself to cook for—but I was ready to do anything so
she would go—

Yesterday Nancy & her sister had me over to their place for dinner and also invited Sara—& Mrs Dr Archer to join me. It was
very sweet of them to think of trying to make my day pleasant—
besides they call up every day to know if I am all right— Also
Chas—calls up & has been out twice to see if he can be of any service[,] so you see I have some nice friends if I am an old lady[.]
Dora Parker & Mrs Canfield where she lives are coming over after
me this week & take me over to spend the day with them[.] ³

It is a very hot day—but there seems to be a breeze springing up
which relieves very much— I miss my neighbor Hurd now they
have left, and the house looks so deserted— She bought or exchanged for a double house on the hts. Ken ⁴ has passed and when
he goes to Columbus for his exam—I expect he will come home
with an M.D. attached to his name— He has improved very much
& is really very likeable and he will fall into much of his fathers
practice. Now I must get busy—much as I like to chat with my
dear Hart, I am so glad for you that you are out of the city heat
and that you feel better—of your fever. We felt awfully after reading your letter and how you were suffering— It was awful here— I
never knew it worse— I thought Mother would surely collapse &
believe if it had held on another day she would—but one thing to
console us is it never lasts but three or four days before there is a
break. Now dear try & lead a quiet life—and a sane one, don't take
or do anything to overstimulate you—for with your trouble you
must avoid that, and watch your diet—for that trouble is a very
treacherous & subtle one, and needs be watched *very* closely[.] I am
sure you will be careful after the experiences you have had—for
what is there for one if your health is gone, money cant bring it

---

³ All those mentioned in this paragraph were friends of Mrs. Hart and Mrs.
Crane.
⁴ Kenneth Hurd, Hart's friend, who was enrolled in dental school at Ohio
State University.

back.— Its a mighty good thing to have in its place but it will not
buy health[.] It fails there—

Write me a good long letter while Mother is away won't you—
and write her as soon as you can & tell her how to address you

Goodbye dear

Love goes with this/ Grandma

you will have a hard time to read this, for I wrote it on my lap on
the porch and with a pencil like stick of wood—

To Elizabeth Belden Hart

[Patterson, New York]
June 17th, '25

Transcript [1]

Dear Grandma:

Your two good letters just reached me today,—the one that was
forwarded from Columbia Heights and the later one direct, containing the enclosed from Grace. It's too damned bad that you had to
be burdened with those Belden bores so long—but I'm glad that
you have been having some freedom lately since they left. The record of the activities in Chicago sounded very pretentious, but the
tiresome and usual thing after all—so much fuss about a very common sort of ceremony. I shall be glad enough, however, if it serves
to entertain Grace a little while, and only hope that it won't tire
her completely out.

As for myself—things couldn't be better. I have great quantities
of fine Guernsey milk every day from a neighboring farm, the finest
butter and eggs and fresh vegetables—and so much outdoor exercise
than I am brown as a nut already with the sun and all greased up
at the joints. Sleep nights like a top and the uric acid trouble has
disappeared completely—at least for the time being. When you consider that this is only about my tenth day out here such results seem
astonishing, don't they? I should have written you more if there had

---

[1] The text of this letter is copied from a copy that John Unterecker made
while doing research for his biography of Crane. The original manuscript is lost.

been a moment, but you have no idea how busy we have all been. There has been a great deal—tons—of wood to clear away from the house, rubbish, also, and a lot of old plaster they threw out in making alterations. Then we have been building bookcases, shelves and tables for the inside, as well as scrubbing and rubbing down floors. Getting up every morning at five-thirty. The air is so fresh and the birds so sweet that you simply can't stay in bed a moment longer. And how good breakfast tastes! We have bought a good oil stove, which works on about 10 cents a day. All our cooking and lamp-oil comes to much less than similar means in the city would cost. Brown has a Ford which he got for 35 dollars! We go marketing about 7 miles away to the nearest town every three or four days. This place, you know, is quite delightfully isolated from other houses. It's about 150 years old—and did I tell you that a lot of wonderful old rope beds and furniture came right along with it? I would like some such place for myself sometime. I certainly prefer it to the city. And it only takes 2 hours from this marvelous country to New York City.

I don't see that it's much use of my re-writing all this for Grace —when she is so busy in Chicago, and besides, considering that she will be back home in a few days probably. So will you either forward this to her or save it for her to read when she returns—as seems to you most appropriate? I wish it were as cool on the porch of 1709 tonight as it is here. We have a bright merry fire in the big fire place (it has a dutch oven along side—do you remember any like that?). It is so high here that I have never had so mild a season of rose fever. Sneezes are very rare.

Here is a good night kiss for you, X

Love—as always,/ HART

I am enclosing some pictures of Bill and Sue and the place.[2] These were taken before anything was done via cleaning up or painting. One shows the house in the distance it sets back from the road. *Please return these to me as soon as Grace has seen them* [.]

[2] These enclosures are lost.

From Elizabeth Belden Hart

[Cleveland]
Monday—1 PM—June 22 / 25

ALS, 3 pp.

My Dear Child:

I wonder if you want a line from Grandma, seing Mother is where she cant write you. I hardly know how to plan you a Sunday letter, but while I am resting a few moments preparatory to cleaning up for the afternoon I can with your permission use a pencil and rest at the same time.

I can not give you any special news—but will try and not be wearisome talking about my self & my "humdrum" duties at home— *1st,* Margarett is here & we are washing curtains and cleaning on second floor so as to have things shining when Grace comes— Do our best, it no doubt will not look very attractive after having 2 weeks stay among so much grandeur.

I rec'd a card this morning saying she could not write any more last week, (this was written last Friday) as every moment was full but thought she would be home about middle of this week—so I will think about Wed—

I have been so busy since she left have hardly missed her— I have put in from 12 to 15 hrs a day— I wonder sometimes how I stand it, for I have been going it that pace for weeks— I suppose, to quote some of the old time sayings that Lillian has ever a ready supply, that "it is better to *wear* out than *rust* out," which whether I care to adopt at my age—or not, it seems my lot, so I try to be reconciled to my fate[.]

I enjoyed your letter *so* much, for *this* reason, that you seemed happy, and that made me feel so too, that you were away from the heat of the city, and where you could get good good food that will build you up—and also the outdoor life and exercise that will fortify you for your work when you return—

I am glad you are sleeping good too, that is Natures great and only restorer—

It seems so strange however that you can be content with such surroundings—one who has been used to being in the rush of city

life so long— I enjoy looking at the pictures you sent and will return them after Grace has seen them. I have not sent them to her,
for she will be at home so soon—

I thought your picture looked a little sad—or thoughtful perhaps
better expresses it, as if you might have been a little homesick—or
thinking of home— Am I right?

Who is the woman & man on the steps. Is she staying there,
doing your cooking, or just a neighbor. I have been wondering who
does your cooking? I thought if you were, and was as efficient in
cooking every thing as you were in making "Bean Soup", I am
afraid you would have to go on your Diet of Buttermilk & crackers
to keep from putting on too much flesh.

Well the Hurds have moved and the Wolseys are moving to
Philadelphia— Kenneth goes to Columbus for last exam, Wed,
when I suppose he will have an M.D. attached to his name— He is
to be bestman at some wedding here June 30th— I don't think you
know the parties, but its quite a swell affair—

I have told you all I know that I think will interest you—and I
must now leave and go to my work— I got your goodnight kiss and
have been sleeping better ever since[,] send more of them, I miss
them so much— I will send Mothers card I rec'd this morning,
maybe it will seem good to see her hand writing—

Much love to my dear Hart.   Grandma—

From Elizabeth Belden Hart

[Cleveland]
[Late June, 1925?] [1]

ALS, 5 pp.

My Dear Boy—

I cannot forego the pleasure of adding a few lines to this already
lengthy epistle.[2] I will try and be very brief however—

The sun is just setting & the afterglow glimmering through the

[1] The reference to the rope bedsteads at the end of the letter suggests that Mrs.
Hart is replying to her grandson's letter of June 17, 1925.

[2] Mrs. Hart very likely included this letter with a letter of Grace's that is now
lost.

beautiful green foli[a]ge of the trees surrounding me, is indeed a very beautiful and inspiring picture— We have had a nice thunder shower which has cooled the air, and made it delightful to sit on the porch but here comes Chas. to take Mother for a ride, so I have all the time I want to talk to you, for she has not finished her letter, and probably won't mail it until morning.

In reading what Mother has written, she has omitted telling you of our trip to Canton last Sunday week.

Bessie Smith came up Friday night with Joe [3] and stayed over night with us—returning Sat— and invited us down to spend Sunday— Chas of course included.

We left here a [t] 9 o'clock—and met the Smiths at Congress Lake Club for dinner.

Elizabeth & Eleanor & her beau were there, by the way, Eleanor is engaged to a young man who lives in Cleveland— We had a nice time there and about 2 P M left for the Smiths, to finish our visit [with] the balance of [the] family[;] Rae, Edith, and her prospective daughter in law, who is on from N York for a visit with Edith. By the way they claim she is quite a writer for several magazines— poetry I believe. She and Kenneth are also engaged—and they all seem to be well pleased over it. She seems like a bright little thing, and very refined— She wants to meet you—after learning you are in the same biz— Well I must hurry on. It ended up by George & his wife inviting the whole bunch to dinner at Springfield Lake Club. From there we bade them all farewell—each going to their homes—& we to Cleveland. We arrived safe & pretty tired at 11— P M—

Dont you think Grandma is a good sport to ride all that distance, visit with so many and *feast twice* in one day—and get up the next morning feeling fine?

We rode 155 miles that day— We had a beautiful day, no dust, just cool enough to enjoy every minute—but dear don't you know we missed having you with us? We miss you *all the time*. It isn't right for us to be separated so long— We must arrange to see each other oftener. These precious years are going so fast, and I want to see you oftener, and [know what?] [4] your Mother feels—

[3] This paragraph and the one below mention Hart's cousins in Canton, Ohio.
[4] These words are illegible.

Well—we will hope that the time will come when we can— I hope you can read this. I sat outside until it got too dark [.] Oceans of love from your old *Gram*

Let me have another good letter like the last *very soon*. It was a veritable tonic for me— I caught the inspiration of the place and also from you. I want to hear from you very often my Dear while you remain there—

Oh you ask me if I knew anything about rope bedsteads. I should say it bro't very vividly to mind when my father had the job house cleaning time of tightening up the ropes, & he would say to me come here "Sis" and walk over these ropes, one at a time and stretch them and then he would stretch each one around the pin in the side of the bed & then over several times until they were tight as a drum

Hart sent a brief letter to his father explaining his new situation. C.A.'s reply, if there was one, is missing.

To Clarence Arthur Crane

Patterson, New York
c/o Mr. Ireland
R.F.D.
June 27th, '25

TLS, 1 p.

Dear Father:

For the last three weeks I have been up here in the Berkshires with some friends who invited me up to a new farm they have bought. I left Sweet's Catalogue as I had expected, about two weeks after your visit. No raise in sight and the heat and rose fever getting on my nerves. There is, to my great relief, none of that pestilence up here—on account of the high altitude, I suppose, and I have been having great days out of doors, working in the garden and painting the house, etc. I feel about made over.

I could stay here indefinitely as far as my hosts are concerned; they have even offered me a strip of land and the timber wherewith to build me a comfortable cabin, but one can't live long on ferns and wintergreen, and so I suppose I'll be jogging back to New York in about three weeks. I'll probably take a boat job then and say good-bye to the U.S. for awhile. If you want ever to get in touch with me after I leave here the only address I can think of at present is 110 Columbia Heights, Brooklyn, where a friend of mine is staying. He will forward my mail wherever I am as long as he is there.

How did your conference and matters pertaining thereto come out—I mean in connection with the visit you were making when I last saw you? Negative, I suppose, as you said you expected that outcome.

Best regards to all the folks.

Your son _____/ Harold

Though Hart was happily settled at Brown's farmhouse in Patterson, New York, Mrs. Crane was experiencing difficulties in Cleveland. For a while she considered moving with her mother to Florida, where she thought she might get a job selling real estate and perhaps take advantage of the land boom under way there. Her letter outlining this scheme to her son is missing, but Hart's reaction to it has survived.

To Grace Hart Crane and Elizabeth Belden Hart

Patterson, N.Y.
care of Ireland,
Rural Delivery
July 10th, '25

TLS, 3 pp.

Dear Grace and Grandma:

I had deferred writing you so long on the daily expectation of hearing from you. As time went on—so long—I found myself, yesterday, in fact, becoming very nervous, but now that my anxieties are so well allayed by this morning's mail I feel on quite friendly terms with you both again. It was nice of you to write me so extensively, and I am especially glad to know that my Grandmother has been disporting herself so vigorously lately and with such healthful results.

Life has been going along here at Brown's farm as pleasantly as anyone could wish excepting that the last few days I have had a considerable touch of the fever. I had expected to evade the whole season, but I guess I'm in for a few days of it here, despite the altitude and other favorable circumstances. We have the house painting almost finished. I've already mentioned how I enjoyed doing that. Brown and I have been making screens the last couple of days and now I defy a mosquito to attack my slumbers or a fly to fall into my soup. Although planted very late in season Brown's garden is about up, peas and beans, and soon will follow a whole menu of delicious vegetables for the table. This is the kind of place I am going to have when I can afford it. Perfect quiet and rolling hills, almost mountains, all around—with apple orchards and lovely groves of trees and rocky glens all about the house. Yesterday afternoon we picked blueberries—about four quarts in an hour—and there's nothing better to eat with cereals for breakfast I can tell you. It's pleasant to pick them, too—great patches of bushes laden to bending with the beautiful milky-blue fruit that looks the freshest thing on earth. The huckleberries will be out later—and there will be simply bushels of them. Brown also has great quantities of raspberries, blackberries, currants and gooseberries—as well as elderberries on his place. Also plenty of sap maples and walnut trees. I haven't yet stopped enthusing about the place, you see, and when you mention buying land in Florida, that dry and tourist-ridden place, I find it hard to agree with you. Brown has even been so nice as to offer me a strip of land as my own and a great pile of cut timber to build me a cabin—if I will stay here with him and Sue. You can't beat his affectionate generosity in any friend on earth. I wish you could know Sue, also. Well, someday you will, I'm sure, as I'm not likely to lose my enthusiasm for them very soon.

This Florida plan of yours prompts me to worry a little, Grace.

You must certainly be cautious about investing your money there the way things are going at present. Of course I have been hearing all that you have about the tremendous sums exchanged there in real estate, and maybe more than you. That information is certainly nothing that one has to be "tipped on" these days. Everyone—even the farmers around here—are scraping their coins together and rushing down to Miami to buy little lots and I know well enough that at least *some people* have made and are making fortunes there. But doesn't such a great campaign of advertising as this now seems to be—doesn't it arouse your suspicions as to the validity of the proposition to the small investor? Remember, Grace, that the stock market is run on the same plan and with the same tactics—and the daily crop of suckers can be reaped in other fields and byways than Wall, and often is. If you had thought of investing in Miami property a year or so ago it would undoubtedly have meant a considerable profit. But—as I see the situation now—the whole proposition there is like a whirling roulette wheel that with every revolution spins a higher figure—but w[h]ich has already begun to slow down. I don't see how the situation can be otherwise when there has been such a wholesale flux of gamblers to the place as there already has been. For certainly there is a limit to the value of property—and there is a limit to the present national craze of flocking to Miami. I may be wrong, of course, but it seems to me that most of the fruit down there has been picked up already. It might net you something to try and sell for others down there, but I would be awfully slow about making any investments myself—at least until after I had been there long enough to ascertain some direct information of my own about matters. In such "gold rushes" watch out for the boom psychology that animates everyone concerned—even the losers—into bursting their voices with salutary legends of their luck and the general prospects of the place. It amounts to as much a conspiracy as though they had all sat down together at a great mass meeting and agreed to swear they each saw Jesus bathing on the beach. Of course I can see your especial interest in going to Miami this winter to make money—but I'm blind to the other advantages of the plan. Especially when you have as lovely a place—only about a day and a half further away—down on the island to go to, and where living expenses will be about one third as much. (Miami is a very expensive place to stay, I understand, especially since this boom). Further—it seems to me you ought to take a run down there—for at least two weeks—regardless of other plans. Or otherwise, after all this time, who is to know what is becoming of the place? I'd jump at the chance to go there myself. Please don't resent my ad[v]ice about these foregoing matters. My opinions on such matters have to be got off my chest naturally—as they are inevitable concommitants to my interest and affection in you both. I certainly have no desire to stand in the way of anything you wish to do.

My trip to South America is as hazy as it's always been. It may be that line of boats or some other across the Atlantic for me when I get back to New York—I won't be able to wait long for employment anywhere as I have only about the carfare back to town. I may even take some other kind of office job. My chiefest concern while I have been out here is to avoid worries of whatever kind for awhile, doing that, you know, takes a kind of discipline after one has been so constantly precautious and apprehensive as I have been for the last five years. With my health and nerves already to snap beneath *that* strain I decided that life wasn't worth continuing. So I am—at least for awhile longer—content to drift a little, let things take care of themselves, reduce my needs and requirements to a minimum and av[a]il myself of as much time for free breathing and meditation as possible. The boat job would—on the South American line—permit me practically three weeks of time (absolutely to myself) out of every eight. This time would be spent in Buenos Aires at one end of the trip, and at New York at the other. I might get some time to write and read again. I really hope very much to make connections with this line for that reason, even though the first job I could get wouldn't amount to more than 65 dollars a month. At least three-fourths of my living expenses while on the job would be gratis, of course. And I even long to be entirely away from the best of friends at times. It gives you a fresh picture of the world. One trip would decided whether I cared for the job or not—six weeks and 12,000 miles. I could probably get a job as night watchman or as engineer's writer. But you have to take what places are open when the ship comes in.

Exactly how much longer I shall stay here isn't decided yet. But it will probably not be more than two weeks from now. In New York I shall stay with either Allen Tate or Emil Opffer,—probably with the latter as Emil is still staying in my old room at Columbia Heights. At any rate that will be the place to write me. I'll let you know more details of course when they are settled. In the meantime I have written to Freeman who is still with the New York office of Corday and Gross if he has any free-lance ad writing which I could do for them while I am out here. That will probably amount to nothing at all, but the idea occured to me and I thought I ought to try it out at least. If I could pay my share in household expenses here I should like to stay all summer as I have certainly been made to feel extremely welcome. Otherwise I can't go on accepting things as they are.

I had a pleasant letter from Kathryn Goettel last week, mentioning that she intended coming to New York in the fall—would conduct some kind of humorous column in The Times—and possibly that a musical comedy she had written would be produced. Raymond Hitchcock, she said, was recommending it to his publishers. When you see Sam I wish you [would] ask him to write me, meanwhile sending me his address from the telephone book. I haven't heard a word from him since he left New York. I'm very very fond of the old bird and it pleases me that you are so fond of him. Now that two publishers have turned down my book (Thomas Seltzer and Boni and Liveright) I have sent the mss to Harcourt Brace & World, where Hal Smith is looking at it. After these rebufs I have decided not to let the vicissitudes of my slender volume interfere at all with my economical program or living plans in the near future. I can promise however, that the book will keep going around until it finds a home somewhere. Meanwhile I may add a poem or so to it from time to time.

Eugene O'Neill wrote me that he was enthusiastic about some recent things I had sent him, and I have enough enthusiasm from other astute and discriminating people in America to make me feel that my writings are justified. Publishers shy at it, of course, because they know it won't make them money. Meanwhile the same flood of mediocrities in verse continues to be printed, bound and sold year after year.

Your story of the Fourth sounded very jolly indeed. Nothing could beat the hilarity of this place—with about an omnibus-full of people here from New York and a case of gin, to say nothing of jugs of marvellous hard cider from a neighboring farm. You should have seen the dances I did—one all painted up like an African cannibal. My makeup was lurid enough. A small keg on my head and a pair of cerise drawers on my legs! We went swimming at midnight, climbed trees, played blind man's buff, rode in wheelbarrows and gratified every caprice for three days until everyone was good an' tired out. The guests are still recovering, I understand, in the separate abodes in the city. It certainly is infintely pleasanter drinking and celebrating on a wide acreage, like this farm, than in the tumult and confusion of the city. Aside from this one blowout I have not had a drop since I have been here—and have not felt like drinking, either. The desire for booze in the city comes from frayed nerves and repressions of the office, I'm sure.

Thanks for the Brooks clipping,[1] which strikes me as rather humorous. If poor Charles didn't have such a mother complex I doubt if there would have been any trouble. I think there is some intensity lacking in both of them, however.

I should like to see your bob, and I'm sure I should like it. You must "save" it for me. And send the kodak picture right along. Don't smile in this picture. I like plain poses, you know. As for the trust paper,[2] it is signed and is probably at the bank by this time (as you read this). Give my best to Helen. And here's my love to you both—

Your Hart

[1] Possibly a newspaper story about Charles Brooks's divorce from his wife, Minerva.
[2] Perhaps a reference to some business concerning the legacy Hart had received from his grandfather Hart, which was being held in trust until his grandmother's death.

⌒ⵡⵑ

The sale of the house in Cleveland took place on July 27, 1925, the day that Hart arrived there from New York. Hart stayed with his mother and grandmother until mid-September, helping them disperse twenty-two years' accumulation of property. Occasionally he and Grace would argue over what he was entitled to, and those effects he managed to get—a desk, a rug, and his books— he sent to Brown in Patterson.

Grace, her mother, and Hart took rooms at the Wade Park Manor, a fashionable hotel and apartment house in Cleveland. Mrs. Crane had not given up her plan to sell real estate in Florida. There, she speculated, was an opportunity to invest her funds accrued from the sale of her mother's Cleveland property and make a considerable profit—and she and her mother would profit as well from a winter in the warm climate. Grace left Cleveland on October 5 for Miami; several weeks later Mrs. Hart followed her to Florida, staying with her friend Marthena Evans in Winter Haven.

To Grace Hart Crane

[July 19, 1925?] [1]
Patterson, N.Y.
Sunday

TLS, 1 p.

Dear Grace:

I await your next letter confirming the sale of the house.[2] In that event I think it will be advisable to follow your suggestion and come to Cleveland until September first. I have wanted to see you and Grandma for a very long time, I would like to say "goodbye" to the property (wherein have occured so many intense experiences of my life) and I would like to sort out a few articles for preservation

[1] Crane probably wrote this letter on Sunday, July 19, 1925, shortly before he left for Cleveland.

[2] Mrs. Hart sold the property on 115th Street to Sabina O'Brien on July 27, 1925.

that have especial personal associations for me. I imagine, also, that I can be of considerable help to you (for your have a complicated job on your hands at the easiest!). As far as my boat job is concerned—that will be just as av[a]ilable (or unav[a]ilable) one time as another. Altogether it seems as though this were the real opportunity to be with you for some time to come: later, with you both floating around in Florida, and myself God knows where, I see few opportunities for meeting.

If the house is sold you can probably afford my carfare for the round trip. Otherwise I simply couldn't come without walking. My present funds include five dollars and loose change—just enough to get back to New York and rely on friends until I find employment. I plan to be back there by next Sunday. If you can do so by that time I wish you would send me about $40.00—addressed to 110 Columbia Heights. I shall, of course, need more than the mere carfare as there is transportation, laundry etc, to take care of. Probably I shan't be able to get away until Wednesday or Thursday—but I'll telegraph you about the exact time later. I think I shall bring my wardrobe trunk home—it has always been too large for me, and you or Grandma may find it more useful in exchange for some smaller trunk around the place. But there is no use starting out on any of my suggestions here—they are too many and perhaps aren't practical anyway. Just one of them, however, is: don't plan on selling any household effects to a dealer—that is in bulk—as I'm told that one gets practically nothing for them that way. Advertising a private sale in the paper is much better (I don't mean an auction) and you get a decent price that way on every piece or item.

Well, I honestly hope that the sale has gone through. If it hasn't I doubt the advisability of my coming at present. I would be more useful later, then, whenever it is finally sold, however much I do long to see you. You'ld better answer this at Columbia Hts. I shall probably have heard from you in the meantime.

This sojourn here has done me a world of good. Wish you could see my tan now—it fades always in about 48 hours after I leave the sunshine. I walked over twenty miles yesterday over the ridges of the hills into neighboring valleys. It made me so sleepy that I went to bed at the fall of darkness.

Love, as ever, to you both—/ Hart

From   Elizabeth   Belden   Hart

#45 Haddam Apts—
Cleveland O.
October 9, 1925—

ALS, 8 pp.

My Dear Grandson:

You see by the above where I have landed. Mrs K.[1] very kindly
invited, yes *urged* me to stop with her until I leave for Florida & it
certainly has made it very nice for me to come here as it has caused
the least possible change & expense[.] If I had gone to Warren, you
see how much trouble the change would have meant & then to
come back to Cleveland to start with all the change back & forth of
baggage Etc— So you see it all—and I feel very grateful for the
kindness shown me— Mother left Tuesday on 12-15 train (noon)
amidst the greatest rush—She was nearly ready to collapse— I
dared not say good bye only at a distance[.] The last I glimpsed of
her she was wiping her eyes— I felt very sorry for her, and for myself also— It was a very trying hour to both of us but we had it to
meet, and so did the best we could to be brave— Under ordinary
conditions it would not have been so hard—I, being at such an advanced age—to go my way & she hers—was not very easy—but I
have been through *many* hard places—and as long as I live I expect to find them all along my pathway—but each one makes me
stronger for the next one[.] Every body is so thoughtful of me &
show[s] it by calling me up every day—& taking me out for a drive
Etc[.]

Dear old Ralph and Margarett[2] are two faithful souls— Ralph
never misses calling me up every day to know how I am and if he
can do anything for me— Yesterday he took me to town on a rush
errand before the man came for the car— Just as Mother had her
hat on she sold her car to a man who answered her *Ad*—& said he
would take it, which was a great relief to us both, so she had to
drive the thing over to Chas, to see to, after she left and deposit the

---

[1] Probably Mrs. Frank Martin Kirk, Mrs. Hart's friend from Cleveland.

[2] Ralph and Margaret had worked for Mrs. Hart when the family lived on
115th Street.

money to her acc— Now we won't have to worry about the expense
of that this winter[.] I had my last ride yesterday in *"Diana"*[.]
Just got back in time to let the man have it. She did not get as
much as she hoped for but it was cash & that was better than to
keep it—

Chas. is a jewel of the first water. He has looked after everything
for us both, regarding our tickets, Insurance on Trunks—
everything, also for Marthena[3] as she changed her tickets to go
with me over the Pennsylvania— The 26th she leaves Warren on
noon train. Chas meets her at 55th street. Erie Depot transfers her
baggage to Pennsylvania Depot 55th & Euclid, gets everything
checked—& then brings her to the Haddam to wait with me until
6:15 PM when he takes us both to station & puts us into a Drawing
Room where we remain without change or delay until we get
within three hours ride of Winter Haven (Marthenas home) then
they switch the Drawing room off and we are furnished a parlor car
for the rest of the trip— Now what could be nicer or more comfortable [?] I am to stay with Marthena until Mother finds a place suitable for us both which may be sometime and it may be that being
on the spot and some leaving who have been there all summer she
may be able to secure something befor the fall rush—any way I
will wait patiently and trust for something good to come to us—
We have been through a whole lot but every time when the way
has seemed the darkest, and no light in sight, something has come
along that has helped us out most wonderfully. The road has been
mighty rough at times and we might have been saved an awful lot
of worry could we only have known the outcome sooner, but it is
something to be thankful for that the clouds lifted at last moment.
My greatest anxiety now is that Grace does not break down now
that its all over—but I think when she gets there and has no one to
depend on only her own efforts she will gather up. She is very determined to get into biz of some kind— She carried with her some
wonderful letters of introduction to the very best and highest influential biz. firms there, including officials also & our Bank here introduced her to two of best Banks there as being a reliable patron
of our bank here—Guardian S. & Trust co—and a very reliable ef-

[3] Marthena Evans.

ficient woman [.] She had no trouble whatever to get a place to stop through Mary Smith Nancys sister, at the Halcyon Hotel 1 room & bath which gave her a place as soon as she landed, until she can look around for something cheaper [.] Edna Moore will get there in a day or two behind her & says she can "bunk" with her if she wishes until better supplied, so that is fine when so many are being turned away, but we must not worry, but know there will be room for *her*—but I do not know where to send this, New York or Jersey —but I will risk it at your country home [.] by the way I have no address unless I can find a letter of yours—I am expecting every minute to get word from Chas. of the night letter he is to receive this morning from Grace as to her arrival—so I will hold this open until I hear—I hope you will not be unmindful that Mother may be made much happier, by frequent letters from her boy—don't wait always until you hear from her. She may be very busy but send a card every day or two— I hope you will keep well & get a nice job very soon [.] Much love from Grandma—

Mrs. Crane sent a long letter to her mother and asked that she send it on to Hart, who had returned to Patterson in mid-September. Though Mrs. Hart's letter is missing, her daughter's has survived.

Hotel Strand—Miami Fla—
Friday Oct 16—1925

My dearest mother:—
Your good letters are beginning to arrive at the Halcyon Hotel, where I go everyday to get them, for as yet your letters addressed to this place have not put in an appearance—but it takes almost a week—sometimes more to get a letter through— Mail from here, like many other things [is] quite overpowering & clogged. Now it makes me very happy indeed & relieves me more than you will ever know to feel that you are well, happy comfortable & are not going to fret over me. This situation down here is like nothing you ever

could imagine, no matter how much you may read—& it simply dazes you at first and I am just beginning to come to, as it were— You know I left home with the idea of selling real estate, & I still hope to, *but* I never would stoop to the kind of selling these women who are down here are doing. They look like freaks—hang around the hotel lobbies & approach men until the whole thing is quite disgusting. I doubt if any of them have been successful, or many of the men either for that matter. There are men men men everywhere, young & old, & it has been my very good fortune to meet a number of very high type ones. One is connected with the Coral Gables outfit—very high type, & is from Cleveland & knows who I am & many of my friends. He stands very close to the powers that be at Coral Gables, is interested in getting me on the sales force in a high type plain & is getting the stage all set to introduce me to his boss at the right time. In the meantime, other things are presenting themselves—& I am trying to let it all soak in & determine if I really have an opportunity, just which is the best. These men have been wonderful to me & I go out to dinner with some of them every night— Last night I went to the Hotel Antilla at Coral Gables & danced & dined until 10:30—later to the beautiful new Coral Gables Country Club for concert & more dancing, & always meeting more people. Well mother, I simply can not tell you how beautifully they are developing that Coral Gables proposition & how perfectly fascinating it is & is going to be out there. Millions & Millions—why Venice isn't going to be a speck beside it—& I wish we could afford to buy a little home & live there forever— But that is another story.

Sunday I am going to drive to Palm Beach, Fort Lauderdale & Boca Racone. We will be gone all day & these two men (young chaps) are simply doing it without any idea of selling me property but simply because I expressed the wish that I could see it. I shall try to locate Ida's house— [1] but it is too soon for her to be there yet—

It is very warm here—perspiration just rolls off of you night & day, but there is always a breeze in the shade on the east side & I am beginning to get used to it.

[1] Ida Skiff, a friend of Mrs. Hart's.

I certainly feel as if God had been with me all of the way & will
be. I am in touch with Dr. Fosteroh[?] by wire & letter & he is a
wonder. I have *every* confidence in his understanding & work. This
situation takes time & I must not rush into anything too quickly. If
I line up with any of the realestate people I am now working with
my residence would be entirely different than if we were here just
for the winter & pleasure—so I must not decide upon an apartment
or anything in the way of living quarters until I come to more definite plans. I would like you to write Bess Frease *immediately,* special delivery, & tell her that I want the first chance at her apartment
if they decide not to take it. I can not tell at this moment anything
—but I am going to Havana & the Isle of Pines about Oct 30th—
They say there is a boom on real estate in Cuba now, & I do not
want to see my price on Villa Casas [2]—until I have learned more of
conditions.

Very prominent Cubans are in Miami at the present time investigating the methods of the Coral Gables development & I may be
able to meet some of them through this Cleveland man. Many other
things are in my mind—& I feel very forcibly that my time for success in some undertaking has come & is right here in Florida. The
brains & the money of the world are here & nothing can stop it— I
wish you could spend just twelve hours in Miami proper. It reminds me of nothing so much as just what hell might be. Buildings
are being built, others torn down—traffic a continual jam, people
run over, ambulances clanging, airaplanes buzzing over head—&
that isn't a beginning. It as as much as your life is worth to cross
the street. Sky scrapers that would do credit to New York City or
Chicago are being erected, & one just can imagine that it will be
anything but a huge city some day. But you would be very lonely
here & entirely too hot at present—so I am so happy that you are
going to Winter Haven among your old friends. Mary has returned
from Tampa & she passed through Winter Haven & says it is the
most heavenly spot in Florida— So that makes me still happier—

Edna Moore has not arrived— A letter she wrote to Mary states
that she was detained & will not arrive until the last of October.
That suits me. Mary is staying at this hotel now—until she can de-

[2] The name of the Harts' house on the Isle of Pines.

termine whether to go to the West Coast again—so I see her every day. She is working independently & I do not know how secure her commissions are. She works very hard & is on the job night & day, but her methods are not mine— That does not mean that she is not right, that I cannot yet determine. As I see it today, it is *most* important to line up with a big reliable development company where methods are straight, even if your commission is less. Mary is plucky at any rate & I certainly hopes she wins.

I had a nice letter from Hart today & a dear one from my beloved Chas. Bless his heart— I think of him so often— There is a side of this he would so love—the wonderful evenings—palm trees flowers moonlight, sea, & dancing. I will write him tomorrow.

Send this letter to Hart. I will write him as soon as I can but time is too valuable now to spend in writing long letters.

Don't worry a moment about me— I have a clean comfortable room, plenty of eat & amusement. I may be able to drive up to see you some time after you get to Winter Haven—because if these men down here like you they will let you lead them around by the nose—

Keep me informed either by wire or letter as to your whereabouts —& remember that letters are a long time on the way.

My love to every inquiring friend & tell Ralph I will write him a letter some day. Send this to Hart—

Devotedly—/ Grace

After returning to Patterson, Hart, with money borrowed from the Rychtariks, bought twenty acres of land from Bina Flynn, who owned the property adjacent to Bill Brown's. He hoped in time to build a cabin on the land, plant a small garden, and sustain himself.

A more immediate problem for the poet was to find work for the winter in New York. In early October Crane returned to the city to begin his usual quest for employment; once again he had no success. He did just miss being hired as a deck yeoman on a ship bound for South America, and then he missed a chance to be a copywriter for an advertising agency. When other opportunities for employment did not materialize, Hart was once again without funds.

To Elizabeth Belden Hart

110 Columbia Heights
Brooklyn, New York
Saturday
Oct. 24th, '25

TLS, 1 p.

Dear Grandma:

Your good letter enclosing Grace's has just reached me. I'm only sorry you have been having such an irritating time with acidosis, and hope that Dr Lytle has improved conditions considerably by this time. I, of course, have not said a thing to Grace about it. But you must be more careful about your diet from now on, even if you have to limit yourself somewhat.

I'm glad to hear that you are going to such a lovely place, and on the other hand I hope you will be able to stay there as long as possible instead of rushing away to Miami—which sounds like a perfect madhouse to me. I don't even like the idea of Grace's staying there very long. It's not the kind of place for people like us. Meanwhile there is plenty to think about with the Isle of Pines property — I hope she stays there long enough to really inspect conditions and rest up a little from the insane flurry of a place like Miami.

I have not found work yet. Meanwhile I'm being taken care of by friends. I'm not discouraged. Don't worry about me; I have still a good deal of self-confidence.

Shall write you next (and soon) at Winter Haven. Meanwhile be good to yourself, and demonstrate your usual cheer and courage.

Love, as always—/ Hart

To Grace Hart Crane

110 Columbia Heights,
Brooklyn, NY
Saturday—
Oct. 24th. '25

TLS, 1 p.

Dear Grace:

It was good to really hear from you at last. I also heard again from Grandma this morning, enclosing another long letter you recently wrote her. She seems to be chipper and in fine order to start out on Monday. I'm convinced that she is going to the right place, too—especially since you describe what a mad place Miami is. It makes me feel, moreover, that she ought to remain away from there all winter—but that's up to you both to decide later—and not me.

There is very little news here, albeit some chance that Waldo Frank has put over my book with Boni and Liveright if Gene O'Neill will consent to write a Foreword. But that has not been settled. No job has eventuated as yet, and I'm obliged to sleep in three different places and always dine as guest. I got all excited about getting a wonderful job on the S. American line last week, but just missed being engaged by 15 minutes. There may be another opportunity Monday.

Whatever happens, write me here. Mail will be forwarded to wherever I am, and should any uncertainties arise otherwise write to Allen Tate, 47 Morton St., New York for news. I shall, of course keep in as constant touch with you as possible.

I hope you will give plenty of time to the Island in preference to this insane Florida territory. If I were you I wouldnt waste another minute or dollar around Miami. It isn't the place for people like us, at all.

Love, and take good care of yourself. I'll write you next at the Island./ Hart

Realizing his mother and grandmother were unable to support him financially, Hart wrote a letter to his father, which is now lost, asking for some money. C.A.'s reply has survived. Though initially argumentative on both sides, their letters eventually became warmer in tone; as if almost against their wishes, Hart and his father found themselves on cordial terms.

In the meantime Grace's Florida adventure had turned into a nightmare. Both Grace in Miami and Mrs. Hart in Winter Haven had succumbed to a series of ailments and were unable to write Hart for six weeks. Regular correspondence was not resumed until his mother and grandmother had returned to Cleveland early in December.

From Elizabeth Belden Hart

[Postmarked November 4, 1925]
[Winter Haven, Florida]
Tuesday 8 PM

ALS, 6 pp.

Dear Hart

Your good letter was a great joy to me today, for it has seemed as if I was deserted by God and man. Instead of the beautiful setting you placed me [in], I have not even been able to step outside the door since I came—and am in bed under a Drs care, and can have suffered more than language can express—and have had no letter from Grace—except a night telegram next morning I got here— I did not let her know my condition for I supposed I would be better very soon—so put the best side on—not to cause her worry—but did suppose she would write me— Every mail I have looked for word from you & her but you say she has gone to the Island, is the reason, & I would suppose she would have informed me before leaving[.] I never want to be caught this way again. imagine how I feel to be here with none of my kin, a care on a friend, who has no girl, but she is very kind to me and Dr says I will have to lie in bed a few days more[,] that it [is] hard to control after it had run so long—but that is nothing very serious, only the suffering is agonizing at times—but I am trying to be brave & sooner get up if I keep quiet. Last night I slept none—but feel easier today & have to rest tonight. Don't worry I'll be all right soon. Write me/ Grandma

Wed 9 AM—

Had a fairly good night, and think I am on the mend—but must keep off my feet until the bladder heals up which depends on how still I keep. it is tedious but not serious Dr says—

The sun is shining and everything is beautiful but quite cool—from the effect of cold up north. I wish I could give you a part of a beautiful boquet of large red roses—half-blown. They are enough to make any one feel well to see them. A young lady sent them to me. They are just gorgeous.

And don't forget to write often. You are the only one I am in touch with[.] Don't worry[.] I am sure I will soon be all right[.] Can you read this?/ Grandma

From Clarence Arthur Crane

[Cleveland]
Nov. 17th 1925

TLC, 2 pp.

Mr. Harold Crane,
110 Columbia Heights,
Brooklyn, N.Y.

My dear Harold:—

I did not reply to your letter of November 4th, as in a letter where you ask money assistance from your own Father, I think it is quite unnecessary that you should stoop to refer to him as a disgruntled, narrow-minded commercialist. In other words I still appeal to the old adage "You cannot catch flies with vinegar".

It seems that we are always to travel different paths, and to have different ideas of what constitutes a wonderful existence. I do not expect to conform you to my way of thinking, neither do I expect that you will ever be able to conform me.

I wish you every success in life and the joys of real prosperity, which you say is only a little ways ahead for you.

I shall be very proud of a son who has achieved the literary success that you claim is already yours.

Unfortunately you have to endure the parents you have until Providence shall provide you with others, but I have never written you a letter which upbraided you for your shortcomings, and I never expect to.

From your viewpoint you have enough sunshine in your life without degrading it with commercialism, and if you find happiness in that sort of an existence, all you have to do is to make the best of conditions that go with it, and not complain to others.

According to my narrowed and bigoted way of looking at things you have pawned your birth right to my accomplishments in life at a very low figure, but fortunately I have found another young man who wants to carry on my work and singularly enough seems to feel that it is worth while.

Whether it is calling at my sisters or elsewhere, I learn your true opinion of my existence, and I have come to accept it as something which I cannot correct, at least at my advanced age.

I read your little article, with much interest, and think it very good advice for a woman to follow. I cannot see where you can get much consultation out of it for she had her husband, and she had children, and the husband was able to support her at home, and to let the children go out and see picture shows and eat good ice cream. Why should a woman want a job when her husband can do so much for her?

Anyway it is a check that you want so I am enclosing you $50.00.

With my good wishes, I am

Very sincerely,

To Clarence Arthur Crane

[New York City]
[November 21, 1925?]

TLD, 1 p.

Dear Father:

I was very glad to hear from you and it was generous of you to thus come to my aid. The only pity is that artificial theories and principles have to come so much between us in what is, after all, a natural relationship of confidence and affection.

You may not believe it, father, but in spite of what opinions you may hear that I have against you (and, not knowing what is told you, I still refuse to acknowledge them either way) I still resent the fate that has seemed to justify them and God Knows how much we all are secretly suffering from the alienations that have been somehow forced upon us. If we were all suddenly called to a kind of Universal Judgment I'm sure that we would see a lot of social defences and disguises fall from each other and we would begin from that instant onward to really know and love each other.

I feel rather strange these days. The old house sold in Cleveland; Grandmother ill in Florida; Mother somewhere in Cuba or the Isle of Pines; and I not hearing from either of them for the past month. Altogether, it's enough to make one feel a little foot-loose in the world. But I'll have a job soon, and will probably be reassured in the mail that everything's alright. At such times, though, I realize how few we are and what a pity it is that we don't mean a little more to each other.

Please let me hear from you when the spirit moves you.

Sincerely and grat[e]fully, your son

From Clarence Arthur Crane

[Cleveland]

Nov. 25th 1925

TLC, 2 pp.

Mr. Harold Crane
110 Columbia Heights,
Brooklyn, N.Y.

My dear Harold:—

On my return home from Chicago, I find your letter of Nov. 21st.

It may be that after a certain time you will get some of the cob-
webs off your eyes and realize that families while broken up and
discarded really do mean something to us after you [1] grow old and
feel the coldness of the outside world.

For the past nine years you have had a very poor opinion of your
Father and you haven't hesitated to feed the flame of discontent
and continually pity yourself for having such an unsatisfactory parent.

For a while you even changed your name, but I note for some
reason or other you have gone back to it.

One thing is certain. Your Father can get along just as well without you as you can get along without him, and that is for you to
find out, if you have not already arrived at that decision.

I am very sorry that your mother and grandmother are ill, and
that you haven't heard from them as you would like to.

They have nothing but my best wishes and always will, and I
will always be glad to know of their happiness, and regret to know
of their sorrow.

No "Fate" has caused you to suffer from any existing conditions
between us. That has just been a matter which you choose to build
up in your own consciousness and if it has gotten now to where it is
difficult to see over it you yourself must tear it down and make the
correction.

You made a statement in your former letter which I unqualifiedly

---

[1] The word "you" is repeated in the text.

denied. I have never said that I was not interested in you. I have told you that I was not interest[ed] in your work, and I am not interested in it because it does not bring you a livelihood. I have used the expression before and again say it. Writing to most people should be an avocation not a vocation.

You came from families on both sides who worked strenuously, perhaps so strenuously that in your eyes it is rather annoying to devote so much time to business and so little to the things which give one pleasure, but you must not forget what Elbert Hubbard once so tritely said "sooner or later in your journey through life your affection will be expressed in beefsteak".

We have to eat and we have to be clothed, and if in our struggle to accomplish things of a material way we overstep the bounds it isn't any wonder for failure often times follows very closely unsuccess and rich to-day and hungry tomorrow has been experienced by untold thousands.

I think you have a very good mind and the ability to express yourself unusually well. It is just a question of whether Harold Crane can make a living following out his pet scheme of life or not. If you can, I would think you are very wise to do as you have done and are doing. So far as the success you claim for yourself having been already attained, and being the greatest in your class since 1852, I can hardly see it that way, but probably I am not informed.

I do hope that you will get better news from your mother, and you can rest assured that any advances you wish to make to me toward getting on more friendly terms with your Father will be met with a hearty response.

Very sincerely your Father,

To Clarence Arthur Crane

110 Columbia Heights
Brooklyn, N.Y.
Dec. 3rd, '25

TLC, 1 p. (reversed image carbon copy)

Dear Father:

Your letter was appreciated in many respects and I don't want you to think that I wasn't glad to hear from you. But there were recriminations in it which assumed a basis for apologies and regrets on my part which I don't feel I at all suggested in my last letter and which I certainly cannot acknowledge now or later. In fact, you always seem to assume some dire kind of repentance whenever I write you or call on you, and so far as I know I have nothing in particular to repent. I simply said I was sorry that you could not see me in a clearer light, and it seems I shall have to go on lamenting that to some degree for the rest of my life. If I began to make recriminations on my behalf there wouldn't be any use writing at all, for though I have plenty to mention, I don't see what good it would be to either one of us to embark on a correspondence of that sort. My only complaint right now is that you seem determined to pursue such a course, and I can only say that if you persist I have no answers to offer. You and I could never restore our natural relationship of father and son by continually harping on all the unnatural and painful episodes that life has put between us via not only ourselves but other people during the last ten years, and if you are not willing to bury such hatchets and allow me, also, to do so, then I'll have to give up.

For the last six weeks I've been tramping the streets and being questioned, smelled and refused in various offices. Most places didn't have any work to offer. I've stepped even out of my line as advertising copy writer, down to jobs as low as twenty-five per week, but to no avail. My shoes are leaky and my pockets are empty: I have helped to empty several other pockets, also. In fact I'm a little discouraged. This afternoon I am stooping to do something that I know plenty of others have done whom I respect, but which I have somehow always edged away from. I am writing a certain internationally known banker who recently gave a friend of mine five thousand dollars to study painting in Paris, and I'm asking him to lend me enough money to spend the winter in the country where it is cheap to live and where I can produce some creative work without grinding my brains through six sausage machines a day beforehand. If he refuses me I shall either ask Eugene O'Neill who is now writing the Foreword to my book and won't refuse me for some help to that end, or I'll take to the sea for a while—for I'm certainly tired of the desolating mechanics of this office business, and it's only a matter of time, anyway, until I finish with it for good. I can live for ten dollars a week in the country and have decent sleep, sound health, and a clear mind. I have already bought ten acres near here in Connecticut and it's just a matter of time until I have a cabin on it and have a garden and chickens. You see I have a plan for my life, after all. You probably don't think it's very ambitious, but I do. As Dr Lytle said to me when I was last in Cleveland, "What does it all amount to if you aren't happy?". And I never yet have had a happy day cooped up in an office, having to calculate everything I said to please or flatter people that I seldom respected.

I wish you would write me something about yourself. Let's not argue any more.

As always,

The "internationally known banker" Hart speaks of here was Otto Kahn, the New York financier and patron of the arts. Late in the afternoon of Sunday, December 6, Hart left Kahn's Fifth Avenue residence with a check for one thousand dollars and the assurance of another thousand when he needed it. He could now pay his debts, provide for his own shelter, and send a check to his mother at Christmas. Since Hart was financially secure he decided to spend his life quietly living with Allen and Caroline Tate in a house they had rented not far from Susan and Bill Brown's in Patterson.

Two days after Hart received his money from Otto Kahn he received a telegram from Grace, who was still in Miami recovering from her illness.

From Grace Hart Crane

MIAMI FLO
DEC 8 1925

TELEGRAM

H HART CRANE
1 1 0 COLUMBIA HEIGHTS BKLYN NY
AM STILL CONFINED TO MY ROOM AT HOTEL STRAND MIAMI
FLO AND AM STARVING FOR SOME NEWS FROM YOU WIRE ME
AT ONCE ANY CHANGE OF ADDRESS AND HOW YOU ARE THAT I
MAY WRITE YOU GRANDMOTHER BACK IN CLEVELAND AT
MANOR ALL MY LOVE / GRACE

To Grace Hart Crane

Brooklyn, New York
Dec. 9" '25

ALS, 4 pp.
LETTERHEAD: HOTEL ST. GEORGE, BROOKLYN

My dear Mother:

For almost six weeks, now, I have not heard from you or
Grandma. Through [Though] Mr. Curtis was thoughtful enough
to notify me that you had been taken ill, the circumstances did not
seem to describe a situation so severe that you could not have taken
pen in hand and at least have written me once yourself during that
time—especially, it seems to me, since you know by my several last
letters that I was having a difficult time and was without funds entirely. I have put off writing you under these conditions; there was
enough reason to so do simply on the basis of your own indifference, or possible disgust with me. And I admit that it was a shock
for me to realize that you needed me so little. I have gone through
a good many realizations of various sorts—during the last six
months—and they are not without echos of certain things you said
to me last summer, trying as I may have been.

I don't know where you may be at this time, but in case you may

for any reason wish to write to me I am writing to say that I shall
be probably for the next year at the following address:

> c/o Mrs. Addie Turner
> Patterson, New York
> R.F.D.

I am unusually well provided for and shall leave for the country
next Saturday. Yesterday afternoon I had the pleasure of being re-
warded in some measure for some of the work I have been doing.
You have probably heard of the banker, Mr. Otto H. Kahn, who
has kept the Metropoltan Opera and various other artistic ventures
endowed for years. After an interview with Mr. Kahn at his home
at 1100 Fifth Ave. I was given the sum of two thousand dollars to
expend on my living expenses during the next year, which time is
to be opened in writing the most creative message I have to give,
regardless of whether it is profitable in dollars or cents or not.

Mr. Kahn was keenly interested in what Waldo Frank and Eugene O'Neill had said about my work, and it makes me very happy
indeed to have this recognition from a man who is not only extremely wealthy and renowned on that account, but who is also
very astute and intelligent. I am very tired now—with all the strain
and effort of the last two months, but I shall probably pick up as
never before when I get into the quiet of the country and have the
first real opportunity of my life to use my talents unhampered by
fear and worry for the morrow.

If you are not too prejudic[i]al about me by this time, you may
also be interested in this turn of affairs.

Let me hear from you sometime soon.

I certainly hope you and Grandmother are feeling better.

Love—/ Hart

From Grace Hart Crane

MIAMI FLO

1925 DEC 11

TELEGRAM

H HART CRANE
HOTEL STGEORGE CLARK ST BROOKLYN NY
YOUR FIRST LETTER IN TWO MONTHS RECEIVED THIS MORNING
AM ALMOST WILD WITH JOY OVER WONDERFUL NEWS AM STILL
BEDRIDDEN AT STRAND I HAVE NURSE SOME TIME YOU WILL
KNOW HOW VERY ILL I HAVE BEEN I ALWAYS WILL LOVE YOU
HOPING TO RETURN TO CLEVELAND FOR XMAS WILL WRITE
SOON WIRE ME ANSWER/ GRACE.

From Clarence Arthur Crane

Cleveland, Ohio
December 16th 1925

TLS, 2 pp.
LETTERHEAD: CRANE CHOCOLATE COMPANY

Mr. Harold Crane,
c/o Mrs. Annie Turner,
Paterson, N.Y.
Putnam County.

My dear Harold:—

Yesterday I received your letter and think you have reason for much rejoicing in the good luck that has come to you.

I carried your last letter around to Chicago, Detroit and other Cities thinking I would have a chance to write you a letter but at Xmas time you realize that the demands upon my time are quite intense.

We have had an unsatisfactory condition in Detroit with Mr. C——. He seems to have proven false to my confidence in him, and has robbed us of considerable money as well as our faith in him.

These things are eternally happening and I guess it is contagious now that business is so difficult to negotiate.

Our Chicago store is not proving out very well to date and I have had to be there several times.

Agreeable to your request I am not referring to any further differences of opinion and now that you are well set for the next few months in what you really want to do, I have nothing but fondest hopes that you will accomplish what you are striving for. Incidental I will endeavor to be helpful.

Yesterday I sent you several boxes of Candy for Xmas and your new address came in just in time as I was preparing a long list of them to go out and had intended to send it to Brooklyn.

Last night, Bessie [1] called me up and told me of the really lamentable condition of the Hart family.

I shall take pleasure in sending Mrs. Hart some Flowers for Xmas and sincerely hope that your mother may recover sufficiently from her illness to return home.

I really feel that you should come out and see them either at Xmas time or early in January and if you feel inclined to do so I will gladly send you your transportation.

There is nothing new this year. Our year's business will be about 15% less than last year, but I think perhaps our goods are distributed among a better clientele.

Your last letter shows a delight in returning to the old surroundings and I hope that every hour of it will come up to your expectations.

Affectionately your Father, / C.A.

Now that Grace and Mrs. Hart were ill, Hart relied more and more on his father for information concerning their condition. C.A. in return became most thoughtful, often acting as an intermediary

1 Bess Crane Madden, Clarence Crane's sister.

between his former wife and his son. Deciding that all his efforts should be devoted to *The Bridge,* Hart remained in Patterson and spent a quiet Christmas with the Tates. On Christmas night he wrote the following letter to C.A.

To Clarence Arthur Crane

Patterson, New York
R.F.D.
December 25th, '25

TL, 2 pp.

My dear Father:

The Day is almost over—and it has been a most happy one. From the window of my study on the second floor I can look out on a valley, white with the moonlight on the snow. Flakes have been falling intermittently all day, then it cleared toward sunset, and a [1] long walk over the hills was about the most pleasant thing imaginable. We had a regular Christmas Dinner at noon, I assisting Mrs. Tate to the extent of making cranberry sauce and plum pudding sauce which I managed to do pretty well considering my lack of previous experience. Maybe I have already mentioned that I am sharing the house with my friend, Allen Tate and his wife, who have also come out here to write. Both from Nashville, Tenn.

Although I've been here a week I'm just beginning to get settled down to work. There was much to pack and settle before leaving New York and I didn't get out here within several days of as soon as I had expected. Bundles and boxes have been arriving here ever since—besides which we may have to get in a large store of food supplies against the strenuous cold weather and snow to come. But once fixed, we'll be as independent as the proverbial pig on ice. Ordering staples and canned goods from Macy's and Charles is cheaper by far than depending on local retail stores in the neighboring towns.

Your candy arrived in splendid condition. I needn't mention how

[1] The word "a" is repeated in the text.

much I appreciated it. The others reiterated the usual praises that always ensue whenever I open up a box of Crane's. I[t] seems to me to be completely up to the old-time standard, and though it isn't especially good for me to eat it I have been indulging myself generously. Let me also thank you for the check remembrance which will of course go a long ways out here. The rush and a[n]xieties incident to the holiday rush didn't, I hope, make Christmas day too much a matter of mere recuperation for you. The flowers you sent to Grandma were much appreciated, I can assure you without even having as yet heard from her, and I only hope that Grace was able to make the trip and be with her today.

I really am terribly worried about them. I had no idea of the state of things until quite recently, when Grace finally wrote me. It seems she had been unable to write before that for a long while, and didn't want to frighten me with telegrams. As I said, I've yet to hear whether or not Grace has reached Cleveland. If she hasn't, of course, there's even more reason to worry. I hope to know tomorrow. And if things are not really imperative at this time I should rather defer my visit until later, in the early spring. Not that I wouldn't prefer to come now, but I feel a certain responsibility about getting started into my work as soon as possible. While Mr. Kahn makes no insistence on immediate results, his generous interest in the work I have in mind makes me want to subordinate most other matters to a particular end. But if I'm really needed I'll of course come. And it's splendid of you to offer me the fare.

I expect to be in New York for a couple of days at a time once a month or so during the winter. When you are writing me, if you are scheduled for any trips there let me know in advance and perhaps I can make it when you, also, are there. We might have dinner and an evening together.

As it isn't too late to wish you a very happy and prosperous New Year, believe me, you have my best wishes. Please convey my greetings to Frances, too. Write me soon.

Affectionately, your son

To Elizabeth Belden Hart

[Patterson, New York]
December 29th, '25

TLS, 1 p.

Dear Grandma:

You haven't written me for a very long time. I'm hoping that you'll soon favor me again—as soon as you feel able, for I love to hear from you and your letters are a treat to me always.

I must mention how glad I am now—not that I wasn't before!—that I brought so many items from home with me last fall when we broke up the house. It is extremely pleasant to have familiar quilts, blankets and comfortors on my bed. Your knitted shawl, of the. many colored insertions, has been admired by legions. I have it hanging outspread on the wall of my bedroom. It is so cheerful and homelike.

Do you remember the old-fashioned kind of "sleigh bed", as they called them? I like the one my landlady is giving me so much that I think I shall bargain with her for it when I get my house built next summer and move it in. This reminds me that it would be fine of Grace to have that small bed sent down here to me now. It would make a splendid couch in the study, and as I'm settled now in this neighborhood, it might as well come now as later.

I think I shall buy one of the small partitional houses that are made in sections by a number of reliable construction companys now. The Bossert Lumber Co. of Brooklyn, for instance, will truck the sections right to your property and erect it for you. I can probably get a four-room cabin and a very comfortable one, for about 600 dollars. That is so much cheaper than any other way that it is the thing for me to do. But more about this later. I shall not begin to think out details until next spring. There is much else for me to do in the meantime.

It is a little warmer than it was—about 12% above zero. I can be sure that you, at least, are warm as toast at the Manor as well as comfortable every other way. I'm so glad you both aren't slaving away in that huge old house!   Love to you both,/ Hart

!XXO XX O!!!

From Clarence Arthur Crane

[Cleveland]
Dec. 30, 1925

TLC, 1 p.

My dear Harold:

I enjoyed reading your letter written on Christmas Day and glad you are in such high spirits and fully enjoying the advantages of your new location.

I am replying immediately so that you may know that your mother arrived here safely and was able to stand at the phone for a half an hour and converse with me last evening. I think she is entirely out of danger. She wrote me a letter, thanking me for the flowers which I sent your mother for Christmas, and knowing she was in town I called her up and had a very enjoyable conversation. I believe your mother is able to be about the hotel but as yet has not ventured out.

There is nothing new with us here. I am busy with the cleanup of the year and Frances has gone to Kansas City for the usual holiday visit with her people.

I have no immediate plans for coming to New York and all will depend on whether or not Hazel comes out here for her arrangements.

With all good wishes, I am

Affectionately, your father,

From Clarence Arthur Crane

Cleveland, Ohio
Dec. 31, 1925.

TLS, 1 p.
LETTERHEAD: CRANE CHOCOLATE COMPANY

My dear Harold:

You and I seem to be entering into quite a correspondence the last few days, but your mother had just called me up and tells me that Mrs. Hart had a very bad night last night and she is very much worried about her. She doesn't want you to come home but wishes you would write your grandmother a good letter immediately and help ease her mind regarding your condition.

Your mother tells me she has heard nothing from you since her return to Cleveland and for that reason Mrs. Hart is much worried. I sent her out your letter and that seems to have helped some.

Grace tells me that I gave you a little wrong impression regarding herself in the letter which I sent you. She says she is not able to be out and is only sitting up at present, but has no fear regarding her own condition as she is slowly recuperating.

So, sit down and write your grandmother a good letter and I think she will appreciate it.

Affectionately, your father,/ CA

Mrs. Crane finally recovered enough from her illness to write Hart a long letter, which outlined briefly the ordeal of caring for her mother.

From Grace Hart Crane

Cleveland
Jan 2—1926—

ALS, 8 pp.
LETTERHEAD: Wade Park Manor/ Cleveland

[*Written at the top of page 1:*] Chas is so interested in your success & good fortune. He is kindness itself to both of us here. His business is coming along fine. You know, he is by him self now—

Dearest Hart:—

This letter is long past due you, but there has been so much on my mind, & I've so little strength these days that I've not been equal to writing. Since Christmas, your Grandmother has had a severe set back, acute indigestion I guess, & I thought for about twelve hours that the end had come. Dr Lyttle came in great haste

& worked to bring her out of it for several hours. Since then, she has had a night nurse, & I care for her daytimes. She is getting along slowly toward where she was a week back. Every bit of food has to be especially prepared, without salt, & all cooked in soft water, & something to be done or prepared all most constantly. Tuesday & Wednesday I came down with a very hard cold & Dr Lyttle ordered me to stay in bed. Wednesday mother has this bad spell, so I had to pile out & do what I could. Our rooms are on the same floor but quite a distance apart, so it makes quite a lot of running back & forth. By Monday, we expect to move into a suite. At present every one is occupied over the holidays—

We both want to thank [you] for the check you sent us for Xmas. I remarked to mother that that was exactly like you—that when you got any spare money to pass it out to your friends. Of course we think & talk of you a great deal—& would love to see you & say many things that I havn't time to write.

Every one who knows anything about it seems to think you are most fortunate to have such a person as Mr Kahn interested in your work. Sally Baker [1] says—tell Hart to play into his hand & try to please him, because if he is satisfied that you are in earnest & he likes you, he will *never* desert you— She knows of some one in Chicago whom he helped—as well as others, & says he is wonderful— So cater to him all you can & be honest to yourself— That is all the advise I'm going to offer *now*—you know everything I could tell you any way.

Yes, it is very amusing & very evident how your father feels—now that you have the interest & support of a prominent person— He said to me over the phone when I was thanking him for the roses —that he sent mother for Xmas,—he said— ["] I understand Harold has a new Daddy"—an expression which revealed a whole lot to me —(both jealousy & fear) [.] I told him I thought it was about time & was of course very happy over it, not any more on account of the money, than for the recognition of your ability by a man of such ["] intelligence & influence."

I think he is just a little bit puzzled as to just how to act. Well, be as it may, I am glad thro & through for your good fortune, &

[1] Very possibly this is Sarah Baker, a friend of Mrs. Crane's.

hope your attitude to all your family will be entirely free from bitterness, as it is a dissapating force you don't want to get into your thoughts now. This next year is a most important year & you want to satisfy your benefactor that you are using his help to the best of your ability—no matter if you do not set the world on fire. I shall hope to meet him some day—

I stay in the house all of the time so the only thing I know about outsiders is what I get over the phone. I don't seem to gain my strength very fast but I think I will as soon as I feel less anxious about mother. I think the doctor has been very doubtful of her recovery—& said if she did she would never be strong again. Her mind has remained perfectly normal through all her suffering & I am so glad. She has been a wonderful woman & were we to lose her we would [2] have many unusual memories— Write her often & tell us if you received our checks—

Much love from us both. Write me again your telegraph address—

All my love/ Grace

To Clarence Arthur Crane

Patterson, New York
Rural Delivery
January 3rd, '26

TLS, 1 p.

Dear Father:

Your two letters relating the state of things with Grace and Grandma came yesterday and I certainly appreciate your concern in informing me so well and so promptly. Of course I have all kinds of faith in Grace's constitution—but the situation with Grandma is possibly precarious.

I have written Grace directions previously for reaching me by phone or wire—but I have found her mislaying correspondence so in the past that it may be well for you to also have the data in case

[2] The words "We would" are repeated in the text.

I am ever needed suddenly. In such event I can be reached by telephone by long distance, *PAWLING (N.Y,) 40F—Ring 2.* Wires should be sent to Patterson, N.Y. c/o J. J. Kessler, who will phone wire message to our house.

As to their not hearing from me—I can't understand it, having written them three letters during the last fifteen days. The last one, addressed especially to Grandma, had possibly not reached her at your time of writing. I certainly would be the last one in the world, however, to wish to deprive the old lady of any comfort, and I'll try for awhile to write her a not[e] every other day or so, even though there isn't much to relate.

Affectionately,/ Harold

To Elizabeth Belden Hart

Patterson

Jan 5th '26

TLS, 1 p.

Dear Grandma:

I was sorry to hear from Grace yesterday that you have been undergoing more pain and illness—and I only hope that this finds you MUCH improved. I wish I could be near you—and have a long talk. We certainly will manage that when I come out to Cleveland next spring.

Yesterday I finally got started into my Bridge poem—really the first full day I have for the work since arriving. And from now on I hope to have the necessary inspiration to keep steadily at it. One really has to keep one's self in such a keyed-up mood for the thing that no predictions can be made ahead as to whether one is going to have the wit to work on it steadily or not.

It is fine to get somewhere where I can sleep soundly again. I'm beginning to feel very much rested. I'm so glad that you both are located in a place where there is nothing more to do than to care for your personal comfort. Grace says that Charles is, as always, a great comfort to you.

There is nothing much to report, the weather has modified a great deal the last two days. It is more like a spring fog—temperature below freezing. I'm glad to hear that you are both moved by this time into a suite together. You probably can't do any writing at this time, and I don't won't [want] you to make any painful efforts, but Grace must write me often about you both.

Love and kisses to you both,—/ Hart

To Grace Hart Crane and Elizabeth Belden Hart

Patterson
Jan. 7" [1926?]

ALS, 2 pp.

Dear Grace & Grandma—

No word from you today—but I am hoping you are both better. It is bedtime—and we turn in early out here—but I wanted you to know that I'm thinking of you—oftener, of course, than I ever write.

There isn't much news—only the good news (to me!) that I've been at work in almost ecstatic mood for the last two days on my Bridge. I never felt such range and symphonic power before—and I'm so happy to have this first burst of substantiation since I had the good luck to be set free to build this structure of my dreams.

I sent New Years greetings to Kahn and in the mail today comes the most cordial answer—wishing as he puts it, "that you will prove yourself a master builder in constructing "The Bridge" of your dreams, thoughts and emotions."

During your many days indoors now, Grace, why don't you get Waldo Frank's novel, "Rahab", and see if you don't find much in it. Or there is another fascinating novel, by a friend of mine, Isidor Schneider, called "Dr. Transit", which deals with one of the myths of the age,—sexology, in a most amusing and unusual way.

Do write me soon—

Love in bushels,/ Hart

From Grace Hart Crane

Cleveland
[Postmarked January 13, 1926]
Wednesday—

ALS, 12 pp.
LETTERHEAD: Wade Park Manor/ Cleveland

My dear Hart:—

It has been so hard to write you anything reliable concerning your grandmother— She is desperately ill, but some days so much worse than others, that I wonder if the end is far away—then again she will revive & be so bright and alert that it does not seem possible than [that] it is the same woman. We are keeping her comfortable with opiates—but unless the condition improves which necessitates them, she will have to continue their use & increase the quantity—which affects the mind & you know the rest of the story — Night before last she decided not to take any & she nearly died with suffering— The doctor said she wouldn't live a week with such agony as that, so you [she?] was glad to take the medicine last night & today she seems better than for several days—but when she takes that opiate regularly she looks awfully & her mind becomes very muddled & she is not herself. She certainly is making a brave fight. She told her day nurse yesterday that if she couldn't get well she never wanted to know it—because as long as she had her mind, she was going to think she would get well— She talks almost constantly to the nurses, principally about Hart & what a wonderfully bright fellow he is, and also about me.

The expense is perfectly terrific and she worries about that—but there's no use—because she must have all that she has in care—& requires constant attention might & day & I could not take care of her a half day or night. I am doing my best when I manage to remain up & dressed all day. Her nurses are two of the finest & are perfectly devoted to her—which is a great relief to me. Oh what a tragic time I have had since leaving 1709—I've wished a good many times I were back in the old home. It is so much harder to be sick in a hotel.

I am so broken down physically & mentally—so depressed & confused that I do not amount to anything, & it is hard for me to believe that I [will] ever take any interest in anything or ever be my self again. I feel so thoroughly whipped that I can't imagine my ever enthusing about anything again. If I can only get strong enough to get to work & earn something in some way that I can become absorbed, I believe that will be my only salvation in the future, and it is going to be work or marry. I have never felt I would be willing to marry to escape work— Chas is wonderful—but he is not young & not rich—& there is going to be little left for me when mother goes—

I guess Katherine Kenny [1] has struck her gait with this work she is doing for Johnson. She is moving here for the rest of the winter on Thursday[.] Her mother also of course—but her mother consented to let her have a room by herself after much argument—so K—— told me Sunday night when she came to my room for a few moments. She is looking fine & is in wonderful spirit.

There is no news—I go nowhere and don't care to.

Had a letter from Helen today— She is not at all well— I can't see why—but she claims she isn't—

Pat Brown called this afternoon & thot it was fine good fortune for you to have Mr Kahn interest himself in you—& wished to be remembered to you. She was extremely handsome[.]

I think Minerva Brooks is in New York—probably associated with Mrs Noyes. Wish you would call her up some time— I cannot bear the way he struts around & advertizes himself in this town— I certainly hope that if success comes to you you won't be completely spoiled—or lose your head as he has— [2]

Aunt Alma [3] had not heard of your good fortune until I told her the other day and she was truly delighted & wished me to tell you that she had always had faith in you, & that now more than ever. A whole lot of your friends are pleased—especially because they resent the attitude your father has taken in the past, & they are delighted

[1] Kathryn ("Kay") Kenney was a friend of Hart's from Cleveland. Just what work she was doing at this time is not known.

[2] These sentences refer to the Cleveland author Charles Brooks.

[3] Alma Crane.

that you are having recognition which is bound in time to make him feel jealous & show him up very badly. Mrs Barnes was *most* emphatic last night at dinner last night in denouncing him in attitude toward you— She hoped you would never have to come to him again—but that the tables sometime would be reversed.

Well I've written much more than I had intended & will send this out right away— Will you *please* answer my two questions of previous letters— What is your telegraph address and did you receive mine & grandmothers checks for Xmas?—

Devotedly / Grace—

Though any direct link between the events in Cleveland and Hart's progress on *The Bridge* would be tenuous, one should not underestimate the influence of Grace's and Mrs. Hart's illnesses on him, for the tensions of Cleveland were certainly enervating. Upon his return to Patterson after five days of relaxation and parties in New York City, he wrote to his mother and Mrs. Hart. Grace replied with further accounts of their health.

To Grace Hart Crane and Elizabeth Belden Hart

Patterson
Jan. 17th, '26 [1]
Saturday

TLS, 1 p.

Dear Grace and Grandma:

I haven't written (although I intended to) because I've been in New York for several days and caught up in a swirl of errands and social engagements. Some friends were driving in last Sunday evening and I was invited to ride in their car. It was a lovely trip through the snow, and it is good to get back, too, I can tell you. I

---

[1] As January 17, 1926, fell on a Sunday, this letter was probably written on January 16.

so much prefer living out here in the peace and beauty of cleanliness. (They are obliged to use soft coal throughout the City now, and great clouds were blowing everywhere, sooty and dark. [)] When I got back last evening I got your letter, Grace, and although it is almost time for the mail man to pass I'm getting off at least these few words. Tomorrow I shall write more. I do hope that dear Grandma is more relieved by this time. It is marvelous the way my brave hearted good Grandmother keeps her character and fibre through everything. I am more proud of her than she knows! Her pictures are around me always. Lovely old daguerrotypes taken at different times—which I snitched from the family archives at various times through the past!

Keep me informed about you both *very* often.

Love and kisses!/ Hart

From Grace Hart Crane

Cleveland, Ohio
Jan 19—[1926?]
Tuesday Noon

ALS, 10 pp.
LETTERHEAD: Wade Park Manor/ Cleveland

My dearest Hart:—

Your letters to us both were most cheering & welcome yesterday, and I hasten to reply as you requested letters more often. I have had such a raft of letters to write & bills to pay that I probably haven't written as often as I should—& then again grandmothers condition has been so distressing that there was always the hope that there would be a change for the better & I could write a better letter.

She is still in bed & has her nurses. The only way she is kept from extreme suffering is by giving her an opiate. She has hopes that she will be herself again—because she is more free from pain. Of course there's a reason for the comfort. We tried to do without it one day, in order to see how her condition was & she nearly lost her

mind with the suffering. Dr Lyttle said *never again*—she must be
kept comfortable & I feel— She looks very badly but is hoping hoping *hoping*. Her mind seems very clear but she has grown very
childish & you would be surprised at the way she carries on some
times, in order to have her way. Its both laughable & most trying.
She is very happy with her day nurse & does not care to have me
stay long—but come *often*. I am expected not to leave the house,
without telling her just how long I'll be gone & what I shall do etc.
She won't let me have a word of conversation with the nurses, unless I speak loud enough for her to hear, & that is louder than it
used to be. She hasn't been able or wanted to pay any of her bills
her nurses or her house expenses—and when I had at last to take
things into my own hands—you would have died laughing if you
had seen her behave. She absolutely refused to let me have her
bank book to get some funds transfered from her savings to checking account—and of all the subterfuges she resorted to—but I finally won.

Friday—Jan 22—

Since starting this I've had a bad attack of acute indigestion in
bed two days—I'm ashamed of myself for having so many things
the matter of me—but I'm in such a condition that anything grabs
me that comes along. Grandmother seems better—sits up about
twice a day—an hour each time. It is hard to tell whether she is
gaining or not—in some ways she seems to be— Has to have her
nurses yet. It is taking a lot of money—but I have not yet been able
to figure out anything any cheaper— You see I can't take care of
her in a house as I once could—some days I can't be on my feet—
only a few minutes at a time—until I percipitate my troubles—
Well enough of this organ recital—

Last night about ten oclock I had a very delightful call from
Charlotte Reichstaric [Rychtarik]. She & Richard are down stairs
attending a lecture, & afterwards she came up to my room. I was in
bed recovering from my indigestion—but was so very glad to see
her. She was marvelously beautiful—and the memory of the lovely
picture of her wonderful face & beautiful shoulders & arms—have
remained with me all day. She should be on the stage— My what a
hit she would make— It seems too bad that such charm & beauty
should have so small an audience.

Well she was very enthusiastic over your good fortune etc. We talked mostly of you of course.

Grandmother loves your letters & reads them to both of her nurses.

Chas. is giving a small dinner party tonight followed by bridge —in which I will be missing of course. I expect to be there for the food.

Your letter of the 21st just received. I will try to do better & write every other day at least. I was hindered by this last sick spell. I know you are anxious—& the time seems long between. Unless something different develops, (which is always a possibility with her in her present condition) there is no *immediate* danger— It looks now she might live for sometime, but will probably have a nurse— maybe always. I do not think the condition of the bladder is improving any—but the opiates keep her comfortable & how long they will be sufficient remains to be seen. Her nurses have to do a great deal for her all of the time, such as duches, irrigation of bladder—baths in alcohol, rubs & she soils constantly so that she seems to have lost almost all control of that organ. She soils about ten sheets during the twenty four hours—so you see how utterly impossible it would be for me to care for her. If she can't be more like her self—& I am sure she will be most unhappy, & I think it would be better for her to pass out now—if she has got to suffer or feel she is not herself— Her mind remains remarkably clear considering the *"codine"* she is taking. I hope your article to "Vanity Fair["] is accepted— [1] I shall be so interested in hearing about everything you are doing & wish to keep closely in touch with you & your interests. Do you see Mr Kahn on your trips to New York—and how do you like him? He certainly has been your saviour, and I want him to like you so much that he always will be.

All my love & write often. If you could manage to get a few kodaks of yourself out there in the snow it would delight grandmother to receive them

Goodbye—from / Grace—

---

[1] The article, which is now lost, was rejected by *Vanity Fair*.

From Grace Hart Crane

Cleveland
Saturday,
Jan—23—'26

ALS, 4 pp.
LETTERHEAD: Wade Park Manor/ Cleveland

My dear Hart:—

Grandmother had a very bad night again— She is weak & tired today from a long night of pain & the effects of the opiate which she had to take more of. I have not seen her yet as she was being bathed and rubbed when I went to her room but I had a talk with her nurse— Dr Lyttle insists upon a bladder irrigation tonight, which is very painful & mother has refused to have one for several days on that account. Consequently she is dreading the ordeal to-night. I have become so sensitive to her suffering that I cannot stand by & see it. It affects me the same way—& besides I cannot sleep or get her out of my mind afterwards.

As I told you in my yesterdays letter I cannot tell whether she is going forward, holding her own, or loosing ground. Some days she seems so much better—

This is a beautifully bright clear winter day—very cold.

Bess Smith of Canton & Mrs Housel who took care of me in Miami, are coming up by auto tomorrow for the day. Tryon & Clara Dunham drove up on purpose to see mother on Thursday & bro't her some beautiful flowers—but we do not let any one in to see her. She makes too much of an effort to talk & it tires her out.

People have been wonderfully kind & attentive & I realize she has many friends & admirers. You do not know how much I miss you now—no one of my own family to talk with or advise. Everything to decide & plan *alone*. I am trying to keep my self in the best possible shape I can, so that if grandmother does pass away, I will be able to do all that I shall have to.

Am enclosing a clipping which appeared in our Plain Dealer the other day—[1] Tho't you might be interested.

[1] The enclosure about Otto Kahn is lost. See next letter.

Write often & mostly to grandmother— Tell her what you are
doing— How things look etc—

Devotedly Grace

To Grace Hart Crane

Patterson
Jan. 26 [1926?] Tuesday

ALS, 3 pp.

Dear Grace:

It *is* a good thing I got your letter yesterday—or I *should* have
been sore. I was so tired last night I simply fell into bed at 10. We
had spent most of the day shopping in town and I later built me
some book shelves which are very simple but extend to the ceiling
—the kind I have always wanted. My study now is a picture to
enjoy. When I was in New York I bought some beautiful and rare
Congo wood carvings—and added to my Sommer paintings—and
your photograph they make a marvelous room.

My hands are so stiff from wood cutting that my writing looks
funny. It is very, very cold today, was yesterday and promises to
continue. We all go about shivering most of the time and I'm sorry
to say get all too little freedom for our writing. Certainly the spring
warmth will be unusually welcome to all of us.

Thanks for the Kahn clipping. The same at greater length was
on the front pg. of the Times recently, indeed, Kahn has been so active lately in promulgating a new site and building for his Metropolitan Opera that the papers have been full of him.[1] We do not
correspond—except at considerable intervals as I hesitate to presume much on his attention. There are so many others whom he is
always helping that his time is largely taken up anyway. What with
two personal secretaries and a whole corps of personal office help—
besides his huge financial machine (his interests occupy a building

[1] As president of the Metropolitan Opera Company, Otto Kahn had proposed
building a new opera house on Ninth Avenue between 57th and 58th streets.
The plan met with such strenuous resistance from many members of New York
society that Kahn had to abandon it.

Patterson
Jan. 26 Tuesday

Dear Grace:

It is a good thing I got your letter
yesterday — or I should have been sore. I was so
tired last night I simply fell into bed at 10.
We had spent most of the day shopping in town
and I later built me some book shelves which are
very simple but extend to the ceiling - the kind I
have always wanted. My study now is a picture
to enjoy. When I was in New York I bought some
beautiful and rare Congo wood carvings - and
added to my Sommer paintings and your photograph they make a marvelous room.

My hands are so stiff from wood-cutting that
my writing looks funny. It is very, very cold today,
was yesterday and promises to continue. We all go
about shivering most of the time and I'm sorry to say
get all too little freedom for our writing. Certainly

First page of letter of January 26 [1926?]
from Hart Crane to Grace Hart Crane

of about 22 stories) he must be a busy man. He wants to hear from "time to time" as he puts it—about how my poem is progressing. But since writing him New Years I shant presume again until March or so. My second thousand is not payable until along in May. At which time I shall probably personally talk to him again. Beyond this money I have no expectations of more assistance, but if my poem when completed seems good enough to him, it may be, of course, that he will be further interested. I'm thankful enough for what I already have, however!

Your news about Grandma is rather heartrending. I do hope she won't have to suffer much longer—and if she does that she will be given enough sedatives to keep the pain dulled, no matter what the consequences. It would be best if she really gives up more—for the remainder of her existance under any conditions—promises her only misery.

I'll have to close now in order to write a brief word to her before the postman comes.

So glad you saw the Rychtariks—and hope you invite them over again when you feel better. Do try to keep yourself in as calm a frame of mind as possible— I know it must be difficult but none of this is surprising to us—after all.

Devotedly,/ Hart

From Grace Hart Crane

Cleveland
Tuesday Jan 26—'26

ALS, 4 pp.
LETTERHEAD: Wade Park Manor/ Cleveland

My dear Hart:

This is a beautiful winter day—the air full of snow flakes and I can see the skaters on the pond in Wade Park as I sit here at my desk.

I've just been over to see grandmother in her room on this same floor. She had a poor night but by noon she gets to feeling more comfortable & likes to talk to me. She reads the papers with as much concern as though she were going to live forever. She is going to loose both of her nurses & I'm in the business of getting some more. One she is firing & the other is resigning—& when mother learns that Miss Wilson is going to leave, I do not know what she is going to do, for she just adores her. Miss Wilson finds the work too hard—& mother *is* a very difficult patient & requires a great deal done for her all through the day & at night too.

Tonight Chas. & I are invited up to Josephine['s] for dinner. I shall enjoy one of her good home cooked meals.

I know very little news because I stay right here most of the time, and shall have to for some time I think. Grandmother is not improving and I do not believe she will because she is requiring more Codine all of the time to allay the pain. She is terribly drawn I think, but her spirit is still unbroken & her will power more determined than ever. I am worn out trying to plan & know what to do for her.

Sid Wilson was here last night just returned from California & invited Chas. and me to dinner with him. He was wonderfully pleased at your good fortune

This all today— Write often—

Loads of love/ Grace

To Elizabeth Belden Hart

Patterson, New York
January 27th [1926?]
Wednesday

TLS, 1 p.

Dear Grandma:

The letter I wrote you yesterday didn't get off until today—as the postman came earlier than usual and had, in fact, slipped by before I had even finished writing to you.

I am hoping to hear from Grace tomorrow all about how you are. Much better, I hope.

We had a brief flurry of snow again today, but not enough yet to permit me to use my scrumptious snow shoes. I have been reading the Journal of Christopher Columbus lately—of his first voyage to America, which is concerned mostly with his cruisings around the West Indies.[1] It has reminded me many times of the few weeks I spent on the Island to hear him expatiate on the gorgeous palms, unexpected pines, balmy breezes, etc. which we associate with Cuba.

I'll have to close now, or I'll get left again with the post. Tell Grace to write often, and give her my love.

Your devoted grandson,/ Hart

To Grace Hart Crane and Elizabeth Belden Hart

Patterson
Jan 31 '26

ALS, 2 pp.

Dear Grace & Grandma:

The cold spell has finally broken—and I'm no longer in the dejected and frigid mood of my last letter. We even welcome the steady drip of rain that has been falling all day,—in preference to the discomfort so long endured.

We had a great celebration up at Brown's home last night— baked ham, mashed potatoes, turnips, squash, pickles, cider and plum pudding. It ended up in a riot of dancing and "carrying on" of all sorts, Bina Flynn and her beau having arrived in their car from New York in the meantime. They had just come back from Montreal and brought me a quart bottle of the finest rum you ever tasted. Made in the province of Quebec and strong enough to send you to Key West!

Next Thursday Bina and her beau with Bill and Sue are leaving for Montreal where they are going to celebrate a "duplex" wedding. If there were only room in the car I should love to go along. It's so beautiful up there now and winter sports are in full swing. With all

[1] It is likely that Crane read the edition of Columbus's journal that was published by Albert and Charles Boni in 1924, with an introduction by Van Wyck Brooks.

the cold weather we've had there hasn't been enough snow to use my snowshoes yet. Yesterday, however, I got some exercise by walking to Sherman Center and back—in all about 12 miles. The sun came out and it almost felt like spring.

On the whole, I'm so happy out here in this lovely landscape and among such pleasant people that I want to live here always. I'm certainly far from regretting my purchase of 20 acres here, and shall erect a charming little house on it someday.

I do hope you are both improving in your respective conditions. Give my very best to Charles— Write often!

Love, as always/ Hart

Aside from an article that he submitted without success to *Vanity Fair* and his negotiations with Horace Liveright over publication of *White Buildings,* Crane concentrated his efforts in the winter months of 1926 on *The Bridge.* Much of his time was taken up reading background materials—New Bedford whaling records, Herman Melville's *White Jacket,* Christopher Columbus's journal of his first voyage to America, and D. H. Lawrence's *Plumed Serpent*—materials with which he slowly and meticulously created the intricate structure of the poem. By early March Mrs. Crane felt sufficiently recovered from her illness of the previous fall to make plans for her second marriage. Hart returned to Cleveland to help with the arrangements.

From Clarence Arthur Crane

Cleveland, Ohio
March 2, 1926

TLS, 1 p.
LETTERHEAD: CRANE CHOCOLATE COMPANY

My dear Harold:

Your letter of February 20th came duly to hand and I have really had no opportunity to write you the last few days.

I saw your mother some four weeks ago. She reported your grand-mother's condition is improving. I think that the strain on your mother has been quite marked for several people have told me that she was not looking at all well and they thought it was only because she had been trying to do too much.

It is good to know that you are feeling so well and that the good farm cooking is entirely to your taste. There is little to write of here. We plod along in our own way and during January and February there are few thrills in business, at least in this climate. It is regretable that one cannot close up shop for those two months and get away for the year's vacation. If it wasn't for rent and the fact that all people have to eat and live I think we would be a lot of money ahead.

From what I know there is no reason for your expecting to be called home right away and of course if you can postpone it until the balmy month of May you will have a much more enjoyable time. I know of nothing else to write of interest and with my best hopes for your continued happiness, I am,

Sincerely, your father,/ C.A.

Crane left Cleveland on a sleeper on March 15, spent the next day on a spree in New York ("I was released from the fond embrace of my relatives in Cleveland—only to fare into rather more than less spasmodic embraces in N.Y."),[1] and returned to Patterson on March 17 to continue working on his poem.

[1] Quoted from Crane's letter of March 28, 1926, to Malcolm Cowley. Published in *The Letters*, p. 242.

To Elizabeth Belden Hart

Patterson [1]
March 18th [1926?]
Wednesday

TLS, 1 p.

Dearest Grandma:

Just a word to say that I'm back. Your dear little note I discovered in my suitcase when I went to bed on the train! It has been so
very nice to see you and talk with you again! I certainly wish I may
be strong and good enough to match the ideals you have for me
someday.

I spent only one hectic day in New York. It was a relief to get
out here, you can be sure. I've been writing letters all day trying to
catch up a little with obligations. A letter came from Ken Hurd,
mentioning how he happened to miss my call, etc. He says it takes a
long time to build up a practice.

I hope your recent wave of improvement continues to continue!
Tell that loving pair (you know who I mean!) to telegraph me
when they grace the altar. Here's my love to you—Grace and dear
Miss Wilson, too!

Devotedly,/ your Hart

To Grace Hart Crane

March 23rd, 1926
Patterson, New York

TLS, 1 p.

Dear Grace:

Bein' that I'm gonna' kinda' gotta sorta write to you I might as
well state that everythin' is well here among the haystacks, that I

[1] As March 18, 1926, fell on a Thursday, this letter was probably written on
March 17.

had a hectic day and night in New York on my way—and was damned glad to get back.

I tried to get you a couple nice Jap prints in that store I rave about in Brooklyn, but nothing could be had short of ten bucks and I didn't have any extra cash on hand at the time. However, you can plan on two *daisies* sometime when "we", Otto and I, can afford it. Of course I caught a cold and sore throat in your city with its steampipes and such appurtanences of civilization. I hope it leaves me soon. Yesterday was very summery, indeed,—but today it looks bleak again and shakes a wicked wind.

I'm back on The Bridge scaffolding again. Temporarily am Christopher Columbus in mid-channel. The poem, as a whole, looks more exciting than ever to me. I wrote Otto a long letter as soon as I got back—describing details of my plan, etc. and expect an answer any day now.

I'll write Grandma again soon. Give her my love. Charles, too. I'm ordering Laukhuff to send you out a copy of Frank's "Virgin Spain"— [1] charged to me, of course, and I hope you'll give it a careful reading.

Yours devotedly,/ Hart

To Grace Hart Crane

[March 28, 1926?] [1]
Patterson
Sunday

ALS, 3 pp.

Dearest Grace:

Your letter came yesterday. And I was *immensely* glad to hear from you. Altogether, the news seemed good, too, and I'm *so* glad

[1] Richard Laukhuff, Crane's friend who operated a bookstore in Cleveland. The full title of Frank's book is *Virgin Spain: Scenes from the Drama of a Great People* (New York: Boni & Liveright, 1926).

[1] Crane's discussion of his visit to Cleveland suggests that he wrote this letter to his mother on the second Sunday after his return to Patterson.

you and Charles have made a definite decision! By *all* means make the Little Church the scene.[2] Then I can be there and we can all take a bus ride afterward. Of *course* you'll be acceptable—who ever heard of such distinctions being made in any Protestant church against widows and widowers, grass or otherwise! Then maybe you could make my humble domicile one of the stops on your celebrations.

I, too, think I made my visit at just the proper time. I'll never forget how really eloquently Grandma looked, how intelligent and fresh. And *you* looked so good to me, too! Remember, that suffering does, if borne without rancour, it does build something that only grows lovelier with time—and it is a kind of kingdom among those *initiated,* a kingdom that has the widest kind of communion. You and I can share our understanding of things more and more as time goes on. I loved you *so much* for many of the things you said when I was with you.

Yes, I hope you never will turn your back on me, as you say. And this is not to say that there may come occasions for it—but there may, after all, be times of temporary misunderstandings as there have been before. I can be awfully proud of *you,* however less occasion I may have to feel similarly about myself. I do some awfully silly things sometimes—most of which you don't know about, but which I sometimes (not always) regret. Don't let this stir your apprehensions any, however, I'm in no particular pickle at present.

We have had another snow—and I'm just disgusted. I had counted on modified weather on my return and instead it's been just one snow flurry after another. Sore throat is some better, but I'm still threatened with tonsilitis. No chance to start gardens yet.

I'm gonna gotta kinda sorta hit the hay now—so good Night. Here's a kiss for you X and one for Grandma X

Give Charles and Miss Wilson my best./ Hart

[2] Mrs. Crane and Mr. Curtis had thought they might be married at The Little Church Around the Corner in New York City. However, they were married at the city hall in New York.

To Elizabeth Belden Hart

ALS, 2 pp.

Dearest Grandma—

As Grace had written me that [2] your scarf was on the way I had expected it sooner—and of course delayed writing until today—when it came. It is indeed a lovely remembrance from you—also the scrumptious hangers which are already in use—and you don't know how grateful I am for all the love and sweetness that went into these gifts.

I'm putting the scarf away carefully for use next winter (I love every "knit-knot" in it) and shall always think of you whenever I wear it. Tell Grace that I think her ties are exquisite, and the very thing to wear when I'm in town.

At last there's hardly a flake of a snowdrift left anywhere—and the sun seems to promise a little belated attention. I got so depressed last week with the endless inflictions of hurricane snow and sleet that I almost beat it for Town for awhile. But as I really can't afford it now it's better not to. I expect one of these fine days you'll be hopping into a motor for a turn around the park. Wish you could go a little further and drop in for tea with us! When you get to feeling like it you must take pencil in hand and write me a little note. I want to hear *directly* from you as often as possible.

I'm getting so fat I almost wobble, and a little sickness, I think, would do me good. However, I think I'll choose something besides bladder trouble this time for a change! I wish you would please keep reminding Grace to return that picture of the house here that my landlady loaned me to send her. Make her miserable, please,

---

[1] There is little internal evidence for the date of this letter. "Grace had written" suggests the letter Hart mentions on March 28. The delay he speaks of suggests he did not write his grandmother until the second Tuesday in April.
[2] The word "that" is repeated in the text.

until she sends it. Mrs. Turner keeps after me about it constantly—
and I did promise to have it returned to here.

Love always—/ your/ Hart

⤫

Confined to their farmhouse as they were for most of the winter, Hart, the Tates, and Mrs. Turner began to get on each other's
nerves. After a particularly bitter confrontation with the Tates during the second week of April, Crane realized he would have to
leave. He sent the following letter to his mother outlining his differences with the Tates and asking permission to stay at the Hart
house on the Isle of Pines.

To Grace Hart Crane

Patterson, New York
April 18th, Sunday [1926?]

TLS, 3 pp.

Dear Grace:

It would be a relief to be able to talk with you an hour or so
today. I'm in such an uncertain position in regard to a number of
things that I feel as though it would be a fitting end to settle it
with powder and bullet. The whole benefit of my patronage from
Kahn, my year of leisure, my long fight with the winter, etc. out
here is about to be sacrificed to the malicious nature of a person I
thought to be friendly—but who turns out to be quite otherwise. I
refer to Mrs. Tate, and Allen.[1] But primarily it has been Mrs. Tate
who has influenced matters until they came to a head the other day,
since which time I have had a note from each of them, respectively,
including insults and malicious remarks to an extent which amazes
me.

I am accused of having victimized their time and their quarters
by intruding without regard to their wishes, etc. This is in part

[1] For the details of this incident, see *Voyager*, pp. 430–35.

justified,—justified, I say because the contingency of such a matter was bound to exist between two families which had agreed on sharing a common water pump. I had to have access to it as much as they did, and had to pass through their kitchen occasionally on my way. When Mrs. Tate—this occured last week—instead of simply telling me that she wished I would avoid such passage in the future—when she bagn [began] putting bolts on her doors, and all that—I could take the *hint* without having to be knocked down by a hammer, and so removed my shaving utensils, etc. which had been beside the pump, into Mrs. Turner's kitchen. Why this should make them mad, I don't know, and why it should make them mad because I immeadiately began avoiding their parts of the house *completely* (not being invited to do otherwise) I can't see, either.

Of course when I encountered them outside, and saw how sulky they behaved, etc. I began to lose all respect for such behavior—made up my mind to ignore them as much as decency permitted, although I realized that with such an atmosphere about the place it would be very difficult to procede with any creative work. Matters came to a climax day before yesterday, shortly after breakfast, I had been talking to Mrs. Turner around on "our" side of the house about some plans for cleaning up some rubbish, etc. when suddenly a door opens from the Tate's kitchen and Allen shouts out, "If you've got a criticism of my work to make, I'd appreciate it if you would speak to me about it first!" Then the door savagely banged, and Mrs. Turner and I (who hadn't mentioned him or anything that concerned him) were left staring at each other in perfect amazement. I can't easily describe how angry I was. I felt myself losing all control—but I managed to address the Tates without breaking anything. Mrs. Turner came in with me and corroborated the facts of the matter, and it turned out that the Tates hadn't heard actually a thing I was saying—their imaginations, they evidently felt, were perfectly justified in building up a perfect tower of Babel out of nothing.

Nothing was touched on at that fiery moment, but the immeadiate circumstances of what I had said and what I hadn't. Tate finally admitting that he was all wrong. My feelings remained little cooled, however. The rest of the time since then has been simply hideous.

The next morning (I, not sleeping) had heard the Tates getting out
of bed during the night and pounding out something on the typewriter I found a couple of the nastiest notes under my bedroom
door that I ever hope to get from anyone. Mrs. Tate began by saying that they had arrived in the house first; that they had invited
me to share quarters with them in the first place because I was penniless in New York at that time, and that as soon as they found out
that I had been fortunate in acquiring funds they immeadiately had
begun to doubt the adviseability of inviting me out, but *of course*
hadn't felt privileged to say anything about such matters before
this. I'm not quoting *insinuations* in any of this, I'm using practically their own words. The[n] she went on to say that they had al-
otted me one room only (this is an absolute lie; they assumed that I
was to have a bedroom and my study besides) and that I had from
the moment of arrival proceeded to spread myself and possessions
all over the house, invading avaery [every] corner; and so on,—
finally ending up with the assertion that I had been busy ever since
I arrived in trying to make them menial servants of[2] my personal
wants! The contents of Mr Tate's letter were about the same, a little more gracefully phrased, that's all.

As a matter of fact, I have never, so long as I've been here, requested a single favor from either of them. You know the story
about the cooking arrangements already—how I changed over to
Mrs. Turner because Mrs. Tate's ill temper made it impossible for
me to perform my share of duties with her in the kitchen. She has
never gotten over that—and all her talk about patronizing me from
motives of "charity", etc. appear very likely to come from a regret
that I didn't continue to buy most of the food, etc. Since then—
even though I derived no benefit from the wood stove that the
Tate's use in their kitchen—I've been careful to go out and help
Allen cut and saw, etc. And made it a point to mention—that while
I couldn't constantly keep after him with questions as to when he
wanted to saw and when he didn't—if he'd let me know about such
occasions I'd be glad to join him whenever possible.

It's all simply disgusting. I don't know how much money they

[2] The word "of" is repeated in the text.

owe me exactly—but I have told them that I was always glad to advance them funds w[he]never needed, and while they haven't been extravagent—they have nevertheless been momentarily relieved from sudden circumstances by frequent access to my funds. On top of all this I have practically given Allen the fare for two trips to New York (on one occasion I was so anxious for him to have the chance to hear a certain opera that I gave him ten dollars to get a good seat), I've had them in to dinner with Mrs. Turner and myself frequently, I gave Carolyn my old typ[e]writer to work on her novel that she pretends to make all this fuss about. She didn't have one herself and would otherwise have had to depend on such moments as her husband wasn't using his to write at all, while I on the other hand, should certainly have been able to make a good discount on my new machine by turning in the old had I not purposely wished to be amiable about the matter. There have been lots of other amenities which I enjoyed extending. And you know me not to obviously hold such things over people's heads. *Doesn't* it all look as though *as Mr. Tate says,* I valued their friendship only for the purpose of exploiting their services to me!

Mrs. Turner has cried for two days and nights about the matter —she hates to have me leave so. She says there is another room in the upstairs which I can use and not be obliged to have anything to do with the Tate's part of the house, their rent or their arrangements. I must say I'm stumped. How can I, on one hand, persist in staying here after such an insulting statement from the Tates to the effect that I was originally their guest and that I was invited on the grounds of charity rather than from any other motives? This is one of the hardest matters I have ever had to decide. For I feel that I owe some sense of economy to Mr. Kahn, who didn't give me money to keep moving about merely out of the way of disagreeable people. My money is very low now. The first thousand is gone—it cost me more than I ever would have guessed to have just got settled here with all my books and materials at hand as they are. I wrote Kahn recently that I needed more money, and he very speedily and kindly replied with a check for five hundred. At the same time the Rychtariks wrote from Cleveland that they needed the money they had loaned me for my land—that they required it for the summer trip to Europe, etc. And so two hundred will have to be taken out of the Kahn money at once.

It really is tragic. The whole fruit of the first opportunity of my life to write an extended poem is apparently about to be blighted by the cankerous bile of a narrow, jealous mind! As I say I don't at this moment know which way to turn. If I remain here (spring is just coming on—and the best time for work, so long waited for, has come!) if I remain here under such unpleasant relations it is very doubtful whether or not I can overcome the hypnosis of evil and jealousy in the air enough to get back into my poem, really just started. But if I move away it means that so much of my slight funds will be wasted in just the cost of travel, etc. that in less than a month I'll be back looking for a job again—and in the middle of the summer, the most devilish and exhausting time to work in the city. I don't feel that I ought to let my indignation and pride effect me so far as the hasty and ill-founded remarks of the Tates are concerned, I would sacrifice all that to my work and remain here if I felt enough assurance of being *able* to work under such circumstances.

If you feel at all sympathetic to this situation of mine I wish you *this time* be generous enough to let me go [to] the Island and finish my poem there. At least I should not have to fear being put off the little land that is still ours in the world. I have ample money to get there and to live economically for some time. It may reasonably be expected that Mr Kahn will come forward with the other five hundred which he promised within a certain time, meanwhile I can't ask him for more before six months without risking the charge of extravagence. I think that I can re-sell the land I bought to Miss Flynn from whom I purchased it. Summer in the tropics isn't of course the paradise of the winter months, but it is a thousand times better than a hall bedroom in New York without light or air, to say nothing of the fact that it might cost me a hundred or so of what I have left just spent in looking for work. You know how long it is sometimes.

If I can't somehow succeed in taking advantage of this one opportunity given me by Mr. Kahn, I don't know how I'll feel about life or any future efforts to live—and if you can't see how it is reasonable for me to request under the circumstances some privileges from my family I shall be amazed. You've already said that you didn't think I'd like Mrs. Simpson,[3] etc. Well do you think *that* is half so important to me or to anyone else after all. I'm not able to reason why this issue should hang on the whimsical temper of an old woman. If I went to the Island I should do my best to preserve the most pleasant relations with Mrs. Simpson, and I haven't much doubt but what I should succeed. I ought to be able to live a few months in the house my grandfather built without being put off by a hired keeper of the place—especially when I am much better fitted naturally, by simply being a male, for keeping up the place than she is.

I'm asking you for this refuge. I've always been refused before. If you deny it now I'm not sure how much farther away I'll go to accomplish my purposes. Perhaps to the orient, even if I have just enough to get there and no more.

I shall go into New York early in the week, perhaps tomorrow. Perhaps several days later. I'll let you know where I settle and what plans are finally adopted. Meanwhile please write me here, as before; Mrs. Turner will be sure to send my mail to whatever address I have at the time.

I'm sorry to have such melancholy news, especially after such lovely letters as renectly [recently] came from you and Grandma, but it can't be helped. It all may be very much for the best in the end. I do hope you'll be generous enough to give me your sanction on the Island matter—that's all I'm requesting. I can always get money enough to get back (from at least 5 people) and go into an office again. But that isn't the issue now. I'm writing a poem that is bound to be a magnificent thing *if* I can escape the wolves (and weazels!) long enough to build it. Won't you help?

With love—/ Hart

[3] Mrs. Simpson was the caretaker at the Harts' house on the Isle of Pines.

༼Ⲯⲯ༽

Shortly after he wrote this letter, Hart went to New York to arrange for his voyage to the island. On April 24 he returned briefly to Patterson in order to gather his belongings. In the meantime he had made arrangements for Waldo Frank to accompany him on his trip.

At first Grace objected strenuously to Hart's plan, saying, among other things, that the house's caretaker, Mrs. T. W. (Aunt Sally) Simpson, was not prepared for his arrival; only when she realized her son's determination to go did she capitulate. Grace and Mr. Curtis made a hasty trip to New York so that Hart could witness their marriage on April 29. Two days later he sailed for the Caribbean.

To Grace Hart Crane

New York
Saturday, April 24 [1926?]

TLS, 2 pp.

Dear Grace:

You have just answered my inquiry about the bank, etc. I'm in such haste to get my train to Patterson that I'm probably missing some of the other necessary queries. Please send me the names and addresses of two or three people or offices in Havana who have some connection with the island and who could be referred to in case I need to ask about transportation, etc. I will have [1] to stay over one day in Havana waiting for the boat to the island and I want to live as cheaply as possible. Their information etc. might be helpful. You must know some such references. I sail, United Fruit Line, S.S. ULUA, May 1st. That's next Saturday, arriving in Havana the following Wednesday. The whole passage costs me less than a cheap room (to say nothing of food, etc) would cost me at some inexpensive seaside resort for 8 weeks. I've made inquiries and know.

---

[1] The word "have" is repeated in the text.

I can live cheaply on the island, and incidentally it will be very well to have me there for awhile in view of what you say about Mrs. Simpson. If she leaves I shall be very glad to take charge of things myself—indefinitely. Anyway, I'm at least a male—and able to do more around the place and keep it up better than any woman, alone as she is. It will be a pleasure for me to keep up repares, etc. and there will still be time left for my other work.

Aside then, from my personal reasons for going, there are very logical reasons for you (and the estate) welcoming it. I've already explained how essential it is for me under present circumstances— and will mention more later when I have more time. I'l write you tomorrow from Patterson. If you answer it quickly on Wednesday it can be answered again before I leave. There will be some other details I'll think of to ask you.

As I said, I'm not going for my pleasure. I have a certain responsibility to Mr Kahn and the funds he gave me. I must do my utmost to perform the work I have undertaken. No arrangements are *perfect,* but I don't want to take the chance again of having to move before I get the work finished. If you'd ever worked two summers in N.Y. offices as I have with hay fever, etc. you'd know that the heat of the island doesn't paralyze me with fear. At least the air will be fresh. But more later. I'm *terribly sorry* that I can't get you to fully agree with me about this matter, but you'll see it work out much better than you may expect.

I wrote Mrs. Simpson a *very* tactful and pleasant letter—explained my sudden haste (no details, but enough to satisfy circumstances) and said that I hoped I would be able to be helpful to her while I was there. I shall give her every deference and consideration. And I shall certainly avoid doing anything which would lead her to think that I might wish her to leave. Will you write her a little note at once? I said that my decision was sudden, that you had not yet had time to write her about it, but that your letter would probably follow on the next boat. I can't take time to write any more now. I'll call at the Waldorf for your letter next Tuesday. Try and not think hardly of me. Life is awfully hard on all of us. I've been in a terrible state of mind—I guess you got that from my letter, and saw the reasons plainly enough. I've tried to give every consideration a thorough test—and while I could bury my pride and beg the Tate's to become reconciled, they really wouldn't you know, and Mrs. Tate especially. I couldn't get any work done in such an atmosphere. Waldo Frank and others of my friends—all agree that the Island is the best solution.[2]

love, hart

To Grace and Charles Curtis

Monday, May 3rd [1926?]
Off Florida

TLS, 1 p.

Dear Grace and Charles:

We are having a wonderful sail; smooth as glass and the usual increasing blue. I've been out watching the flying fish this morning. Waldo is still tired, but I'm picking up wonderfully today. This is a fine line, meals and service perfect, and our cabin has been very comfortable. We get into Havana tomorrow noon—a day earlier than I had expected. Probably take the boat for the Island Wednesday evening.

As we have so little time in Havana I thought this might serve for a letter from there—although I'll drop you some word anyway. Your lovely flowers are still fresh on our table in the saloon. I'm very happy. We've had a little drink, but not much. What we have had has been straight from Europe and openly served on our table. Makes you feel rather civilized to have some genial real St. Julian and a cordial in the smoking room afterward.

The boat is only half filled—and half of that Cuban. One senorita that Waldo says looks typical Castilian, but she doesn't send any thrills up my spine. Tell Grandma I shall deliver her hangers to Mrs. S. in perfect condition. Have her write me as soon as possible. Can't think of any more news now. The sudden heat effects you with a pleasant drowsiness.

Love,/ hart

[2] In typing the word "solution," Hart spaced the letters over several lines in a descending order.

Once on the island, Hart busied himself with repairing the house that had been neglected for almost a decade, work that helped him forget the events in Patterson. He was now secure with the knowledge that his mother was married, that his grandmother was improving, and that the problems in Cleveland had eased considerably since Christmas. Hart found in Mrs. Simpson a companion who was loyal to him and interested in his writing. In his new environment Crane went through a period of prolific activity: outlining the major sections of *The Bridge,* writing and revising the "Powhatan's Daughter," "Ave Maria," "Proem," and "Cutty Sark" sections of that work, as well as writing other poems about the island and the Caribbean including "The Air Plant," "Royal Palm," and "O Carib Isle!"

Efforts to publish his book *White Buildings* kept Crane busy as well. After receiving pressure from O'Neill, Cowley, and Frank, Horace Liveright committed his firm to publishing the volume, and at the end of July sent Hart an advance of one hundred dollars. Perhaps even more important was Allen Tate's offer—in a gesture of reconciliation as well as a display of genuine interest in Crane's poetry—to write a preface for the volume.

To Grace Hart Curtis

Nueva Gerona [Isle of Pines]
Villa Casas
Saturday, May 8th [1926?]

TLS, 2 pp.

Dear Grace:

Well, here we are! We got in Havana Tuesday (a day earlier than expected—it seems the Ward line is faster) and Wednesday night we were on the boat leaving Batabano. We enjoyed Havana immensely while we were there, but wouldn't have stayed longer for the world. Waldo's Spanish proficiency carried us everywhere—Cuban hotel (Isla de Cuba) and Cuban cafes and theatres. We kept entirely away from American haunts, and I discovered that Havana gives you a better impression from that angle. But it's too noisy everywhere, and we were glad to get away. A knowledge of Spanish surely does save one money here.

I am constantly being su[r]prised at the novelties the island has to offer. I'm astonished that I carried away such vague impressions before—but being only 15 and being here so short a time accounts for it, I spose. First of all—the approach in the early morning was simply gorgeous, then all the varied plant life, the fruits etc. I discover I never really got acquainted with. This is only our third day here, but it has meant more vivid and exact impressions than would be easy for me to enumerate.

The weather has been wonderful—and except for the fact that May is the worst month in the year for mosquitoes everyt[h]ing would be perfect. Breezes have kept up, and the only rain we've had was last night. The sky is somewhat different though; you'd know it was the rainy season. I've been again surprised at the spaciousness of the house—much larger than I had remembered. The bathroom, etc. is of course entirely new to me. I have your old room on the front west corner, and Waldo has the room next to it. Mrs. Simpson has been goodness itself, and while she was very much surprised at our early arrival, she has been pleased, I think, at the prospect of some company about the place. She has written you, she says, and you will probably gain from her letter the impressions she has formed of Waldo and me. I hope they are as favorable as we have of her.

Waldo is having the time of his life. I was so worried for fear I had perhaps gotten him into a perfect furnace—but his ease and comfort is evident—he even felt like putting on a coat for supper yesterday—it seemed so cool to him. He has only 20 more days to stay—even less, I guess—so Mrs. S won't be especially burdened, especially as we are making a point of performing numerous chores for her, etc. I haven't yet settled on the amount of board I am to pay, but we had an immeadiate understanding that such was to be the general arrangement. It is sure to be settled satisfactorily, and I thought it would be better to wait a few days before discussing such matters in complete detail. A little acquaintance with our tastes, requirements, etc. I thought would better determine in her mind what money was needed.

All my baggage arrived in perfect condition, I didn't have to pay duty on anything, even the Lachaise bird. Which reminds me that we had some good hours and happy ones together in NY. Charles was such a good sport and you looked so scrumptious! The flowers we took from the cabin to our table. We also had a moderate amount of good wines on [or?] cordials for a reasonable price (all French) served right on the table. Apparently the Am. boats aren't bound so tight as they were for awhile. And how good the cigars were in Havana! I find I don't feel like drinking much in hot climates, though; it's too heating.

Herrin is about the only person I've met yet whom you recommended me to. I was introduced very hastily to a number of others by Mrs. S. on Wednesday morning when we went to town, but I haven't wanted or had the need to go around much yet. Waldo and I walked over to the coast nearest the house the other day—and had a pleasant swim. The water is almost too warm, however, by afternoon. They really have discovered a little beach there, and people do bathe there often, it seems. I've been too tired to attempt such sudden or strenuous exercise in the heat.

Besides, I suspect that I ought to be rather careful for a week or so, after coming right out of a long severe winter. It taxes the body to make such sudden changes.

Waldo has been having the best time with a baby owl which flew on the porch the other morning—we all have, in fact. Mrs. S. is very sociable and jolly, doesn't mind my smoking a bit, she says. We really like her very much, her wit, her good sense and lack of all sentimentality. She and Waldo have just come back from town —with the mail. It will interest you to know that it contained a letter from the Dial (forwarded, of course) accepting a poem of mine [1] which I sent them recently. There is another of mine in the current issue [2] which I brought down with me.

My navy pants, etc. have proved to be just the right thing here. I

[1] Probably "To Brooklyn Bridge."
[2] Hart speaks of his poem "Again," published in *The Dial*, LXXX (May, 1926), 370.

bought some hemp-soled shoes at Waldo's recommendation at one of the Cuban shops. They are the kind the peasants of Spain have worn for centuries and they are the coolest thing on a hot road that you ever tried. Mrs. Simpson knows a native woman who will launder for me.

I reserve comments on conditions, etc. until later—naturally I haven't been able to make any especial observations as yet. Before this goes to the boat I may have a picture or so to send you—taken on the boat. Next boat I expect a letter from you. Give Grandma my deepest love and Charles my very very best.

Yours devotedly,/ Hart

From Clarence Arthur Crane

[Cleveland]
May 10, 1926.

TLC, 1 p.

Mr. Harold Crane,
Nueva Gerona,
Isle of Pines,
Via Cuba.

My dear Harold:

This morning I have your postal card sent me from Havana, and am glad to note that you have negotiated a pleasant trip.

Your being in New York and your sailing for the Tropics was quite a surprise to me as was also your Mother's marriage. I had a very pleasant visit with them and think she has chosen very wisely.

My not being at the boat to see you off was not on account of not wanting to see you but I had an engagement with a Wall Street firm for 9:00 o'clock that morning and I could not put it off without getting in touch with them, which was impossible to do at that late hour. You have not written me since you returned to New York and you are also aware that I had no idea that you were going South. Even now I do not know the real reason. Your Mother told me something over the phone, but you had better tell me just what condition exists.

I have been away from home quite a bit of the time lately and have just made another trip to Atlantic City with the idea of putting in a demonstrating booth on the Board Walk. However, that has not been closed as yet.

Write me when you can.

With love,/ Your father,

To Grace Hart Curtis and Elizabeth Belden Hart

Nueva Gerona [Isle of Pines]
Friday
May 14th [1926?]

TLS, 1 p.

Dear Grace and Grandma:

We haven't had altogether more than 3 hours of rainfall since arriving. Rather less than usual, Mrs. Simpson says, for the rainy season. Today the sky is overcast, making it much cooler than usual, and the rain of last night promises repitition at any moment. When there is a good wind, like today's, it sweeps the bugs away somewhat—but otherwise they are terrific,—especially around Casas Villa, which so far as I have been able to judge by contrast with other places is become the buggiest place on the island. This is mostly due to the thick growth of trees and shrubbery surrounding the house—which hardly lets a zephyr through and which harbor and incubate millions of insects. It is, of course, a great mistake to have planted so many fruit trees so close to the house. They give practically no shade—and simply stifle every breeze that approaches.

Yesterday we rented a car from Herrin and I drove Mrs S and Waldo over to the Jones' Jungle. Mrs. S. had prepared a wonderful picnic lunch which we finally shared with the Jones's in their bungalow. Both Waldo and myself went quite wild about the beauties of the place, the marvelous work they have accomplished there is equalled, I'm sure, by nothing else in the West Indies or N America. Waldo says he remembers visiting a place in the Azores, owned by a wealthy Portuguese prince which was something like it, but I have never seen anything so amazing before.

The Jones's are by far the pleasantest and most cultured people I have met on the island. The tragedy of their life here is pitiable to the point of tears. After twenty-three years of unremitting toil on their place, to have it all brought to naught—as it is now, since the treaty matter, makes them the saddest kind of jests of fate. Jones says that the Cuban bureaucrats may seize his place at any moment without offering more than five dollars an acre, and he can have no recourse whatever. Furthermore, they are both quite penniless, and live entirely on what he can gather as a taxi-driver and the little fee they charge for visiting the jungle. But Jones is no worse off than others—in many ways. He is only too old to ever hope to take hold anywhere else again.

People seem to have trouble in even giving away their places down here now. I may have gotten a particularly dark picture from Jones, however, so it may not be so bad. At any rate people like Miller are said not to have sold any real estate for about two years, and it seems plausible enough in view of the circumstances under which Americana are allowed to hold property now.

There has been great excitement lately on account of the escape of two convicts from the penitent[i]ary here. Guards stop you wherever you go and search the car. Mrs Simpson seems to be rather glad to have some company out here—in fact she tells me that she had been expecting to have some woman friend of hers come out here and live with her in the near future. She certainly has been lovely to us in many ways and I don't think there is any doubt about her staying. She wants to sell her own place as soon as possible, but that won't be very soon, I guess.

Waldo is leaving a week sooner than expected. He finds he has some work to do in New York before leaving for Maine and needs the privacy of his apartment to concentrate. I think he has enjoyed his stay, however, and looks much rested. We are going swimming at Bibihagua Sunday. He sails Tuesday night.

Why haven't you written me a line or so? Do write soon and tell me about all the excitements in Cleveland.

Love—my best to Charles—/ Hart

To Clarence Arthur Crane

Box 1373
Nueva Gerona
Isle of Pines
May 20th, 1926

TLS, 2 pp.

Dear Father:

Just two weeks since I arrived. Waldo Frank, who came down with me, left two days ago and will spend the rest of the summer in Maine. We had a fine sail down and a couple of very pleasant days in Havana—which I found to be quite a different place than the average American sees. Frank speaks Spanish fluently and we stayed at a Cuban hotel and dined in the more typically Cuban places than would be convenient without the advantage of the language. It's a funny little metropolis, just the same, and more like a toy city than a real one. The Cubans seem such trashy bastard people—without any sense of direction or purpose. We enjoyed the tobacco, however, and the Bacardi.

At present I'm peeling. Mrs. Simpson, widow of the caretaker that has been on the place since the Wattles's, arranged a picnic at one of the beaches last Sunday and I received my first real coat of tan. After Grace's warnings I was quite dubious about getting along with Mrs. S., but I find her very pleasant indeed and things promise well.

You have my gratitude for writing. I had intended several times to write you before leaving Patterson, but being for some time in an unsettled state of mind I kept deferring it—also I was deep in my work for quite awhile after my Cleveland visit. The Tate's baby proved very annoying in the household, a continual hubbub and upset, where a bachelor like myself felt not only in the way but distracted from work. Hence the Island popped into my mind, not only as being quiet but cheap, and although the expense of getting here was rather steep, it could be at least planned on .as a decent place to work until my present work is finished. I shall not risk sharing a common household with anyone again, I can assure you.

Grace was glad to have me come on account of the real need for some one of us to acquire some first-hand information on conditions here. It has been five years since Grace was here—and certainly there have been many changes, I can see that already. .

I am astonished to find how little of the Island I really saw when I was here before. The variety of vegetation, fruits, flowers and woods in general—all is the more amazing now because of the season. Everything but the citrus fruits is in full harvest or approaching it. For instance, I never had any ripe mangoes when I was here before. It would take millions of dollars to advertise them enough in the north (as with any new fruit) to make them initially acceptable even as a gift—but once tasted, people would come back for them like wildfire! They're the most delicious fruit I ever tasted. I haven't eaten meat more than once since I hit the island, and I don't want it again. Not that the cut wasn't good, but such an abundance of fruits and vegetables makes it completely superfluous.

The first shock of the sudden hot weather after our lingering winter-spring in the north gave me some prickly heat, but I am much better already. I'm told that we are now in maximum heat, which isn't half so bad as midsummer heat in a NY office building, not to mention subways! I can't say how long I'll be here. Possibly until next year at this time; at least until my book is finished.

Grace's marriage was a su[r]prise to us all. I hadn't known a thing about such a definite plan until two days before my sailing— when even her presence in NY was a distinct surprise to me. But I have always liked Mr. Curtis and I feel that the occasion was pleasant all around. It surely was a coincidence that you were in NY at the same time! I didn't hear of it until boat time.

Please give Bess, Byron [1] and my Grandparents my most tropical greetings—and write me again soon.

With love,/ Harold

[1] Bess Crane Madden and Byron Madden.

To Elizabeth Belden Hart

Box 1373
Nueva Gerona [Isle of Pines]
May 26th, 1926

TLS, 2 pp.

Dear Grandma:

I have been somewhat slow in writing, but I've been waiting for more word from Grace—the little post-card is all she has committed herself to since May 1st. Of course she is very busy, and there has been much excitement, but I'm all the more anxious to hear all about it. Especially do I want to know how *you* are.

Waldo left about ten days ago. He had Mrs S and me "down town" to dine with him (at Tom Upton's place) the evening of departure, Mrs. S even indulged us by taking a sip or so of Spanish wine with us, and everything was quite merry. He certainly made himself liked by both of us; I also feel sure that he had a restful and enjoyable time.

I am getting used to the heat and bugs now, and the Island looks better to me than it did the first few days. Much recent rain has kept Mrs. S and me busy lugging pots, pans and tubs to and fro [m] the attic—for the roof is so rotted in several places that the water comes right down into the living room. New roofing will certainly have to be put on, soon, unless the place is to be abandoned—for it won't take much more leaking to rot out the timbers below the shingles and gradually undermine the entire roof structure. Something is wrong with the water tank pump or rather the pipe end that extends into the well. We can run the engine perfectly but no water! And the structure is so rotted that it threatens to let down tank and all on anybody that dares to stand under while it fills. This structure should never have been built of wood in such a climate. The native Cuban tanks of cement that one sees everywhere are the only sensible kind of thing. But comments and reports such as these had better be deferred to later times, Mrs S says she has already written you about these details anyway.

Two Sundays ago we all went over to Bibijagua Beach to swim, taking three young Austrian boys with us who are at present living in Mrs S's house. Mrs. Saxe invited us to use their bathing houses,[1] and we ended up by eating the [2] picnic lunch which Mrs. S had prepared on the Saxe porch—and ferocious appetites we had! Mrs Saxe and her mother, Mrs. Wick impressed me as being very amiable people. They are leaving for the north in a few days. Their place is decidedly the most beautifully and comfortably situated of any on the island; I am wild about it. For the sea and bathing are the best part of things here.

The mangoes are coming on now, and I'm wild about them. The finest fruit I ever ate—excepting grapefruit, which are impossible to get now. When I was here before it wasn't mango season, so I had my first taste recently.

I see by the Times that you aren't having any very torrid weather north yet. Almanacs predict a cold summer north, this year and next, which ought to be rather preferable to the usual. I'm enclosing some pictures taken at the beach.[3]

with love to all—/ Hart

To Grace Hart Curtis

Nueva Gerona [Isle of Pines]
June 1, 1926

TLS, 2 pp.

Dear Grace:

Albeit yourself has been too ferociously busy to indite me your own most intimate thoughts and doings, at least I must compliment you on your success in persuading the others of your household to perform this office for you. Charles and Grandma have done admirably in picturing your preoccupations; so much so that I see you surrounded with telegrams, flowers, cand[e]labra, silver pheasants, salt cellars, pin-money pickles, brooches, white elephants and what not, and the room densely floating with tissue paper. Well, I don't

---

[1] Mrs. Mary Alfred Saxe, a friend of Grace's from Cleveland.

[2] The word "the" is repeated in the text.

[3] The enclosures are not filed with the letter. However, there are several pictures in the Columbia collection taken on the Isle of Pines.

blame you for not writing, but you must break the silence soon.

Mine own true self has been chewing its cud, mostly, i.e. trying to imagine itself on the waters with Cristobal Colon and trying to mend the sails so beautifully slit by the Patterson typhoon. The Island grows more attractive to me as I get more acclimated and we have had constant breezes and cool weather ever since Waldo left, just two weeks ago today. There are many things that need to be done about the place, but I am attacking them with some deliberation—one has to respect the ferocity of the sun and the insects not a little. I have succeeded in eradicating the carcasses of several dead and dying orange trees in the front yard, putting young royal palms in their places. How I wish you had thought of planting some of these perfect delights when the place was being built; they are the one perfect sort of tree to have round a house, their ornamentation, stateliness and openairyness can't be surpassed.

Mrs. Simpson is going to help me put up some new gate posts of rocks and cement. The entire fencing directly in front of the house is ready to collapse and there are so many breaches in the line down by the grove which we need repair at once, (pigs can't be kept out, but some of the cattle can be) that something should be done as soon as possible. I'm constantly at a loss to know what attitude to take about these and other highly necessary repairs,—not knowing what you really intend doing about the place. Most important of all, of course, is an entirely new roof for the house. I don't think you'll ever get pin money for the sale of the place until this, at least, is done, for it's the first and outstanding fault to be noticed even from the road.

Moreover, the inside of the house—its whole structure, in fact—will soon begin to deteriorate so rapidly for the want of dry sheltering that whatever value the place has now will be sacrificed. If I were you, and relished the tropics during the winter as much as you do, I'd economize in some way or other so as to afford a new roof as soon as possible. The house is really so comfortable and so very well built that it's a shame to let it run down. A few shingles and patches here and there won't meet the situation at all. The whole roof is rotted, loosely assembled and full of perforations. And, as I said, it looks it. Patches would only make it look a little worse.

Mrs. S and I think that tile roofing, while costing a little more than the cheap shingles that we put on first, is the proper thing for the climate, exigencies of grass fires, etc. Asbestos shingling would be good, but not so permanent—and although I don't know for certain as yet, I think it would be about as expensive as tile. Tile would also look better. Now we are going to ask Mr Jones, whose honesty and disinterestedness is unquestionable, to make an estimate on what tile roofing would cost, also what he would charge for his services in undertaking the job. As soon as possible I'll write you about the figures, or Mrs S will. It can do no harm to go this far, anyway. And as the Island is so infinitely superior to Florida, California or any other place you might go for the winters—and *so much cheaper a place to live when you get here*—I think you will agree with me that investments in repairs on the place here are ultimately cheaper than hotel rooms at ten to fifteen dollars a day with nothing to keep when you leave. A new roof, some new screening and a fresh coat of paint are all this house needs for years to come if someone like Mrs Simpson or myself stays here. I don't forget the water tank, but that isn't so crucial; water can, after all, be pumped by hand. Let me know a little more of your present attitude about the property here, then I can better judge whether or not you want my reports, advice, etc.

Thursday (June 3rd) I'm sailing on the schooner for Grand Cayman. There are two days on the water each way, and I may spend a week on the island if the boat stays that long. I'm looking forward with great glee to my first real sail—and they tell me that Cayman is lovlieer than anything around. Bread, cheese and cookies are to be packed by Mrs Simpson and I'm hoping not to feed the fishes. If I do,—well then I'll have at least found out that I'm a goodfor-nothing landlubber. The trip will be worth while from any standpoint.

With love—/ Hart

From Clarence Arthur Crane

[Cleveland]
July 7, 1926

TLC, 1 p.

Mr. Harold Crane,
Box 1373,
Nueva Gerona,
Isle of Pines.

My dear Harold:

I have, of course, been very dilatory in answering your letter received here on the First of June, but I have been extremely busy and out of town much of the time. I have just now returned from a western trip and confidently hope that the Kansas City plant has been sold to my employees there. If that is the case I shall be very glad, for the Plant has been a burden in more ways than one and to be relieved of it will please me more than I can tell you.

Since you were in Cleveland we have opened two new stores, and while we are contracting in a wholesale way, we aim to expand in a retail direction.

The family are all well, and while I do not hear from your Mother, I take it that she is happy in her new environment and I most certainly hope so.

We have had a very cool June with a fair amount of candy business for summer. All in all business is about equal to last year, which, under conditions, is not bad.

I hope you are enjoying the climate of the Isle of Pines. I will never forget the rustle of the leaves in the late afternoon when the trade winds come up the bay. If absolute rest were imposed upon me, I should like very much to spend some time there.

We went out to Bessie's last evening and the children are off today for their summer camp in Toronto.

Write me when you feel the urge and I shall always be glad to know that you are happy and contented with your surroundings and prospects.

Affectionately/ Your Father.

To Grace Hart Curtis

Box 1373
Nueva Gerona [Isle of Pines]
July 8th, 1926

TLS, 2 pp.

Dear Grace:

Well,—after two months of absolute silence I'm glad to hear from you—and sorry to know that you are so disturbed and worried as you are, and sick in bed. Despite two very pleasant letters that Charles has written me—I've delayed answering, first because I was led to expect some direct news from you with almost every boat, and second, because lately I've been in too much misery to concentrate on anything whatever. I hope you'll write oftener. Do you know that it's been two months since I heard directly from you about anything.

The trip to Cayman I'm still trying to get over. Everyone (I don't know why native Americans here should tell such stories) had been telling me how charming the little island was. More than that, the sea-sailing to and fro had interested me. Being in a very dull mood (the intense and sudden heat here had made me torpid and inactive) I thought the trip would spur me, stimulate me a little toward continuing my writing on the Bridge poem, not a line of which I had been able to add since I came down here.

Instead of a two days trip over, it took four. Headwinds all the way. It was not until the island was cleared that I realized how many were on that sixty-foot schooner. Thirty-five! and all of them niggers who proved to have no idea of ordinary decent cleanliness, and the crowd made it almost impossible to find a place to stand, lie or sit for ten minutes at a time—not to mention the fact that there was no shade from the intense blaze of the sun unless one could brave the stinks and fumes of a dozen odd sick and wailing nigger females below decks. Most of these never emerged from their hole there during the entire voyage, but pots, bowls, basins, fruit peelings and a thousand shrieks and wails were raised up every hour of the day and night to be emptied on the deck, my nose and ears being kept busy, I can tell you!

When we at last hove in sight of the island we were greeted (even three miles out) with such droves of savage mosquitoes as I had never imagined outside of Bon Echo, Canada. And when I was landed I found them to be far, far worse. There was only one place on the island (no hotel) where I could be accommodated. A sort of boarding house kept by a woman who used to cook over at Santa Fe. Whether they were her's or not, I don't know, but the house was packed with infants and children who kept up a constant racket and screaming. All the negroes on the island were very pious, and about the time the children would quiet down a whole band of them in the house next door would raise their voices to God in Hymns that would scrape the varnish off the woodwork. Worst of all, there was not an inch of screening on the house. I spent liter- ally dollars buying insect powders and keeping a constant smudge going in my room so that my eyes were in a constant stream of tears from the smoke and my lungs nearly burst with suffocation.

Even then, one side of my face and neck were so badly poisoned from the constant bites that they were quite swollen. The beautiful beaches that I had heard about on the island I never saw. To walk more than half a mile from your doorstep was almost to court mad- ness, St. Vitus dance, or death. The very arm with which you were attempting to beat off the regiments of insects would become so covered with them (even while in violent action) that you gave up any hope of relieving yourself of their company.

You can picture me, then, pacing back and forth in my room, very much in the mood of old Mrs. Johnson,[1] in our kitchen at 1709—with a hand pressed on the top of my head, whispering to myself that I would soon be quite insane and relieved of my tor- ments.

Someday I'll tell you more about this famous "vacation" and "holiday" in the picturesque West Indies. I had *ten* days and long nights of it before the boat captain finally pulled anchor and started back to Gerona again. The load this time was as heavy as before and equally dirty. The trip was equally long. We lay for two whole days in midocean and a dead calm, the water so still that you could see yourself in it like a mirror. The sun was terrific and the decks

[1] Mrs. N. B. Madden remembered that Mrs. Johnson was a cleaning lady who worked for the Crane family.

scorched your feet. Not a bit of shade, and I couldn't go below decks without nausea. Our island seemed like Paradise and Mrs Simpson like the goddess of Liberty when I finally got home. Two days later I was taken with abscesses in both ears, and I am still suffering night and day, though they seem to be on the mend.

Added to this, during the first week home, I had such difficulty in breathing, especially at night—with pains in the chest and terrific sweats—that I became seriously alarmed. Mrs. S and I both agreed that I had better go at once to Havana and consult with an able physician. Which I finally did. Doctor A. Agramento, Vedado—a grad. of Columbia University, etc.

He pronounced me alright except a slight infection of the throat, which may have been contracted from the common water supply on the boat, so musty and contaminated that at the time I almost parched my system by attempting to avoid all drinking. The ear trouble he said was probably due to sun exposure. I was given some prescriptions and returned on the next boat. Mrs. Simpson has been goodness itself in douching my ears and in giving me whatever other attentions I have needed. The last three days it has almost disappeared and then come again, by turns. I am hoping that nothing chronic ensues. The pain has been nerve wracking and my whole system is at present functioning "below par". . . . So much for the Cayman trip.

Mrs. Simpson has lately taken a friend of her's, widow of a grove owner here, Mrs. Durham, to live with us. This plan was concerted, it seems, previous to my arrival here, or Mrs. S's expectancy of it. She was careful to ask me, shortly after I came, if I approved of it, explained that Mrs. Durham was left quite alone as she was, etc. and I saw no reason to object. Mrs. Durham has made us several visits meanwhile, and though she vacillated long, and still trembles a little —I guess she is going to be a permanent fixture. She's company for Mrs. S (which I fear I'm not especially) and helps her with the work. The two of them leave me to my side of the house (the two west bedrooms) when I want to be alone—and without there being, so far as I know, any misunderstandings about my occasional withdrawals, silences, etc. Mrs. Simpson, has displayed the most unusual sensibility and tact in many ways, and while I thought for awhile that her voice and her parrot (which sounds the same) would become unbearable in time I find that altogether I couldn't hope to find a greater aggregate of sense, understanding and goodwill in any woman I know of.

Since my ear trouble started I haven't thought of much of anything but possible relief. So the investigations regarding the re-roofing, re-painting, etc. have been neglected. Mrs. Simpson, however, has not been inactive, and she will write you herself in more detail. The following considerations will have to be met with, however; this much I do know. . . That tile roofing (alas!) is out of the question, because the structure is not strong enough to support the weight. Two authorities, already, have told us this much. Thus, we are left the choice of asbestos shingles or plain shingles of pine or some other wood. Asbestos is more expensive, but almost as permanent as tile. Now there is no contractor on the island, so we can't get any estimate on the cost that way. This makes it best for you to call on the Johns-Manville people in Cleveland or Mr. A. E. Brown, at Carey's and find out what the cost of their asbestos shingles would be,[2] including shipment to Gerona, *via. Tampa,* which bring them directly here on a schooner from the States, simplifies tracing, rate payments, etc.

Installation costs can't be accurately gauged, it's simply a matter of hiring day labor from anyone we can find here who is competent. I should plan on that cost as probably not less than $200., however I don't know, haven't made inquiries yet, and it might be considerably cheaper. In any case the roofing couldn't be done until the dry season starts, the sudden rains, otherwise, with the house left unprotected with work in process, would be fatal. But even so, it's not too soon to order materials, as it would take them possibly two months to get here after ordering.

I shall also try to find out about the painting. None of this should be done until the roof is repaired, however, as considerable trim and other woodwork is rotted and must be replaced before painting. I could probably paint the house myself, thus saving labor costs. But more about this later. The pump and tank are finally working, some of the pipe was rotted and only slight repairs were

[2] Abner E. Brown, vice president of the Carey Building Materials Company of Cleveland.

necessary. The platform of the tank may fall anytime, however,— but more about this later. I'm glad you sympathise with me about the king-orange trees. We won't take all of them out, but I intend to weed out several, which will improve the yard a lot. However, I'm going to be very light in my physical labors for awhile. The sudden heat down here has been a great shock to me, and the natives tell me that this is the hottest summer they have had here in years. It's strange, that the more energy you have down here—the more difficult it is for you to do anything—it sort of works against itself inside you. Of course I'll be glad when winter comes, if I'm still able to be here it will be fine. However, with my finances as at present I'm uncertain about everything. The trip took far more than I expected, then the doctor and the trip to Havana—I'm sending to Patterson to collect the money I had placed in Miss Flynn's hands for the 20 acres I had there. But in all probability, money or not, I'll be here until next spring.

This long tirade of mine has continued about long enough for today—so I'll close. Do give my love to Grandma, and tell her that I'll write her soon. Charles, too. Frankly, I haven't answered him because I knew that as long as you could still get news of me by depending on the efforts of others—you might *never* write! I hope you are already much better and rested. Write soon.

Love,/ yr./ Hart

PS—What has become of Kathryn Kenney? She hasn't written me a word since my visit to Cleveland last March, and was rather cool just before I left. I'm wondering—not brokenheartedly, but what has happened to her? So much seemed brewing—anyway.

My book will be out in the fall, positively. Waldo cabled me that it has already been entered in Boni & Liveright's fall catalogue, and contract is on its way to me here. Liveright is offering me 10% royalties on the first thousand copies. No use to mention terms on the second thousand, as there'll never be that many sold—not in my lifetime. Anyway,—I'm glad the "event" has at last "occured". Haven't seen the O'Neill introduction yet, but it's being set up.

To Elizabeth Belden Hart

Box 1373
Nueva Gerona [Isle of Pines]
July 29th [1926?]

TLS, 1 p.

Dear Grandma:

I've meant to write you for a long time, but about the time I got over my ear agonies I began to swarm with ideas and I've been writing like mad for the last two weeks. I'm so glad I don't know what to do—for I began to fear that I never would be able to work done [down?] here. I'm sorry your birthday slipped by without my thinking of it in time—but I wasn't thinking of much of anything those days with hayfever, earache, backache and everything else at once.

I'm wondering how you are and hoping that Grace won't wait so long this time before writing, I've only had one letter from her since I came to the Island. It's so hot its impossible to sleep some nights, occasionaly there is an hour that's delightful. I don't go around much. It's too hot—and I've been busy nearly every minute I haven't been laid up. So there's practically no news. I got a hundred dollars advance from my publisher recently—and other odd checks from magazines, so I'm not as worried as I was in that way either.

Tell Grace to write, and drop me a note yourself, dear, if you feel at all up to the exercise. Mrs Simpson asks me to send you her love

with my own—Love/ Hart

To Grace Hart Curtis

Gerona [Isle of Pines]
Friday   July 30th [1926?]

TLS, 2 pp.

Dearest Grace:

Last boat brought your splendid letter from NY—welcome news, all of it. I'm so glad that you were invited, went and had the chance for a little rest and diversion. Thank you for the birthday gift, the best form in which you could have remembered me. Everything new sent down here now incurs terrific customs duty, so don't send me any luxuries—or necessities either until I ask for them. Waldo sent me some ointment for bug bites after he went north—and the duty came to over the original price in NY; I was so angry I threw it back into the post office and refused to have anything more to do with it. (by which please understand I *didn't* pay the duty)

You already have most of the news from Grandma's letter, and Mrs Simpson's letter also must have arrived explaining the cable matter. I wasn't worried about it because I was certain that you had received my letter almost immeadiately afterward—couldn't have *before* or else how could my *whereabouts* have been questioned in the cable. I am feeling quite well now—all but sleep, and whether that's due to the heat, chronic insomnia or my present ferment of creative work, I don't quite know. Certainly the hayhennies and crowing roosters (at all times of nights) and the breathlessness of the "air" don't encourage one to slumbers. In a number of ways, however, I'm better acclimated, and I don't need to memorize your advice to know enough to keep out of the sun and physical work! My spasm of hay fever seems to have gone—at about the same time it leaves in the north, that is, the spring session.

In all other ways this is the most ideal place and "situation" I've ever had for work. Mrs. S—— lets me completely alone when I'm busy; lets me drum on the piano interminably if I want to—says she likes it—and has assumed a tremendous interest in my poem . . . She reads and sews a great deal and just talks enough to keep on splendid and equable terms with me. She's a perfect peach, in other words. The result is—that now that my health's better I'm simply immersed in work to my neck, eating, "sleeping", and breathing it. In the last ten days I've written over ten pages of the Bridge—highly concentrated stuff, as you know it is with me—and more than I ever crammed in that period of time before. I can foresee that everything will be brightly finished by next May when I come north, and I can make a magnificent bow to that magnificent structure, ["] The Brooklyn Bridge" when I steam (almost under it) into dock! For the poem will be magnificent.

Meanwhile my other book "White Buildings" will have been published. It comes out sometime this fall. I have my contract and the $100. advance royalties mentioned in Grandma's letter. O'Neill finally backed out on the foreword, as I thought he would. He's enthusiastic about my work, I've never doubted that, but he didn't have the necessary nerve to write what his honesty demanded—a thoroughly and accurate appraisal of my work. He can't write criticism, never has tried even, and I foresaw the panic that this proposal on the part of our mutual publisher would precipitate in his bosom . . . None other than Allen Tate! it seems is to write the foreword. I was informed by my publisher of all this—along with the acceptance. Has written it, in fact . . . And (mums the word on this!) I was very much touched to hear from Waldo, who knows all the inner workings on this, that Allen offered his foreword under O'Neill's signature when he heard that O'Neill had backed out. Of course O—— wouldn't think of anything like that—so the foreword goes back to its own name.[1] I'm very glad things have turned out this way. My umbrage toward Allen is crushed by the fidelity of his action, and I'm glad to have so discriminating an estimate as he will write of me.

We'll try to find out as much as possible about the roofing details. You must write Mrs. Simpson—what do you mean by saying that she owes you and the bank in correspondence!—she hasn't had any answer to her last *five* letters, that note I brought down was all

[1] O'Neill wrote and signed a short note for the jacket blurb of *White Buildings* that read: "Hart Crane's poems are profound and deep seeking. In them he reveals, with a new insight, and with unique power, the mystic undertones of beauty, which move words to express vision." Tate wrote and signed the preface to the book.

she'd heard from you this winter. Wake up! Remember to take your blue-prints of the house along with you when you talk to AE Brown, for the area to be covered, etc.

My best to Charles

Love/ Hart

To Grace Hart Curtis and Elizabeth Belden Hart

Gerona [Isle of Pines]
Aug 13 [1926?]

ALS, 1 p.

Dear Grace & Grandma:

Hope you will like these snaps.[1] I think them about the best ever taken of me. I've been trying to get something to send to my publisher to use.

Work continues at a high pace. I'm quite happy these days.

Love—and my best to Charles / Hart

Just had a fine letter from Kahn [2] and sold another poem to the *Dial*.[3] Watch for my work there from time to time. There should be one in the current issue.

By mid-August Hart grew disturbed by his mother's long periods of silence; neither he nor Mrs. Simpson had received answers to their numerous questions regarding the house. While Crane was out of touch on the Isle of Pines, Grace's marriage was foundering in Cleveland. At the end of August he sent her this short note before traveling to Havana for a brief vacation.

[1] Quite possibly some of these photographs are in the Crane collection at Columbia. However, they are not filed with the letter. See the photograph of Crane on the Isle of Pines in *Voyager*, following p. 358.

[2] See Kahn's letter of August 6, 1926, in the Columbia collection.

[3] Possibly "To Brooklyn Bridge," published in *The Dial*, LXXXII (June, 1927), 489–90.

To Grace Hart Curtis

[Postmarked August 28, 1926]
Box 1373
Nueva Gerona
Isle of Pines
Cuba

TLS, 1 p.

Grace,—you naughty old thing!

Why don't you write me a line or so: *stingy!* You'ld think you had some choice secret or so—that you wouldn't part with for the world!—while I sit here sweating out masterpiece after masterpiece! Well, I've got the [1] main outline sections of the *Bridge* already done, and I'm going to Havana for a week, even though I can't afford it; just for the change of scene. One can't even take a walk here or budge out of one's corner without being consumed by bugs; this for the summer, anyway . . . My hayfever has reached a crisis lately, on top of which I'm very tired from doing more writing than all the last three years together (a glorious triumph!)—so I think I deserve a little variety. I'm going to see a few bad shows—and come back next week.

Under seperate cover I'm sending you the best photo ever taken of me. It's an enlargement from several I had take[n] for my publisher. And now, for God's sake, take out that greasy looking libel that Pierie Macdonald [2] did—take it out from the frame, replace it by this,—and never let me see that soft-centered artichoke of mis-repres[e]ntation again!

And write me sometime during the 30th century!

Love to Grandma, you—and my best to Charles—/ Hart

Mrs. Simpson sends you her best, and she's a dear, AND you owe her *seven* letters!

---

[1] The word "the" is repeated in the text.   [2] A Cleveland photographer.

By this time Crane's money was getting low. Having spent all the funds Kahn had given him before he was due to receive another installment, he decided to ask his father for a loan of fifty dollars.

To Clarence Arthur Crane

Habana,[1]
Sept. 2 '26

ALS, 1 p.
LETTERHEAD: ISLA DE CUBA HOTEL

Dear Father:

I've been up here a few days to get away from the hay fever season on the Island. It's really as bad (for *me* at least) as anywhere north—in spite of all they say about its absence there. Well, it *has* been a relief—and I'm going back tomorrow quite refreshed.

I hope there'll be news from you waiting me. You haven't written for quite a while. Could you advance me fifty dollars or so—until I get my next installment from Mr. Kahn? It would help me out with the cost of this little vacation.

Havana is lovely despite many drawbacks. Excellent food if you go to the best Cuban places—and avoid American imitations. Of course you wouldn't like this summer heat—but I'm so used to it by now—anyway—that it doesn't bother me.

It's great fun walking the quaint old streets and alleys—you don't need any company. Last night I took a long cool drive along the Malacon—by the sea, you'll remember.

Write soon—with love,/ your/ Harold

[1] Hart was staying at the "Nuevo Hotel, Restaurant Y Cafe 'Isla de Cuba,'" which had "Grandes Departamentos Con Servicio Sanitario Privado Y Elevador."

To Elizabeth Belden Hart

Nueva Gerona
Isle of Pines
Sept 6th, 1926

TLS, 1 p.

Dearest Grandma:

I'm sorry to hear that you have been having such a tough time with the heat and your sickness. Well, now that the cooler weather is on its way you'll be more relieved.

I spose you got my card from Havana. I had an awfully good time; a complete relaxation after the strenuous work I have been putting into my poem. *The Bridge* is about three quarters done now, and I'm very happy about it. Waldo Frank writes me praises about the sections he has seen—praises which are the highest imaginable. He leaves his little island in Maine for New York again—about the 15th of this month. It has been cold and wet there, he says,—which certainly sounds different than any report I should make out for the Island during the same period.

They are beginning to ship much fruit again, now—but they won't let it stay on the trees long enough to ripen thoroughly. Same old story,—and it keeps on doing the Island considerable harm.

My love to you, and best hopes for immeadiate relief. Mrs. Simpson also sends her love—

your/ Hart

To Grace Hart Curtis

Nueva Gerona [Isle of Pines]
Sept. 6 '26

TLS, 1 p.

Dearest Grace:

I was awfully glad to get your two letters on my return from Habana last Saturday, though I am deeply effected by many of the facts therein. I think you are very brave, I'm proud of your spirit, and you must not fail to maintain it steadily.

I've just finished a long letter to Mr. Stockwell,[1]—which you will see yourself, of course,—you should confer again with him at once, as there are issues (you will see by the letter) which ought to be attended to. Mrs. S had evidently noticed the address of the letter from the Bank, and has been somehow upset and curious ever since I came back. She will be satisfied, I *think,* with less than formerly, and I think will stay. She has been having much trouble with some people in her place, however, whom she cannot collect on rent, etc., and is [in] a stew a good deal of the time. I have not confided with anyone, naturally, on what you wrote.

Mrs. S says she wrote you about confering with Heeren about the roofing. He hasn't been out yet—I haven't snubbed anyone on the Island, but I've simply been too gloriously busy to play in any society—but I spose he will be soon. At any rate, we can get some good paper roofing through him which will last at least 5 years,—and maybe this cheaper method is better under present circumstances. It certainly should be done this winter, anyway,—or else abandon all hope of the place during next year's rainy season.

The little Havana excursion was a great relief to my hay fever and the long confinement of the house here these last four months. I indulged myself in some marvelous Cuban resaurants, superb wine, a ride or so to Mariano-by-the-sea, took long strolls, etc. I'm wild about the place, at least for short periods of stay. It's cooler there than the Island, too,—a constant breeze; this summer has been stifling here, people say unusually bad. Well, two more months of it—and then I hope to enjoy myself and get better sleep. The Bridge will also probably be finished. And I am going to study Spanish—the most beautiful language ever invented.

I've had so much correspondence to catch up with today, I can't write more now, but if I've left out anything I'll acquit myself of more immediately. Your reference to the young "darling" is amusing; nothing I ever heard about him thrilled me very much. I'm glad you have the good sense to take the matter as you do. Keep as

[1] Edward A. Stockwell, assistant secretary of the Guardian Trust Company in Cleveland.

cool as possible, mentally, I mean, and stop thinking about everything being "all over" for you! A good long rest (it's coming someday) and you'll think differently. Meanwhile, let it just be "all
over", perhaps,—that's one way of most economically bearing the
burden. Both of us are too strong-fibred to die easily, or resign
under any circumstances, even though we think we have sometimes.

Love always—I'm anxious to see the pictures—/ Hart

To Grace Hart Curtis

Nueva Gerona [Isle of Pines]
Sept. 19th, [1926?]

TLS, 1 p.

Dear Grace:

It's hard to answer your last two letters with any real equanimity,
I'm too sympathetic to all you're going through. There isn't much
to say except that it's all evidently got to be faced, and the calmer
the better for you, and what you'll gain after all, by having braved
it. And you will gain something out of it, if you face it in the right,
square way, one always does. I think of you a great deal these days,
and if I sometimes seem indifferent, remember that I'm attempting
a titanic job myself, and if anything of that is to be accomplished
there must be some calm and detatchment sought for.

I'm glad that your correspondence with the Heerens has settled
the roofing details in your mind. You have had all the blueprints,
etc. up there with you, it was impossible for me to gauge the pitch
of the roof, etc without them. I still recommend paper instead of
shingles (considering your finances at this time) and invite you to
consider the matter thoroughly before deciding on shingles.

It won't be necessary for you to inquire any about my book because I have already left an order with Laukhuff to deliver you a
copy as soon as it appears, which probably won't be until December. I haven't even had my proofs yet for correction.

Everybody seems to like that picture of me, and I'm especially
glad that you do. It may or may not be flattering, but to my mind

it looks more like "me" to "myself" than any other picture I ever had.

I like the section of town you have chosen for the new apartment and can picture it quite clearly in memory.[1] There are some nice trees along in there, aren't there? You may be glad to get a little away from the rather public air of the Manor lobby, after all. Thanks for the clippings by Kathryn K. Oddly enough, they are remarkably funny in patches. But so mechanical, of course, that one can't thoroughly enjoy any one of them. That stuff she isn't writing to us, or our kind, anyway. I'm glad she has found herself somewhere out side that family of her's, anyway.

I'll write again soon. Brace up, dear, and don't think so much about melodramatic things like old ladies homes. This is a stiff year for both of us.

Love, and love to my dear Grandma—/ Hart

[*Written in the margin of the page:*] The heat and bugs here the last two weeks have been perfectly awful. Hottest summer she ever remembers says Mrs. Simpson.

Grace's separation from Charles Curtis meant the end of any monetary support she would be able to give her son. Hart had spent all the money he had received from Otto Kahn, and as the banker was traveling, requests for another installment of five hundred dollars went unanswered. To add to his mounting problems, the Hart house on the Isle of Pines (already in disrepair) was severely damaged by a fierce hurricane that battered the island in early October. The poet had no choice but to borrow money from Mrs. Simpson and return to the United States.

When Hart arrived in New York in the final week of October, he learned that Grace, under the duress of the impending divorce, had been taken ill and in desperation had approached Otto Kahn for financial help and information about her son. After an interview

[1] Hart's mother had moved from the Wade Park Manor to an apartment on Superior Road.

with Kahn, who had returned to New York, Hart received his final payment of five hundred dollars.

From Grace Hart Curtis

CLEVELAND, OHIO
1926 OCT 30 AM

TELEGRAM

HART CRANE. HOTEL ALBERT
NEW YORK NY.
YOU WILL NEVER KNOW HOW RELIEVED I AM IN RECEIVING YOUR WIRE FROM NEW YORK HAVE BEEN PROSTRATE IN BED FOR 2 WEEKS IN HOSPITAL THINGS IN TERRIBLE SHAPE HERE SEE KAHN HES BEEN WONDERFUL NO ONE INTERESTED HELPING ME BUT BANK AND KAHN WRITE DETAILS WHEN YOU FEEL ABLE. / GRACE.

To Clarence Arthur Crane

New York
Oct. 31st, '26

TLS, 1 p.
LETTERHEAD: Hotel Albert, New York

Dear Father:

It is, of course, quite possible that you have not cared to answer any of my letters to you this summer, addressed from the Isle of Pines. Since my return to New York this week, however, I discover from various friends of mine that many of my letters have not reached their destination, and that much mail addressed to me on the Island was never delivered. This is due, I understand, to the corrupt manners of the Havana postoffice. Letters are often opened in the hope of finding American currency, and not reforwarded . . .

So, in view of this, I feel prompted to at least express my regrets to you—in case you have been as mystified at *my* silence as I have been at yours. If you care to write me, I'll be here another week in all probability.

Sincerely, your son,/ Harold

Hart's cordial letter to his father brought a swift reply in which C.A. explained his silence and enclosed a check for twenty-five dollars. His wife's long illness had been diagnosed as cancer; she was near death. As C.A. was consumed with concern for his wife's health and Grace was consumed with bitterness over her second divorce, Hart decided it would be best not to visit Cleveland immediately but to return to Mrs. Turner's farmhouse in Patterson. There he hoped he would have the peace he needed to continue his work on *The Bridge*. As the following letters show, he spent a melancholy Thanksgiving and Christmas unable to escape thinking about his parents' difficulties.

The one pleasant event of the winter was the publication of *White Buildings*. Hart received the first copies from Boni and Liveright in late December, 1926, and in the first months of 1927 he wrote lengthy accounts of the reviews to his mother.

From Clarence Arthur Crane

[Cleveland]
Nov. 2, 1926.

TLC, 1 p.

Mr. Harold Crane,
Hotel Albert,
11th St. & University Place,
New York City.

My dear Harold:—

I have your letter of October 31st. I did not answer your letter to the Isle of Pines. It came to me at a time when I first discovered that my Frances could not recover from her present illness, and I have been so nearly crazed with grief from that day to this that I am in no condition now to write you a very satisfactory letter.

I believe your mother is passing through a very serious and unsatisfactory condition herself, both mentally and physically. I think you should come home and see her, and perhaps be helpful.

As far as I am concerned I am so nearly broken that I don't know whether I can bear up through the valley that is ahead of me or not. Your letters have always been sent to your mother for she requested that.

Am glad to know that you escaped any misfortune in the Isle of Pines disaster, and I hope you are well and happy. If so, you are the only member of the Crane family who is. I am enclosing you a check for $25.00 in case you care to come home, and will be glad to know what your plans are.

With much love/ Your Father,

From Clarence Arthur Crane

[Cleveland]
Nov. 10, 1926.

TLC, 1 p.

'

Mr. Harold Crane,
Patterson, N.Y.

My dear Harold:—

Your letter of Nov. 3rd was duly received. When you have settled down to work at Patterson, tell me what your immediate needs are and I will try and help you out. I have heard nothing more from your mother.

My own condition remains as despairing as ever, and I have nothing to say which is either comforting or cheerful.

You might tell me when your new book is coming out, and what your prospects are. I know that you will recover your physical and mental poise as soon as you get in the quietude of your old haunts, and I only hope that things look brighter for you than they do for me.

With love,/ Your father,

To Grace Hart Curtis

Patterson—N.Y.
Dec. 22 '26

ALS, 4 pp.

Dear Grace:

Your letter came yesterday and I am glad that you can once more write. Yes—it is a very melancholy Christmas for all of us. . . . I am certainly anything but joyful.

Insomnia seems now to have settled on me permanently—and when I do "sleep" my mind is plagued by an endless reel of pictures, startling and unhappy—like some endless cinametograph.

Am making as much effort as possible to free my imagination and work the little time that is now left me on my Bridge poem. So much is expected of me via that poem—that if I fail on it I shall become a laughing stock and my career closed.

I take it that you would not wish this to happen. Yet it may be too late already, for me to complete the conception: My mind is about as clear as dirty dishwater—and such a state of things is scarcely conducive to successful creative endeavor. If it were like adding up columns of figures—or more usual labors—it would be different . . . Well, I'm trying my best—both to feel the proper sentiments to your situation and keep on with my task. "The Bridge" is an important task—and nobody else can ever do it.

My "White Buildings" is out. A beautiful book. Laukhuff has been instructed to send you out a copy as soon as he receves his order.

Do write to Mrs. Simpson—Box 1373 Nuva Gerona—and tell her what to do with the house. She has written you many times asking. There won't be a timber of it left in a few weeks if someone doesn't live in it.

I'm glad you have taken up C.S. again. You never should have dropped it. But it seems to me you will have to make a real effort this time—with no half-way measures. It isn't anything you can play with. It's either true—or totally false. And for heaven's sake—don't go to it merely as a *cure*. If it isn't a complete philosophy of life for you it isn't anything at all. It is sheer hypocrisy to take it up when you get scared, and then forsake it as soon as you feel angry about something. Anger is a costly luxury to you—and resentment and constant self-pity. I have to fight these demons myself. I know they are demons—they never do me anything but harm. Why look at yourself as a martyr all the time! It simply drives people away from you. The only real martyrs the world ever worships are those devoted exclusively to the worship of God, poverty and suffering—you have, as yet, never been in exactly that position. Not that I want you to be a martyr. I see no reason for it—and am out of sumpathy with anyone who thinks he is—for the *real* ones don't think about themselves that way—they are to[o] happy in their faith to ever want to be otherwise.

If this sounds like a sermon it's the last I offer sincerely. I'm not well and still have the tonsilitis. Write me again as soon as you feel able.

Love,/ Hart

if you see Grandma give her my love—I don't know where to write her . . .

I can't understand why you have to move at once. Chas. wrote me that he was paying the rent on your aptmt. until next *Oct*. And isn't a husband *obliged* to pay the expenses—or half his income—until at least such time as a divorce has been enacted?

In the early months of 1927 Hart's mood roughly paralleled his mother's. (Frances Crane died on January 3; Clarence was so preoccupied with his own affairs that he sent no letters to Hart between November, 1926, and the final day of March, 1927.) When Grace sent bitter and despairing letters to her son, Hart's own mood would become melancholy and he would not be able to work on *The Bridge*. When she sent more cheerful notes, he too would become more ebullient, and even enclose copies of his poems in his letters to Cleveland.

To Grace Hart Curtis

Patterson, NY
Sunday—
Jan 23, '27

TLS, 2 pp.

Dear Grace:

Your good letter and the ph[o]tographs arrived in the same mail —yesterday. I was awfully glad to hear from you; and your letter was a perfect volume of news. I had heard nothing about the death of Frances until Grandmother's letter reached me, last Friday, I think. CA did not trouble to answer the letter I wrote him in November, and though I shall probably not hear from him, even now, until God knows when—I wrote him a short note of condolence as soon as I heard.

I liked the pictures, especially the one with the hat, and the frame is beautiful. I shall take them with me into NY when I get the job (whatever it shall turn out to be) that I'm at present fishing for. I am trying to get a line on something before going in, as I have scarcely any money left, and I would like to avoid any charities from my friends on this occasion if possible.

Meanwhile I am doing what writing I can, and studying Spanish.

I'm very much amused at what you say about the interest in my book among relatives and friends out there in Cleveland. Wait until they see it, and try to read it! I may be wrong, but I think they will eventually express considerable consternation; for the poetry I write, as you have noticed already, is farther from their grasp than the farthest planets. But I don't care how mad they get —*after* they have bought the book! It is going to get some excellent and laudatory reviews. Waldo Frank's in the New Republic (a full page) ought to be out any day. Matthew Josephson is reviewing it in the NY Herald, Yvor Winters in the Dial, Archibald MacLeisch in Poetry, A Magazine of Verse (Chicago), etc.[1]

Yvor Winters, who is a professor of French and Spanish at the Moscow University, Idaho, writes me the following:

"Your book arrived this evening, and I have read it through a couple of times. It will need many more readings, but so far I am simply dumfounded. Most of it is new to me, and what I had seen is clarified by its setting. I withdraw all minor objections I have ever made to your work—I have never read anything greater and have read very little as great." Etc. So you see what kind of a review he is apt to write.

Waldo Frank ends his article in the New Republic by saying:

"At present Hart Crane is engaged in a long poem that provides him with a subject adequate for his method: the subject indeed which Mr Tate prophecies in his introduction. Yet already White Buildings gives us enough to justify the assertion, that not since Whitman has so original, so profound and—above all, so important a poetic promise come to the American scene."[2]

In a way it's a pity that none of the Crane family are readers of anything more important than such magazines as the Saturday Evening Post and Success. Which reminds me, in contradistinction to all this, that Clara Risdon wrote me a jolly little Christmas card,[3] mentioning the fact that she had been inquiring for White Buildings, having seen it advertised. I wonder what her address is; I should like to return the greeting somehow.

You are probably getting tired of all this egotism and lit'ry news, but this is the last for the present . . . A publisher in London (Wishart & Co.) has written me proposing a London edition of the book;[4] and I think that arrangements will be concluded within a few weeks. Mail is slow, of course. But I am glad to have the book

---

[1] Actually Josephson and MacLeish never reviewed the book. Winters's review was published in *Poetry*, XXX (April, 1927), 49–51.

[2] This paragraph was deleted from the published version in the *New Republic*.

[3] Clara Risdon, a cousin of Hart's.

[4] *White Buildings* was never published in an English edition.

re-issued there, as I may live abroad sometime and a reputation in London might help me.

You asked about my 'domestic arrangements' here . . . Well, the Tates are in New York for the rest of the winter, and so are the Browns. I have the house to myself, and Mrs. Turner has forsaken her Aunt's 'part' for the time being, and cooks, washes and mends for me—all for the round sum of seven dollars a week! If I had the slightest sort of income I could live on here forever at such a rate. One would simply have to make an expedition to NY once in two months or so for a few days, however, as there are some limitations to the fascination of the 'scene'.

Grandmother's letter to me was a perfect marvel of lucidity after all she's been through. I was amazed! I gathered from it—as well as from your letter—that you are both seeing a good deal of Bess and Byron lately. I suppose the unusual proximity of your present loca- tion to theirs makes visiting easy. I've always thought that Bess was pretty good company, and so is Alice Crane.[5] I'm glad that they have proved their friendship and given you a somewhat grateful su- prise at this time. I'm wondering what has become of the Rychtariks—true, I had a Christmas card from them, but for some reason they have written me only one letter in the last eight months. Do you see them any—lately?

The delay in the divorce procedings may mean that Charles is reconsidering—and it might be just as well all around if he did. I have the idea that you both care for each other more than you thought you did. Such thoughts are neither here nor there, how- ever, and I'm in no position to form judgements or advise. I've never been able to figure out what the quarrel was 'all about'—i.e. the issue involved. I think you had probably better keep your mind off the subject as much as possible, assuming the issue as closed. But you must get something to do as soon as you are physically able . . . I mean—that without some kind of activity you'll remain in a morbid condition—and your viewpoint will become more warped all the time. People just have to have some kind of activity to re- main healthy-minded.

---

[5] Clarence Crane's sisters, Alice and Bess, and his brother-in-law Newton Byron Madden.

But you seem to [be] already much better; and I'm enormously glad. Don't think I don't care for you,—I can't help it, no matter how I feel about some things. I must write Grandmother a letter now. I hope you'll write me again soon.

Much love,/ Hart

p.s.—I enclose the Dedication to my long poem, The Bridge,—the Dial bought this part last summer, but so far it hasn't appeared.[6]

DEDICATION
TO
BROOKLYN BRIDGE

How many dawns, chill from his rippling rest
The seagull's wings shall dip and pivot him,
Shedding white rings of tumult, building high
Over the chained bay waters Liberty—

Then, with inviolate curve, forsake our eyes
As apparitional as sails that cross
Some page of figures to be filed away;
—And elevators heave us to our day . . .

I think of cinemas, panoramic sleights
With multitudes bent toward some flashing scene
Never disclosed, but hastened to again,
Foretold to other eyes on the same screen;

And Thee, across the harbor, silver-paced
As though the sun took step of thee, yet left
Some motion ever unspent in thy stride,—
Implicitly thy freedom staying thee!

Out of some subway scuttle, cell or loft
A bedlamite speeds to thy parapets,
Tilting there momently, shrill shirt ballooning,
A jest falls from the speechless caravan.

Down Wall, from girder into crowd noon leaks,
A rip-tooth of the sky's acetylene;

[6] "To Brooklyn Bridge" was published in *The Dial*, LXXXII (June, 1927), 489-90.

All afternoon the cloud-flown derricks burn.
Thy cables breathe the North Atlantic still.

And obscure as that heaven of the Jews,
Thy guerdon . . . Accolade thou dost bestow
Of anonymity time cannot raise:
Vibrant reprieve and pardon thou dost show.

O harp and altar of the fury fused,
(How could mere toil align the choiring strings!)
Terrific threshold of the prophet's pledge,
Prayer of pariah, and the lover's cry,—

Again the traffic lights that skim thy swift
Unfractioned idiom, immaculate sigh of stars,
Beading thy path—condense eternity:
And we have seen night lifted in thine arms.

Under thy shadow by the piers I waited;
Only in darkness is thy shadow clear.
The City's fiery parcels all undone,
Already snow submerges an iron year . . .

O Sleepless as the river under thee,
Vaulting the sea, the prairies' dreaming sod,
Unto us lowliest sometime sweep, descend
And of the curveship lend a myth to God.

To Grace Hart Curtis

[Patterson, New York]
[Postmarked January 27, 1927]

TMS, 4 pp.

[*This handwritten note appears at the top of the manuscript:*]

Dear Grace: You've already seen the dedication. Here is the first section of the Bridge— Columbus meditating at the prow on the return from his first trip—he thought he had found the way to India, you know. It's been hailed as a masterpiece by more than one. I wrote it on the Island.

AVE MARIA

Be with me, Luis de San Angel, now—'
Witness before the tides can wrest away
The word I bring, O you who reined my suit
Into the Queen's great heart that doubtful day;
For I have seen what now no seasoned breath
Of clown or courtier riddles or gainsays;
And you, Fray Juan Perez, whose counsel fear
And greed adjourned,—I bring you back Cathay!

Here waves climb into dusk on gleaming mail;
Invisible valves of the sea,—locks, tendons
Crested and creeping, troughing corridors
That fall back yawning to another plunge.
Slowly the sun's red caravel drops light
Once more behind us . . . It is morning there,—
O where our other cities, mountains steep
White spires in heaven, yet hammocked in this keel!

I thought of Genoa: and this truth, now proved,
That made me exile in her streets, stood me
More absolute than ever—biding the rain
Til dawn should lift that darkened coast to us
—The Chan's great continent . . . And nightingales
Nigh surged me witless, voices far swept near.
I, wonder-breathing, kept the watch,—saw
The first palm chevron the first lighted hill.

And lowered. And they came out to us crying,
"The Great White Birds!" (O Madra Maria, still
One ship of these thou givest safe returning;
Assure us through thy mantle's obscure blue!)
—All this,—far more floats written in a cask,
Was tumbled from us under barepoles scudding;
And other hurricanes may claim more pawn.
For yet between two worlds, another harsh,

This third, of water, tests the word; lo, here
A mutiny and malice wield some fierce

Delight, and shadow cuts sleep from the heart
Almost as though the Moor's flung scimitar
Found more than flesh to fathom in its bed.
Yet under lashings of a million gales
Some inmost sob, half-heard, tolls the abyss,
Is lifted by the breeze into the wave

Series on series, infinite,—until the eyes,
Long bleached on chartless winds, accrete,—foreclose
This turning rondure whole, this crescent ring
Sun-rimmed and zoned with modulated fire
Like pearls that whisper through the Doge's hands
—Yet no delirium of jewels! O Fernando,
Take of this eastern shore, this western sea,
Yet give thy God and Virgin verily!

—Rush down the plenitude, and you shall see
Isaiah counting famine on this lee . . !
      . . . . . .
An herb, a stray branch among salty teeth,
The jellied weeds that drag the shore,—perhaps
Tomorrow's eve will bring us Saltos Bar—
Palos again,—a land cleared of long war.
Some angelus environs the cordage tree;
Dark waters onward shake the dark 'prow' free.
      . . . . . .
O Thou who sleepest on thyself, apart
Like ocean, athwart lanes of death and birth,
And all the eddying breath between dost search
Cruelly with love thy parable of man,—
Inquisitor! incognizable Word
Of Eden and the enchained Sepulchre,
Into thy steep savannahs, burning blue,
Utter to loneliness the sail is true.

Who grindest oar, and arguing the mast
Subscribest holocaust of ships, O Thou
Within whose primal scan consummately
The glistening seignories of Ganges swim;—
Who sendest greeting of the corposant
And Teneriffe's garnet,—set it in a cloud
Burning through night the passage to the Chan,
Te Deum laudamus Thy teeming span.

Of all that amplitude that time explores,
A needle in the sight, suspended north,—
Yielding by inference and discard, faith
And true appointment from the hidden shoal;
This disposition that thy night relates
From Moon to Saturn in one sapphire wheel;
The orbic wake of thy once whirling feet,—
Elohim, still I hear thy sounding heel!

White toil of heaven's cordons, mustering
In panic rings all sails charged to the far
Hushed gleaming fields and pendant seething wheat
Of knowledge,—round thy brows unhooded now
—The kindled Crown! Acceded of the poles
And biassed by white sails, meridians reel
Thy purpose—still one shore beyond desire!
The sea's green crying towers a-sway, Beyond

And kingdoms
                    naked in the
                              trembling heart—
          Te Deum laudamus
                    O Hand of Fire

                              Hart Crane

To Elizabeth Belden Hart

                                   Patterson
                                   New York
                                   Feb 28th
                                   1927

TLS, 1 p.

Dearest Grandma:

I'm much later in writing you again than I expected to be. But there is awfully little to write about.

I am writing some, chopping wood for the stove, going to a neighboring farm for wood, studying Spanish—and waiting for some money to come from some things which I have submitted to editors. It's the devil to be so 'broke'—but I'm getting used to it. Mrs Turner, the 'landlady' is very kind indeed, and says I can stay on as long as I want to—on credit—; but I don't intend to victimize her. As soon as I get enough money again for a trial at finding a job in the city I shall go in. Right now I haven't the carfare to get there.

For over a week we have had no mail delivery. The great storm which hit all the eastern seabord (and I guess it swept over Ohio, too) left such snowdrifts all through this section that it's only today that the mail delivery man is getting through. I've had a slight return of the tonsilitis lately, and your lovely gift has come in very handily and comfortably!

I hear nothing from anyone in Cleveland but you. C.A. hasn't written me a line since November; and I suppose, or am left to suppose, that the publication of my book has so angered him that I need not expect to hear from him again. I have written him two letters, neither of which he has answered, so I can't do more. Grace also does not write; but I suppose feels like anything but writing if she's depressed. It's hard at such times to write. But I should love to hear from her. . . . You are my old standby! I do hope that you are comfortable. I wish I could do something for you, but in the long ponderings—sometimes very painful—which I've gone through lately, I don't see how I am, or can be, much good to anyone.

Please write me again when you feel strong enough. This is a beautiful day with the sun pouring down showers of gold on the spotless snow over hill and dale. Here are some hugs and kisses for you—OXXOXXOX

Love always,/ Hart

To Grace Hart Curtis

Patterson
March 1 '27

ALS, 3 pp.

Dear Grace:

Just a line before the postman comes. I wrote all the news to Grandma yesterday.

I dont want you to think that you haven't my sympathy these days. You don't know how horribly upset I am—and have been for many months. I could not with[h]old my sympathies from you—no matter how much I might disagree with you on the question of your judgement etc. which brought about the present state of affairs. Affection is something that overules reason always—and I suffer with you much more than you think.

There seems to be only one thing to do. Face the situation, and make it as simple as possible by putting all essentials out of mind.

By this I mean—put out of your thoughts the reactions of all your former "friends"—ignore them. I know it isn't easy. But you are not going to have to live in Cleveland always.

Get up your ire enough to dominate the court. You ought to get some alimony—don't urge any lump settlement. But get so much per month if you can.

For the present we'll have to be separated. I can't ever get enough money together to get to Cleveland at present. And what would I do when I got there! It takes weeks to get work, you know that. If I can get anything in N.Y. I'll send you something from that. I'm trying as best I can to get a connection.

Wish you would write me soon.

Love,/ Hart

P.S.—Mrs Simpson wrote me—and said she had also written you—that she had a chance to sell the island place. I *can't* understand why you didn't use this opportunity to get some cash for the present crisis—an extra thousand or so—when you seem to be so worried. But I wrote you about this before. You never trouble to explain to me why you don't do something about it however.

To Grace Hart Curtis

Patterson

March 12th '27

TLS, 1 p.

Dear Grace:

Your splendid long letter of last week will have to be answered a little later when my eyes are better. For the last three days I've been half blind with conjunctivitis—better known as 'pink-eye', and I can't see to either read or write very well. I [am] immensely glad to know—and the tone of your letter shows it—that you are facing things with energy and courage. It helps me a lot, and I may be able to get to work again on my poem when I get rid of this eye trouble. I walked to a neighboring town and saw a doctor Friday. Have medicine and will probably recover in a few days.

I enclose review clippings of White Buildings. All are not out yet. Frank's review is out this week in the New Republic, I hear, though I haven't a copy yet. You can get it at numerous news stands in Cleveland—at University Book Store at 105th for one place. I'll write you again in a few days. Mrs Turner would love to have any dresses, coats, shoes or what-not that you don't want to keep. She's about your size, and needs clothing very much.

Here's loads of love to you—and to my dear Grandmother!

as ever/ Hart

[*Written in the margin:*] *Please* take care of all these clippings—and *return* within 2 weeks! They're my *only* copies.

To Grace Hart Curtis

Patterson
Tuesday
[March 15, 1927?] [1]

TLS, 1 p.

Dear Grace:

The enclosed letter from Mrs Simpson tells its own story. Hadn't you better write her—as I advised some time ago—and give her license to sell what's left of the house furniture before it's *all* stolen? You might get sixty or seventy dollars out of it. Better than nothing!

My eyes aren't any better today—so I'll close for the time. Am sending you on a copy of the New Republic with Frank's article in it.

Love,/ Hart

[*The letter from Mrs. Simpson is printed below:*]

Nueva Gerona
Jan 9 1927

Dear Hart

The book came yesterday and I thank you very much for it. Tis a very pretty little book and I shall prize it very highly for both the donor & the writer's sake. I showed it to several and they all admired it and send you congratulations[.] they all also wish to borrow it but I am going to ask them why not buy a copy for themselves? Miss Kennedy said she would send for a copy [;] she often sends to Boni & Liveright for books. There is nothing new to write about[.] every body still digging among the debris (caused by the late hurricane) to salvage what they can. I am all alone now and can do just as I please and not wonder if I am shocking two fussy old females; not that I cared very much if I did.

[1] References to his eye trouble and to Waldo Frank's article (which was probably his review of *White Buildings* published in the *New Republic*, March 16, 1927, pp. 116–17) suggest that Crane wrote this letter on Tuesday, March 15, 1927.

Ben and Mary have gone back to New York [.] they didn't even
say good bye to me [.] they were gone a week before I knew it [.]
cant imagine what was the matter with them unless they were jealous of a young poet who came to the Isle last summer [;] if so I
should worry. We are having some quite cool weather now. had to go
to bed last night early to keep warm. I am going over to visit the
"House house" tomorrow to see how things are [.] I go over once a
week to let people know that some one is looking out for it so the
house will not be carried away. quite a few people are coming down
from Canada now and we may have a chance to sell it [;] the house
and what land goes with it [.] any way if I only knew what they
will take for it I might be able to do something. I went out with a
man one day to look at it [.] he asked the price but I couldn't tell
him & he couldn't wait for a letter from Cleveland [.] that is just the
way things stand [.] I could have sold some of the furniture but they
didn't say whether or not [,] so I've not tried but if something is not
done soon 'twill all be stolen if left over there and I haven't room for
it all over here. I believe Margaret Miller will buy the piano if they
dont want too much for it. I am not sure but think I've sold one, and
maybe both your trunks [.] will let you know just as soon as I do.
I've not been feeling quite myself lately [.] think I've worked a little
too steadily and such hard work but I'll slow up for a few days and
be all right again soon. Hope you keep well [.]

With much love/ Aunt Sally

Tuesday Gee but it is cold [.] woke up with a cold nose.

To Grace Hart Curtis

Patterson, NY
19th March 1927

TLS, 2 pp.

Dear Grace:

My eyes are so much better today that I'm able to type a little
without straining. I had to order a pair of glasses—and that seems
to have done more good than medicine. I lost my old pair down on

the Island, but really have not worn them for more than a few days
at a time for years. Nervous crises always affect my eyes, however,
and it may be that this present case of conjunctivitis was caused as
much by that as by wind and sunglare on snow. At any rate there's
no snow left around here now, and the air is as balmy as you could
wish. I do hope that the season has definitely arrived—and no more
snow! My spirits react entirely too much to the endless gloomy days
we've had for so long.

As I said before, your letter was a perfect marvel to me, and so
well organized that I'm sure you are in a much improved state. I
am immensely relieved that you are getting alimony—and I feel
certain that you are going to get at least a modest amount as a regular monthly stipend. I think you have a right to that, regardless of
the question as to whether or not Curtis is wealthy or not. People
don't undertake marriage in these days without assuming some responsibilities. Considering his slight income, however, I wouldn't
ask for much.

I never see Kent's name—nor have ever read a line he wrote,[1]
but I don't happen to see the magazines he writes for. There is
probably even less danger of his ever hearing of me! I am so glad
that you enjoyed the Columbus part. It is coming out next September in The American Caravan,[2] a yearbook of American letters, just
started by Paul Rosenfeld, Alfred Kreymborg and VanWyck
Brooks, and published by the Macaulay Co. When I was last in NY
the owners of the Macaulay Co gave a large party to all the contribu-
utors up in a huge but unbelievably vulgarly furnished and expensive apartment on West End Avenue. There seemed to be everybody there I'd ever heard of. Enormous quantities of wine, cocktails
and highballs were served. I had just landed in town after three
months with the bossy cows—and I had my share. It would take me
ages to tell all the amusing things that happen at such parties. But
to come back to the poem: Rosenfeld was so excited about it that
he called me up long distance and urged me to let them have it. I
had thought to have to deny it to them on account of some compli-

[1] Kent Curtis.
[2] "Ave Maria" was published in *The American Caravan* (New York: Macaulay
Company, 1927), pp. 804–6.

cations on the copyright, conflicting possibly with my terms with Liveright (he has first option on my next two books) but after some concessions were made I was glad to have them take it.

The Dial has just informed me today that they have taken the main section of Part II, Powhatan's Daughter.[3] This is an indian dance—and will run about 4 Dial pages. I'll be glad to have the cash to pay my arrears with Mrs Turner and the doctor . . . I have for some strange reason, heard nothing yet from London regarding the projected British edition of White Buildings. What you say about the reactions to it on Cornell Road are both amusing and touching.[4] And when I read about Mrs Jackson taking a copy to read to the Garrettsville Federated Women's Clubs I rocked with laughter! The poor dears will never, NEVER know what in hell to make of it all! I'm awfully grateful to Aunt Alma for having sold so many. I had almost written her—at Burrows. Is she there, or at Korner and Woods?[5]

Heard from Kathryn Kenney lately. She has been divorced—or rather divorced her husband. Her job fell through also—I think the whole syndicate collapsed, though she doesn't say anything except that she was 'double-crossed'. As usual she is foaming to get away from Cleveland, thinks of coming to NY—and also wants to get to Europe. Also heard from William Wright. He was married last Fall, and apparently hasn't been well for the last several years. He is just now returning from some sanitarium in Clifton Springs, NY where he's been undergoing treatment for nerous indigestion and complications. That nervous breakdown he had at Yale seems to have permanently crippled him. He wrote me a rather pathetic letter congratulating me on my book—which he said he'd seen and bought.

I took enough veronal powders on the Island during those mad last days to convince me that there's nothing worse. And they didn't even give me sound sleep! The feelings next day were weird in the extreme. I hope that CA won't keep them up very long. His atti-

---

[3] "The Dance" section, with the title "Powhatan's Daughter," was published in *The Dial*, LXXXIII (October, 1927), 329–32.

[4] Hart's grandparents, Arthur and Ella Crane, lived on Cornell Road in Cleveland.

[5] Alma Crane, Hart's cousin, worked as a saleslady in the Burrows bookstore. She was responsible for selling many copies of *White Buildings*.

tude and emotions toward life would probably make one gasp if one could get a cross section of them. For a long time he has seemed to me as thorough a specimen of abnormality as I have ever heard of. I've given up even trying to imagine how he sees or thinks. I probably shall continue to not write him until he answers some of my former letters—or gives some sign that he wants to hear from me. I sent him a copy of the recent New Republic, but without any note or comment. He probably likes to build up the picture that he he's creeping around in utter disgrace on account of the public 'disgrace' his son has made of himself. Well, the thirty thousand people that read the New Republic probably wouldn't give him much sympathy—regardless of their estimate of my particular value.

That was a happy thought—sending me the picture of the Kinsman house.[6] It is particularly beautiful. What of Zell and Helen these days? I haven't, of course, corresponded with Zell since our little blow-up of nearly two years ago. Every once in awhile I have a dream with Warren scenes in it. Hall Kirkham, Donald Clarke, Katherine Miller, Leanard Bullus, Mrs Potter with her great heart-shaped bosom—and Mrs Gilbert gasping with her goitre—what has become of them all.[7] I wonder. I once wrote a poem with Mrs Potter as the subject—but it didn't turn out to be much of anything but a sentimentality, and I guess I threw it away. You are right; I should write some prose. But to date I've never been able to think of things with plots to them. Somehow just can't. When I do, there won't be any particular difficulty in expressing myself. We'll see what happens when I get through with this long Bridge poem. Right now I'm too occupied with *it* to think of other themes.

I must write Grandma a letter soon. I hope she'll forgive me for not writing her a special letter now. This is a stupid enough letter for one day without adding more. I'll do better when I'm better organized. I do hope to get something accomplished next week.

Let me hear from you soon—both of you.

LOVE,/ Hart

[6] The Kinsman house is one of the oldest surviving homes in Warren, Ohio.

[7] Mrs. Helen Hart Hurlburt was unable to identify any of these people, who were very likely Hart's childhood friends. It is not known what was the cause of Hart's "little blow-up" with his Aunt Zell.

[*Written in the margin of page 2:*] The enclosed letter may interest you. I am also enclosing the poem referred to—O Carib Isle— which is one of three of mine which Jolas has translated into French to appear in a French anthology of American poems coming out this fall.[8] Carib Isle was written one hellish hot day on the Island—but the *scene* of the poem and its inspiration was *Cayman!* It is coming out soon in "Poetry" in this country.[9] It's not a bad poem. I'm crazy about those Caribbean waters and skies—even if they are hot! There's a lot of feeling they give you in the Columbus poem—don't you think? *Please return the letter.*

[*The enclosed letter from Eugene Jolas written on the stationery of* Transition *magazine is printed below:*]

Feb. 24, 1927

Dear Mr. Crane:

Thank you for your prompt answer to our cable. It was for Tran- sition I wanted to use Carib Isle. It will appear in the first number to be published March 15, since your cable clarifies the situation.[10]

My translation of Carib Isle will appear in a French version in the anthology sometime this spring. The house of Kra will bring out the book.

Please let us see any future poem you may wish to send us. I have read White Buildings and thank you very much for thinking of me. It's immense. I agree absolutely with Tate. We expect to review it.

I am just now trying to have the French version of Carib Isle published in a French review here. I hope it will be O.K. with you.

Wont you ask Mr. Tate and Mr. Cowley to send us something, if they care to?

With many good wishes to you,/ Eugene Jolas

---

[8] "O Carib Isle!" was published in Eugene Jolas, ed., *Anthologie de la Poésie Américaine* (Paris: Simon Kra, 1928).

[9] "O Carib Isle!" was published in *Poetry*, XXXI (October, 1927), 30.

[10] The poem was published in *Transition*, I (April, 1927), 101.

O CARIB ISLE!

Grand Cayman, June '26

The tarantula rattling at the lily's foot,
Across the feet of the dead, laid in white sand
Near the coral beach,—the small and ruddy crabs
Flickering out of sight, that reverse your name;

And above, the lyric palsy of eucalypti, seeping
A silver swash of something unvisited . . . Suppose
I count these clean, enamel frames of death,
Brutal necklaces of shells around each grave
Laid out so carefully. This pity can be told . . .

And in the white sand I can find a name, albeit
In another tongue. Tree-name, flower-name deliberate,
Gainsay the unknown death . . . The wind
Sweeping the scrub palms, also is almost kind.

But who is Captain of this doubloon isle?
Without a turnstile? Nought but catchword crabs
Vining the hot groins of the underbrush? Who
The Commissioner of mildew throughout the senses?
His Carib mathematics dull the bright new lenses.

Under the poincianna, of a noon or afternoon
Let fiery blossoms clot the light, render my ghost,
Sieved upward, black and white along the air—
Until it meets the blue's comedian host.

Let not the pilgrim see himself again
Bound like the dozen turtles on the wharf
Each twilight,—still undead, and brine caked in their eyes,
—Huge, overturned: such thunder in their strain!
And clenched beaks coughing for the surge again!

Slagged of the hurricane,—I, cast within its flow
Congeal by afternoons here, satin and vacant . . .
You have given me the shell, Satan,—the ember,
Carbolic, of the sun exploded in the sea.

From Grace Hart Curtis

Cleveland,
, Mch 20—1927

ALS, 6 pp.

Dear Hart:—

I am still looking for a good long answer to that last long letter of mine—do not forget that your excuse for delay was the "pink eye." I hope your eyes are well by this time but be careful about the way you use them for awhile[.]

Now I want you to know that we are enjoying reading the clippings you sent and will send them back before the two weeks limit. They are all very interesting & most of them complementary— But the New Republic of Mch 16—is certainly all one could ask, and I am quite jubilant over it.

It is making Clevelanders sit up & take notice, and is going to do you a world of good everywhere it is read.

You know what a high brow, Mrs Wolf (Sara Bakers sisterinlaw) is? Well she called Sara on the phone as soon as she read it & was much excited over it, as was Sara, who called me immediately & told me to be sure to secure a copy.

Mr Frank has been most unstinted in his praise & has really paid you a wonderful tribute.

The jewish womans book club of this city are discussing you at their meetings, and considerable local interest is manifesting itself.

I met Glenn Whis[t]ler on the car the other night, and he rode on out here with me. He had read your book & the criticism in the New Republic—and was very much pleased.

Mrs Kenney told me that Kathryn had been reading aloud some of your poems to her & one or two others and that the way Kathryn read them clarified them immensely.

The charming lady of Boston who has been here for her confinement case, has also read them & everything about you, & left for home yesterday with the parting words to me, that she should certainly look with interest in the future for anything concerning you or your writing.

I was so gratified with the way Mr Frank treated your book. It puts it in the place it belongs & explains why, so that any one reading your verses will be better guided, if they need guiding, & most of us do.

But the wonder of wonders to us—was that letter from Mrs. Simpson— Her loving interest in you & your work & her ability & desire to read & reread your White Buildings shows that there is a depth of intelligence & appreciation of the fineness of things that one just meeting or knowing her casually, would never believe.

You certainly have a warm place in her heart, and I am going to write her very soon & tell her how I appreciate all she did for you.

Sara is so enthusiastic since reading that article in the Republic that she says she is going to write you a letter. She is a wonderful friend of mine—& all th[r]ough this last months tragic experience she has stood right by my side. Believe me, if you knew all, you would realize I needed my friends. Such stories as got circulated concerning me by that crazy E—— M——[,] rattle headed A—— S——,[1] & scared Chas Curtis would make one lose faith in every one.

Did you know that Geniveve Taggart,[2] is Mrs Wolf's daughter in law. She married Robert Wolf, and has written a book of verses[.]

It is raining hard here to day and such weather makes my spirits very low. I am feeling stronger, looking better everyday, & I am trying to forget the recent unhappy past, as fast as I can. I often wonder what all this struggle amounts to—but it seems to have to be—and it no doubt has its purpose.

You must tell me, when you next write something about the financial terms with your publisher, & etc etc.

My divorce case is liable to come up any day now, & I am just sitting on the edge all the time—nervous & unsettled & still dazed somewhat at the whole turn of affairs.

I wish I didn't have to live here in Cleveland another day— I just despise the place, in every way—but I can't budge on account of mother. She has *no one* but me. My mind is so confused about

---

[1] Mrs. Crane refers to several people who she thought had turned against her.

[2] Genevieve Taggard (1894–1948), the poet and biographer, was married to Robert Wolf from 1920 to 1934. The book of poetry that Mrs. Crane refers to is *Words for the Chisel* (New York: Knopf, 1926).

things pertaining to myself that I can't see anything clearly, can't formulate any plan that seems right or that will solve my problems.

I certainly wish I might have a visit with you—

Love by the bushel—/ from/ Grace.

To Grace Hart Curtis and Elizabeth Belden Hart

Patterson—
March 28 [1927?]

ALS, 2 pp.

Dear Grace & Grandma:

I've been slow writing—but the Browns and others have been back and forth— I've had a lot of letters from all sorts of people to answer—and the last few days Mrs. Turner has been in bed on the verge of la grippe. She's up today, however, and I guess isn't going to succumb.

Thanks for the travel supplement. I'm wild to travel. A sailor friend of mine in the Navy writes me cards from the Mediterranean. I've been getting them now for nearly a year—and it keeps me stirred up and "rarin' to go" most of the time. I want to go to Spain —then Paris—and when things have cooled down there perhaps live in Mexico for a year or so.

My typewriter's on the bum—and I'm just lost. One gets so used to one that you're very dependent. I've been reading little and fretting much—but my eyes are better. Glad you liked Mrs. Simpson's letter. She was good as gold to me—and I have a very high opinion of her—shall always do what I can to liven up the rather bitter monotony of her position there on the Island. Very few people understand—and I suppose if we hadn't been thrown so very close together I shouldn't have discovered so much to love and admire.

By the way—if you really meant what you suggested about sending Mrs. Turner some old things I hope you wont forget about it. Some old house dress—even under wear—you've no idea how tattered and forlorn she looks. It's really kind of hard to look at her. But don't send anything the least bit fancy! You can't imagine how awful that would make her look—she's absolutely toothless and a kind of brownish-grey complexion.

Your last letter was so welcome—and I'm so glad to know you are facing things so bravely. I feel sure that with your recent attitude you'll fare a thousand times better.

There is so little happens here that I *have* to talk about my literary news whether or not it bores you. Last Sunday's N.Y. Times had a fair review of my book along with several others.[1] They often bunch them that way. Then I just got a letter from Wilbur Underwood containing a very nice review from the London Times—[2] it was short, but they don't give much space to any American editions anyway. The Nashville-Tennesseean is running a long review, etc. I may send some of these later—meanwhile don't loose the ones I have already sent. Keep the Frank one . . . Harriet Monroe has bought another section of The Bridge for Poetry, etc.[3] I have lately been travelling on the Mississippi—in that part of The Bridge, I mean.

Spring has turned out to be slower than at first it promised. But I [am] grateful for what we have. It's at least a month ahead of last year—which was awful! I was leaving here—and that was around May 1st with snow still melting in some parts of the wood. Forgot to mention that Claire looked me up when I was in N.Y. over a month ago. As beautiful as ever—but not very happy. Plenty of money of her own—and was about to leave for a trip to Haiti to paint. Pat [4] has become a Wall Street wizard, etc.

Will write more soon. Lots of love to you both—/ Hart

[1] *White Buildings* was reviewed by Herbert S. Gorman in the New York *Times*, March 27, 1927, section iii, p. 2. The other books included in the review were: John Crowe Ransom, *Two Gentlemen in Bonds* (New York: Knopf, 1927); Langston Hughes, *Fine Clothes for the Jew* (New York: Knopf, 1927); James Rorty, *Children of the Sun* (New York: Macmillan, 1926); Humbert Wolfe, *News of the Devil* (New York: Henry Holt, 1926); Richard Aldington, *The Love of Myrrhine and Kallis* (Chicago: P. Covici, 1926); John Drinkwater, *Persephone* (New York: Rudge, 1926); and Ford Madox Ford, *New Poems* (New York: Rudge, 1927).

[2] This review was published in the *Times Literary Supplement*, February 24, 1927, p. 130.

[3] "Cutty Sark" appeared in *Poetry*, XXXI (October, 1927), 29–31.

[4] Claire Spencer and her brother Pat.

From Clarence Arthur Crane

Cleveland, Ohio
March 31, 1927.

TLS, 2 pp.
LETTERHEAD: CRANE CHOCOLATE COMPANY

Mr. Harold Crane,
Patterson, Putnam County, N.Y.

My dear Harold:

I have not written you for more than weeks. There is little to say. We are all of us trying to make the best of a bad situation and Fredericka,[1] Frances' brother and myself are living at the apartment. I have been paying but little attention to business, some days working less than two hours, and have been putting in most of my time where roads were good and trying to get my mind on something besides my troubles.

The first of May I am going up into the far North; well up toward Hudson Bay, and investigate a mining property which I have acquired a small interest in, hoping that it would offer me some relief from my mental strain and, perhaps, I would so like the wilds of that country I could remain there for two or three months this summer. If I do this we will close up the flat when I go away, and then I will decide when I am gone what I will do on my return, but before we do this it occurs to me you might want to come home for two or three weeks, and now is a good time for you to do it. There is plenty of room in the house and you could spend as much time with me as you wished, for time hangs heavily on my hands. I am enclosing you a check which will enable you to find your way here if you are so inclined; if not, you can use it for things which you need.

I should have written you under ordinary circumstances long ago that your book of poems has raised much favorable comment from my friends who are capable of understanding it. As for myself, I

1 Fredrica Crane, Clarence's niece. She came to live with C.A. after the death of his second wife.

have not read it for my mind is only on my troubles and even a magazine article has failed to interest me, or anything which pertains to outside matter.

Mr. Morgan [2] was in the office Tuesday and said he would soon write you a congratulatory letter. I showed him the article by Mr. Frank and he thought it an excellent one.

I hear from your mother through Bessie and Byron [3] and they tell me she is in a much better frame of mind and, no doubt, will be glad to see you, for Bessie told me not more than an hour ago she is very lonely and has little to take up her time. All things considered, it looks like an advantageous hour for you to come back, and if you are so inclined I shall be glad to furnish the accommodations of coming and while you are here.

Your father has had a blow that has staggered him, and I shall be glad to have you put in some time with me, for I am lonesome enough even under conditions which could not be bettered, or with friends who help all they can.

> With much love, I am/ Your father,/ C.A.

⟨✦⟩

Hart decided to take the trip that he had dreaded for so many months, and he returned to Cleveland to console both of his parents. This time, though, he did not stay with Grace. For the first time since December, 1916, when C.A. and Grace were separated, he spent a night in his father's house.

Hart ended his visit with his father by accompanying him on April 18 to New York City. Once they had checked into the Roosevelt Hotel, each went his separate way—Clarence to try to consummate a business proposition concerning a machine that would make reproductions of oil paintings, and Hart to visit his numerous friends. After a day and a half in the city, Hart left for Patterson (probably on April 20). Before Clarence left later on the same day for Cleveland he sent the following note to his son. A short fragment of a letter (perhaps written on Saturday, April 23) Hart sent

[2] Edward Morgan, a business friend of Mr. Crane's.
[3] Clarence's sister Bess, and her husband, Newton Byron Madden.

to his father reveals how warm his feelings were about his recent visit.

From Clarence Arthur Crane

New York City
[April 20, 1927?]

ALS, 2 pp.
LETTERHEAD: The Roosevelt Hotel, New York

Dear H:

I found the enclosed on my return to the hotel.[1] Am leaving for home on the 6:30 and so ends the N.Y. trip. I am none the worse or no better for it unless it has in a small measure contributed to your joy.

Nothing developed at 501—when a jew has something that many want—its no time to get a good deal out of him.

They will forward their contract but I shall expect a foolish proposition. Am leaving without seeing anyone for my mind isnt in accord with things in general. Write me once a week & I'll do the same.

Much love

Your father/ C.A.

To Clarence Arthur Crane

[Patterson, New York]
[April 23, 1927?]

TLC, 1 p. Fragment

I am still thinking about some of the pleasant hours we had together recently. Altogether it was the most satisfactory visit we have ever had together. And this, despite the fact that, as I well realize, you were far from gleeful much of the time. If I was able to alle-

[1] Whatever Clarence did enclose, it is no longer filed with the letter.

viate, even for only a short period, some of [the] depression that you were struggling under, I shall feel very happy—for it is a good thing to be of some use to one's father, especially when he's been so good to me as you have.

I hope you won't change your mind about the Canadian trip, for I think it will do you a world of good to get out of cities for awhile. Be sure to take plenty of woolens, though. We're back to the normal chilly April weather again, at least in these parts. Give my best to Bessie, Freddie, Joe and Sing [1]—write me soon.

                                        With much love,/ Harold.

On Tuesday, April 19, the day after Hart and his father left Cleveland, Grace's suit for divorce came before the Common Pleas court. After the divorce was granted (but before the alimony was settled), Mrs. Crane made a short visit to her friends Frank and Blanche Ross in Chicago.

From Grace Hart Curtis

                                        [Cleveland]
                                        Sunday Night
                                        April 24—1927

ALS, 3 pp.

Dearest Hart:—

I was very glad indeed to get your letter & to know you were happy back in Patterson, once more. I suppose you received my night letter—sent Wednesday— I *never* put in such a day as I did on Tuesday—all day from 9 to six in that court room on & off of the witness stand— I was a rag & Mr Payer stayed right there all of the time. Since then, I have been expecting hourly to receive the

1 Bess Crane Madden; Fredrica Crane; Joe was a man who worked for C.A.; Sing was Clarence Crane's dog.

verdict from Judge Ewing, but Saturday came & went & no word.
So I am still on the anxious seat & nervous is no name for it. I feel
I must scream— Ever since last Oct. I've been thinking of this
night & day, & never dreamed of all this trouble at the last. Mr
Payer is trying *so* hard to get a good alimony—but he said he never
had worked so hard for a little. The trial was a very tense nerve
wracking thing. I was on & off the witness chair three times, & it
certainly was hard to be composed when they told things that were
untrue. Bud was mean & Payer got after him & put him where he
belonged— Also their stenographer. We proved that Chas. made
last year $8000.00 just as I had said, altho in his statement to Mr
Payer before going to court he said it was only 4000.00.

I am enclosing a clipping which is as rediculous as it is false.[1]
You know I never asked Chas to drive his car in all my life, nor

---

[1] The article Mrs. Crane refers to appeared in the Cleveland *News*, April 19,
1927. Though not filed with the letter, the clipping is worth reprinting here:

DENIED CAR, SHE SEEKS DIVORCE

Wife of Wade Park Manor Insurance Adjuster Holds $250
Insufficient

Complaints by Mrs. Grace Hart Curtis 51 that her husband Charles E. Curtis
67 wouldn't allow her to use his automobile, thus compelling her to use taxicabs
and pay for them out of the $150 a month "pin money" he gave her, featured a
contested divorce hearing Tuesday before common pleas Judge Ewing.

The two were married April 29, 1926, and their marital venture went on the
rocks Nov 10, 1926, when the wife filed a divorce petition charging neglect and
cruelty. The husband countered with a cross petition which made like charges in
his own behalf.

Mrs. Curtis who now lives at 2057 E. 100 St. testified that Curtis, an insurance
adjuster, left her Nov 9, 1926. In his cross petition he asserted he came home
from a business trip about that time to find she had left their Wade Park Manor
home and quartered herself in Hotel Statler for 2 days.

That seemed to have angered him, altho she says she explained that she had
been ill and she felt she could get better attention at the downtown hotel.

Curtis, she testified, paid all the bills at the Wade Park Manor home and allowed her the sum of $150 a month as "pin money." Since their separation she
testified he has paid her $250 a month which she finds insufficient.

Declaring that she lives in "a garrett" and in a manner such as she never has
been accustomed to she has asked the court to fix alimony comparable to her
needs.

Curtis now lives at 3290 Warrington Rd., Shaker Heights. He is represented by
Attorney Rees Davis. Att. Harry Payer is Mrs. Curtis' counsel.

wanted to. The judge asked me if I did, & I said no—I used the street car or taxi as the occasion demanded.

The Press notice was different but equally silly & untrue.[2] I feel so humiliated I can hardly look up & yet I do not intend to show it. It all is an awful strain—& I am showing it in the last few days — Alice Crane stayed right in court all day with me & testified as to my condition when she came to my home after Chas. had left. I hope to hear the outcome tomorrow.

Blanche wired me today to be sure to be in Chicago by Wednesday of this week—the 27th for some big ball. I don't see how I can make it. I am so weary I feel like hiding.

Will wire or write you as soon as I know my fate.

We miss you—all of us— A week ago today you were here— Grandma is about the same— She stands my suspense very well— wonderfully in fact— Hear that C.A. is home—have no other news—

Love from/ Grace.

Grandmother & Margaret send love—

[2] The following article appeared in the Cleveland *Press* on April 19, 1927:

SAYS MATE 67 LET LOVE COOL

Cooled ardor of a 67 year old husband drove Mrs. Grace H. Curtis 51, from a palatial suite in E. 100th St. to a one room apt. at 13732 Euclid Avenue according to Mrs. Curtis.

Hearing of her suit for alimony against her husband, Charles E. Curtis, opened Tuesday before Common Pleas Judge Harrison W. Ewing.

Curtis is in the insurance business with offices in the Keith Bldg. Mrs. Curtis says his income is 10,000 a year.

The Curtises were married April 29, 1926. They stayed for a time at Wade Park Manor, then moved to a 7 room suite at 2057 E. 100th St. where Mrs. Curtis says she had $100 a month "just for pin money."

Last Oct Mrs. Curtis was ill. Her son Hart Crane, former Cleveland newspaper man, was in the Isle of Pines, there was a storm there. Mrs. Curtis charges Curtis refused to get a message from her son for her.

Mrs. Curtis went to Hotel Statler where she says her husband came to tell her he no longer loved her. She sued for alimony Nov 10. Curtis entered a cross-petition for divorce charging neglect and extreme cruelty. The case was still in progress Tuesday afternoon.

From   Clarence   Arthur   Crane

[Cleveland]
April 25, 1927.

TLC, 1 p.

Mr. Hart Crane,
Patterson, N.Y.,
Putnam County, R.F.D.

My dear Son:

I have your letter, written Saturday, and rejoice that you are back where you seem to be so happy. I would suggest that you remain there forever; in other words, follow the advice that John Kendrick Bangs many years ago gave his audience—"Go and live in a houseboat; I never heard of anyone dying in [a] houseboat." [1]

After you left New York I was seized with one of those periods of depression which have been manifesting themselves for the past few months, and, without waiting for any more business conferences, or without seeing Hazel, I boarded the train and came home immediately. I would have done well to have kept you in New York another day, for I seem to be no good at all when I am left alone. Nothing further has developed regarding the picture machine.

Bessie and Byron came down to see father yesterday on his eighty first birthday, and volunteered the information that the judge had not yet handed down his decision regarding your mother's case. Of course, I have made no further inquiries and that is all I can tell you regarding it.

I greatly enjoyed your visit home and I am going to see to it that you come back before very long.

The Canadian trip will probably bob up for attention within the next two weeks. I had a letter from one of the directors Saturday, saying the weather was unusually warm there and he thought within ten days the river and lake would be free from ice to enable us to make the trip by motor boat. It is my understanding the trip

---

[1] John Kendrick Bangs (1862–1922), the American humorist, was the author of *A House-Boat on the Styx*.

has to be made in May on account of the mosquitoes and black flies holding conventions there regularly by the first of June.

Father Crane was quite ill for three days the past week, but plans on getting out for a walk today. I know of no further news.

Write me often and I will answer promptly.

With love./ Your father,

To Grace Hart Curtis

Patterson, Thursday
[April 28, 1927] [1]

TLS, 1 p.

Dearest Grace:

By this time, even though I have of course not heard, you must have received the judge's verdict: and whatever it is, I hope you will go out to Chicago with Blanche and Frank for a couple of weeks—hop on the train as soon as you can pack, and let Cleveland go hang for awhile. You probably didn't miss anything by failing to arrive before the great ball refered to in your letter, in fact I imagine the less pretentiously social the visit is—the better you will enjoy it.

The clipping you enclosed from the News was actually not as bad as I feared it might be. It seems worse to you than it would naturally seem to others—especially in view of the fact that both News and Press are generally recognized as very sensational papers of dubious honesty. At least nothing was said about 'dope'—by which I take it that no such fool accusations came up in court. They certainly would have been liable for a charge of slander and libel if they had dared to bring it up. You must write me a few details—such as whether or not Edna's testimony was offered—what Curtis based his main charge on, etc. But don't bother to do this now. Get your mind off the whole affair as much as possible—and as I said, slip off to Chicago for awhile.

[1] Hart's reference to his father's letter suggests that he wrote this on the last Thursday in April.

A nice letter from CA came along with yours of yesterday. I can scarcely believe that he has so revived his interest in me. The skies are again blue today, after several gloomy days of unbelievable cold and rain. We all ought to be thankful that we're not living beside the Mississippi! I am glad to hear that Grandma is keeping up so well. Give her my love. And Margaret, too. As I mentioned before, I am planning on a visit from you here—whenever you feel like coming. I'm pretty sure to have the whole house to myself all summer—an unexpected delight—and the peace and quiet would be very good for you.

The woods are full of shad-blows and the lovliest cowslips! Mrs. Turner has been cooking me bushels of fresh dandelion greens! Write soon.

Love ever,/ Hart

From Clarence Arthur Crane

[Cleveland]
April 30, 1927.

TLC, 1 p.

Mr. Harold Crane,
Patterson, N.Y.

My dear Harold:

I have your letter of April 28, and I am just dropping you a hurried note this morning to tell you we have not yet shipped your boxes and you need not look for them until next Thursday. Moving the Hanna restaurant has kept our truck busily employed and, for that reason, they have not gotten out to the house as I asked them to do over a week ago. I know you are worried over their non-arrival, and that they may have gone to Patterson, N.J., but such is not the case.

Father Crane is improving and I took him for a short ride on Thursday.

I have heard nothing more from your mother's case, and I suppose she will write you when she knows about it.

I am expecting to hear very shortly that my people are ready to visit the mine, and I shall go along with them whenever it is.

I will write you at greater length in a few days.

With love./ Your father,

To Elizabeth Belden Hart

[Postmarked April 30, 1927] [1]
Patterson—
Saturday

POSTCARD

Dear Grandma:

So glad to hear about Grace's victory I could whoop for joy! This is just a little whoop to tell you I'll do better & write you a letter soon. "Everybody" is up here this weekend and the country is beautiful.

Love/ Hart

To Grace Hart Crane [1]

Patterson
Saturday
[April 30, 1927?]

TLS, 1 p.

Dearest Grace:

Your telegram—and the letter following—have made me fairly whoop for joy! And I am *so* glad that you started off for Chicago at once. It was just the thing for you to do. With such a decision as

---

[1] The postcard, from the Cleveland Museum of Art, has a picture of a Buddhist triptych on the obverse.

---

[1] Even though she was not legally divorced until July, 1927, Hart's mother resumed using the name Grace Hart Crane after the trial.

you have received—you certainly can hold your head in as fair a way as you ever have—and I think you are fairly certain to get as much as 150 per month. Payer *is* alright, isn't he? I think I shall write him a little note sometime soon.

I had just written you quite a little letter before getting your telegram. I suppose it has been forwarded to you. There isn't much more news, excepting that the Tates have decided, after all, to come up during June and July, and so that sort of puts an end to our little plans for visiting here *then*. But August and Sept are equally lovely,—so we'll see.

I'm sure you are having a good time by now—and the lovely attentions of the Ross's will go a long way toward making you smile again. Write me soon.

Love always,/ Hart

From Clarence Arthur Crane

Cleveland, Ohio
May 3, 1927.

TLS, 2 pp.
LETTERHEAD: CRANE CHOCOLATE COMPANY

Mr. Harold Crane,
Putnam County, R.F.D.,
Patterson, N.Y.

My dear Harold:

Yesterday the truck brought down the two cases from the house. I am on the point of sending them to you; however, there is a new star up in the horizon. For a long time I have thought of a road house as another link in the Crane stores, and I have lately been negotiating for the Old Tavern at Welchfield, Ohio, which is on the beautiful, paved highway exactly one-half way between Youngstown and Cleveland, twelve miles from Chagrin Falls, and located on the top of one of the most picturesque hills in the Berkshires of Ohio. This tavern is very old—more than one hundred years. Your grand-

Form 29 3M 1/27

THE CRANE CHOCOLATE COMPANY
522 EAGLE AVENUE

CLEVELAND, OHIO **May 3, 1927.**

IN REPLY PLEASE REFER TO

Mr. Harold Crane,
Putnam County, R. F. D.,
Patterson, N. Y.

My dear Harold:

   Yesterday the truck brought down the two cases from
the house. I am on the point of sending them to you; however, there
is a new star up in the horizon. For a long time I have thought of
a road house as another link in the Crane stores, and I have lately
been negotiating for the Old Tavern at Welchfield, Ohio, which is on
the beautiful, paved highway exactly one-half way between Youngstown
and Cleveland, twelve miles from Chagrin Falls, and located on the top
of one of the most picturesque hills in the Berkshires of Ohio. This
tavern is very old - more than one hundred years. Your grandfather
and grandmother attended dances there before they were married. During
the past two years it has been put in very good shape by a new owner,
and if one wants an old tavern I have never seen a better one. Surrounding it are sixteen acres of splendid land, part of it in fruit. The
frontage is small, about the size of the Nelson place, if you can
remember back that far. The through buses from Cleveland and Pittsburgh
pass the tavern every half hour, and I am almost inclined to close the
deal. There are fifteen rooms, which probably would not be in great
demand, but it is a marvelous place for you to live and if I buy it
I am going to ask you to come back and make that your home. You can
earn your board and keep in any number of ways. Be assured of a jolly
life, with woods and acres to roam in and write all the poetry you want.
We would take Sing there for his home, provide him with a wife and
insist on a family. I would not give up a Cleveland room, but would
expect to spend most of the time there myself.

   The tavern can be made as beautiful as one wishes. The
frontage is at least four hundred feet and, I suppose, sets back from
the road fully two hundred and fifty feet. We shall have as fine
chicken dinners as is possible to produce and bid for the high class
business in this section of the country. There are many things to
be worked out, but it looks to me as though I were going to do it.

   I can think of no reason why you would not think this an
admirable place for you. Ed Morgan went out with me yesterday and
then walked three and one-half miles over the hills to his home in
Hiram. You are not much interested in stores, but this might be
something your father could leave you that you would appreciate.

   I would not ask you to do the cooking or to milk the cow,
but you would probably have to earn your board and keep by attending
to certain duties. Among them we are going to have the best barbecue
that was ever built.

"In All the World No Sweets Like These"

First page of letter of May 3, 1927,
from Clarence Arthur Crane to Hart Crane

father and grandmother attended dances there before they were married. During the past two years it has been put in very good shape by a new owner, and if one wants an old tavern I have never seen a better one. Surrounding it are sixteen acres of splendid land, part of it in fruit. The frontage is small, about the size of the Nelson place, if you can remember back that far. The through buses from Cleveland and Pittsburgh pass the tavern every half hour, and I am almost inclined to close the deal. There are fifteen rooms, which probably would not be in great demand, but it is a marvelous place for you to live and if I buy it I am going to ask you to come back and make that your home. You can earn your board and keep in any number of ways. Be assured of a jolly life, with woods and acres to roam in and write all the poetry you want. We would take Sing there for his home, provide him with a wife and insist on a family. I would not give up a Cleveland room, but would expect to spend most of the time there myself.

The tavern can be made as beautiful as one wishes. The frontage is at least four hundred feet and, I suppose, sets back from the road fully two hundred and fifty feet. We shall have as fine chicken dinners as is possible to produce and bid for the high class business in this section of the country. There are many things to be worked out, but it looks to me as though I were going to do it.

I can think of no reason why you would not think this an admirable place for you. Ed Morgan went out with me yesterday and then walked three and one-half miles over the hills to his home in Hiram. You are not much interested in stores, but this might be something your father could leave you that you would appreciate.

I would not ask you to do the cooking or to milk the cow, but you would probably have to earn your board and keep by attending to certain duties. Among them we are going to have the best barbecue that was ever built.

Think this over and write me if you are willing to come out and assume some share of the burden, if I undertake it.

Our work for a year would be in revamping the place inside and out, building huge fireplaces and getting the ground in shape for out door entertainment.

It really seems to me this is the answer to the wearisome days ahead of me, and as we can drive into Cleveland in an hour and a half, and I am an early riser by nature, there is nothing to hinder my carrying on my present business, leaving the office at three or four in the afternoon and really living in the country. It would not have to make a lot of money to satisfy me, and the chances are I will go ahead with it.

Nothing new here; have no news to report.

With love, I am/ Your father,/ C.A.

From Grace Hart Crane

Oak Park, Illinois
Thursday May 5—1927

ALS, 8 pp.
LETTERHEAD: Frank P. Ross/ 531 North East Avenue/ Oak Park,
Illinois

My dear Hart:—

Your two nice letters have been received and they were entirely welcome I assure you—even though I am visiting & supposed to be enjoying life. If I do not its my own fault—as the whole Ross family are kindness itself— But I doubt if any of them or you either, with the conditions both mental & physical that I have to contend with, would be very conscious of anything but *self*—& all of the complications that seem to be present. I think I have *never* been so restless and uncertain of everything—especially myself. One of the worst things that can happen to one I think, is to lose self confidence. That is what I seem to have done—and I just feel like a know nothing in my own estimation most of the time.

The weather is *cold* again & yesterday was more like fall than spring. Blanche's yard is very attractive with the spring flowers and bushes blossoming, and there are a great many different kinds of birds around here, that sing early in the morning. Many more than we have in Cleveland any where Ive been.

I suppose your father will soon be on his way to Canada if he is not already. Gee, it makes me shiver to think of it—it is plenty cool enough for me *here*. I am so pleased over the conditions which seem [to] exist between you and your father, & I really believe the war is over for you two. If you can only keep him from marrying now, & prevent a new state of affairs & complications from arising, from having a wife's whims to cater to & be influenced by.

As for myself—I cannot imagine anything worse than marriage. I feel toward that subject, as I do when I've been made ill by overeating. It nauseates me and I still agree with your poetess friend—"They make me sick, they make me tired." I view all men, at present at least, with entirely new eyes—totally incredulous as to actions or sayings toward women. I certainly have not an illusion left in that respect, but I must not show it I suppose—but go on listening & pretending to believe the *darlings!*

No, there was no audible mention made of any dope business on the witness stand. In fact Chas. side of the testimony was *very weak,* & mine none too strong—as it struck me, & in fact the judge looked most of the time as if he wondered what it was all about, or why we were taking up his time. Really I never felt so chagrined & thoroughly ashamed of myself as I did that day. All so silly & childish for grownups. If there was any mention in Chas. written petition about "dope", Im sure the judge must have been convinced it was not true—for I certainly didn't look it or act it.

Chas. grounds he claimed were "Gross Neglect & Extreme Cruelty". When I told Byron Madden that he said, "The old——— he ought to be hit over the bean." Those were also my grounds you remember.

I feel pretty much ashamed of the newspaper clipping I sent you —but in a way I suppose you couldn't blame them. We fooled around all day trying to make a case. I suppose they were in a hurry to get away and couldn't wait any longer.

I am still in doubt as to the amount of alimony the judge has decided upon—altho I left word with Miss Brown to forward the news to me here. Margaret writes that she has seen nothing more in the paper nor heard anything. I wish I knew. He didn't pay last month's alimony either. I am afraid I shall have difficulty in collecting the monthly payments—for he has shown privately to me where no one could observe him, that he is *mad* & can be mean as can be.

But outwardly & to the world he is the perfect gentleman, bruised and long suffering—*silent*.

Bud was nasty with his testimony—& I had a chance to go back & contradict his statements. Chas's lawyer was not bad at all— In fact he really had not any case at all.

It just seems to me I've written you all of this before—if so please forgive. Im so full of the thought of it & its memories that I don't remember whether I [have] written you my thoughts or not.

I hope you will send grandmother a telegram for Mother's day, the eighth, on Sunday. I feel just like crying every time I think of her— Although she's been *such* a trial & so difficult *always* for me, & has been responsible for so much trouble, yet I realize she didn't do anything maliciously & she now sits alone in a strange place—so many many hours in which to reflect—& nothing around her to remind her of the long life she's almost ended, except *me,* & you, & what we can bring to her from the world outside, of which she still is so fond. I wish with all my heart that I could see my way clear to put her in a little home again & surround her with the old things that are so familiar & with which she has seen around her for so many many years. I, too, miss my home—& never shall be happy until I can have another, no matter how modest. In fact that is about half what is the matter of me— I *can't get adjusted to this way of living in some one else's house!* You will feel that way too, some day when you grow older. It is my strongest sense of security —a place that is mine to manage & be what I want to within its four walls.

I shall leave here either Sunday or soon after—& probably return by day light as there is a fast train between here & Cleveland & excellent service.

I shall hope & expect to hear from you *often* & what you are doing—

Keep me posted on reviews of your book & everything you write that appears in Magazine's.

Will send Mrs Turners things as soon as I can after I return—It has been too cold for her to need those summer dresses yet.

Loads & loads of love/ from/ Grace—

To   Clarence   Arthur   Crane

Patterson, NY
May 7th, 1927

TLC, 2 pp.

Dear Father:

Your good letter of the third came yesterday, and I have been thinking over your kindness in offering me so pleasant a domicile in the Ohio hills as the tavern plan would seem to present. There is one big bugbear, in my case a permanent one, which you probably didn't think of; and this in addition to a rather temporary but nevertheless important consideration make me feel that it would be inadvisable to adopt the rôle of Ohio innkeeper, especially now.

I am refering to such divers matters as hay fever and 'bridges'. I'm sure I've mentioned more than once that this particular valley out here—for God knows what reason—does, however, as a proven fact furnish me almost complete immunity from that nightmare affliction. It has so happened that for a number of years you haven't seen me under the benign influence of Ohioan pollens during the months of June, July, Sept. & October,—so you probably don't so sharply recollect what a miserable looking critter I become during those twelve or so weeks every year. Cleveland is severe enough, but what those months would mean right out in the hayfields—I dread to contemplate. And, wouldn't those be the most active months of all the year for a hostelry? I'm sure you will see my point and realize as well that I wouldn't be much good to you, either, at such periods. I used to be asked to remain away from the office—often for several days—during my hay-fever period with Corday & Gross. The fact is that I'm unusually susceptible. The altitude and extreme woodedness of these parts are probably what make the difference here.

The other drawback is the urgency of getting my Bridgepoem completed by next fall. It will take all the concentration I can give it to accomplish this. And if I came out behind-hand on it I would disappoint Boni & Liveright, my publisher, very much: he wants it to appear by next spring. So you see how things stand . . . It would be folly for me to add complications, however fine it would be to live in such a lovely place as you describe and be with you. Get the farm though, I think it's a fine idea, and you will get a great deal of pleasure and relaxation out of it. One doesn't lose money often on that kind of real estate, and as for someone good to run it—the range of your acquaintance will probably suggest a number of capable people: Morgan has the necessary personality, as well as Fredericka, and the latter could be completely trusted, I'm sure, to hold her head much better than the average female. Besides, she would be able to make it a homelike place for you. Then I will visit you at some sneeze-less time—like midsummer or late fall—and tell you about all the latest farm improvements in New York and Connecticut!

Grace has gone to Chicago, after winning a complete victory in the court. The judge finally asked her to choose whether or not she wanted a divorce, and at the judge's recommendation, she chose to have one. She's awfully tired, and I hope that the Rosses succeed in cheering her up a little before she returns next week. Details as to alimony had not been settled at her last writing.

There is little news here excepting wonderful weather and continued application to my work. We have ploughed the garden and I am about to plant. It is colder here than around NY and Cleveland, and frost has up to very recently delayed us. I looked for the May check in today's letter. Hope you won't forget it before plunging into the Canadian wilds as I have obligated myself somewhat for oil and other supplies on the pleasant prospect of being solvent. The Tates are definitely decided against coming out here this summer, so that makes it possible for you to comfortably visit me here whenever you feel like it. I wish you would consider it and come!

With much love,

One thing other than his "hay fever" and work on *The Bridge* prevented Hart from returning to Ohio. Hart was, as he wrote to an intimate friend, "in love again" [1]—this time with a sailor (identi-

[1] Quoted from Crane's letter of May 4, 1927, to Wilbur Underwood, in Columbia University collection. Underwood was the only person to whom Hart confided the details of his new relationship.

fied in letters only as "Phoebus Apollo") whom he had met on April 19 in New York City. In the spring and summer of 1927 Hart made many trips to the city in order to meet Phoebus, and these trips (always concealed from his parents) were at least partially responsible for the extensive "obligations" he mentions so frequently in letters to C.A.

From Elizabeth Belden Hart

[Cleveland]
Sunday
May 8, 1927
3, PM.

ALS, 4 pp.

My Dear Boy:

Dinner just served, and with it came your welcome telegram, for which I want to thank you for your loving remembrance of Grandma.

I also rec'd a special Delivery from Grace before I had my breakfast. I think I will send it on to you. I am so grateful for all this, for no one knows how heavily time drags, when I can't go out, or change my environments.

I read, awhile, then sew awhiles & then try writing, and so the days go on, and yet what a blessing it is to be able to do this much — If I only had my hearing wouldn't it be a joy? I never shall cease to be grateful to the Rosses for their kindness to your Mother. It has meant more to her mentally to go there and have this visit with them and change her current of thought, then if they had given her a sum of money, & she stayed at home— She has certainly rec'd much besides their company—besides— I suppose she has told you how Blanche insisted on ordering a dress for her, also paid out otherwise for other things.

I see *you* are having company. I think the Card you sent shows the country you live in, which I'm sure must be beautiful now[.] Today is partly cloudy, and looks if it might rain any minute, &

then clears up. Mother had Margarett get me a lovely plant for today a large Pink Geranium—and some roses for Grandma—and all three of us S.D. letters. She certainly has been thoughtful of us— Grandma feels so proud over her letter[.] She poor soul has no relative to send her anything[.] [1] Margarett has her car repainted looks like new. She has gone out to show it off—now. I have not heard from any of the Cranes since Grace left.

[*Written vertically on the first page:*] I can't hatch up any more news, so will stop & let you tell me some[.]

Love from Grandma

I guess I will not enclose Mothers letter, I like to read it over. She has probably written the things to you—

[*Written vertically on the third page:*] No news yet from Mr Payer —have you? How are your books selling? and how about the Bridge?

To Grace Hart Crane

Patterson, N.Y.
May 9th, 1927 [1]

TLS, 1 p.

Dearest Grace:

   Your second letter from Chicago came yesterday, announcing your return to Cleveland early this week—so maybe this will be on hand at your arrival. By this time—or soon, in any event—you will know what your alimony is to be: then it will be easier to devote your mind to other matters—and to some extent forget all the unpleasant details of the last eight months. I hope you will not think about it any more than you can avoid: bitterness will only warp

---

[1] Mrs. Hart is somewhat confusing here. Margarett (sometimes spelled with one "t") was Margarett Lloyd, whom Mrs. Hart lived with at this time. The occasion for the "lovely plant" was Mother's Day. "Grandma" is Mrs. Keith, who also lived with Margarett Lloyd.

---

[1] Crane's references to Mother's Day indicates that he wrote this letter on May 8, 1927.

your viewpoint and make matters all the harder for you. If you feel like coming east here with me for a visit you'll be very welcome. The Tates are not coming out here, after all—it is now definitely decided.

I have just sent off a little telegram to Grandma with the greetings of the day. I hope she is keeping quite well, and I look forward to seeing her when I come out to Cleveland again in the fall. CA keeps writing me letters about twice a week. He has not gone to Canada yet—and probably won't. In the meanwhile he has almost dragged me into two other different enterprises of his, but I keep fighting shy—and it has so happened that in both cases the propositions finally failed to interest him.

The weather now is gorgeous here. There's a whip-poor-will that sings until about ten every evening. Just now the 'Tate's part' (for a week) is rented to the Vail family—six in all,[2] including two governesses—and Mrs Turner is turning six somersaults every hour trying to feed them, etc. Mrs Vail is one of the Guggenheims, and as soon as her husband gets his book finished up [3] they are going back to their villa on the Riviera—where I'm invited to come and visit them as soon as possible. They are great friends of a number of my friends, and I've known them somewhat before. Give great wine parties at the Brevoort, etc. I'll be glad when they're gone, however, as it is impossible to get any work done with so many about, especially children.

Write me soon, and tell me all the news. Tell Margaret I loved her letter—and will answer as soon as I get a chance. This book of mine has brought more correspondence down on my head than I can ever keep up with. Love to you—and Grandma and Mart/ Hart

[2] The author Laurence Vail, who at this time was married to Peggy Guggenheim.
[3] Vail very possibly was working on his book *Murder! Murder!* (London: P. Davies, 1931) at this time.

From Clarence Arthur Crane

[Cleveland]
May 10, 1927

TLC, 1 p.

Mr. Harold Crane
Putnam County, R.F.D.,
Patterson, N.Y.

My dear Harold:

I have yours of May 7, and note that you have very good reasons for not wanting to join the tribe in the country. Under some circumstances I intend to make an offer for the place in about a week, but I will not be disturbed if I do not get it.

I went up to the tailors this morning and gave him your present address, so I suppose you are soon to have your suit.

It is refreshing to know with what enthusiasm you are entering into your work on your return to the old lady and the cats.[1]

I have been looking for advice relative to the Canadian trip, but as yet have received no word they are ready to go.

I am enclosing you a check to help you along for a little while. With much love, I am/ Your father,

From Elizabeth Belden Hart

[Cleveland]
May 11—27
Wednesday 4–30 Pm—

ALS, 2 pp.

Dear Hart:

I have just got this letter from Grace[1] and she wants me to forward to you—which I know will do you lots of good to see what a

[1] C.A. refers to Mrs. Turner, who kept many cats.

---

[1] Mrs. Hart enclosed a five-page letter from her daughter dated May 10, 1927. It contained news of the Ross family and of the family's kindness to Grace: "I am

nice time she is having—oh it means a great deal to me—much as I wanted to see her come in tonight, as she had planned.

This trip has been her *salvation*— I got such a lovely letter from her Sunday morning. I think I sent it on to you— I cannot think of any thing new about myself or surroundings that is new—but when I see others happy—who have had deep sorrow that makes me happy too. Friends such as the Ross'es have been to her, are the *real* friends—one can rely on—

She went to a PsychoAnalysist and had an interview of an hour to have him tell her what her vocation she was best fitted for, and you see what she says about it—and Blanche paid him $10.00 for it, may be I told you in my Sundays letter. I had so much company that I have forgotten what I did tell you—Now I am waiting for that long letter you promised me— I cant give you much this time for I have to write Mother yet tonight.

We are about through house cleaning[.] Margarett has worked very hard late & early[.] It just looks lovely here now, trees all out, grass green flowers coming up. She got 11 baskets of beautiful pansies, and fixed up a beautiful dish for Mothers room[.] She says tell Hart she appreciated his Post Cards very much, and also to say she hopes you won't get on any more *"Sprees"* & *disgrace* especially with the old ladies[.]

> With our best love—/ Margarett & As ever Grandma

---

beginning to feel better both mentally and physically and they are just the personification of goodness." In addition, Mrs. Crane reported on the results of her recent interview with a psychoanalyst: "I got my physoanalysis report today and I am so thrilled & proud of it, & I believe it is going to be a great help to me in getting into my right work. I have the privilege of consulting with this man at any time for advise or guidance, and if I were here in Chicago he no doubt could get me located, because big business seems to recognize the advantage of people who have been studied, vocationally. He may be of service to me even in Cleveland."

From Clarence Arthur Crane

[Cleveland]
May 19, 1927.

TLC, 2 pp.

Mr. Harold Crane
Patterson, N.Y.

My dear Harold:

I have your letter of May 12, and I am enclosing you a check
which will clean up your obligations.

This is another rainy morning and I hope that you are not having the same weather that we are here. It has rained a little nearly
every day this month, and sunshine would be a very welcome com-
modity in this vicinity.

Things at home are about the same. This morning I am going to
Chagrin Falls to write the checks for two adjoining pieces of property I have lately purchased there instead of at Welchfield, and
where we are going to build the tavern. I believe you will find we
have discovered something quite interesting and the location promises to be a mighty good one. For many reasons we gave up the
Welchfield project. If the old tavern had burned down we would
have had nothing to show for our investment of $17000.00, for the
land represents no value to me. At Chargrin Falls we have purchased in the very heart of the village two lots which give us a dimension of 110 by 120; one very interesting, old house and another
old house which has been made modern by additions. Two sides of
the lot are surrounded by splendid maple trees and now we are
going ahead to build a real edifice in the back of it which will connect the two. I am planning on putting in several rooms in the new
part and to live there permanently when it is completed. This
seems to be the best escape yet suggested for my troubles, and with
a declining wholesale business it is very possible that I can spend
quite a bit of my time out in the village.

Chagrin Falls has had a great impetus, owing to the rapid transit
and 200 foot boulevard from Cleveland being extended to this

point. I am hopeful that it will all materialize and that the tavern will secure a liberal patronage once it is established. Just how soon I start the new building depends entirely on the cost of it, and these estimates should be in by tomorrow or the next day.

I have heard nothing from your mother, so I have no news to report.

Father Crane has not been feeling well for a couple of weeks, but true to form he walks around the house every day and tries to think that his troubles are largely imaginary. Called by another name he would have been a great Christian Scientist.

I hope that you are well and enjoying the springtime as your letter indicates.

With love, I am/ Your father,

From Grace Hart Crane

Cleveland—

May 21—1927

Saturday—A.M.

ALS, 19 pp.

My dearest:—

I've been home since last Monday night, and found your letter and postal here—of course I was very happy to hear from you.

My three weeks away from Cleveland, and spent with Blanche were very beneficial and I look much better for the change. But I am still sitting on the edge on account of no decision by Judge Ewing. I went away thoroughly expecting that in a very few days everything would be fixed up and I would know what I could depend upon from Curtis. It kept me anxious all of the time I was gone, and in fact I returned several days sooner than I would have, just because I wanted to find out what was going on. I've had no alimony from Chas. since March, and won't have until things are settled.

I went to see Payer the other day and he said Ewing had been holding off hoping he could get the other side to agree to a fair settlement as to alimony. He and Payer are very good friends, and I feel they are working for my good—altho Mr Payer said, that at best the amount wouldn't be much.[1] The moral side of it remains as I wrote you before—I can keep him from getting a divorce, or can have one granted me. Mr Payer asked me the other day which I wanted to do—if I wanted to punish him or let him go— I replied that which ever way worked out best financially for me, was the way to decide. He said, "well suppose you just leave it to me". Then he inquired very nicely about you. He is very busy working on a big case, and I suppose is not staying awake nights over my affairs. I suppose there is nothing to do but wait, and I feel pretty certain that it soon will be settled. You spoke once of writing him— I think it *would* be a very nice thing and might help. You certainly know how to write letters that can make one feel good if you care to, & the opposite, too.

As I requested mother to forward you all my letters written to her from Blanche's—there is not much to tell you about my visit. They were wonderfully kind and I enjoyed the latter half of my stay very much. At first I was too upset over matters here to take much notice. They wanted me to go to their physician & be diagnosed but I was afraid of his report, and knowing I've no money for treatments or hospitals, I kept out of it. However I did become convinced of the presence of toxic poison in my system from what cause I'm not sure—but I believe that is the trouble with my leg. So at Blanche's advise, I adopted a few simple rules which I think are helpful. I am taking large quanities of oil for my bowels, drinking quarts of water when I am where I can relieve myself when I need to, drinking two or three glasses of buttermilk, and refraining from meat almost entirely.

I do look & feel better, and if I sleep better I think my nerves would get stronger. The greatest trouble now is that I have no indurance at all—get so exhausted that I would like to lie down on the street or anywhere—& my leg swells terribly at times, even up to my hip. I think it is going to be necessary for me to get to earning something very soon, and I am wondering how I am going to

[1] When the settlement finally was made, Mrs. Crane received $150.00 a month for two years.

stand up under it. I shall have to live elsewhere, as this is costing me too much, and besides its too long a ride on the car. It takes too much time, & too much out of me as it is. I suppose grandmother will have a fit when I leave. She has not been so well—pain in back of neck & eyes very blood shot. I think she's been using her eyes too steadily.

I've neither seen nor heard from C.A. & do not care. I do hope you will not take him seriously in regard to his promises, but will keep right along your line of work & accomplish what you've started & what your friends are expecting you to. You'll have a life of regret if you do otherwise. Youve made a fine beginning—your father has many good qualities and much real talent, but he is so very unreliable in his plans that he is very unsafe to *listen* to, even. I really feel sorry for him. He is getting nothing out of life—doesn't understand himself or anything—just working hard and hitting wild. I really wonder where he will end up. He hasn't any philosophy, no plans, no friends, no love and no hobbies. I've never seen any one like him. I really think you can do more for him today than anyone. You know how to give advise without his discovering that it is advise or that you are questioning his wisdom.

Today is very beautiful—the first real nice day since my return. My room is very charming up here, almost in the very boughs of the trees and overlooking a nice bed of tulips in the back yard. Margaret nearly killed herself cleaning house while I was gone but things certainly do shine. She certainly is *queer* and *most difficult* at times. Her beau, from Chicago, was visiting her when I returned. He went back that night & expects to return for Decoration.

No word from Zell. She was up for the Warren Society but never called up or came near mother. I was glad I was away at that time.

I know it must be beautiful out where you are, and I wish I could spend the summer months out in the country with you. I get so tired in the city, especially Cleveland. I just seem to wilt when I come back here. I think a large part of it is mental—I've been so before the public lately that I shrink from seeing any one I know. Blanche is just determined I spend a couple of months out there

with you, but I am afraid it will be necessary for me to start to earn
something before then.

Hazel had a letter here for me when I returned. She was quite
disgusted with "C.A." that he had not seen her or some of their
good mutual friends while he was in New York last time.

I went down to see Bess the other night after my return, and she
was suffering from one of her spells of jealousy because of my nice
time in Chicago & what was done for me. You know how sarcastic
she can be and she made me feel so uncomfortable I was glad to get
away. It doesn't make any difference how much she apparently
thinks of you you are never exempt from those occasional attacks. I
understand perfectly how C.A. feels about going there. Her mode of
advising & interference is most untactful and disagreeable, to say
the least. One resents it through & through, & certainly has no desire to remain in that liability. I think she could have anything she
wants from C.A. if she just knew how to treat him.

Before I finish this I want to tell you how interested Blanche &
Stella, Verna & Mildred [2] are in your book and the attention or
rather comment it is receiving. Blanche never lost an opportunity to
speak of your work to strangers to me when I was with them. I took
the New Republic with me and that article in there by Waldo
Frank made a big hit with her. You would be surprised how much
reading Blanche does in the more radical publication. She reads the
Nation & the American Mercury—etc. and has a very open mind
on *most* things.

Stella returned from nine months in Italy just a few days previous
to my return home. She is out on her farm in Wheaton, Ill. and I
am sure you would be *greatly* pleased to see how much interested
she is in your success. She said she was so thrilled when she was in
Paris to find one of your poems in the Dial, or else the American
Mercury, she couldn't remember which. She said, "you know they
print only the most select high brow things".

Now I told Blanche I would have you send her an autographed
copy of White Buildings, & *I do hope you will.* They were *so* kind

---

[2] Blanche Ross; her daughters, Verna and Mildred; and Stella Jannotta.

to me, I hope you will do this, & write something besides your name in the book—something like you put in Margaret's.

Verna told me to tell you that they were very proud of you—Both of the girls have splendid minds—especially Mildred. She has very little to say, but that is general [ly] worth listening to. Frank [3] is the typical successful business man—talks nothing but dollars and cents, and is as uneasy as can be when he isn't rushing around after business. I feel sorry for such people but it seems to be inevitable— I will say this for him though, that he does many things and goes places that he doesn't care to, just to please Blanche and the girls.

Well I've written you a long letter and you know now about [4] all there is to know of my situation. I shall expect a long letter from you *soon,* and in the meantime don't let C.A. side track you with any of his overtures for getting you to live with him or be employed by him, and don't count a great deal upon his help— Work & plan independently, and then anything he gives you will be that much extra. I wonder what has become of his Canada plans.

With all my love and wishing I could see you today,/ I am yours devotedly/ Grace.

P.S. One of these days I will send you my physoanalysis "vocation-gram" for you to read & study—but you must not lose it, & please do not keep it long.

To Clarence Arthur Crane

Patterson, N.Y.
May 24, 1927.

TLS, 1 p.

Dear Father:

Dull and cold here: we have now had four days of steady down-pour. I scarcely dare look over the garden, for every thing I planted must have been washed away. And it still continues. I should have

---

[3] Frank Ross.   [4] The word "about" is repeated in the text.

answered your letter sooner, but I've been immersed in the Bridge at which times personal matters are always neglected.

I hope by this time you have secured your property at Chagrin Falls, for it strikes me as even better than the Welchfield plan. It will give you as much as you probably want of the country, going back and forth to the office, and the rest of the time you will have a real home, built exactly as you would wish it, with just enough business in connection with it to make it seem additionally "home-like" to you.

Just yesterday I had a long letter from Grace, the first I have heard from her since her return from Chicago. She certainly has devoted and affectionate friends in the Rosses and seems to have been benefited a great deal by her visit.

I hope to hear that Father Crane is on the mend soon. And though I hear nothing in particular about your state of being—I assume that "no news is good news." I enclose a recent report from The Times regarding the death of your friend Morgenthau. The time[s] seems a little ironical in it's report regarding the strict purity of the Mirror candies at one time.[1]

I can't help including some rhymes coined recently by a number of us at a cider party.[2] They might be called "Sweeney's Answers to the Sphinx."

> *Did you ever see Amanda Swope*
> *Riding in a calliope—*
> *Eating iced cantalope?*
> . . . . Nope
>
> *Did you ever see old England's Queen*
> *All dressed up in bombazine—*
> *Riding in her limousine?*
> . . . . Nope
>
> *Haven't you seen Edwardus Rex*
> *Wearing his new gold-rimmed specs—*

[1] Menge L. Morgentheau, president of the Mirror Candy Company. The walls of Mr. Morgentheau's stores were lined with mirrors, which reflected both the cleanliness of the store and the purity of the ingredients in his candy.

[2] It was actually Malcolm Cowley who wrote these lines. See *Voyager*, Notes, p. 496.

Riding into Waco, Tex?
. . . . Nope

Your check came just in time to stave off a suit on account of an old bill for books. Thanks.

With much love,/ Harold.

To Grace Hart Crane

Patterson
May 27th 1927

TLS, 2 pp.

Dear Grace:

We've had four days of continued downpour with such disastrous effects on my garden, newly planted, that I guess I'll have to put new seeds in. There are several brooks and lakes floating around over the bean and corn rows, and I can almost swear there's a geyser or so!

Your long letter was very welcome. It does seem strange that Ewing can't come to some speedier decision about the alimony. I should be glad to write Payer, but about my only excuse for writing him is to thank him for his work for you—and until that is done (which includes alimony, certainly) I don't see what there is to say. It seems as though he should certainly be able to collect what was due you before the proceedings, however, and I should really keep after him a little.

I'm in a considerable stew about money myself. CA's fine promises have already shown their vacancy. The worst was—that on the strength of his word (I certainly thought he wouldn't fail the very first month!) I went ahead and put in a wholesale supply of a number of commodities necessary here, and have been worrying ever since how I was going to pay for them. Meanwhile he has kept me so busy writing him successive excuses first for not going with him here, or managing some new tavern of his there, or what-not—ever since, that I've had no time to settle down to work or anything! DAMN it all!

This next month *must* see something accomplished on the Bridge or I shall be completely discouraged. I have done nothing but insignificant parts since last July, no *major* work has been done since then. And I must have it ready to hand over to my publisher this fall. I've got to clear my head of a lot of things, pleasant and unpleasant, and dig.

I don't know what to tell you about your leg or work or anything. For so much depends on your alimony. If there were something you could work at for awhile, like library work, where you would not have to remain standing for long I should recommend it. But you said you didn't care for that. I want you to come here and visit me later on in the summer when it gets hot and when there are some nice green things to be had from the garden. Meanwhile, can't you make ends meet? While you are here your expenses won't amount to more than ten dollars a week. Please understand me right: you are certainly welcome here at any time. I have the whole house to myself and shall continue to have it—there is a bedroom for you, etc. And the country around here is simply gorgeous. I never saw such profusion of wildflowers. And it is cool here at night throughout the whole year. The best thing in the world for you would be to spend long days of comparative solitude here—away from all the hubbub of life in the city, and in a totally new environment. I think that your nervous feelings are mainly responsible for your swelled leg—disordered nerves generate all kinds of poisons—and you must plan to come here awhile at least some time during the summer.

I am glad that the Rosses are such faithful friends. I wrote and told them so, thanking them for their constancy to you, etc. Also sent them White Buildings with a suitable inscription. I've spent at least twelve dollars worth of presentation copies of that book already, and expect to put in about at least a dozen more before I get through. Please don't think this is any slant at the Ross copy: I was only too glad to do it.

If this letter sounds kinda crabby please don't mind. I'm feeling in fine shape—all too well—but you can't blame me for having a conscience and getting a little upset at times at the slow progress my work seems to be making! And if I don't always answer as promptly as you like, you'll realize, I know, that a letter generally means losing a whole day's work—I don't care how slight it is, or to whom, it demands a completely different adjustment and takes one completely out of one's creative subject matter.

I've heard an amusing bit of gossip lately by people who know— about Bob Wolff's novel and it's results on the family in Cleveland.[1] It seems he caricatured them all, and the result is that they have cut him off from the $200.00 a month allowance he has had for years! His wife, Genevieve Taggard, is publishing a snotty review of White Bldgs in the Literary Supplement of next Sunday's Herald-Tribune,[2] so I hear. Just sold three more poems to the Calendar, London.[3]

Love to Grandma and Margaret, / hugs and kisses, / Hart

From Clarence Arthur Crane

[Cleveland]
May 31, 1927.

TLC, 1 p.

Mr. Harold Crane,
Patterson, N.Y.

My dear Harold:

I received your letter just as I was leaving for Atlantic City. I was down there three days with Hazel, and came home yesterday. Did

[1] Crane probably is referring to Robert L. Wolf's *Springboard* (New York: Albert & Charles Boni, 1927).

[2] "An Imagist in Amber," Genevieve Taggard's review of *White Buildings*, was published in the New York *Herald Tribune*, May 29, 1927, section vii, p. 4. The review was uncomplimentary. "Mr. Crane," Miss Taggard wrote, "is an Imagist in the amber of rich sound. . . . But so far as I can see he has not written a poem. *White Buildings* is made up of fragments that are not a part of each other. . . ." In addition to these comments Miss Taggard rewrote "At Melville's Tomb."

[3] Crane is referring to "National Winter Garden," "Southern Cross," and "Virginia," which were published under the title "Three Songs from the Bridge," in *Calendar*, No. 4 (April–July, 1927), pp. 107–10.

not get much kick out of it, but it was my first time away for pleasure and, maybe, the next time will be more successful.

We have secured our property at Chagrin Falls and as soon as I can get George am going down to watch the corner stone laid. I hope I won't tire of this venture for I must roost somewhere and up to now I have thought it the best of any guess I have been able to make. Anything is most unsatisfactory, so I must be content to go ahead with some plans, hoping that the future will find it reasonably successful. With fair weather they think they will complete the project in about six weeks, so that I imagine around August 1 I will be about ready to move down there and again become a citizen of small town caliber. I have already discovered who the village jester is and he has suggested that I would make a very good mayor. No telling what honors await your father during his reclining and decadent years. You may yet be glad to come home and find him enrobed in honor and distinction.

This is really a good letter for a duffer who cried all the way to town this morning on account of depression, and who is getting away from his desk as soon as he can so he won't have another attack. To me, life is just one big, black cloud but I hope that some day I may emerge from it.

With love./ Your father,

From Clarence Arthur Crane

[Cleveland]
June 6, 1927.

TLC, 2 pp.

Mr. Harold Crane,
Patterson, N.Y.

My dear Harold:
I have your letter written Saturday. It is probably to be expected that I will occasionally have a fit of the blues, for my outlook on

life is not as it was once and something very important has been taken from it.

I gave up the Canadian excursion because it promised a few minor hardships, which I did not feel able to undertake, but I will probably go later.

Enclosed please find my check, and I do not think you have quite gotten my viewpoint regarding the money. I do want to keep you from seeking other employment for such time as you are completing your "Bridge", and the amount which you mention is correct. You told me that you were able to get along on even less than ten dollars a week; I think you stated seven dollars as the amount you pay the lady. When you came home I gave you a good setting out for clothes; paid your expenses, etc., and for that reason I thought you were not in need of money and sent you no more for the month of May. Had I not done these other things, putting you in complete order, I would have done differently, but during the month of May I think I gave you considerably more than the hundred dollars. I do not want you to be financially embarrassed, and do not want you to think that your father is stingy; I only thought I had more than made up the difference in the other things and sent you home in good shape to care for everything.

You do not have to borrow money from your father. As long as I have any I shall be glad to see that you are provided for, and your idea of giving your mother a little diversion by living with you is not out of line at all. So let your mind rest easy regarding this matter for the time being, and I will do the needful.

I am enclosing a copy of an article which appeared in The Press Saturday night.[1] If you have not already had it I think you will read it with a great deal of interest.

This week we shall complete making the excavation for the cellar at Chagrin Falls, and from now on I think our property will show

[1] The article Clarence Crane enclosed was a review of *White Buildings* that appeared in the Cleveland *Press* on June 4, 1927, p. 6. The article, entitled:

"HART CRANE BON-BONS ARE ACCLAIMED
They're in Verse You May Think a Bit Obscure;
Fine Book of them is Newly Published"

was written by George Davis, whom Crane had met when he worked for the Cleveland *Plain Dealer*.

progress. It is hardly likely we will open it before the first of September, but there is every reason to believe that it will, in time, pay the interest on the investment and, perhaps, provide me with a diversion and a roof over my head when other things may have failed. Most anything which gives my mind employment and the semblance of a thrill is worth the price these days.

All are usually well here. My father has started to make over the flat where we have been living, and when you are again in Cleveland I presume I will have no abode in the city.

I do not believe I have seen anyone lately in whom you would be interested.

With much love, I am/ Your father,

In early June, 1927, Mrs. Hart became seriously ill and required the services of a nurse. Grace wrote a letter to her son, which is now lost, telling him just how grave his grandmother's condition was. Hart replied immediately with the following two letters.

To Grace Hart Crane

Patterson
June 7th, 1927

TLS, 1 p.

Dearest Grace:

Your letter announcing the moving came yesterday.[1] I am glad to hear that you have found such a comfortable place at so reasonable a price. And it's good that you didn't try to get out any furniture of your own at this time. Although I don't know the details of your difficulties with Margaret I myself felt that she gave one a feeling of strain—and it will be a relief to you, I'm sure, to escape that.

There is little news here. I have written a letter to CA which ought to be fairly decisive. My patience is worn thin with such con-

---

[1] Mrs. Crane and her mother moved into an apartment on Superior Road.

duct; and I have finally written asking him for at least a loan—
since he, by insincere promises, has succeeded in getting me so
deeply in debt as I am at present.

I am having the usual June attack of hay-fever, a little severer
than I expected in this usually-favorable district. Otherwise am in
good enough shape. As your alimony will not be settled until July I
take it that you will not visit me here until sometime later, but I
am still planning on a visit from you at least by August. I have not
yet received Grandma's latter, mentioned in your last, but it will
probably come in today's mail—which takes this along to you.

Give her my love, and also please give my best regards to Mrs
Archer,[2] who, I'm so glad to hear, is with you.

Love always,/ Hart

To Grace Hart Crane

[Patterson, New York]
[June 7, 1927?]
Saturday

TLS, 2 pp.

Dear Grace:

I write two notes—because I want you to be able to read the
other one to Grandma without frightening her. I recognize from
your letter how serious things are.

This is terrible for you—I realize how you feel. And I wish I
could write more at once, but the mail-man is due. Now don't lose
these directions the way you seem to have lost them before. If you
do—remember C.A. has them—and you can phone him for them.
You can reach me directly by telephone—long distance—Call
PAWLING (N.Y.) 40-F, Ring-2. The phone is right in our house.
Otherwise wire me at Patterson, care of J. J. Kessler—who will
phone me message from town.

Your checks came, and I turned them in to the bank, which I
would not have done had I known that you had not at the time of

---

[2] Mrs. Hart's nurse.

sending them already received the ones I sent. From your long silence on the subject I supposed that you chose to ignore my gift, or had some objections to it—I'll explain more about the matter later. Of course it was lovely of you to send me the money. And I want you to *use* my checks—even though they practically offset each other. In the true sense however, they aren't self cancelling, *are* they?

I am very much moved by the state of things—and you must believe that I am ready to do anything I can. Don't let [it] blind you with its weight and shock, however, to the rest of your life and the many thoughts and experiences that it can hold for you. You have the Hart courage and beauty of attitude—which that marvelous Mother of both of us has to such a great degree. The victory of life is love, I know it more each year.

Do write me oftener!

All my love—/ Hart

To Clarence Arthur Crane

Patterson, New York
June 9th, 1927

TLS, 1 p.

Dear Father:

Your good letter with check came yesterday. I'm certainly relieved to know that I can now meet my obligations and continue the Bridge with a free mind and imagination. You certainly have my enthusiastic gratitude for your loyalty and the general attitude you have toward my work. I venture to predict that you will not be disappointed in the final results.

Thanks for sending the Press clipping. It *was* amusing! I met the writer, Davis, years ago when I was working on the P.D. He is still hired, I see, to represent whatever "highbrow" tendencies the Press dares express.

I'm having a much severer tussel with hayfever than I expected. As one grows older it seems to get worse,—or perhaps it's bad this

year on account of my recent long siege of it on the Isle of Pines.
I've heard it said that if you can escape a season or so of hayfever
via the sea or pine woods the membranes heal sufficiently to practically cure one from future susceptibility. But this experiment remains in the future for me.

I'm glad to hear that ground has been broken at the Crane's
Nest. This isn't a particularly good name for the Chagrin Falls
property—but I think you should christen it with some sort of poetical appellation. I'll scratch my head a little longer over the matter, and maybe come forward with a better name.

The blue suit, I forgot to mention in my last letter, arrived in
good shape and fits me perfectly. What's-his-name was so slow in
sending it that I began to think he'd forgotten the order. Could you
have a few pounds of either hard or soft candy sent to me? The old
woman is pining for a taste and pesters me continually. Her daughter and son-in-law are now here from Florida and they all have
sweet tooths.

Do write me soon. And give my best to that prodigy of dogdom,
Sing!

Love always,/ Harold

To Grace Hart Crane and Elizabeth Belden Hart

Patterson
June 14th, 1927

TLS, 1 p.

Dear Grace and Grandma:

It has been good to hear from you. And I'm so glad you are happily in your nice new rooms—with a sort of home atmosphere
again.

The news about the Halle job certainly sounds good.[1] I can think
of nothing more likely to please you, Grace, in any line, nor nothing at which you would be more competent. I hope you keep in
touch with them about it, for it's a splendid chance.

---

[1] For a short time Grace considered the possibility of taking a job at the Halle
Brothers department store.

I'm writing no more than a word today. I've been in a productive mood—the usual kind of dream state—for several days, and for the first time in a long while am getting some real work done on the Bridge. I know you will understand my mood. I'll write more later when my head is less busy.

CA finally came forward, after a sharp letter from me, and helped me out somewhat. I'm glad at least for that. I have another month, anyway, in which to work without worry.

Bushels of love to you all—/ Hart

From Clarence Arthur Crane

Cleveland, Ohio
June 15, 1927

TLS, 1 p.
LETTERHEAD: CRANE CHOCOLATE COMPANY

Mr. Harold Crane,
Putnam County, R.F.D.
Patterson, N.Y.

My dear Harold:

There is very little to write you of. I have been unusually busy the last few days, for the prevailing reports of our business continue most unsatisfactory, and I have been getting ready for some changes, managers, etc.

We have located a certain lady whom we think will be satisfactory at Chagrin Falls, and while we know little of her real capabilities, her references are most excellent and her personality most unusual.

I am wondering from your letter whether you ever thought we intended to call it Crane's Nest. The name is Canary Cottage; nests get foul so easily.

I will have some candy sent you today.

Sing and the rest of the family are doing well, and that is about all there is to say.

Affectionately,/ Your father/ C.A.

From Grace Hart Crane

13800 Superior Rd—
Suite 5—
Cleveland, O.
June 16—1927

ALS, 4 pp.

Dear Hart:—

Your short letter came yesterday afternoon and we were of course very very glad to hear from you. I do not ask for long letters but frequent ones—if only a few lines. It pleased me to know that you were again beginning to do some work on your book which to *me* seems *so important,* and comes first of all. Was also glad C.A. came across. I never see him, but that is all right. I only am concerned about his treatment of you.

There was a long piece about you in the Press of June 4th—which I missed at the time but later secured 4 copies—thinking to send one to you. However I understand your father sent you one—so will not bother. There was also a short piece in Sunday Plain Dealer by Ted Robinson.[1] *Very good*— I will send it if you say to. Was surprised that he is coming around so to your style—

The weather is bright but cold, & it has affected grandmother unfavorably—the first few days she came over here she was very much keyed up & excited over making her escape from Margaret's into a place where she could move about and not be criticized all the time. She was like a child over Santa Claus— But for two or three days back she has let down & the cool weather has kept her in bed where she is more comfortable & warmer— It will be so nice for her to sit here in this sun parlor & see the lovely trees across the street that are apart of the Rockefeller estate.[2] Our little apartment is just *ideal* for this summer—excepting there is a great deal of noise on the street. Superior Rd is the main artery for traffic between Euclid & the lights & there is a constant stream of auto's day & night— But mother does not mind noise—she likes the sight of activities.

---

[1] Ted Robinson, a Cleveland writer and an acquaintance of Crane's.
[2] This was John D. Rockefeller's large house on Euclid Avenue.

I am having a hard time to write this as my finger is sore & done up in a cloth—

I am glad of a few weeks to rest before going to work— I have not any positive assurance of that position at Halles, but they are regarding me favorably for the position, which is a new one in their plan of things, & I've interviewed them twice. Mr Stockwell [3] who knows both the Halle Bros. *very* well has written them a letter, & I can think of nothing else to do to secure it just now, as they do not intend to innaugerate it until August or Sept. In the meantime I am alert to anything else that seems to look good or have possibilities. I certainly have not overlooked any thing & I feel sure that before many weeks I'll find something. My divorce ought to be granted sometime next month so Payer says—and I am satisfied with what he has secured for me is more than any one else would of under the conditions. Chas is nearly 70 & we were only married 5 months & the court doesn't do much more than grant a divorce in such cases. When it becomes a fact and a matter of court record I will tell you the details and I am sure you will feel like I do that I had a wonderful lawyer & that I should be grateful, indeed, even if it isn't very much— He has asked me not to tell any of this to anyone as it is not yet on file in the courts—but if all goes well by the middle of July *I* will have been granted an absolute divorce from Chas. my former name restored, & a small monthly allowance for two year's— Chas will have court costs & the larger part of my attorneys fees to pay besides. *Tee hee!* Now keep this to yourself[.] Don't tell C.A or anyone—and wait to write Mr Payer, when it becomes a fact. He is tremendously interested in you, & much so in me & my future I believe. My greatest desires now are to see mother through, get out of debt, take care of myself & not be a burden in any way to anyone.

Write often & soon, with much love/ from/ Grace.

Mrs Archer is here & is a great help—

[3] Edward Stockwell of the Guardian Trust Company.

To Grace Hart Crane

Patterson, NY
June 18th, 1927

TLS, 1 p.

Dearest:

I'm enclosing a fragment of the Bridge, part of the River section that I'm working on now, the end of it, in fact, where you suddenly find yourself adrift on the vast flow of the Mississippi. I think it one of the finest things I've written, and I think you will enjoy the epic sweep of the thing—like a great river of time that takes everything and pours it into a great abyss. After this comes a great Indian dance which I wrote on the Island but which is too long for me to take time to copy now. The Dial has taken it.[1] The Brooklyn Bridge dedication is out this month, in the June Dial.

I've been so pleased to hear about the divorce terms, though a little sorry that they could not have covered a longer period than two years. But I'm sure that Payer has done everything possible. I shall write Payer soon and thank him, without revealing any exact knowledge of the terms, or violating your tact.

I am glad that you have a location where you can have a view of trees and some natural scenery. Just now my hay-fever is unexpectedly bad for this locality, and I'd just as soon not have so much 'natural scenery'—nor tall grass either! I am immensely surprized that Ted Robinson should have noticed me. Yes, send the clipping on; and also the notices you have never returned which I left with you on my visit. Please remember them before they get lost! CA sent me the amusing Press clipping. It was a better ad for him than for me, and of that I was genuinely glad. I think his vanity is becoming a little tickled.

I wish you would give Bess, Byron and the rest of the Crane family my best when you see them. I don't get time to write these days, but I often think of them. The same might be said to Grandma.

[1] *The Dial*, LXXXIII (October, 1927), 329–32, published "The Dance" under the title "Powhatan's Daughter."

But all my letters to you—include her too, of course. Can't you make me a visit before the job begins?

Love ever,/ Hart

FROM THE BRIDGE: Section II, Powhatan's Daughter, 3

THE RIVER

You will not hear it as the sea, though stone
Is not more proved by gravity . . . But slow,
As loth to take more tribute—sliding prone
Like one whose eyes were buried long ago

The River, spreading, flows—and spends your dream.
What are you, lost within this tideless spell?
You are your father's father, and the stream—
A liquid theme that floating niggers swell.

Damp tonnage and alluvial march of days—
Nights turbid, vascular with silted shale
And roots surrendered down of moraine clays:
The Mississippi drinks the farthest dale.

O quarrying passion, undertowed sunlight!
The basalt surface drags a jungle grace
Ochreous and lynx-barred in length'ning might;
Patience! and you shall reach the biding place!

Over De Soto's bones the freighted floors
Throb past the City storied of three thrones.
Down two more turns the Mississippi pours
(Anon tall ironsides up from salt lagoons)

And flows within itself, heaps itself free.
All fades but one thin skyline 'round . . Ahead
No embrace opens but the stinging sea;
The River lifts itself from its long bed,

Poised wholly on its dream, a mustard glow
Tortured with history, its one will—flow!
—The passion spreads in wide tongues, choked and slow,
Meeting the Gulf, hosannas silently below.

*

Byron & Bess ought to like this better than my earlier stuff—

From Elizabeth Belden Hart

[Cleveland]
Monday 8 P.M.
June 20/27

ALS, 5 pp.

My Dear Hart.

Just two weeks ago at this hour we were leaving 13732 to come over here, and I can truthfully say it has been a happy change. We never have been so comfortably and beautifully situated [.]

I only wish you could step in now and see for yourself. This lovely sun set and the view from the third story, on top of this hill [.] It is past describing.

It has been so cloudy & cold & rainy for days that we have had to keep fire going in the grate much of the time, but the weather man says we may now expect a decided change & warmer and we are all glad, although we have never for a moment been homesick.

We have wonderful cross ventilation, and our sleeping rooms are so large and cheerful, all outside rooms—so at night we have all the breeze we want, or shut it off [.] Truly we are fortunate for the coming summer at least. Grace says its play to work in this kitchen where she can stand and reach every thing she uses— A back door opens onto a (small porch) which takes all the heat and odor outside.

We rec'd your sweet letter today—and its contents made us very happy. This being Monday, Grace and Mrs Archer have washed and ironed, our table linen, hdkfs, etc, so I told them they would sleep better, to go for a walk, or the movies—which they did, so Grace says Mother you write Hart, and so put in your evening.

When Herrick returns from Paris, for his vacation [,] Cleveland is preparing for a great reception for he and Lindenburgh, but this is no special news.[1] They are doing it every where: He is famous the world over, these days, but there are others, who, though in a more

[1] Myron T. Herrick, the U.S. ambassador to France, had a large estate at Chagrin Falls, Ohio. When Lindbergh did visit Cleveland on August 1, 1927, Herrick was recovering from an operation and could not welcome the aviator.

quiet way, may be as much appreciated along another line in the literary world. Oh my dear boy I would like to express myself and interest in you, but I feel sure you understand me at least.

Every night of my life I offer my earnest prayer for you that you may have health and determination, not to let anything come into your life to side track you from your career [.]

I am feeling perfectly well except one affliction which I have not gotten rid of entirely. It is sure very amazing, but I still have faith that I will be healed of this, also my deafness.

Mrs Archer is certainly a great comfort, and while it costs to keep one extra, yet its not like paying what I did over to Mrs Lloyds [2]— & by putting what little income I have and my pension with what Grace can do—we will be far happier this way & also making a home for Mrs Archer & if she takes up C.S. practice she will make quite a little extra.

I judge from your letter, Grace has told you all about Mr Payer, and I think time will prove it has all been for the best. She is look-ing fine now and every body says the best for years.

She is a very *bright, capable* woman & I think if she has a rest, & an opportunity to do something that she likes will be a great suc-cess.

I had a beautiful large boquet of Roses bro't me today 12 differ-ent colors, you would admire them. Mrs Chamberlain [3] and her Mother bro't them over. They were grown in their own garden. Then from another party one dozen of white Peonias—so I have them beside me as I sit in the sun room. Awful pretty I know you would say.

Now I'm sure you must be tired of reading this long drawn out affair, but just read part today & the rest some other time.

I am going to bed now, and let the folks come when they get ready—

Tuesday, AM—

The girls didn't go to see Lindy but took a Comedy show, which Grace says she laughed her head off—

[2] Mrs. Archer was Mrs. Hart's nurse. Mrs. Margarett Lloyd was the lady with whom Mrs. Hart had lived earlier in the year.
[3] Mrs. Chamberlain was a friend of Mrs. Hart's.

Let us hear as often as you find time to write, and God speed you on road to fame.

Lovingly Grandma

A letter from Zell yesterday, first since Xmas, saying she was coming up soon & bring baby, but awful busy— Mother better, but very frail, could not be left alone. That Helen was *far from well* but they would try & come up very soon—

Quite a nice letter. We just left her alone—she finally has come round very nice— I had no ill feeling—but nevertheless can't quite forget.[4]

To Clarence Arthur Crane

Patterson,
June 21, 1927

TLS, 1 p.

Dear Father:

We have just had a long twenty-four hours of rainfall, and it being Sunday besides, I'm in one of those rather bluish hazes that such conditions usually induce. Besides I'm itching, tickling and sneezing incessantly with the fever, always worst in damp weather. When I get through my present enterprise I'm in for a life on the sea. I'd rather swab decks than keep on swabbing my face all the time!

I don't wonder that business is depressed. For over a month we haven't heard, read, eaten or been permitted to dream anything but airplanes and Lyndberg. After reading a good deal about it I've decided that the world is quite mad. I'm sure it will take months for people to get their eyes out of the sky and their necks uncrooked and back to their stomachs. Time and Space is the myth of the modern world, however, and it's interesting to see how any victory in that field is heralded by the mass of humanity. In a way my

[4] Mrs. Hart and Mrs. Crane had had a minor disagreement with Mrs. Zell Deming early in the year.

Bridge is a manifestation of the same general subject. Maybe I'm just a little jealous of Lindy!

Canary Cottage is a fine name for the Inn, much better than the Nest, which I wasn't particularly enthusiastic about, if you noticed. I'm glad that you've got a line on a good caretaker and hostess. There's no particular news here, either, but I'll write again soon anyway. The old woman is all up in the air with expectancy now that the chocolates are on the way!

With love always,/ Harold

From Clarence Arthur Crane

[Cleveland]
June 29, 1927.

TLC, 1 p.

Mr. Harold Crane,
Putnam County, R.F.D.
Patterson, N.Y.

My dear Harold:

I duly received your letter of June 21, but on inquiry I found out your chocolates have not gone forward yet; I will take care of this today.

Nothing very startling has happened here. Our Chagrin Falls project is moving along very rapidly. I think the carpenters and the plasterers will be out of the building by July 1.

Father Crane is feeling better, and for that reason has been anxious to start with the re-arrangement of the flat. Charley and his wife start in today to pack up our belongings, and while I may sleep at the apartment a few weeks longer, we are going to move our furniture into the front room and give the carpenters full sway. Freddie [1] is going to room outside and Joe [2] is leaving Friday, so

[1] "Freddie" is Fredrica Crane.
[2] "Joe" is the name of a man who worked for Mr. Crane.

when you next return to Cleveland the only lodging I will have to offer you will be at Chagrin Falls.

Our weather has been about the same as yours, but today promises to be of summer heat.

For some reason or another I am having quite a bit of annoyance from Rose fever this year. I have been so free from this malady for the past several years that I thought it had disappeared.

Write me when you have time. / Your father,

From Grace Hart Crane

> 13800 Superior Rd.
> Suite 5—Cleve. O.
> Friday, July 1—1927—

ALS, 3 pp.

My dearest:

It is the hope that this will reach you before you have begun to worry over my long delay in writing, that prompts me to get this off today—because the heat has been so intense that it has been impossible to do any thing for the past three days, other than the absolute necessities [.]

When it is cool & we do not have to open all of these windows & let in this constant traffic noise, this is a very charmingly situated apartment—but the heat & the noise are a very trying combination. I've delayed writing from time to time for one reason or another. Of course housekeeping keeps me a lot busier than I've been for two years, & then the care of mother is quite a task—3 meals aday —baths etc—but just the same we are all enjoying the freedom of our own home again & Mrs Archer is a very great comfort & help in every way.

Today, mother has been almost overcome with the heat several times, & has not left her bed only to go to the bathroom. We have kept ice packs on her head most of the day, & she has slept a good deal—but she has such a terrible fear of death that she just can't let herself relax for fear something will happen & she will slip away. It

is written all over her face, & it seems just terrible to me to have her
have such thoughts at her time in life, under circumstances such as
hers have been for two years & knowing as she *ought* to, that she
never will be herself again—or entirely free from pain— With
every one of her own family, fathers, and her most intimate friends
gone—she looks very badly today, eyes blood shot, & face red &
drawn. It would not shock me if this weather if it continued would
be too much for her to bear— She certainly has enjoyed being over
here in this apartment & having just everything and all she wants of
freedom & food. We are very comfortable, aside from the heat &
noise, but of course there is always something[.]

Last Sunday night I had the Maddens for supper—and called it
Jack's going away party as he left for Canada the next day to be
gone for 8 weeks.[1] He has a job at some summer resort up there beyond Perry Sound, running motor boats for the hotel. We had a delicious supper & they all seemed to enjoy the food & being here.

I am glad you have a writing spell on & that you are really accomplishing something. It [is] the *important* thing with you & has
been delayed, long enough. I bought the Dial with your poem in &
am in love with it. Have read it many times & like it better every
time. That is the test of the quality of your verses— They always
give give give no matter how many times I go to them— I am enjoying the other contributions in the Dial also—Padriac Colum,
Henry McBrides "Modern Art" Malcolm Cowley's article etc— [2] I
wish I had more time to read, but mother always insists upon conversing when I do have a little time. It [is] just a hopeless situation.

I've no invitations or plans for the fourth of July[.] My fourth
will be advanced about 5 or 6 days, when my divorce will become a
reality and my independence a legal fact— At least that is the date
that Mr Payer gives me as the one which my divorce will be
granted & made a court record. I cannot tell you how glad I shall
be to be my old self again—

[1] John Madden was the son of Byron and Bess Madden.
[2] The June, 1927, issue of *The Dial*, Vol. LXXXII, included "To Brooklyn
Bridge," pp. 489–90; Padraic Colum's article on Stendahl, pp. 470–75; Henry
McBride's criticism of Gaston Lachaise, pp. 530–32; and Malcolm Cowley's review of Archibald MacLeish's *Streets in the Moon*, pp. 516–17.

Let us hear from you more at length when you feel that you can write without interference with your work & let me know how you spend the Fourth. Remember to plan your future independent of any help from C.A. You certainly must learn not to count upon his promises—

Lovingly—/ Grace.

To Grace Hart Crane and Elizabeth Belden Hart

Patterson, N.Y.
July 4th, 1927

TLS, 1 p.

Dear Grace and Grandma:

The date carries me back to the Fourth on the Island last summer, when I felt pretty lonely and dejected. I certainly feel a lot better these days, even though I haven't any beer to add to my sorrows (and joys!). It looks as though it were going to be a pretty dry Fourth up here with not only myself but all my friends. No firecrackers—no firewater, not even Crane's ch[o]colates, although after my third mention of it, CA wrote a few days ago that he had sent some on.

I'm especially happy lately on account of having finished up one of the long sections of the Bridge which has been bothering me for a long time, the difficulties seemed unsurmountable. I enclose it for you to read.[1] What I'm trying to do is tell the pioneer experience of our forefathers in terms of the present, and finally via the hobos get back to an entrance into the original world of the American Indian, symbolized by Pocahontas. The hobos are really just "psychological ponies" to carry the reader along without mention of mares and prairie schooners, etc. I think I do it pretty smoothly, so that the reader is really led back to the primal physical body of America (Pocahontas) and finally to the central pulse and artery, the Mississippi. The description of that great river of time is one of the statli-

---

[1] This enclosure, very likely the "Powhatan's Daughter" section of *The Bridge*, is no longer filed with the letter.

est things I've done, I think. Read it carefully, and tell me what you think of it. The introductory speedy vaudeville stuff (what comes before the line beginning "The last bear . . ." is a kind of take-off on [2] all the journalism, advertising, and loud-speaker stuff of the day.

I'm looking forward to a letter from you in the mail that takes this. Miss Gracie hasn't written her son for quite awhile, and I'm wondering what new things she is up to. As for me—I have so little news beyond my day-to-day writing (and I think about little else) that it's no wonder I write you scantily. I'm in a heated spell of brain fever again, and hope I can keep in it for awhile, for that's the way I was during that great month of work last summer down on the island. Which reminds me that you must write Mrs Simpson soon. It's not fair to neglect her kindnesses. She wrote me recently —was awfully poor and tired—and as usual said she could get no answer whatever from you, despite several urgent proposals she had submitted to you.

It's awfully hot in Cleveland, I hear. But around here we still have a comforter on the bed every night. Let me know the new Payer developments, and write soon.

Love always,/ Hart

To Grace Hart Crane and Elizabeth Belden Hart

Patterson, New York
July 8th, '27

TLS, 1 p.

Dear Grace and Grandma:

Just a line to say hello. I have just come in from hoeing my corn and beans. Can't tell you how I revel in having some green things to eat. And it is fun to see them grow from day to day. I eat a great plate of lettuce and radishes twice every day, have lettuce in all stages of maturity so that when one sowing is done I can start in on another. Most of the other things are still quite a ways from bearing

---

[2] The word "on" is repeated in the text.

as we have had such cool weather. But there isn't much that the ordinary gardener has that I haven't planted.

Got a long letter from Kathryn Kenney today. She has been in Paris for some time, and seems to like it very much. She saw my Bridge dedication in the Dial on the Paris newstands and bought it. She says that she meets quite a number of people who are enthusiastic about White Bldgs. I certainly am surprised the way it has impressed the world in general. I only see about half the written notices. It seems there was a long essay by Antonio Marichalar in the recent number of *Revista de Occidente* (Review of the Western World) on my poetry.[1] This review is published in Madrid and is the most authoritative and respected literary and cultural organ in the Spanish speaking world. I had a copy sent them, but I hardly expected such attention as I have apparently received. So it goes,— there was an editorial in The Nation recently in which I was mentioned as one of three or four others who are recons[t]ituting the art of poetry in this country,[2] and Edmund Wilson (a very fastitidious sceptic) recently began his review of the season's poetry in The New Republic by saying: "When one looks back on the poetry of the season, one is aware of only two events which emerge as of the first interest: "The King's Henchman", by Miss Millay, and "White Buildings", by Mr Hart Crane." [3]

I'm glad you liked the Brooklyn Bridge Dedication. And hope you like the Emily Dickinson thing I sent you in The Nation,[4] and especially the recent River section. I guess I haven't been wandering around entirely in the dark all this time. The sincerity of my vision and technique evidently has made an impression. It certainly takes work though, and unflagging self-criticism. I was so glad to get such a good letter from you, and to know how you enjoy your place these days. Also that you and the Maddens are on good terms again.

[1] Antonio Marichalar, "La estética de retroceso y la poesía de Hart Crane," *Revista de Occidente*, XV (February, 1927), 260–63.

[2] Crane is mistaken here. No editorial published in the *Nation* in 1926 or 1927 mentioned him.

[3] Quoted from Wilson's article "The Muses Out of Work," *New Republic*, L (May 11, 1927) 319–21. Other passages in Wilson's article were not as favorable.

[4] "To Emily Dickinson" was published in the *Nation*, CXXIV (June 29, 1927), 718.

I can't help liking them all—the whole family. Give them my best, won't you, when you see them.

continued—How about sending Mrs Turner those dresses now, that you had laid aside for her when I was out with you? Would it be much trouble? And, dear me,—I wish you *would* think to send me back those reviews and notices I send you long, long ago!

Love always, Hart

From Clarence Arthur Crane

Cleveland, Ohio
July 12, 1927.

TLS, 2 pp.
LETTERHEAD: CRANE CHOCOLATE COMPANY

Mr. Harold Crane,
Patterson, N.Y.

My dear Harold:

I received your letter the middle of last week, and the enclosure was, I believe, the best I have ever seen of your work.[1] When I say the best it more nearly approached that low standard which I could understand. Something of this nature, in my humble opinion, would sell better than other things I have seen; it does not leave quite so much to the imagination.

We are progressing nicely as of this morning at Chagrin Falls. The plastering will be finished this week and I think by the first of August I shall be able to move. It is high time that I did so, for the old house has lost all semblance of a home, and the carpenters and plumbers are making it over into a domicile for someone else.

I hope that your troubles may be less acute than mine. I could not help but think this morning as I wandered around in the new

---

[1] Hart had sent his father a copy of "The River."

partitions of that verse of the Rubaiyat, which runs—"It is but a tent where makes [h]is one day's stand." [2]

I am enclosing you [r] check for $50.00, and regarding finances I have this to say. I am not in as good shape for money as I used to be. Things won't be easy for me inside of a year, unless I stumble into something unexpected at the present time. When you were home you told me your expenses were six or seven dollars a week. This $50.00 a month will take care of these things. You are well provided with clothes and you tell me you are receiving some checks from your publishers, so if this $50.00 keeps you writing and does away with the need of your taking up employment in the city, I shall be glad to keep it up indefinitely and give you a chance to show your mettle as a writer. Write and tell me how you feel about it and we will make an adjustment.

Business continues very quiet in the wholesale, but the retail has been helped out this month by two rather good conventions.

Freddie [3] has moved across the road, but comes over for her breakfast.

Sing sleeps with me in the one room in the house that is not upset and is anxiously awaiting the promised vacation at the Falls.

I have neither seen nor heard from your mother since you were in Cleveland, but I suppose you are advised of her welfare.

                    With much love, I am/ Yours truly,/ C.A.

Monetary problems seem at this time to dominate the correspondence of all three members of the family. Mrs. Crane was to receive $150.00 a month alimony for two years, but often her payment would not arrive on schedule. Hart still depended on his monthly "allowance" of $50.00 from his father, yet this sum was insufficient to support his trips to New York City. And C.A. himself hints increasingly in his letters that the profits from his business ventures were not what he had expected them to be.

[2] C.A. misquotes from stanza 45 of the *Rubáiyát of Omar Khayyám*. The line should read: " 'Tis but a Tent where takes his one-day's rest/ A Sultán to the realm of Death addrest."

[3] Fredericka Crane.

Throughout the summer of 1927, while Clarence Crane was preoccupied with the construction of his Chagrin Falls restaurant, Hart and Grace were attempting to formulate some plans for the future. Hart's ideas were numerous: he would find a job in New York City; he would travel to the Isle of Pines, or Martinique, or Mexico, or Spain, or Majorca. By August he had decided that there was little choice but to go to New York and seek an office job. Grace's situation was somewhat more desperate than her son's. She had to plan not only for herself but also for her mother—and she had to plan with no real assurance that her alimony checks would continue.

From Grace Hart Crane

13800 Superior Rd—
Suite 5—
Cleveland O.
July 19—1927—

ALS, 8 pp.

Dearest:—

A Billious attack, work, some unexpected worries etc have deferred my long past due letter to you, being written. The weather has been terribly hot also & its so noisy here I almost lose my mind when we have to have all of the windows open letting in the noise & dust, for the sake of a breeze.

Thursday is your birthday & I have no material gift to send but I *do* send you a great deal of *love* & my *sincerest* wishes for your *success, happiness & health* and a *long useful life*. I am also very happy that I am your mother & that I have a dear son of whom I am so proud & who I know loves me—

I am sending you a box of clothes for Mrs Turner and in it is the rug that your grandmother has finished & lined, every stitch her own. I think it is very beautiful and am pretty sure you will enjoy it tacked up on the wall. Brush it off once in a while & keep the moths out of it— If you should ever leave there I think you would

better send it to me to keep for you for I'm sure that in the years to
come you will prize it very greatly—along with your great grandmothers four poster bed & some other old things that will be yours
when you settle down, in a home of your own. I feel that with the
completion & publishing of the "Bridge" you will want to go
abroad—and sometimes I am inclined to think that once over there
the life will be so much to your liking that you will stay quite con-
tentedly for a long time. So many Americans are over there now—
more every year—& especially the artist type that you will hardly
feel any real separation & still have the romance & beauty that only
those countries can give. I am just *longing* to go myself—but how
can I now?

I received your card yesterday but you did not mention my last
note— The weather is cooler & that helps a lot—

I enjoyed reading about your wonderful press notices and soon I
will write you more along that line. I'm very busy getting the tan-
gles out of mothers & my business & money affairs; things that happened during the past nine months. I wouldn't care to write you
the details—they would make you so mad—especially some of the
things mother let happen— But it is all over & too late to do anything but accept now.

I hear from Bess that C.A. is wretched with hayfever— I never
see him, or in fact anyone. You would might thing I'd had small-
pox, the way people avoid me. But I am getting on top of that too
—and afterwhile I shall either die of exhaustion, or be so tough
from mental struggles that nothing will ever phase me.

My divorce papers are at the Court house signed by both parties
but not by Judge Ewing—Why God only knows—& I went to see
Payer yesterday & he said all was up to the Judge. He no doubt
would when he got ready but might be on his vacation or refused
to be overworked at this time of year—

In the meantime the check from Chas. has not arrived yet this
month and I nearly went wild trying to locate enough money to
pay the rent gas ice etc here. It makes me fearful of the future with
Chas. and while of course I can send him to jail—for "contempt of
Court" if he fails, that is not what I want to do & takes a lot out of
me, besides. However I won't cross that bridge until I have to & I

can't believe he will continue to do this when all papers are signed & he knows as well as *I* do his obligation & the penalty for not fulfilling it.

Mrs Archer is still with me & a big help, altho things are sometimes pretty tense. Your grandmother is still very dominating & often very difficult— She is not happy anywhere & never will be, neither is she grateful or appreciative & I've long ago decided she never will be in this world— I really do not know what to do with her—she is so difficult & completely spoiled. Its my biggest worry & problem. Physically she is much stronger & better—

Well enough of this— Write me a long letter as soon as you can & may your birthday be a very happy satisfactory one—

Devotedly—/ Grace

Tell Mrs Turner Im sorry things are so mussed but they are all clean— The linen robe will looked better when pressed & could be tinted.

Let me know if the shoes fit—there may be more later on.

From Elizabeth Belden Hart

[Cleveland]
Thurs 7:30 PM July 28, 27.

ALS, 5 pp.

My Dear Grandson:

Just as I was going to bed last night Mother says Ill go down to the letter box and see if there is any mail. I sure thought we would hear from Hart to day. She soon came in with your letter, and says here it is.

Well we certainly were glad, and thoroughly enjoyed it, especially your dancing party.

I am glad you like your Rug. It is only just some thing to remember Grandma by— I could do better with another one, but I'm quite satisfied not to try it again. Most too heavy work for hands that have been idle so long.

We are having another hot wave for past two days, but have promise of showers tonight & cooler weather again. A sheet over us last night was unbearable.

Grace has gone out to Randall Tavern, (Painesville) tonight with Mrs Archer's new beau (Grandpa Harmon,) who is taking Sallie & Guy Livingston. You saw him the time you came home Xmas & was invited up to M. J. Mandebaum's to Breakfast.

This Mr Harmon (City Park Director) is quite wealthy, owns a beautiful home on Heights, also a large stock firm in Boston. His wife died about two years ago, but his daughter & Mother keep house for him here on Hts. He is a great big fat fellow, not very attractive, nor very smart, I don't believe, but he seems to be smart enough in a big way—well I started to say Grace invited him with two other friends of Mrs Archers who were here in town from California—to a supper last Sunday night—& this dinner tonight is in return for that I suppose.

He has a Chauffeur and nice Car any way & goes in good shape & Mrs Archer has lost her head as Mother says "Old Fools are the biggest fools"—and gets very much disgusted sometimes— You see Mother has no use for men, only as for some one to take her out once in a while. Her recent experience has cured her for ever trusting to marriage again— She was finally notified to day that she was divorced and once more a free woman— Mr Payer called her to day & told her the judge signed the Bill as long ago as July 7th, but never said a word before. What object he had in keeping it until this time no one knows only he objects to divorces—and their having trouble so soon, probably thought she would only try it again before long. I don't ask her any questions. She only tells me anything when she feels like it, but she has been & is on a terrible mental strain all the time to know what to do about the future. She could not get any position because no one wanted to hire any one who is in the courts. They want some one who they know will stay with them, and has had experience so I don't or can't see what is in future for us— God alone knows. I am trying to be brave and know there will be some way open for us—if Grace could only get rid of some of the resentment & bitterness out of her system, she would have better health & be happier.

Every body is seeking a job, even that Dorothea Lewis. She has had another windfall of thousands come to her, & she is or has been here & applied for the position at Halles that Grace has hoped to get, but I feel sure that something good will come to Grace if she can only hold out, & not get sick. She looks well & eats well but her leg still has spells of swelling, showing that poison is not all out of her system yet.

I am looking for Bess every minute to come over. She told Grace she would come over after supper if she could get away— She had a big disappointment about her vacation. Got started & fairly settled at the Hotel & little Arthur [1] was taken sick & Dr sent them Home fearing he was to have scarlet fever, but he is all over it and romping around as ever—so every body has some trials. Don't they. Oh I must not forget how much I liked your Poem to "Emily Dick[in]son." [2] Grace saw in a magazine who she was—and her history so it was doubly interesting to us— Your last Poems, I don't quite grasp yet, but Mother says she does & likes them.

It was indeed very sweet in Mrs Simpson to remember you on your birthday, bless her dear heart. I feel sorry for her.

Your father has left his apt, at his fathers & gone to the Alcazar to stay until his country home is ready. Mr Crane is very poorly, suffers greatly from his old trouble. Bess says he is very hard to manage— Alice [3] has gone back to her home in New Jersey— I guess we are not the only ones who have trouble, and the worst of it is half of our worry is over things that never happen— Now you must not think that because I wrote you all this is to complain, no! I know we have a great deal to be thankful for and dont think we are snufling & wailing, we are cheerful & full of fun much of the time.

I have sat here and wrote everything I could think of to put in the time waiting for Bess—but I have given her up, so if I don't have time to rewrite this and leave out some that is not necessary, I will try my best to do better next time—

Hope your housekeeper will enjoy the things we sent her. That

---

[1] Arthur Madden, son of Bess and Byron Madden.
[2] "To Emily Dickinson." See Hart's letter of July 8, 1927.
[3] Alice Crane, C.A.'s sister.

white silk dress you will recognize as mine. The girls laughed &
said she may be would use it for a wedding dress. The others I
thought would be good for her around the farm. Too heavy for me
now—

I guess I'll seal this before Mother sees it. She will be ashamed I
wrote such trash—but you will not mind I know. Write often if
only a few words to Mother. It is such a comfort to her to know you
are thinking of her. She says I don't expect him to write much—

She would like to see your garden [.]

With love now as ever/ Grandma.

From Clarence Arthur Crane

Cleveland, Ohio
August 6, 1927.

TLS, 2 pp.
LETTERHEAD: CRANE CHOCOLATE COMPANY

Mr. Harold Crane,
Patterson, N.Y.

My dear Harold:

I think I have not replied to your last good letter which was received here on July 20. It found me in the midst of moving to Chagrin Falls and the peak-load of work at the new place. I have devoted every day for the past month trying to get things straightened
out there. The carpenters have left and now the painters,
electricians and plumbers are having their innings. I think by the
end of this week we will be rid of nearly all of them, and then find
time to straighten things up. I am trying to get it all set before September 1 for I shall have to give my time to wholesale after that.

Business has been terrible; the worst I have ever known, and unless we do get something going in the wholesale for the coming of
fall I shall be very much discouraged over that branch of my business. Retail has not been bad in Cleveland, but the outside stores
have been far from good.

We took Sing out into the country a week ago to spend a month with Ed Morgan, and I think he will enjoy it and, perhaps, put on a little weight. The last I heard of him he was checking up all the rabbit holes and had found a convenient spot for his mornings' ablutions.

I am living at the Alcazar and will remain there until the painters are through and there is a chance to set my furniture.

Father and mother were well when I saw them last.

Your mother called up a week ago and said she would enjoy a trip to Chagrin Falls, but I have not yet had the time to do any visiting.

We are still without a hostess for the new place, but I am devoting tomorrow and this afternoon to the job, and have in mind two prospects I intend interviewing.

Hay fever is manifesting itself in this vicinity and while I am not as yet severely distressed with it, there are times when I know on which side of my face the nose is located.

I am enclosing a check which will keep you out of the poor house for a little while, and hope by this time the publishers have done their part to keep the authors working.

Affectionately, your father/ C.A.C.

To Clarence Arthur Crane

Patterson, N.Y.
August 12th, 1927

TL, 1 p. Fragment

Dear Father:

You certainly have had an active summer, all of which has probably been salutary in staving off the blues; but it is too bad that your wholesale business has become so doubtful an issue. I think it can't help but pick up some from now on, however, as we are certainly having a cool time of it here—almost cold—and the worst of the summer heat (which means candy depression) must be over elsewhere as well. Your good letter was certainly welcome, and though it seemed unusually long in coming, I imagined that you were just very busy rather than laid up with any sickness.

You'll feel a lot better, hay fever and all, when you can ring a doorbell that's your own again. I'm glad to hear that the Falls place is so far advanced. I'll bet no details of comfort or good taste are lacking!

Life goes on here pretty evenly and monotonously. I have managed to do a good deal of writing, but not as much of it is on The Bridge as I would have liked to have finished by this time. Difficult is no word to describe the sort of things I'm trying to 'put across' in that poem, and I've been rather too much on a tension of worry lately about a number of things to give it the requisite concentration. Grace and her present pathetic circumstances is one cause and my own arrangements for the coming fall and winter is another. It's obvious that I must get a job in town, and I'm casting-out lines now even—for it generally takes ages to get something definite worked up. I'm not asking for reassurances, but I do hope that I can count on your assistance to the extent of the monthly amount until I can get something on my hook—for otherwise I may not have the necessary carfare to ride in when the time comes for the preliminary interview!

I certainly never fancied that my poems would suffice to keep me 'going' anywhere, but my market returns have certainly been much less for this summer than I had expected. One magazine in England that owed me about $50. has just suspended publication, and it doesn't look as though I'd get anything from them, and I've saturated most of my American market for some months to come, occasionally five or ten dollars will drift in, but not much.

From Clarence Arthur Crane

[Cleveland]
August 17, 1927.

TLC, 2 pp.

Mr. Harold Crane
Patterson, N.Y.

My dear Harold:

I received your long letter yesterday and read it on the way out to Chagrin. It is my belief that in about a week everything will be in readiness to start in with our help. The painters and carpenters have been away, but are coming back again to finish a few days work that is necessary, and it has taken quite a little time to tie in all the loose ends. Yesterday I thought the place looked worse than ever, but I suppose by night it will be straightened up and look more encouraging. Whatever happens to it after it is done, I can truthfully say it has helped me this summer in keeping my mind occupied, which otherwise would have been in a sorry state.

I am sorry to know that your mother is not getting sufficient alimony to care for her needs. I hear nothing from her except what you write me.

Now regarding yourself, which is the paramount issue. I am perfectly willing to continue for an indefinite period the allowance of $50.00 a month. If I understand you correctly this pays for your board and gives you an overage of $20.00 a month. You have, at different times, written me of sales of your articles, but I note from your letter that they are not forth coming as expected. I do not want to say anything more than I have in the past regarding your mode of living, but it is necessary that people earn a livelihood, and if writing will do it then you have chosen a much better vocation than I: If it won't do it, then a job is the right thing to think about. I know you are not interested in things I am doing and so much of my life is now in a ship-wreck I cannot say the example is a good one for you to follow. About all that the Lord can do with my soul when it comes to the final accounting is to say that I worked hard and accomplished little.

I read a very interesting article in the morning paper. J. Ogden Armour died yesterday in London. From the second richest man in the world his fortune dwindled until less than $20000.00 of it remained at the time of his death, but through it all he stood up like a soldier and took his medicine which was dealt out to him.[1] I have not been as brave as that with my calamity, but I have been dealt a bitter blow for some reason or other and if you can avoid those things in life I do not blame you for roaming the wild wood and getting all there is in the broad expanses of nature. However, we are born under a certain star and are probably influenced naturally by conditions not altogether under our control. The great thing in life is to be able to chose the right way; the way that leads to peace and comfort and satisfaction to yourself when you reach the declining years.

I can think of no reason why I cannot keep up the allowance I am giving you, providing it adds to your comfort and helps you do the things you want to do.

I took a room at the Alcazar for about a month. That will be over on the 28th and I hope to be living out at Chagrin Falls by that time and driving in in the mornings at any time that suits my pleasure.

Affectionately,

[1] J. Ogden Armour, heir to the Armour Packing Company fortune, suffered several financial reversals in World War I and lost most of his money. C.A. was perhaps thinking of his own financial troubles when he wrote this paragraph.

From Clarence Arthur Crane

[Cleveland]
September 1, 1927.

TLC, 1 p.

Mr. Harold Crane,
Patterson, Putnam County, N.Y.

My dear Harold:—

Your last letter came duly to hand, and I read it at Chagrin Falls. I am now firmly settled there, and your letters can be addressed to the Canary Cottage at that point.

We are having our opening on Monday, and I wish you were here to see what we have accomplished in the days that I have worked out the problem. It won't be done for a long time, but we have sufficient accomplishments so that it may be opened.

I won't write you a long letter today for I have just run into the office for an hour, and I am going back to fight it out with the plumbers and painters.

I am enclosing you your check, and I hope that things are well with you.

With much love,/ Your father

Hart decided by this time to return to New York and to ask Otto Kahn for another "loan" to enable him to complete *The Bridge*. Kahn responded to his request with assurances that he would be "willing to advance [1] the poet another $500.00, and he offered to help Hart find a job with the Metropolitan Opera Company. Before Hart received the money, however, Grace's plans interfered.

By mid-September Grace decided that she must go immediately

[1] Quoted from Otto H. Kahn's letter of September 19, 1927, to Crane. Kahn continued in his letter: "I shall look around among my friends and acquaintances to ascertain whether any other opening can be found for you."

to California with her mother, where she would be near relatives who lived in Los Angeles. She wrote C.A. asking that he send Hart money so that he might visit her in Cleveland before her departure with her mother. As the next letter shows, C.A. was skeptical; Hart, however, felt he had no alternative but to return for a visit and help his mother pack for California.

From Clarence Arthur Crane

[Cleveland]
September 21, 1927.

TLC, 1 p.

Mr. Harold Crane,
Putnam County,
Patterson, N.Y.

My dear Harold:

This morning I have a letter from your mother, asking if I will furnish the money to have you come home because she expects to go to a far away city very shortly and does not expect to have the opportunity of seeing you again for a long time.

I do not take much stock in this, for her obligation to her mother is such that she could not do this without bringing much criticism upon herself. I think this is simply a case of an idea which will probably disappear as soon as she gives it more sober thought.

However, if she writes you she is positively going and wants to see you, you can act on your own judgment about coming home and I will be glad to pay your fare out and back, if you desire to come.

I think I received a short letter from you last week. I say I think because the days are so crowded with things I have to do in order to get my new venture running smoothly that I do not know much about what is going on around me.

The Chagrin Falls problem is being slowly worked out and is

filled with lot of troubles that are not apparent when you start in on the job.

With much love, I am / Your father,

From Clarence Arthur Crane

[Cleveland]
Sept. 26, 1927.

TLC, 1 p.

Mr. Harold Crane,
c/o Miss M. E. Fitzgerald,
Provincetown Playhouse,
McDougal Street,
New York City, N.Y.

My dear Harold:

I have your letter this morning and note that you really desire to come to Cleveland to see your mother before she departs for her new location.

I am enclosing you [r] check, which will cover your expenses out, and any time you find it convenient I will be glad to see you.

I have not been informed when she expects to go, or whether, but I suppose these are dark secrets that will, in time, be revealed.

With much love. / Your father,

On his return to New York from Cleveland in early October, Crane stayed with Sam Loveman at his old apartment in Brooklyn, which Loveman had taken over. He again contacted Kahn, who agreed to give him $300.00 so that he might travel to Martinique. Grace, however, once more foiled his plans. This time she became alarmed at the thought of her son being so far away when both she and her mother were in ill health. After a short period of indecision, Hart canceled his plans and took a job as a clerk in a small bookstore on 57th Street.

To Clarence Arthur Crane

110 Columbia Heights,
Brooklyn, New York
October 11th, 1927

TLS, 1 p.

Dear Father:

I have just had an interview with Otto Kahn, following his reading of the manuscript of 'The Bridge'. Kahn is very enthusiastic about what I have accomplished and is most anxious that I keep on with the composition without interruption until it is finished. I told him about your willingness to extend me the assistance of the monthly allowance of $50. and he has come forward with an additional $300. which will provide me with the neccesary boat-fare to Martinique for the winter. That is a much pleasanter island than the Isle of Pines and I will also be able to learn French and Spanish there, which will make it possible for me [to] earn my living up here later by translation work.

I know enough about Martinique from people who have recently been there to be sure that the allowance you have been giving me will cover my living costs there. The winter season will insure me against any of the excessive heat that I experienced on the Isle of Pines and I shall be able to get much more accomplished.

I shall probably sail on the 20th (Furness-Bermuda Line) and arrive about 8 days later. Am busy now seeing about my passport. Please let me hear from you soon.

Much love,/ Harold

From Clarence Arthur Crane

[Cleveland]
October 13, 1927.

TLC, 1 p.

Mr. Harold Crane,
110 Columbia Heights,
Brooklyn, N.Y.

My dear Harold:
   I found your letter on the desk at Chagrin Falls last night, on my
return from Cleveland, and I know you are very happy to have this
opportunity to spend the winter in a tropical climate. I hope that
Mr. Kahn will be happy over your accomplishments, and I will be
glad to have you write me often.
   In order that you may have plent[y] of cash to start off with, I
am giving you two month's allowance now and hope to hear from
you frequently when you are established in your winter home.
   There is nothing new to write of. Our trade is dropping off at the
Cottage and probably will continue until winter sets in.
   All the family are well.
                                    With love, I am/ Your father,

From Clarence Arthur Crane

[Cleveland]
October 17, 1927.

TLC, 1 p.

Mr. Harold Crane,
110 Columbia Heights,
Brooklyn, N.Y.

My dear Harold:
   I was very much surprised to receive your letter this morning,
saying that your trip to Martinique has been given up, owing to

news from your mother that she is in very bad health, and while I am not advised as to her ailment or anything that has passed between you, if she is in as bad shape as you say I do not think you should go so far from her.

I am leaving here tomorrow night and will be in New York at the Waldorf-Astoria Thursday morning. You can drop over there at ten or eleven and we can have a chat.[1]

Affectionately, your father

Just when Hart felt trapped by this turn of events, Eleanor Fitzgerald, the business manager of the Provincetown Playhouse, introduced him to Herbert A. Wise, a young stockbroker. Wise had been advised by his doctor to spend six months in California and invited Hart to accompany him as his "secretary and companion." On Thursday, November 17, Hart left by train for the West Coast.

To Grace Hart Crane

110 Columbia Heights,
Brooklyn, NY
Nov. 3rd, 1927

TLS, 2 pp.

Dearest Grace:

My letters recently have been pretty meager, but when you have finished all I have to tell you in this one you will see to a large extent why this has been so. For until circumstances took some more or less definite sort of shape I haven't wanted to say anything about them, for the news is exciting, I warn you, and even though there is *still* some chance of a miscarriage, still I can't suppress it any longer. All this has occupied my mind so completely during the last ten days that I haven't been able to think of much else to write you. So draw in your breath now and hear!

[1] Hart missed this appointment with his father. See his letter of November 10, 1927.

On the fourteenth of this month I am leaving for Pasadena. This was decided yesterday in a final conference with Herbert A Wise, a Wall Street millionaire, who has been ordered by his physician to spend at least six months in Pasadena to recuperate from a nervous breakdown. I am to be his secretary and companion. He is a very cultured man, interested in my work, and is giving me almost complete freedom to pursue my inspiration, though I have been cautioned by his physician and nurse to exercise as sedative an effect on him as possible.

I have been most excited, I assure you, while my probation period has been progressing! Dinners, luncheons and rides with him during as much time as I have been able to spare from my bookshop duties. He has travelled everywhere, and if our friendship proves to be a success there is a possibility of its including such things as travel with him in Europe, etc. On the other hand, if either of us at any time feels that we are getting on each others nerves the understanding has already been established that we can part immeadiately without argument or strain. This includes economic provisions for me, however, which guarantee me a certain amount of independence in the matter. And it is still possible, as I have already said, that I may not go along with him. He must, at all costs, secure a minimum of irritations—and if his physician should recommend it, I might well be left behind. But so far as I can see I am going to see you soon—and under the most amazing circumstances.

Yesterday I saw the pictures of the estate he has rented in Pasadena. It is simply marvellous! A huge bungalow with patio arrangement, every room with private bath and private heating system, etc. It is the winter home of the president of the American Express.

He is taking his car and chauffeur along, as well as his valet and wine cellar. A regular 'establishment', in fact. I certainly shall have every comfort imaginable, probably too much. I have the privilege of ordering a great quantity of books for our reading and I shall have the chance to play all the tennis I've been longing for so long. *But* don't think that I haven't some responsibilities, all the harder because they are indefinite in that I really have a 'patient' on my hands!

Now you have most of the points on the situation. Almost incredible, isn't it? A mutual friend brought us together, I guess you've

heard me speak of 'Fitzi' (Miss Fitzgerald, of the Provincetown Theatre). I shall not say anything about this matter to CA for awhile
yet. It is possible that I may be able to finger my nose at him some
day! He seems to have dropped me completely lately, though he
may have been just too busy to write. Also, please say nothing to
the Harts or anyone else out there until I tell you to. I have had to
use tact—a great deal of it—in this affair, and you must be ready to
observe a certain amount of discretion along with me. I have not
even mentioned that I knew anyone on the West Coast as yet,
though in due time I intend to tell him that my mother is in Los
Angeles. I can't explain now why these points are important, except
that until he understands me better I don't want to introduce any
features into the situation which might complicate matters. On the
other hand, please don't feel the least bit uncomfortable—there will
be no difficulty in my spending a fair amount of time with you. I
shall probably tell him about that side to the situation before we arrive.

Also, remember to be prepared to hear that this has been suddenly called off, in which case I'll wire you. —But I've just had to
tell you! *Ain't we got fun!!!!* I'll be at the above address until 'sailing'.

Love, love and more love!/ Hart

To Clarence Arthur Crane

110 Columbia Hts.,
Brooklyn, NY
November 10th, 1927

TLS, 1 p.

Dear Father:

I was sorry to hear that I had put you out waiting for me when
you were last in New York. I had supposed, however, that you
would be *registered* at the Waldorf, and that I should first get in
touch with you over the telephone. After three efforts—each time
being told that no such name was registered—I concluded that you

simply hadn't come, or else had gone to another hotel. The calls were all made between the hours of 9 and 12 on the announced date of your visit. Perhaps the Desk or the phone girl were to blame. Anyway, I certainly was most sorry to miss you.

As to Mother—she hasn't been seriously ill at any time since leaving Cleveland, but she has been so near the edge of collapse as to cause me concern. I think that California and the kindness of the Harts are doing a great deal for her recently, and I should not now feel the same qualms about removing myself to such a distance from her as Martinique as I did at the time when I reversed my decision and took the book store job instead. Meanwhile events have taken a most unexpected turn, and it looks as though I should be almost within whistling distance of her for a while, at least.

Mr. Herbert A. Wise, a Wall Street broker, has asked me to accompany him to Pasadena for the winter as his private secretary. His interest in literature and the arts in general has led him to choose a person like myself in preference to the professional secretary. And his interest in the work I am doing will permit me a good deal of free time for the completion of my present project. My salary is slight, but with all my living expenses 'prepaid' I'm more likely to profit by these circumstances than by any other opportunities presently offered . . . . We are leaving on the 17th—valet, chauffeur, and whole shebang—and shall go straight through to Los Angeles. He has taken the home of the president of the Am. Express, which, from the pictures, looks like anything but a hovel.

I wrote H[a]zel [1] during my stay at the book store and asked her to drop in some day when she was passing. She didn't get around, but sent some very pleasant couple—friends of hers and yours, whose name slips me; at any rate they were with you at Atlantic City not long ago. They made minute enquiries regarding you, and asked to be remembered when I wrote you. You will probably place them.

If you write before next Tuesday the present address will be good. Otherwise I'll be at 2160 Mar Vista Ave., *Altadena,* Cal.

Love always,/ Harold

[1] Hazel Hasham.

From Clarence Arthur Crane

[Cleveland]
November 14, 1927

TLC, 1 p.

Mr. Harold Crane,
110 Columbia Heights,
Brooklyn, N.Y.

My dear Harold:

Your letter of November 10 was a big surprise to me, and it is certainly very marvelous that you can go to California the way you have outlined it. You will be with your mother, which is another satisfaction, and yet nicely situated I imagine from what you tell me. I hope everything will come out well and I shall look forward to hearing from you after you have arrived and gotten located.

Your letter does not say whether you are motoring through or going by rail. If you do motor I imagine you will be going through Cleveland.

There is nothing more to say except that I am enjoying a cold in my head; otherwise, the same.

With much love. / Your father,

Though at first impressed by Wise's opulent house in Altadena, which Crane characterized in a letter to friends as "all bad furniature and bathrooms," [1] he soon was revolted by the homosexual orgies and alcoholic binges that took place there. In spite of his boasts to friends, the frenetic life that Wise led was too much for him. On March 20, 1928, Hart resigned his position and joined his mother and grandmother in Hollywood.

[1] From Hart's letter of December 15, 1927, to Isidor and Helen Schneider. Quoted in *Voyager*, p. 519.

From Clarence Arthur Crane

[Cleveland]
March 28, 1928.

TLC, 2 pp.

Mr. Harold Crane,
2160 Mar Vista Avenue,
Altadena, California.

My dear Harold:

Your card of March 7 has been on my desk awaiting reply. In the meantime I have been down to New York for a few days, but nothing very important has happened.

We are getting out an entirely new line of chocolates, which has taken much of my time and attention. Your father is now Mr. Cartier, a Frenchman with a gay moustache and several years lopped off his countenance in order to make him more attractive to the buying public.

Mr. Cartier lives in New York. The father whom you have known is residing at Canary Cottage, Chagrin Falls Village. We have at last gotten around to impersonating Doctor Jekyl and Mr. Hyde. You will not be surprised to know that I have a grown family in New York, and chow pups in Chagrin.

The financial situation in business is such that most anything could happen without alarming us greatly. I see that General Motors stock has climbed from a low of twenty-five to a high of two hundred, but your father's stock seems to be hovering around the zero mark.

I had a letter from your mother, in which she indicates she is roaming around among flower beds and enjoying life to the fullest in Hollywood. I hope she won't pick up a bumble bee in her quest for happiness.

Father and mother remain about the same. Sing gives me a welcome whenever I bring home fresh bones, and now and then some stranger knocks at our door and we serve a ham and egg dinner to a traveler.

Your postcard indicates that you have fallen victim to the California climate, and I can easily understand how that could be.

Write me when you have the time, and until I get more money, and have time to roam, my address will be the same.

With love./ Your father,

In the months of April and May, Hart realized more than ever before the unbearable constriction of living with his mother and grandmother. Grace was ill much of the time; his grandmother was near death. By this time there was little money left. Hart had hoped to take a job in the motion picture industry, but even an introduction from Otto Kahn (whom Hart saw briefly when the banker was in Los Angeles) could not get him employment. In addition to these problems, Hart had told his mother that spring of his homosexuality—a revelation that he soon regretted, since it sometimes caused their quarrels. At the end of May, 1928, Hart decided to return to the East. He made his plans stealthily. First he would steal away in the night. Then he would go by train to New Orleans, from which he would take a boat to New York City. "Well," he wrote his aunt Zell Deming from New York, "I carried it through—packing by infinitesimal degrees and labyrinthine subterfuges (it sounds like a comedy, but I was ill and nearly dead for sleep) until on the appointed hour the taxi drove up with darkened lights—and I was on my way—'home'—the only one I ever hope to have—this supposedly cruel city, but certainly better for me than either of my parents." [1] The morning after his departure his mother found only a brief note: "gone East." [2] Grace Hart Crane never saw her son again.

[1] Horton, p. 244.   [2] Horton, p. 243.

To Clarence Arthur Crane

Patterson, New York
June 14th, 1928

TLS, 2 pp.

Dear Father:

It's going on to three weeks since I got back here in the country, and in spite of my sincere fondness for certain features of the Coast I can certainly say that I feel more in my element here in the East. Maybe it's my room—with my desk and my books—or old friends nearby—or the more stimulating mental atmosphere. But at any rate I don't miss the parade of movie actors nor a lot of other artificialities of Hollywood, though for a time I was rather amused by such matters.

I should have stayed on however, according to my announced intention, had I finally felt that there was any opportunity to be of help to Grace. But as the employment situation out there seemed only to grow worse with time and as I didn't above all want to become a burden to the household I decided to go while the going was good—and the remainder of my savings went toward carfare. Living isn't so cheap as it's cracked up to be out there, and though Grace was very generously inclined and urged me to stay I felt that it was taking too big a chance. So when you come down to New York next time perhaps we can get together for an evening.

As it was just as cheap I took a southern route back: across Texas to New Orleans and thence by boat to New York. I had a day in New Orleans and was treated like a senator by some writers on the *Times-Picayune* who had a considerable enthusiasm for my poetry. It's a beautiful old town, full of history and with the kind of mellowness which I prefer to all the boomed-up modernity of Los Angeles and environs. And the boat ride down the delta of the Mississippi (we were from 10 till 5 p.m. completing it) was one of the great days of my life. It was a place I had so often imagined and, as you know, written about in my River section of *The Bridge*. There is something tragically beautiful about the scene, the great, magnificent Father of Waters pouring itself at last into the oblivion of the Gulf!

Then five days on the boat. As I don't seem to get sea-sick any more I was grateful that the meals had been included in my ticket, for I only had $2. and an entirely disproportionate appetite. Although I'm not as keen about New York as I once was, it looked damned good to me. People aren't as indifferent and impersonal there as they are in the west despite all the slogans and catchwords to the contrary. I soon had the carfare to complete my journey out here—and here I've been ever since, thanks to my good credit with the old woman and the famous cat! There seems to be no possibility of finding any kind of work until after election, but at least I can live here at the most utter minimum of cost imaginable. I hope you can help me out a little as you did last summer. It's just a question of your interest in the matter, for I'm not claiming that you necessarily ought to. I hope to have some advance royalties on my new book within a couple of months.

I neglected to mention how much I enjoyed your last letter. You must be getting a lot of real satisfaction out of your country retreat *this* summer, now that it is really a completed article and in all probability running pretty smoothly. Recently I came across the enclosed poem by Guest in a newspaper.[1] I don't know whether or not it tells of *all* the trials of a confectioner or not, but at any rate it certainly suggested that Eddie had recently been sampling some of *Crane's Best*. Which reminds me that I'm sort of candy-hungry these days, as well as the old woman. And I can't help recalling the delicious assortment we received from you last summer.

Please give my best to all the folks including Joe [2]—and do let me hear from you real soon.

With love, as ever—/ Harold

[1] This enclosure is lost.   [2] "Joe" worked for Mr. Crane.

From Clarence Arthur Crane

[Cleveland]
June 18, 1928.

TLC, 3 pp.

Mr. Harold Crane
Putnam County, R.F.D.,
Patterson, N.Y.

My dear Harold:

You surprised me very much with your letter this morning. I had always imagined that California, with its limpid climate, moving picture stars and shady nooks, was an ideal stamping ground for a vagabond. I can't imagine you ever leaving that for the wild country around New York City.

Perhaps you had the same experience that I had. Thirty days at Mr. Hart's palatial residence cured me of ever wanting to live there. Of course, anyone of us would like to be adopted by George Hart and enjoy some of the fruits of his wonderful prosperity. I am not referring to the hospitality, but only to the continual sunshine; the same bird perched on the same spot every morning, singing the same song. In a short space of time I grew weary of such a methodical climate. However, I would imagine with your desire to write, and with your willingness to do so, entertaining a great many privations, that the California climate would appeal.

Your letter is very interesting, and I envy you your many experiences.

I built the Cottage as sort of a sink hole for all my troubles and [to] get away from the methodical humdrum life which has been mine since 1922, when my business began to show depression. It has certainly served its purpose in giving me something else to think of. Every week I find myself getting to the office later, and find much to do to keep pace with the demands the Cottage is making on me. If not too tired I enjoy part of it, but once in a while I feel I shall have to install an elevator to get to my room.

You know I always went to bed very early, and for that reason set eight-thirty for the last minute to get into the dining room. Even with this restriction some of our guests stay on until ten, and after I have looked at every switch and gas socket it is often twelve or twelve-thirty when I get settled in my bed for the night.

As a consequence I am not arising until about eight in the morning, which you know is not my custom, but my whole life was changed when Frances passed on so I am making the best of things as they come along.

Father and mother were down to the Cottage yesterday and told me that Uncle Cassius [1] was advised by his physician to come home immediately, and he will be leaving California in a few days. I suppose he is not as well as he should be and feels that he should be near his daughter, if possible. This may keep Eva from going to Florida to live this winter, as she had intended.

The candy business continues to decline and the store business is not as good as it should be, and falling steadily behind last year.

The Cottage has had an immediate promotion to prosperity and I think we will more than break even the first year, which is quite flattering. Yesterday our receipts were seven hundred dollars, and for one day of the week they are generally surpass any store we have ever built. I have done much to improve it since you were here and shall now call it a completed job, and await developments.

I bought Sing a little sister in November, and I think he has enjoyed life after he got used to having company. He, however, was raised a selfish dog, and it took him quite a little while to like his companion. I think, however, it gradually dawned upon him that his little playmate was a female and at a mature age would probably occupy the same house.

All are usually well here and Joe is still my secretary. I will ask him to prepare a two pound Cartier La France and forward to you today.

Yesterday was Father's Day, so it is opportune that I should enclose a check to help you get settled again in the old home.

Your letter does not indicate what you intend to do, but I suppose you will resume your writing and chop wood for the coming winter. Don't get to thinking that we don't have one. I have burned

[1] Cassius Crane, C.A.'s uncle. Eva was Cassius's daughter.

more coal in the last year than I ever knew was mined, and for a while, from the receipts of the Cottage and the months of zero, it looked as though we would have to burn up the furniture.

You are getting to be a big boy now, so don't go around with your pants unbuttoned, and write your old decrepit father whenever you have a stamp with which to mail it.

With my love, I am

As ever,

Write me how your mother and grand-mother are getting along. Is Mrs. Hart confined to her bed, and do they intend remaining in California indefinitely. You never refer to them in your few letters, and I am commencing to think it is a secret.

Once he had returned to Mrs. Turner's farmhouse in Patterson, Hart did not continue his work on *The Bridge*. Instead he embarked on a steady round of parties in an effort to forget his turbulent California experiences. The country around Patterson was now his only anchorage in the East, so it was not unusual for Hart to entertain thoughts again of owning property there. This time he wrote C.A. asking for a loan to purchase a small farmhouse. Remembering his grandfather's legacy of $5000, which was being held in trust until Mrs. Hart's death, Hart offered it as security for the loan. Though Hart's letter is missing, Clarence Crane's strong refusal has survived.

From Clarence Arthur Crane

[Cleveland]
July 5, 1928.

TLC, 2 pp.

Mr. Harold Crane,
Putnam County, R.F.D.,
Patterson, N.Y.

My dear Harold:

I have your two letters this morning, one of June 30 and the
other of July 3, and am pleased to know that you are enjoying your
surroundings at the old stamping ground, and that everything is
moving on well with you.

On Saturday we buried Uncle Cassius. He was operated on
Wednesday. I went to Ravenna to see him on Friday, but without
being admitted to his room. On Saturday at 11 PM he passed away.
His funeral was well attended by the old timers and some splendid
things were said of his life among the people of Garrettsville.

I am interested in your criticism of the Cartier package. I am
glad that you like it so well. We cannot afford to make it too
Frenchy, but I think we have approached it better than I can
truly appreciate myself, and, if there are one or two loop holes
suggesting that it was made and concocted on Eagle Avenue in
Cleveland, maybe it will be just as well for the package.

Father and Mother Crane are just the same as ever, but my
mother is failing noticeably. Father, of course, was deeply grieved at
Cassius' passing but I think he realizes their time is all measured at
his age and the inevitable must be submitted to.

Now, Harold, your second letter dwelling on the purchase of a
home cannot possibly gain my interest at the present time. There
are many reasons for it. Since 1922 my business has consumed at
least one-half of what I was worth. During the war period we built
a very satisfactory enterprise, but through taxes, falling off of business, mis-judgment in a lot of matters, it is keeping my nose well to
the grind stone now to meet the pressing demands of the present.

Canary Cottage was built as a heart ease for a very strenuous time in my life. It has taken much more money than I anticipated and, of course, is not yet in position to pay any of it back. While we are very much elated at the prospect of doing so, it still is a very great expense to me in the matter of equipping and getting ready for the business we expect later on.

Besides, I question very much the advisability of your investing your anticipated five thousand dollars in that locality. There are always homes for sale. It may not be this one, but one that will amply suffice for your requirements.

When you get your money from the Hart estate you can invest it as you see fit. I surely have little ownership or interest in that treasure.

If you are suffering from hay fever there as badly as you do here, why don't you pick out a place in Michigan where the weather might be more propitious and equally as pleasurable.

I never owned any real estate until I was fifty-one years old. That is not an argument for not doing so; in fact, I think it is a mistake not to own your own home and have a place where your feet are firmly planted on the ground, but I cannot take on anything new as long as I have a sizable mortgage and a bank loan to face every three months.

Our business is nothing to be happy about. We are all hoping that the Cartier Idea may help get us back on the sunny side of the street, but it won't do much but get a beginning this year.

Now I am sorry that I cannot write you more encouragingly regarding your acquiring a home, but this is the first indication I have ever had that you had a tendency toward settling down, and maybe by the time you have fully convinced me that you want to I will be in better shape.

With much love, I am/ Your father,

In mid-July, after one of his more violent parties, Mrs. Turner forced Hart to leave her farmhouse. Crane moved to Eleanor Fitzgerald's house in nearby Gaylordsville, Connecticut, for a few days, and then went to visit Charmion von Wiegand and her husband, Hermann Habicht, at Croton-on-Hudson in New York. Realizing by this time that he would have to find some employment, Hart decided to go to New York City. Another friend came to his aid: Malcolm Cowley offered him the use of his apartment when Crane arrived in the city in early August.

To Clarence Arthur Crane

c/o M. E. Fitzgerald
Gaylordsville, Conn.
July 25th, 1928

TLS, 1 p.

Dear Father:

Thank you for your early answer to my last. I'm sorry that hay fever has bothered you so much this year. But it isn't the roses, for if they had anything to do with it I should have "died the death", as Mrs Hurd used to say, in California. I lived surrounded by them in the Pasadena villa. Which reminds me that I might have missed a good many of this year's sneezes if I hadn't lingered on out there after my boss left—with the vain delusion that I might be of some help to Grace. Just had a letter from him recently from one of the mountain resorts in the Swiss Alps. And at present I haven't a place to lay my head.

I oughtn't to say that, I suppose, for I really have been made perfectly welcome. However, I'm far from comfortable and really don't know where to turn. Mrs Turner decided that she couldn't extend my credit any longer although I had paid her up to the last three weeks and she has never suffered from her trust in me in the past. So here I am at Fitzi's place trying to get a job working on the roads around here as soon as possible, for I haven't enough cash to even get into New York, regardless of what I might find there to do after a canvass of the possibilities. I've never felt quite as humiliated. I can't ask you for anything more, and I'm not. The above is about all the news there is, however, and it might have been better not to have written you at all just now, I don't know.

Love, and all best—/ Harold

From Clarence Arthur Crane

[Cleveland]
July 27, 1928.

TLC, 2 pp.

Mr. Harold Crane,
c/o M. E. Fitzgerald,
Gaylordsville, Conn.

My dear Harold:

I have your letter this morning and note your new address and new conditions.

Now, Harold, it was not more than three or four weeks ago that I sent you fifty dollars and I don't see why you should be in such urgent need of help or should be in arrears with your lady landlord. I know you have to have some money for yourself, but I had been lead to believe always that your necessities in the country were very meager.

Of course you don't know where to turn. You don't seem to have enough of the earnest side of life in your make-up. You and I agree now as never before that your father has made a failure of his life because he has paid too much attention to hard work and not enough to play. I have been too ambitious for things that really did not amount to anything at all, and now when I analyze it all I cannot quite understand why I have been so foolish.

I stood at the bed-side the other day of our good friend Charley Streich. For eleven years Charley has suffered from a condition which he has tried to make better with drugs, and the last year with

Christian Science. He has worked too hard; been on his feet too much, and to the best of my knowledge, has never even seen New York or Chicago, in the devotion to his drug stores.

When they operated last month they found an incurable cancer of the bladder. Charley thinks he is going to get well, but he does not know the truth. Aside from the news of that, I wanted to tell you what he said when I told him that he had unquestionably worked too hard: He said he did not regret it at all; that he had money enough to care for his illness, and something to leave his wife if he did not recover.

It was born in my father to be saving and energetic. All of my younger life he kept me at it until I got the same impression of things. Then as it happened I was not in the maple syrup business and did not have to use the weather as a brake on my ambition, so I kept at it and at it.

Now, I don't want you to do this way, for I have lived to see the folly of it all, but I want you to get it out of your head that you can live in this world and be a good citizen without paying your way in the legal tender of the realm. People may laugh at your jokes; they may regard you as a prodigy; they may occasionally buy a book, but old Elbert Hubbard has it right, and I quote it very often—"Sooner or later your affections are expressed in beef steaks".

You tried to work with your father, but you didn't want to work. You didn't see the sense of it all. Now it happens with you as it does with the young man who just left my office—searching for a job at an inopportune time. The world does not seem to need any-one ver[y] bad, and yet the tried and true employees are, in the main, being protected against conditions.

I think you write well, and unquestionably have better than an average ability for it, but no business is any good unless it pays a dividend and if writing does not pay a dividend then you have to do something else.

You know I would not be very happy to have you hungry, or have you go along and not pay your honest obligations. I am trying my best to do that much, if nothing more.

I am enclosing you another check for fifty dollars, which will help you out of the present calamity, and I urge you to do something to make a living outside of your writing, and to create if you can an interest that will put you on a better footing financially.

I cannot tell you what to do. On that subject my advice has been all wrong for many years. I would have turned from my own business many times in the past seven years could I have done so, but like the shoemaker I must stick to my last and not follow strange Gods during poor times at least.

Now, Harold, write me often how you are and you are doing, and if there is anything I can do to help you I stand ready now and at all times to do so.

Affectionately,/ Your Father

To Clarence Arthur Crane

Croton-on-Hudson
August 2nd, 1928

TLC, 1 p.

Dear Father:

The Habichts (Hermann & Charmien) have been after me all summer to make them a visit so I'm stopping off here at Croton at their lovely place for a day or so on my way into town. The huge barn and stables of the old Horace Greeley estate have been made over into a long, L-shaped or rather U-shaped villa, with an ample court and patio garden within. And I haven't had such good food since I left Pasadena.

Your check alleviated my distress and extreme embarassment. After paying up, I had about $15.00 left, and decided I had better clear out before I repeated any of my obligations. I am going into the City without any prospects whatever, and as my funds won't last very long I shall have to take anything on land or sea that I can grab. Patterson is the only address I can give as I don't know where or with whom I shall bunk. But the old woman will always forward my mail wherever I may be.

Thank you a great deal for the help. Someday I shall have a little place of my own away from all the contention and fret that have beset me so the last three years. Then maybe I can hang up my few pictures, lay down my rug, set my books on a shelf—and know that I can really sit down and concentrate on my work for awhile. I'm tired of having to leave my few possessions scattered in all corners of the western hemisphere. I know, you think I'm just lazy. But there are other sides to the matter which are evidently impossible to make clear. Anyway, I'm grateful for your affection, and maybe I'll someday be able to prove myself less trivial and inconsequential than you think.

With love,/ Harold

To Clarence Arthur Crane

501 East 55th Street,
New York City
c/o Malcolm Cowley
August 14th, 1928

TLS, 1 p.

Dear Father:

Your letter, forwarded from Patterson, reached me yesterday. I have been offered the use of the flat of a friend of mine who is spending the summer in the country, and I'm fortunate enough to have it for several weeks. I've been cooking my own meals and doing my best without the help of a flatiron to keep myself looking spruce, but my shoes are giving out as well as the several small loans that friends have given me—and so far I haven't been able to make any connections with ad. work. I guess I'll have to give that up.

I agree with you completely in what you say about learning a trade; in fact I have wanted to learn some regular trade like typesetting, linotyping, etc. for a long time back. However, connections that pay anything whatever while learning these trades are hard to find out about. And, of course, I need something more than air to live on in the meantime. I'm going to do my best during the next few days to find a job as a plumber's or mechanic's helper. The work is physically heavier than I have been used to for a long time, but I fancy I can make the adjustment in due time. The way things are now I'll consider myself lucky to get anything.

Last week was terrific here in New York, but we got relief Sunday. Now the heat is in full blast again, and I suppose you are also getting some of it out in Cleveland. I'll be at the above address for awhile, at least, and hope I shall hear from you again soon. Did you hear that Joe Smith of Canton recently died?[1] Bess is simply prostrate with greif, so I hear.

Yours, with love,/ Harold

Clarence Crane was so alarmed by Hart's letter of August 14 that he immediately sent his son money to return to Chagrin Falls. Hart, however, decided to remain in New York and was fortunate to find a part-time position in a bookstore.

From Clarence Arthur Crane

CLEVELAND OHIO AUGUST 16 1928

TELEGRAM

HAROLD CRANE
c/o MALCOLM COWLEY
501 EAST FIFTY FIFTH STREET
NEW YORK CITY NY

AM SENDING YOU THE MONEY TO COME HOME AT ONCE / FATHER

[1] A cousin of Crane's.

From Clarence Arthur Crane

[Cleveland]
August 16, 1928.

TLC, 1 p.

Mr. Harold Crane,
c/o Malcolm Cowley,
501 East 55th Street,
New York City, N.Y.

My dear Harold:

I have your letter of August 14. I judge that you are coming to realize that one has to have some money to get along in this world, and that they cannot eternally borrow from their friends and remain in good standing.

Your letter indicates that you are so nearly on your uppers that I am sending you the money to come home and try a job I have for you here. In that way I think you will be well cared for, have enough to eat and a good place to sleep.

I am enclosing [a] check for forty dollars and will expect to see you either Saturday or Sunday morning.

With love./ Your father,

To Clarence Arthur Crane

501 East 55th Street,
New York City
August 19th, 1928

TLS, 1 p.

Dear Father:

I hope you won't blame me for utilizing the check enclosed in your letter for some immediate necessities, without which my first pay day would seem even longer away! I can refund the money to you later. Meanwhile it will seem good to have something definite to do—as well as something definite to eat.

As I wired you, I start in tomorrow. The job isn't much, but it can tide me over to something better. A former Cleveland acquaintance of mine has opened a book store here. He needs to be out a good deal collecting stock, rare editions, etc. and I'm coming in as clerk, besides which I shall have some work to do on his catalogues, make-up, etc. The offer wasn't made until last Friday, else I should have let you know sooner.

This may strike you as a rather poor alternative to your invitation to return to Cleveland, but as there are two or three real possibilities hanging fire here—and of considerable ultimate importance, —I feel that I am justified in staying on the ground. One in particular, the editorship of a magazine, I should hate to risk missing. Thank you a lot though, Father, for your interest and help!

There isn't much other news. I shall be at this same address for probably a month or more, for I might as well save rent as long as I can, especially as I'm not, under the circumstances, imposing in the least on anyone.

With much love,/ Your son,/ Harold

From Clarence Arthur Crane

[Cleveland]
August 21, 1928.

TLC, 1 p.

Mr. Harold Crane,
501 East 55th Street,
New York City, N.Y.

My dear Harold:

I have yours this morning and you should have advised me promptly on receipt of my telegram and letter why you did not come to Cleveland. I have been expecting you every day.

However, if there is agreeable work in sight, that is all right as far as I am concerned. I hope things will turn out as you imagine they will, and shall be pleased to have you write me of your progress.

With love, I am / Your father,

After several weeks at the bookstore, Hart located a temporary position writing copy for the Griffin, Johnson, and Mann advertising firm. Once again with funds, he was able to move from Cowley's apartment to a room at 77 Willow Street in Brooklyn.

It was at his new address that Hart received the following telegram.

From Grace Hart Crane

LOS ANGELES CALIF
SEPT 6 1928

TELEGRAM

MOTHER PASSED AWAY TONIGHT FUNERAL HERE ADVISE LATER / GRACE

According to Philip Horton, Crane's first biographer, Hart "immediately sent her [Grace] telegrams, flowers, and letters of genuine sympathy. Furthermore, knowing that she herself would receive almost nothing from the estate, he wrote his father to persuade him to make some provision for her welfare." [1] Hart's letters to his mother (like all of his correspondence with her after he left California) and his letter to his father have not survived. C.A.'s reply, which is printed below, has; it left Hart unable to communicate with his father for more than a year.

[1] Horton, p. 247.

From Clarence Arthur Crane

Cleveland, Ohio
September 12, 1928.

TLS, 1 p.
LETTERHEAD: CRANE CHOCOLATE COMPANY

Mr. Harold Crane,
77 Willow Street,
Brooklyn, N.Y.

My dear Harold:

I have your letter of September 9, and on my return home from a business trip last Sunday my sister Bessie told me of the passing of Grandmother Hart.

Of course, this had to be expected for she had long since lived out her usefulness, either to herself or to others. I think your mother will be much relieved now that she does not have the responsibility of Grandmother Hart to reckon with.

Now, regarding finances: I appreciate the fact that your mother is having a hard time, but I am not disposed to send her funds for she has all kinds of relatives in Warren who are abundantly able to take care of their own family. Matters with me are not easy at all. I have tried to tell that to you in a frank manner, and your mother's future existence will have to be worked out by herself, without any support or advice from me.

I am glad that you have found work which is more pleasing to you, and will be glad to know of your progress whenever you feel inclined to write.

I am having the hay fever worse this year than for five years past, and will be anything but comfortable until frost.

With love.

Your father,/ C.A.

Most evidence suggests that Hart corresponded with his mother for a short while after Mrs. Hart's funeral.[1] Hoping that her son would return to her in California, Grace told him she was physically incapable of coming East and that she would be unable to sign the papers granting her son his inheritance. When Hart refused her request to return, Mrs. Crane simply stopped writing. Then in mid-October Hart received the following telegram.

From Grace Hart Crane

LOS ANGELES CALIF
1928 OCT 15

TELEGRAM

COME AT ONCE DESPERATELY ILL AT HOME ALONE ONLY YOU CAN HELP ZELL IN NEW YORK ANSWER AT ONCE / GRACE.

Again, Hart refused to leave New York. Instead, he tried to determine from mutual friends in Cleveland if his mother's claim of illness was genuine, and if she actually was incapable of signing the legal papers. All evidence Crane could gather led him to believe his mother was resorting to fiscal and emotional blackmail to force his return.

In the meantime Hart was planning to go to Europe—if he received his inheritance of $5000. By the end of November he was desperate enough to call the Guardian Trust Company (which served as executor for Mrs. Hart's estate) and demand that the legacy be released. But he learned that Grace still had not forwarded the necessary papers. The poet sent his mother a sharp telegram threatening legal action if she did not sign. Grace in turn replied with an equally sharp telegram saying she had signed the papers,

---

[1] Because there are no letters, we are forced to rely on the account Grace Hart Crane gave Philip Horton. See Horton, p. 250.

and threatening "to urge his father to use his influence with the bank against paying him his inheritance on the grounds of his drinking habits."[1] Fully understanding just what his mother could reveal to C.A. about his drinking and sexual predilections, Hart began a desperate flight: first to London, and then in January, 1929, to Paris.

Much has been written of Hart's months in France, and it is not the purpose of this narrative to recount the numerous parties the poet attended or beatings he suffered. Europe gave Hart a chance to "cut all cables"[2] with his family. He would never see Grace again; and he was not to correspond with C.A. until late October, 1929.

The most important event that happened while Crane was in France was not a party or a fight but his introduction to Harry and Caresse Crosby, the owners of the Black Sun Press. Harry Crosby had an enormous sum of money at his disposal and a genuine interest in modern letters. Now Crane's name would be added to the Black Sun Press's distinguished list of authors. And even more important for Crane, the Crosbys would pressure the poet into completing *The Bridge*. Hart went to their country house in early February to work on the "Cape Hatteras" section of the poem. By March 1 he had substantially completed it.

The next four months were spent at parties and on trips to Collioure and Marseilles. By July, Hart decided he must return to New York. After a spectacular fight in the Café Select in Paris and a week's incarceration at La Santé, Hart knew it was time to leave. Several days before his thirtieth birthday, the poet embarked for New York on the *Homeric*.

Before he left Paris, the Crosbys set a deadline of November 1 for receipt of *The Bridge* manuscript. When his boat landed, Crane went directly to Brooklyn, found a room at 130 Columbia Heights, and began what he hoped would be his final work on *The Bridge*. He wrote steadily, finishing first drafts of "Quaker Hill" and "Indiana" and revising the "Cape Hatteras" section. As always, periods of intense work were followed by an equally intensive round of parties. By October 30, in spite of his diligent effort, Hart realized he

---

[1] Horton, pp. 249–50.
[2] Quoted from Crane's letter to William Wright. See *Voyager*, p. 582.

would not make the deadline. He postponed publication until February, 1930.

To add to his depression over his inability to complete the poem on time, Hart learned through a mutual friend of his mother's impending trip East to see him. The news put him into a state of panic. In desperation he placed a long-distance call to Chagrin Falls; even though Hart had not communicated with his father for over a year, Clarence understood immediately that his son was in trouble. "Harold," he said, "come right home." [3]

In Chagrin Falls, Hart again found the security he longed for. C.A. was planning to marry Bessie Meachem, the woman who worked as a hostess at Canary Cottage, and his mood was one of unusual ebullience. Yet the peace and security Hart found in Chagrin Falls was shattered in mid-November with the news that Grace was expected shortly in Cleveland. Fearful of her visit to Canary Cottage, and even more fearful of what she might tell C.A. about him, Hart left immediately for New York. It was probably with no small sense of relief that Hart read the following letter from his father.

From Clarence Arthur Crane

Cleveland, Ohio
November 26, 1929.

TLS, 2 pp.
LETTERHEAD: CRANE CHOCOLATE COMPANY

Mr. Harold Crane,
130 Columbia Heights,
Brooklyn, N.Y.

My dear Harold:

I have your letter this morning and am glad to know that you are well again and the two packages you received you can put to good use.

---

[3] Quoted from Mrs. Bessie M. Hise in an interview with the editor, June, 1972. Mrs. Hise said substantially the same thing to John Unterecker in 1961. See *Voyager*, p. 605. Mrs. Hise, formerly Bessie Meachem, was Clarence Crane's third wife. After his death she married Donald Hise.

I imagine you are very busy with the Crosbys in arranging for the new book, and I hope your week will be full of pleasure.

I have very little to report to you in regard to the other matter, except that the second morning after arrival in Canton she called me on the 'phone and asked me to come there for a conference, which I stoutly refused to do.

Then she asked if I was not interested in her future welfare, and I told her I was not in any particular. That's about all there was to the conversation.

Later Helen called and advised Bess Smith was going to call, but she did not and I am not even aware where Grace is at the present time.

She asked for your address, and I gave it as Patterson, N.Y., thinking to follow out your desire in not having your home molested for the time being, at least.

I think as matters now stand, she without any money whatever, and a liability to her friends, she should submit to an examination and get in better health, both mentally and physically, and I think you are fully justified in signing such papers as would help clear up the atmosphere.

Write me when you can.

With much love, I am/ Your father,/ C.A.

Even though Crane returned to New York to avoid meeting his mother, he did not brood for long over his problems with her. Instead he worked steadily to bring *The Bridge* to completion. The Crosbys visited New York in December and naturally their presence meant more parties; but even these diversions did not deter Hart from his resolve to finish the poem. There was one serious interruption. On December 10, three days before he and his wife were to return to France, Harry Crosby committed suicide. On December 26, Hart was satisfied enough with *The Bridge* to send the final revisions to Caresse Crosby (who had assured him that even her husband's death would not prevent the poem's publication).

Now that *The Bridge* was complete Hart was literally adrift with nothing to do. While waiting for its publication by the Black Sun Press in February, 1930, and by Boni and Liveright in April, Hart spent his time in New York, or Patterson, or with E. E. Cummings in New Hampshire. By this time he had spent his inheritance and could expect only meager support from the sales of his books, yet he was not desperate. He was simply relieved at the thought of having finished his ambitious poem, which had taken nearly seven years to complete.

Since his hasty departure from Chagrin Falls, Grace Crane had not tried to contact her son. After visiting Cleveland and Warren briefly in November, 1929, Mrs. Crane went to her friends the Rosses in Oak Park, Illinois. There she found work at the local hotel. She could not resist the temptation to try again to make peace with Hart. This time she used the occasion of his thirty-first birthday to send what was probably her final letter to him.

From Grace Hart Crane

Oak Park Ill.
July 19—1930

ALS, 3 pp.
LETTERHEAD: The Carleton, Oak Park, Ill.

My dear Hart:—

This is to convey to you my love and congratulations on your birthday. Last year was the first time you ever failed to receive a message from me, and that was because I did not know where to address you, but you were in my thoughts just the same.

This time my congratulations are twofold, because of the publication of your book, "The Bridge". I have been reading it as well as some of the reviews and criticisms. You should be happy, proud, and highly gratified.

It is a fine achievement, beautifully presented, and I trust you are going to continue right along with more of such work. I am intensely interested in your plans and ambitions, and whenever you feel disposed to write me of them, I shall be greatly pleased. You have never answered my last letter written you sometime in May and addressed to Patterson. Well my dear, your heart will change toward me someday I am sure, and in the meantime I can and shall wait.

I hope there has been some sort of a celebration planned for your birthday, and that there will be lots of fun—and many pleasant things to recall.

My love, & best wishes go with this as well as the enclosed small recent photo which I hope you will be pleased to receive.[1]

I am quite well, pleasantly located and reasonably happy—

Affectionately Yours,/ Mother—

Hart refused to reply to his mother's letter.

In early August Hart decided to apply for a Guggenheim fellowship, and he spent most of the month filling out the application form. He was not without prospects of work. *Fortune* magazine commissioned him to write two articles, one on the George Washington Bridge, which was then nearing completion, and the other on J. Walter Teagle, president of the Standard Oil Company. However, Hart found writing prose equally as difficult as writing poetry; he was unable to complete either article.

By mid-December all of Hart's funds were gone, so he decided to return to Chagrin Falls for Christmas. Arriving in the middle of the month and staying until mid-March, Hart spent some of the most peaceful days of his adult life with his father and stepmother. He and C.A. had come to mutually respect each other, and Hart enjoyed the company of his father's new wife, Bessie. When he was not doing odd jobs around the Canary Cottage, Hart visited his Aunt Bess and the Rychtariks in Cleveland.

On March 15, 1931, Hart heard from Henry Allen Moe, the secretary of the Guggenheim Foundation, that he had received a fellowship for the coming year. He returned to New York City and made plans to go to France. However, after talking with Malcolm Cowley, Hart decided he would be wiser to travel to Mexico. C.A.

[1] The enclosure is lost.

was delighted at this decision, for his former office manager in New York, Hazel Hasham, had recently married Arthur Cazes and was now living in Mexico City, where she and her husband operated a candy business.

When he arrived in Mexico City in mid-April, Crane was without funds. Though the Guggenheim grant was for $2000, the money was not given in a lump sum and Crane quickly spent his allowance. Once again in debt, Hart turned to his father.

From Clarence Arthur Crane

Cleveland
May 1, 1931.

TLS, 1 p.
LETTERHEAD: Clarence A. Crane/ Cleveland/ 522 Eagle Avenue

My dear boy:

I have not had a stenographer for several days, so my last two letters to you were rather unsatisfactory notes.

Sending money by wire is a new experience to me. I suppose it can be done very satisfactorily, but I believe it would be expensive to a foreign country, and it occurred to me that in an emergency you might go to Mr. Cages [1] and get quick relief, so I wired you to proceed that way, and I would send check, which I did immediately. However, it might be you were waiting at that hotel for your wire, and I made the mistake to send you a check to the hotel address. I have advised you of that, so that you could call there and get it.

I do not believe I understood just how often your money was coming to you, but you should be very careful of your expenditures so that your receipts and debts will sort of meet, and I did not quite approve of your going to a new acquaintance and borrowing, as you suggested. You know, Harold, more friendships are lost by the intrusion of financial obligations than anything else, and you might have sacraficed the friendship of one who could do you plenty of good if this element were not present.

[1] Arthur Cazes.

I can appreciate the fact that you had the expense of getting to Mexico, but your apartment could wait a little while for embellishment without going to such means of getting it.

I would like to have you write me who this Miss Porter [2] is that you are living with. I sort of believe that she is a New York friend, and perhaps an author. You are starting out in a new country where you say you hope to live, and I hope that your decision will be wise, so that your ambitions may be reached.

We were all very much amused at your letter and enthusiasm, etc., but you must have tripped a little when you said that poverty was respected. There isn't any place in the World that I have ever heard of where we get along without paying our way, but there are sections of the World where it costs less to do that. I would like to have you write me Cage's address or the address of the house. I want to write him and I want to answer Hazel's letter.

There is nothing new to tell you here. The past week has been cold and the cottage has not done very well. Uncle Fred is back from Florida semi-enthusiastic over the country, but I notice he fails every time I meet him. Bess and those at the cottage are all well, and want to be remembered to you.

We opened up our place at Hudson two weeks ago, but the weather has kept it from having many visitors. I suppose you will soon be buckling down to your work, and I hope that the inspirations will come thick and fast. With much love,/ Your father,/ CA

From Clarence Arthur Crane

Cleveland, Ohio
June 2, 1931.

TLS, 1 p.
LETTERHEAD: Clarence A. Crane/ Cleveland/ 522 Eagle Avenue

My dear Harold:

In this morning's mail I have a letter from Hazel telling me that you have entirely recovered from your illness and that a little Amer-

[2] Hart stayed at Katherine Anne Porter's house for two weeks after he arrived in Mexico.

ican cooking has straightened you out again. With your tendency towards indigestion and its far-reaching consequences, you should be very careful with your diet. This really is not hard to do if you only stop to think what you are doing, as I have had to do for many years.

Hazel writes me that she advanced you $50.00 again and I have sent her a check for this. In your previous letter you wrote me that the Guggenheims had given you a drawing account on your next donation and that you felt you could now meet your expenses without further help, so I have written Hazel that she need not advance you more money until she hears from me, for I want you to live within your income now that you are adjusted. This should be very easy to do, as you are in Mexico to work and study and not to entertain.

Matters in a business way do not improve with us; in fact, the stock market yesterday must have been very disappointing to those people who make their living that way. The Van Sweringen issues which were put out at $25.00 and rose to $35.00, were selling yesterday at $4.00. U.S. Steel, which a year ago was around $240.00 a share sold for the lowest point in recent years—$81.00 a share. Of course we shall not have any more candy business until Fall, but if the weather would ever settle, I think our Cottage would do fairly well.

I write you about what I told Hazel so that you would not be embarrassed. I asked her to do this as I really think you don't need it. I know full well that at the expiration of the time the Guggenheims are supplying you with money you will have need of advances from me which are not apparent to you just now.

We are all well and send our love,/ C.A.

Mr. Hart Crane,
15 Michocan,
Mexcoac, D.F.,
Mexico.

To Clarence Arthur Crane

Michoacan 15,
Mixcoac, D.F.
Mexico
June 5th, 1931

TLS, 1 p.

Dear C.A.:

I really owe you answer for two letters. The postcard was about all I could get time for the other day, and regardless of time, there happens to be very little more to report even now—without going far beyond a letter, in fact, clear into a couple of books, in order to describe some of the places, villages, rug factories, museums, etc. that I've been busy visiting. In any case, such descriptions will have to be postponed. It takes a while even to digest it all,—let alone relay it!

Regarding money—I shall economize and make out probably very well from now on—without any outside help. You know how grateful I am to you for seeing me installed here, and ultimately with the accepted indispensibles. I'm feeling very well, am getting well into the language study and my work. And—in a certain way —the less news there is for awhile, the better it really is.

I don't see much of American papers here, so anything about the stock market would surprise me. But I'm sorry to hear that the weather has been so inclement as to keep people away from the Cottage. April & May are always great lotteries, however. But you'll be sure to find more luck in June—and thereafter. You can't lose . . . Don't you remember the "Bright" prediction?

How is Sherlock Holmes these days? From over the wall I occasionally hear American programs from Los Angeles and other stations in California. But by and large, I enjoy my portable Orthophonic and a few symphony records much more. There are some wonderful native Mexican dances, Saints' Day songs, etc. that you would enjoy very much. And situated as I am—I can play them as late at night as I like. That's all to the good of my inspiration, as you may remember my saying.

More anon. Meanwhile send the next letter airmail, like the last. It only took two days en route.

Much love to you, and to all,/ Hart

[*Crane wrote the following note at the top of the page:*]
PS—The enclosed photo was taken on a special occasion, the bard being gifted with a very old and rare solid silver pony bridle, from the period of the Conquest. The shirt and pants are part of my previous wardrobe—a French sailor's outfit—from my days "over there". I don't look very sick however, do I?[1]

From Clarence Arthur Crane

Cleveland, Ohio
June 29, 1931

TLS, 2 pp.
LETTERHEAD: CRANE CHOCOLATE COMPANY

Hart Crane
15 Michocan,
Mixcoac, D.F.
Mexico

My dear Harold:

After a lapse of three weeks, we are very glad to have your letter this morning. It isn't surprizing to me that after a stay of a few months in Mexico that you would find that in this world it isn't all "tit that titters". All of us find out that there are certain illusions that we make and later discover that there are strange conditions in our lives.

We often speak of you at the Cottage. It is wonderful how you are getting along. Drop me a line about once a week.

Friday we had a violent storm that approached a hurricane and did about a million dollars worth of damage in the city and more of that outside. It is the first time in my life that I have ever been stuck on the road. The wind and rain were almost undiscribable.

[1] The enclosure is lost.

I am sorry to hear that Hazel is not feeling her best and that her husband is losing his job. Everywhere you go this same condition prevails.

We had 230 at the Cottage yesterday, but we don't know yet that we are more than breaking even because of the reduced prices. It makes a big difference in the revenue.

I am going ahead with a picture deal which I have thought of myself and it promises very well.[1] Whether or not it will come through remains to be seen.

Tell Hazel that I sympathize with her in any trouble which she is enduring and when she comes north and looks around, I feel, perhaps that the way times are that she would be much more successful with moderate priced chocolates like we have than her old at $1.50 per pound. She can think about this and tell her I would like to talk with her before she does anything definite.

Father spent Sunday with us at the Cottage and while he fails I think he is a wonderful man for 86 years.

Jack [2] was home from college a few days, but has now gone on to the camp, which he is compelled to go to for four weeks. I understand that he is going to put in the summer in Canada with Mr. Ely as usual.

Now try and keep well and when you are through with Mexico, I am sure you will be glad to come back to the best place on earth. Every morning at breakfast I tell to the girls that there are a lot worse places than Canary Cottage and a lot worse men than your old father. I don't know whether it sinks in or not.

When you write always send your regards to Dorothy.[3] She is just about as much our family as anyone could be and is always interested in you.

With much love,/ Your father/ C.A.

[1] C.A. is referring to his plans to manufacture and distribute copies of famous oil paintings.
[2] John Madden, Clarence's nephew.
[3] A worker at Canary Cottage.

Much has been written of Crane's behavior in Mexico, behavior which certainly is not revealed in his letters to his father. While Hart presented one side of himself to his family in Chagrin Falls, he presented quite another side to those around him in Mexico. By spring, 1931, stories of Crane's conduct drifted back to Henry Allen Moe at the Guggenheim Foundation in New York. On June 29, Moe wrote a strong warning to Crane saying: "stay sober, keep out of jail, and get to work."

"There's no use or sense in getting mad at this letter; protests have been made in several governmental channels and I cannot ignore them, which I have no desire to do anyway. So I put my cards on the table and tell you that you are making yourself liable to deportation; and, if that happens, your support from the foundation must cease. . . ." [1]

On July 6, 1931, several days after Hart received these letters from his father and Moe, he received two telegrams from his stepmother, Bessie Crane. The first urged his immediate return to Chagrin Falls, for his father was seriously ill. The second telegram arrived several hours later: Clarence Crane was dead.

On reading the news of his father's death Hart left immediately by plane for Albuquerque, and from there he went by train to Cleveland where he arrived on July 11. The next day Clarence Arthur Crane was buried in the Crane family plot at Garrettsville. Since Hart had not spoken with his mother in over three years, and had no intention of doing so now, his only anchorage with his family was lost. He could take some consolation in the knowledge that he and his father had spent the previous winter together in Chagrin Falls; as he wrote to his friend William Wright: "I'm so glad that I had a chance to *know* him before he died." [2] However, financial and personal problems lay ahead.

The first problem involved Clarence Crane's legacy, and the financial difficulties of the Crane company. For the rest of July and well

[1] Quoted from *Voyager*, p. 674.   [2] Quoted from *Voyager*, p. 678.

into August Hart stayed with his stepmother at Canary Cottage and acquainted himself with the day-to-day operation of his father's business ventures. What he learned was not encouraging. C.A. had left the Crane business to his wife; Hart was to receive an annuity from his father's extensive stockholdings, which he hoped would yield two thousand dollars a year. However, the outlook for all of C. A. Crane's ventures was bleak. The Crane Chocolate Company's revenues had been declining steadily since World War I; though the Canary Cottage was successful, C.A. had borrowed heavily to begin the restaurant; his third business, manufacturing and distributing reproductions of famous paintings, was just beginning. Perhaps the greatest surprise for Hart concerned his father's stocks; the depression had made them virtually worthless. Aside from an initial payment of five hundred dollars from his father's estate, Crane would receive little.

In late August, after a short stay in New York, Hart returned to Mexico. News of Crane's activities in Mexico had filtered up to Patterson and New York City, and these rumors, coupled with the despondency over his father's death and his meagre production of poetry, led Crane to avoid those whom he knew in the city.

Once back in Mexico, Crane kept up the distinction between that side of his personality he presented in his letters to Chagrin Falls and the side he presented to his friends. His letters to Bess Crane discuss business matters, describe the Mexican countryside, and sometimes contain genteel hints of the drinking (but not of its severity), as well as intimations of his growing relationship with Peggy Cowley (who was living in Mexico while her divorce from Malcolm Cowley became final). While he was drinking heavily at times, he also was writing one of his finest poems, "The Broken Tower," a fusion of his experiences in Mexico and especially his experiences in Taxco and Tepotzlan.

By February, 1932, Hart's friendship with Peggy Cowley had grown into love. "You might have guessed I'd fall in love again!" [3] he wrote in a postcard to Charlotte and Richard Rychtarik on March 1. The following letter to his stepmother perhaps best illustrates Crane's mood.

[3] Quoted from *Voyager,* p. 732.

To Bessie M. Crane

15, Calle Michoacan
Mixcoac, D.F.
March 8th, 1932

TLS, 2 pp.

Dear Bess:

Peggy and I have been together in Puebla for several days, and that accounts for my delay in answering your good letter. Puebla is one of the most beautiful places I have ever seen; wide streets, pink, blue and terra cotta houses with balconies of wrought iron; a main plaza with lofty trees of a dozen native varieties; the second largest cathedral on this continent, whose interior blazes with enough gold railings and gold leaf ornament to pay off Germany's reparation debts. Besides that (believe it or not) the city contains 364 other churches—one for every day in the year. I can't say we visited more than a few of those. A good Catholic, however, might easily wear out not only shoe leather but his eyes also in trying to do justice to all. The streets of Puebla would put the average American city to shame with their immaculate cleanliness. And if you could have seen the main market—where not only food but clothing, rugs, pottery, toys and every conceivable article in the world is sold, you would have raved for weeks! Peggy has an income of her own, and we both bought some of the most beautiful sarapes, glass ware (hand blown), pottery and leather work that you ever laid eyes on. Really, Bess, you can't conceive the beauty of the arts and crafts of these Indians. Our house is now a delight to the eyes.

Our garden is abloom with white iris, calendulas, nasturtiums, calla lilies, a dozen varieties and colors of geraniums, sweet alyssum, daisies, candytuft, cassas, roses, violets, begonias, larkspur, crysanthemums, and a number of native flowers and shrubs whose names I really don't know. I've never had half my fill of flowers before and I can't resist reiterating my satisfaction now. There is never an inch in Mexico where flowers aren't cultivated and loved. Yesterday in Puebla I came back to the hotel with an armful of violets, cornflowers, white carnations and carmine poppies for Peggy,—four bouquets in all, and the total cost not being more than 15 cents in US money. It certainly is delightful to look over the balcony of one's hotel room in the morning and see an indian walking along with a basket twice the size of any of our laundry baskets full of fresh flowers balanced on his head. But that's a common sight in most Mexican cities.

Now about the allowance . . .[1] I'm just expressing my wishes and needs. I leave the arrangements to you as you see fit. I don't feel like asking for more than the $125. per month which I mentioned in my last letter. However, I'll need all of that, and I think it may be highly important to feel the assurance that I can plan on getting it regularly at monthly intervals. If it isn't too much trouble I wish that Miss Brooks would plan on mailing me a chasier's check on the 25th of each month, dated for the 1st of the following month. I have recently opened up a small checking account with a bank here in Mexico on what remained of my letter of credit from the Guggenheim Foundation. That will obviate any necessity for the expensive form of wiring money—barring some extraordinary emergency. I would like to plan, however, on arrival of funds promptly on the first of each month, especially as I must maintain enough of a balence in my account here to draw on the new check to some extent, perhaps before it is confirmed through the mails. When my lease on this house expires I hope to be able to cut down on my present expenses to some extent; I want to travel more, for after all, seeing the country is one of the reasons for my being here. But even so, I can't yet know what exactly I can save, and I must plan on having at least the amount I have mentioned. So unless I hear otherwise from you, I'll expect receipt of the first "installment" on April 1st.

Yes, Bess, I'm really getting to work on one of the strongest pieces of poetry I've ever written. Being with Peggy is doing me a great deal of good. No kinder, sweeter, more unselfish person have I ever known. Her companionship is removing that exhausting sense of loneliness that has been a great handicap to me for years. I don't need to tell you what love and devotion mean. You have responded,

---

[1] It was thought that Hart could have a small allowance from his father's estate.

and how beautifully! to those instincts yourself. You have one of the most beautiful understandings that I know of. And if you ever felt reason to worry about me certainly there is less reason now than ever before.

I do hope that my "Auntie Bess" is thoroughly through with all recent maladies, and that all the Maddens are well and happy. Do give them my love! And my sympathy to Mr. Church, toward whom I really felt a sincere attachment. I think his worries and strain may have had a great deal to do with his present condition. Isn't Ethel back? Anyway my love to her, and to Dorothy and Anne! None of you probably realize how often I picture you all by the fireside, the daily program at the Cottage—and how, in spite of all my interest in this vast and exotic country, I always think of your environment as my home. Thanks to you, Bess!

We are giving a tea this afternoon to two of the 1932 Guggenheim scholars who are here in Mexico with their wives. Both are historians; but I seem to get along fairly well with them. About that express matter, Bess;—I can't yet figure it out; but I don't think it's anything to worry about unless you have sent me something else since Xmas. At least you've never mentiond it, if you have. I got everything you sent—and all was prepaid and delivered to the house here without my even having to sign for it. Then later I got a notice from the Mexican Railways, Inc. saying that what I had already eaten and enjoyed was still waiting for me up at the border! And wouldn't I please send certain duty charges! I've just laughed that off long ago. There must have been some ludicrous mistake; but I know that you had already paid all charges in advance as I got a receipt to that effect from the shipping agency. . . .

Lots of love,/ Harold

Unfortunately this was one of the last rational letters Crane wrote. From mid-March until his death on April 27 the Hart Crane of legend reigned, with fights, long drinking bouts, wild Easter celebrations, and several visits to Mexican jails. Numerous events precipitated his behavior. His Guggenheim fellowship ended on March

31; his father's death left him with little family to return to; his meagre output of poetry raised in his mind serious questions about his writing ability; and finally, he quarreled frequently with Peggy Cowley.

By mid-April Crane and Peggy Cowley decided that they had to return to New York. They booked passage on the *Orizaba,* the ship that had brought Hart to Mexico. Hart wired Chagrin Falls for money for his passage. On April 22, the day the money arrived, he sent his last letter to his stepmother.

To Bessie M. Crane

Mixcoac, DF
April 22nd '32

TLS, 2 pp.

Dear Bess:

Pardon me for wiring Byron about money, but so many difficulties came to a head at once here, and with myself weak from a fever and dysentery I had to use every way of impressing on you the urgency of my immediate needs. And I imagine that you well may have been too preoccupied to realize the situation here anyway—even in part.

Altogether I've had a terrible time lately. I can't begin to write the details now in the finalities of packing. I leave for Vera Cruz tomorrow night and sail Sunday morning on the Orizaba for New York. I was planning to return to Ohio even before the shocking news came about the Wilson matter.[1] But with that having happened I wouldn't have thought of staying here another minute anyway. I may be able to be of some help to you this summer. Anyway I want to make the effort, especially since you must be quite crippled (at least at the Cottage) without Dorothy's help.

You can't imagine how difficult the Mexicans make it for any foreigners to remain here—comfortably. I love the country and the

---

[1] Hart refers to a serious auto accident that took the life of an employee of Canary Cottage and seriously injured several other employees.

people (Indians) but certainly have had my fill of passport difficulties, servant problems and other complications for awhile. I have been not only ill—but frightened nearly out of my wits because I happened, in all innocence, to put my passport-renewal problem in the hands of a lawyer crook. It's all right; I have clearance papers; but it involved me in a lot of expense, consultations with innumerable people and just endless worry. Then at the last moment my servant got roaring drunk and left, and came back and shook the gate to its foundations, yelling threats against my life, terrorizing us for days, until we had to call on the American Embassy for special police service. Etc. and so on . . . Do you wonder I've been anxious to get off as soon as possible. Thank God the lease on my house is already expired—and there can be no further complications that I know.

I have hated to draw on you so heavily for money lately, but after all, I had no way of knowing how matters would turn out with the estate; and the expense of coming home now certainly seems justified in view of the possibility of economizing later on. There are many things highly important for us to discuss together, and besides that I am looking forward to seeing you and the rest of our friends and relatives again. I am bringing back a lot of very interesting things, some very beautiful, that you'll enjoy seeing, I'm sure.

A case of books had to be sent collect (Wells Fargo) direct to the factory. Please be on the watch for it. The other things are all in a large hamper which will go with me on the boat and will be expressed to the factory later on from New York. I'll be in New York a couple of days as I simply must see some of my old friends after so long a time. I'll telephone you on the first night of my arrival around ten o'clock when the rates are reduced.

Please give my love to poor little Dorothy. I haven't had a moment to write to anyone lately or I should have written her long ago. Had to spend all day yesterday running around trying to get the telegraphed money cashed. Wasn't your fault, nor mine. Peggy nearly went crazy with her's sent from her former husband, too. The telegraph office paid us off in six hundred and some odd "Tostons" (about like getting it all in dimes) and neither the Ward Line office nor the official Banco de Mexico would accept them . . . It seems there's a law against paying out any such currency beyond a certain small amount. But how should we know—and besides what does a government agency like the telegraph here mean by paying you in currency which the government itself, through its own official bank, turns around and refuses! We finally had to arrange a special interview with the president of the bank himself. I was already to complain to the embassy. So you see how slow things move here and what incessant obstacles one has to fight for the simplest sort of transactions. It certainly has about made a nervous wreck of me. But I'll rest up on the boat.

Lovingly,/ Harold

The *Orizaba* sailed from Vera Cruz on April 24 and on April 26 stopped for a day at Havana, Cuba. Details of what happened that day in Havana or that night aboard the ship are sketchy and much must be left to conjecture. There was a lot of drinking both in Havana and on the boat that evening, and very likely Hart found his way to the sailors' quarters before the evening was over. A few minutes before noon on April 27, Hart stopped at Peggy Cowley's cabin to say: "I'm not going to make it, dear. I'm utterly disgraced." From her cabin he proceeded to the ship's deck and jumped into the sea. One passenger, Gertrude Vogt, remembered in 1969 Hart's death:

> "On that ill-fated morning, one of the ship's officers told us that Crane had been in the sailors' quarters the previous night, trying to make one of the men, and had been badly beaten. Just before noon, a number of us were gathered on deck, waiting to hear the results of the ship's pool—always announced at noon. Just then we saw Crane come on deck, dressed . . . in pajamas and topcoat; he had a black eye and looked generally battered. He walked to the railing, took off his coat, folded it neatly over the railing (not dropping it on the deck), placed both hands on the railing, raised himself on his toes, and then dropped back again. We all fell silent and watched him, won-

dering what in the world he was up to. Then, suddenly, he vaulted over the railing and jumped into the sea. For what seemed like five minutes, but was more like five seconds, no one was able to move; then cries of "man overboard" went up. Just once I saw Crane, swimming strongly, but never again." [1]

At about eleven o'clock on April 28, Bess Crane received a call from her brother-in-law, Byron Madden, with news of the "tragedy" —as she called it more than forty years later.[2] Grace Hart Crane, who had been working at the Carleton Hotel in Oak Park, Illinois, since her mother's death in 1928, read of Hart's suicide in the newspaper. From that time until her own death fifteen years later Grace Crane labored to perpetuate her son's memory, and she tried desperately to reconstruct Hart's last years. "About three years ago," Mrs. Crane wrote to Charlotte Rychtarik on May 3, 1932,

"we had a cruel experience which has separated us ever since, altho I have made repeated efforts to get in touch with him by letter & other ways. I had been living in hopes that perhaps this summer something would bring us together when I knew everything would be forgotten instantly. Knowing him as I did, I was certain he was suffering remorse over the affair. But now he is gone—forever—and those past years will be a blank to me, regarding his movements and actions. Would you *please* write me what you know of his life during that time & if he ever talked of me." [3]

In the years before her death she gathered his correspondence, helped Philip Horton with his biography of Crane, and assisted Waldo Frank in the preparation of the *Collected Poems*.

The end of Grace Hart Crane's life was not without its own tragic elements. After her mother's death in 1928, financial difficulties forced her to take a succession of jobs, sell her possessions, and move from California, to Oak Park, to Leonia, New Jersey, and fi-

---

[1] Quoted from *Voyager*, Notes, p. 759.
[2] From an interview with the editor, June, 1972.
[3] This letter is filed in the Columbia University collection.

nally to New York City. At the time of her death on August 30, 1947, she was living in a single room on East 38th Street. At her request, Sam Loveman, one of Hart's closest friends, who was with Mrs. Crane when she died, had her body cremated and scattered the ashes from the Brooklyn Bridge.

CALENDAR OF LETTERS

The following abbreviations are used in the calendar of letters and the index:

CAC   Clarence Arthur Crane   EBH   Elizabeth Belden Hart
GHC   Grace Hart Crane   *WB*   *White Buildings*
HHC   Harold Hart Crane

The following letters are the property of Mrs. Donald Hise:

December 31, 1916	to CAC	June 6, 1927	from CAC
January 3, 1917	from CAC	June 9, 1927	to CAC
January 17, 1917	from CAC	June 21, 1927	to CAC
January 20, 1917	from CAC	June 29, 1927	from CAC
January 29, 1917	from CAC	August 12, 1927	to CAC
February 2, 1917	from CAC	August 17, 1927	from CAC
March 23, 1917	to CAC	September 1, 1927	from CAC
March 29, 1917	from CAC	September 21, 1927	from CAC
April 16, 1917	from CAC	September 26, 1927	from CAC
May 5, 1917	to CAC	October 11, 1927	to CAC
May 15, 1917	to CAC	October 13, 1927	from CAC
May 16, 1917	from CAC	October 17, 1927	from CAC
June 5, 1917	to CAC	November 10, 1927	to CAC
August 1, 1917	from CAC	November 14, 1927	from CAC
August 8, 1917	to CAC	March 28, 1928	from CAC
September 18, 1917	to CAC	June 14, 1928	to CAC
December 30, 1925	from CAC	June 18, 1928	from CAC
January 3, 1926	to CAC	July 5, 1928	from CAC
May 10, 1926	from CAC	July 26, 1928	to CAC
May 20, 1926	to CAC	July 27, 1928	from CAC
July 7, 1926	from CAC	August 2, 1928	to CAC
October 31, 1926	to CAC	August 14, 1928	to CAC
November 2, 1926	from CAC	August 16, 1928	from CAC
November 10, 1926	from CAC	(telegram)	
April 25, 1927	from CAC	August 16, 1928	from CAC
April 30, 1927	from CAC	August 19, 1928	to CAC
May 10, 1927	from CAC	August 21, 1928	from CAC
May 19, 1927	from CAC		

The following letters are the property of Ohio State University:

January 9, 1924   to GHC   November 9, 1924 to GHC and
                                                               EBH

The following letters are the property of The University of Texas:

May 25, 1923   to GHC and EBH   January 12, 1924 to GHC and EBH
October 14, 1924 to GHC and EBH   April 13, 1925   to GHC and EBH
October 25, 1924 to GHC and EBH   March 23, 1926   to GHC

The rest of the letters are the property of Columbia University Libraries.
Illustrations of letters on pages 5, 101, 254, 468, and 553 are reproduced
through the courtesy of Columbia University Libraries.

INDEX

146–47; with Crane Chocolate Company (1919–21), 143, 147–49; with Corday and Gross (1922–23), 149, 151; with Stanley Patno (1923), 151; with J. Walter Thompson (1923), 151, 165–66, 222, 225; possibility of position at Harcourt, Brace and Company (1923), 225, 232; offered job at Crane Chocolate Company, (1924) 246, 248–50, (1925) 392; with Pratt and Lindsay (1924), 267, 279–80; with Sweet's Catalogue Service, 280, 297, 299–300, 408; considers taking job on boat, 295, 438; offered job at Corday and Gross (1925), 392, 405–6; offered job by CAC (1927), 552–55, 558–59; secretary and companion to Herbert A. Wise (1927–28), 612–16 passim; looks for employment in Los Angeles (1928), 618; part-time position in N.Y. bookstore (1928), 631; with Griffin, Johnson, and Mann (1928), 634; see also Sweet's Catalogue Service; Thompson, J. Walter, Advertising Agency

——finances, 170; CAC's maintenance of HHC in N.Y. (1917), 17, 28, 30, 33, 55–57 passim, 60–61, 77, 83–85 passim; schedule of payments for HHC in parents' divorce settlement, 40n–41n; spends money entertaining GHC (1917), 48, 52; owes money to Charles Brooks (1917), 81; CAC's and GHC's maintenance of HHC in N.Y. (1919), 109–10, 117–18, 119–32 passim, 127–28, 130–31, 134–38 passim, 143; borrows money from Rychtariks, 203, 436, 481–82; GHC sends HHC money (1923), 205–6, 221, 226, 228, 236, 243, 245; HHC complains of lack of money to GHC and EBH (1924), 252, 336; GHC and CAC promise to send money (1924), 256, 263, 266; HHC's financial difficulties (1924), 279–81, 336; Stewart Mitchell gives HHC money (1924), 292; HHC asks GHC to mention his financial situation to her friends the Rosses (1925), 412; CAC's support of (1925) 439, 441, (1926–27) 516–17, 563, 576, 578–79, 581, 596, 605–6, (1928) 626–29 passim, 631–33; describes his financial situation to CAC (1925), 445–

46; sends checks to GHC and EBH, and receives checks from them (1925), 456–57; asks CAC for loan (1926), 510; asks CAC for advance on expected legacy from EBH estate (1928), 623–25; receives legacy from EBH, 636–37, 641; financial arrangements in Mexico (1931–32), 642–45 passim; legacy from CAC estate, 648–49, 651; asks for money to return to U.S. from Mexico (1932), 653–54; see also Kahn, Otto

——relationship with family: hopes for GHC's happiness (1917), 18; pledges not to forget GHC (1917), 32; writes of love for GHC (1917), 46; entertains GHC in N.Y. (1917), 48–49; concern over divorce (1917), 56; possibility of reunited family (1917), 57–58; lives with GHC in N.Y. (1917), 58–62 passim; reports on GHC's health to CAC (1917), 60; speaks of "foundation of sincerity" in relations with CAC (1917), 67; asks CAC not to speak distastefully of GHC (1917), 67; censures CAC (1917), 69–70, 74, 79; advises GHC about nerves (1917), 80, 88; angry at possibility of reconciliation between GHC and CAC (1918), 95; arguments with GHC while living in Cleveland (1918), 108; writes to GHC about Christian Science (1919), 120–21, 125–26; speaks of his life as a "battleground" for parents' sexual problems (1919), 136; complains to GHC about CAC (1919), 139; comments to GHC on his relationship with CAC, (1919) 141–42, (1923) 178–79; fears GHC may come to N.Y. (1923), 180; discusses GHC in letter to Charlotte Rychtarik (1923), 217–18; tells GHC of need to write poetry (1923), 242–43; discusses meetings and correspondence with CAC to GHC (1924), 273–74, 296, 308–10, 338; advises GHC he cannot tell her more about CAC (1924), 289; GHC's prospects for remarriage and its relation to him (1924), 341, 343–45, 383, 390; feelings about CAC (1925), 383–84; concern for GHC's health (1925), 404; disturbed by